Zits alternative

Also by Jerry Scott and Jim Borgman

Zits: Sketchbook 1
Growth Spurt: Zits Sketchbook 2
Don't Roll Your Eyes at Me, Young Man!: Zits Sketchbook 3
Are We an "Us"?: Zits Sketchbook 4
Zits Unzipped: Zits Sketchbook 5
Busted!: Zits Sketchbook 6
Road Trip: Zits Sketchbook 7
Teenage Tales: Zits Sketchbook 8
Thrashed: Zits Sketchbook No. 9
Pimp My Lunch: Zits Sketchbook No. 10
Are We Out of the Driveway Yet? Zits Sketchbook No. 11
Rude, Crude, and Tattooed: Zits Sketchbook No. 12

Treasuries
Humongous Zits
Big Honkin' Zits
Zits: Supersized
Random Zits
Crack of Noon

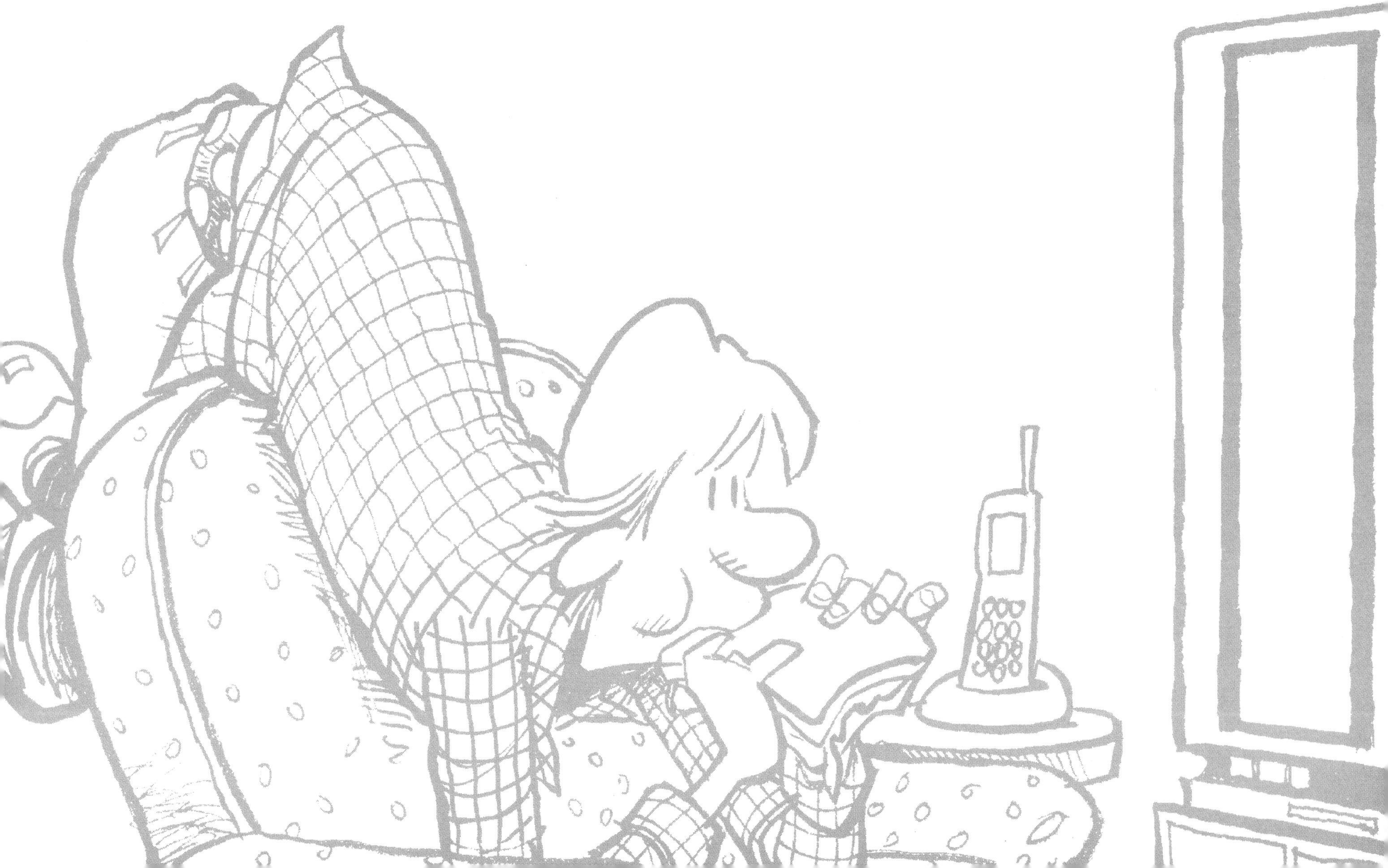

Zits

alternative

Jerry Scott and
Jim Borgman

Andrews McMeel
Publishing, LLC

Kansas City

Zits® is syndicated internationally by King Features Syndicate, Inc. For information, write King Features Syndicate, Inc., 300 West Fifty-Seventh Street, New York, New York 10019.

07 08 09 10 11 BAM 10 9 8 7 6 5 4 3 2 1

ISBN-13: 978-0-7407-6848-4
ISBN-10: 0-7407-6848-4

Library of Congress Control Number: 2007925340

Zits® may be viewed online at
www.kingfeatures.com.

www.andrewsmcmeel.com

─── **ATTENTION: SCHOOLS AND BUSINESSES** ───

Andrews McMeel books are available at quantity discounts with bulk purchase for educational, business, or sales promotional use. For information, please write to: Special Sales Department, Andrews McMeel Publishing, LLC, 4520 Main Street, Kansas City, Missouri 64111.

For Jay

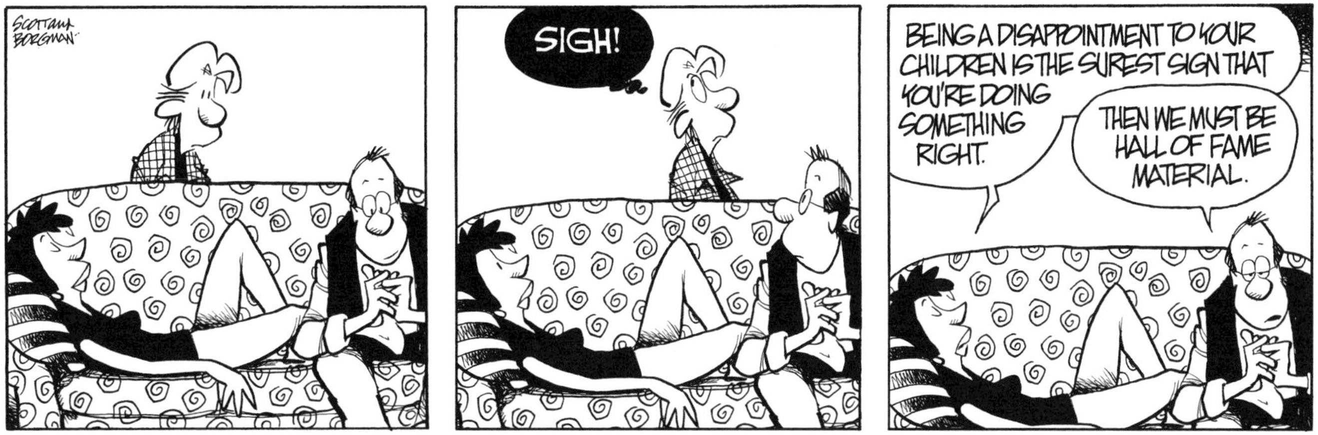
SIGH!
BEING A DISAPPOINTMENT TO YOUR CHILDREN IS THE SUREST SIGN THAT YOU'RE DOING SOMETHING RIGHT.
THEN WE MUST BE HALL OF FAME MATERIAL.

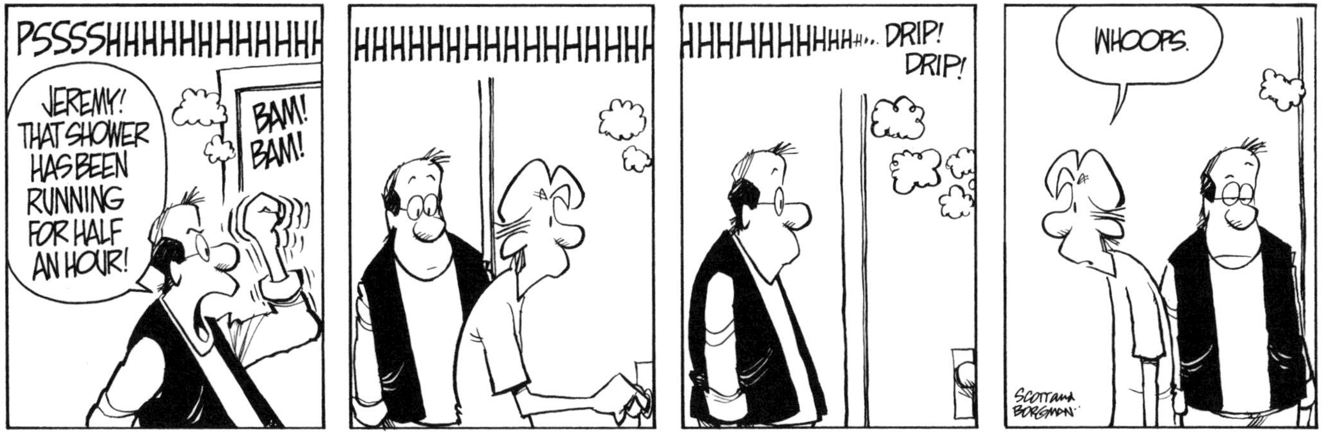
PSSSSHHHHHHHHHHHH
JEREMY! THAT SHOWER HAS BEEN RUNNING FOR HALF AN HOUR!
BAM! BAM!
HHHHHHHHHHHHHHHHH
HHHHHHHHHHHH... DRIP! DRIP!
WHOOPS.

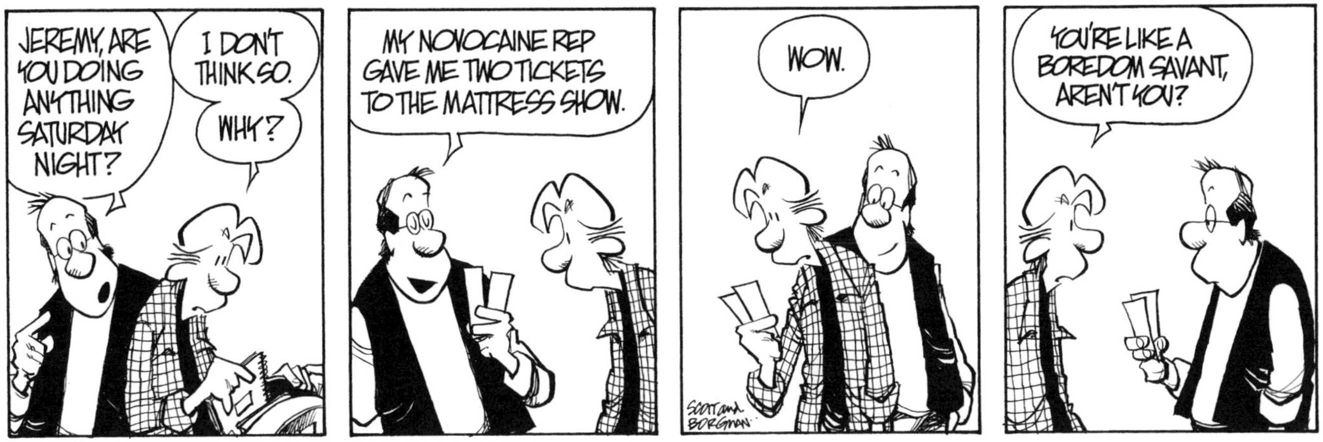
JEREMY, ARE YOU DOING ANYTHING SATURDAY NIGHT?
I DON'T THINK SO.
WHY?
MY NOVOCAINE REP GAVE ME TWO TICKETS TO THE MATTRESS SHOW.
WOW.
YOU'RE LIKE A BOREDOM SAVANT, AREN'T YOU?

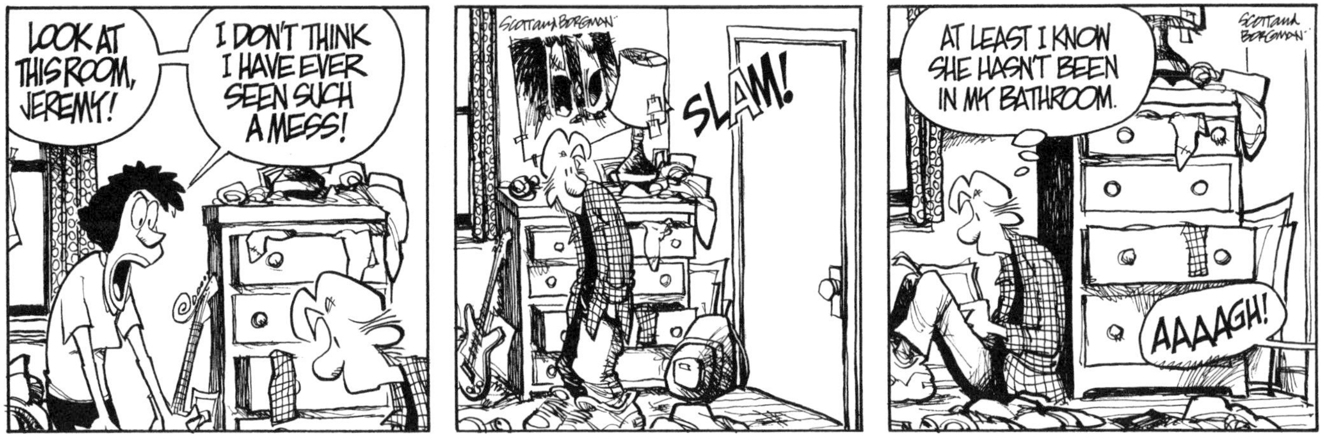
LOOK AT THIS ROOM, JEREMY!
I DON'T THINK I HAVE EVER SEEN SUCH A MESS!
SLAM!
AT LEAST I KNOW SHE HASN'T BEEN IN MY BATHROOM.
AAAAGH!

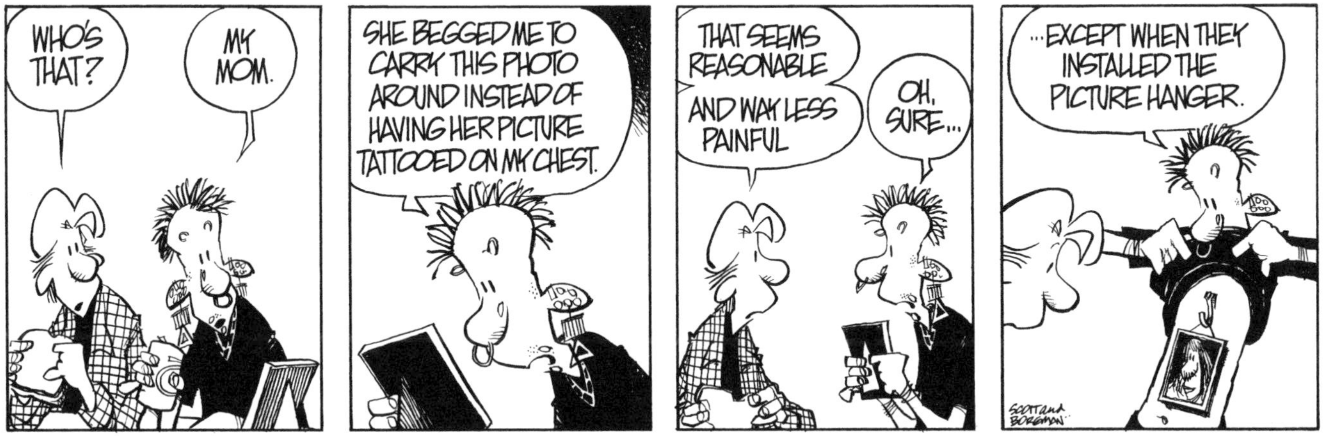
WHO'S THAT?
MY MOM.
SHE BEGGED ME TO CARRY THIS PHOTO AROUND INSTEAD OF HAVING HER PICTURE TATTOOED ON MY CHEST.
THAT SEEMS REASONABLE
AND WAY LESS PAINFUL
OH, SURE...
...EXCEPT WHEN THEY INSTALLED THE PICTURE HANGER.

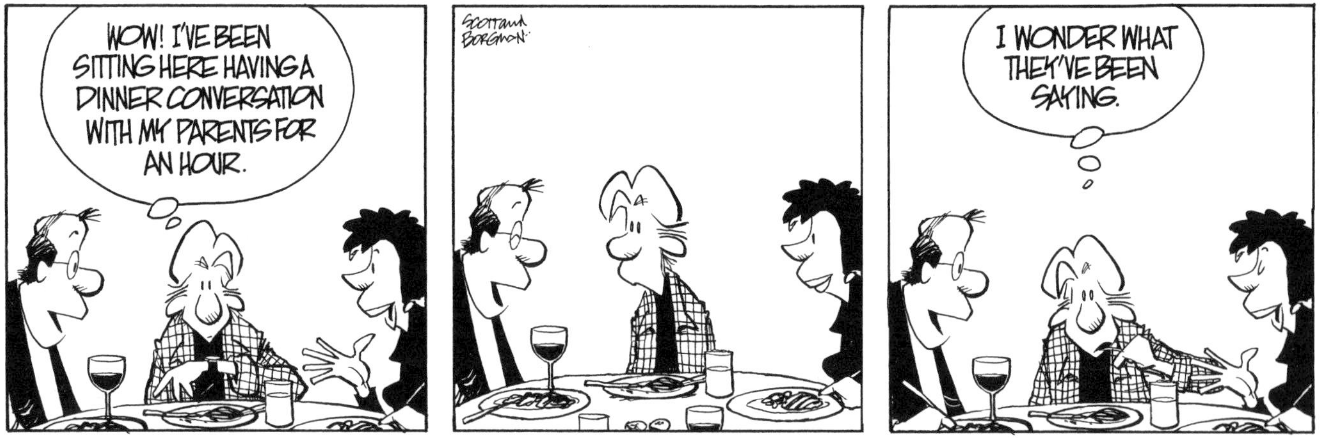
WOW! I'VE BEEN SITTING HERE HAVING A DINNER CONVERSATION WITH MY PARENTS FOR AN HOUR.
I WONDER WHAT THEY'VE BEEN SAYING.

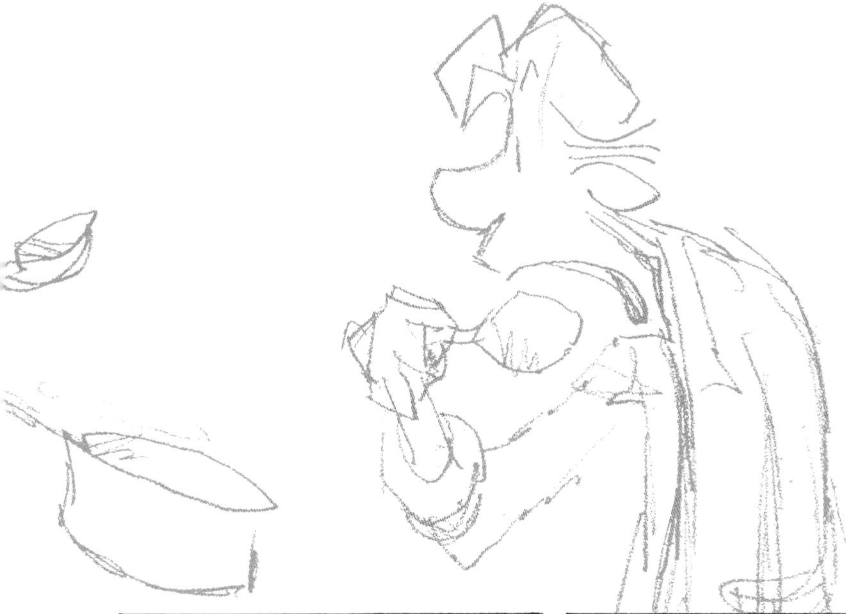

Zits

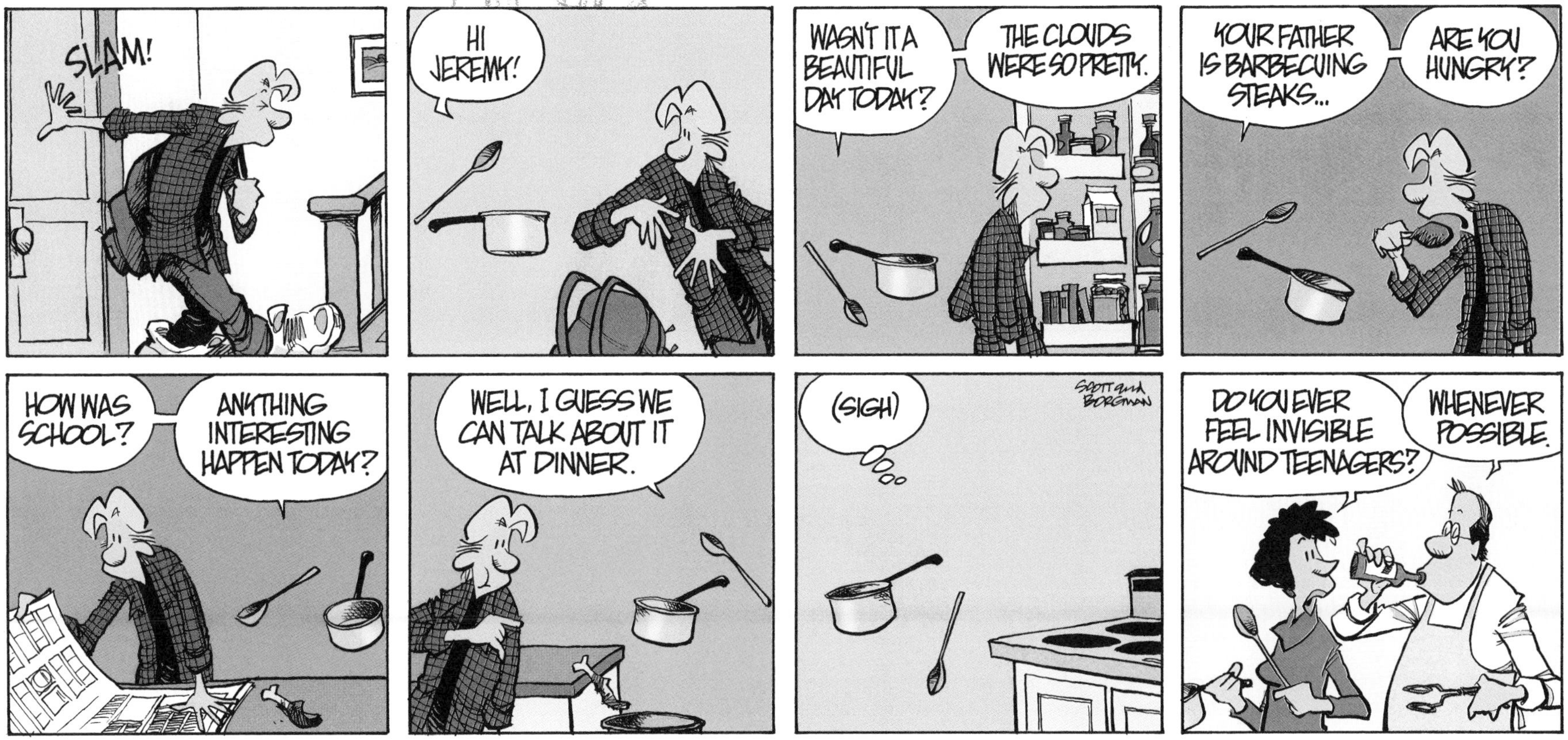
SLAM!
HI JEREMY!
WASN'T IT A BEAUTIFUL DAY TODAY?
THE CLOUDS WERE SO PRETTY.
YOUR FATHER IS BARBECUING STEAKS...
ARE YOU HUNGRY?
HOW WAS SCHOOL?
ANYTHING INTERESTING HAPPEN TODAY?
WELL, I GUESS WE CAN TALK ABOUT IT AT DINNER.
(SIGH)
SCOTT and BORGMAN
DO YOU EVER FEEL INVISIBLE AROUND TEENAGERS?
WHENEVER POSSIBLE.

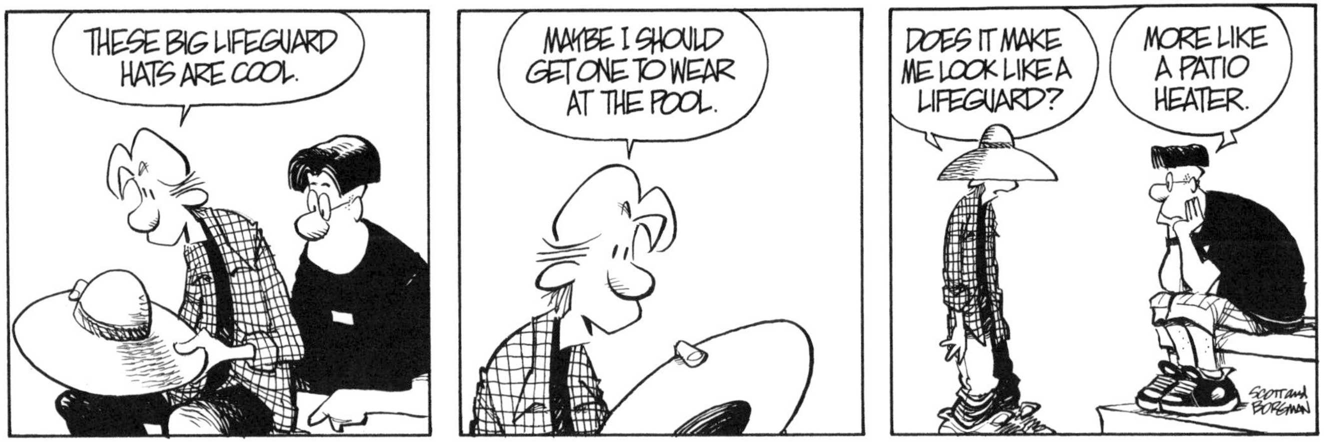
THESE BIG LIFEGUARD HATS ARE COOL.
MAYBE I SHOULD GET ONE TO WEAR AT THE POOL.
DOES IT MAKE ME LOOK LIKE A LIFEGUARD?
MORE LIKE A PATIO HEATER.

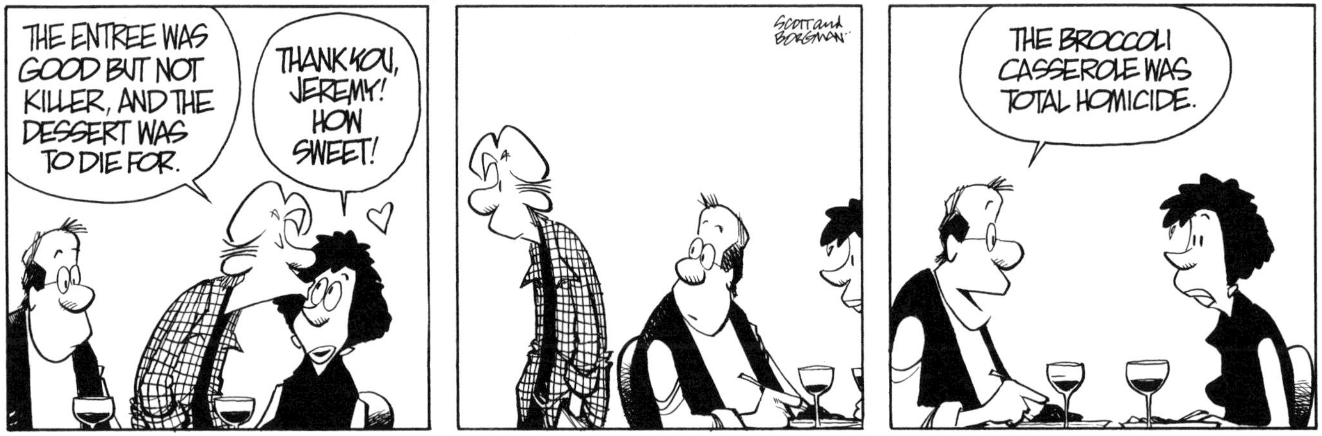
THE ENTREE WAS GOOD BUT NOT KILLER, AND THE DESSERT WAS TO DIE FOR.
THANK YOU, JEREMY! HOW SWEET!
THE BROCCOLI CASSEROLE WAS TOTAL HOMICIDE.

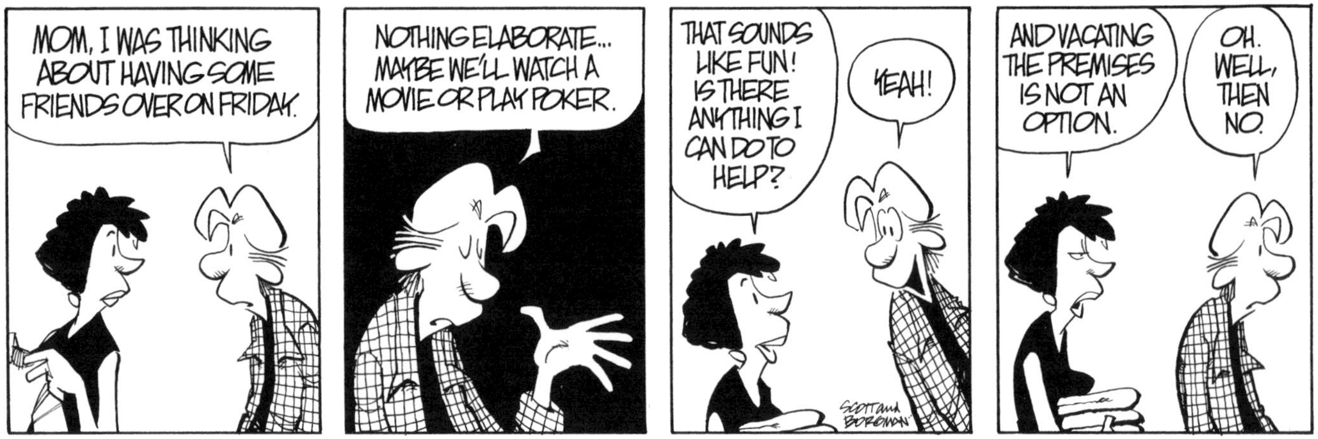
MOM, I WAS THINKING ABOUT HAVING SOME FRIENDS OVER ON FRIDAY.
NOTHING ELABORATE... MAYBE WE'LL WATCH A MOVIE OR PLAY POKER.
THAT SOUNDS LIKE FUN! IS THERE ANYTHING I CAN DO TO HELP?
YEAH!
AND VACATING THE PREMISES IS NOT AN OPTION.
OH. WELL, THEN NO.

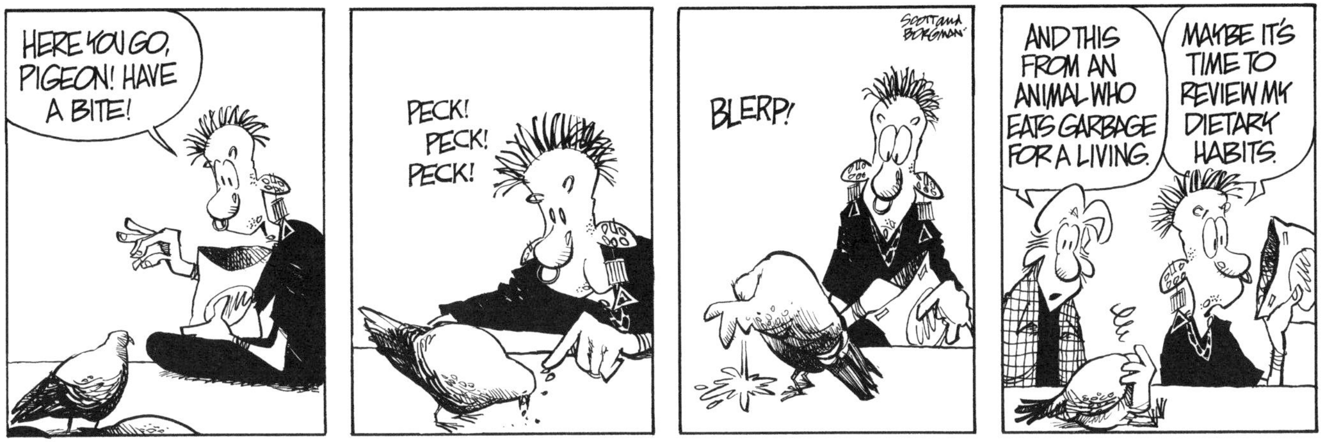
HERE YOU GO, PIGEON! HAVE A BITE!
PECK! PECK! PECK!
BLERP!
AND THIS FROM AN ANIMAL WHO EATS GARBAGE FOR A LIVING.
MAYBE IT'S TIME TO REVIEW MY DIETARY HABITS.

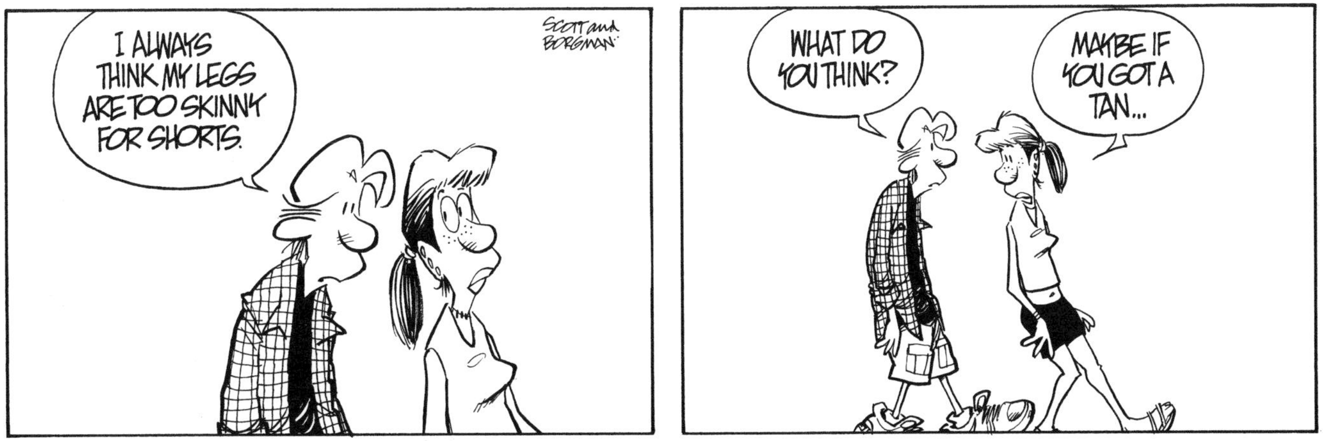
I ALWAYS THINK MY LEGS ARE TOO SKINNY FOR SHORTS.
WHAT DO YOU THINK?
MAYBE IF YOU GOT A TAN...

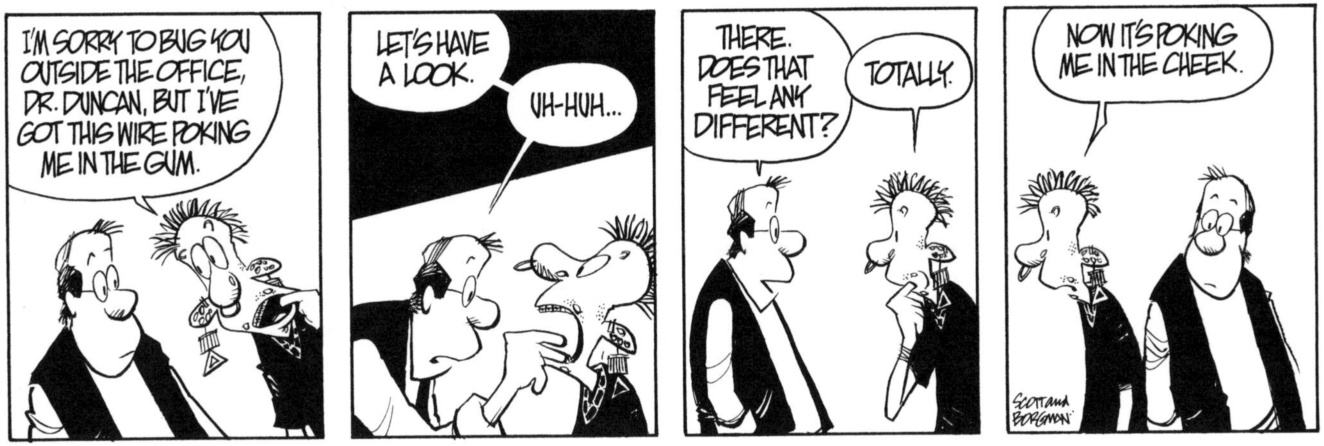
I'M SORRY TO BUG YOU OUTSIDE THE OFFICE, DR. DUNCAN, BUT I'VE GOT THIS WIRE POKING ME IN THE GUM.
LET'S HAVE A LOOK.
UH-HUH...
THERE. DOES THAT FEEL ANY DIFFERENT?
TOTALLY.
NOW IT'S POKING ME IN THE CHEEK.

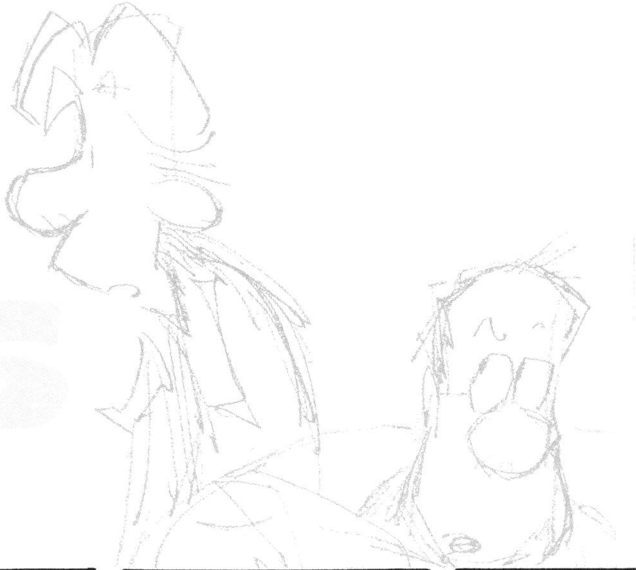

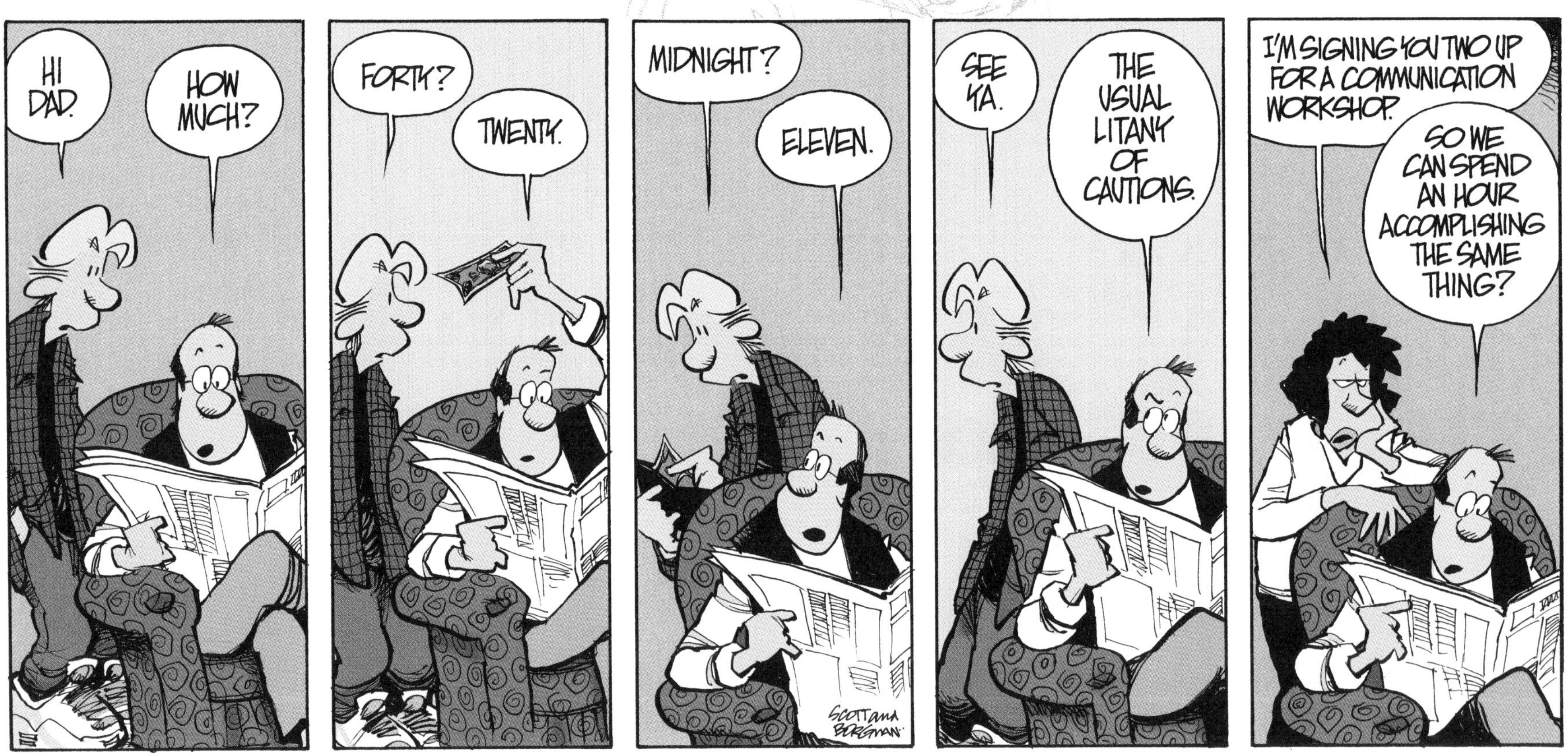
HI DAD.
HOW MUCH?
FORTY?
TWENTY.
MIDNIGHT?
ELEVEN.
SCOTT and BORGMAN
SEE YA.
THE USUAL LITANY OF CAUTIONS.
I'M SIGNING YOU TWO UP FOR A COMMUNICATION WORKSHOP.
SO WE CAN SPEND AN HOUR ACCOMPLISHING THE SAME THING?

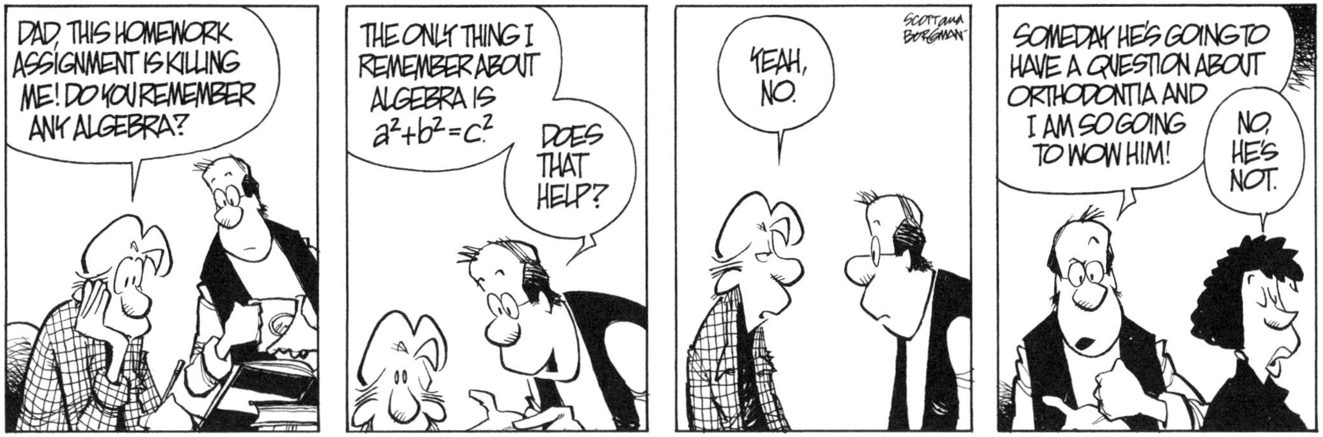
DAD, THIS HOMEWORK ASSIGNMENT IS KILLING ME! DO YOU REMEMBER ANY ALGEBRA?
THE ONLY THING I REMEMBER ABOUT ALGEBRA IS $a^2+b^2=c^2$
DOES THAT HELP?
SCOTT and BORGMAN
YEAH, NO.
SOMEDAY HE'S GOING TO HAVE A QUESTION ABOUT ORTHODONTIA AND I AM SO GOING TO WOW HIM!
NO, HE'S NOT.

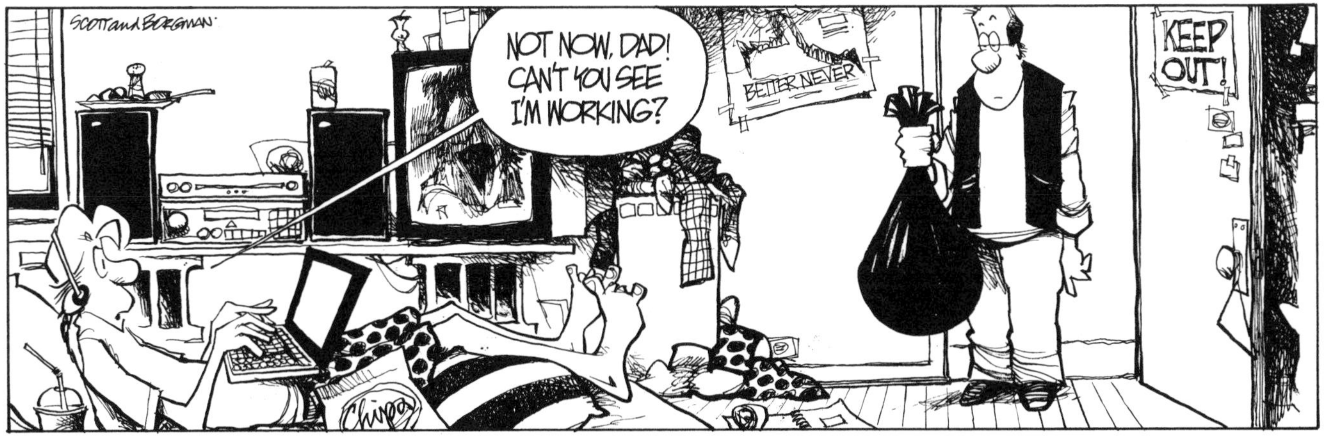
SCOTT and BORGMAN
NOT NOW, DAD! CAN'T YOU SEE I'M WORKING?
BETTER NEVER
KEEP OUT!
Chips

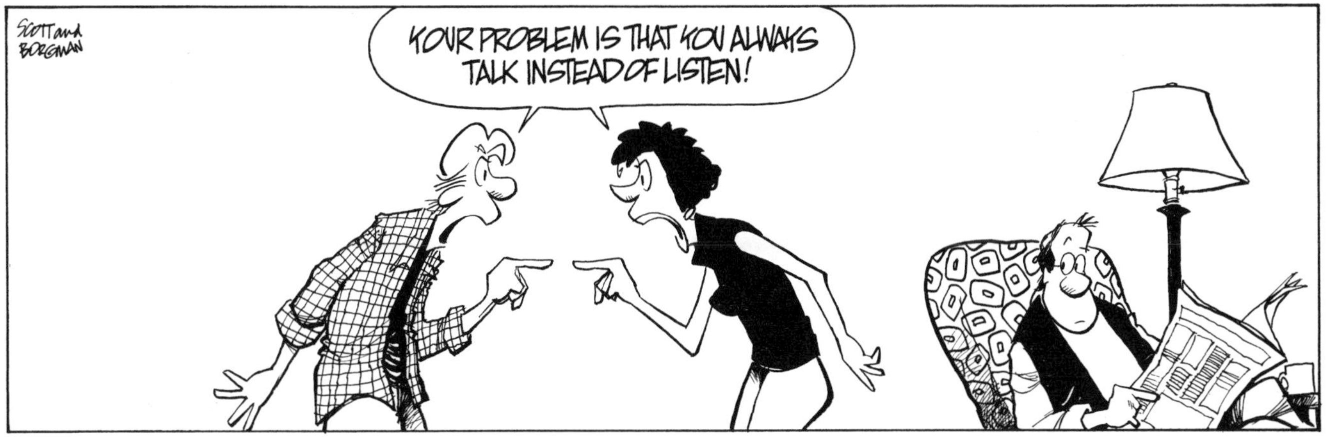
SCOTT and BORGMAN
YOUR PROBLEM IS THAT YOU ALWAYS TALK INSTEAD OF LISTEN!

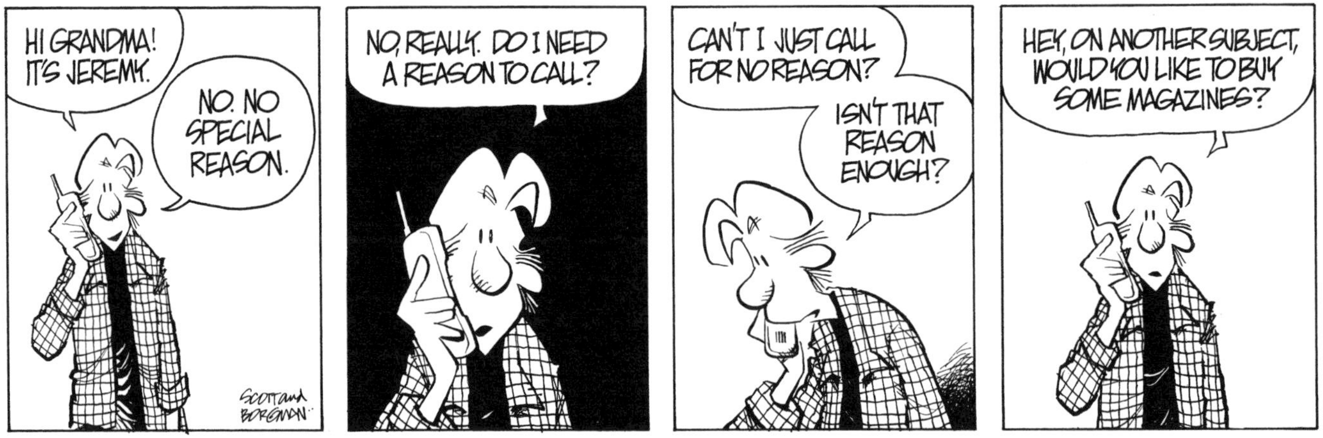
HI GRANDMA! IT'S JEREMY.
NO. NO SPECIAL REASON.
NO, REALLY. DO I NEED A REASON TO CALL?
CAN'T I JUST CALL FOR NO REASON?
ISN'T THAT REASON ENOUGH?
HEY, ON ANOTHER SUBJECT, WOULD YOU LIKE TO BUY SOME MAGAZINES?
SCOTT AND BORGMAN

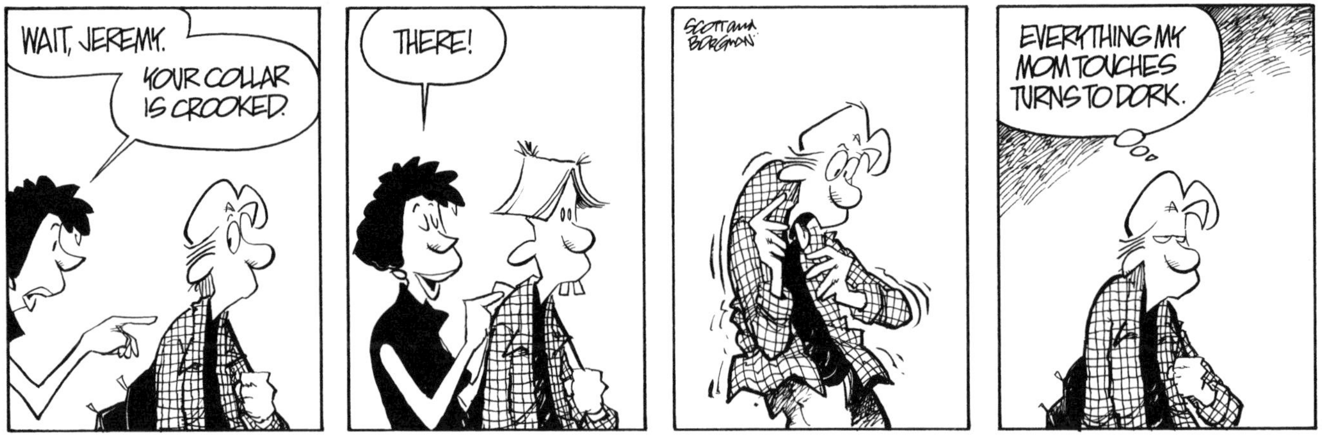
WAIT, JEREMY.
YOUR COLLAR IS CROOKED.
THERE!
SCOTT AND BORGMAN
EVERYTHING MY MOM TOUCHES TURNS TO DORK.

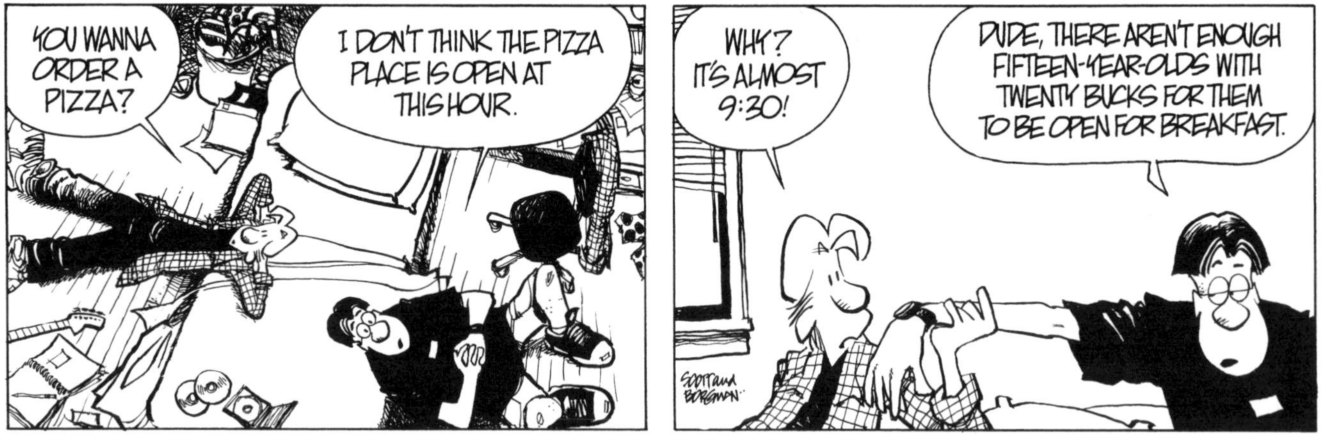
YOU WANNA ORDER A PIZZA?
I DON'T THINK THE PIZZA PLACE IS OPEN AT THIS HOUR.
WHY? IT'S ALMOST 9:30!
DUDE, THERE AREN'T ENOUGH FIFTEEN-YEAR-OLDS WITH TWENTY BUCKS FOR THEM TO BE OPEN FOR BREAKFAST.
SCOTT AND BORGMAN

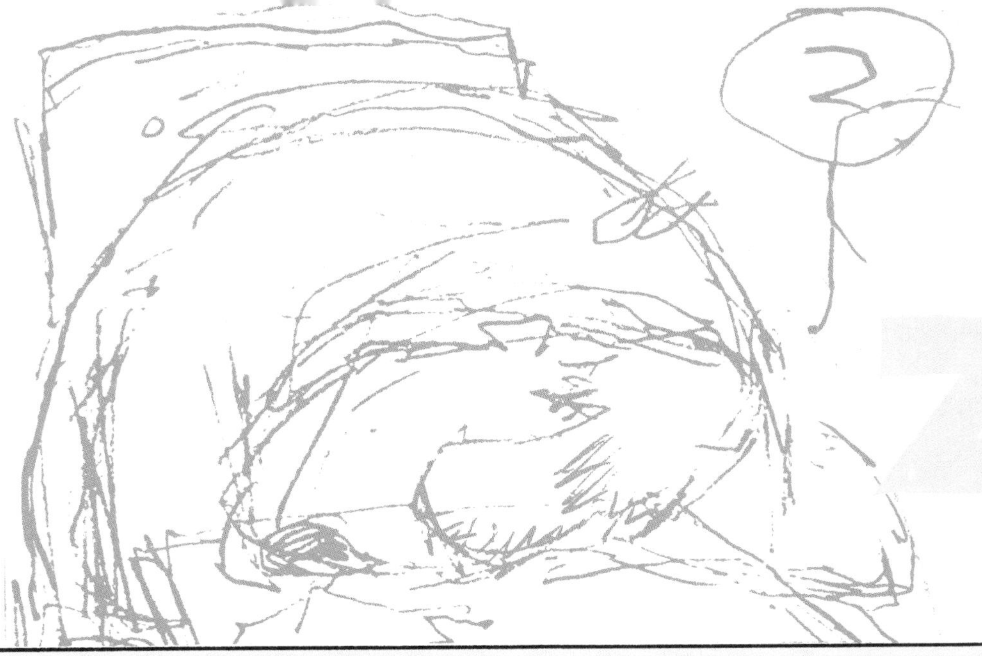

Zits

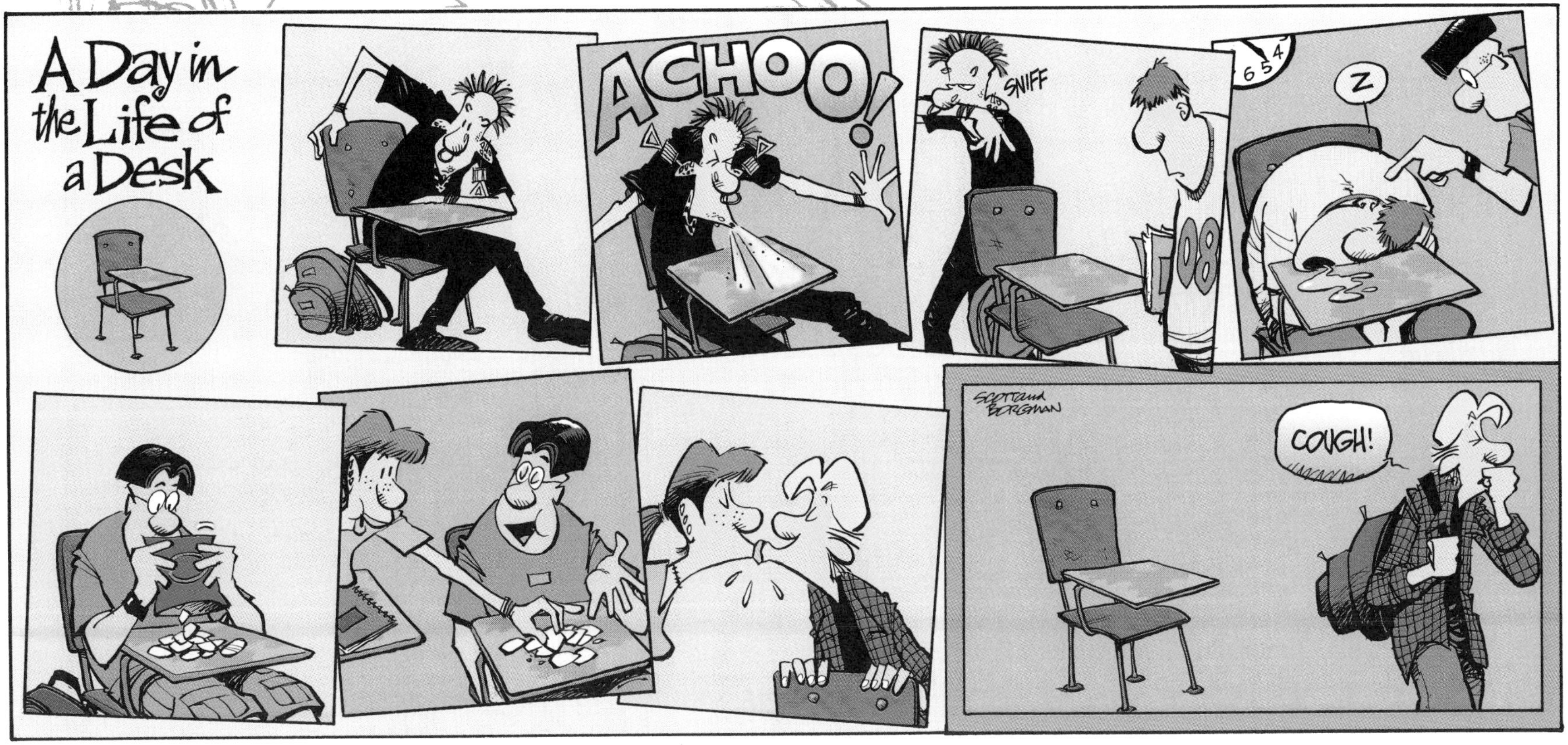

A Day in the Life of a Desk
ACHOO!
SNIFF
6 5 4
08
Z
COUGH!

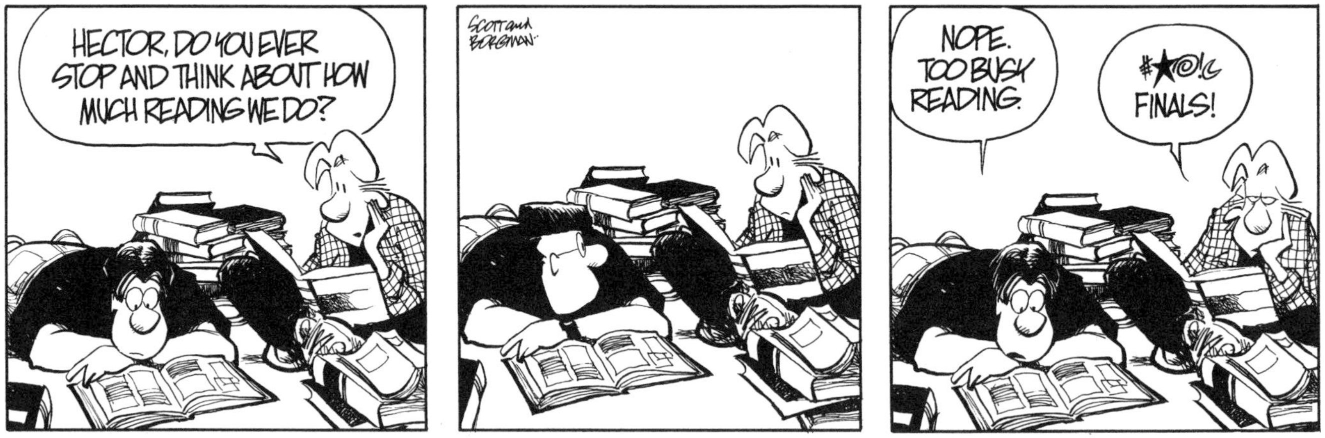
HECTOR, DO YOU EVER STOP AND THINK ABOUT HOW MUCH READING WE DO?
NOPE. TOO BUSY READING.
#★@!& FINALS!

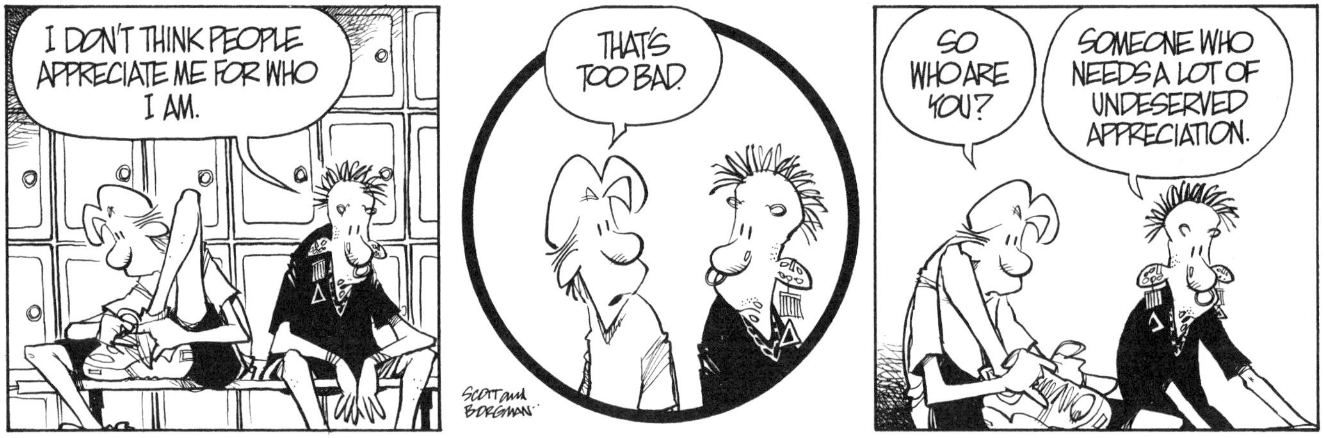
I DON'T THINK PEOPLE APPRECIATE ME FOR WHO I AM.
THAT'S TOO BAD.
SO WHO ARE YOU?
SOMEONE WHO NEEDS A LOT OF UNDESERVED APPRECIATION.

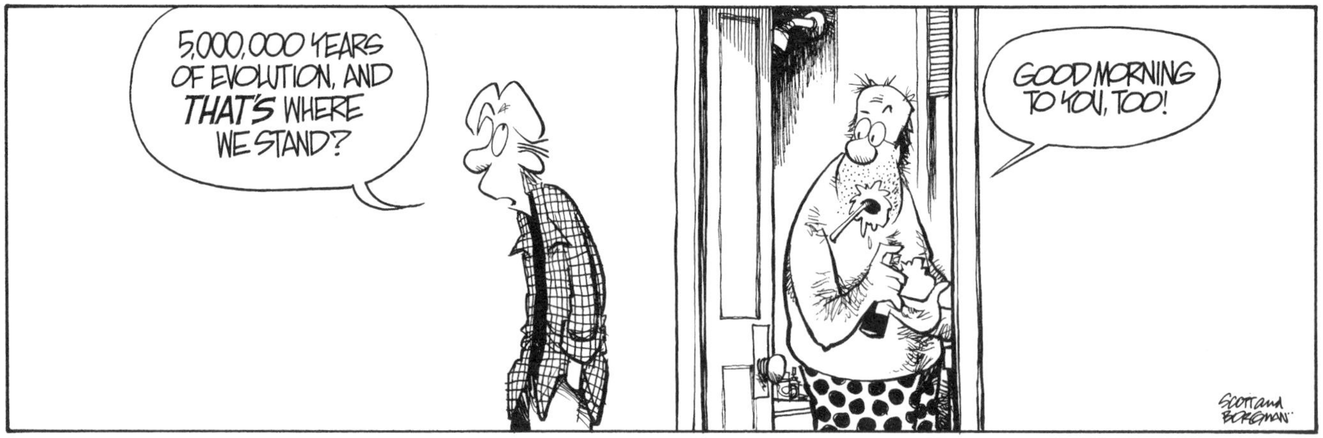
5,000,000 YEARS OF EVOLUTION, AND ***THAT'S*** WHERE WE STAND?
GOOD MORNING TO YOU, TOO!

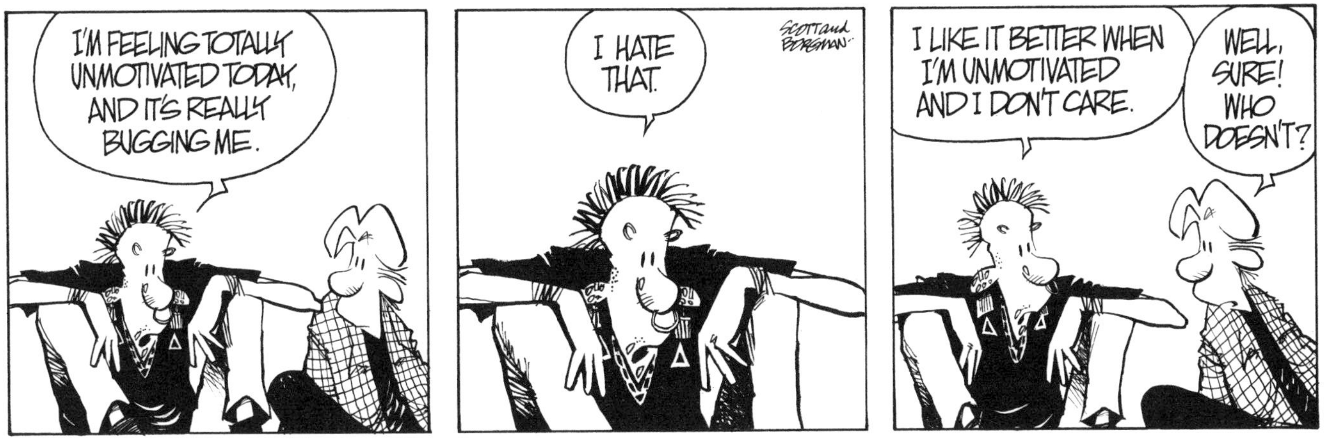
I'M FEELING TOTALLY UNMOTIVATED TODAY, AND IT'S REALLY BUGGING ME.
I HATE THAT.
SCOTT and BORGMAN
I LIKE IT BETTER WHEN I'M UNMOTIVATED AND I DON'T CARE.
WELL, SURE! WHO DOESN'T?

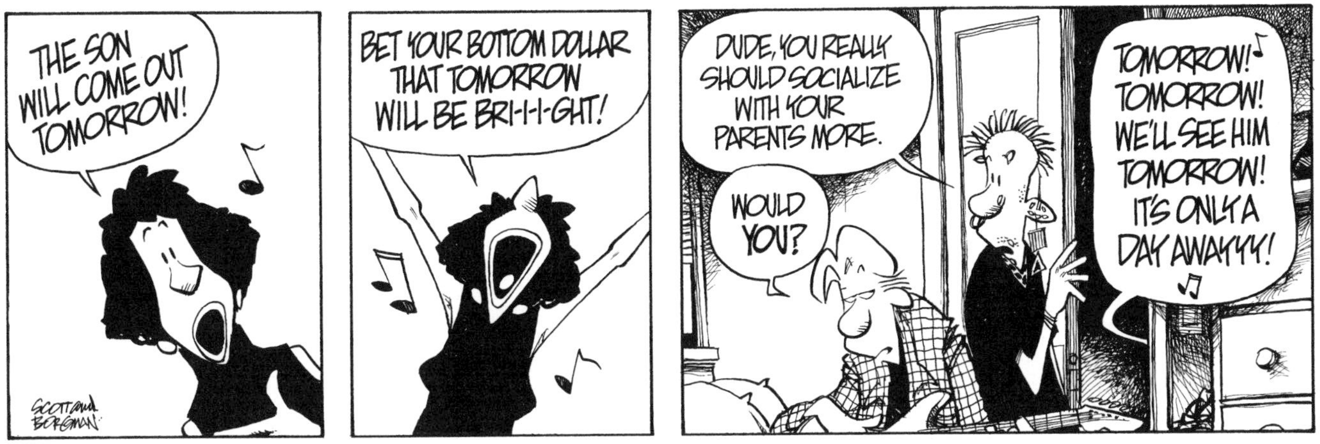
THE SON WILL COME OUT TOMORROW!
SCOTT and BORGMAN
BET YOUR BOTTOM DOLLAR THAT TOMORROW WILL BE BRI-I-I-GHT!
DUDE, YOU REALLY SHOULD SOCIALIZE WITH YOUR PARENTS MORE.
WOULD YOU?
TOMORROW! TOMORROW! WE'LL SEE HIM TOMORROW! IT'S ONLY A DAY AWAYYY!

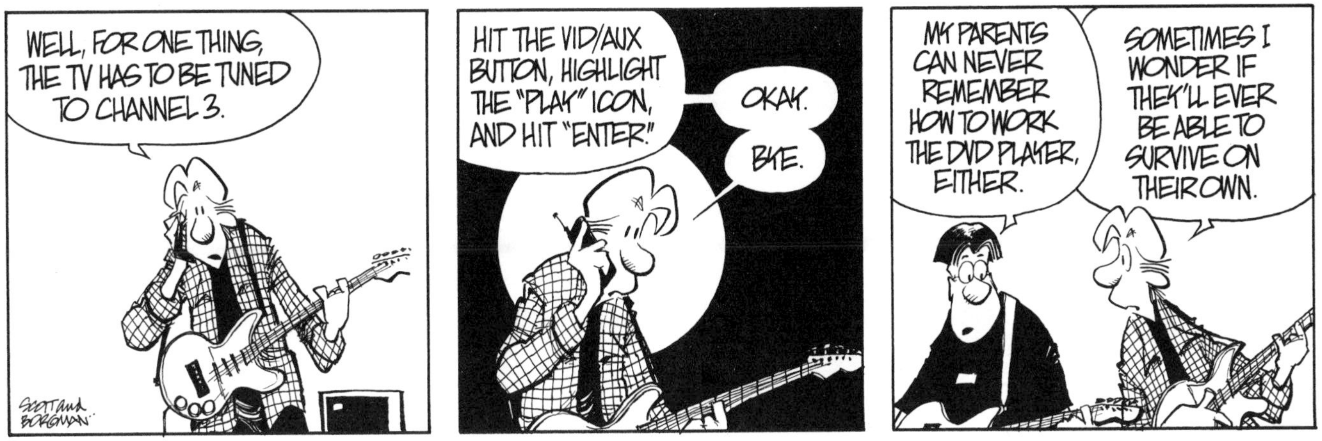
WELL, FOR ONE THING, THE TV HAS TO BE TUNED TO CHANNEL 3.
SCOTT and BORGMAN
HIT THE VID/AUX BUTTON, HIGHLIGHT THE "PLAY" ICON, AND HIT "ENTER."
OKAY.
BYE.
MY PARENTS CAN NEVER REMEMBER HOW TO WORK THE DVD PLAYER, EITHER.
SOMETIMES I WONDER IF THEY'LL EVER BE ABLE TO SURVIVE ON THEIR OWN.

Zits

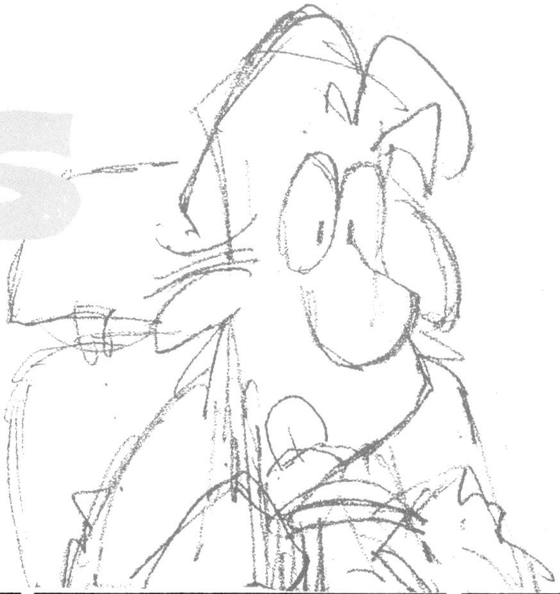

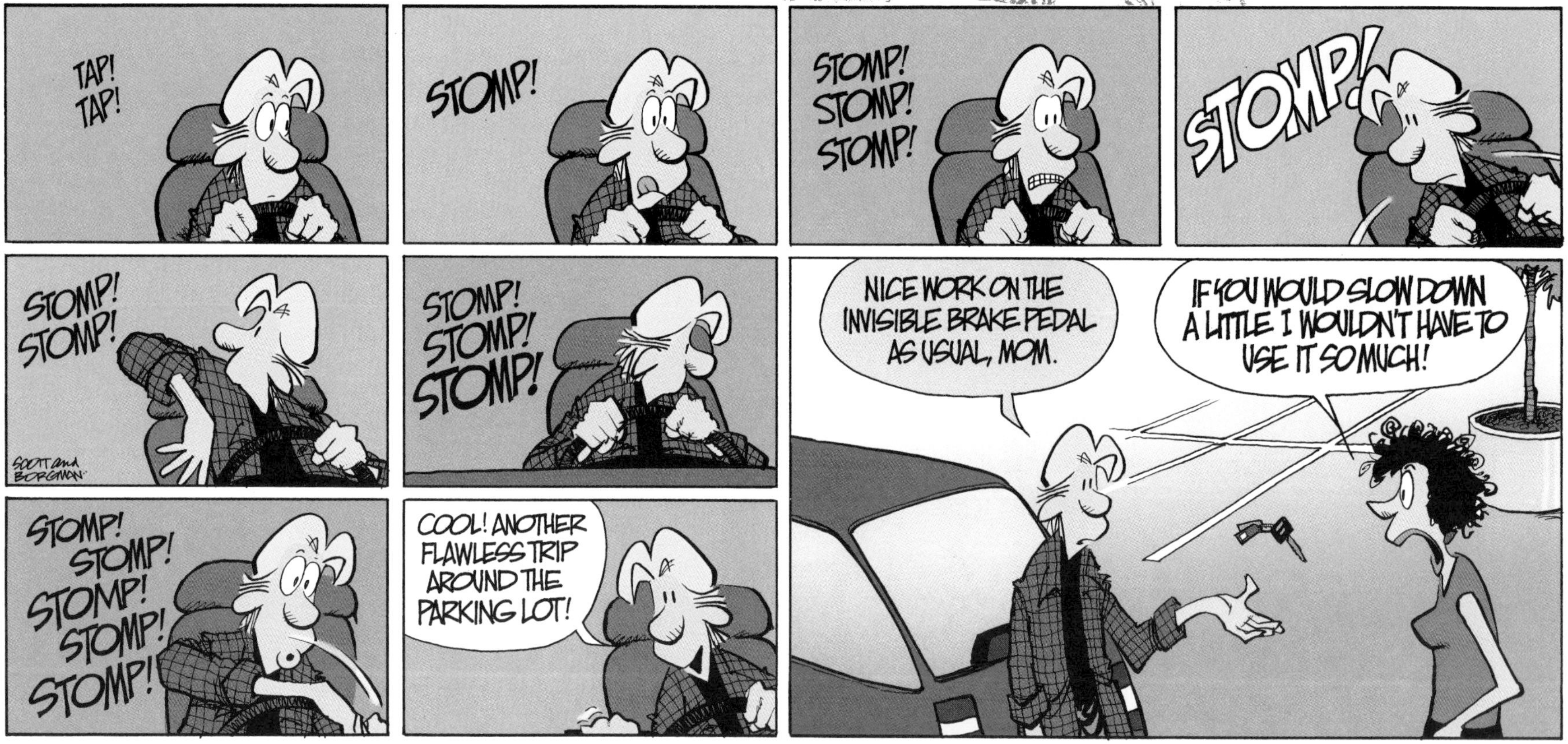

TAP! TAP!
STOMP!
STOMP! STOMP! STOMP!
STOMP!
STOMP! STOMP!
SCOTT AND BORGMAN
STOMP! STOMP! STOMP!
STOMP! STOMP! STOMP! STOMP! STOMP!
COOL! ANOTHER FLAWLESS TRIP AROUND THE PARKING LOT!
NICE WORK ON THE INVISIBLE BRAKE PEDAL AS USUAL, MOM.
IF YOU WOULD SLOW DOWN A LITTLE I WOULDN'T HAVE TO USE IT SO MUCH!

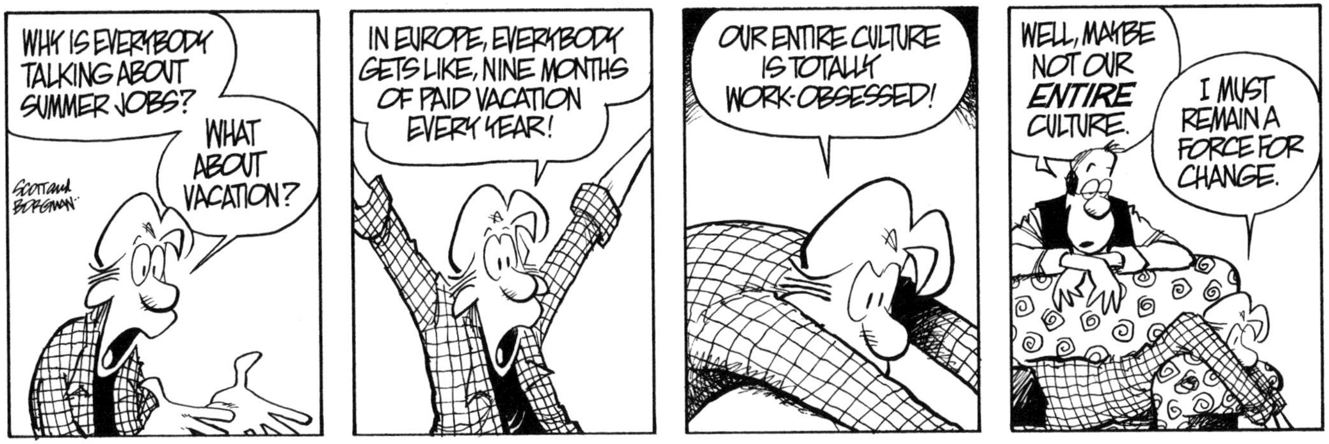
WHY IS EVERYBODY TALKING ABOUT SUMMER JOBS?
WHAT ABOUT VACATION?
SCOTT AND BORGMAN
IN EUROPE, EVERYBODY GETS LIKE, NINE MONTHS OF PAID VACATION EVERY YEAR!
OUR ENTIRE CULTURE IS TOTALLY WORK-OBSESSED!
WELL, MAYBE NOT OUR ENTIRE CULTURE.
I MUST REMAIN A FORCE FOR CHANGE.

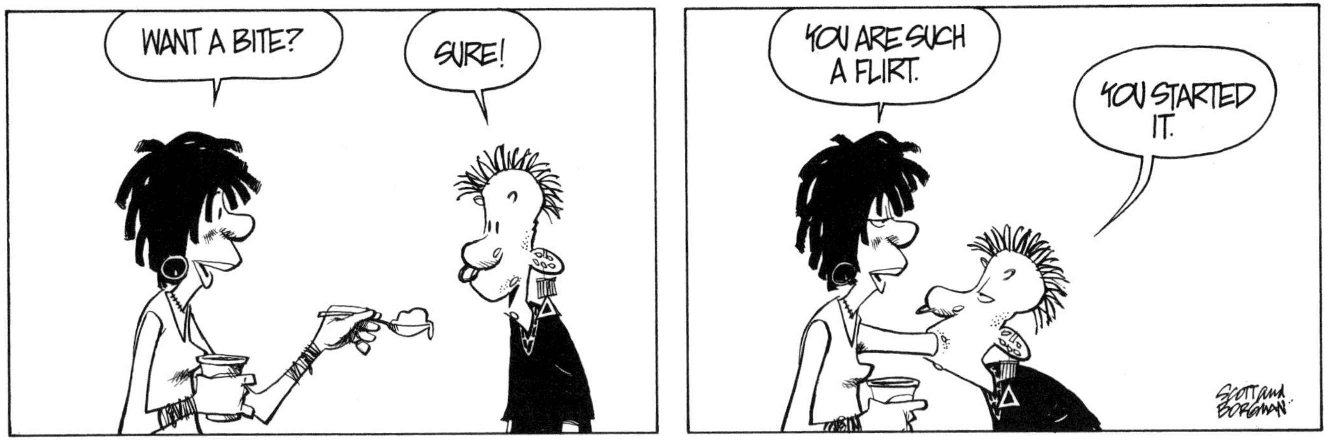
WANT A BITE?
SURE!
YOU ARE SUCH A FLIRT.
YOU STARTED IT.
SCOTT AND BORGMAN

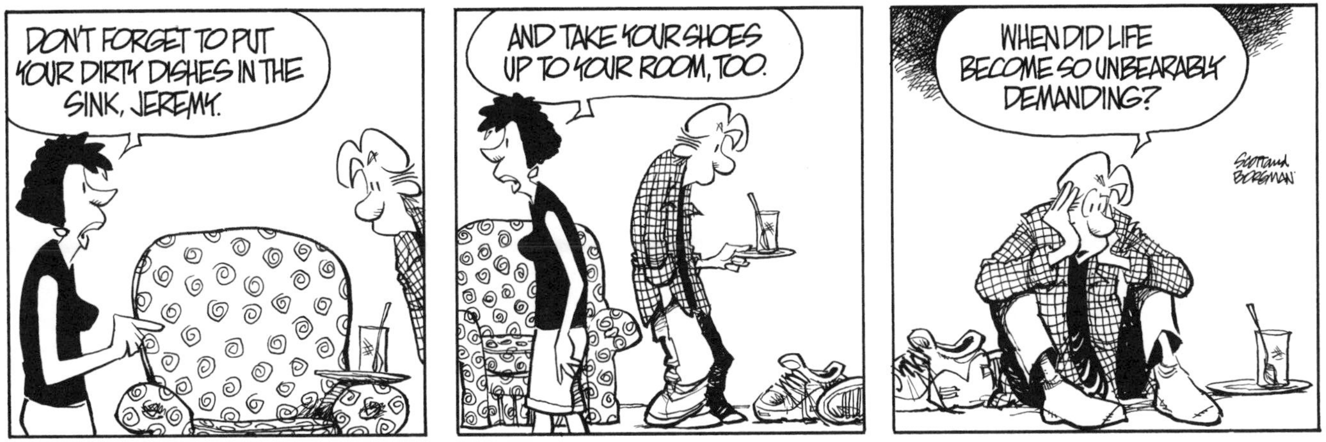
DON'T FORGET TO PUT YOUR DIRTY DISHES IN THE SINK, JEREMY.
AND TAKE YOUR SHOES UP TO YOUR ROOM, TOO.
WHEN DID LIFE BECOME SO UNBEARABLY DEMANDING?
SCOTT AND BORGMAN

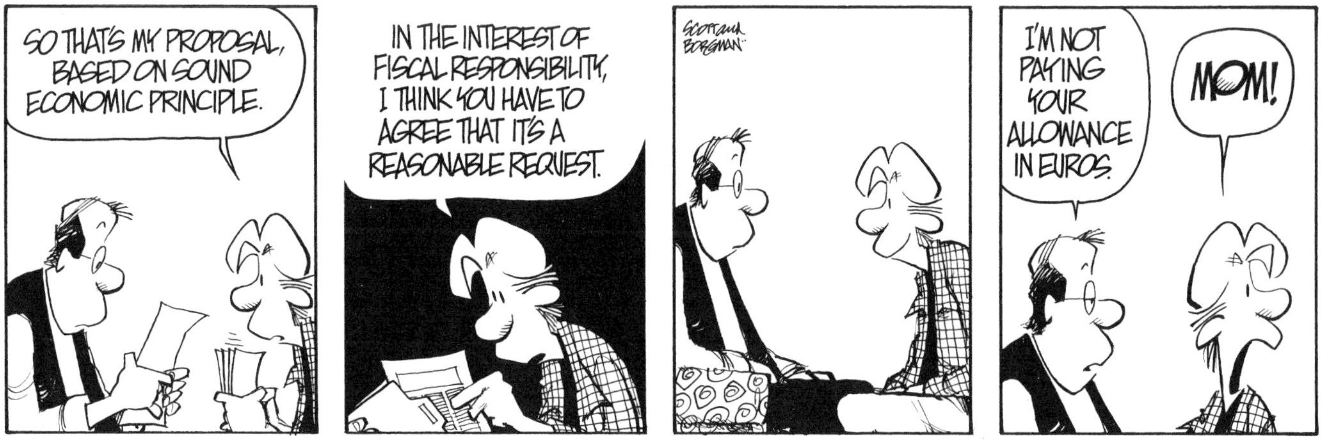
SO THAT'S MY PROPOSAL, BASED ON SOUND ECONOMIC PRINCIPLE.
IN THE INTEREST OF FISCAL RESPONSIBILITY, I THINK YOU HAVE TO AGREE THAT IT'S A REASONABLE REQUEST.
I'M NOT PAYING YOUR ALLOWANCE IN EUROS.
MOM!

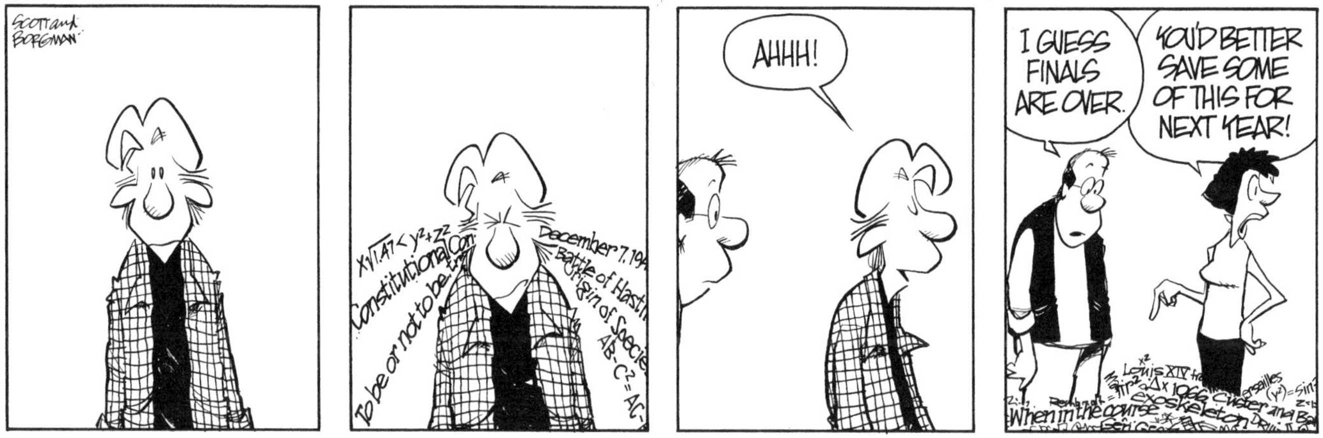
AHHH!
I GUESS FINALS ARE OVER.
YOU'D BETTER SAVE SOME OF THIS FOR NEXT YEAR!

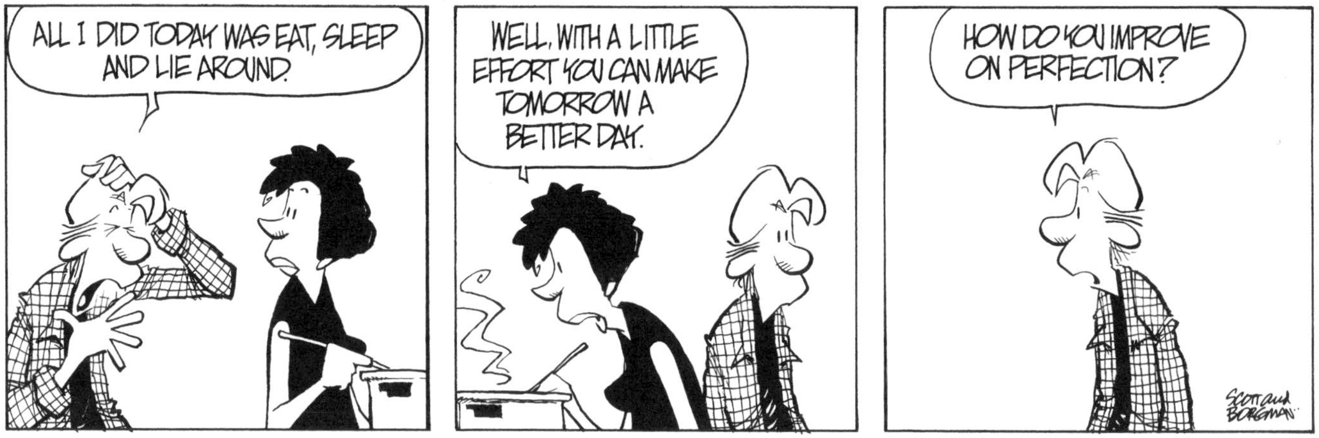
ALL I DID TODAY WAS EAT, SLEEP AND LIE AROUND.
WELL, WITH A LITTLE EFFORT YOU CAN MAKE TOMORROW A BETTER DAY.
HOW DO YOU IMPROVE ON PERFECTION?

Zits

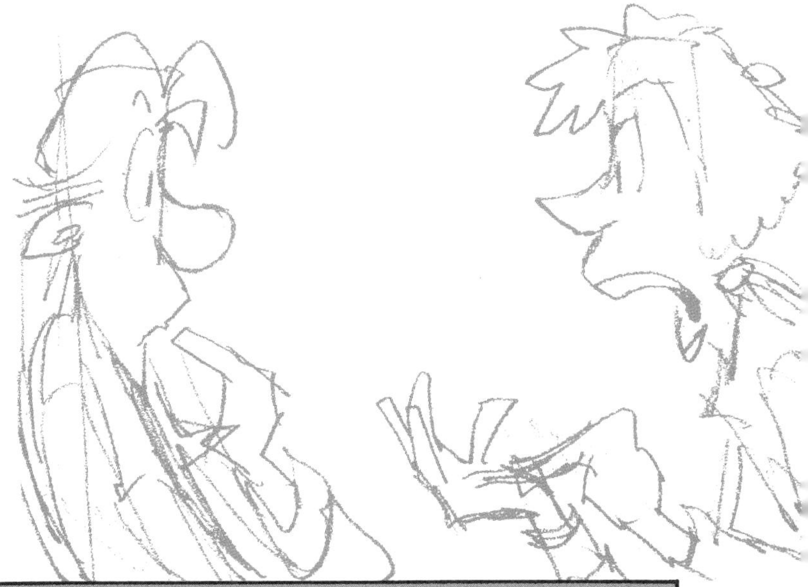

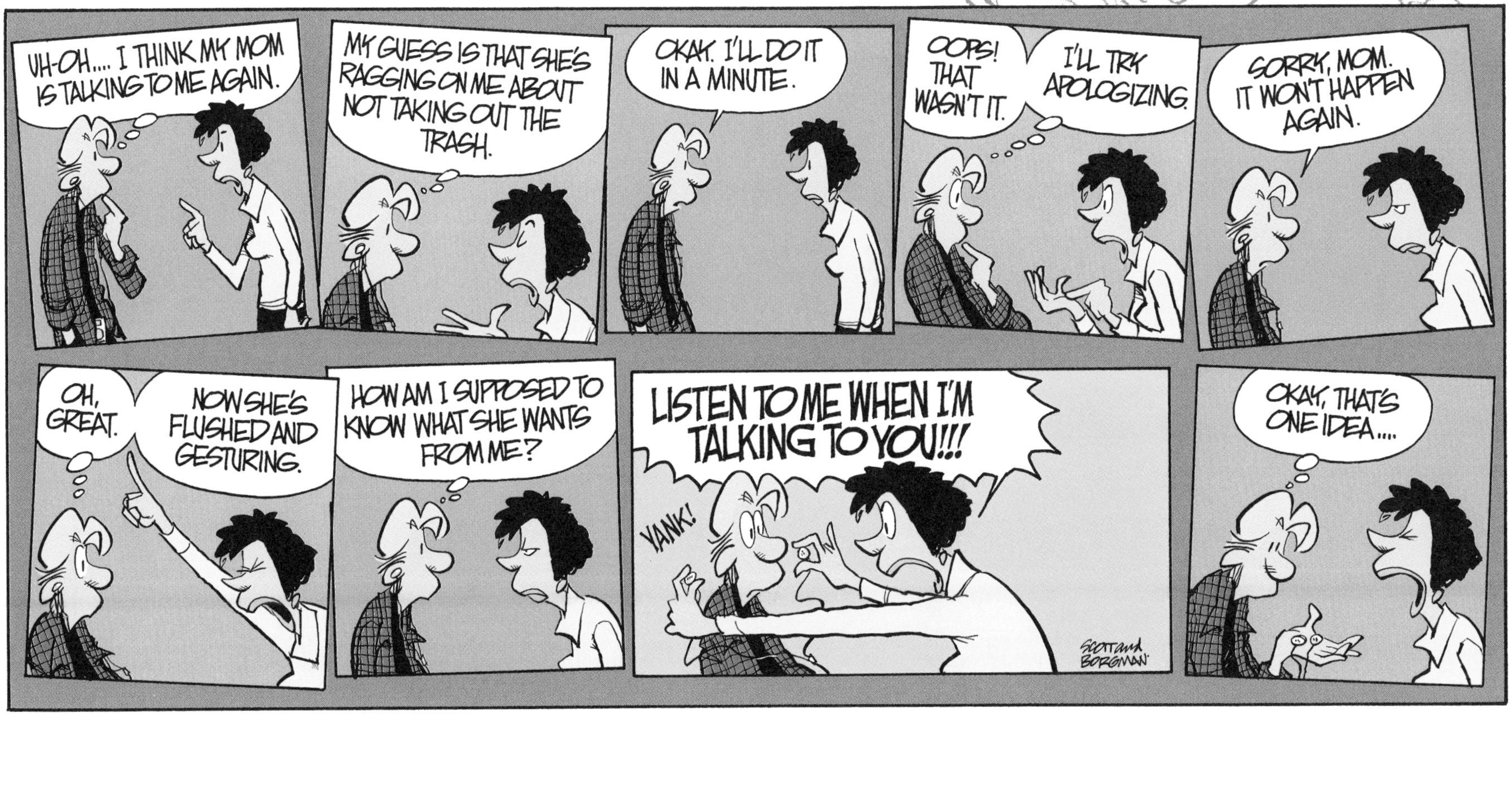
UH-OH.... I THINK MY MOM IS TALKING TO ME AGAIN.
MY GUESS IS THAT SHE'S RAGGING ON ME ABOUT NOT TAKING OUT THE TRASH.
OKAY. I'LL DO IT IN A MINUTE.
OOPS! THAT WASN'T IT.
I'LL TRY APOLOGIZING.
SORRY, MOM. IT WON'T HAPPEN AGAIN.
OH, GREAT.
NOW SHE'S FLUSHED AND GESTURING.
HOW AM I SUPPOSED TO KNOW WHAT SHE WANTS FROM ME?
LISTEN TO ME WHEN I'M TALKING TO YOU!!!
YANK!
SCOTT AND BORGMAN
OKAY, THAT'S ONE IDEA....

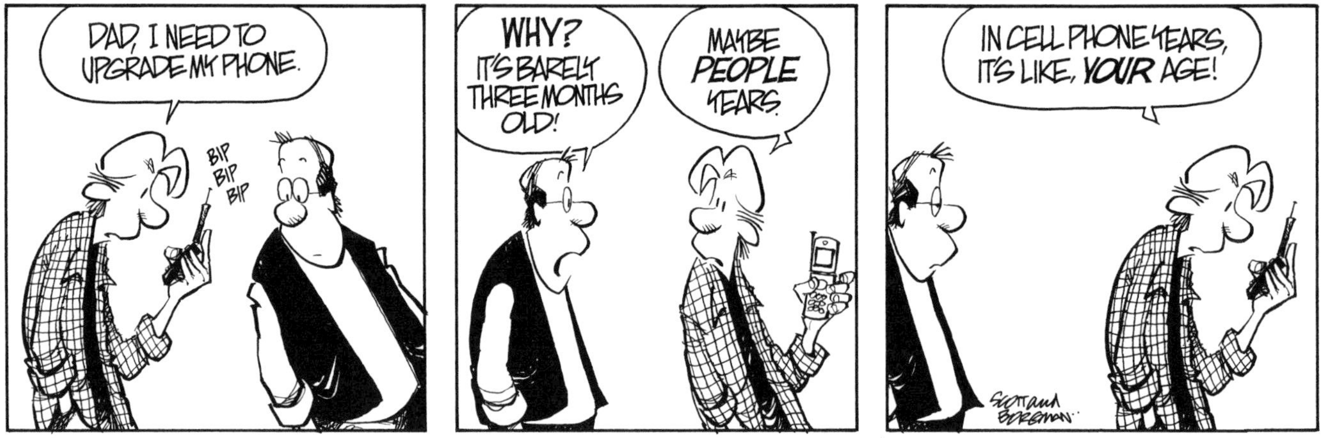
DAD, I NEED TO UPGRADE MY PHONE.
BIP BIP BIP
WHY? IT'S BARELY THREE MONTHS OLD!
MAYBE PEOPLE YEARS.
IN CELL PHONE YEARS, IT'S LIKE, YOUR AGE!
SCOTT and BORGMAN

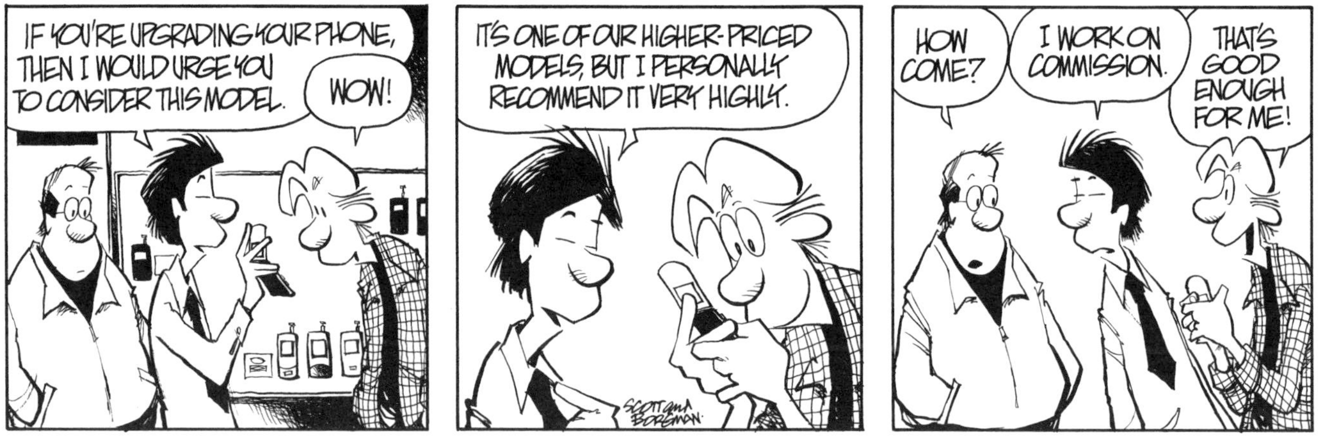
IF YOU'RE UPGRADING YOUR PHONE, THEN I WOULD URGE YOU TO CONSIDER THIS MODEL.
WOW!
IT'S ONE OF OUR HIGHER-PRICED MODELS, BUT I PERSONALLY RECOMMEND IT VERY HIGHLY.
SCOTT and BORGMAN
HOW COME?
I WORK ON COMMISSION.
THAT'S GOOD ENOUGH FOR ME!

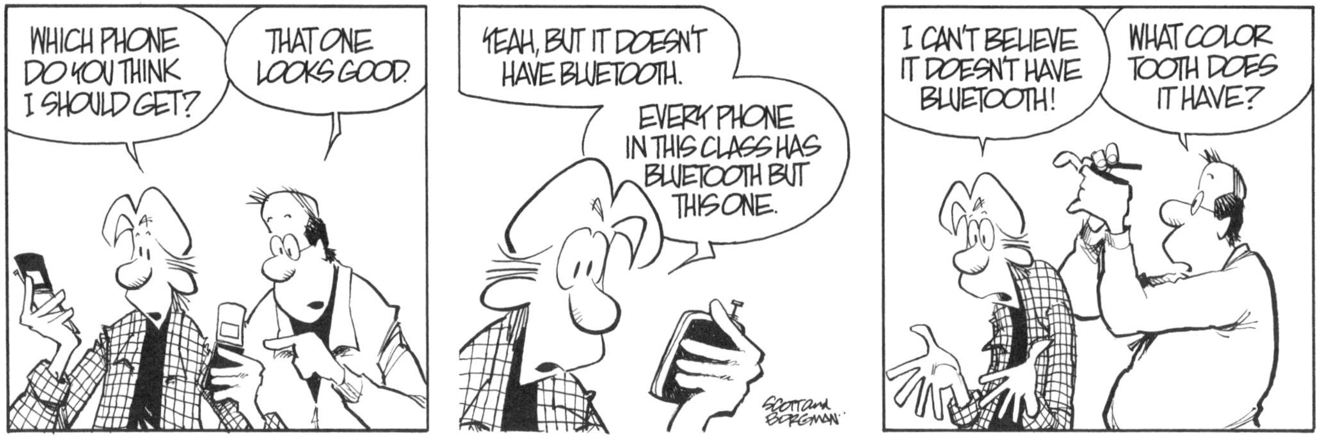
WHICH PHONE DO YOU THINK I SHOULD GET?
THAT ONE LOOKS GOOD.
YEAH, BUT IT DOESN'T HAVE BLUETOOTH.
EVERY PHONE IN THIS CLASS HAS BLUETOOTH BUT THIS ONE.
SCOTT and BORGMAN
I CAN'T BELIEVE IT DOESN'T HAVE BLUETOOTH!
WHAT COLOR TOOTH DOES IT HAVE?

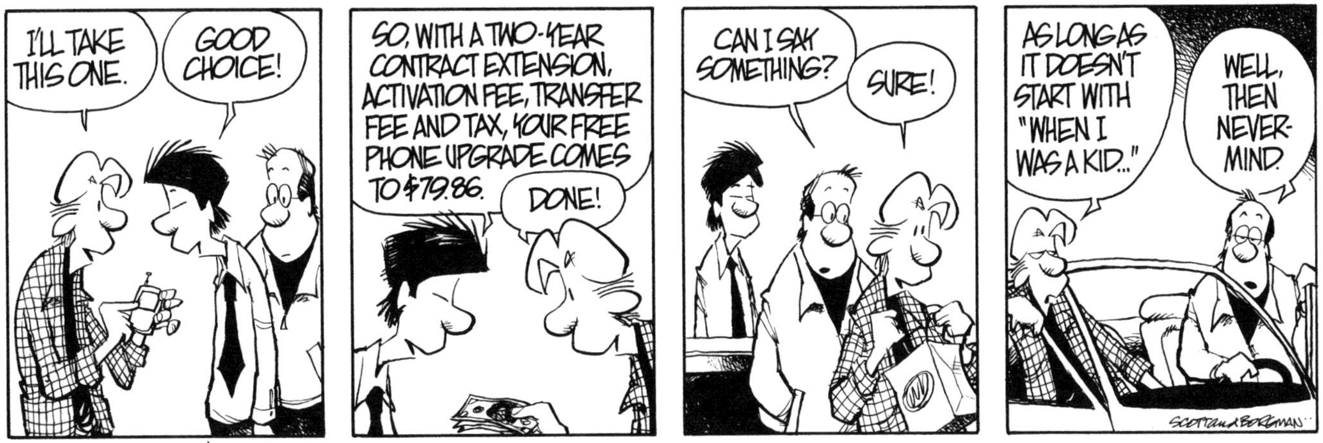
I'LL TAKE THIS ONE.
GOOD CHOICE!
SO, WITH A TWO-YEAR CONTRACT EXTENSION, ACTIVATION FEE, TRANSFER FEE AND TAX, YOUR FREE PHONE UPGRADE COMES TO $79.86.
DONE!
CAN I SAY SOMETHING?
SURE!
AS LONG AS IT DOESN'T START WITH "WHEN I WAS A KID..."
WELL, THEN NEVERMIND.

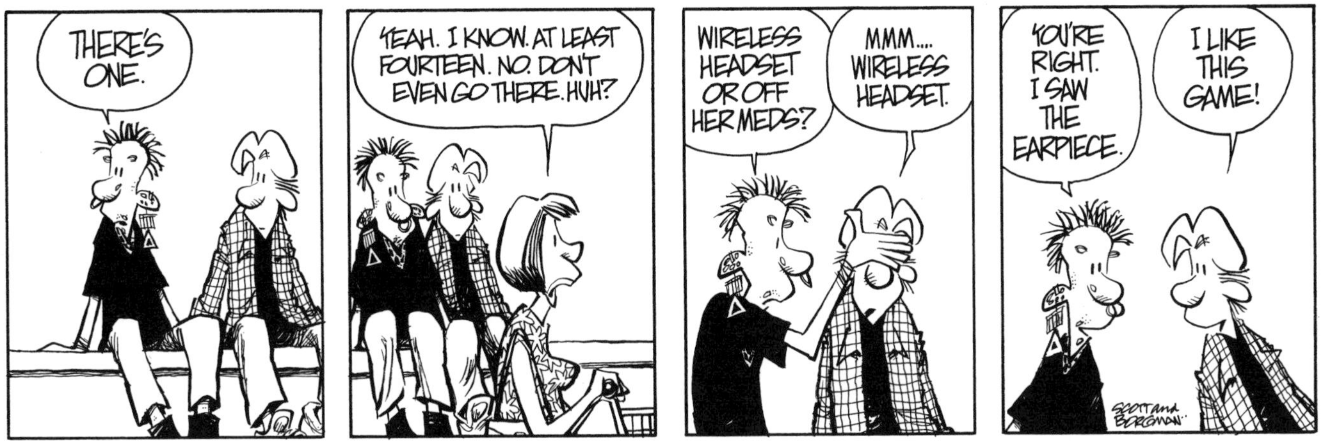
THERE'S ONE.
YEAH. I KNOW. AT LEAST FOURTEEN. NO. DON'T EVEN GO THERE. HUH?
WIRELESS HEADSET OR OFF HER MEDS?
MMM.... WIRELESS HEADSET.
YOU'RE RIGHT. I SAW THE EARPIECE.
I LIKE THIS GAME!

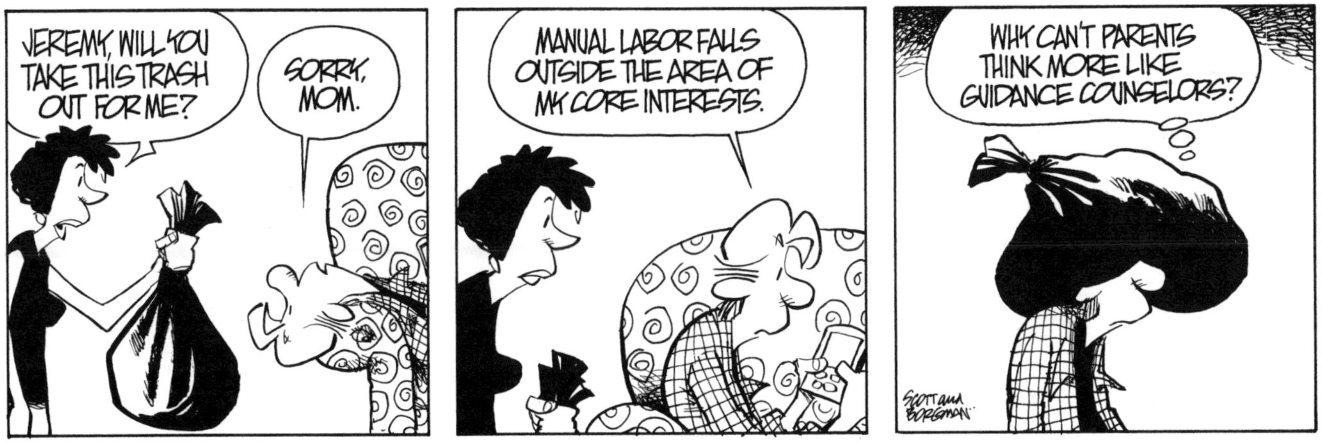
JEREMY, WILL YOU TAKE THIS TRASH OUT FOR ME?
SORRY, MOM.
MANUAL LABOR FALLS OUTSIDE THE AREA OF MY CORE INTERESTS.
WHY CAN'T PARENTS THINK MORE LIKE GUIDANCE COUNSELORS?

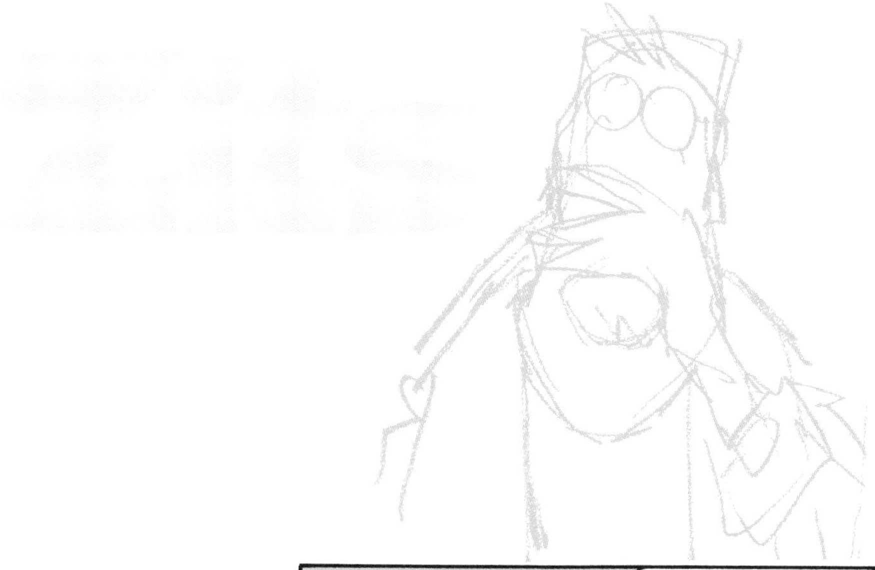

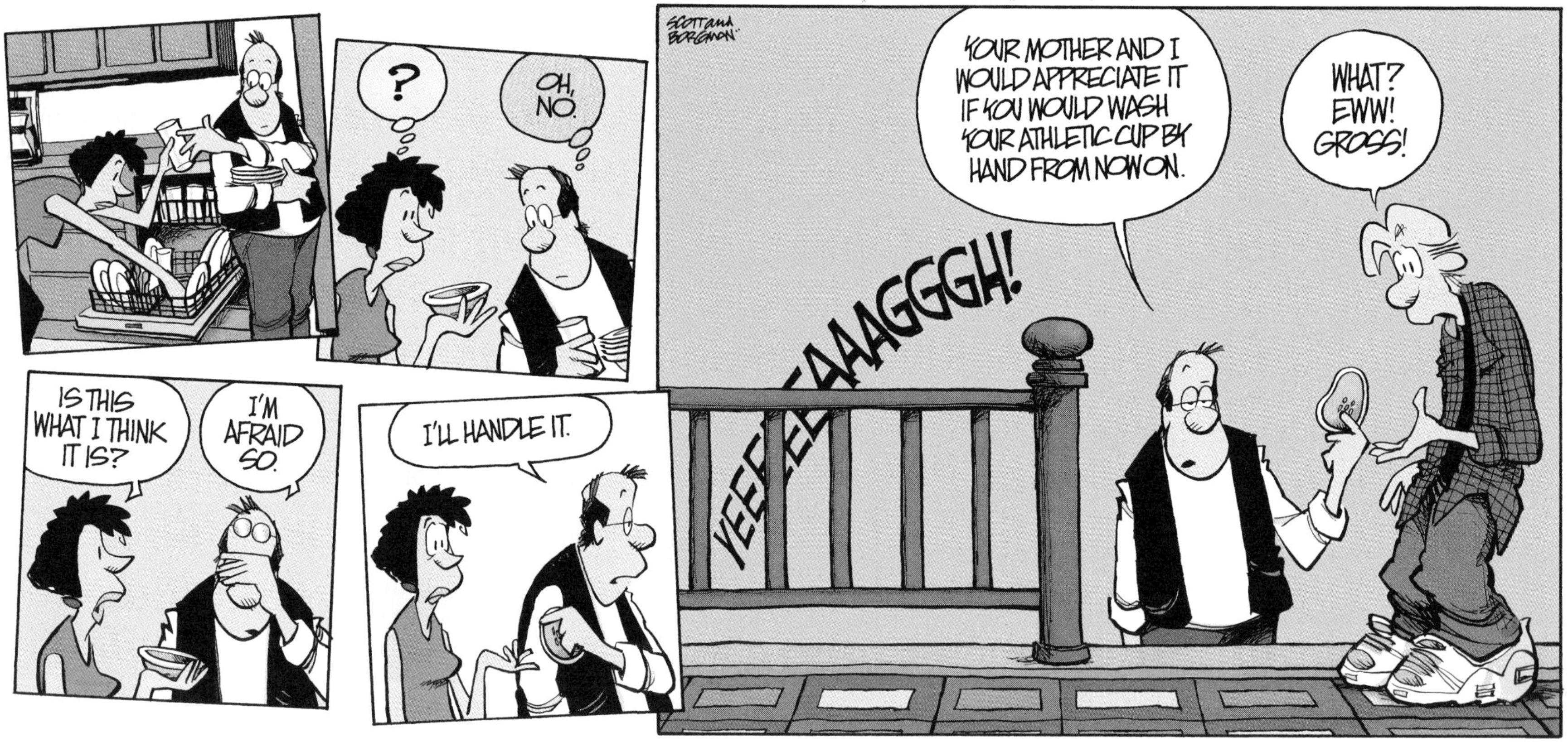

?
OH, NO.
IS THIS WHAT I THINK IT IS?
I'M AFRAID SO.
I'LL HANDLE IT.
YOUR MOTHER AND I WOULD APPRECIATE IT IF YOU WOULD WASH YOUR ATHLETIC CUP BY HAND FROM NOW ON.
YEEEEEEAAAGGGH!
WHAT? EWW! GROSS!

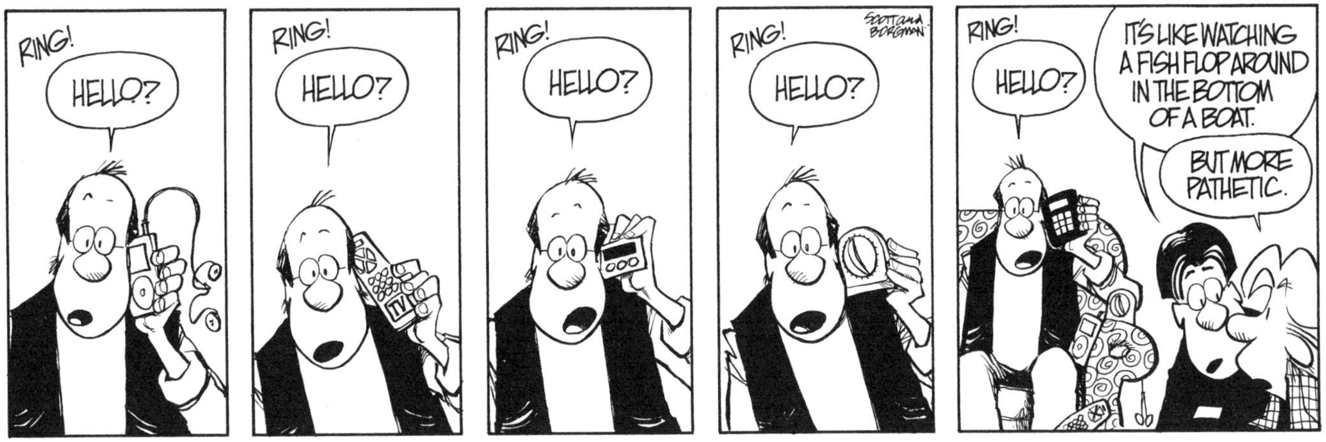
RING!
HELLO?
RING!
HELLO?
RING!
HELLO?
RING!
HELLO?
RING!
HELLO?
IT'S LIKE WATCHING A FISH FLOP AROUND IN THE BOTTOM OF A BOAT.
BUT MORE PATHETIC.

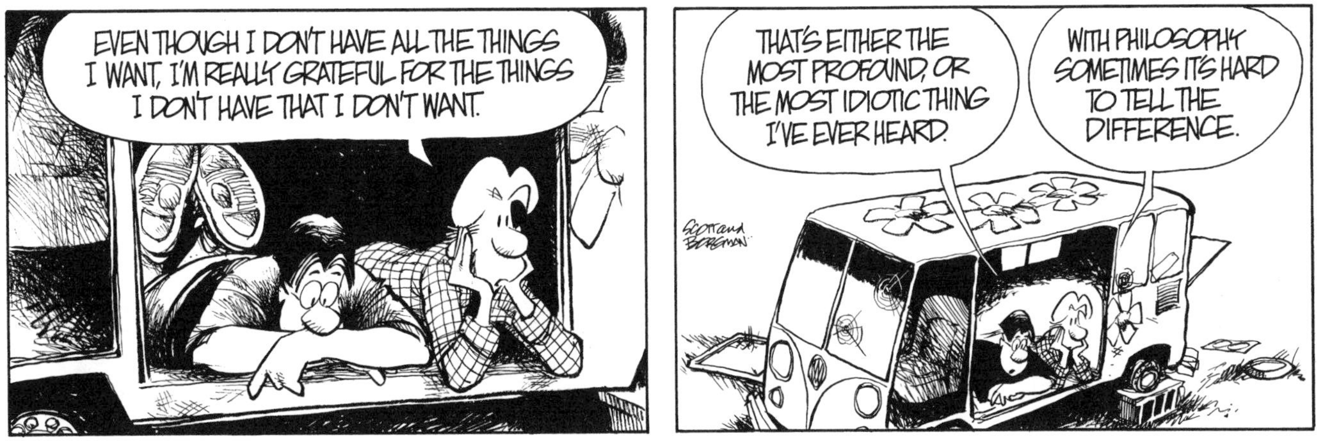
EVEN THOUGH I DON'T HAVE ALL THE THINGS I WANT, I'M REALLY GRATEFUL FOR THE THINGS I DON'T HAVE THAT I DON'T WANT.
THAT'S EITHER THE MOST PROFOUND, OR THE MOST IDIOTIC THING I'VE EVER HEARD.
WITH PHILOSOPHY SOMETIMES IT'S HARD TO TELL THE DIFFERENCE.

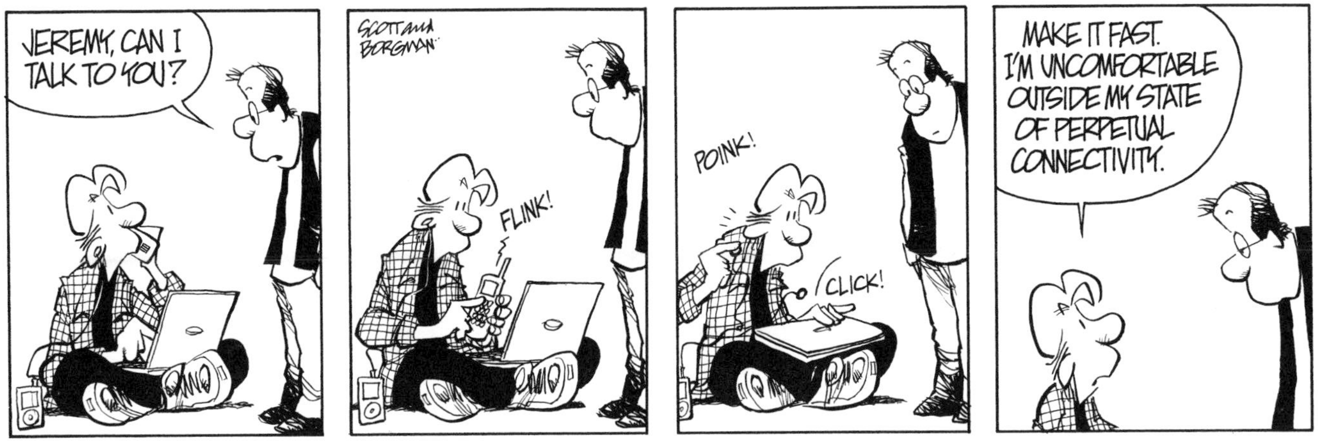
JEREMY, CAN I TALK TO YOU?
FLINK!
POINK!
CLICK!
MAKE IT FAST. I'M UNCOMFORTABLE OUTSIDE MY STATE OF PERPETUAL CONNECTIVITY.

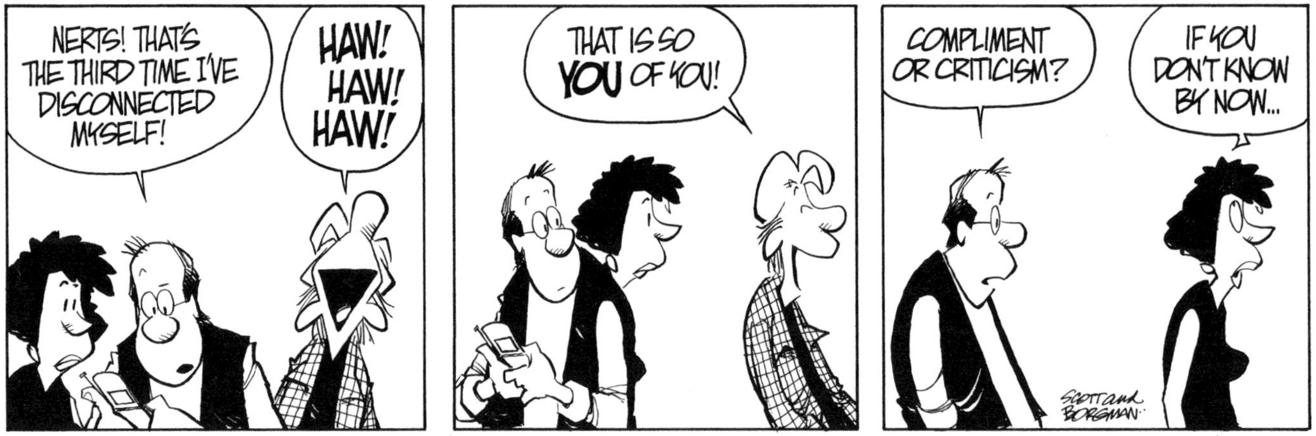
NERTS! THAT'S THE THIRD TIME I'VE DISCONNECTED MYSELF!
HAW! HAW! HAW!
THAT IS SO YOU OF YOU!
COMPLIMENT OR CRITICISM?
IF YOU DON'T KNOW BY NOW...
SCOTT and BORGMAN

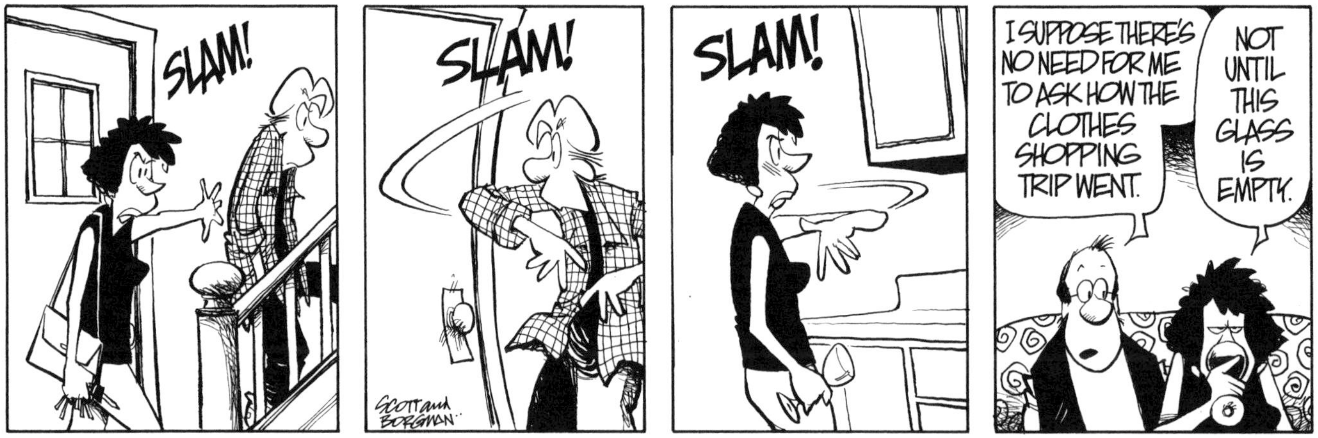
SLAM!
SLAM!
SCOTT and BORGMAN
SLAM!
I SUPPOSE THERE'S NO NEED FOR ME TO ASK HOW THE CLOTHES SHOPPING TRIP WENT.
NOT UNTIL THIS GLASS IS EMPTY.

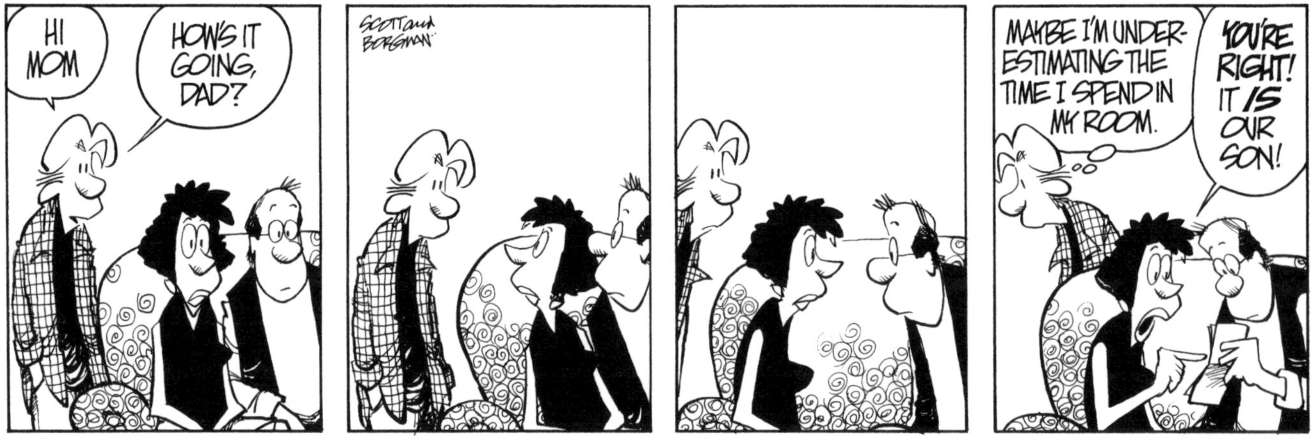
HI MOM
HOW'S IT GOING, DAD?
SCOTT and BORGMAN
MAYBE I'M UNDER-ESTIMATING THE TIME I SPEND IN MY ROOM.
YOU'RE RIGHT! IT IS OUR SON!

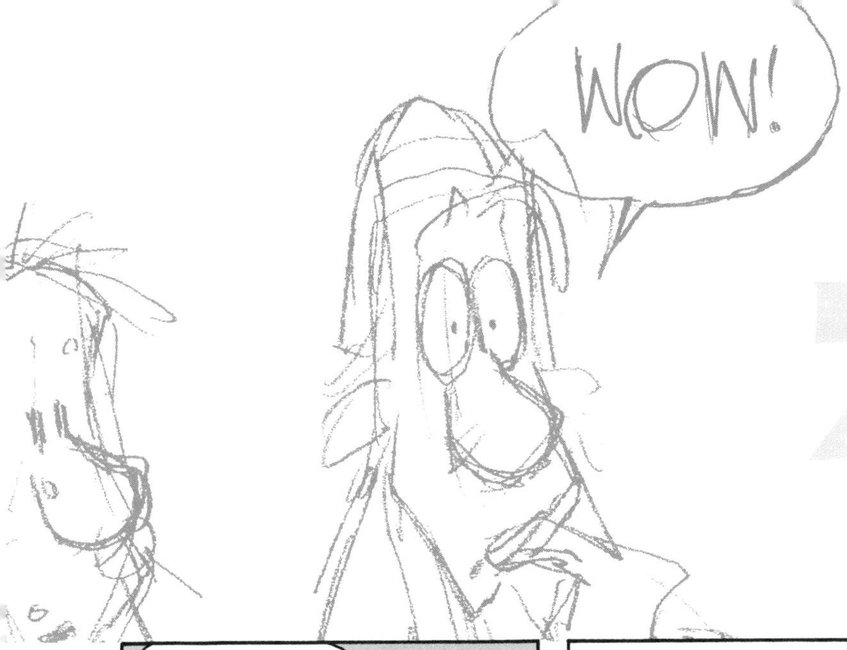
WOW!

Zits

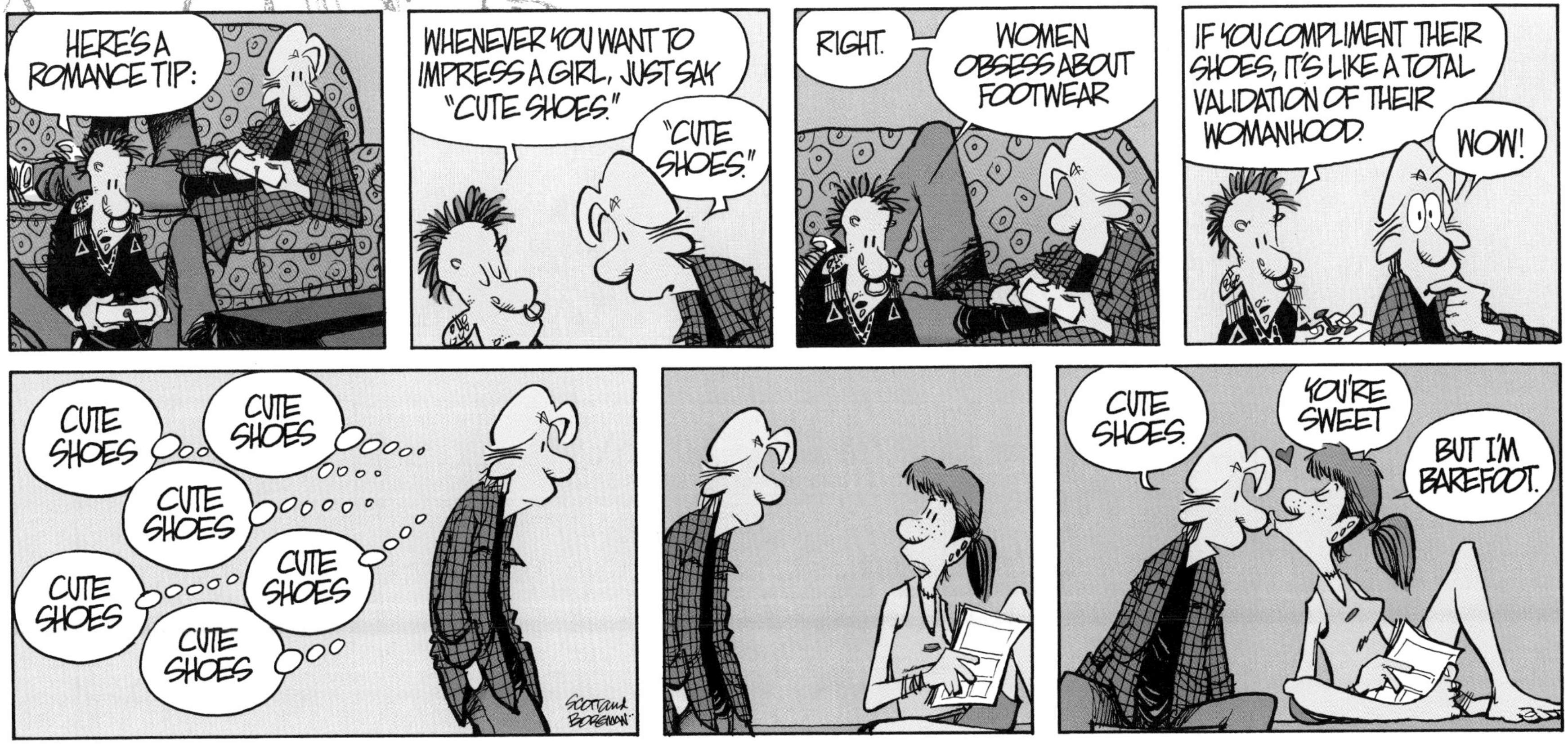
HERE'S A ROMANCE TIP:
WHENEVER YOU WANT TO IMPRESS A GIRL, JUST SAY "CUTE SHOES."
"CUTE SHOES."
RIGHT.
WOMEN OBSESS ABOUT FOOTWEAR
IF YOU COMPLIMENT THEIR SHOES, IT'S LIKE A TOTAL VALIDATION OF THEIR WOMANHOOD.
WOW!
CUTE SHOES
CUTE SHOES
CUTE SHOES
CUTE SHOES
CUTE SHOES
CUTE SHOES
CUTE SHOES.
YOU'RE SWEET
BUT I'M BAREFOOT.

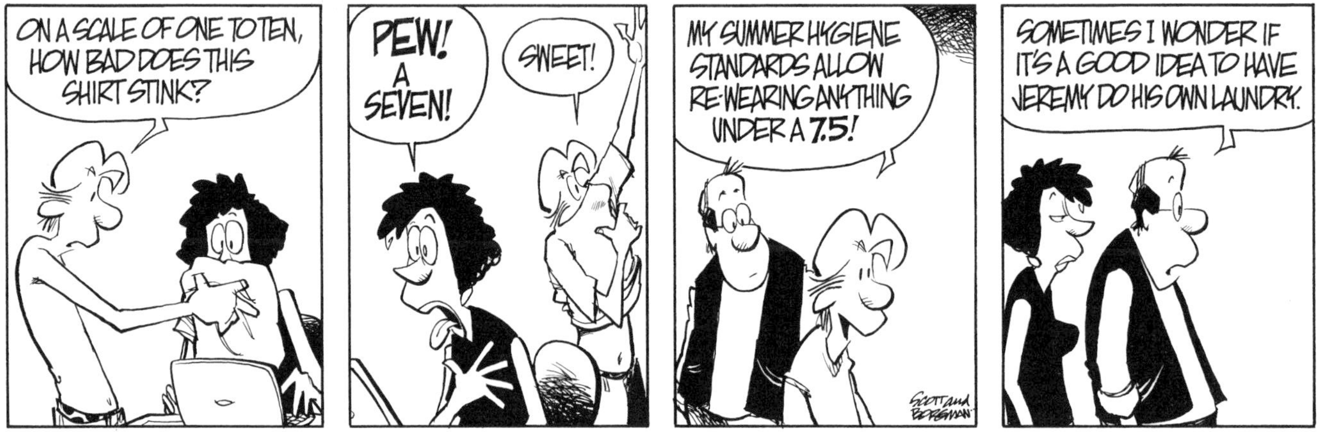
ON A SCALE OF ONE TO TEN, HOW BAD DOES THIS SHIRT STINK?
PEW! A SEVEN!
SWEET!
MY SUMMER HYGIENE STANDARDS ALLOW RE-WEARING ANYTHING UNDER A 7.5!
SOMETIMES I WONDER IF IT'S A GOOD IDEA TO HAVE JEREMY DO HIS OWN LAUNDRY.

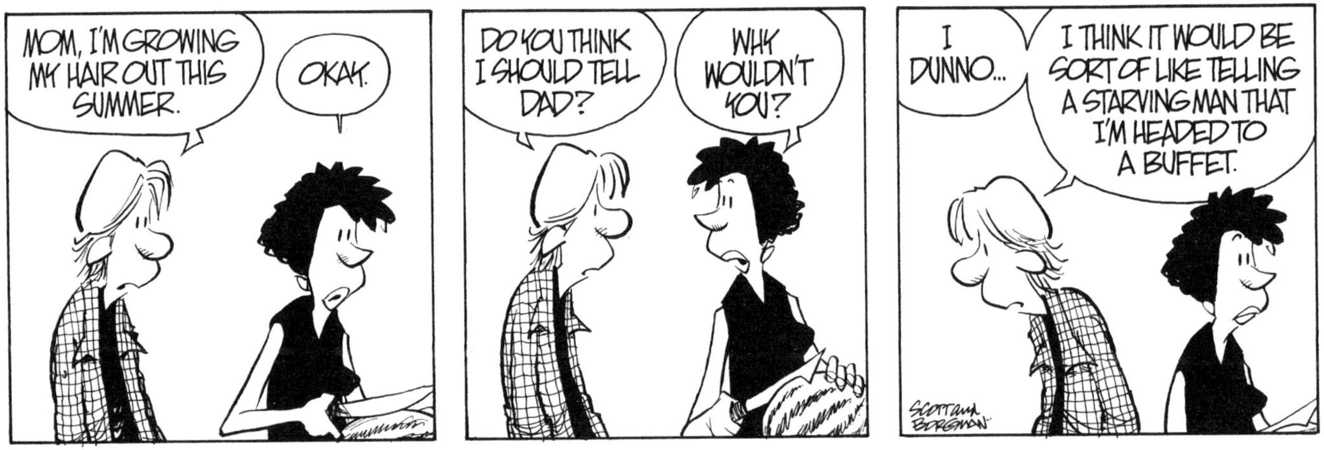
MOM, I'M GROWING MY HAIR OUT THIS SUMMER.
OKAY.
DO YOU THINK I SHOULD TELL DAD?
WHY WOULDN'T YOU?
I DUNNO...
I THINK IT WOULD BE SORT OF LIKE TELLING A STARVING MAN THAT I'M HEADED TO A BUFFET.

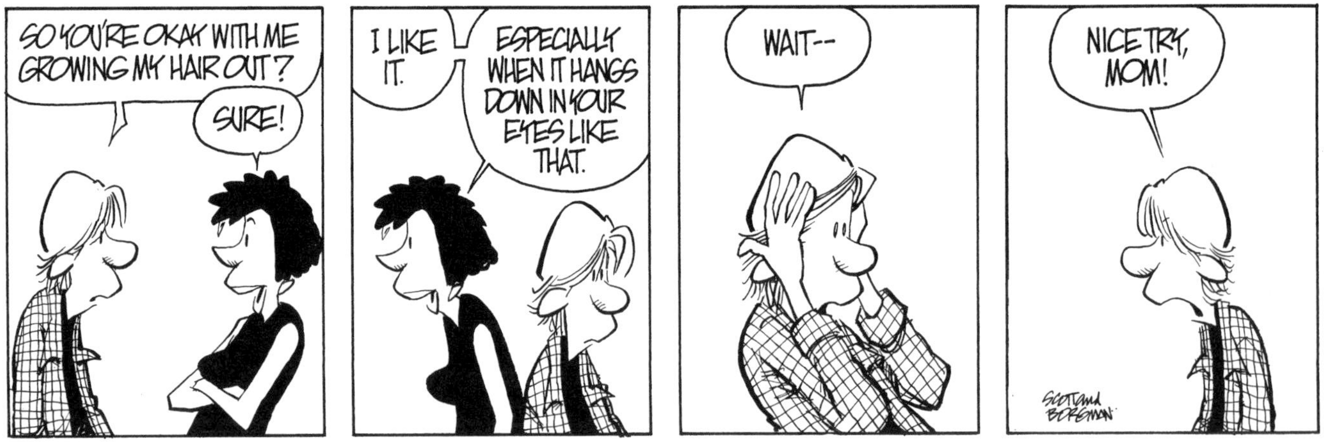
SO YOU'RE OKAY WITH ME GROWING MY HAIR OUT?
SURE!
I LIKE IT.
ESPECIALLY WHEN IT HANGS DOWN IN YOUR EYES LIKE THAT.
WAIT--
NICE TRY, MOM!

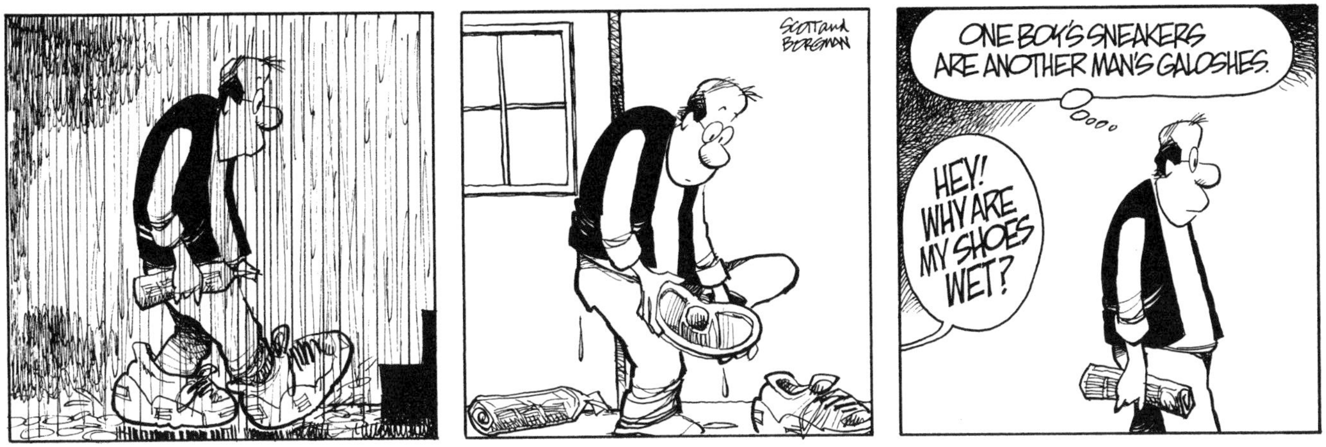
HEY! WHY ARE MY SHOES WET?
ONE BOY'S SNEAKERS ARE ANOTHER MAN'S GALOSHES.

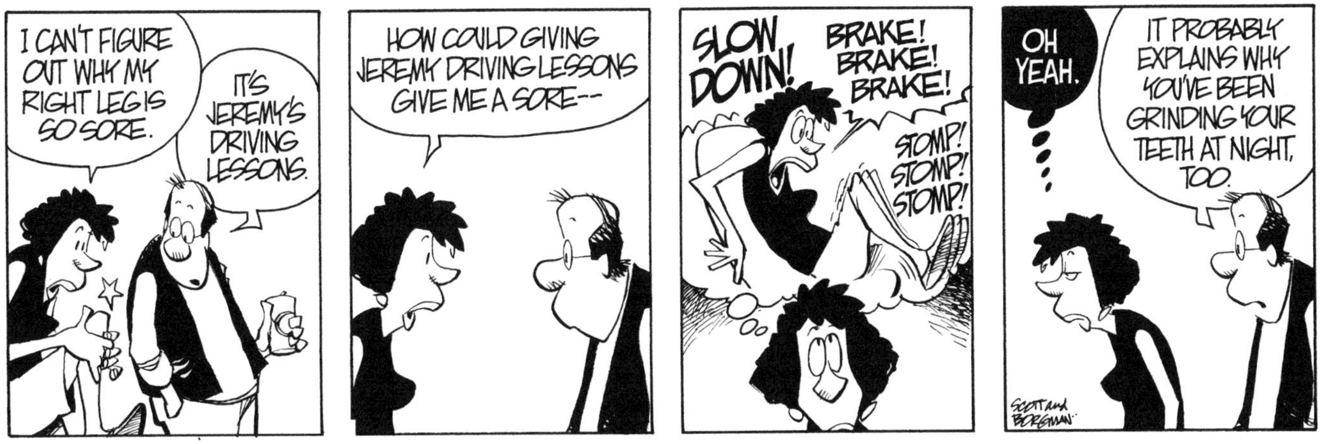
I CAN'T FIGURE OUT WHY MY RIGHT LEG IS SO SORE.
IT'S JEREMY'S DRIVING LESSONS.
HOW COULD GIVING JEREMY DRIVING LESSONS GIVE ME A SORE--
SLOW, DOWN!
BRAKE! BRAKE! BRAKE!
STOMP! STOMP! STOMP!
OH YEAH.
IT PROBABLY EXPLAINS WHY YOU'VE BEEN GRINDING YOUR TEETH AT NIGHT, TOO.

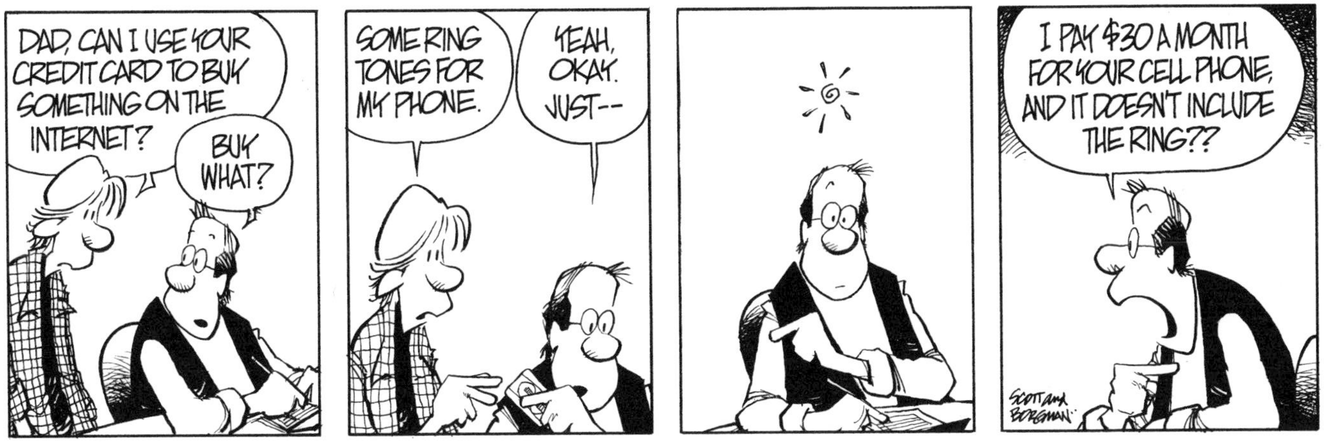
DAD, CAN I USE YOUR CREDIT CARD TO BUY SOMETHING ON THE INTERNET?
BUY WHAT?
SOME RING TONES FOR MY PHONE.
YEAH, OKAY. JUST--
I PAY $30 A MONTH FOR YOUR CELL PHONE, AND IT DOESN'T INCLUDE THE RING??

Zits

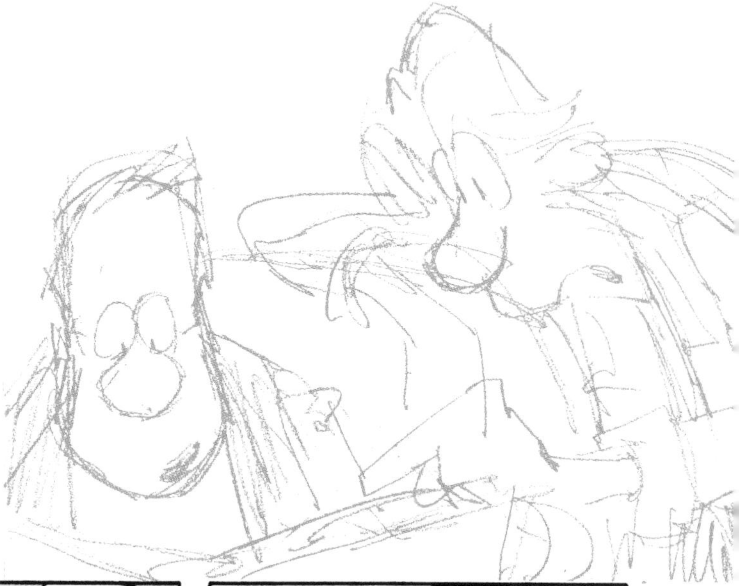

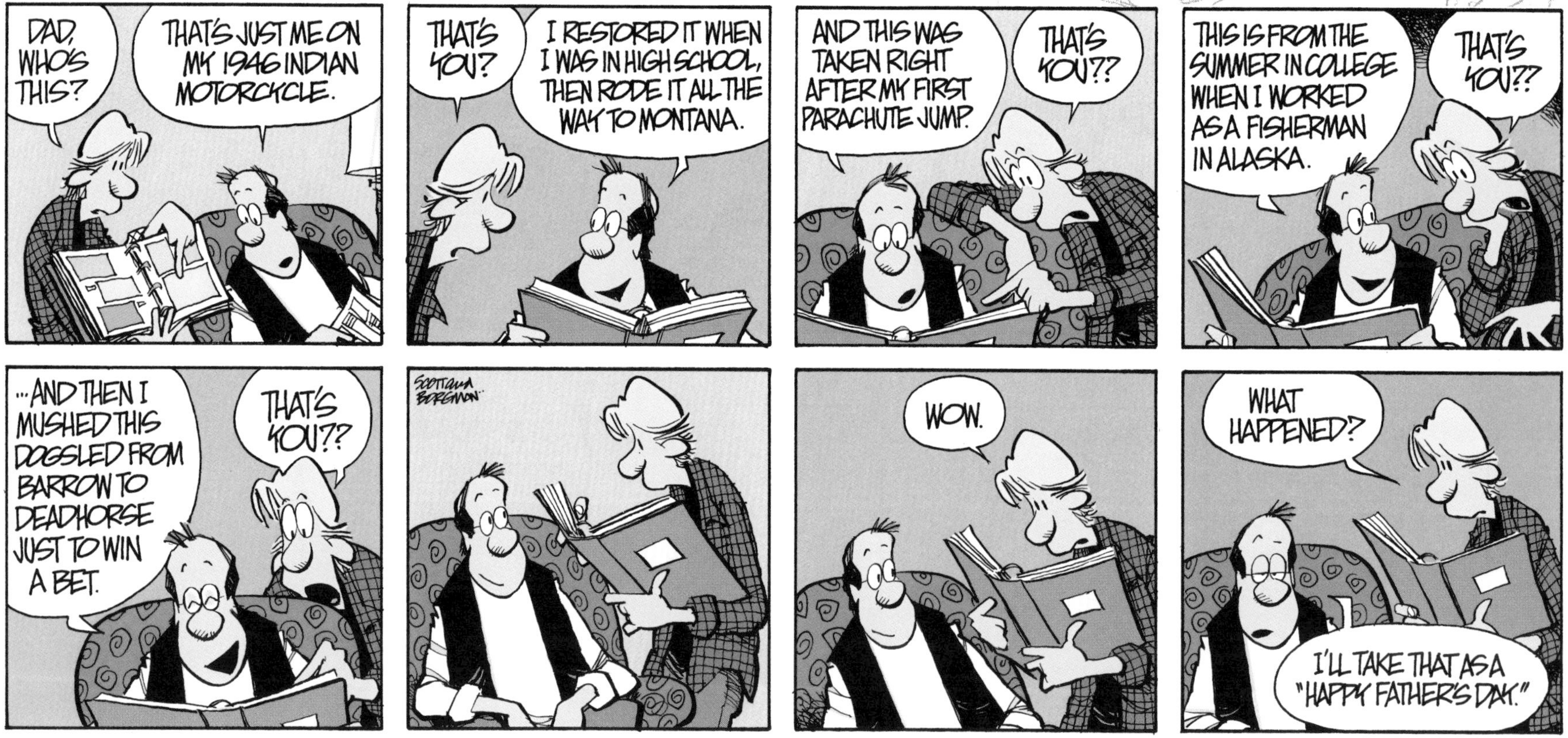

DAD, WHO'S THIS?
THAT'S JUST ME ON MY 1946 INDIAN MOTORCYCLE.
THAT'S YOU?
I RESTORED IT WHEN I WAS IN HIGH SCHOOL, THEN RODE IT ALL THE WAY TO MONTANA.
AND THIS WAS TAKEN RIGHT AFTER MY FIRST PARACHUTE JUMP.
THAT'S YOU??
THIS IS FROM THE SUMMER IN COLLEGE WHEN I WORKED AS A FISHERMAN IN ALASKA.
THAT'S YOU??
...AND THEN I MUSHED THIS DOGSLED FROM BARROW TO DEADHORSE JUST TO WIN A BET.
THAT'S YOU??
WOW.
WHAT HAPPENED?
I'LL TAKE THAT AS A "HAPPY FATHER'S DAY."

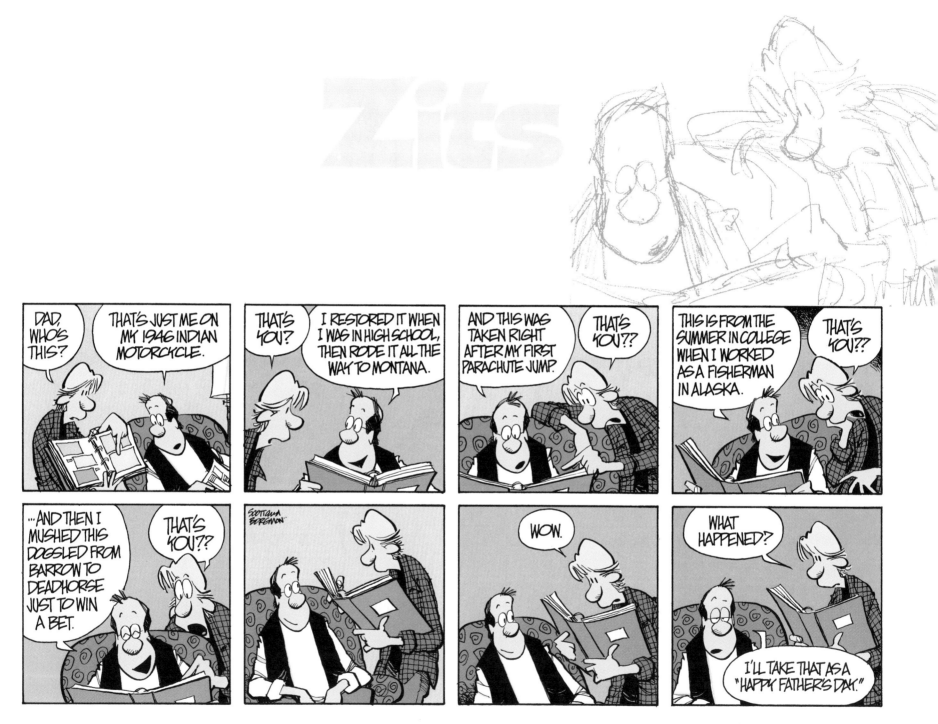

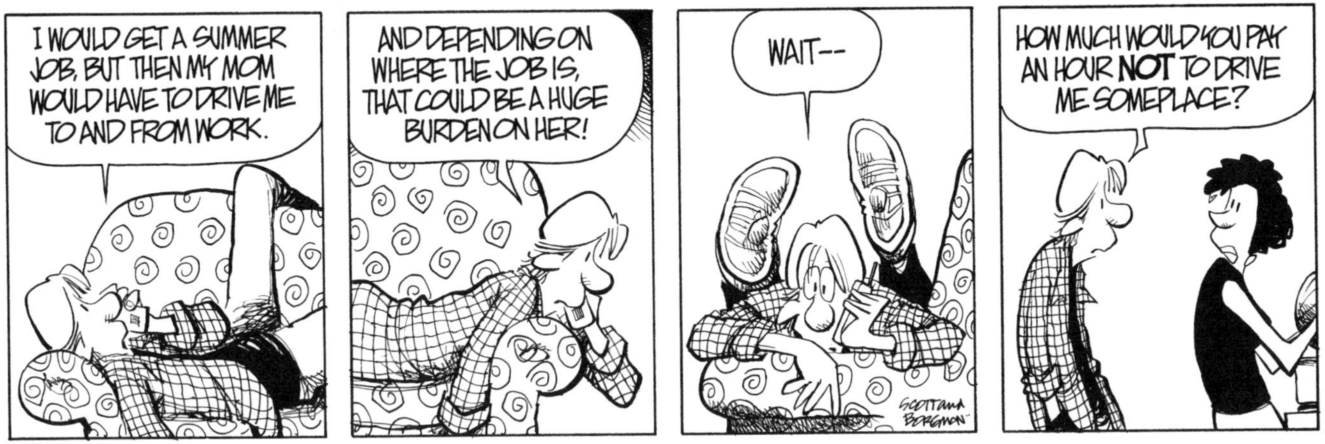

I WOULD GET A SUMMER JOB, BUT THEN MY MOM WOULD HAVE TO DRIVE ME TO AND FROM WORK.
AND DEPENDING ON WHERE THE JOB IS, THAT COULD BE A HUGE BURDEN ON HER!
WAIT--
HOW MUCH WOULD YOU PAY AN HOUR **NOT** TO DRIVE ME SOMEPLACE?

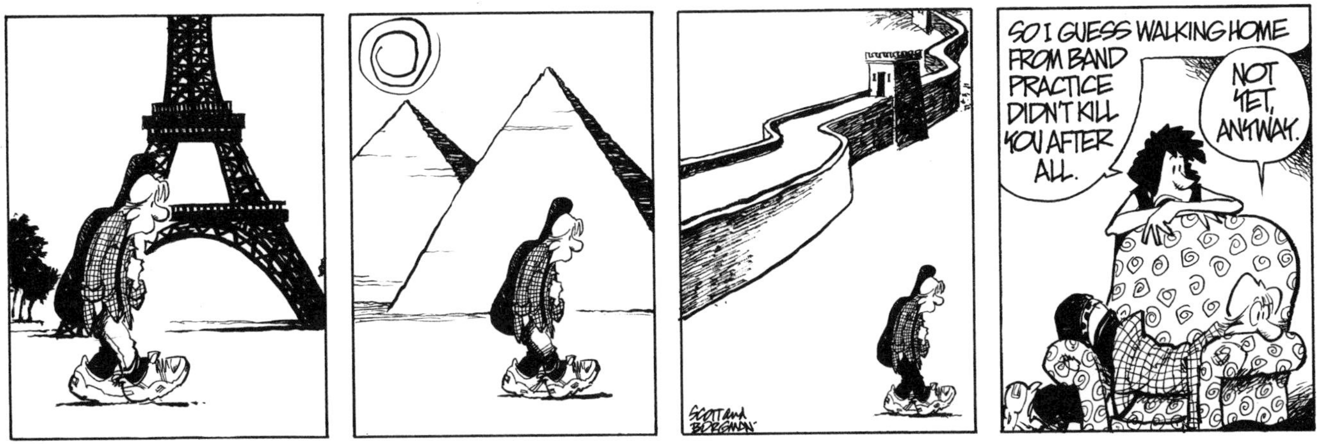

SO I GUESS WALKING HOME FROM BAND PRACTICE DIDN'T KILL YOU AFTER ALL.
NOT YET, ANYWAY.

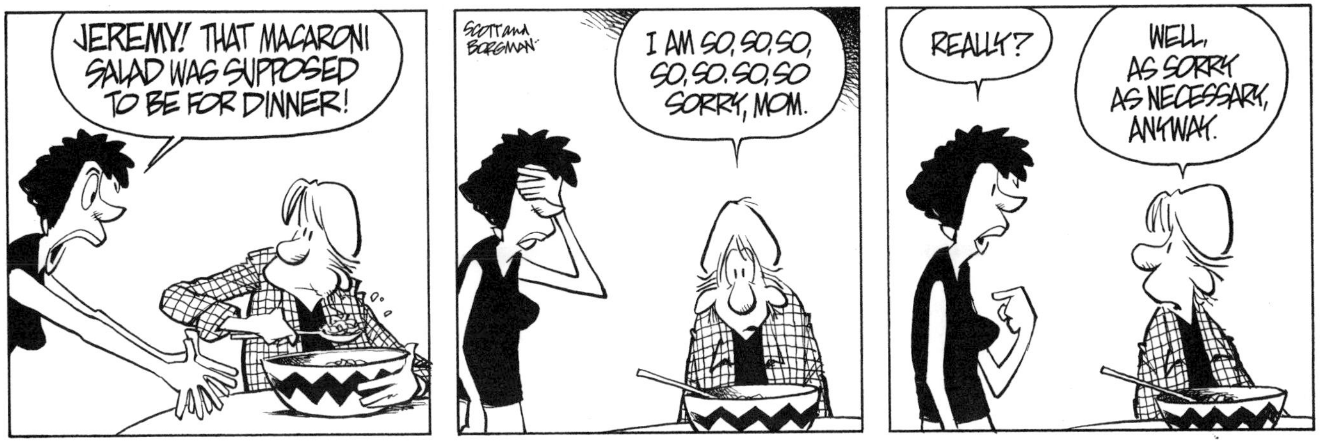

JEREMY! THAT MACARONI SALAD WAS SUPPOSED TO BE FOR DINNER!
I AM SO, SO, SO, SO, SO. SO, SO SORRY, MOM.
REALLY?
WELL, AS SORRY AS NECESSARY, ANYWAY.

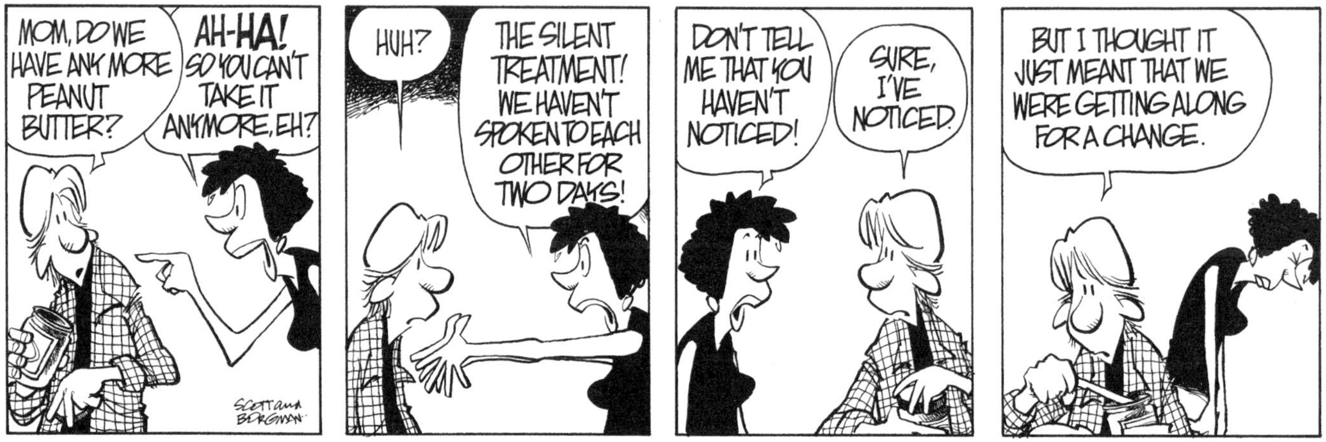
MOM, DO WE HAVE ANY MORE PEANUT BUTTER?
AH-HA! SO YOU CAN'T TAKE IT ANYMORE, EH?
SCOTT and BORGMAN
HUH?
THE SILENT TREATMENT! WE HAVEN'T SPOKEN TO EACH OTHER FOR TWO DAYS!
DON'T TELL ME THAT YOU HAVEN'T NOTICED!
SURE, I'VE NOTICED.
BUT I THOUGHT IT JUST MEANT THAT WE WERE GETTING ALONG FOR A CHANGE.

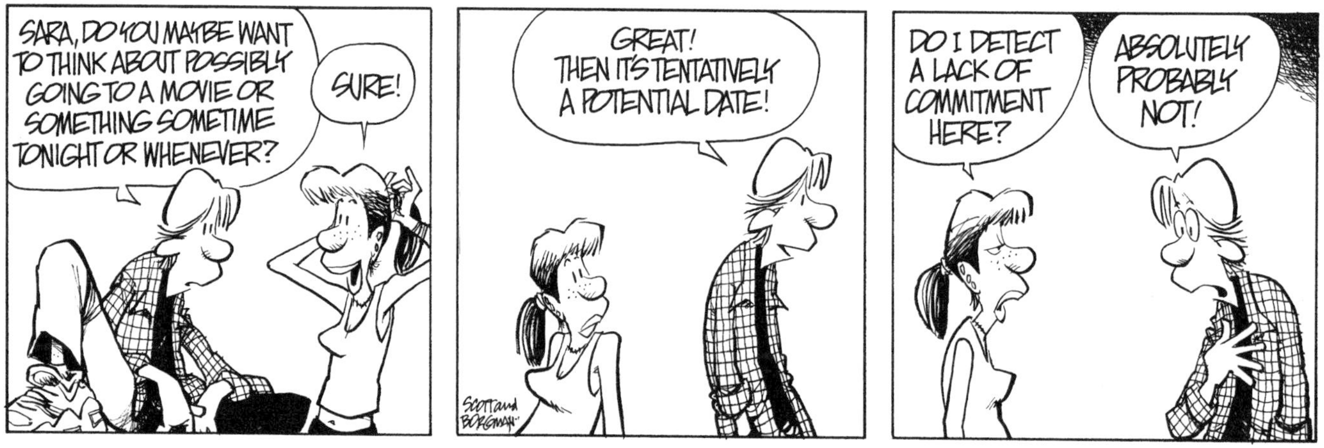
SARA, DO YOU MAYBE WANT TO THINK ABOUT POSSIBLY GOING TO A MOVIE OR SOMETHING SOMETIME TONIGHT OR WHENEVER?
SURE!
GREAT! THEN IT'S TENTATIVELY A POTENTIAL DATE!
SCOTT and BORGMAN
DO I DETECT A LACK OF COMMITMENT HERE?
ABSOLUTELY PROBABLY NOT!

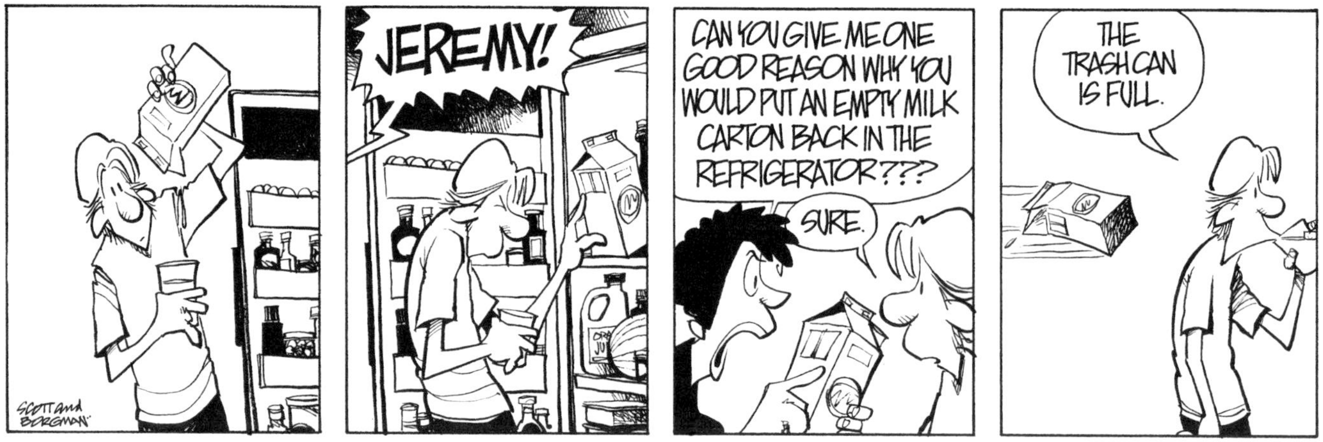
SCOTT and BORGMAN
JEREMY!
CAN YOU GIVE ME ONE GOOD REASON WHY YOU WOULD PUT AN EMPTY MILK CARTON BACK IN THE REFRIGERATOR???
SURE.
THE TRASH CAN IS FULL.

Zits

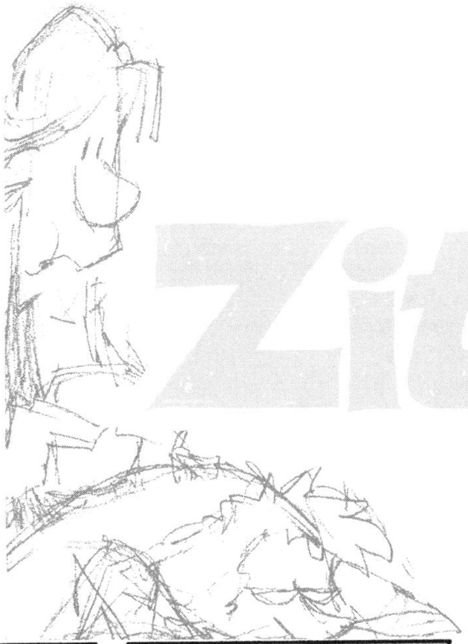

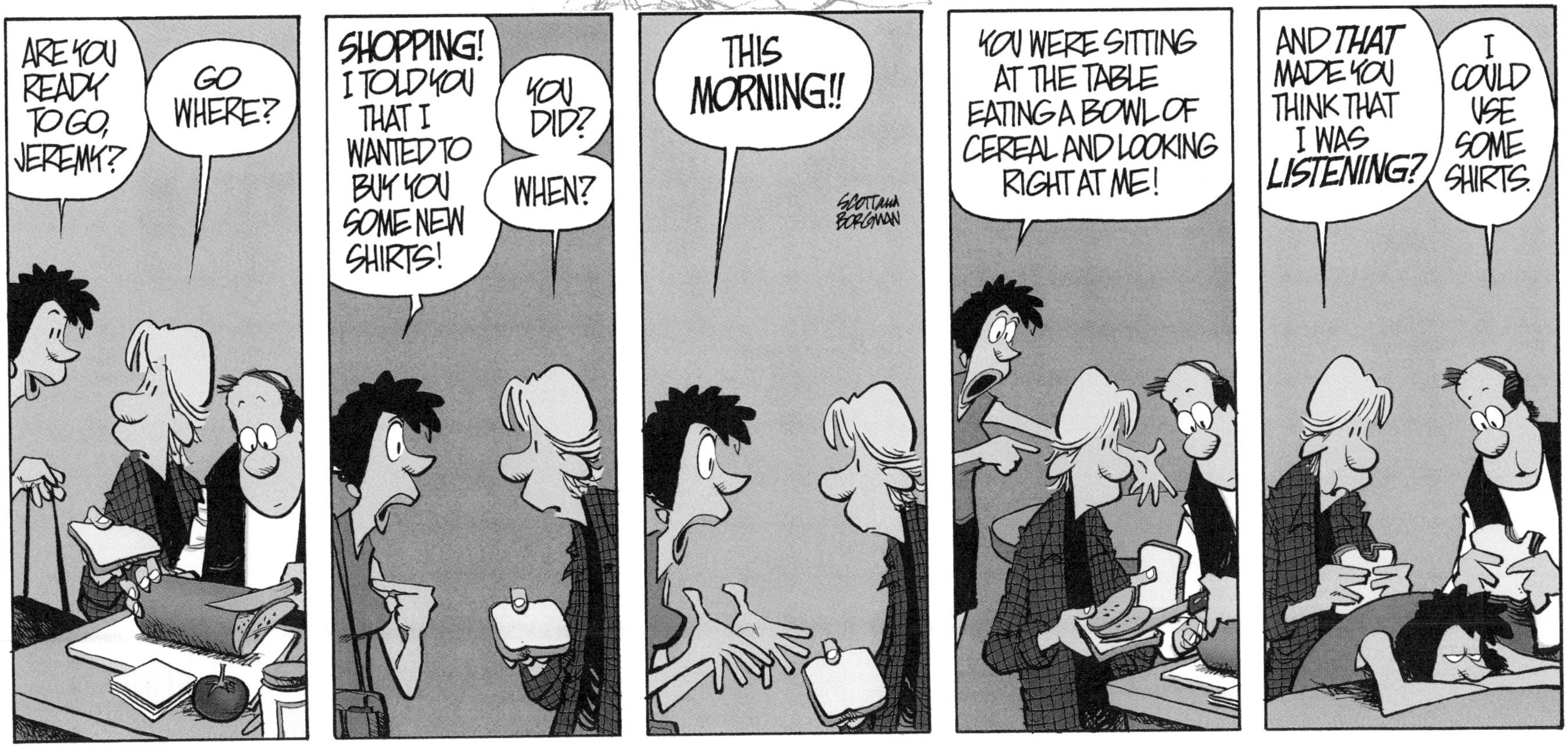
ARE YOU READY TO GO, JEREMY?
GO WHERE?
SHOPPING! I TOLD YOU THAT I WANTED TO BUY YOU SOME NEW SHIRTS!
YOU DID?
WHEN?
THIS MORNING!!
YOU WERE SITTING AT THE TABLE EATING A BOWL OF CEREAL AND LOOKING RIGHT AT ME!
AND THAT MADE YOU THINK THAT I WAS LISTENING?
I COULD USE SOME SHIRTS.

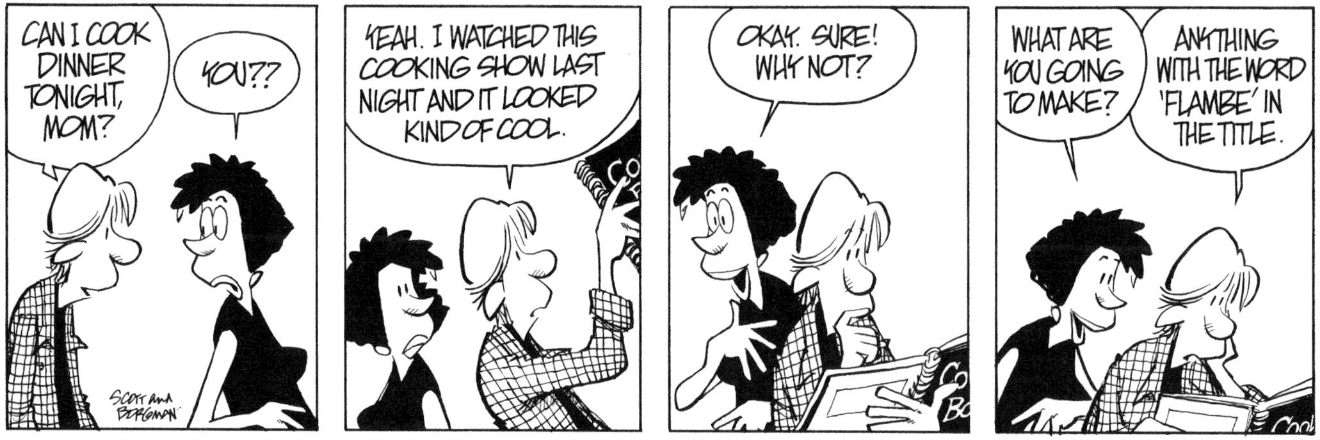
CAN I COOK DINNER TONIGHT, MOM?
YOU??
YEAH. I WATCHED THIS COOKING SHOW LAST NIGHT AND IT LOOKED KIND OF COOL.
OKAY. SURE! WHY NOT?
WHAT ARE YOU GOING TO MAKE?
ANYTHING WITH THE WORD 'FLAMBE' IN THE TITLE.

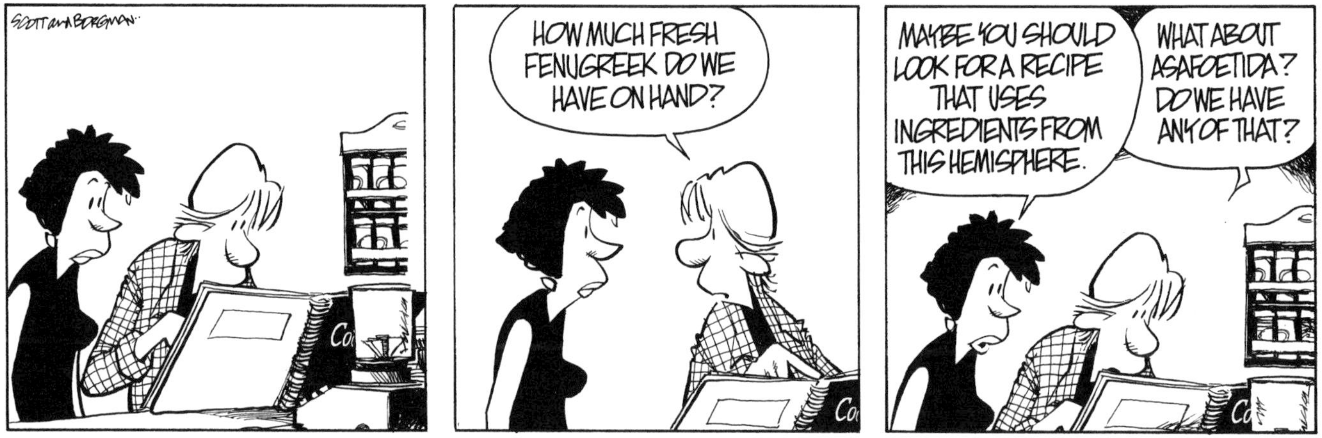
HOW MUCH FRESH FENUGREEK DO WE HAVE ON HAND?
MAYBE YOU SHOULD LOOK FOR A RECIPE THAT USES INGREDIENTS FROM THIS HEMISPHERE.
WHAT ABOUT ASAFOETIDA? DO WE HAVE ANY OF THAT?

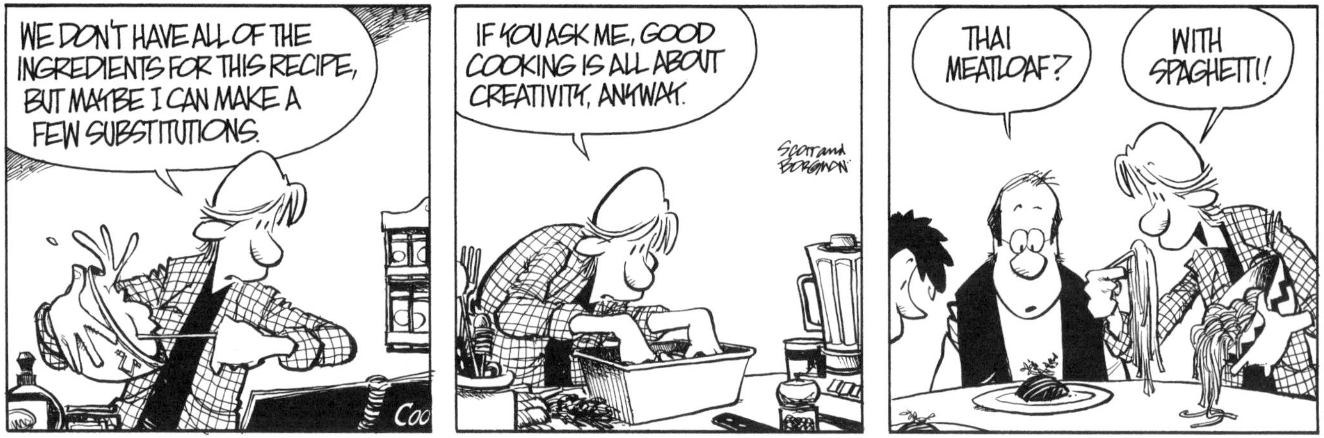
WE DON'T HAVE ALL OF THE INGREDIENTS FOR THIS RECIPE, BUT MAYBE I CAN MAKE A FEW SUBSTITUTIONS.
IF YOU ASK ME, GOOD COOKING IS ALL ABOUT CREATIVITY, ANYWAY.
THAI MEATLOAF?
WITH SPAGHETTI!

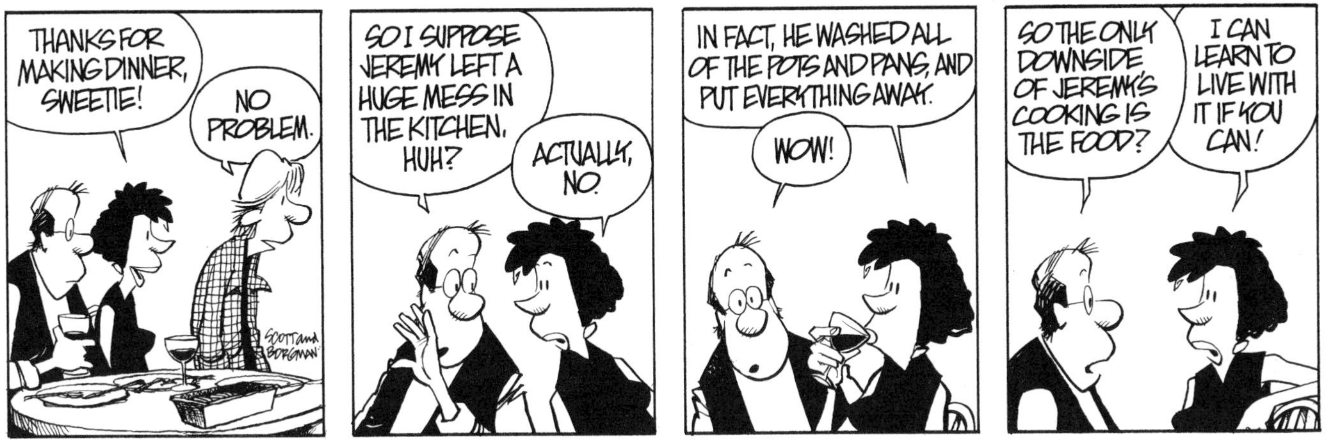
THANKS FOR MAKING DINNER, SWEETIE!
NO PROBLEM.
SCOTT and BORGMAN
SO I SUPPOSE JEREMY LEFT A HUGE MESS IN THE KITCHEN, HUH?
ACTUALLY, NO.
IN FACT, HE WASHED ALL OF THE POTS AND PANS, AND PUT EVERYTHING AWAY.
WOW!
SO THE ONLY DOWNSIDE OF JEREMY'S COOKING IS THE FOOD?
I CAN LEARN TO LIVE WITH IT IF YOU CAN!

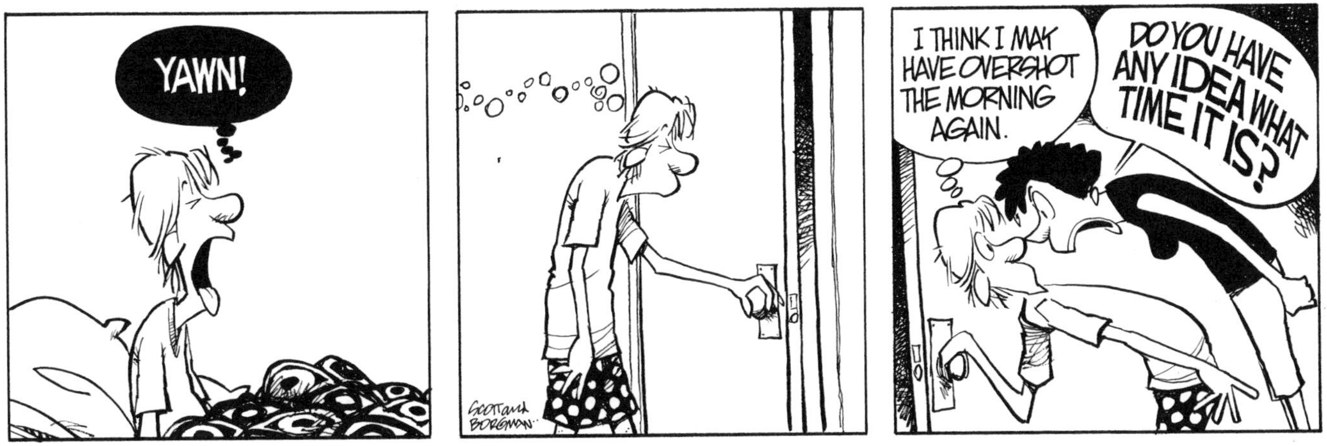
YAWN!
SCOTT and BORGMAN
I THINK I MAY HAVE OVERSHOT THE MORNING AGAIN.
DO YOU HAVE ANY IDEA WHAT TIME IT IS?

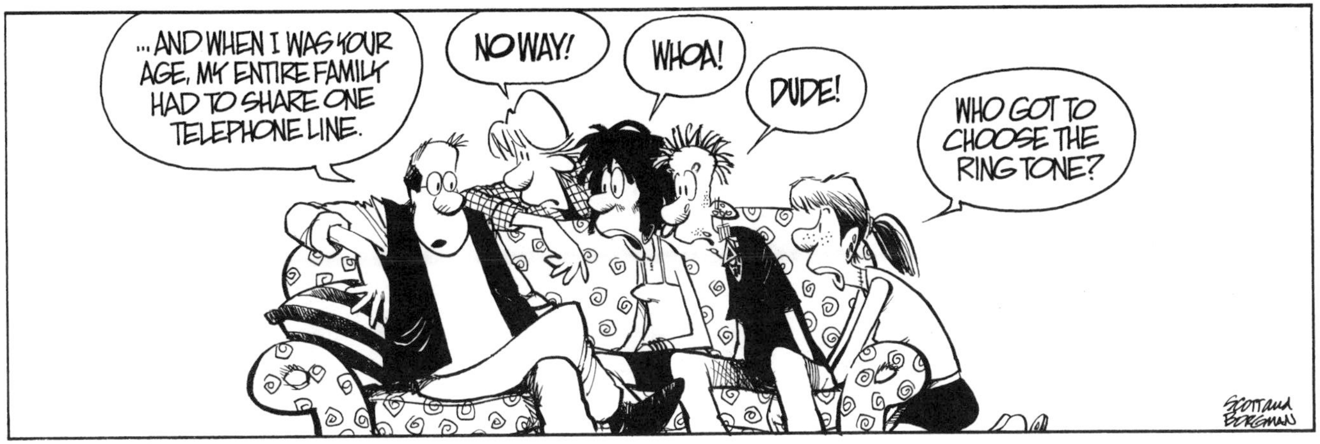
...AND WHEN I WAS YOUR AGE, MY ENTIRE FAMILY HAD TO SHARE ONE TELEPHONE LINE.
NO WAY!
WHOA!
DUDE!
WHO GOT TO CHOOSE THE RING TONE?
SCOTT and BORGMAN

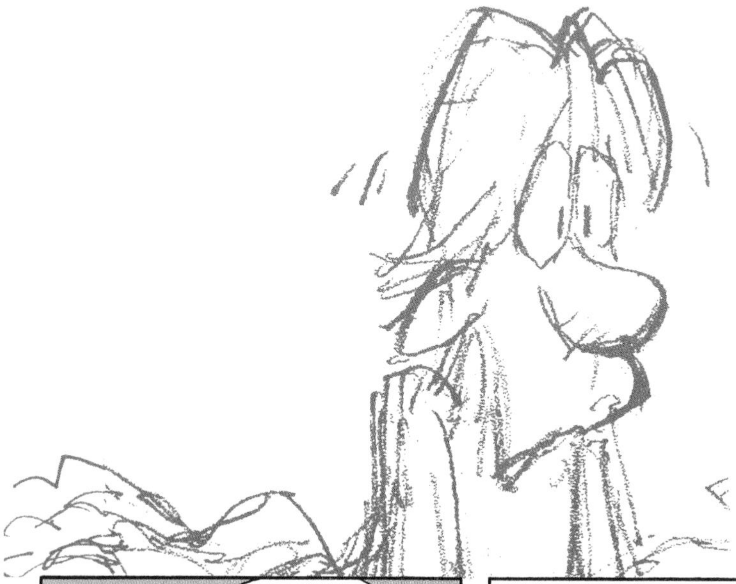

Zits

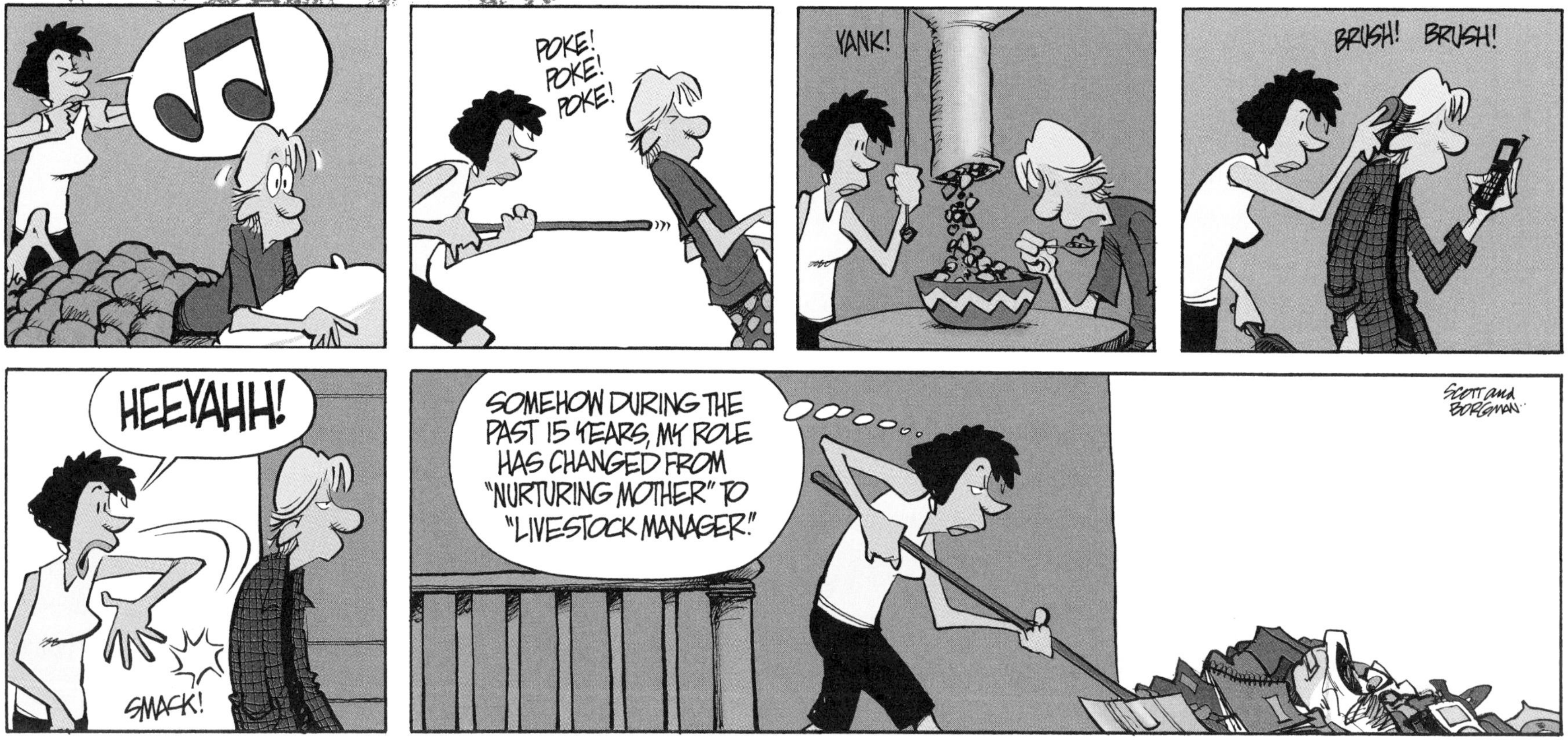
POKE! POKE! POKE!
YANK!
BRUSH! BRUSH!
HEEYAHH!
SMACK!
SOMEHOW DURING THE PAST 15 YEARS, MY ROLE HAS CHANGED FROM "NURTURING MOTHER" TO "LIVESTOCK MANAGER."
SCOTT and BORGMAN

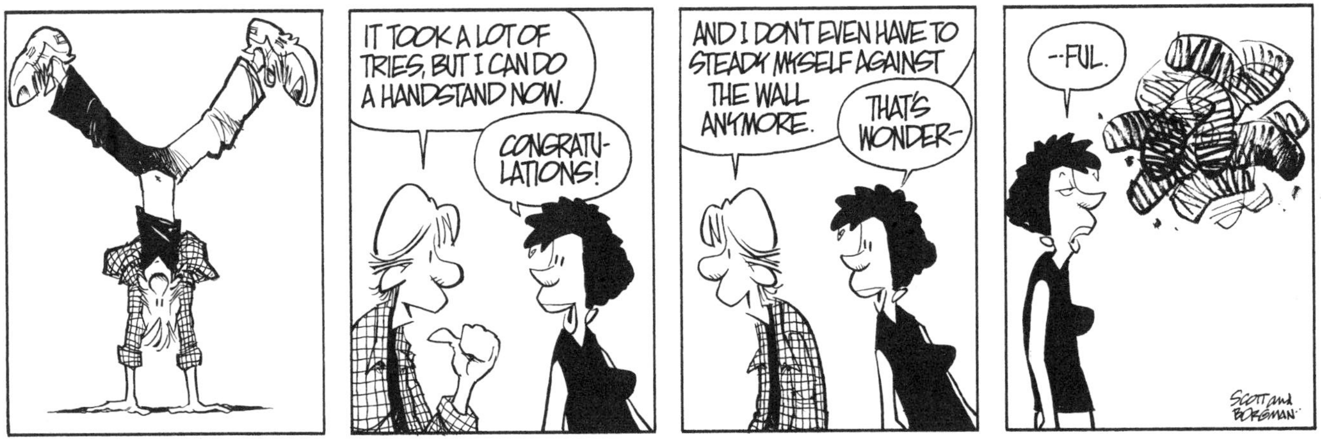
IT TOOK A LOT OF TRIES, BUT I CAN DO A HANDSTAND NOW.
CONGRATULATIONS!
AND I DON'T EVEN HAVE TO STEADY MYSELF AGAINST THE WALL ANYMORE.
THAT'S WONDER-
--FUL.
SCOTT and BORGMAN

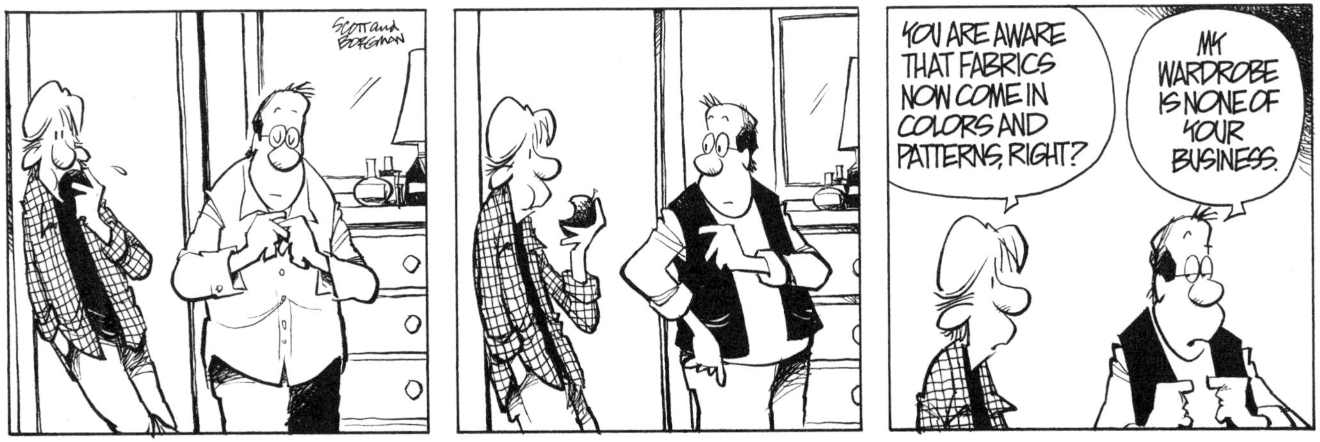
SCOTT and BORGMAN
YOU ARE AWARE THAT FABRICS NOW COME IN COLORS AND PATTERNS, RIGHT?
MY WARDROBE IS NONE OF YOUR BUSINESS.

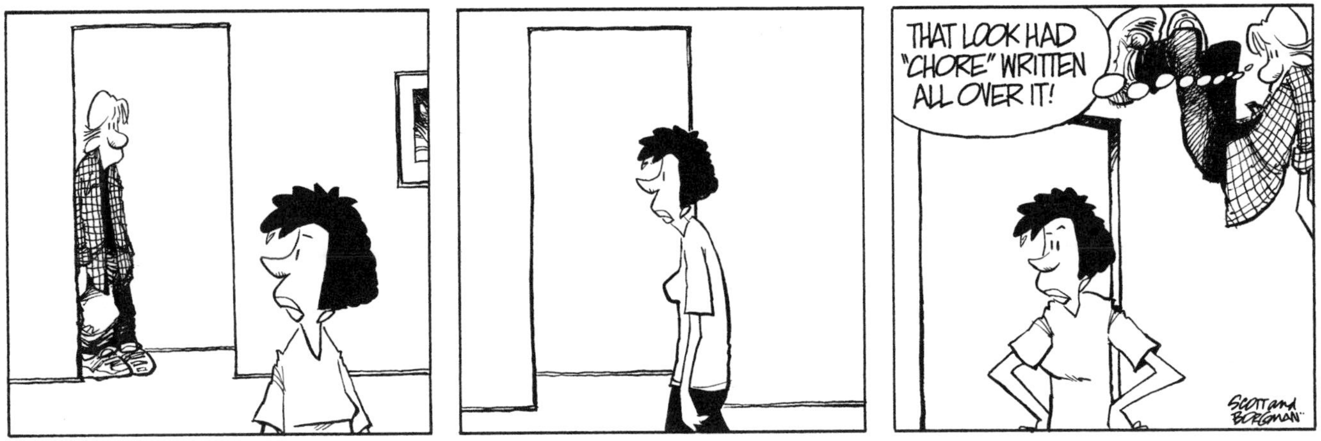
THAT LOOK HAD "CHORE" WRITTEN ALL OVER IT!
SCOTT and BORGMAN

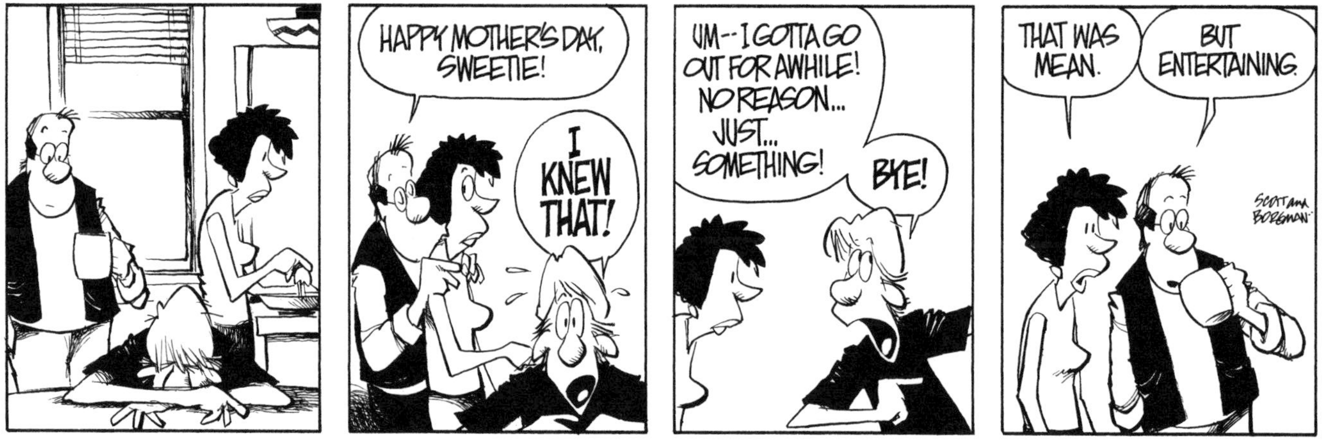
HAPPY MOTHER'S DAY, SWEETIE!
I KNEW THAT!
UM-- I GOTTA GO OUT FOR AWHILE! NO REASON... JUST... SOMETHING!
BYE!
THAT WAS MEAN.
BUT ENTERTAINING.

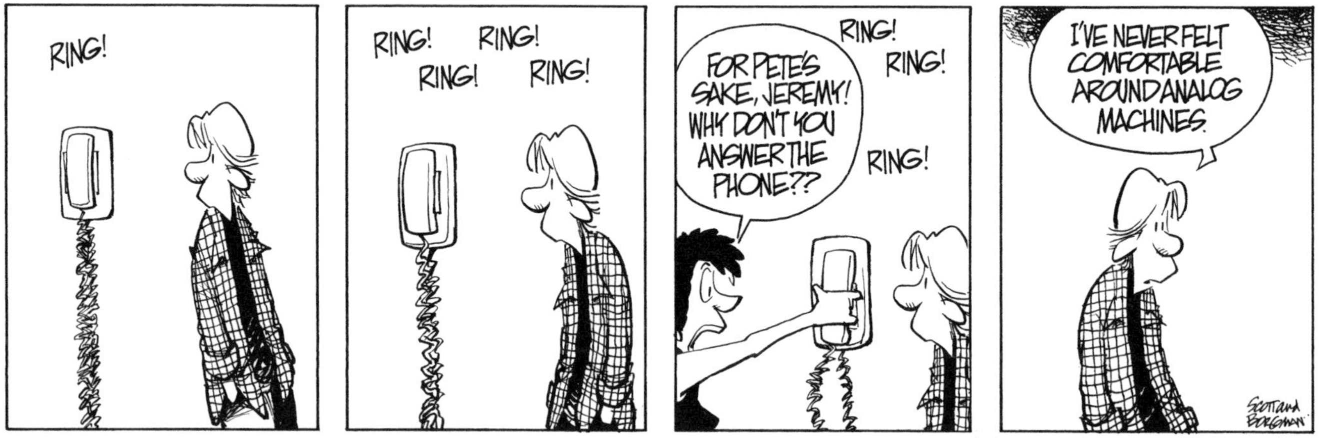
RING!
RING! RING!
RING! RING!
RING!
RING!
FOR PETE'S SAKE, JEREMY! WHY DON'T YOU ANSWER THE PHONE??
RING!
I'VE NEVER FELT COMFORTABLE AROUND ANALOG MACHINES.

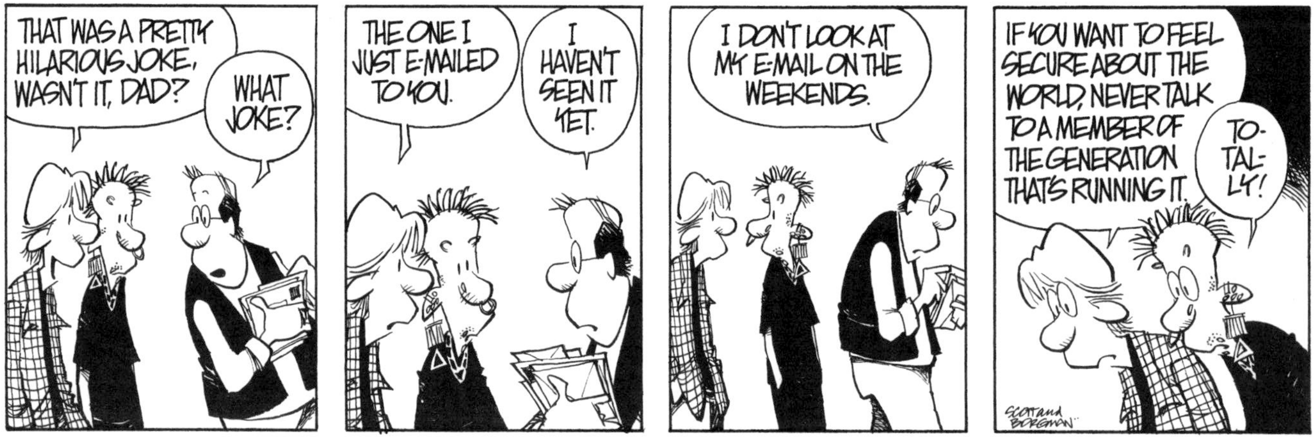
THAT WAS A PRETTY HILARIOUS JOKE, WASN'T IT, DAD?
WHAT JOKE?
THE ONE I JUST E-MAILED TO YOU.
I HAVEN'T SEEN IT YET.
I DON'T LOOK AT MY E-MAIL ON THE WEEKENDS.
IF YOU WANT TO FEEL SECURE ABOUT THE WORLD, NEVER TALK TO A MEMBER OF THE GENERATION THAT'S RUNNING IT.
TO-TAL-LY!

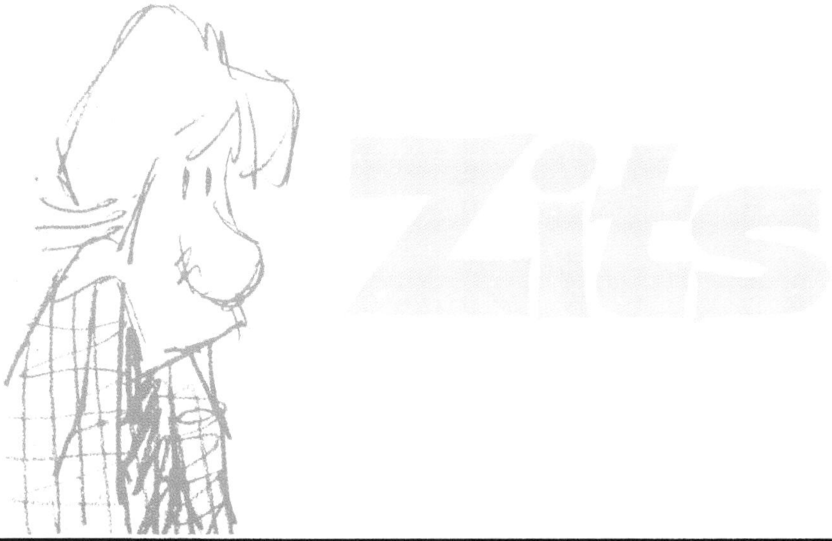
Zits

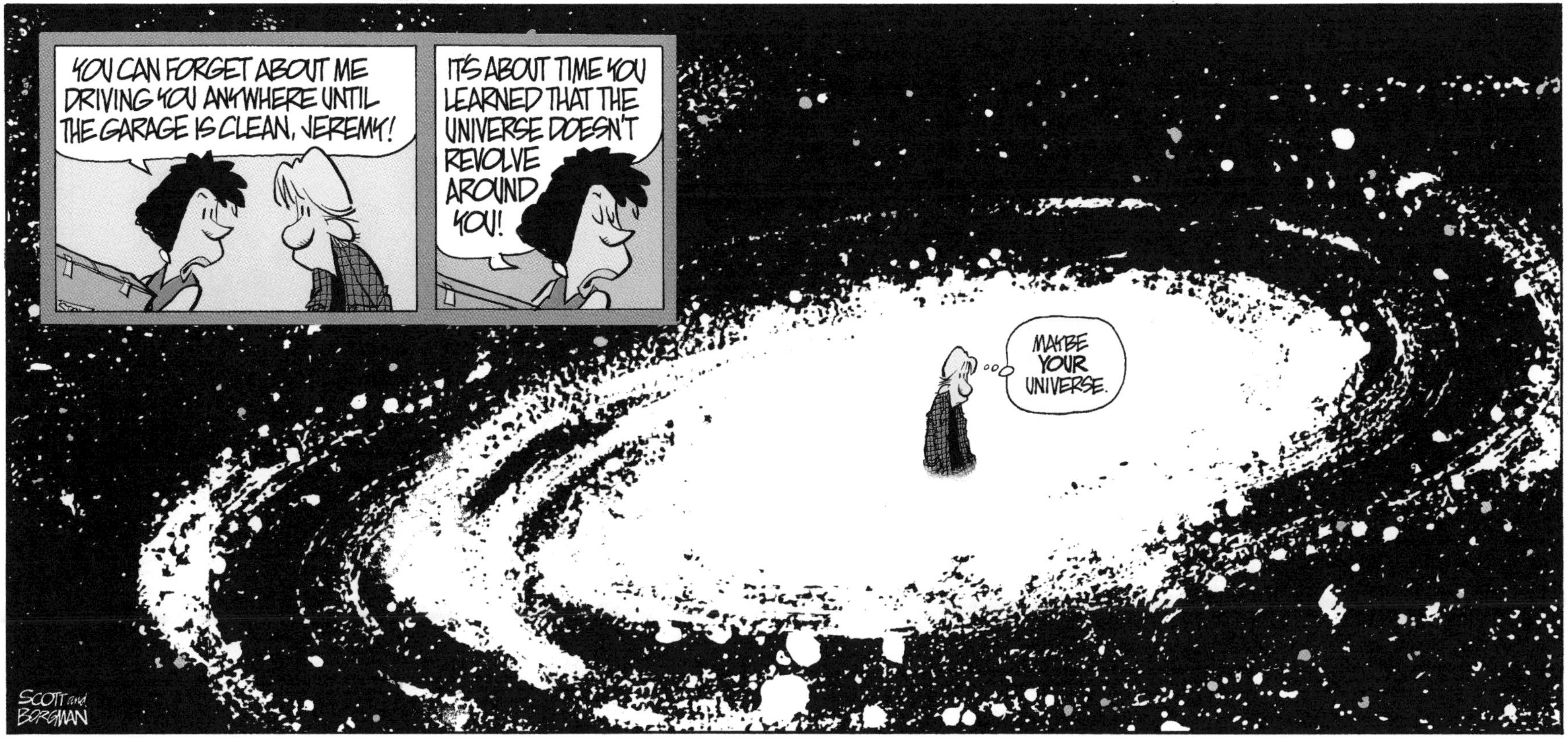
YOU CAN FORGET ABOUT ME DRIVING YOU ANYWHERE UNTIL THE GARAGE IS CLEAN, JEREMY!
IT'S ABOUT TIME YOU LEARNED THAT THE UNIVERSE DOESN'T REVOLVE AROUND YOU!
MAYBE YOUR UNIVERSE.
SCOTT and BORGMAN

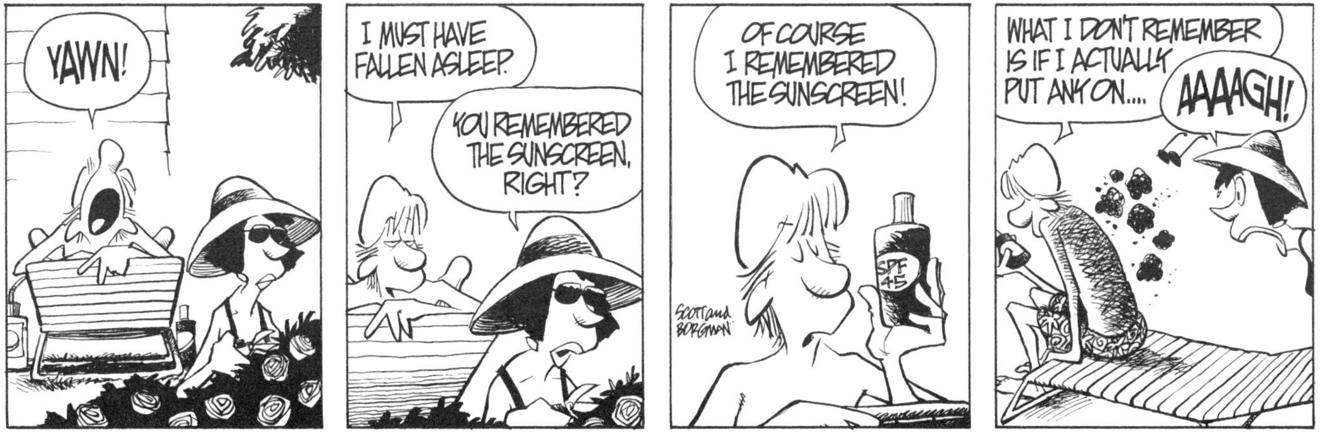
YAWN!
I MUST HAVE FALLEN ASLEEP.
YOU REMEMBERED THE SUNSCREEN, RIGHT?
OF COURSE I REMEMBERED THE SUNSCREEN!
SPF 45
SCOTT and BORGMAN
WHAT I DON'T REMEMBER IS IF I ACTUALLY PUT ANY ON....
AAAAGH!

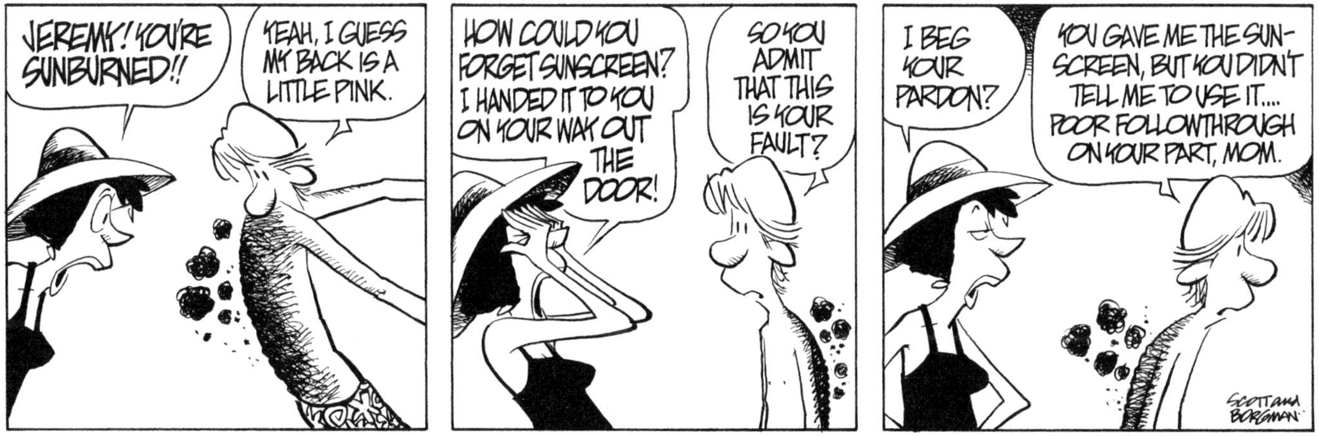
JEREMY! YOU'RE SUNBURNED!!
YEAH, I GUESS MY BACK IS A LITTLE PINK.
HOW COULD YOU FORGET SUNSCREEN? I HANDED IT TO YOU ON YOUR WAY OUT THE DOOR!
SO YOU ADMIT THAT THIS IS YOUR FAULT?
I BEG YOUR PARDON?
YOU GAVE ME THE SUN-SCREEN, BUT YOU DIDN'T TELL ME TO USE IT.... POOR FOLLOWTHROUGH ON YOUR PART, MOM.
SCOTT and BORGMAN

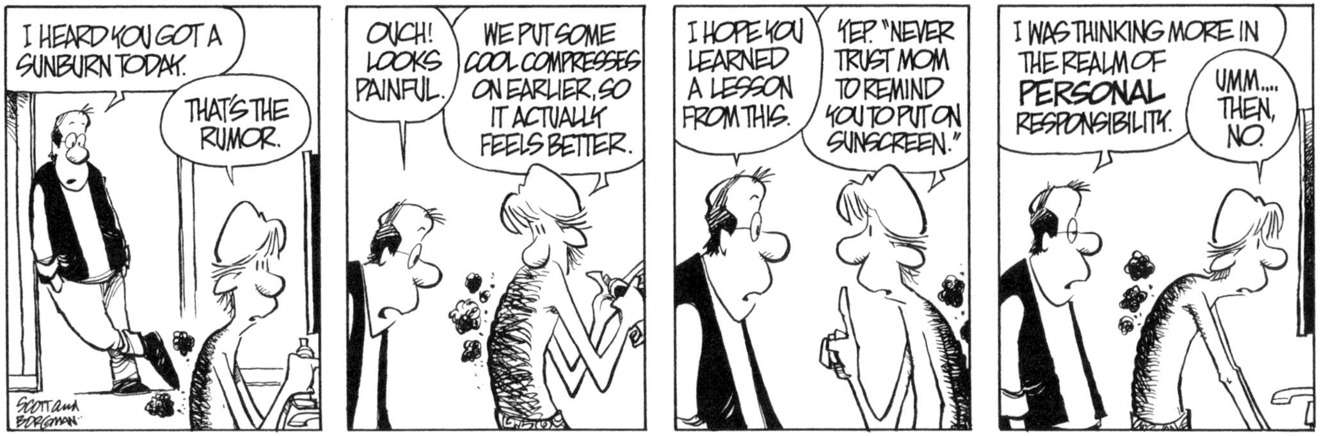
I HEARD YOU GOT A SUNBURN TODAY.
THAT'S THE RUMOR.
SCOTT and BORGMAN
OUCH! LOOKS PAINFUL.
WE PUT SOME COOL COMPRESSES ON EARLIER, SO IT ACTUALLY FEELS BETTER.
I HOPE YOU LEARNED A LESSON FROM THIS.
YEP. "NEVER TRUST MOM TO REMIND YOU TO PUT ON SUNSCREEN."
I WAS THINKING MORE IN THE REALM OF PERSONAL RESPONSIBILITY.
UMM.... THEN, NO.

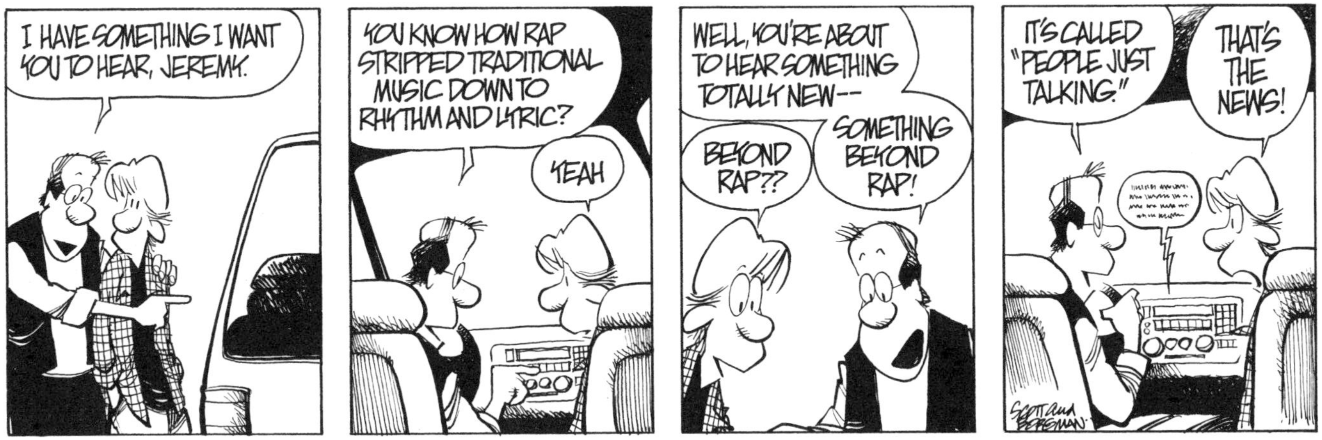
I HAVE SOMETHING I WANT YOU TO HEAR, JEREMY.
YOU KNOW HOW RAP STRIPPED TRADITIONAL MUSIC DOWN TO RHYTHM AND LYRIC?
YEAH
WELL, YOU'RE ABOUT TO HEAR SOMETHING TOTALLY NEW--
BEYOND RAP??
SOMETHING BEYOND RAP!
IT'S CALLED "PEOPLE JUST TALKING."
THAT'S THE NEWS!

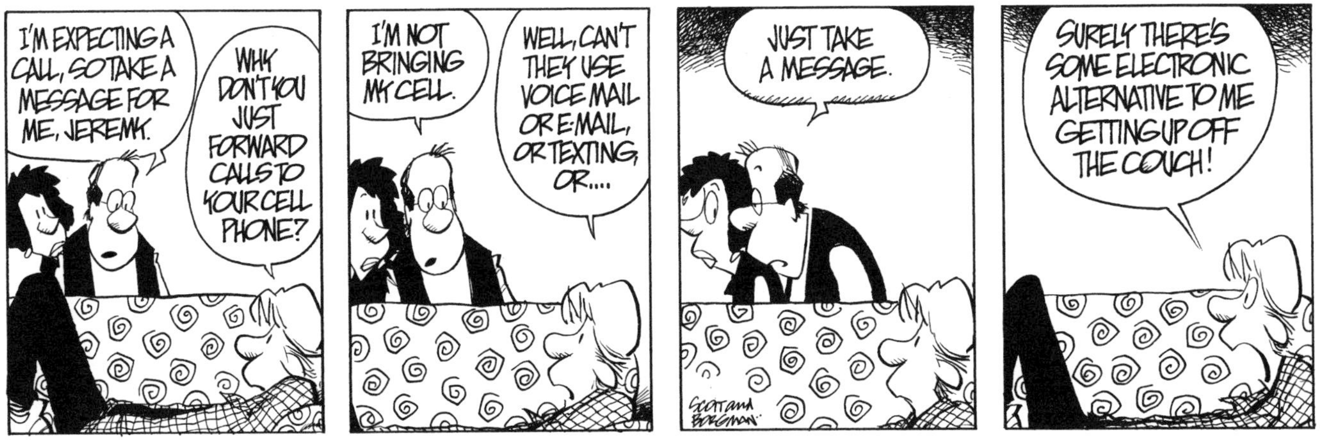
I'M EXPECTING A CALL, SO TAKE A MESSAGE FOR ME, JEREMY.
WHY DON'T YOU JUST FORWARD CALLS TO YOUR CELL PHONE?
I'M NOT BRINGING MY CELL.
WELL, CAN'T THEY USE VOICE MAIL OR E-MAIL, OR TEXTING, OR....
JUST TAKE A MESSAGE.
SURELY THERE'S SOME ELECTRONIC ALTERNATIVE TO ME GETTING UP OFF THE COUCH!

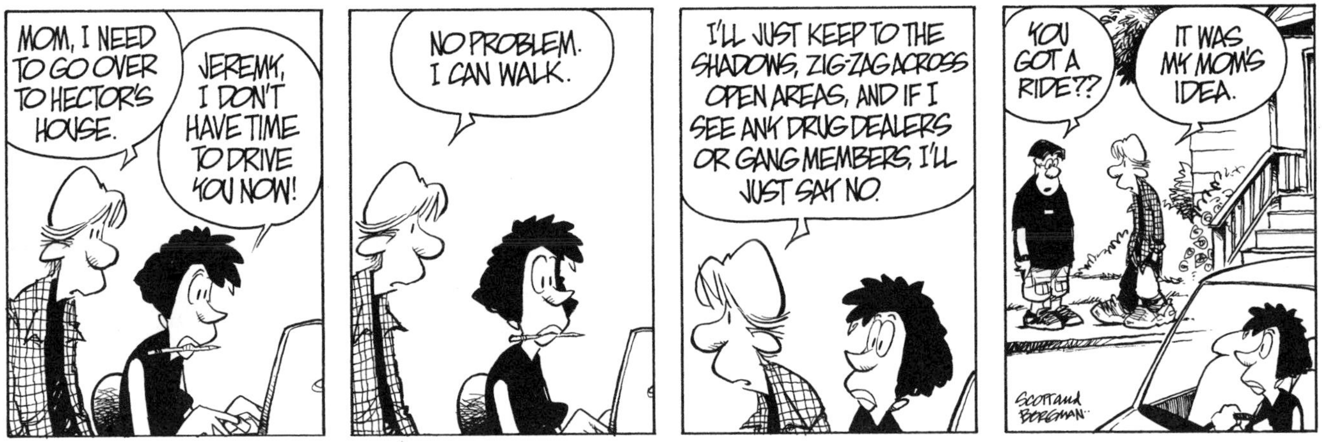
MOM, I NEED TO GO OVER TO HECTOR'S HOUSE.
JEREMY, I DON'T HAVE TIME TO DRIVE YOU NOW!
NO PROBLEM. I CAN WALK.
I'LL JUST KEEP TO THE SHADOWS, ZIG-ZAG ACROSS OPEN AREAS, AND IF I SEE ANY DRUG DEALERS OR GANG MEMBERS, I'LL JUST SAY NO.
YOU GOT A RIDE??
IT WAS MY MOM'S IDEA.

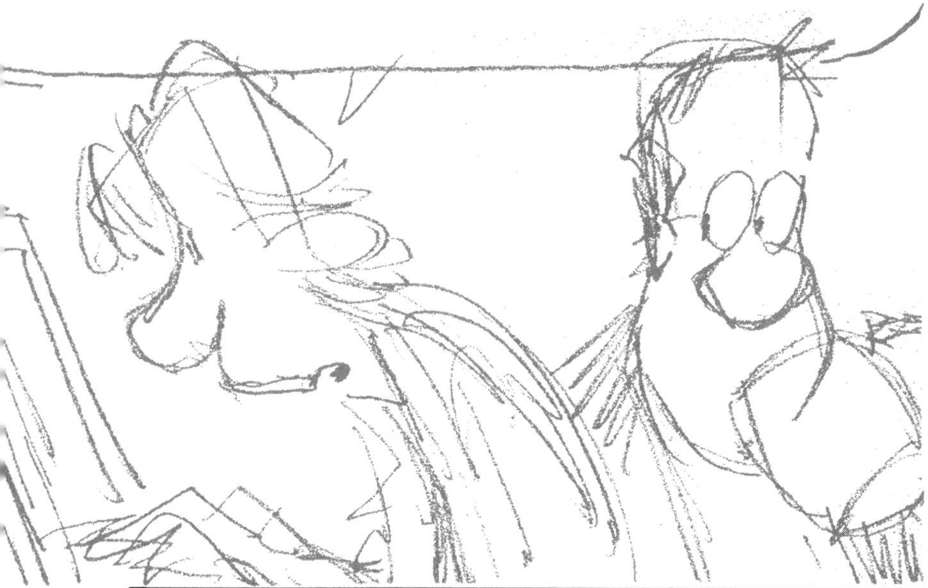

Zits

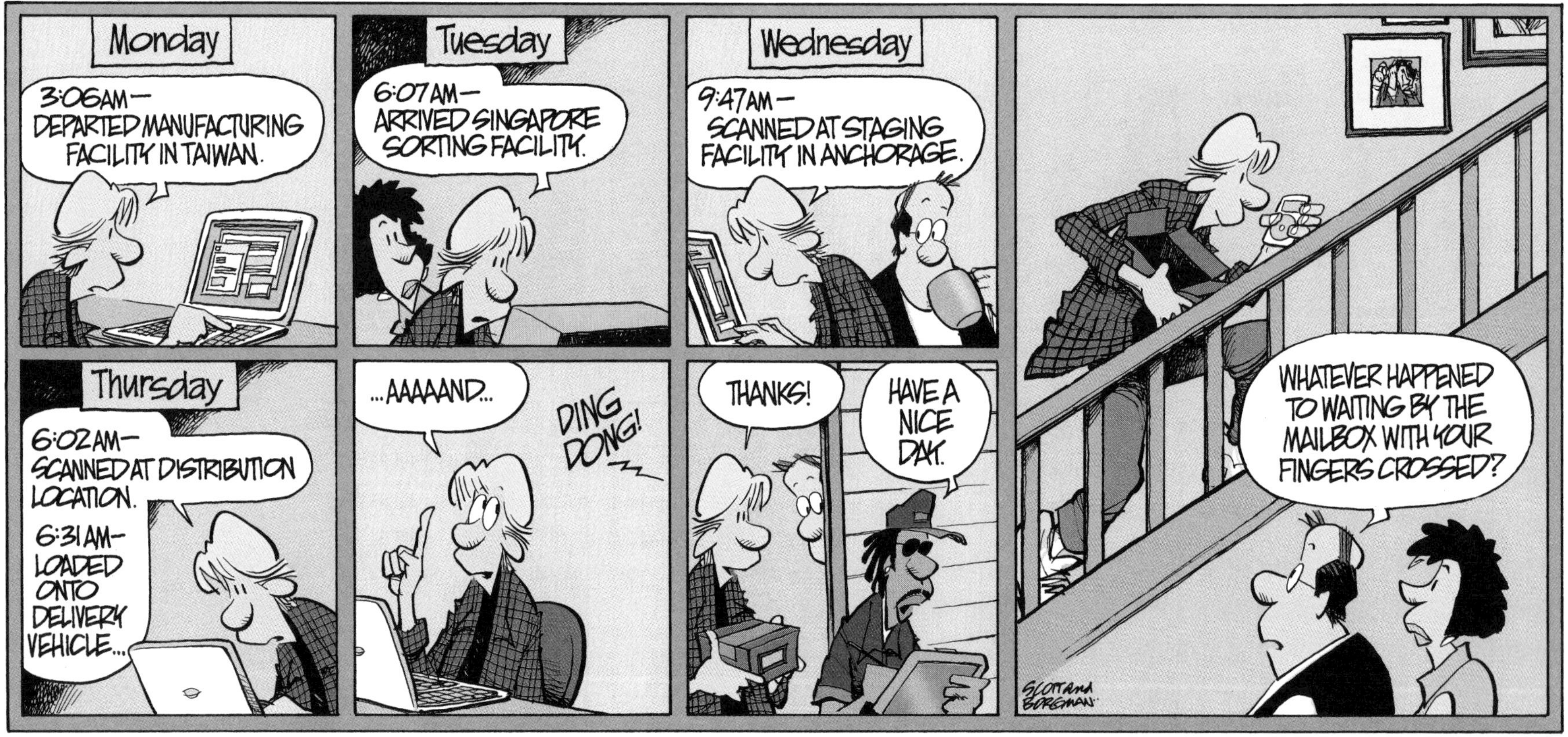

Monday
3:06AM— DEPARTED MANUFACTURING FACILITY IN TAIWAN.
Tuesday
6:07AM— ARRIVED SINGAPORE SORTING FACILITY.
Wednesday
9:47AM— SCANNED AT STAGING FACILITY IN ANCHORAGE.
Thursday
6:02AM— SCANNED AT DISTRIBUTION LOCATION.
6:31AM— LOADED ONTO DELIVERY VEHICLE...
...AAAAAND...
DING DONG!
THANKS!
HAVE A NICE DAY.
WHATEVER HAPPENED TO WAITING BY THE MAILBOX WITH YOUR FINGERS CROSSED?
SCOTT AND BORGMAN

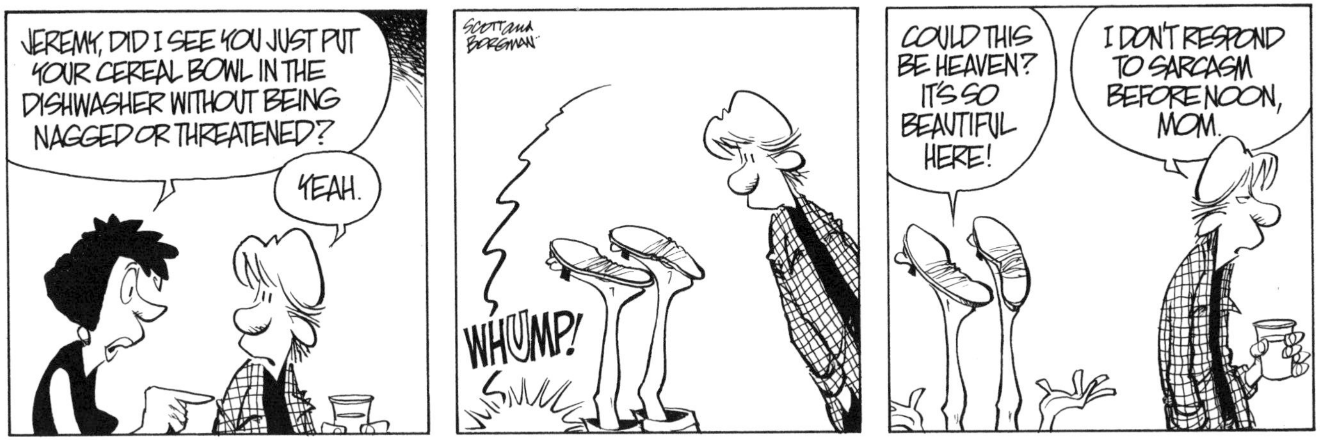
JEREMY, DID I SEE YOU JUST PUT YOUR CEREAL BOWL IN THE DISHWASHER WITHOUT BEING NAGGED OR THREATENED?
YEAH.
SCOTT and BORGMAN
WHUMP!
COULD THIS BE HEAVEN? IT'S SO BEAUTIFUL HERE!
I DON'T RESPOND TO SARCASM BEFORE NOON, MOM.

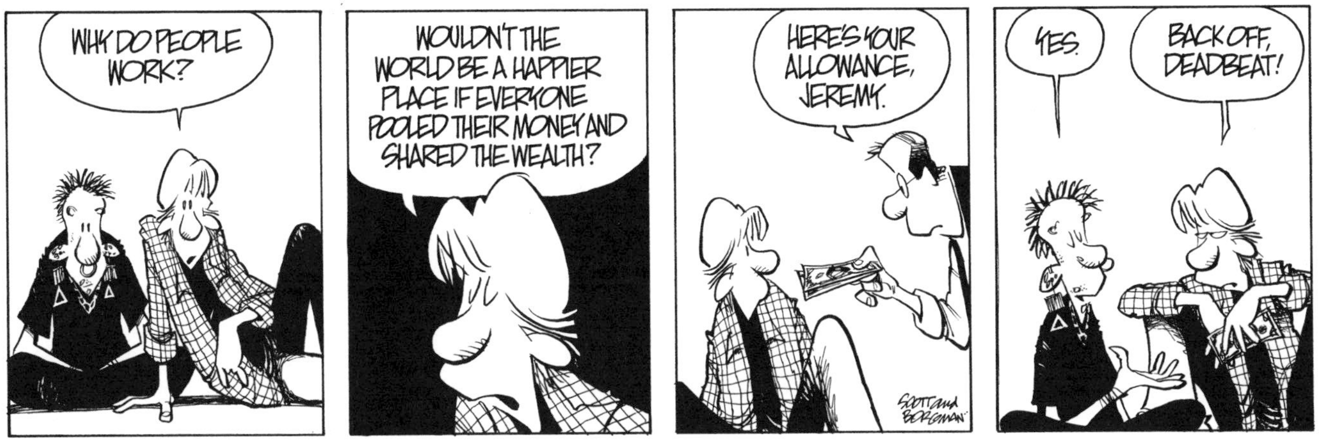
WHY DO PEOPLE WORK?
WOULDN'T THE WORLD BE A HAPPIER PLACE IF EVERYONE POOLED THEIR MONEY AND SHARED THE WEALTH?
HERE'S YOUR ALLOWANCE, JEREMY.
SCOTT and BORGMAN
YES.
BACK OFF, DEADBEAT!

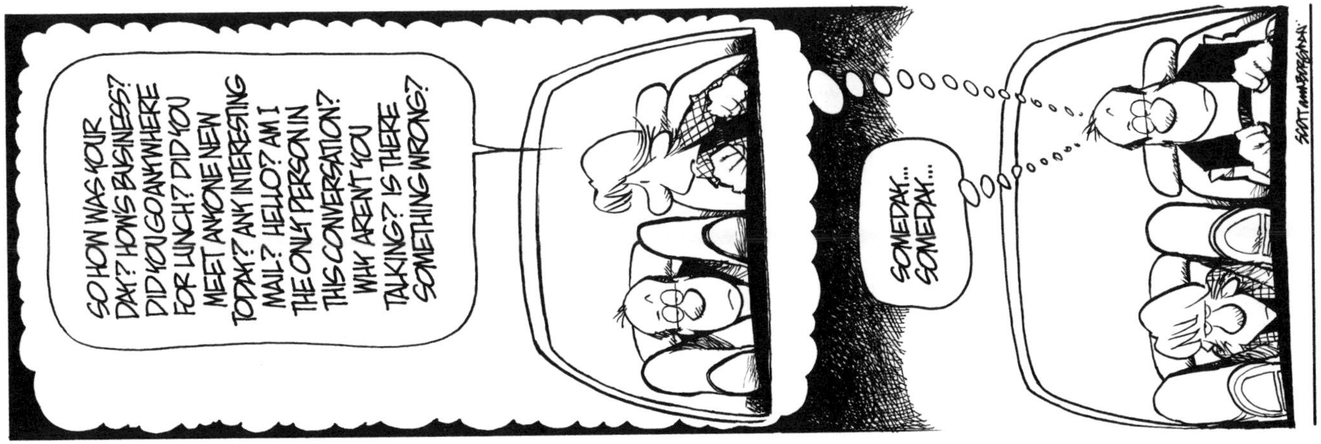
SO HOW WAS YOUR DAY? HOW'S BUSINESS? DID YOU GO ANYWHERE FOR LUNCH? DID YOU MEET ANYONE NEW TODAY? ANY INTERESTING MAIL? HELLO? AM I THE ONLY PERSON IN THIS CONVERSATION? WHY AREN'T YOU TALKING? IS THERE SOMETHING WRONG?
SOMEDAY... SOMEDAY...

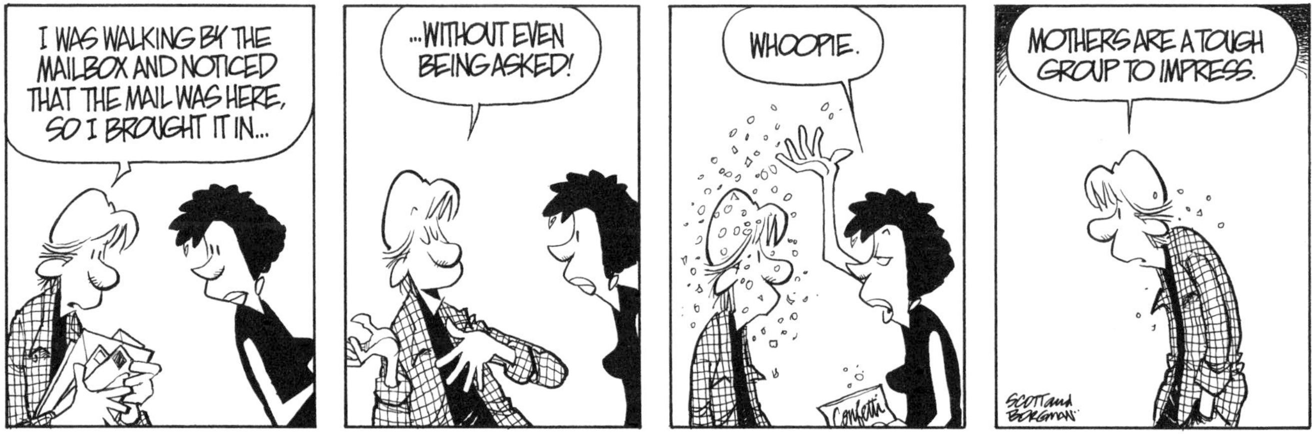
I WAS WALKING BY THE MAILBOX AND NOTICED THAT THE MAIL WAS HERE, SO I BROUGHT IT IN...
...WITHOUT EVEN BEING ASKED!
WHOOPIE.
Confetti
MOTHERS ARE A TOUGH GROUP TO IMPRESS.
SCOTT and BORGMAN

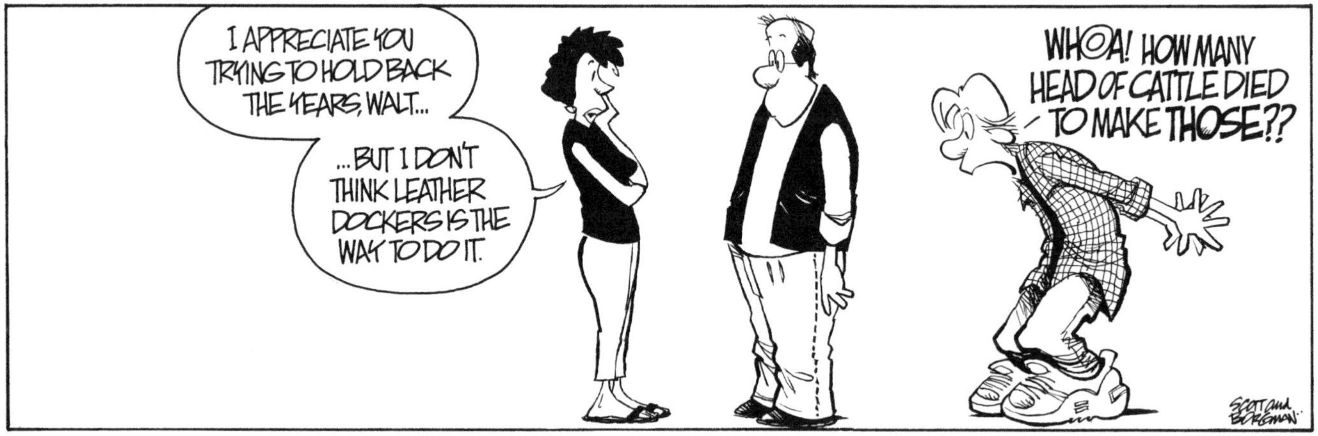
I APPRECIATE YOU TRYING TO HOLD BACK THE YEARS, WALT...
...BUT I DON'T THINK LEATHER DOCKERS IS THE WAY TO DO IT.
WHOA! HOW MANY HEAD OF CATTLE DIED TO MAKE THOSE??
SCOTT and BORGMAN

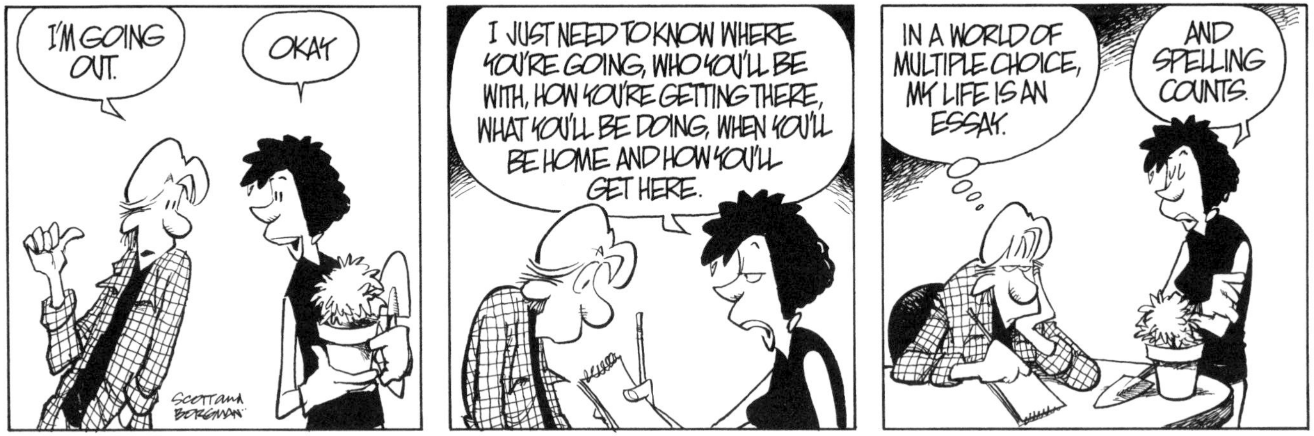
I'M GOING OUT.
OKAY
SCOTT and BORGMAN
I JUST NEED TO KNOW WHERE YOU'RE GOING, WHO YOU'LL BE WITH, HOW YOU'RE GETTING THERE, WHAT YOU'LL BE DOING, WHEN YOU'LL BE HOME AND HOW YOU'LL GET HERE.
IN A WORLD OF MULTIPLE CHOICE, MY LIFE IS AN ESSAY.
AND SPELLING COUNTS.

Zits

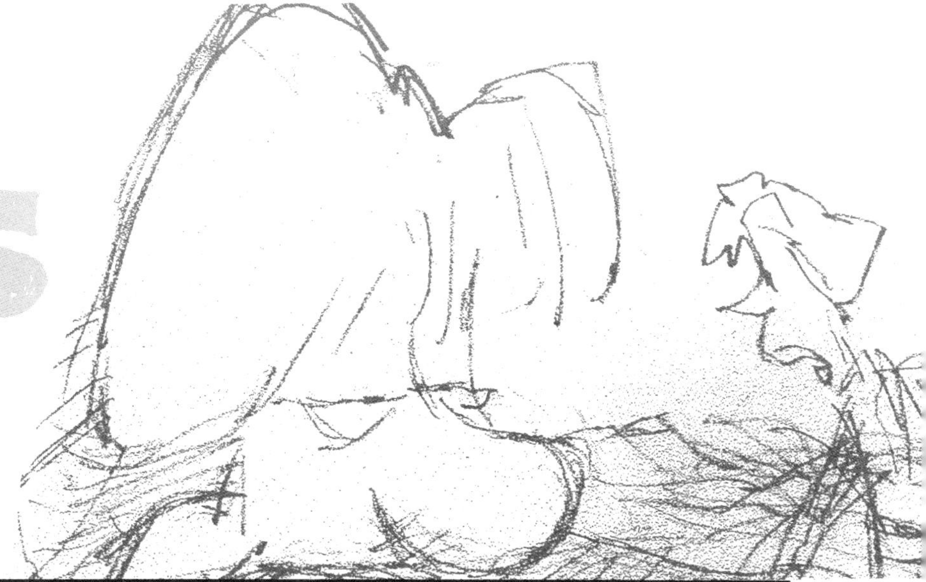

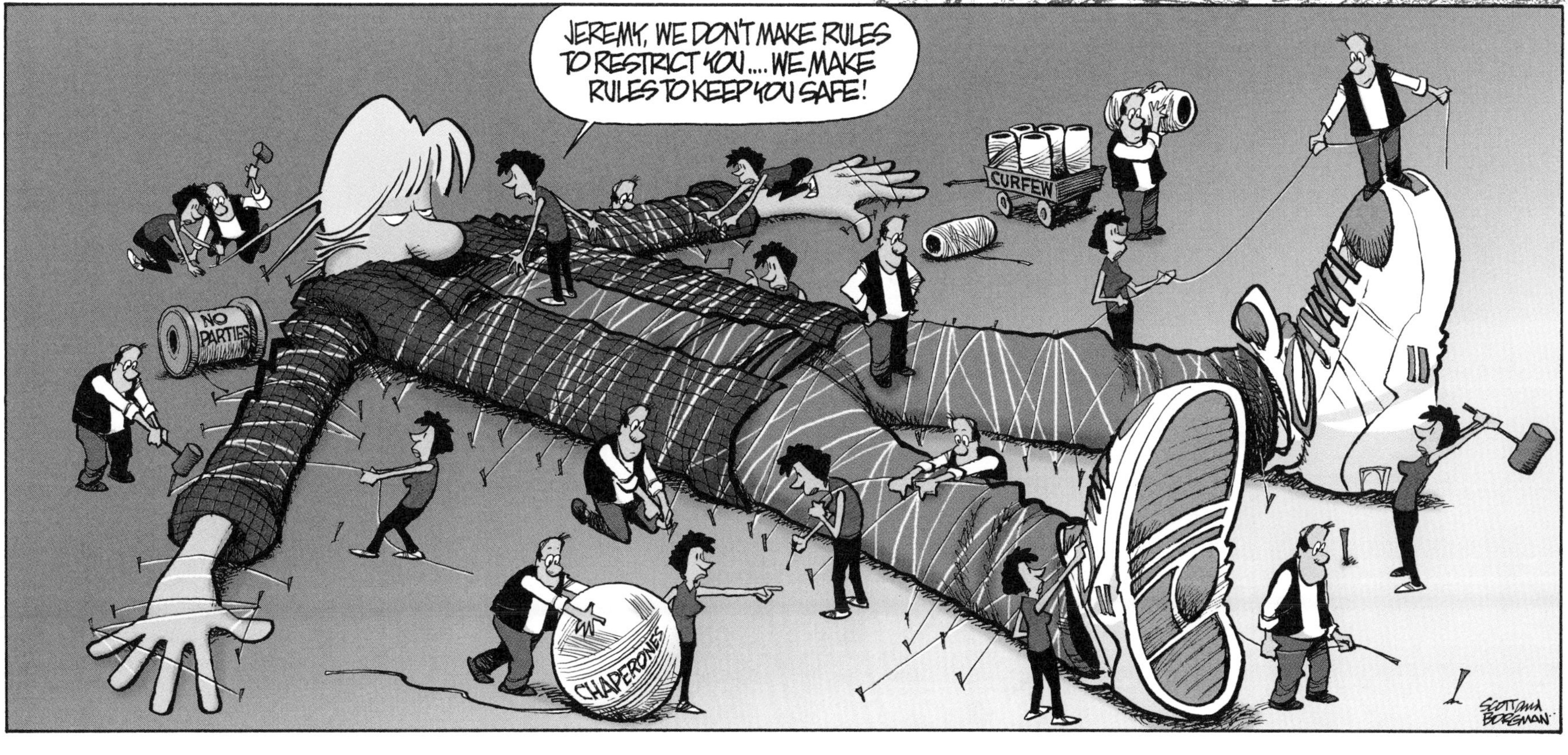

JEREMY, WE DON'T MAKE RULES TO RESTRICT YOU.... WE MAKE RULES TO KEEP YOU SAFE!
CURFEW
NO PARTIES
CHAPERONES
SCOTT and BORGMAN

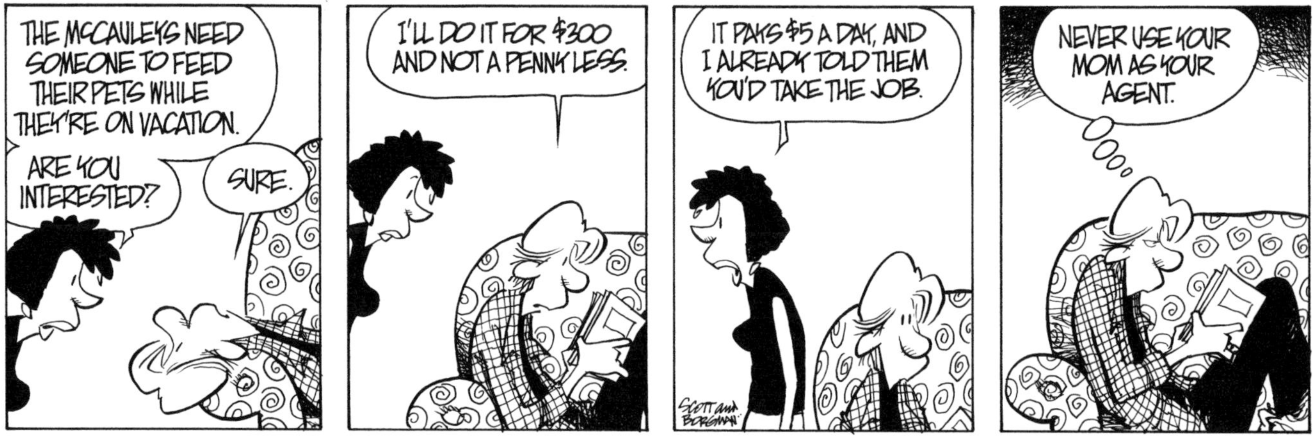
THE McCAULEYS NEED SOMEONE TO FEED THEIR PETS WHILE THEY'RE ON VACATION.
ARE YOU INTERESTED?
SURE.
I'LL DO IT FOR $300 AND NOT A PENNY LESS.
IT PAYS $5 A DAY, AND I ALREADY TOLD THEM YOU'D TAKE THE JOB.
NEVER USE YOUR MOM AS YOUR AGENT.

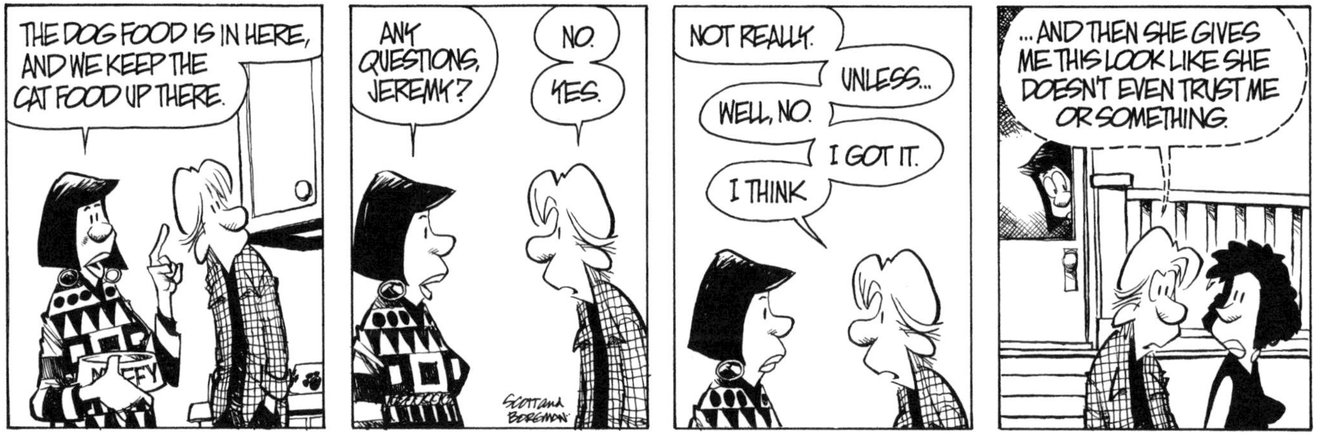
THE DOG FOOD IS IN HERE, AND WE KEEP THE CAT FOOD UP THERE.
MIFFY
ANY QUESTIONS, JEREMY?
NO.
YES.
NOT REALLY.
UNLESS...
WELL, NO.
I GOT IT.
I THINK.
...AND THEN SHE GIVES ME THIS LOOK LIKE SHE DOESN'T EVEN TRUST ME OR SOMETHING.

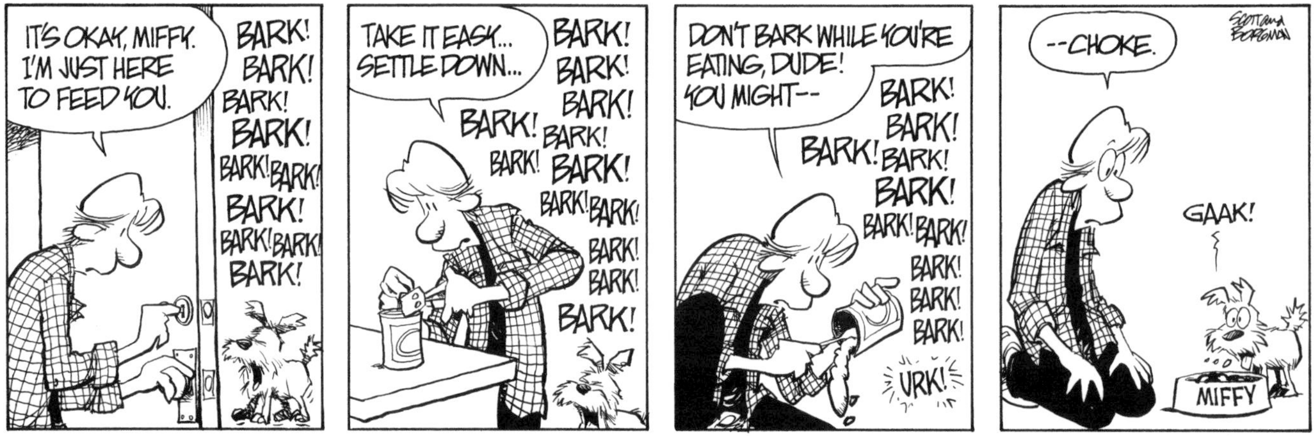
IT'S OKAY, MIFFY. I'M JUST HERE TO FEED YOU.
BARK! BARK! BARK! BARK! BARK! BARK! BARK! BARK! BARK! BARK!
TAKE IT EASY... SETTLE DOWN...
BARK! BARK! BARK! BARK! BARK! BARK! BARK! BARK! BARK! BARK! BARK! BARK! BARK!
DON'T BARK WHILE YOU'RE EATING, DUDE! YOU MIGHT--
BARK! BARK! BARK! BARK! BARK! BARK! BARK! BARK! BARK! BARK!
URK!
--CHOKE.
GAAK!
MIFFY

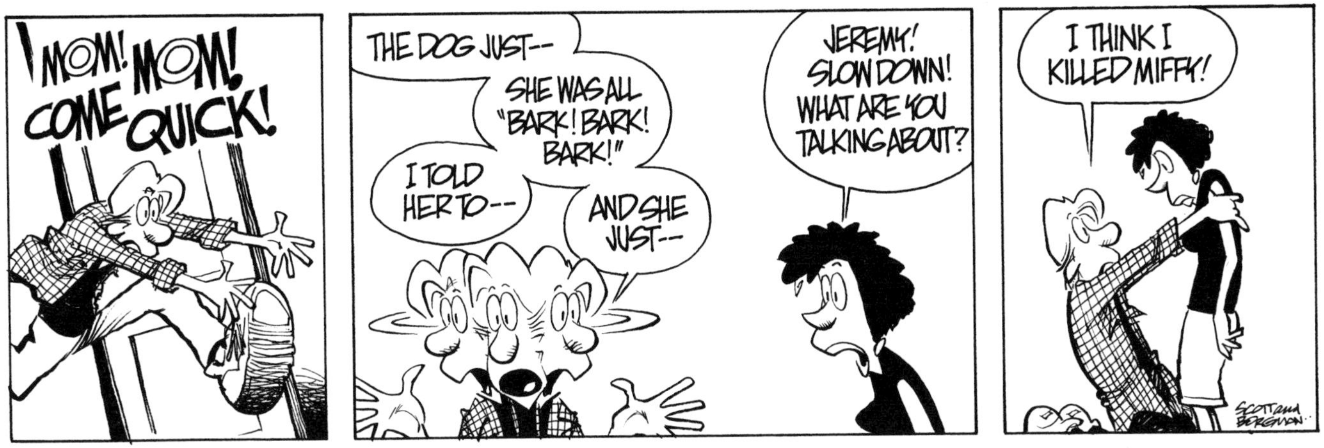
MOM! MOM! COME QUICK!
THE DOG JUST--
I TOLD HER TO--
SHE WAS ALL "BARK! BARK! BARK!"
AND SHE JUST--
JEREMY! SLOW DOWN! WHAT ARE YOU TALKING ABOUT?
I THINK I KILLED MIFFY!

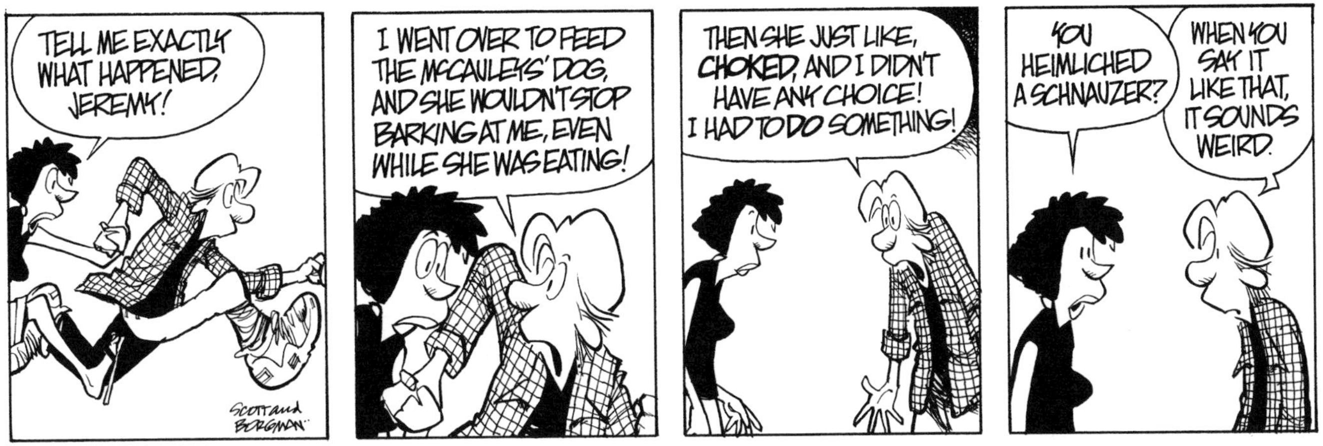
TELL ME EXACTLY WHAT HAPPENED, JEREMY!
I WENT OVER TO FEED THE McCAULEYS' DOG, AND SHE WOULDN'T STOP BARKING AT ME, EVEN WHILE SHE WAS EATING!
THEN SHE JUST LIKE, CHOKED, AND I DIDN'T HAVE ANY CHOICE! I HAD TO DO SOMETHING!
YOU HEIMLICHED A SCHNAUZER?
WHEN YOU SAY IT LIKE THAT, IT SOUNDS WEIRD.

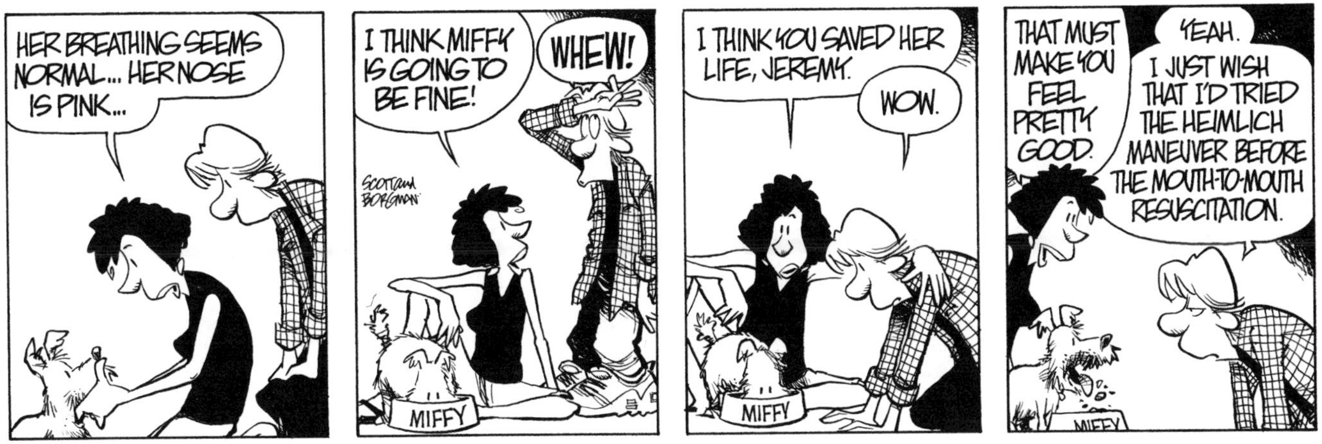
HER BREATHING SEEMS NORMAL... HER NOSE IS PINK...
I THINK MIFFY IS GOING TO BE FINE!
WHEW!
MIFFY
I THINK YOU SAVED HER LIFE, JEREMY.
WOW.
MIFFY
THAT MUST MAKE YOU FEEL PRETTY GOOD.
YEAH. I JUST WISH THAT I'D TRIED THE HEIMLICH MANEUVER BEFORE THE MOUTH-TO-MOUTH RESUSCITATION.
MIFFY

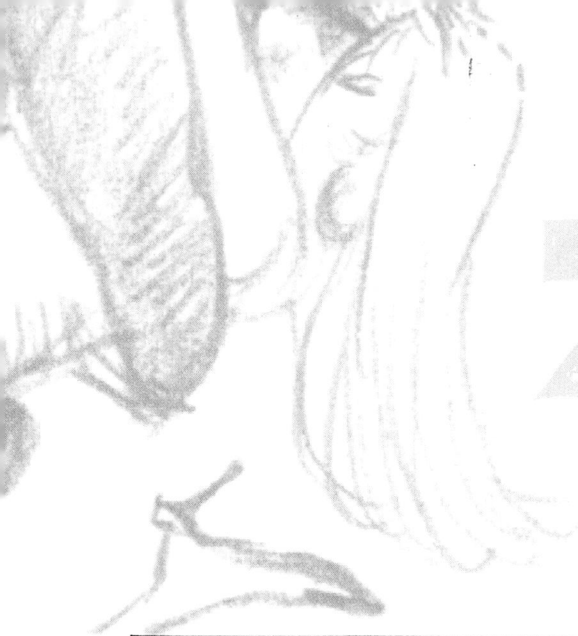

Zits

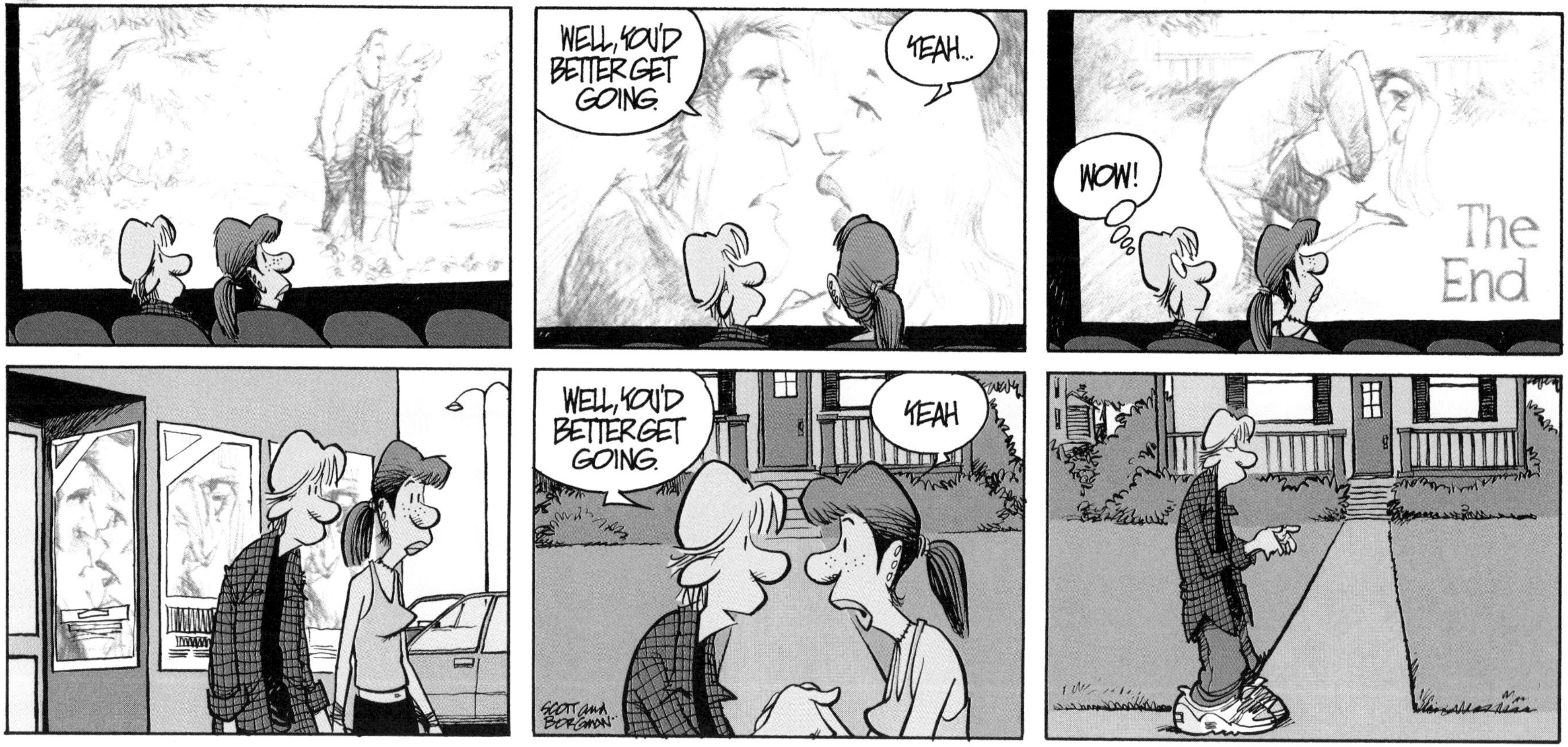

WELL, YOU'D BETTER GET GOING.
YEAH...
WOW!
The End
WELL, YOU'D BETTER GET GOING.
YEAH
SCOTT AND BORGMAN

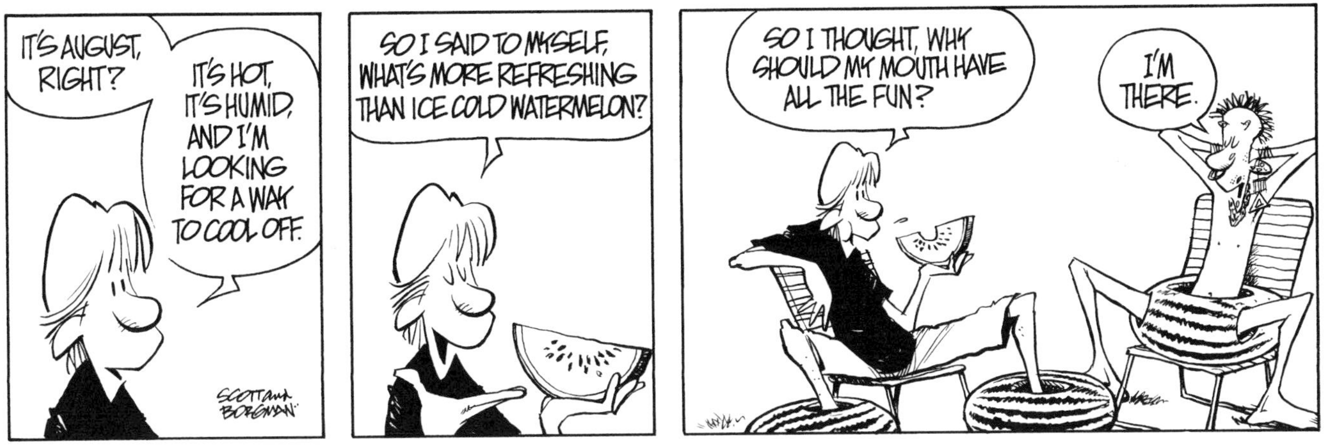
IT'S AUGUST, RIGHT?
IT'S HOT, IT'S HUMID, AND I'M LOOKING FOR A WAY TO COOL OFF.
SCOTT and BORGMAN
SO I SAID TO MYSELF, WHAT'S MORE REFRESHING THAN ICE COLD WATERMELON?
SO I THOUGHT, WHY SHOULD MY MOUTH HAVE ALL THE FUN?
I'M THERE.

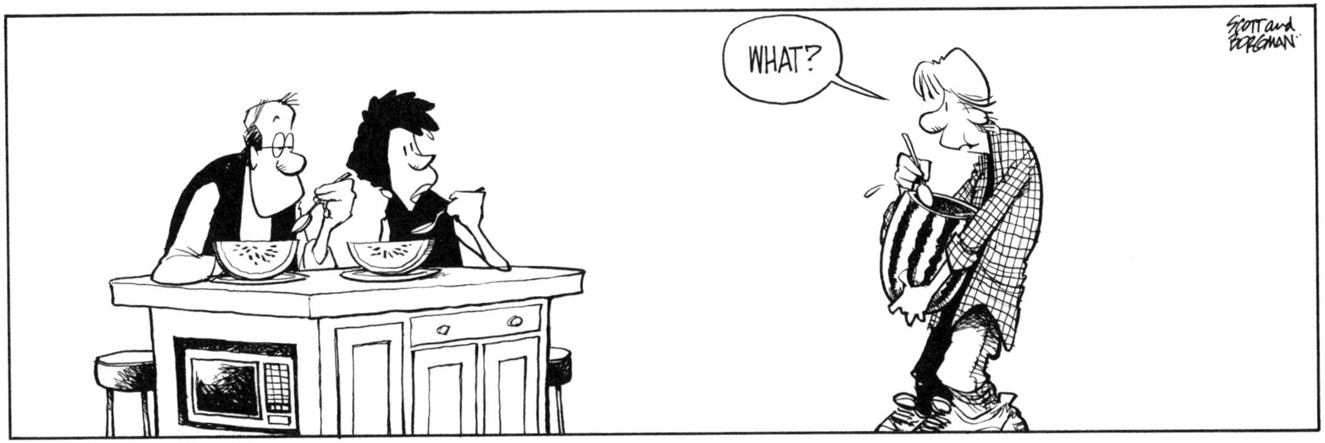
SCOTT and BORGMAN
WHAT?

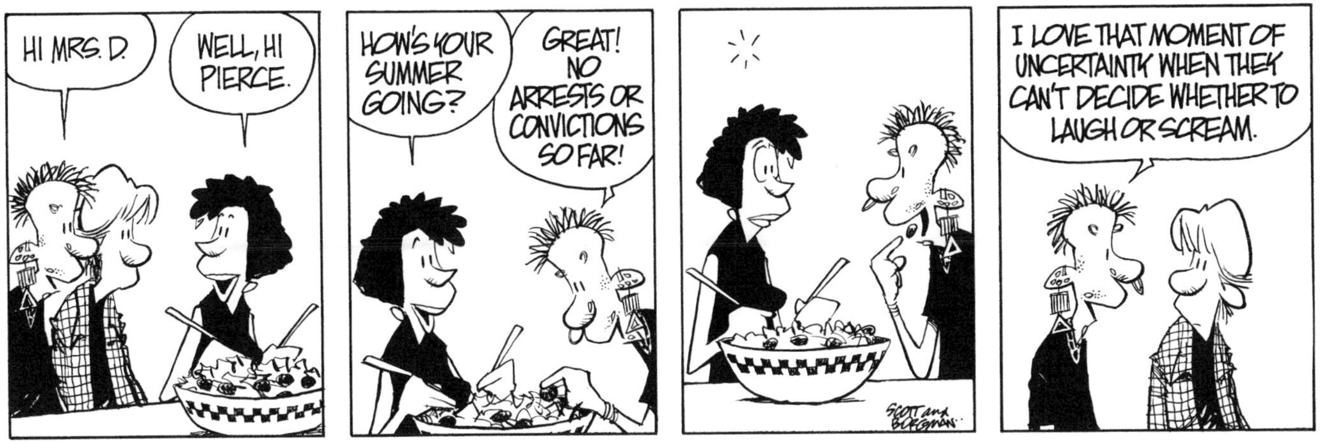
HI MRS. D.
WELL, HI PIERCE.
HOW'S YOUR SUMMER GOING?
GREAT! NO ARRESTS OR CONVICTIONS SO FAR!
SCOTT and BORGMAN
I LOVE THAT MOMENT OF UNCERTAINTY WHEN THEY CAN'T DECIDE WHETHER TO LAUGH OR SCREAM.

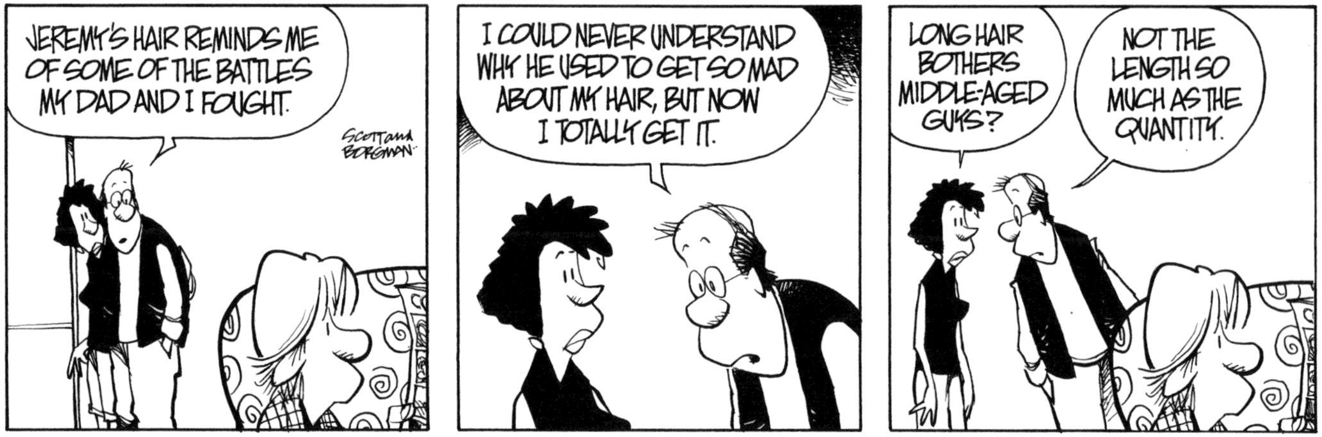
JEREMY'S HAIR REMINDS ME OF SOME OF THE BATTLES MY DAD AND I FOUGHT.
I COULD NEVER UNDERSTAND WHY HE USED TO GET SO MAD ABOUT MY HAIR, BUT NOW I TOTALLY GET IT.
LONG HAIR BOTHERS MIDDLE-AGED GUYS?
NOT THE LENGTH SO MUCH AS THE QUANTITY.

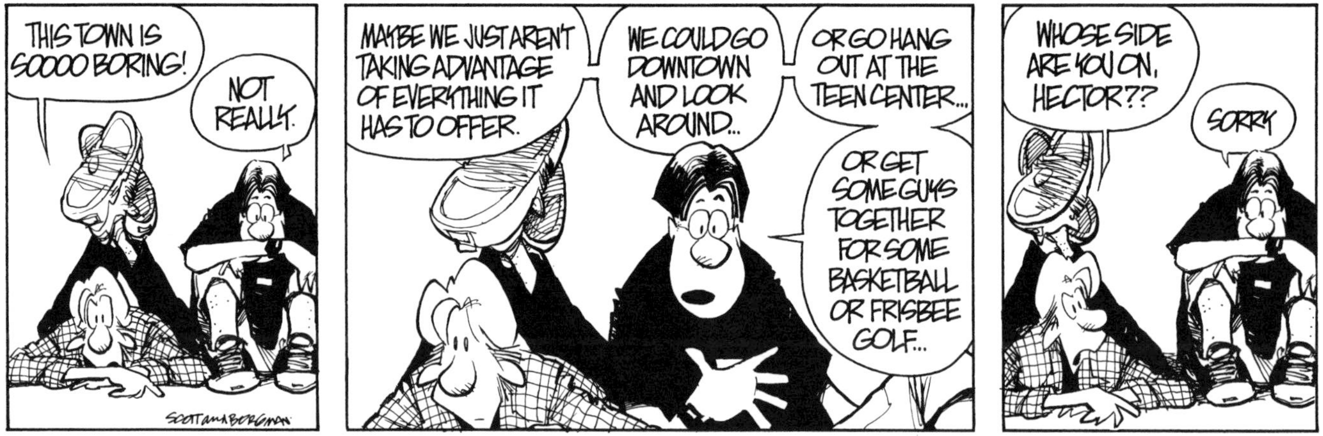
THIS TOWN IS SOOOO BORING!
NOT REALLY.
MAYBE WE JUST AREN'T TAKING ADVANTAGE OF EVERYTHING IT HAS TO OFFER.
WE COULD GO DOWNTOWN AND LOOK AROUND...
OR GO HANG OUT AT THE TEEN CENTER...
OR GET SOME GUYS TOGETHER FOR SOME BASKETBALL OR FRISBEE GOLF...
WHOSE SIDE ARE YOU ON, HECTOR??
SORRY

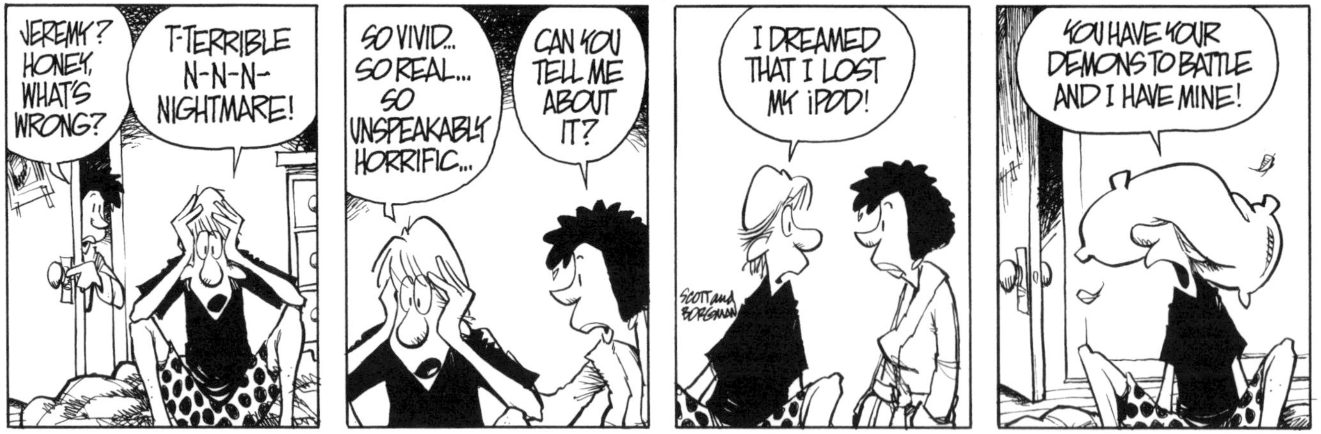
JEREMY? HONEY, WHAT'S WRONG?
T-TERRIBLE N-N-N-NIGHTMARE!
SO VIVID... SO REAL... SO UNSPEAKABLY HORRIFIC...
CAN YOU TELL ME ABOUT IT?
I DREAMED THAT I LOST MY iPOD!
YOU HAVE YOUR DEMONS TO BATTLE AND I HAVE MINE!

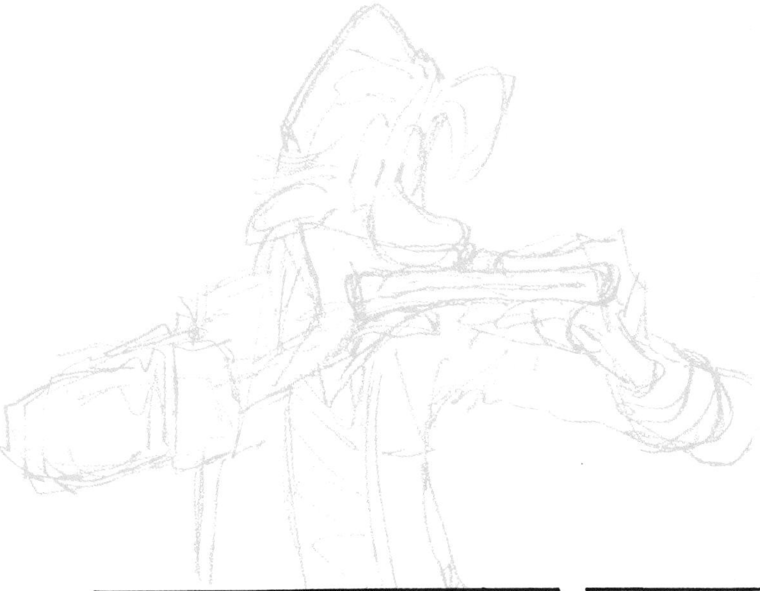

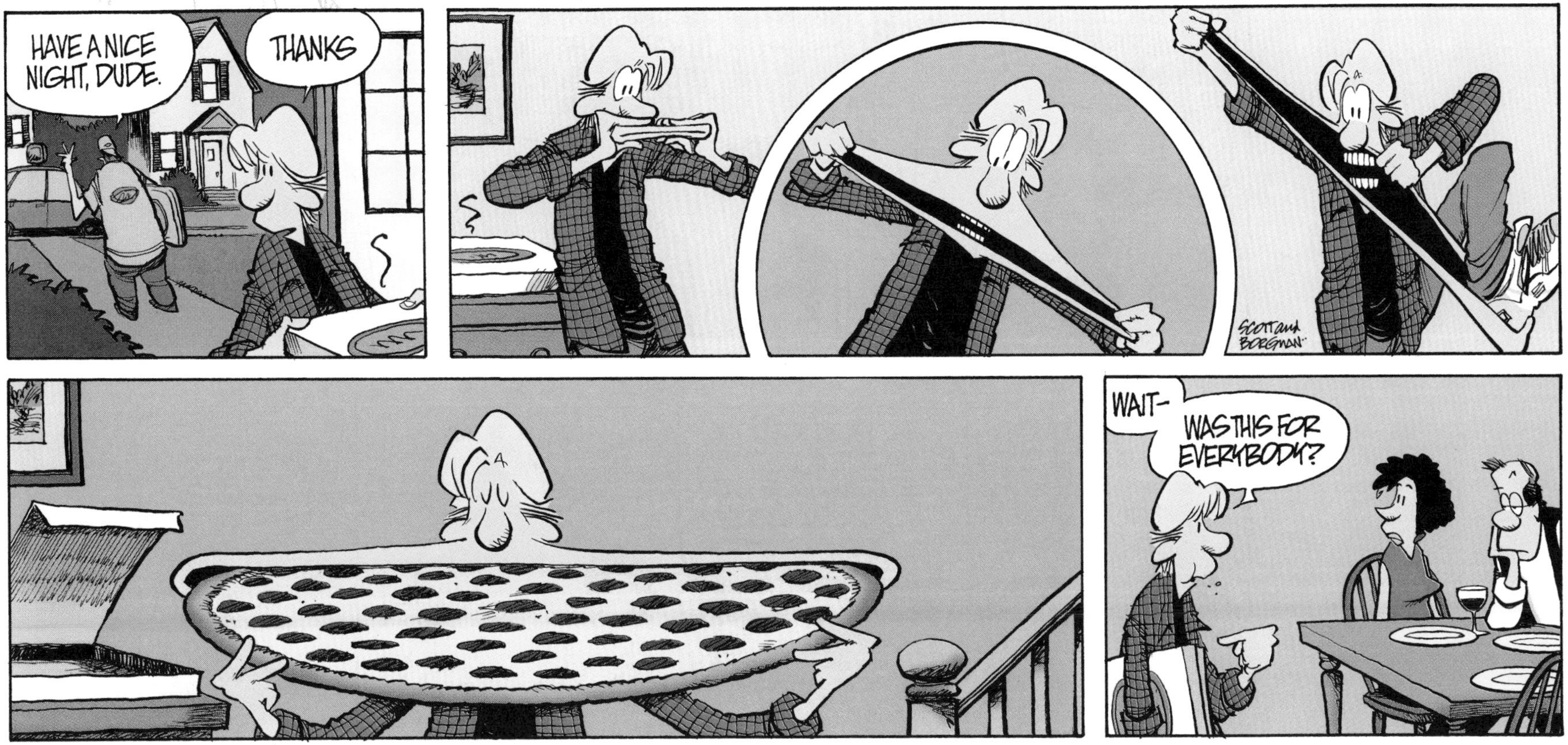
HAVE A NICE NIGHT, DUDE.
THANKS
WAIT-
WAS THIS FOR EVERYBODY?

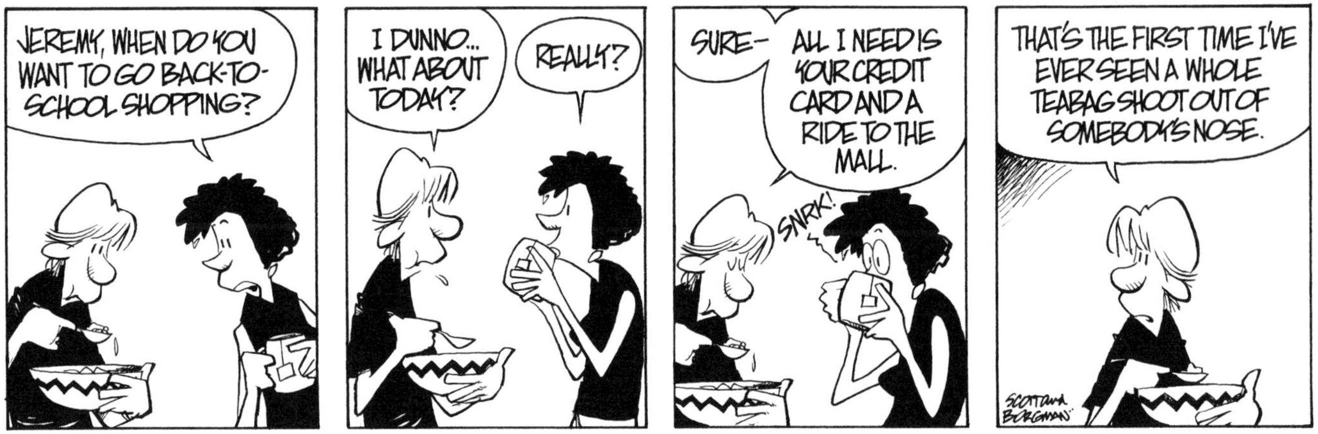
JEREMY, WHEN DO YOU WANT TO GO BACK-TO-SCHOOL SHOPPING?
I DUNNO... WHAT ABOUT TODAY?
REALLY?
SURE-
ALL I NEED IS YOUR CREDIT CARD AND A RIDE TO THE MALL.
SNRK!
THAT'S THE FIRST TIME I'VE EVER SEEN A WHOLE TEABAG SHOOT OUT OF SOMEBODY'S NOSE.

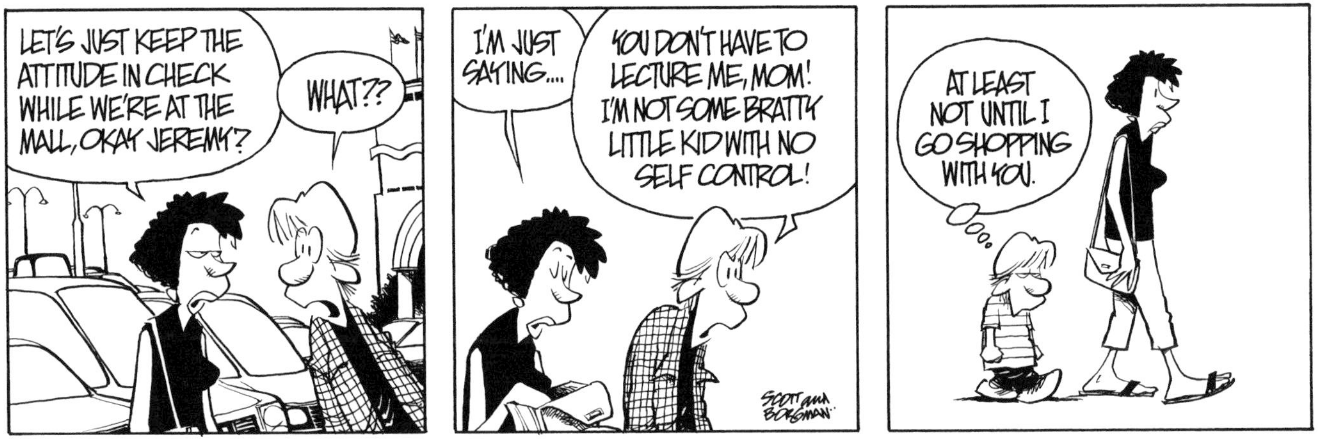
LET'S JUST KEEP THE ATTITUDE IN CHECK WHILE WE'RE AT THE MALL, OKAY JEREMY?
WHAT??
I'M JUST SAYING....
YOU DON'T HAVE TO LECTURE ME, MOM! I'M NOT SOME BRATTY LITTLE KID WITH NO SELF CONTROL!
AT LEAST NOT UNTIL I GO SHOPPING WITH YOU.

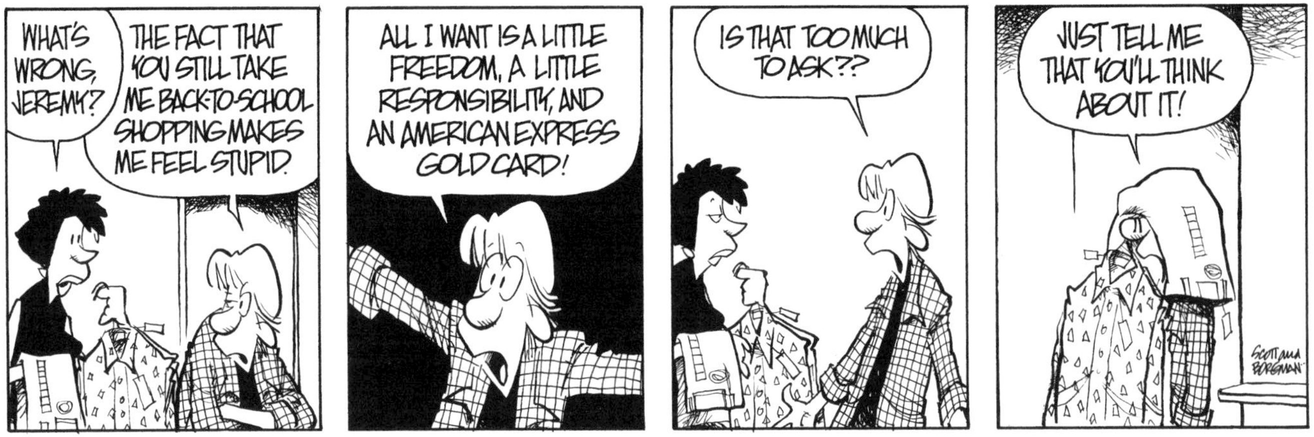
WHAT'S WRONG, JEREMY?
THE FACT THAT YOU STILL TAKE ME BACK-TO-SCHOOL SHOPPING MAKES ME FEEL STUPID.
ALL I WANT IS A LITTLE FREEDOM, A LITTLE RESPONSIBILITY, AND AN AMERICAN EXPRESS GOLD CARD!
IS THAT TOO MUCH TO ASK??
JUST TELL ME THAT YOU'LL THINK ABOUT IT!

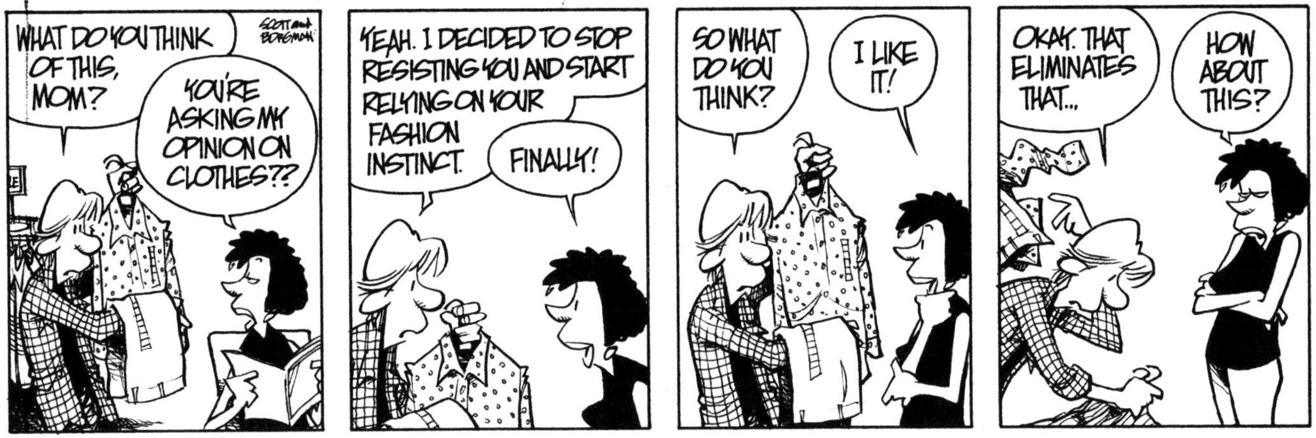
SCOTT and BORGMAN
WHAT DO YOU THINK OF THIS, MOM?
YOU'RE ASKING MY OPINION ON CLOTHES??
YEAH. I DECIDED TO STOP RESISTING YOU AND START RELYING ON YOUR FASHION INSTINCT.
FINALLY!
SO WHAT DO YOU THINK?
I LIKE IT!
OKAY. THAT ELIMINATES THAT...
HOW ABOUT THIS?

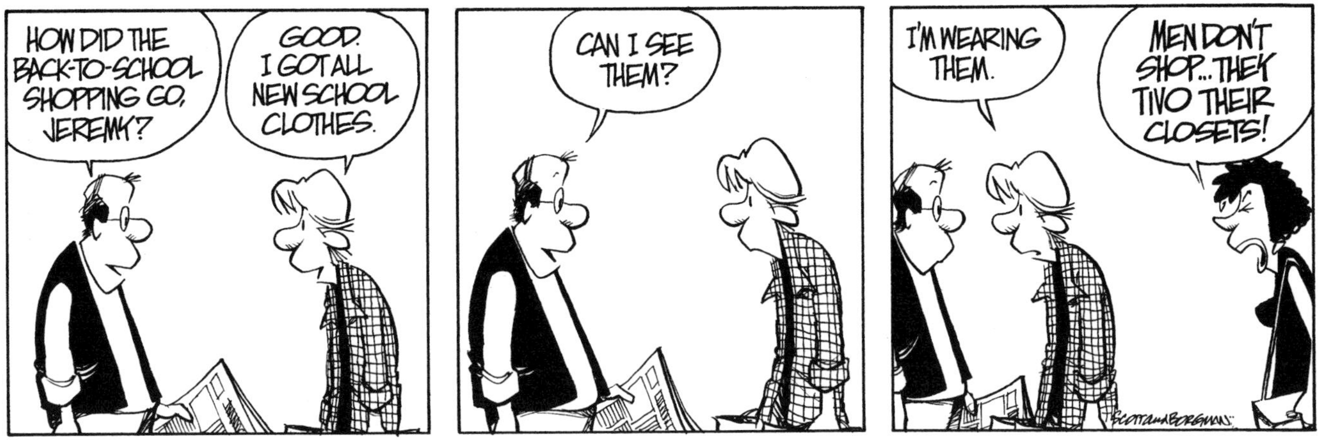
HOW DID THE BACK-TO-SCHOOL SHOPPING GO, JEREMY?
GOOD. I GOT ALL NEW SCHOOL CLOTHES.
CAN I SEE THEM?
I'M WEARING THEM.
MEN DON'T SHOP... THEY TIVO THEIR CLOSETS!
SCOTT and BORGMAN

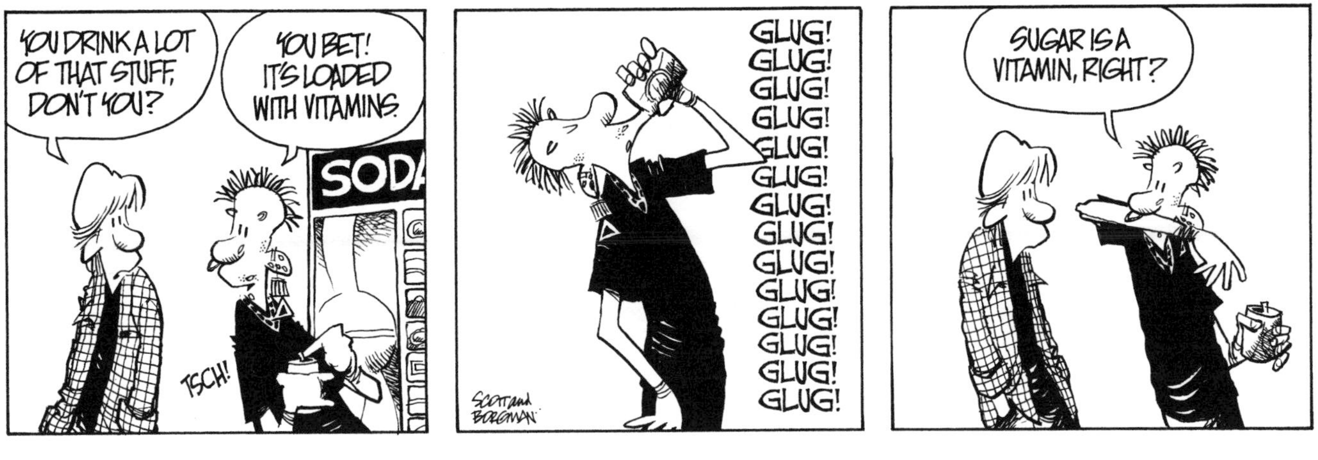
YOU DRINK A LOT OF THAT STUFF, DON'T YOU?
YOU BET! IT'S LOADED WITH VITAMINS.
SODA
TSCH!
GLUG! GLUG! GLUG! GLUG! GLUG! GLUG! GLUG! GLUG! GLUG! GLUG! GLUG! GLUG! GLUG! GLUG!
SCOTT and BORGMAN
SUGAR IS A VITAMIN, RIGHT?

Zits

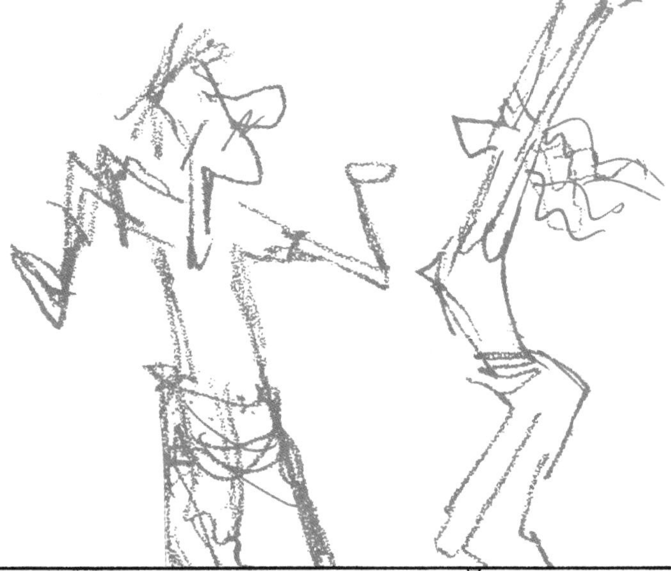

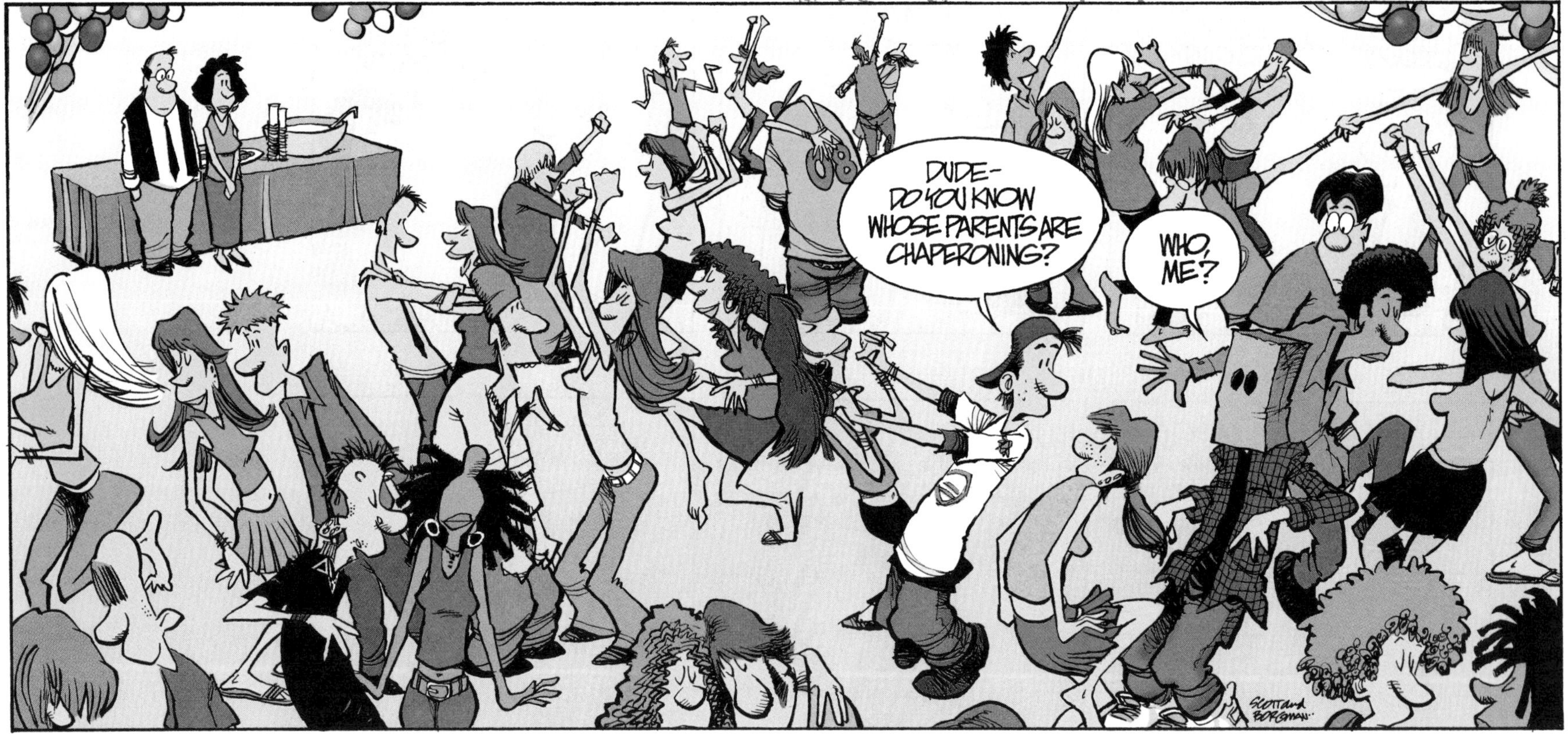
DUDE- DO YOU KNOW WHOSE PARENTS ARE CHAPERONING?
WHO, ME?
SCOTT and BORGMAN

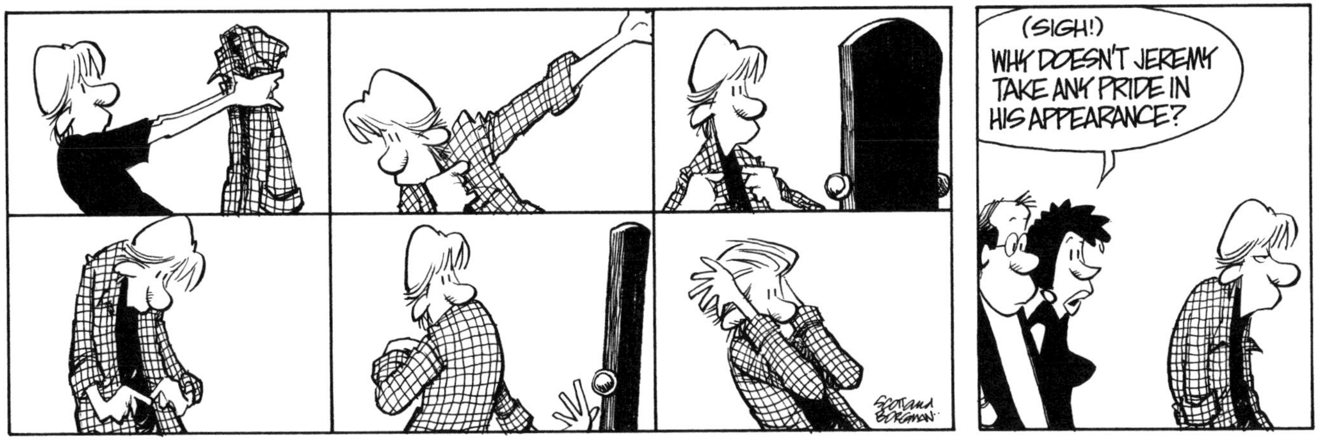
(SIGH!)
WHY DOESN'T JEREMY TAKE ANY PRIDE IN HIS APPEARANCE?

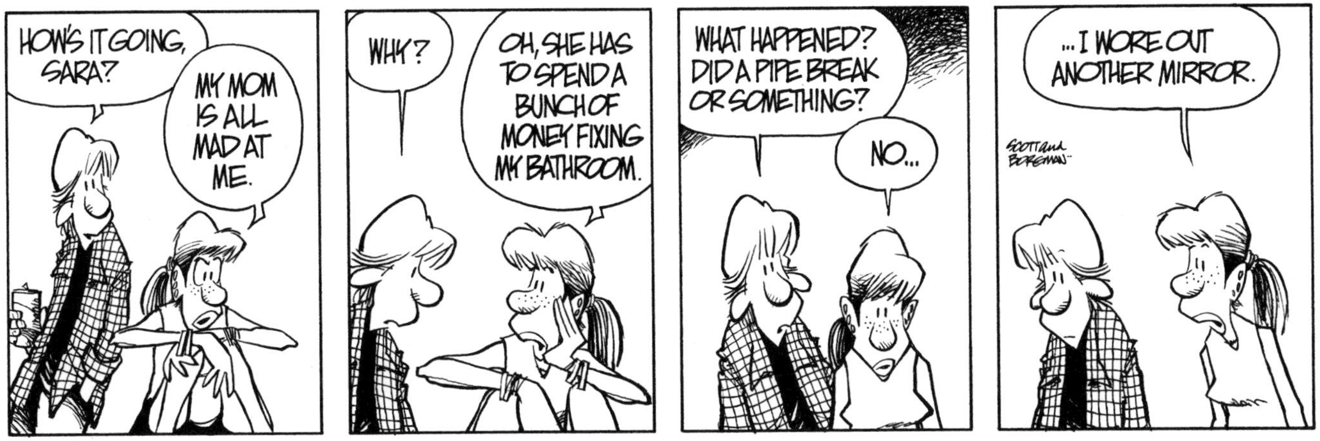
HOW'S IT GOING, SARA?
MY MOM IS ALL MAD AT ME.
WHY?
OH, SHE HAS TO SPEND A BUNCH OF MONEY FIXING MY BATHROOM.
WHAT HAPPENED? DID A PIPE BREAK OR SOMETHING?
NO...
...I WORE OUT ANOTHER MIRROR.

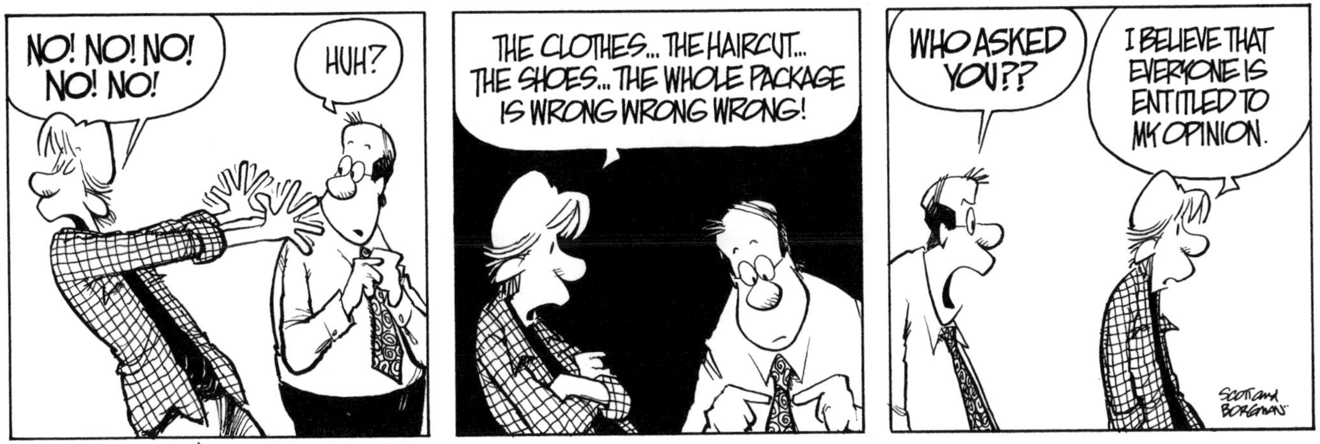
NO! NO! NO! NO! NO!
HUH?
THE CLOTHES... THE HAIRCUT... THE SHOES... THE WHOLE PACKAGE IS WRONG WRONG WRONG!
WHO ASKED YOU??
I BELIEVE THAT EVERYONE IS ENTITLED TO MY OPINION.

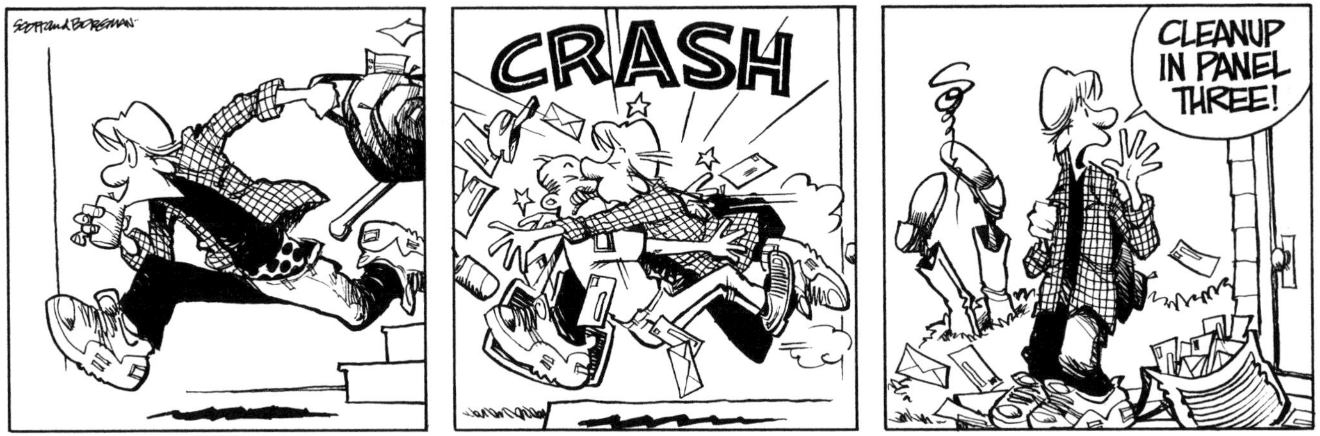
CRASH
CLEANUP IN PANEL THREE!

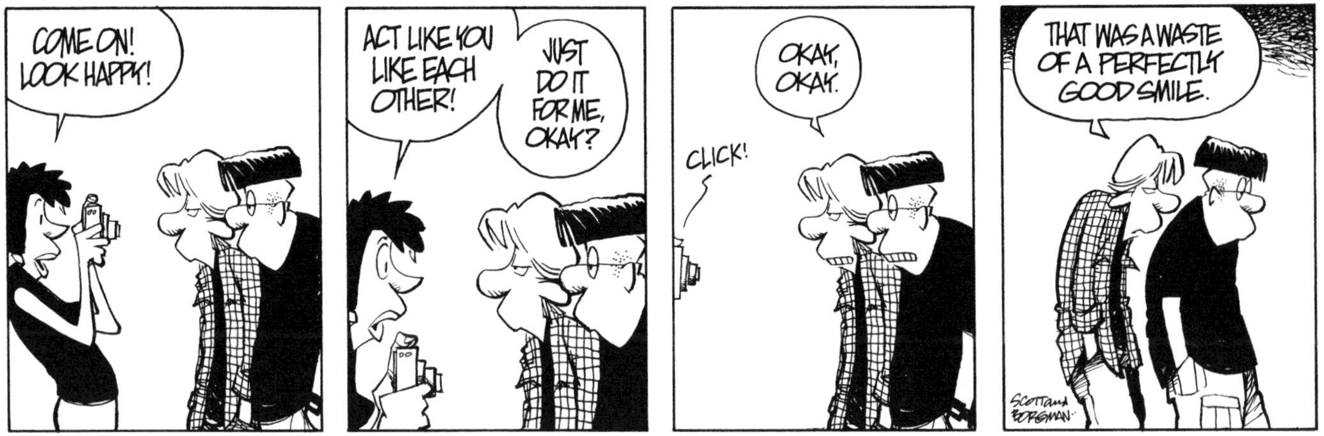
COME ON! LOOK HAPPY!
ACT LIKE YOU LIKE EACH OTHER!
JUST DO IT FOR ME, OKAY?
CLICK!
OKAY, OKAY.
THAT WAS A WASTE OF A PERFECTLY GOOD SMILE.

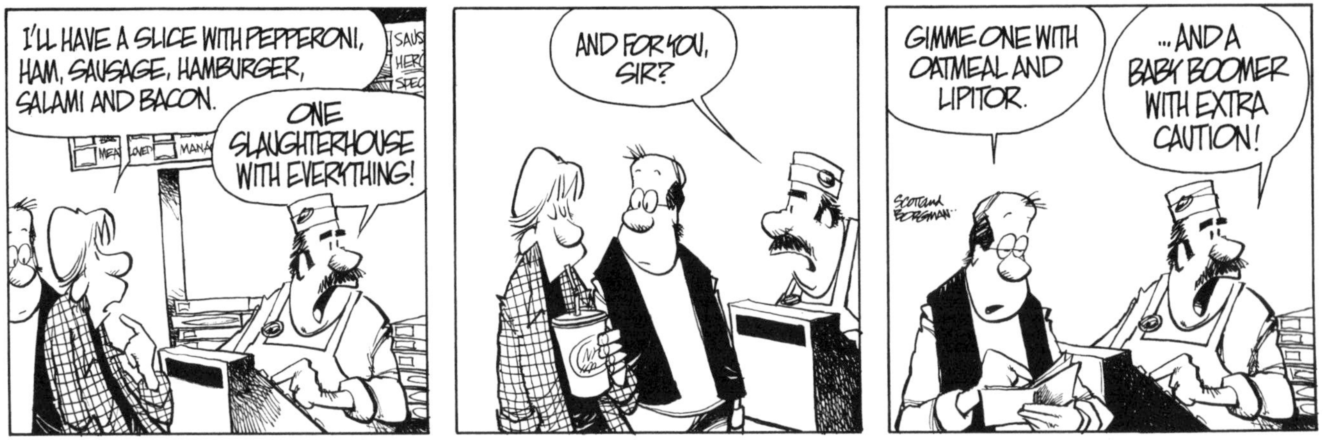
I'LL HAVE A SLICE WITH PEPPERONI, HAM, SAUSAGE, HAMBURGER, SALAMI AND BACON.
ONE SLAUGHTERHOUSE WITH EVERYTHING!
AND FOR YOU, SIR?
GIMME ONE WITH OATMEAL AND LIPITOR.
...AND A BABY BOOMER WITH EXTRA CAUTION!

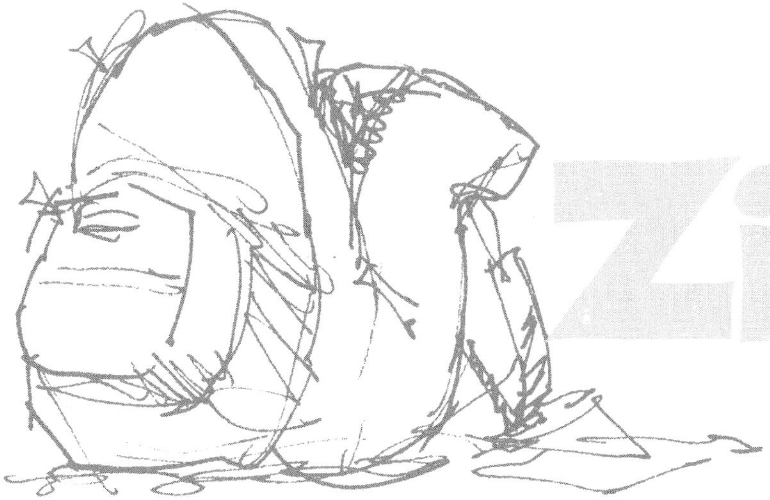

Zits

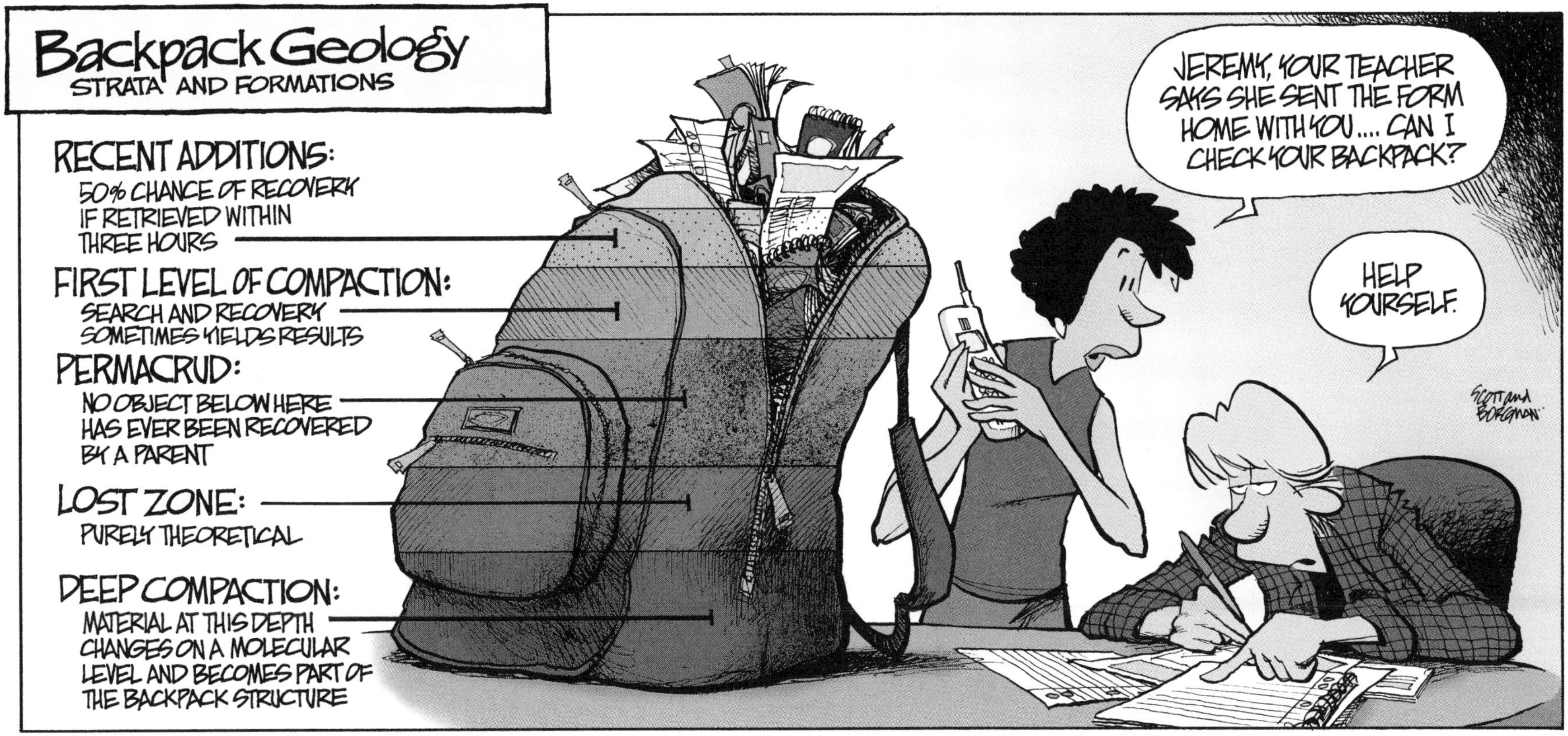

Backpack Geology
STRATA AND FORMATIONS
RECENT ADDITIONS:
50% CHANCE OF RECOVERY IF RETRIEVED WITHIN THREE HOURS
FIRST LEVEL OF COMPACTION:
SEARCH AND RECOVERY SOMETIMES YIELDS RESULTS
PERMACRUD:
NO OBJECT BELOW HERE HAS EVER BEEN RECOVERED BY A PARENT
LOST ZONE:
PURELY THEORETICAL
DEEP COMPACTION:
MATERIAL AT THIS DEPTH CHANGES ON A MOLECULAR LEVEL AND BECOMES PART OF THE BACKPACK STRUCTURE
JEREMY, YOUR TEACHER SAYS SHE SENT THE FORM HOME WITH YOU.... CAN I CHECK YOUR BACKPACK?
HELP YOURSELF.
SCOTT AND BORGMAN

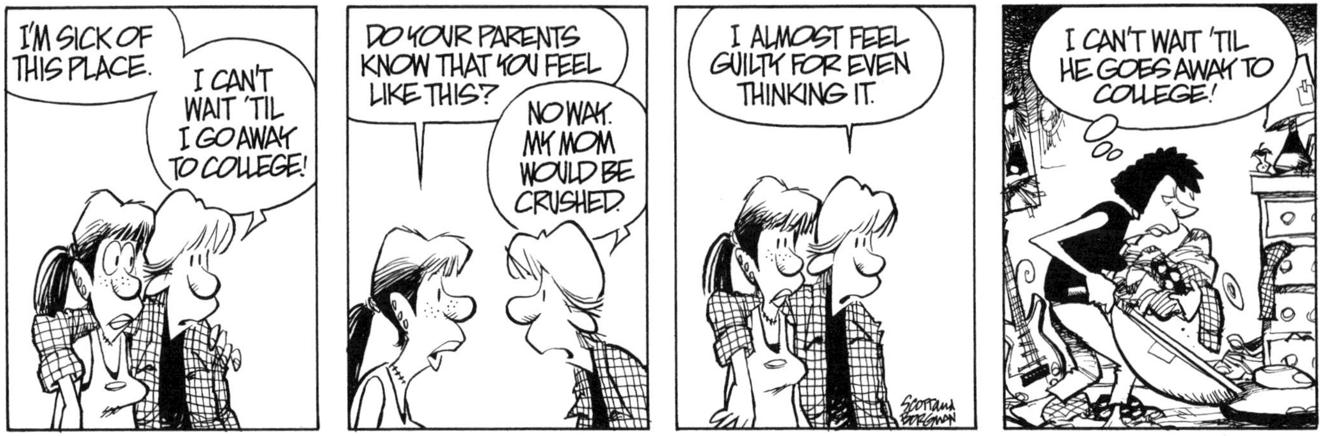
I'M SICK OF THIS PLACE.
I CAN'T WAIT 'TIL I GO AWAY TO COLLEGE!
DO YOUR PARENTS KNOW THAT YOU FEEL LIKE THIS?
NO WAY. MY MOM WOULD BE CRUSHED.
I ALMOST FEEL GUILTY FOR EVEN THINKING IT.
I CAN'T WAIT 'TIL HE GOES AWAY TO COLLEGE!

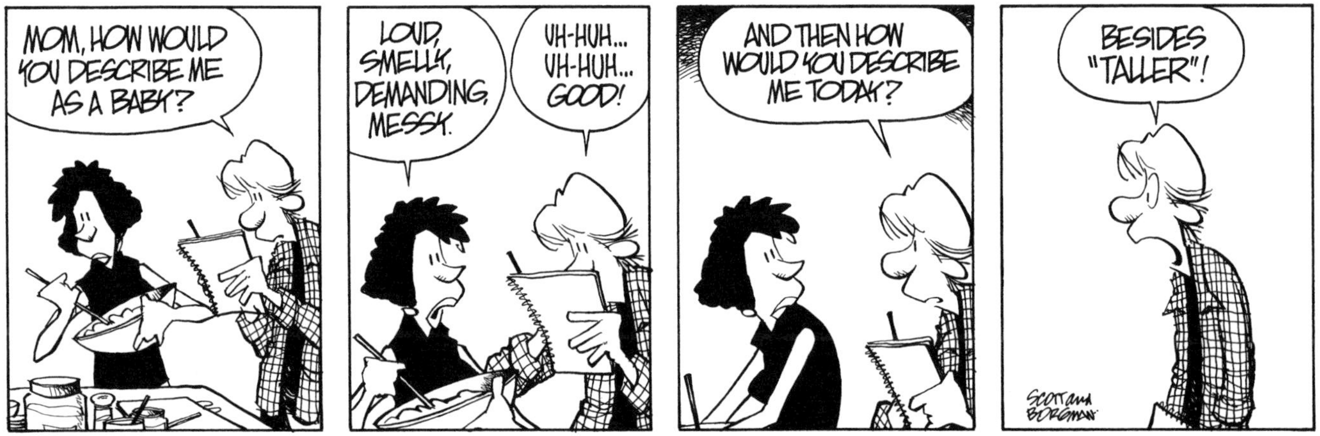
MOM, HOW WOULD YOU DESCRIBE ME AS A BABY?
LOUD, SMELLY, DEMANDING, MESSY.
UH-HUH... UH-HUH... GOOD!
AND THEN HOW WOULD YOU DESCRIBE ME TODAY?
BESIDES "TALLER"!

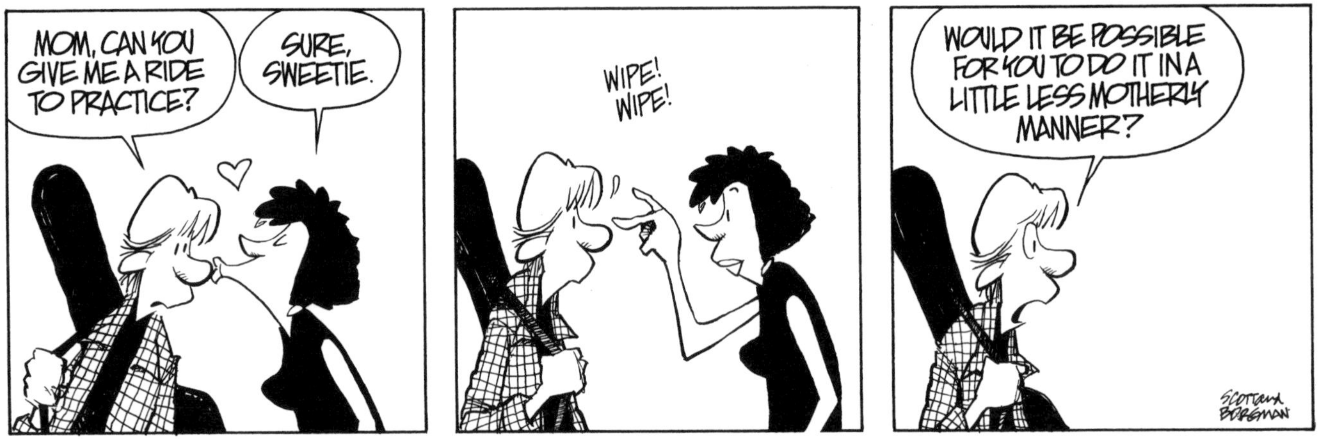
MOM, CAN YOU GIVE ME A RIDE TO PRACTICE?
SURE, SWEETIE.
WIPE! WIPE!
WOULD IT BE POSSIBLE FOR YOU TO DO IT IN A LITTLE LESS MOTHERLY MANNER?

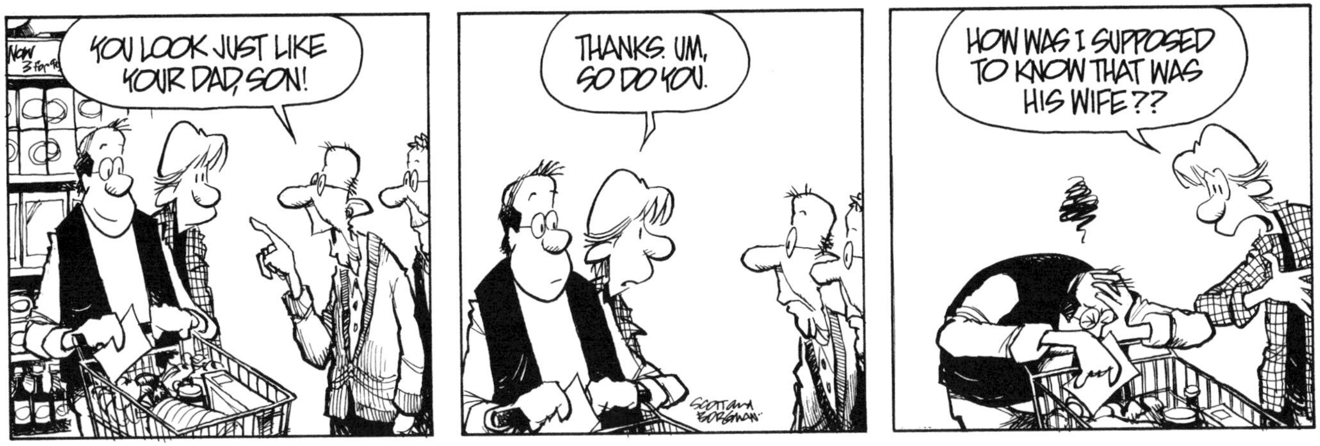
YOU LOOK JUST LIKE YOUR DAD, SON!
THANKS. UM, SO DO YOU.
HOW WAS I SUPPOSED TO KNOW THAT WAS HIS WIFE??

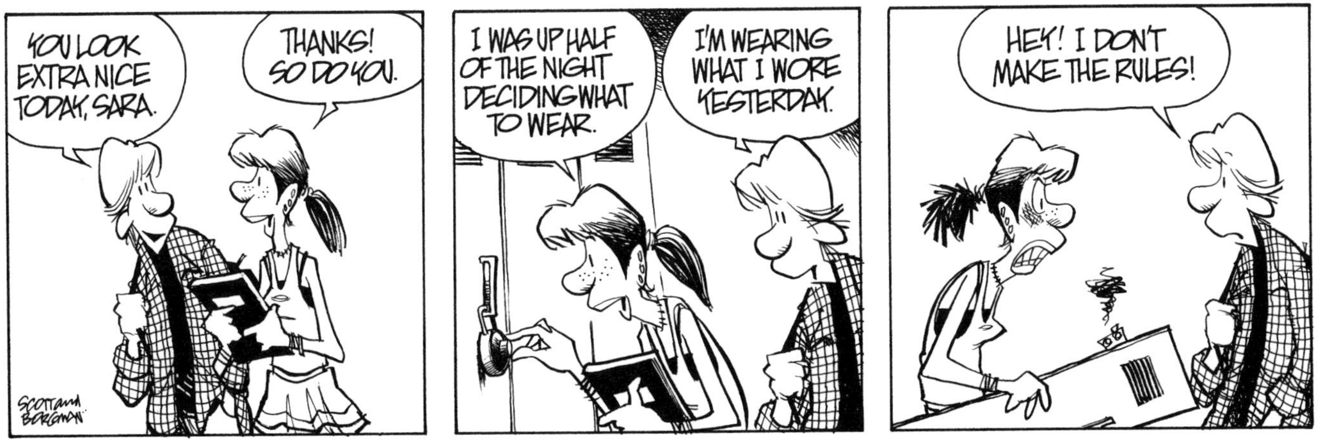
YOU LOOK EXTRA NICE TODAY, SARA.
THANKS! SO DO YOU.
I WAS UP HALF OF THE NIGHT DECIDING WHAT TO WEAR.
I'M WEARING WHAT I WORE YESTERDAY.
HEY! I DON'T MAKE THE RULES!

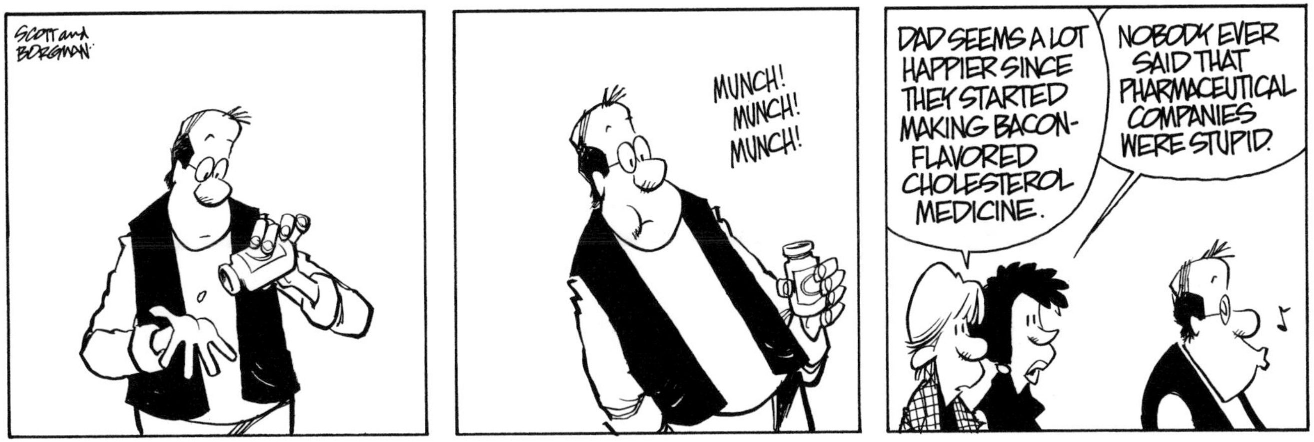
MUNCH! MUNCH! MUNCH!
DAD SEEMS A LOT HAPPIER SINCE THEY STARTED MAKING BACON-FLAVORED CHOLESTEROL MEDICINE.
NOBODY EVER SAID THAT PHARMACEUTICAL COMPANIES WERE STUPID.

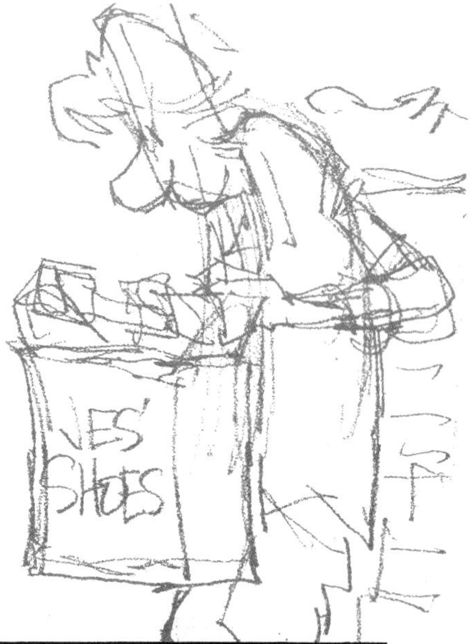
JES'
SHOES

Zits

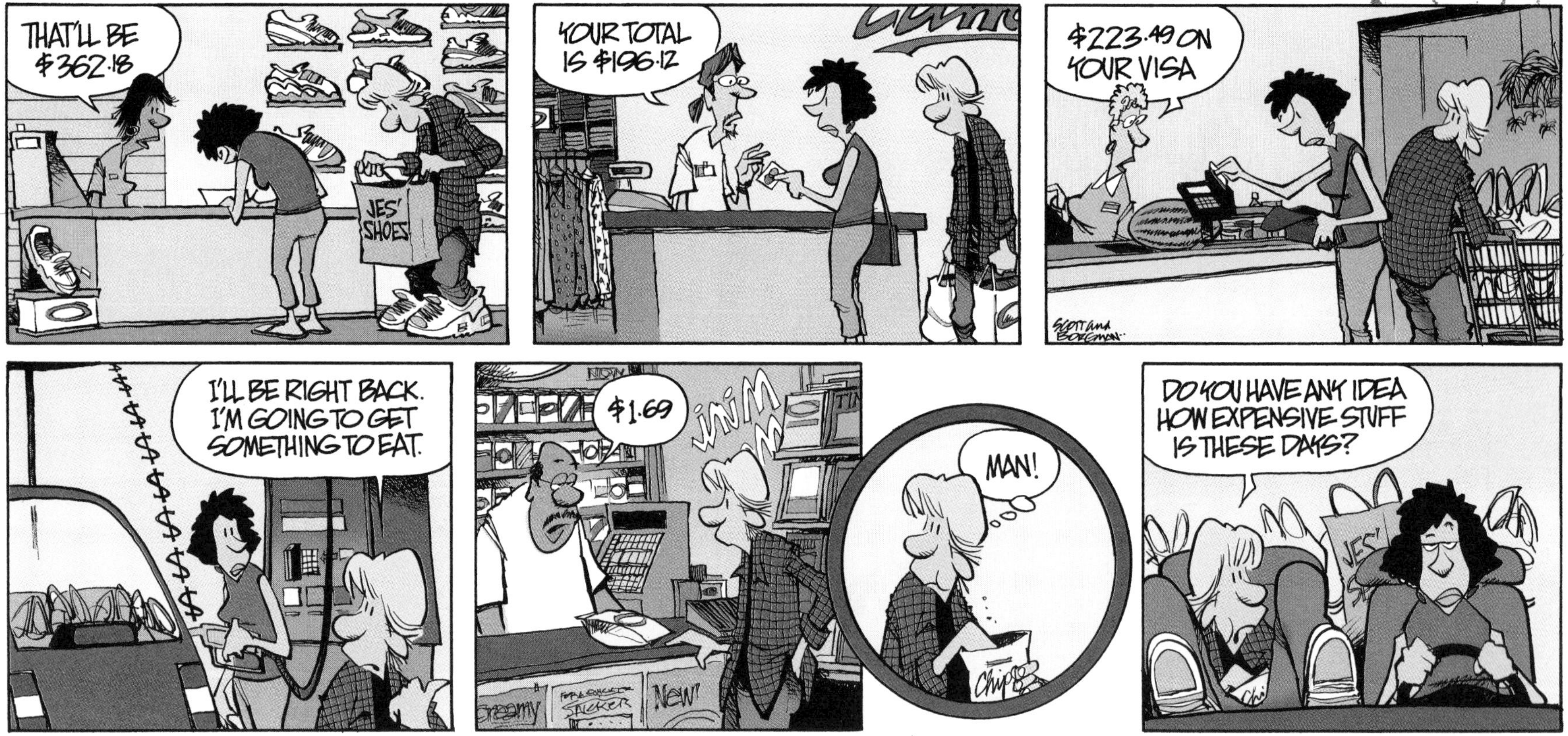
THAT'LL BE $362.18
JES' SHOES
YOUR TOTAL IS $196.12
$223.49 ON YOUR VISA
SCOTT AND BORGMAN
I'LL BE RIGHT BACK. I'M GOING TO GET SOMETHING TO EAT.
$1.69
MAN!
DO YOU HAVE ANY IDEA HOW EXPENSIVE STUFF IS THESE DAYS?

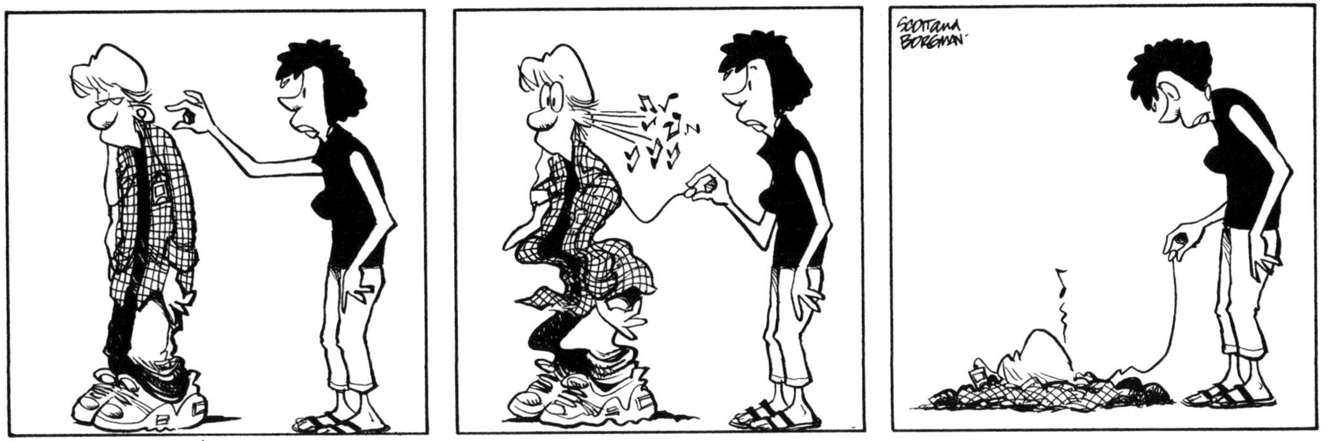

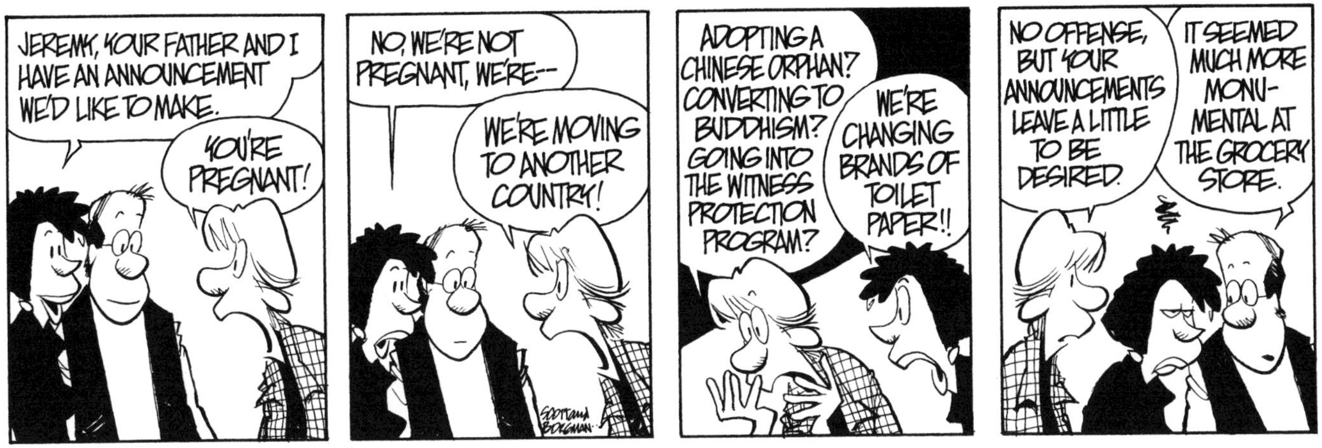
JEREMY, YOUR FATHER AND I HAVE AN ANNOUNCEMENT WE'D LIKE TO MAKE.
YOU'RE PREGNANT!
NO, WE'RE NOT PREGNANT, WE'RE--
WE'RE MOVING TO ANOTHER COUNTRY!
ADOPTING A CHINESE ORPHAN? CONVERTING TO BUDDHISM? GOING INTO THE WITNESS PROTECTION PROGRAM?
WE'RE CHANGING BRANDS OF TOILET PAPER!!
NO OFFENSE, BUT YOUR ANNOUNCEMENTS LEAVE A LITTLE TO BE DESIRED.
IT SEEMED MUCH MORE MONU-MENTAL AT THE GROCERY STORE.

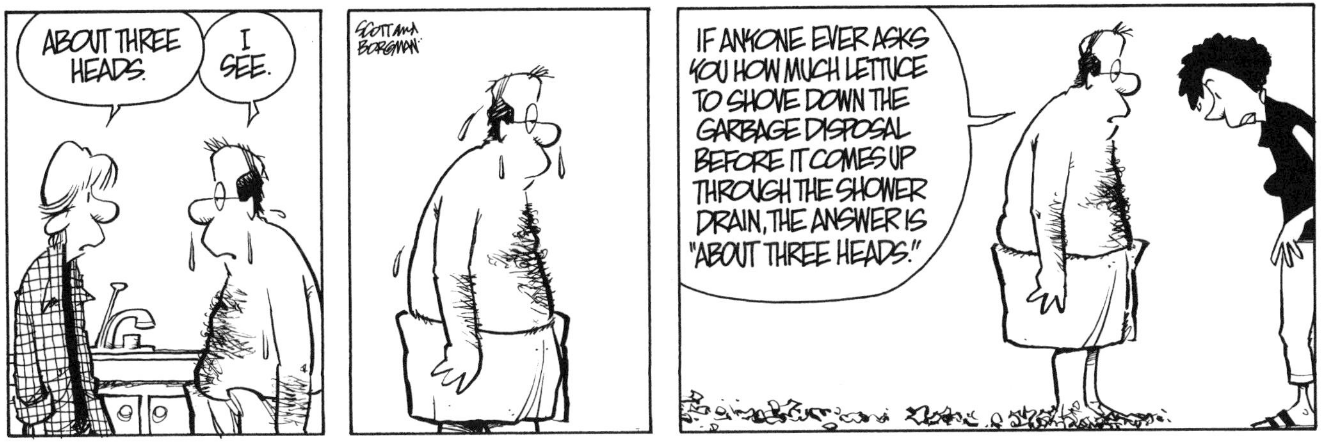
ABOUT THREE HEADS.
I SEE.
IF ANYONE EVER ASKS YOU HOW MUCH LETTUCE TO SHOVE DOWN THE GARBAGE DISPOSAL BEFORE IT COMES UP THROUGH THE SHOWER DRAIN, THE ANSWER IS "ABOUT THREE HEADS."

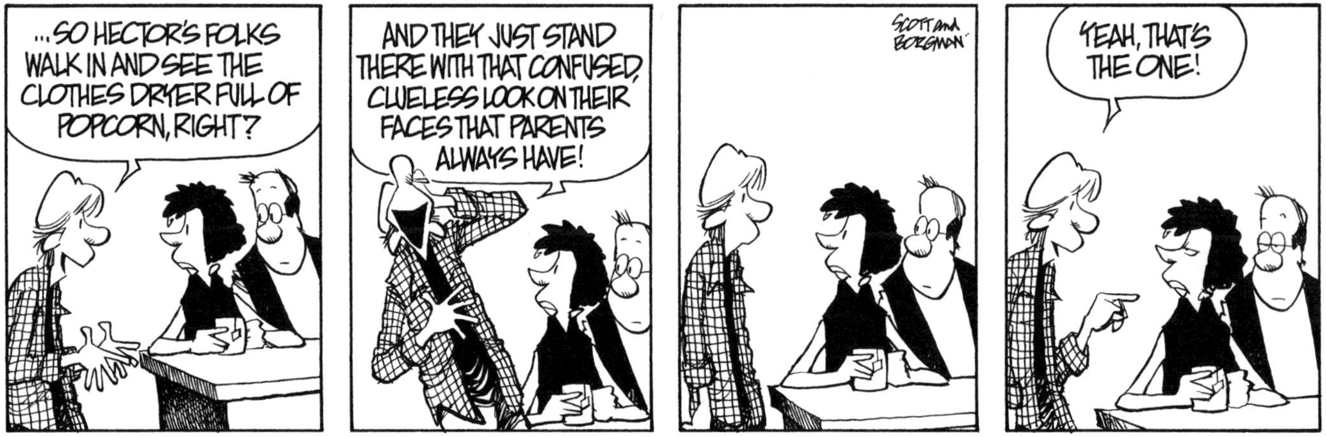
...SO HECTOR'S FOLKS WALK IN AND SEE THE CLOTHES DRYER FULL OF POPCORN, RIGHT?
AND THEY JUST STAND THERE WITH THAT CONFUSED, CLUELESS LOOK ON THEIR FACES THAT PARENTS ALWAYS HAVE!
YEAH, THAT'S THE ONE!

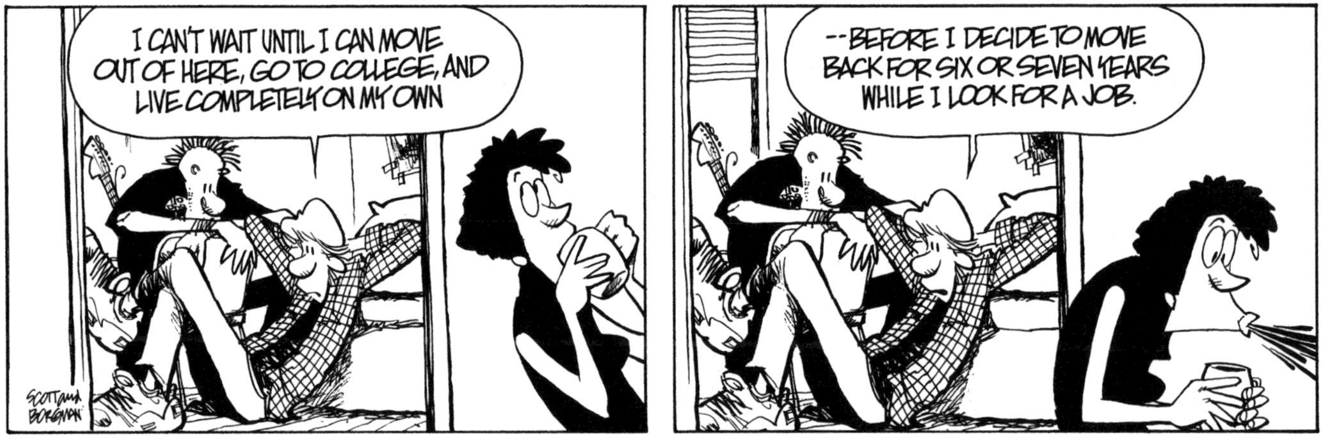
I CAN'T WAIT UNTIL I CAN MOVE OUT OF HERE, GO TO COLLEGE, AND LIVE COMPLETELY ON MY OWN
--BEFORE I DECIDE TO MOVE BACK FOR SIX OR SEVEN YEARS WHILE I LOOK FOR A JOB.

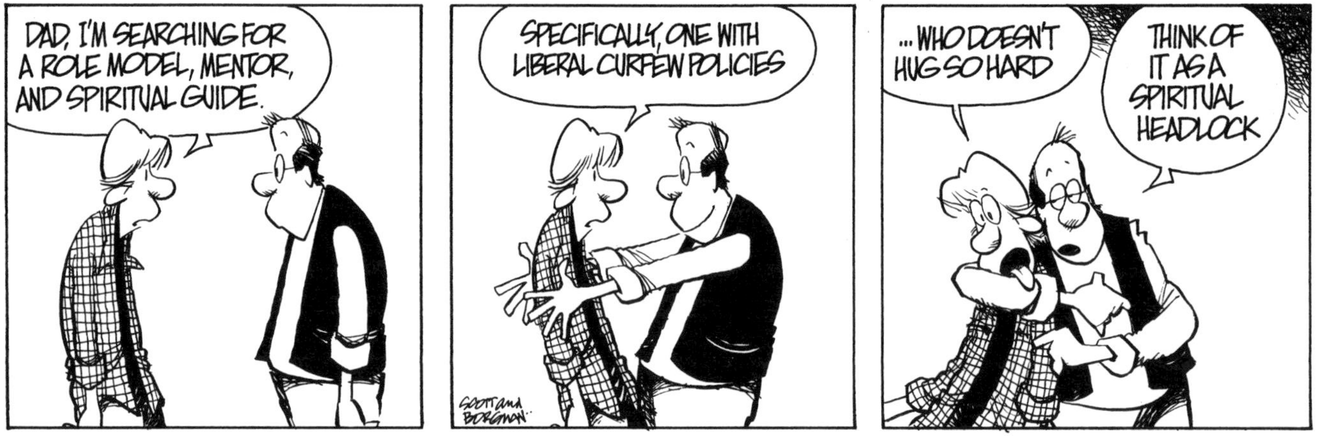
DAD, I'M SEARCHING FOR A ROLE MODEL, MENTOR, AND SPIRITUAL GUIDE.
SPECIFICALLY, ONE WITH LIBERAL CURFEW POLICIES
...WHO DOESN'T HUG SO HARD
THINK OF IT AS A SPIRITUAL HEADLOCK

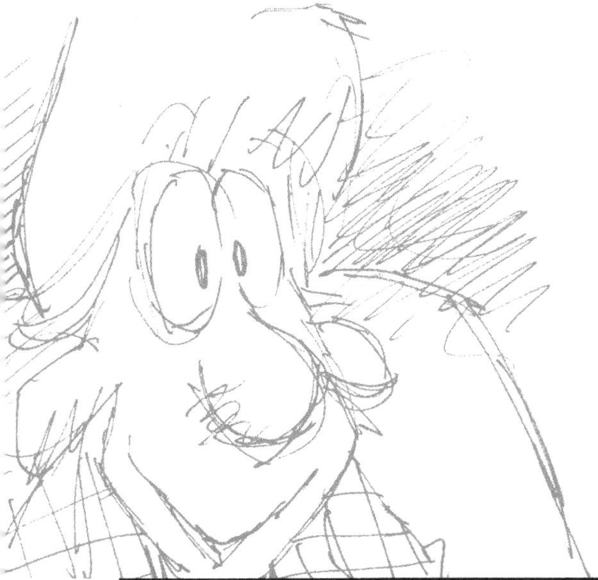

Zits

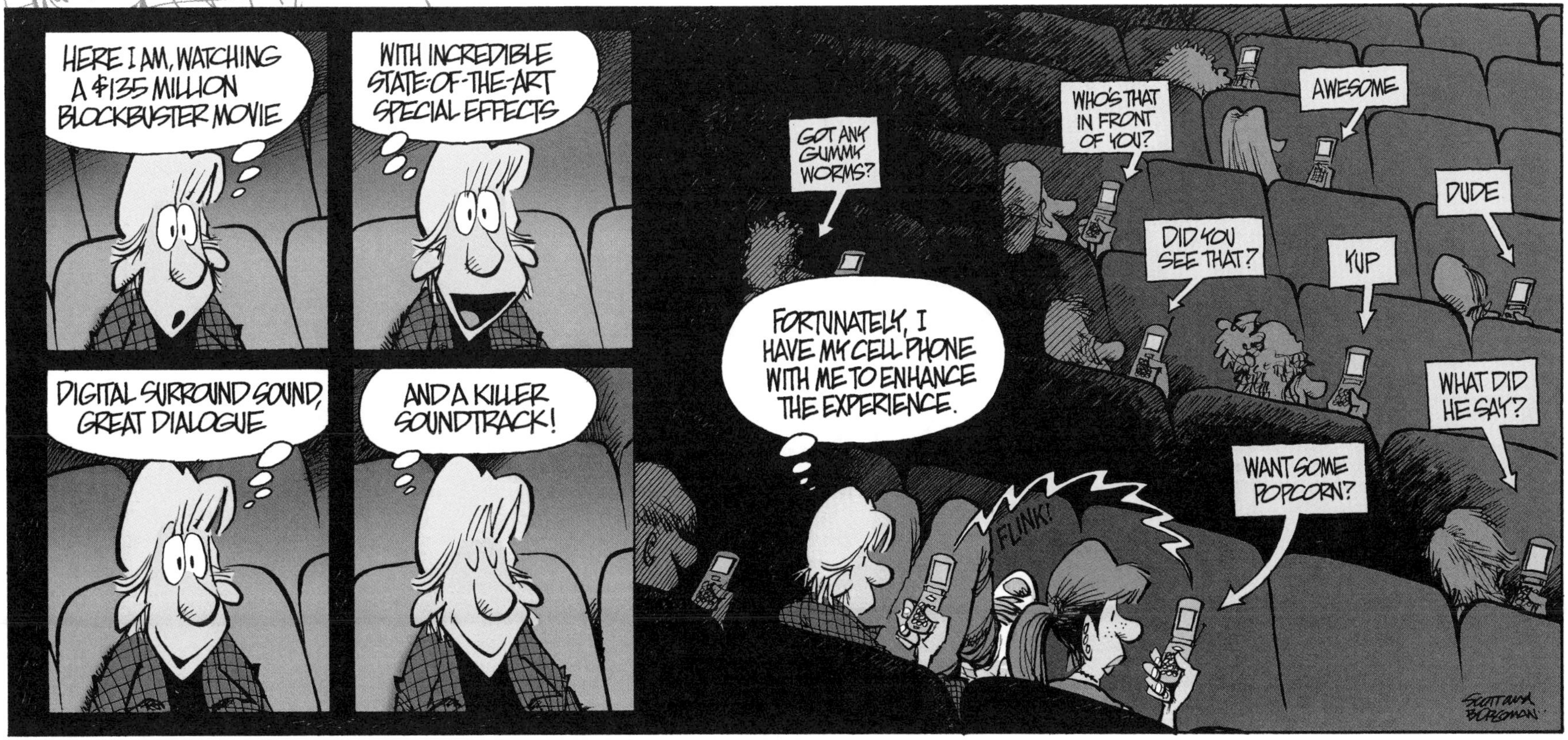
HERE I AM, WATCHING A $135 MILLION BLOCKBUSTER MOVIE
WITH INCREDIBLE STATE-OF-THE-ART SPECIAL EFFECTS
DIGITAL SURROUND SOUND, GREAT DIALOGUE
AND A KILLER SOUNDTRACK!
GOT ANY GUMMY WORMS?
WHO'S THAT IN FRONT OF YOU?
AWESOME
DUDE
DID YOU SEE THAT?
YUP
FORTUNATELY, I HAVE MY CELL PHONE WITH ME TO ENHANCE THE EXPERIENCE.
WHAT DID HE SAY?
WANT SOME POPCORN?
FLINK!

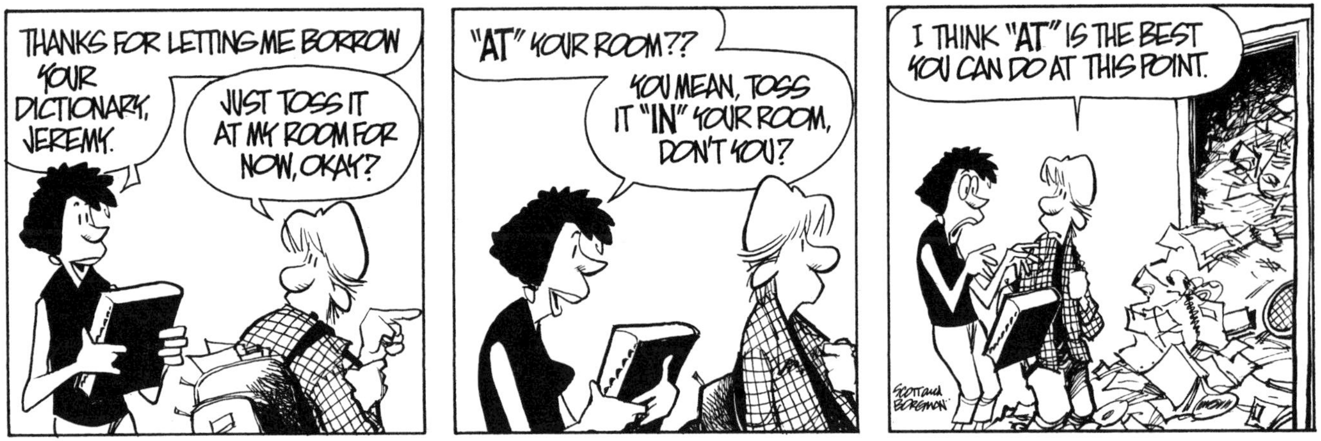
THANKS FOR LETTING ME BORROW YOUR DICTIONARY, JEREMY.
JUST TOSS IT AT MY ROOM FOR NOW, OKAY?
"AT" YOUR ROOM??
YOU MEAN, TOSS IT "IN" YOUR ROOM, DON'T YOU?
I THINK "AT" IS THE BEST YOU CAN DO AT THIS POINT.
SCOTT AND BORGMAN

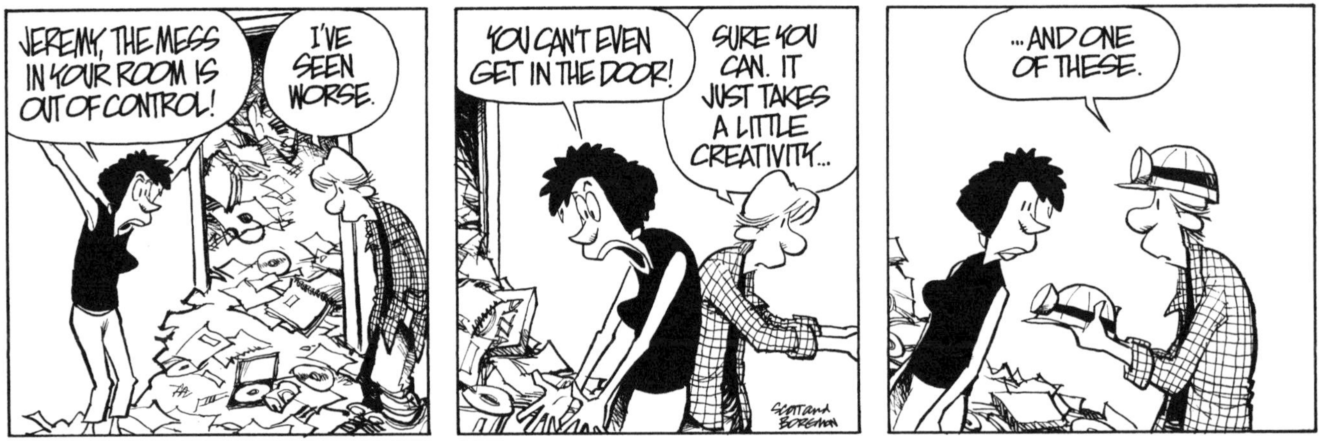
JEREMY, THE MESS IN YOUR ROOM IS OUT OF CONTROL!
I'VE SEEN WORSE.
YOU CAN'T EVEN GET IN THE DOOR!
SURE YOU CAN. IT JUST TAKES A LITTLE CREATIVITY...
SCOTT AND BORGMAN
...AND ONE OF THESE.

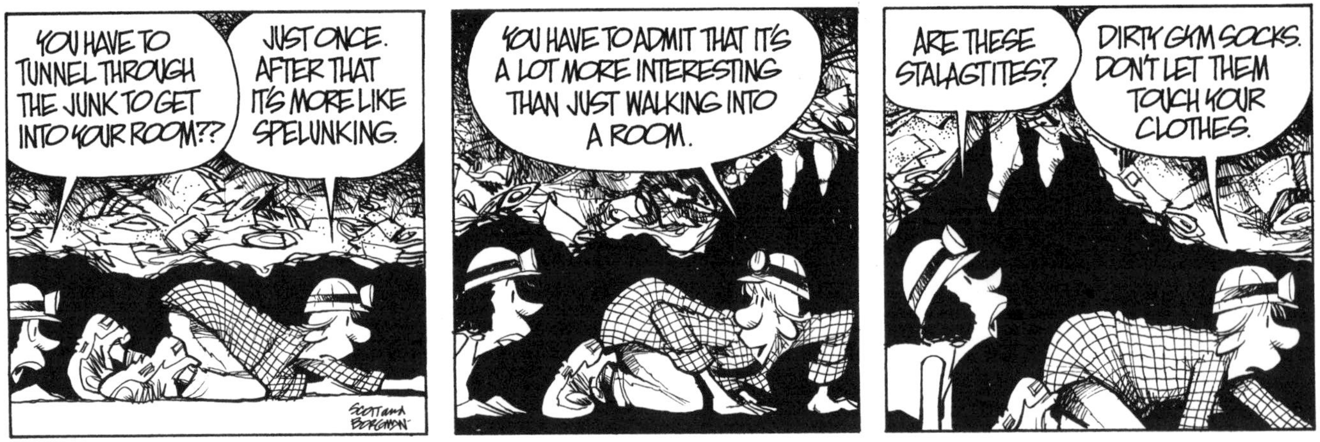
YOU HAVE TO TUNNEL THROUGH THE JUNK TO GET INTO YOUR ROOM??
JUST ONCE. AFTER THAT IT'S MORE LIKE SPELUNKING.
SCOTT AND BORGMAN
YOU HAVE TO ADMIT THAT IT'S A LOT MORE INTERESTING THAN JUST WALKING INTO A ROOM.
ARE THESE STALAGTITES?
DIRTY GYM SOCKS. DON'T LET THEM TOUCH YOUR CLOTHES.

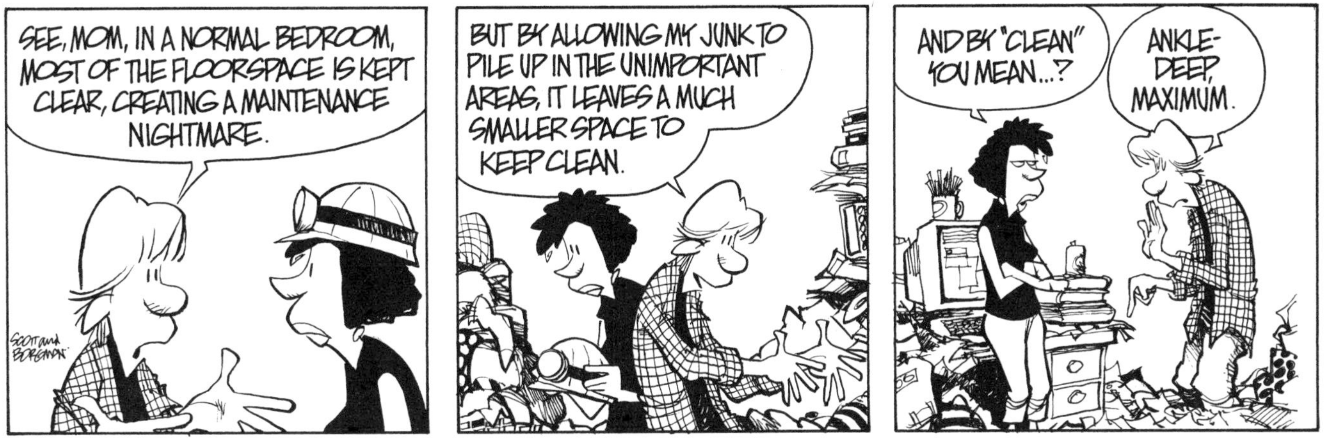
SEE, MOM, IN A NORMAL BEDROOM, MOST OF THE FLOORSPACE IS KEPT CLEAR, CREATING A MAINTENANCE NIGHTMARE.
BUT BY ALLOWING MY JUNK TO PILE UP IN THE UNIMPORTANT AREAS, IT LEAVES A MUCH SMALLER SPACE TO KEEP CLEAN.
AND BY "CLEAN" YOU MEAN...?
ANKLE-DEEP, MAXIMUM.

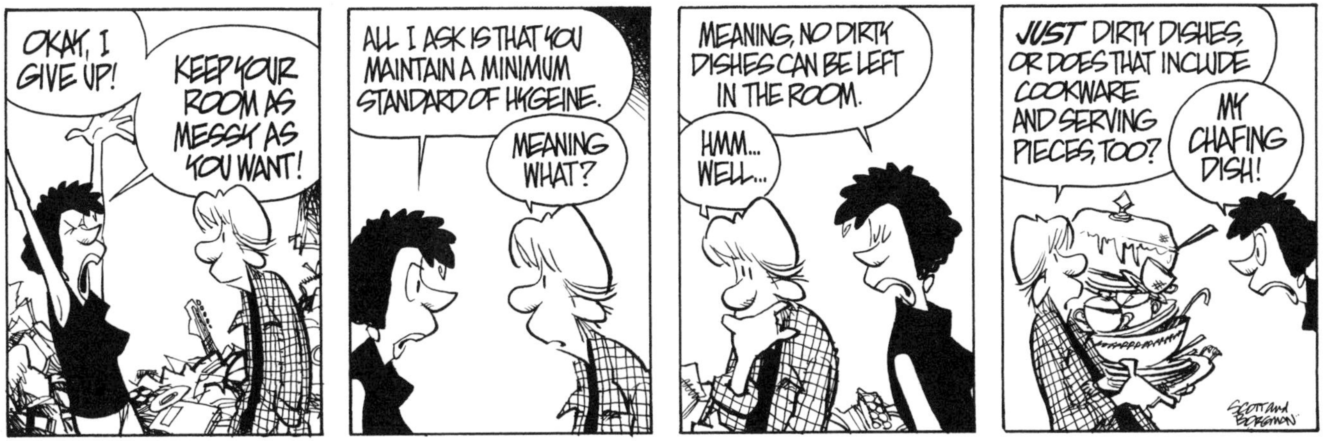
OKAY, I GIVE UP!
KEEP YOUR ROOM AS MESSY AS YOU WANT!
ALL I ASK IS THAT YOU MAINTAIN A MINIMUM STANDARD OF HYGEINE.
MEANING WHAT?
MEANING, NO DIRTY DISHES CAN BE LEFT IN THE ROOM.
HMM... WELL...
JUST DIRTY DISHES, OR DOES THAT INCLUDE COOKWARE AND SERVING PIECES, TOO?
MY CHAFING DISH!

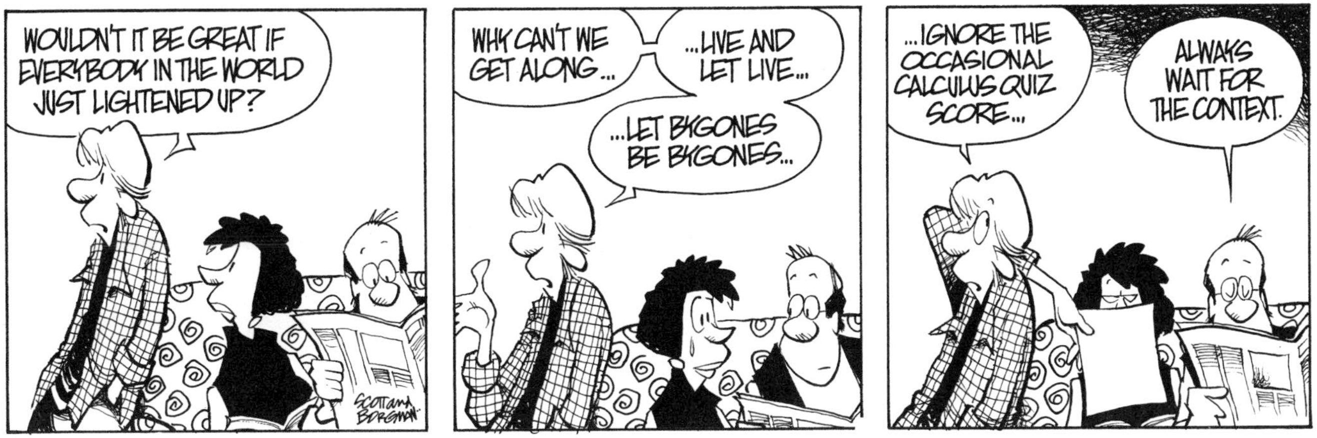
WOULDN'T IT BE GREAT IF EVERYBODY IN THE WORLD JUST LIGHTENED UP?
WHY CAN'T WE GET ALONG...
...LIVE AND LET LIVE...
...LET BYGONES BE BYGONES...
...IGNORE THE OCCASIONAL CALCULUS QUIZ SCORE...
ALWAYS WAIT FOR THE CONTEXT.

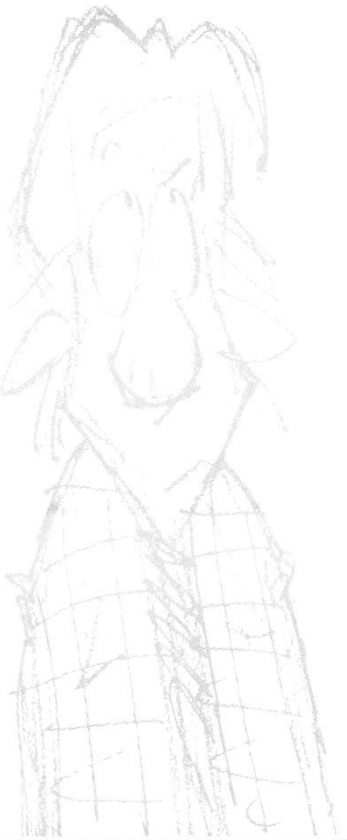

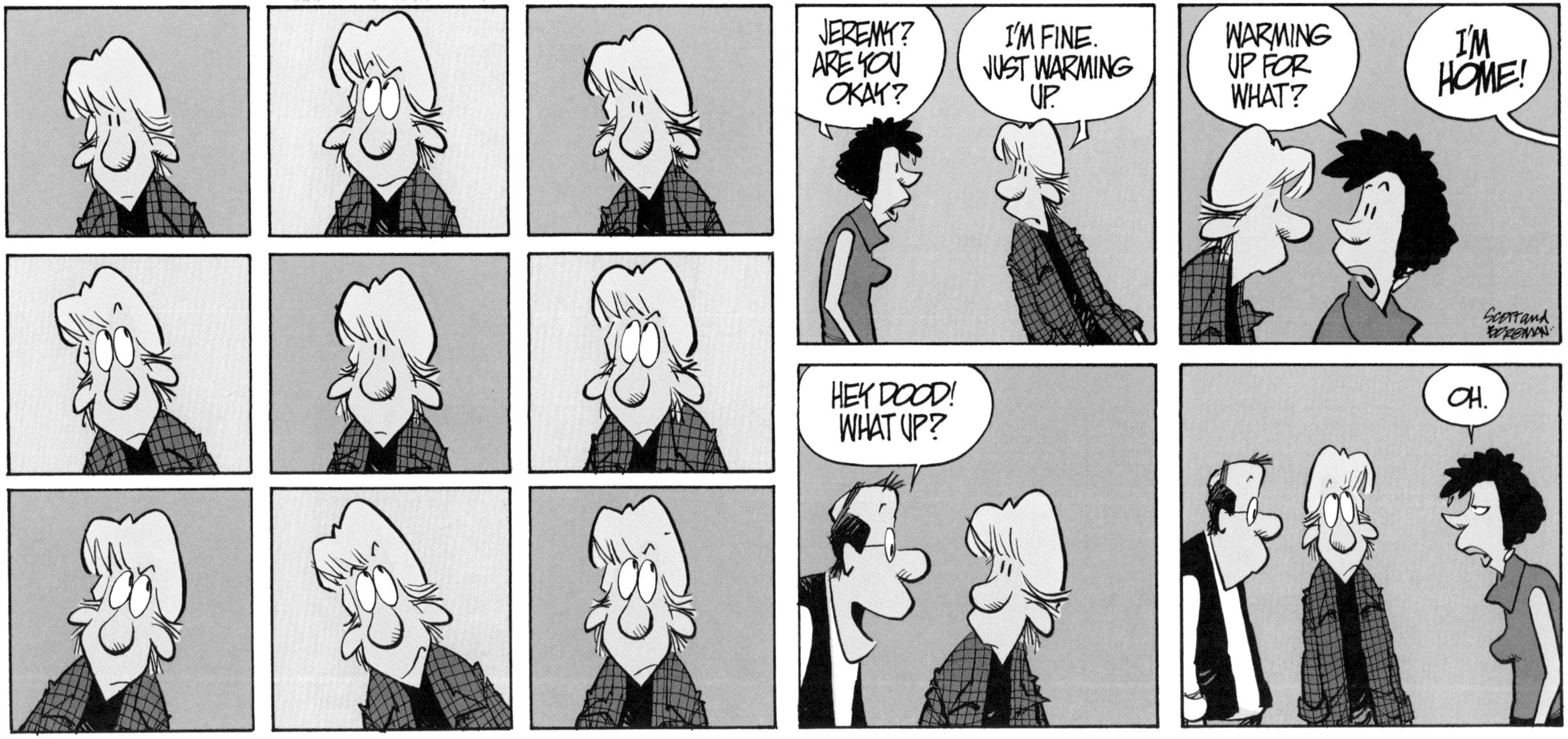
JEREMY? ARE YOU OKAY?
I'M FINE. JUST WARMING UP.
WARMING UP FOR WHAT?
I'M HOME!
SCOTT and BORGMAN
HEY DOOD! WHAT UP?
OH.

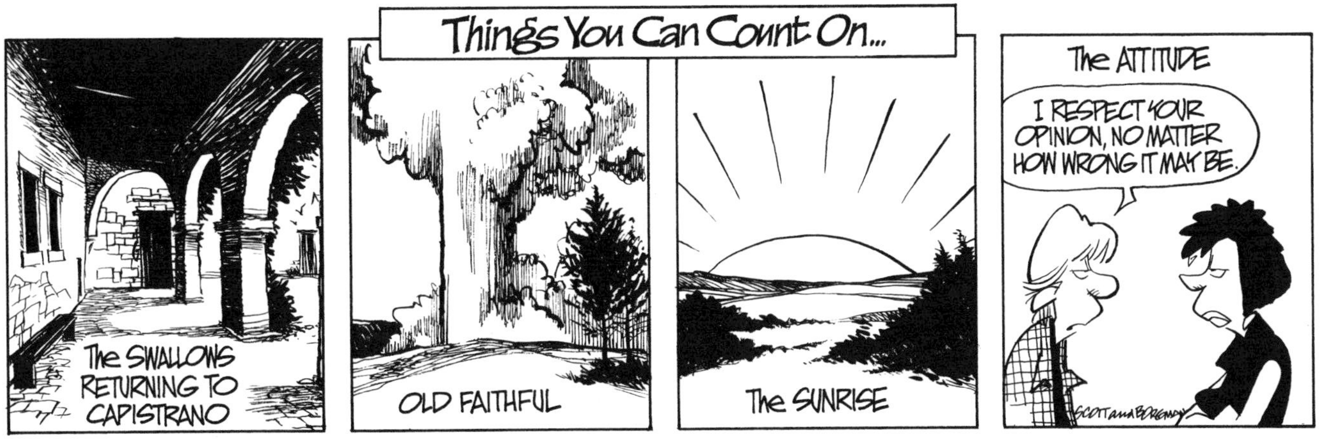
Things You Can Count On...
The SWALLOWS RETURNING TO CAPISTRANO
OLD FAITHFUL
The SUNRISE
The ATTITUDE
I RESPECT YOUR OPINION, NO MATTER HOW WRONG IT MAY BE.

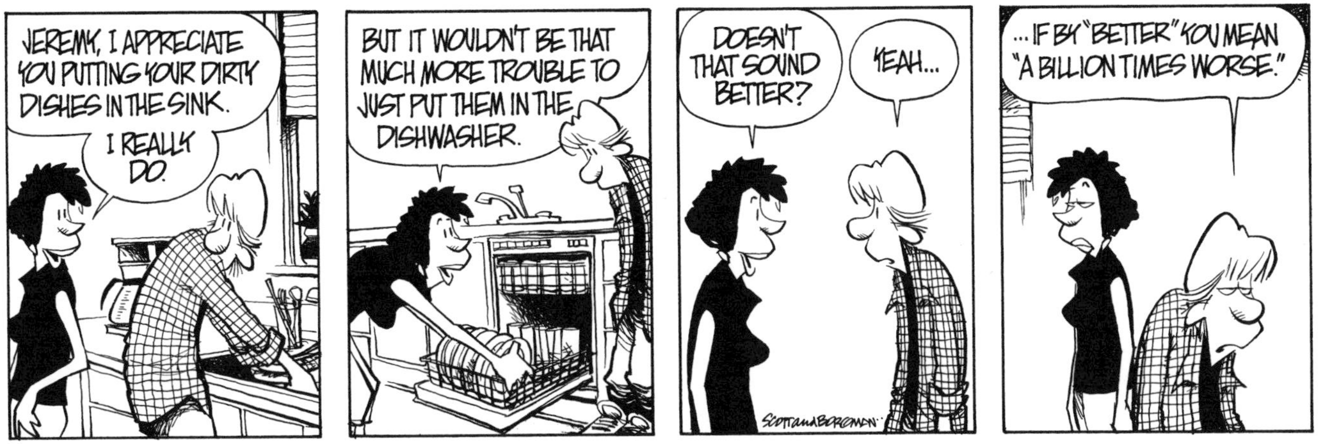
JEREMY, I APPRECIATE YOU PUTTING YOUR DIRTY DISHES IN THE SINK.
I REALLY DO.
BUT IT WOULDN'T BE THAT MUCH MORE TROUBLE TO JUST PUT THEM IN THE DISHWASHER.
DOESN'T THAT SOUND BETTER?
YEAH...
...IF BY "BETTER" YOU MEAN "A BILLION TIMES WORSE."

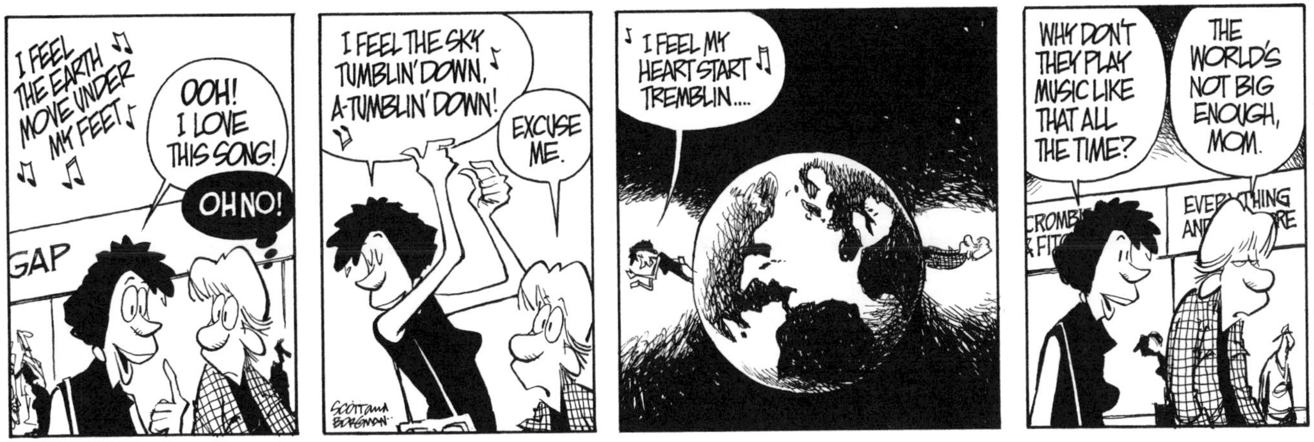
I FEEL THE EARTH MOVE UNDER MY FEET
OOH! I LOVE THIS SONG!
OH NO!
GAP
I FEEL THE SKY TUMBLIN' DOWN, A-TUMBLIN' DOWN!
EXCUSE ME.
I FEEL MY HEART START TREMBLIN....
WHY DON'T THEY PLAY MUSIC LIKE THAT ALL THE TIME?
THE WORLD'S NOT BIG ENOUGH, MOM.

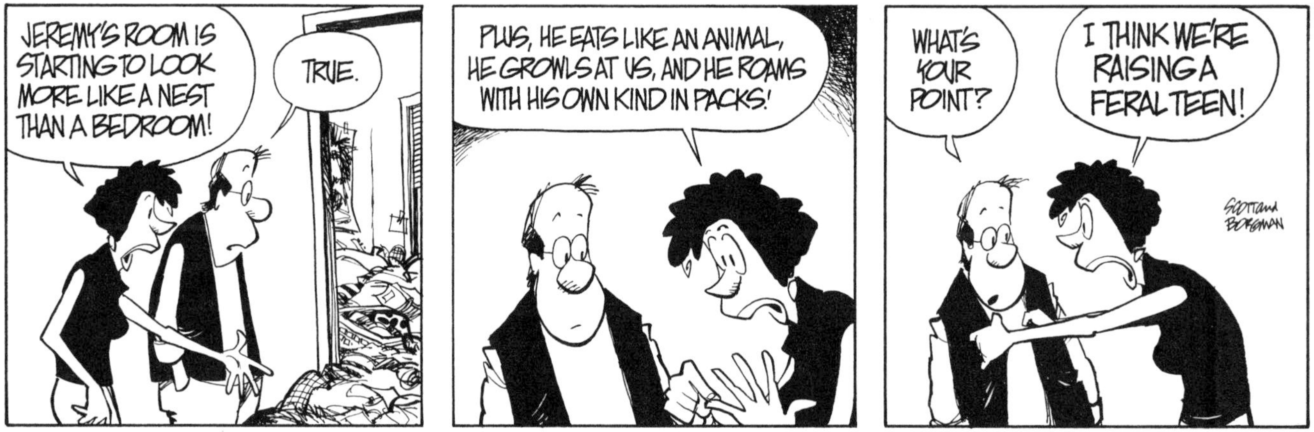
JEREMY'S ROOM IS STARTING TO LOOK MORE LIKE A NEST THAN A BEDROOM!
TRUE.
PLUS, HE EATS LIKE AN ANIMAL, HE GROWLS AT US, AND HE ROAMS WITH HIS OWN KIND IN PACKS!
WHAT'S YOUR POINT?
I THINK WE'RE RAISING A FERAL TEEN!

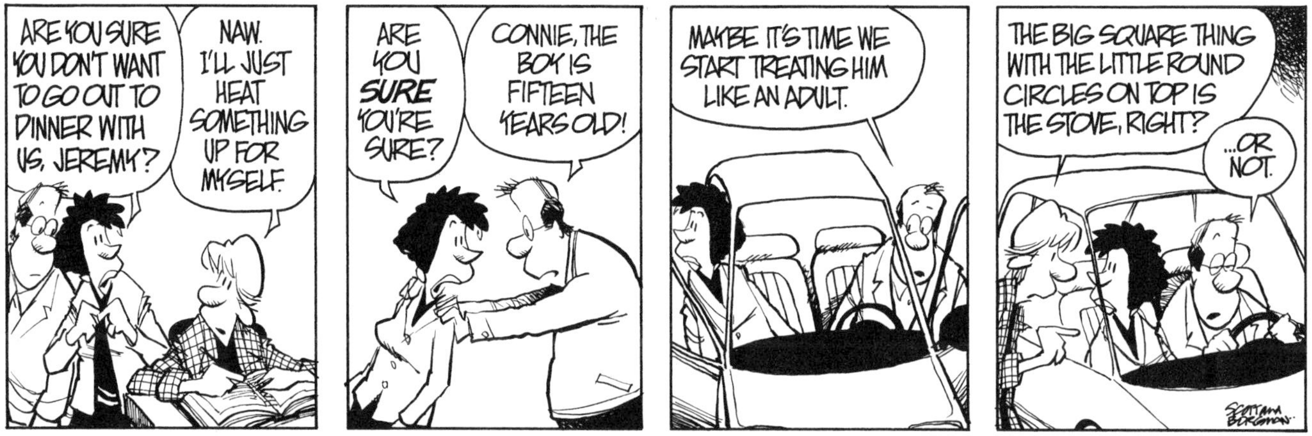
ARE YOU SURE YOU DON'T WANT TO GO OUT TO DINNER WITH US, JEREMY?
NAW. I'LL JUST HEAT SOMETHING UP FOR MYSELF.
ARE YOU *SURE* YOU'RE SURE?
CONNIE, THE BOY IS FIFTEEN YEARS OLD!
MAYBE IT'S TIME WE START TREATING HIM LIKE AN ADULT.
THE BIG SQUARE THING WITH THE LITTLE ROUND CIRCLES ON TOP IS THE STOVE, RIGHT?
...OR NOT.

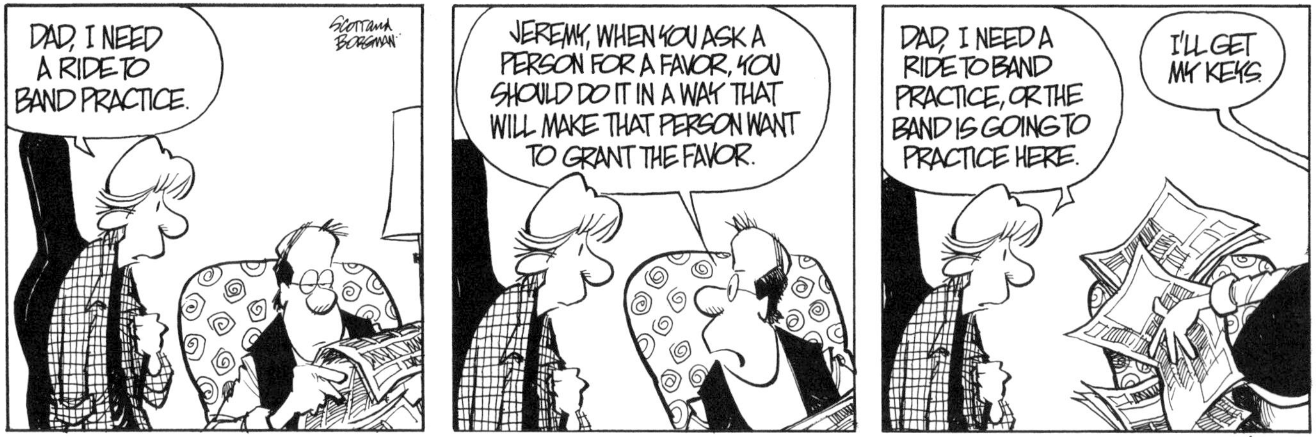
DAD, I NEED A RIDE TO BAND PRACTICE.
JEREMY, WHEN YOU ASK A PERSON FOR A FAVOR, YOU SHOULD DO IT IN A WAY THAT WILL MAKE THAT PERSON WANT TO GRANT THE FAVOR.
DAD, I NEED A RIDE TO BAND PRACTICE, OR THE BAND IS GOING TO PRACTICE HERE.
I'LL GET MY KEYS.

Zits

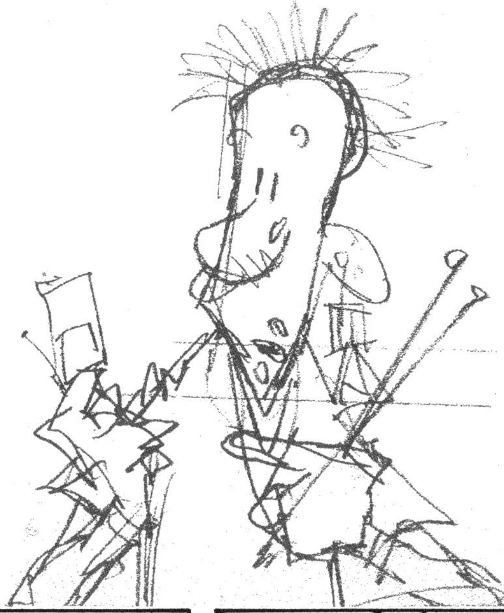

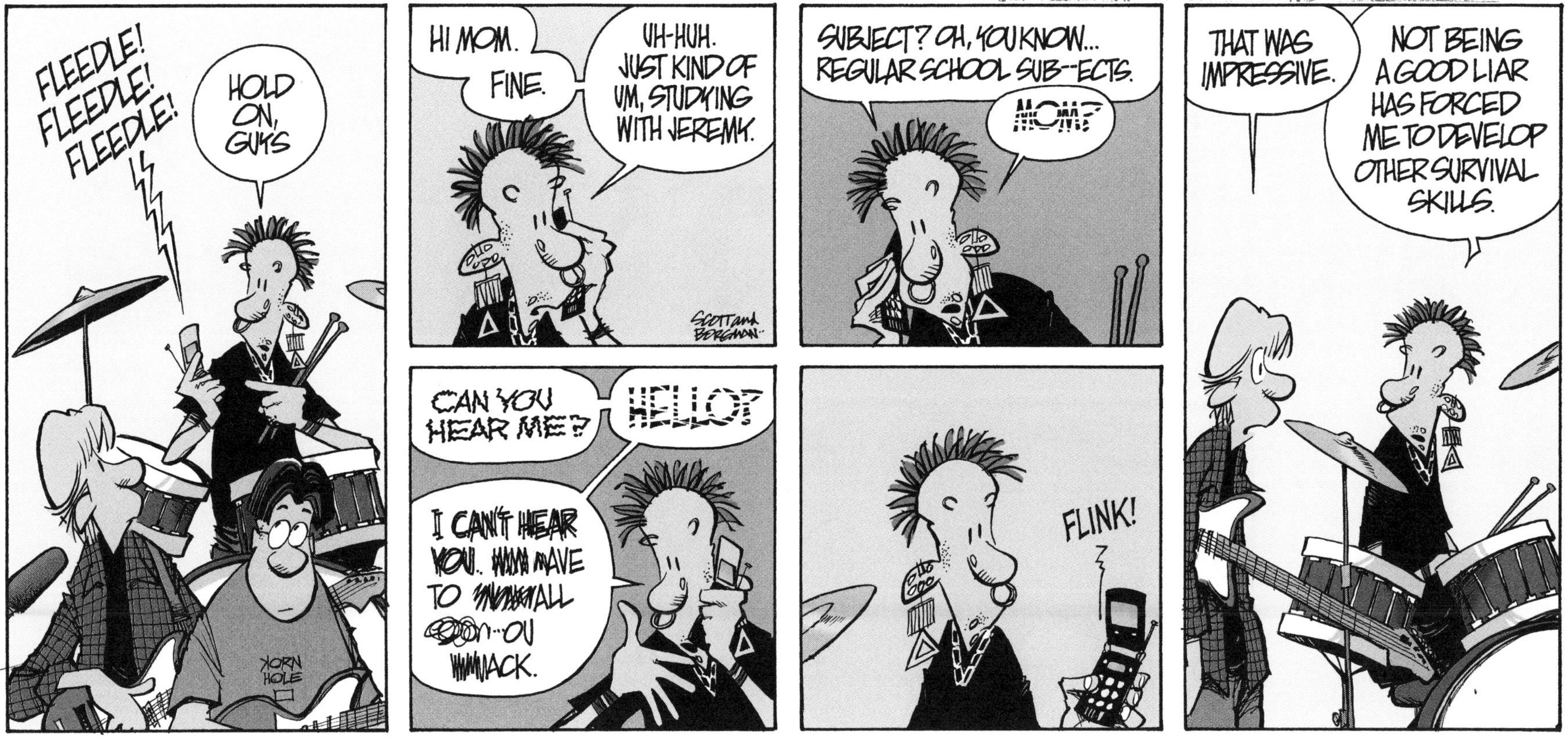

FLEEDLE! FLEEDLE! FLEEDLE!
HOLD ON, GUYS
HI MOM.
FINE.
UH-HUH. JUST KIND OF UM, STUDYING WITH JEREMY.
SCOTT and BORGMAN
SUBJECT? OH, YOU KNOW... REGULAR SCHOOL SUB--ECTS.
MOM?
CAN YOU HEAR ME?
HELLO?
I CAN'T HEAR YOU.. HAVE TO ALL ..OU ACK.
FLINK!
THAT WAS IMPRESSIVE.
NOT BEING A GOOD LIAR HAS FORCED ME TO DEVELOP OTHER SURVIVAL SKILLS.
KORN HOLE

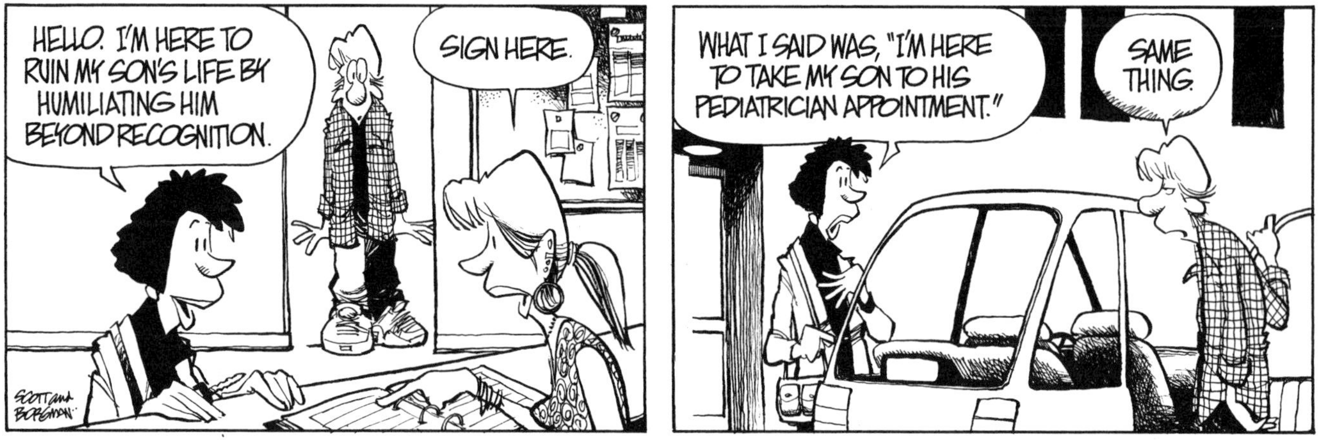
HELLO. I'M HERE TO RUIN MY SON'S LIFE BY HUMILIATING HIM BEYOND RECOGNITION.
SIGN HERE.
WHAT I SAID WAS, "I'M HERE TO TAKE MY SON TO HIS PEDIATRICIAN APPOINTMENT."
SAME THING.

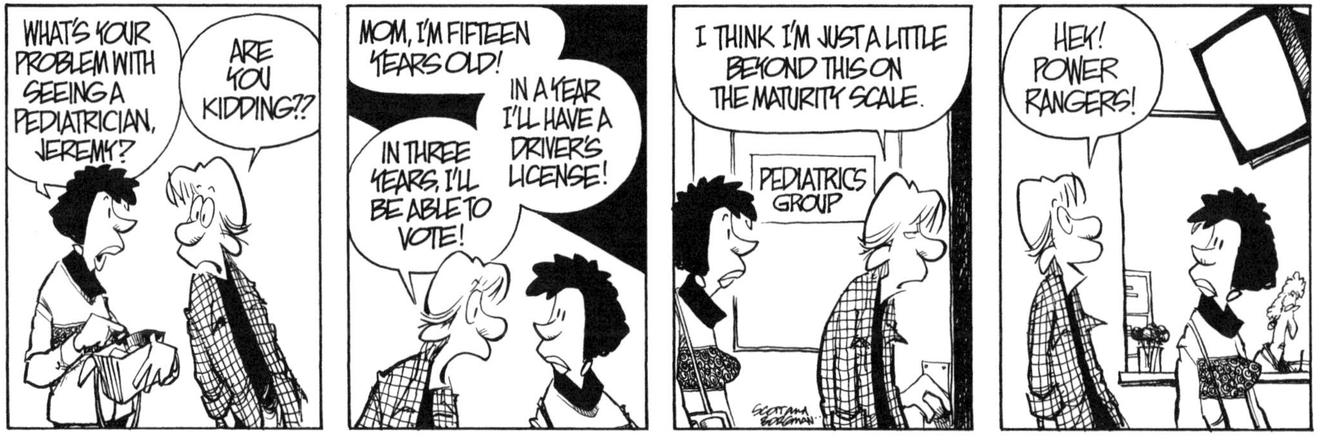
WHAT'S YOUR PROBLEM WITH SEEING A PEDIATRICIAN, JEREMY?
ARE YOU KIDDING??
MOM, I'M FIFTEEN YEARS OLD!
IN A YEAR I'LL HAVE A DRIVER'S LICENSE!
IN THREE YEARS, I'LL BE ABLE TO VOTE!
I THINK I'M JUST A LITTLE BEYOND THIS ON THE MATURITY SCALE.
PEDIATRICS GROUP
HEY! POWER RANGERS!

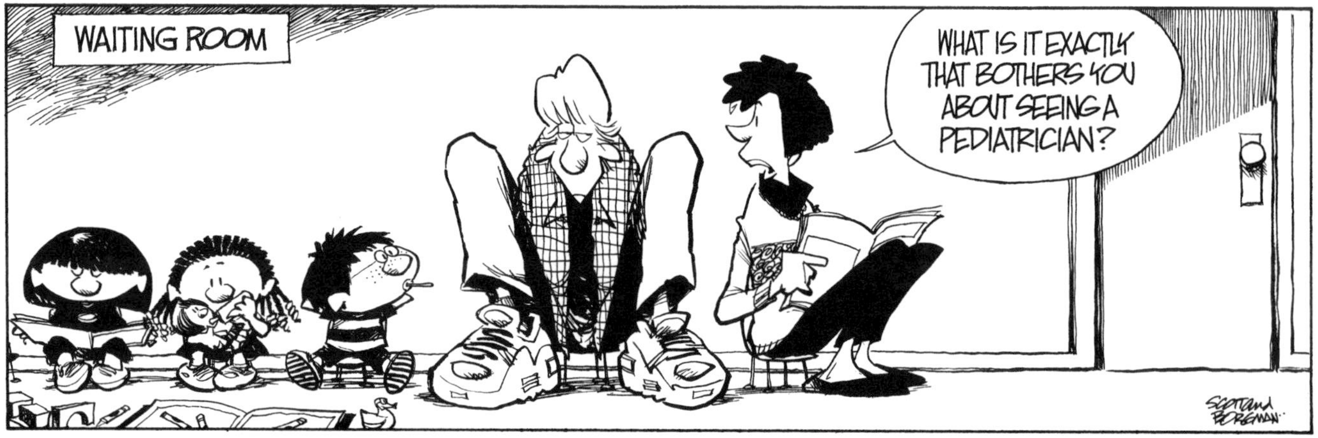
WAITING ROOM
WHAT IS IT EXACTLY THAT BOTHERS YOU ABOUT SEEING A PEDIATRICIAN?

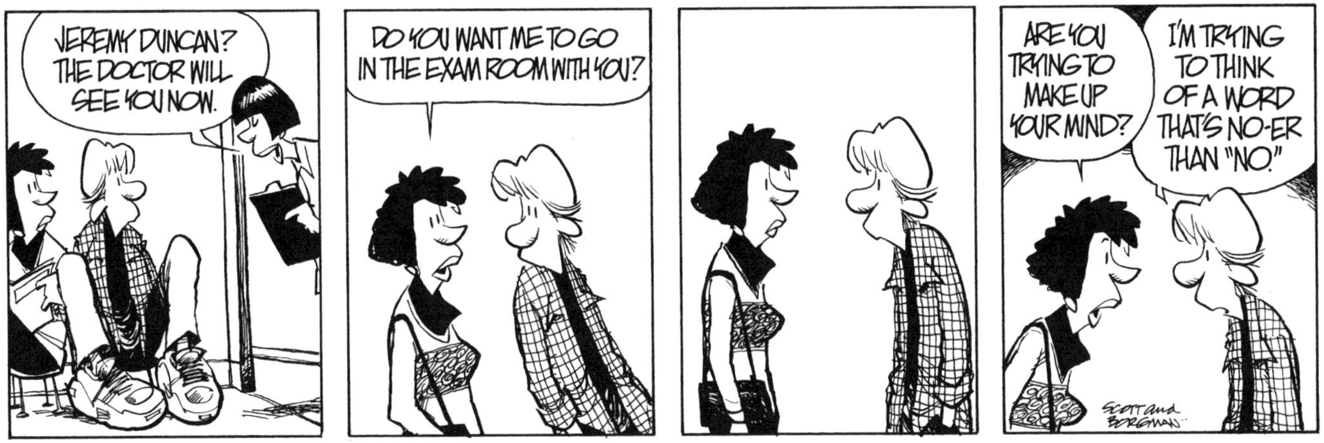
JEREMY DUNCAN? THE DOCTOR WILL SEE YOU NOW.
DO YOU WANT ME TO GO IN THE EXAM ROOM WITH YOU?
ARE YOU TRYING TO MAKE UP YOUR MIND?
I'M TRYING TO THINK OF A WORD THAT'S NO-ER THAN "NO."
SCOTT and BORGMAN

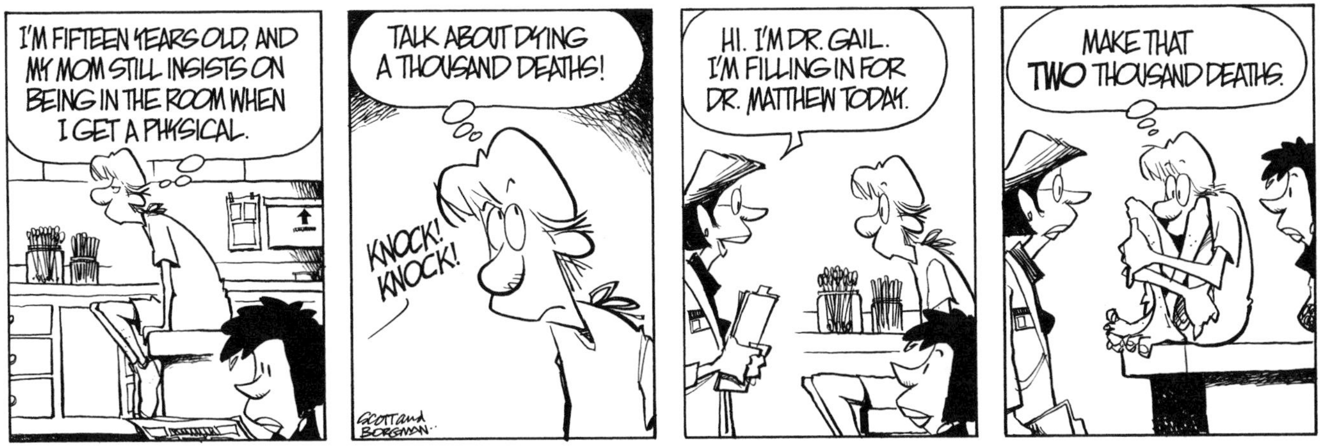
I'M FIFTEEN YEARS OLD, AND MY MOM STILL INSISTS ON BEING IN THE ROOM WHEN I GET A PHYSICAL.
TALK ABOUT DYING A THOUSAND DEATHS!
KNOCK! KNOCK!
SCOTT and BORGMAN
HI. I'M DR. GAIL. I'M FILLING IN FOR DR. MATTHEW TODAY.
MAKE THAT TWO THOUSAND DEATHS.

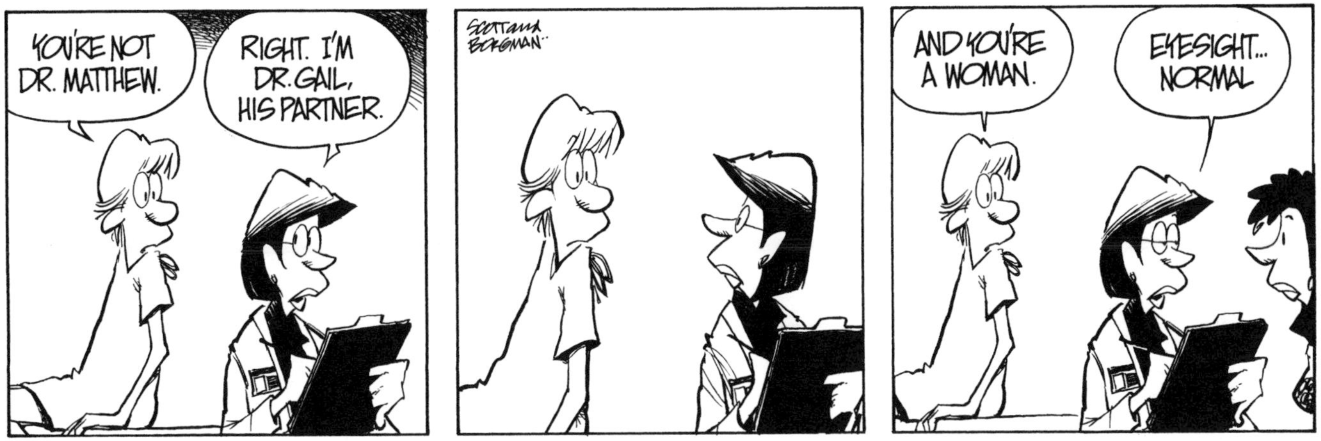
YOU'RE NOT DR. MATTHEW.
RIGHT. I'M DR. GAIL, HIS PARTNER.
SCOTT and BORGMAN
AND YOU'RE A WOMAN.
EYESIGHT... NORMAL

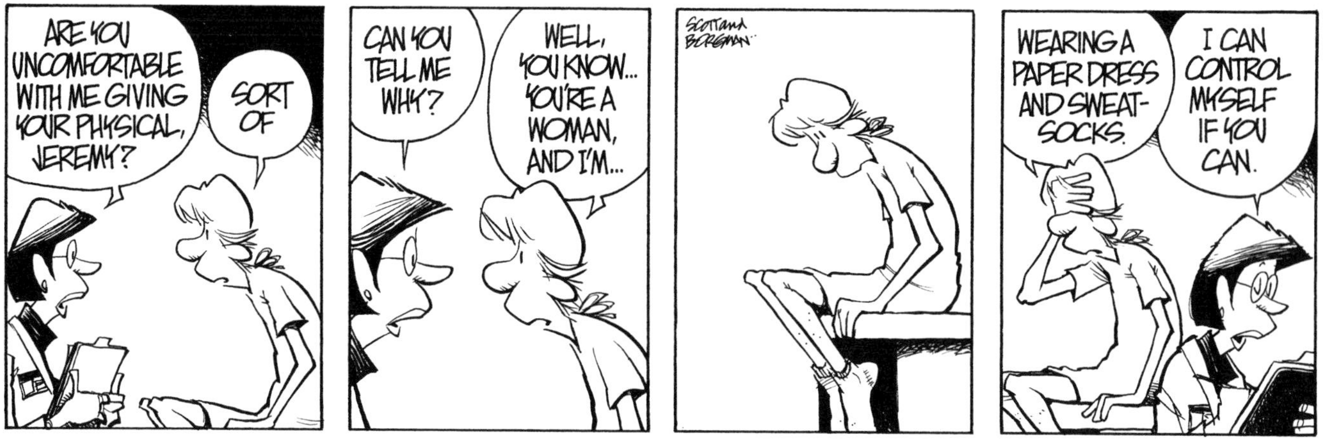
ARE YOU UNCOMFORTABLE WITH ME GIVING YOUR PHYSICAL, JEREMY?
SORT OF
CAN YOU TELL ME WHY?
WELL, YOU KNOW... YOU'RE A WOMAN, AND I'M...
WEARING A PAPER DRESS AND SWEAT-SOCKS.
I CAN CONTROL MYSELF IF YOU CAN.

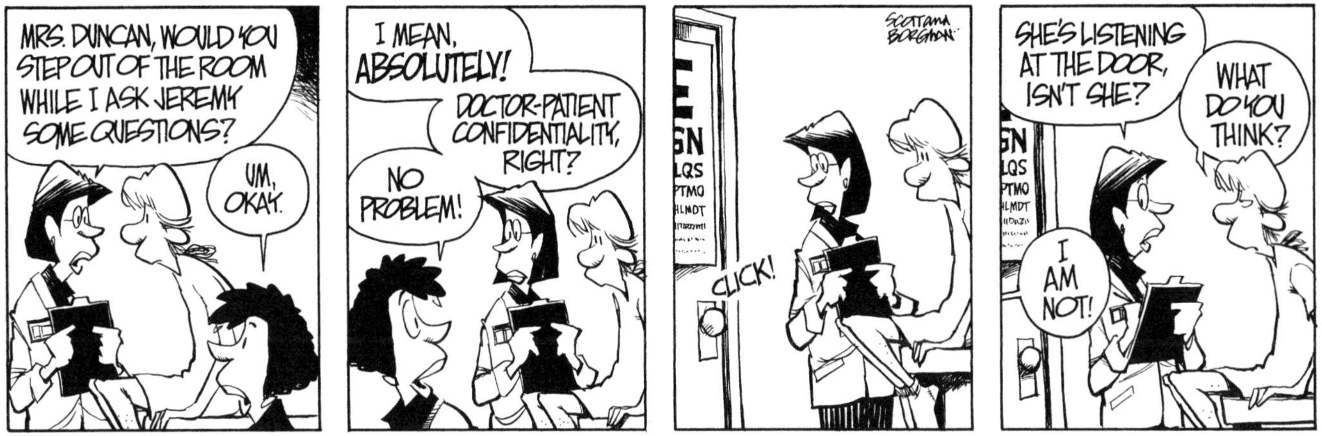
MRS. DUNCAN, WOULD YOU STEP OUT OF THE ROOM WHILE I ASK JEREMY SOME QUESTIONS?
UM, OKAY.
I MEAN, ABSOLUTELY!
DOCTOR-PATIENT CONFIDENTIALITY, RIGHT?
NO PROBLEM!
CLICK!
SHE'S LISTENING AT THE DOOR, ISN'T SHE?
WHAT DO YOU THINK?
I AM NOT!

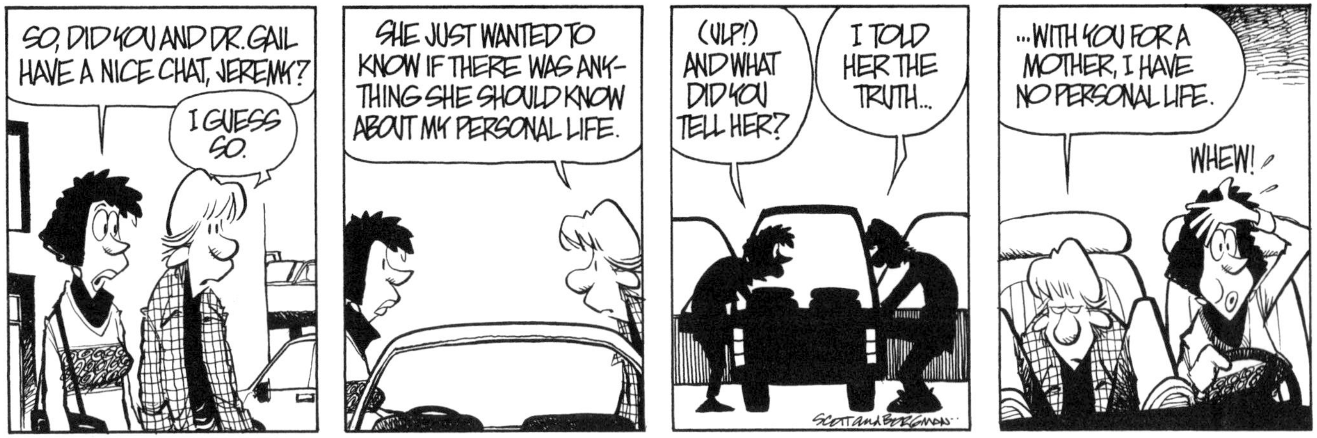
SO, DID YOU AND DR. GAIL HAVE A NICE CHAT, JEREMY?
I GUESS SO.
SHE JUST WANTED TO KNOW IF THERE WAS ANYTHING SHE SHOULD KNOW ABOUT MY PERSONAL LIFE.
(ULP!) AND WHAT DID YOU TELL HER?
I TOLD HER THE TRUTH...
...WITH YOU FOR A MOTHER, I HAVE NO PERSONAL LIFE.
WHEW!

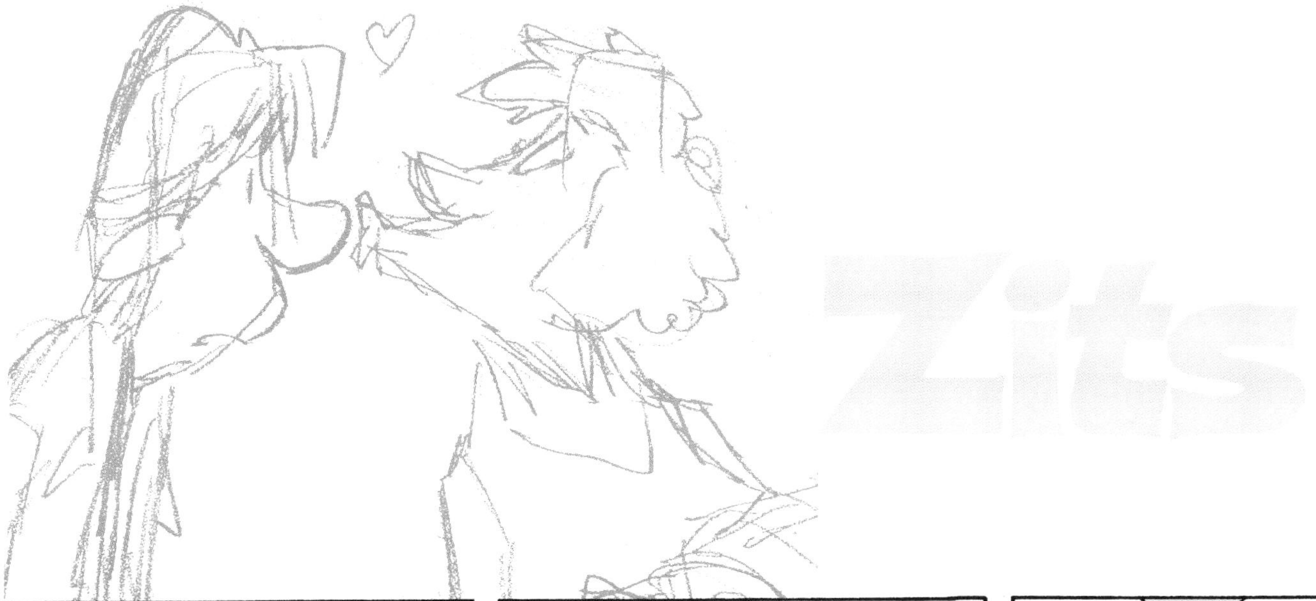

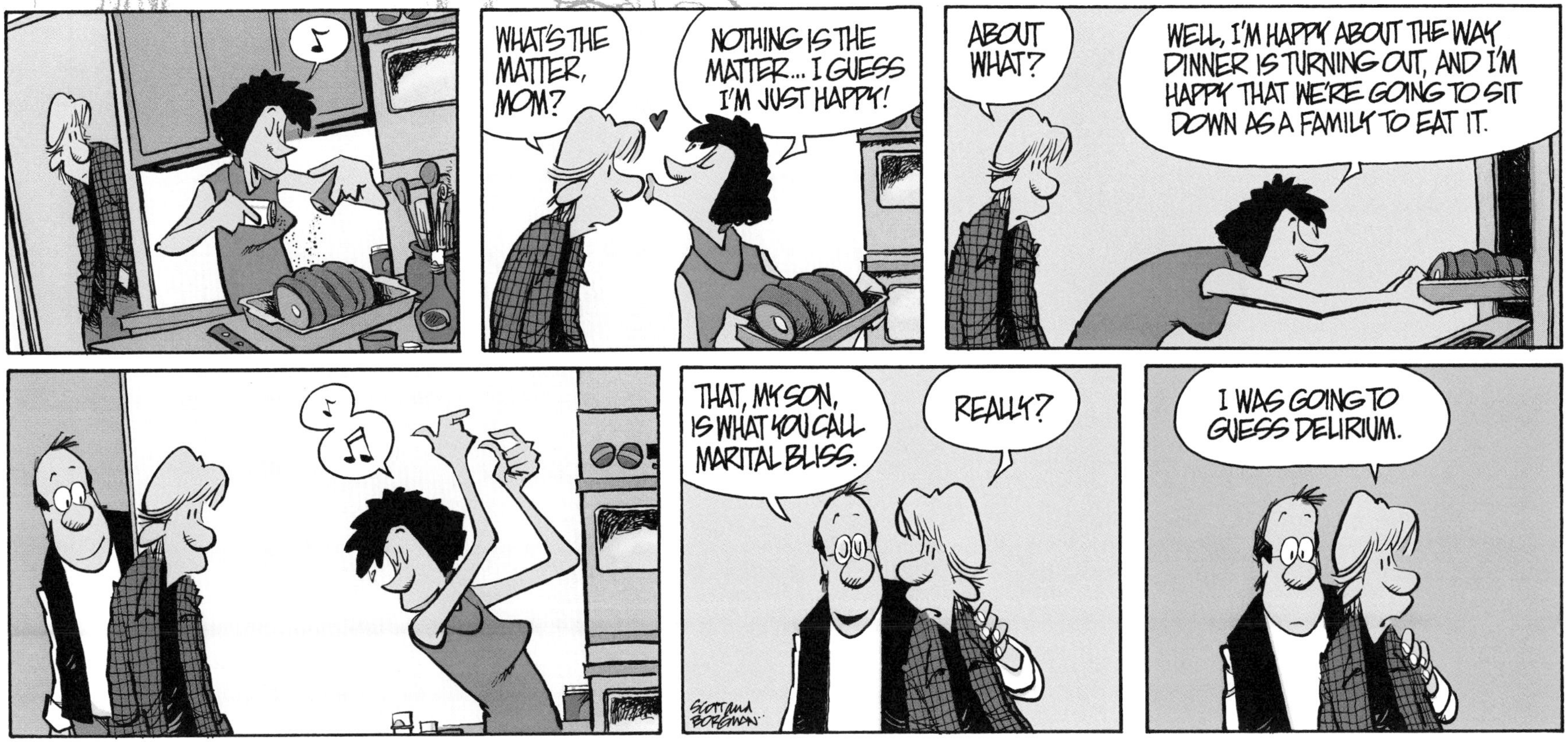
WHAT'S THE MATTER, MOM?
NOTHING IS THE MATTER... I GUESS I'M JUST HAPPY!
ABOUT WHAT?
WELL, I'M HAPPY ABOUT THE WAY DINNER IS TURNING OUT, AND I'M HAPPY THAT WE'RE GOING TO SIT DOWN AS A FAMILY TO EAT IT.
THAT, MY SON, IS WHAT YOU CALL MARITAL BLISS.
REALLY?
I WAS GOING TO GUESS DELIRIUM.

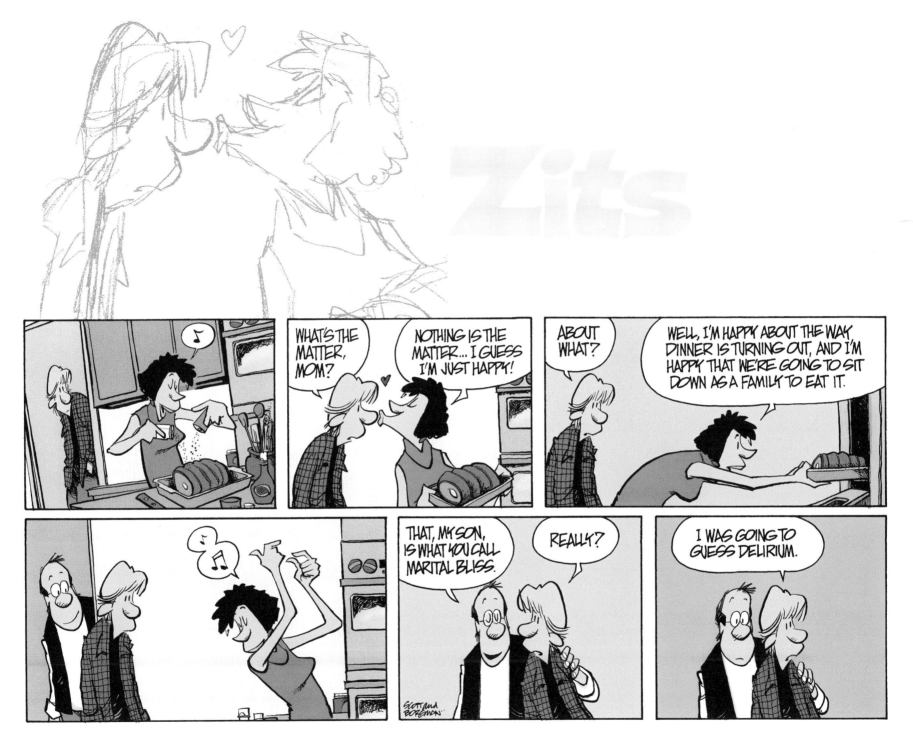

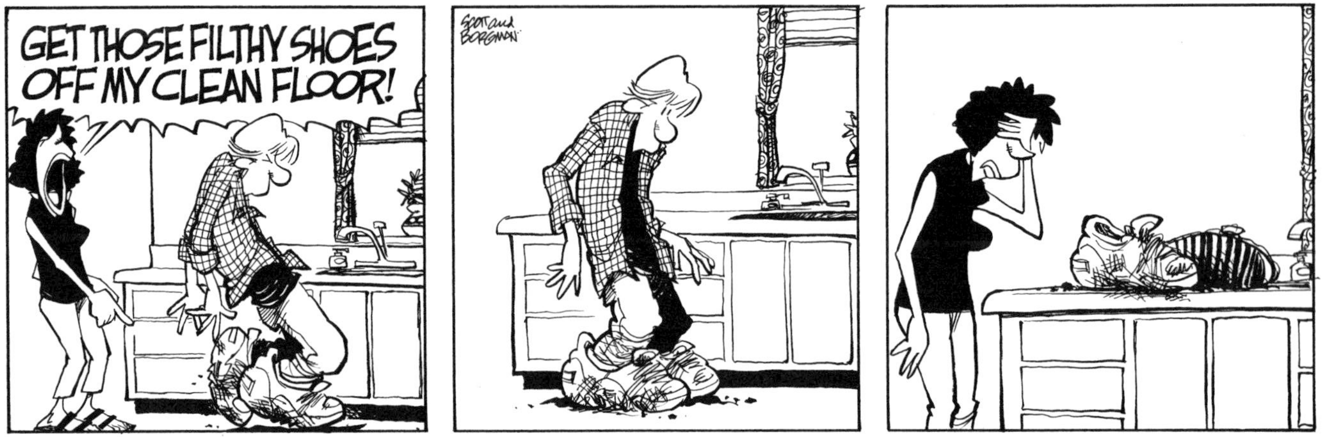
GET THOSE FILTHY SHOES OFF MY CLEAN FLOOR!

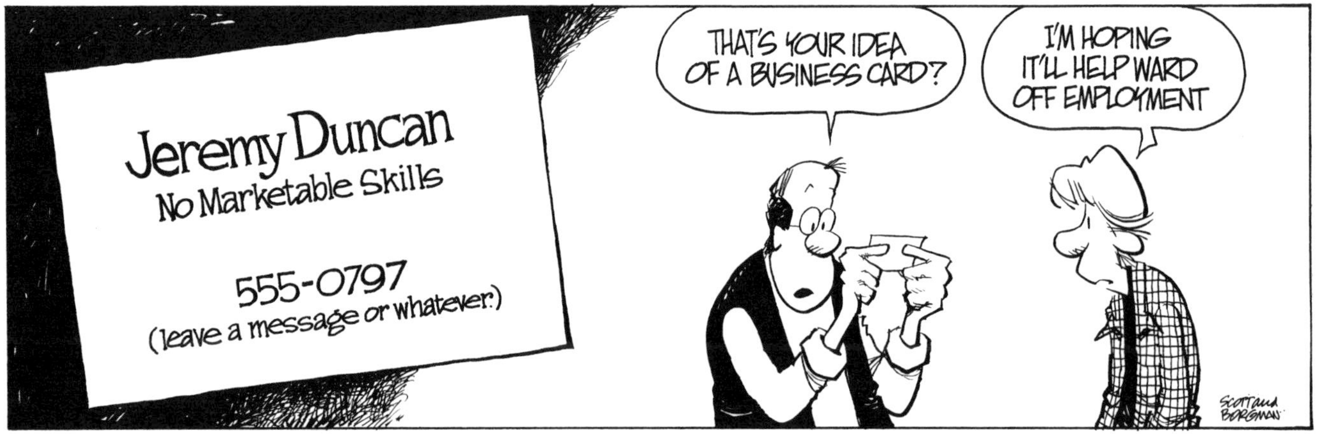
Jeremy Duncan
No Marketable Skills
555-0797
(leave a message or whatever.)
THAT'S YOUR IDEA OF A BUSINESS CARD?
I'M HOPING IT'LL HELP WARD OFF EMPLOYMENT

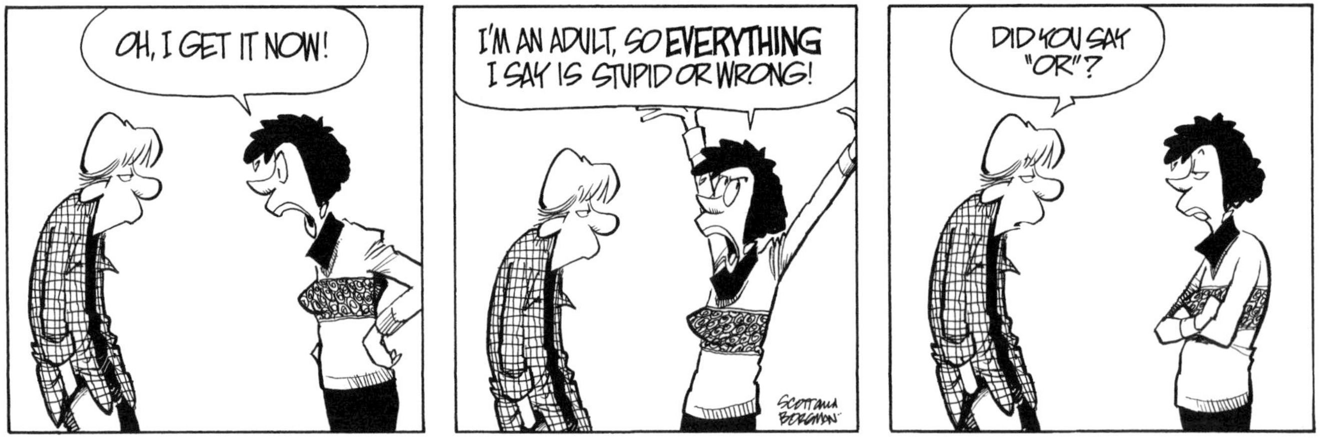
OH, I GET IT NOW!
I'M AN ADULT, SO **EVERYTHING** I SAY IS STUPID OR WRONG!
DID YOU SAY "OR"?

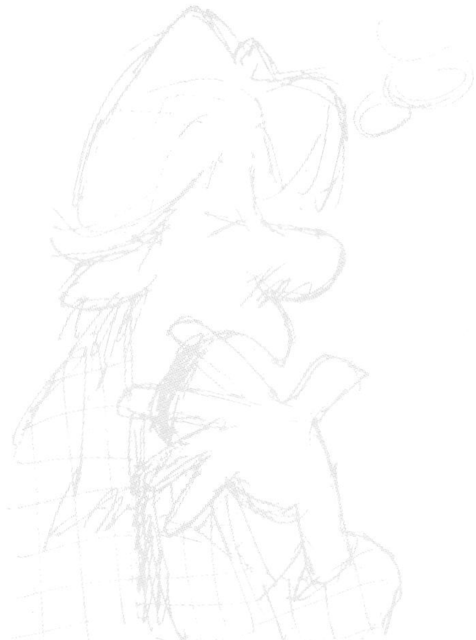

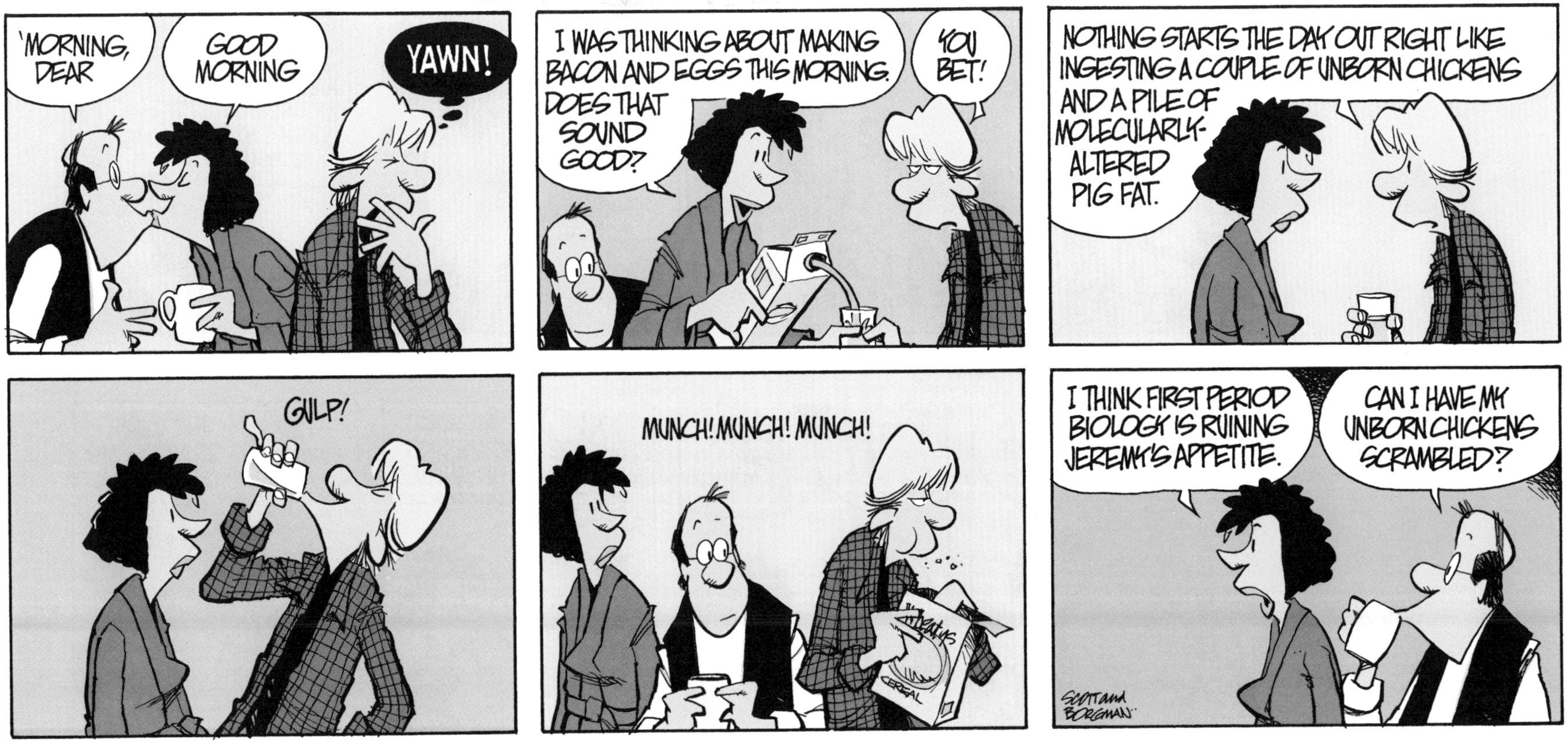
'MORNING, DEAR
GOOD MORNING
YAWN!
I WAS THINKING ABOUT MAKING BACON AND EGGS THIS MORNING. DOES THAT SOUND GOOD?
YOU BET!
NOTHING STARTS THE DAY OUT RIGHT LIKE INGESTING A COUPLE OF UNBORN CHICKENS AND A PILE OF MOLECULARLY-ALTERED PIG FAT.
GULP!
MUNCH! MUNCH! MUNCH!
CEREAL
I THINK FIRST PERIOD BIOLOGY IS RUINING JEREMY'S APPETITE.
CAN I HAVE MY UNBORN CHICKENS SCRAMBLED?
SCOTT AND BORGMAN

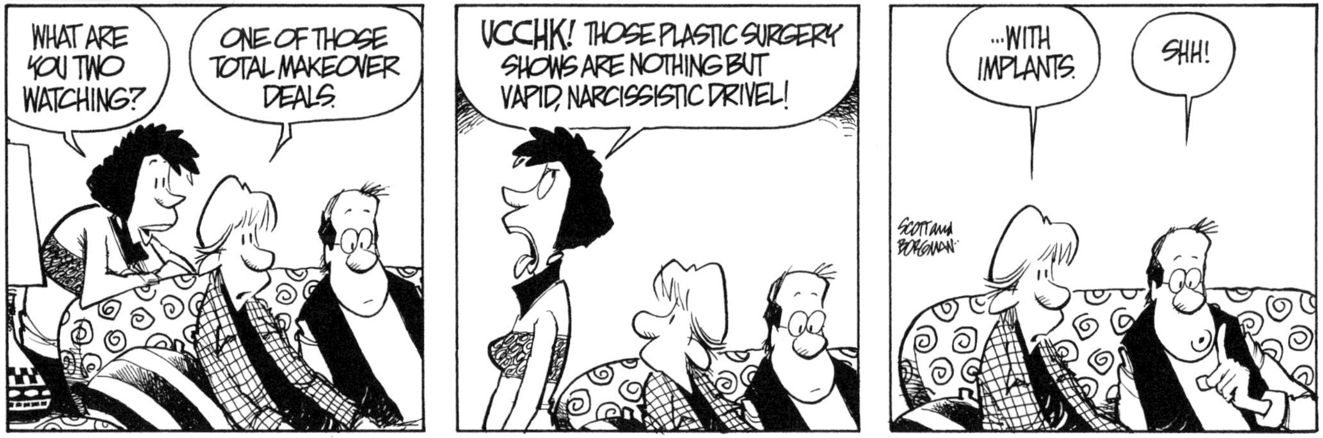
WHAT ARE YOU TWO WATCHING?
ONE OF THOSE TOTAL MAKEOVER DEALS.
UCCHK! THOSE PLASTIC SURGERY SHOWS ARE NOTHING BUT VAPID, NARCISSISTIC DRIVEL!
...WITH IMPLANTS.
SHH!

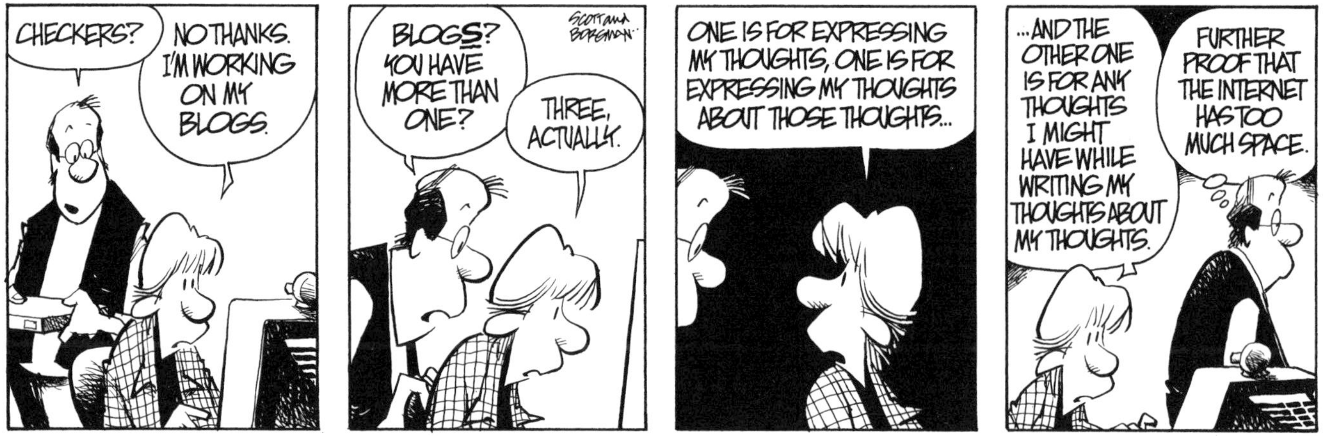
CHECKERS?
NO THANKS. I'M WORKING ON MY BLOGS.
BLOGS? YOU HAVE MORE THAN ONE?
THREE, ACTUALLY.
ONE IS FOR EXPRESSING MY THOUGHTS, ONE IS FOR EXPRESSING MY THOUGHTS ABOUT THOSE THOUGHTS...
...AND THE OTHER ONE IS FOR ANY THOUGHTS I MIGHT HAVE WHILE WRITING MY THOUGHTS ABOUT MY THOUGHTS.
FURTHER PROOF THAT THE INTERNET HAS TOO MUCH SPACE.

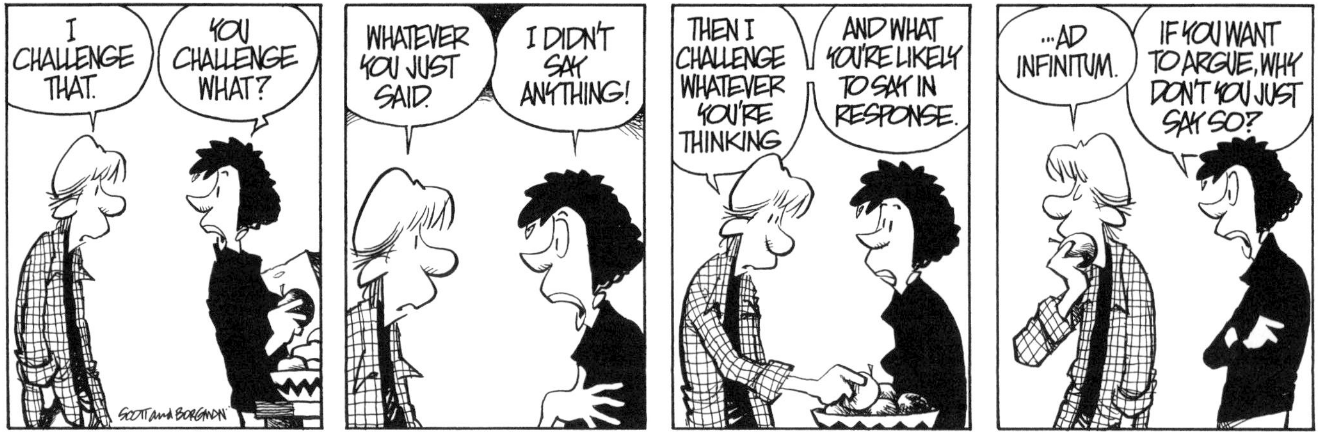
I CHALLENGE THAT.
YOU CHALLENGE WHAT?
WHATEVER YOU JUST SAID.
I DIDN'T SAY ANYTHING!
THEN I CHALLENGE WHATEVER YOU'RE THINKING
AND WHAT YOU'RE LIKELY TO SAY IN RESPONSE.
...AD INFINITUM.
IF YOU WANT TO ARGUE, WHY DON'T YOU JUST SAY SO?

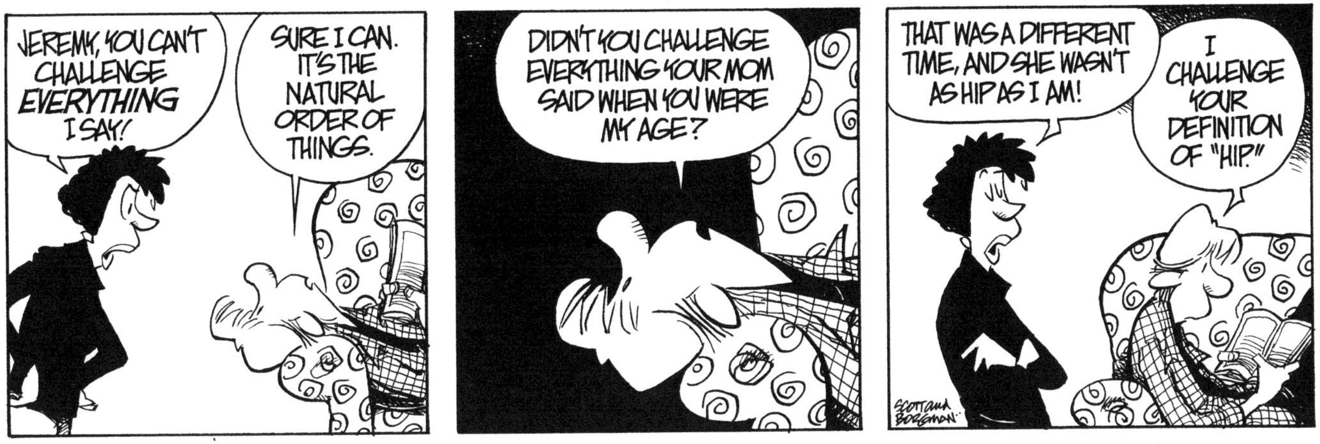
JEREMY, YOU CAN'T CHALLENGE **EVERYTHING** I SAY!
SURE I CAN. IT'S THE NATURAL ORDER OF THINGS.
DIDN'T YOU CHALLENGE EVERYTHING YOUR MOM SAID WHEN YOU WERE MY AGE?
THAT WAS A DIFFERENT TIME, AND SHE WASN'T AS HIP AS I AM!
I CHALLENGE YOUR DEFINITION OF "HIP."

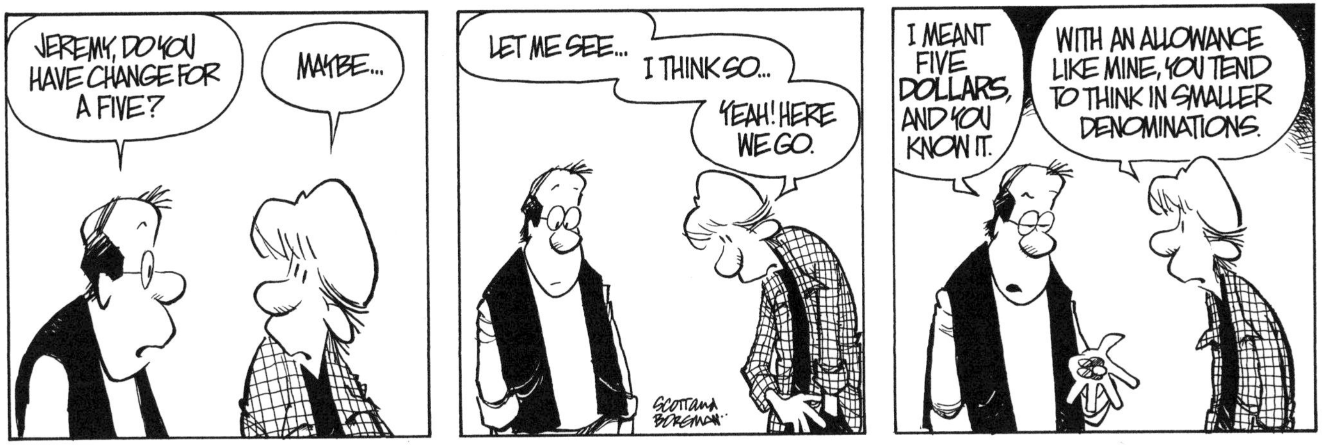
JEREMY, DO YOU HAVE CHANGE FOR A FIVE?
MAYBE...
LET ME SEE...
I THINK SO...
YEAH! HERE WE GO.
I MEANT FIVE **DOLLARS**, AND YOU KNOW IT.
WITH AN ALLOWANCE LIKE MINE, YOU TEND TO THINK IN SMALLER DENOMINATIONS.

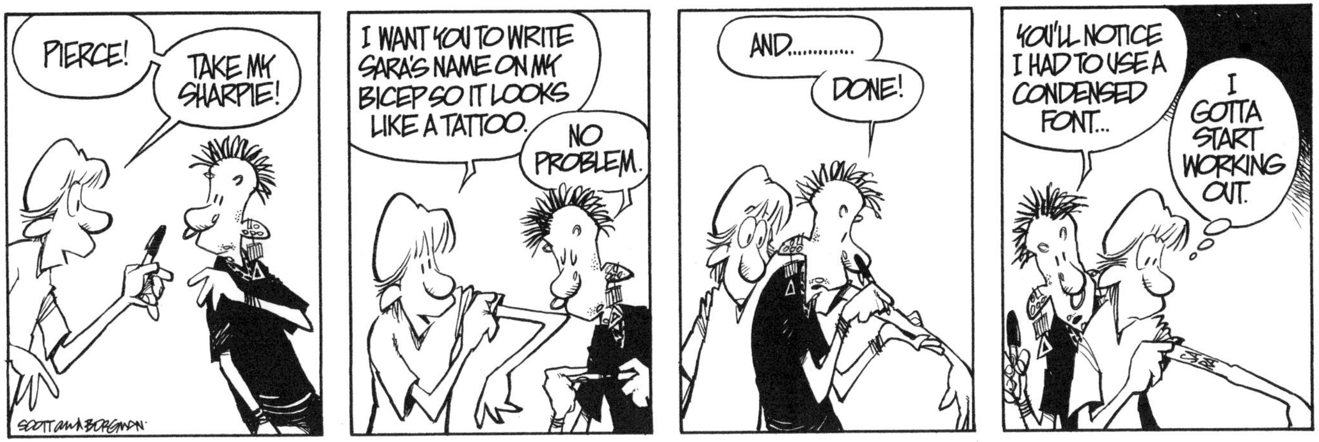
PIERCE!
TAKE MY SHARPIE!
I WANT YOU TO WRITE SARA'S NAME ON MY BICEP SO IT LOOKS LIKE A TATTOO.
NO PROBLEM.
AND............
DONE!
YOU'LL NOTICE I HAD TO USE A CONDENSED FONT...
I GOTTA START WORKING OUT.

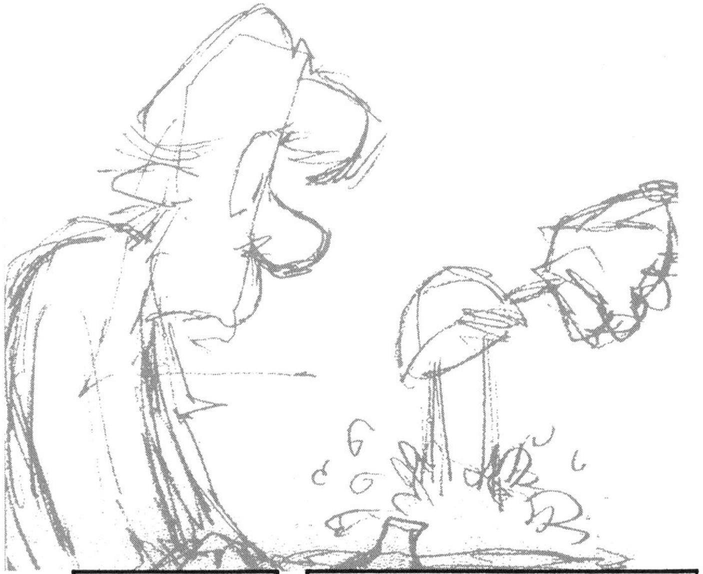

Zits

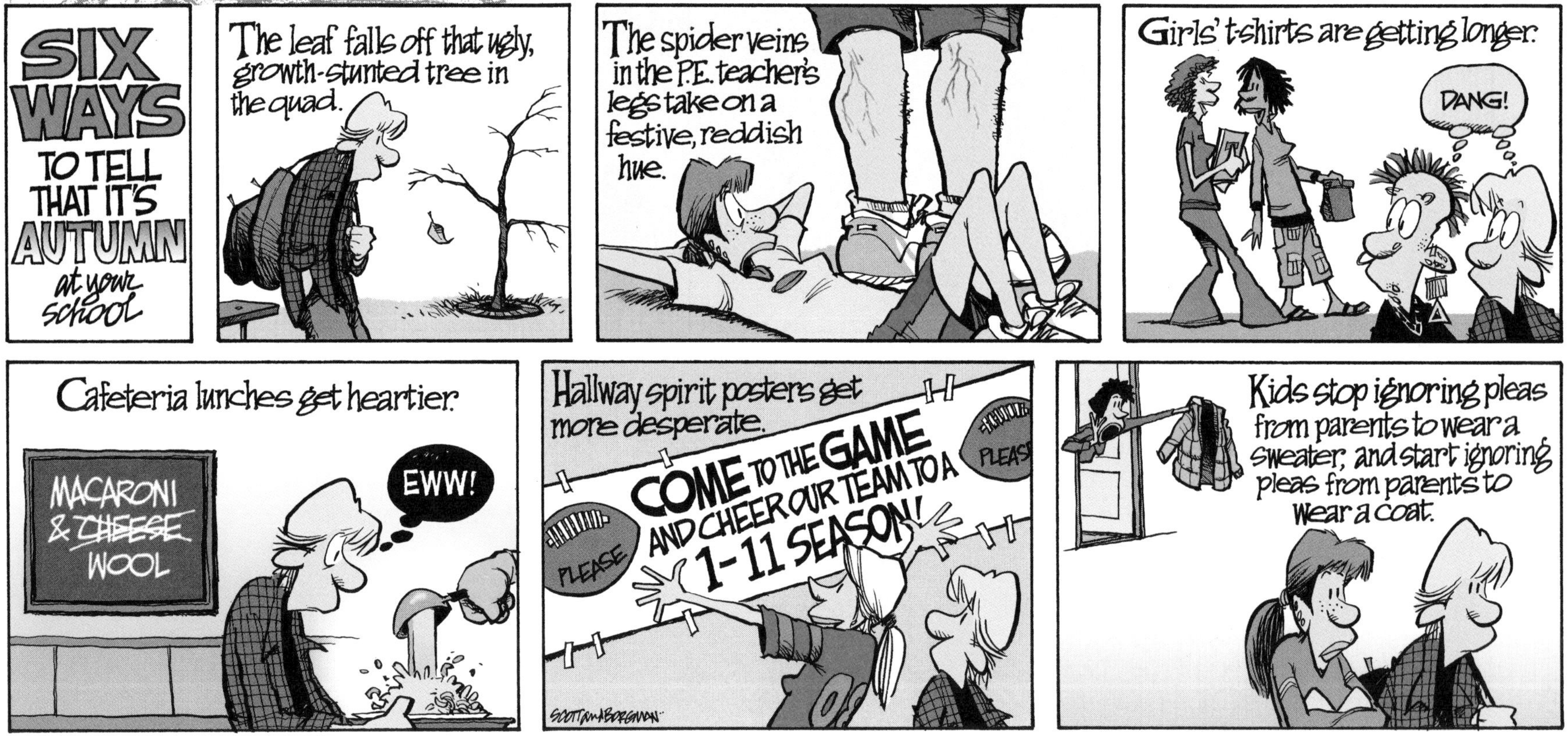
SIX WAYS TO TELL THAT IT'S AUTUMN at your school
The leaf falls off that ugly, growth-stunted tree in the quad.
The spider veins in the P.E. teacher's legs take on a festive, reddish hue.
Girls' t-shirts are getting longer.
DANG!
Cafeteria lunches get heartier.
MACARONI & CHEESE WOOL
EWW!
Hallway spirit posters get more desperate.
COME TO THE GAME AND CHEER OUR TEAM TO A 1-11 SEASON!
PLEASE
PLEASE
Kids stop ignoring pleas from parents to wear a sweater, and start ignoring pleas from parents to wear a coat.

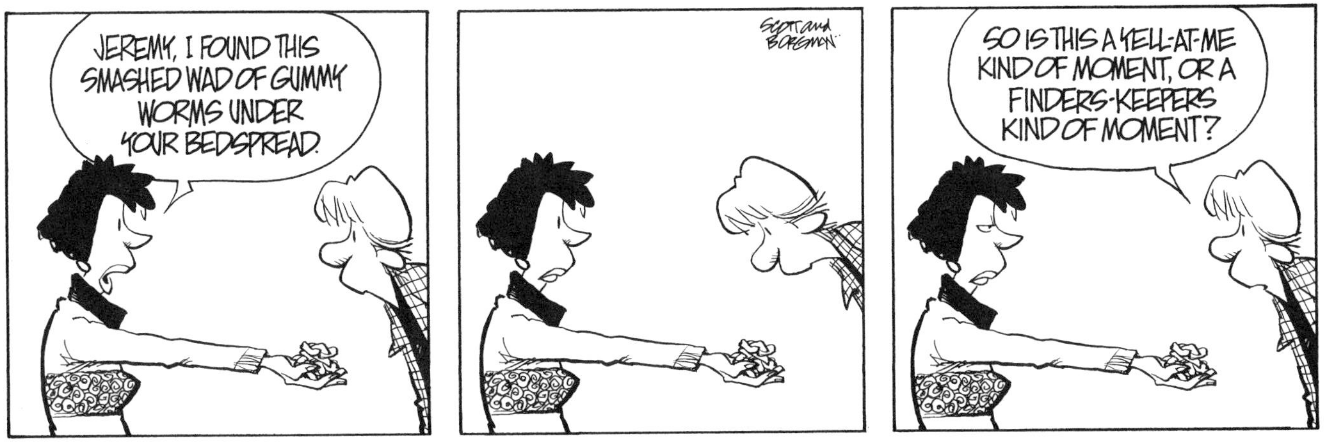
JEREMY, I FOUND THIS SMASHED WAD OF GUMMY WORMS UNDER YOUR BEDSPREAD.
SCOTT and BORGMAN
SO IS THIS A YELL-AT-ME KIND OF MOMENT, OR A FINDERS-KEEPERS KIND OF MOMENT?

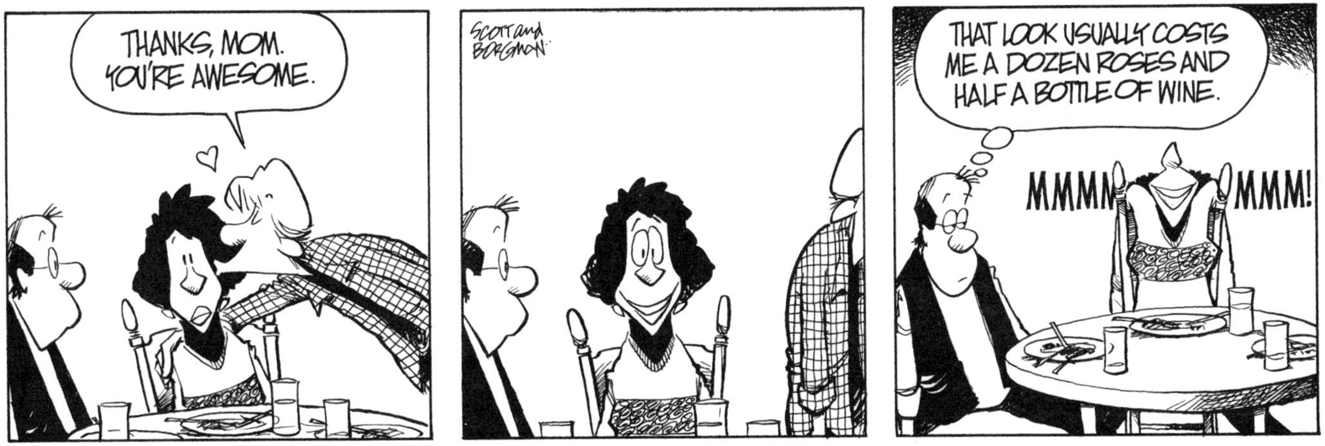
THANKS, MOM. YOU'RE AWESOME.
SCOTT and BORGMAN
THAT LOOK USUALLY COSTS ME A DOZEN ROSES AND HALF A BOTTLE OF WINE.
MMMM
MMM!

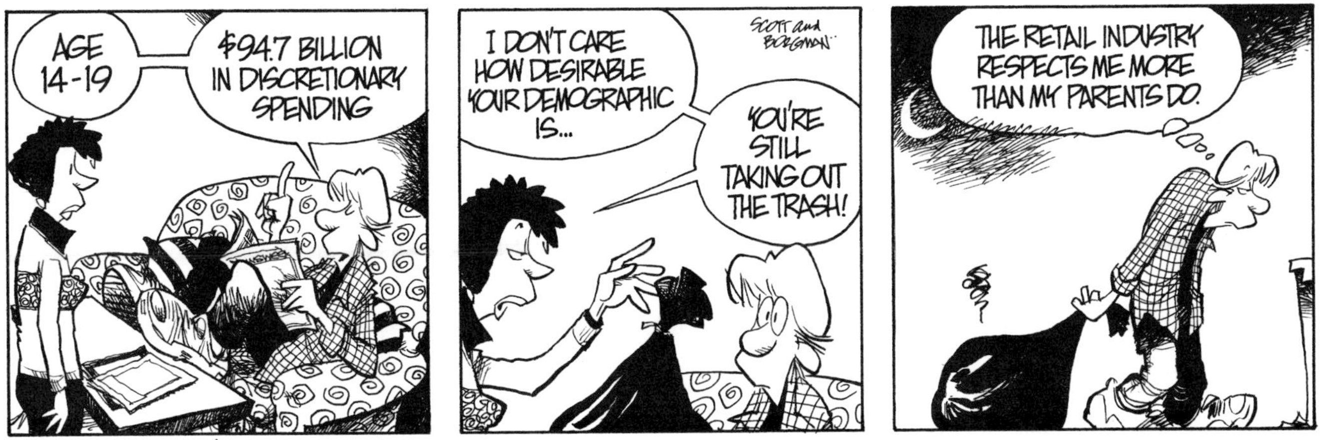
AGE 14-19
$94.7 BILLION IN DISCRETIONARY SPENDING
SCOTT and BORGMAN
I DON'T CARE HOW DESIRABLE YOUR DEMOGRAPHIC IS...
YOU'RE STILL TAKING OUT THE TRASH!
THE RETAIL INDUSTRY RESPECTS ME MORE THAN MY PARENTS DO.

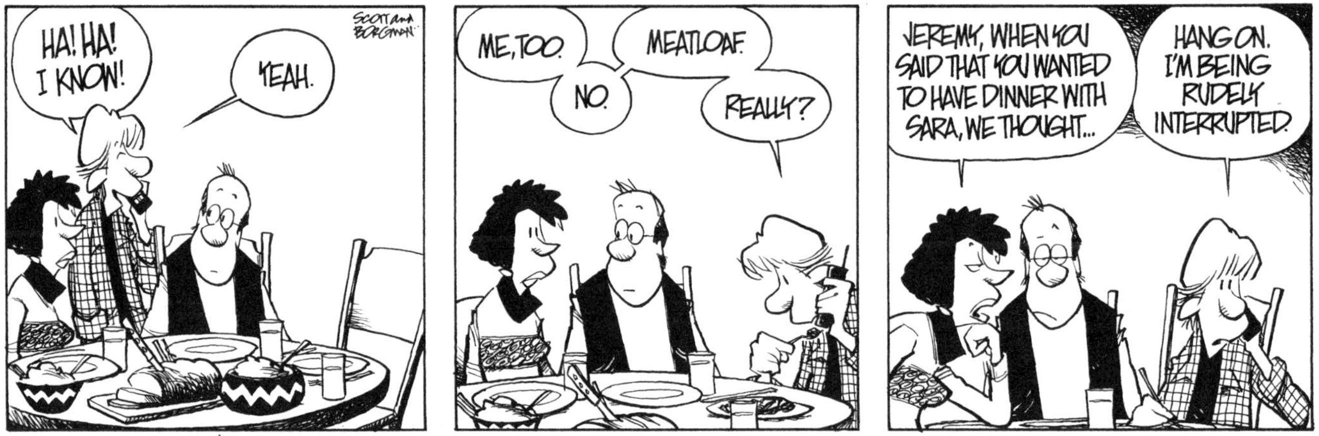
HA! HA! I KNOW!
YEAH.
ME, TOO.
NO.
MEATLOAF.
REALLY?
JEREMY, WHEN YOU SAID THAT YOU WANTED TO HAVE DINNER WITH SARA, WE THOUGHT...
HANG ON. I'M BEING RUDELY INTERRUPTED.

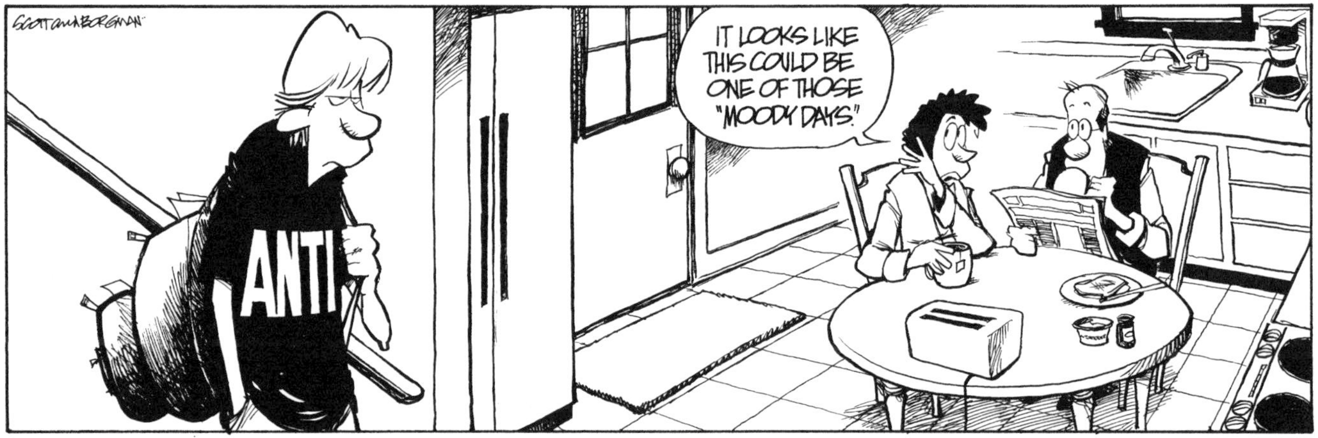
ANTI
IT LOOKS LIKE THIS COULD BE ONE OF THOSE "MOODY DAYS."

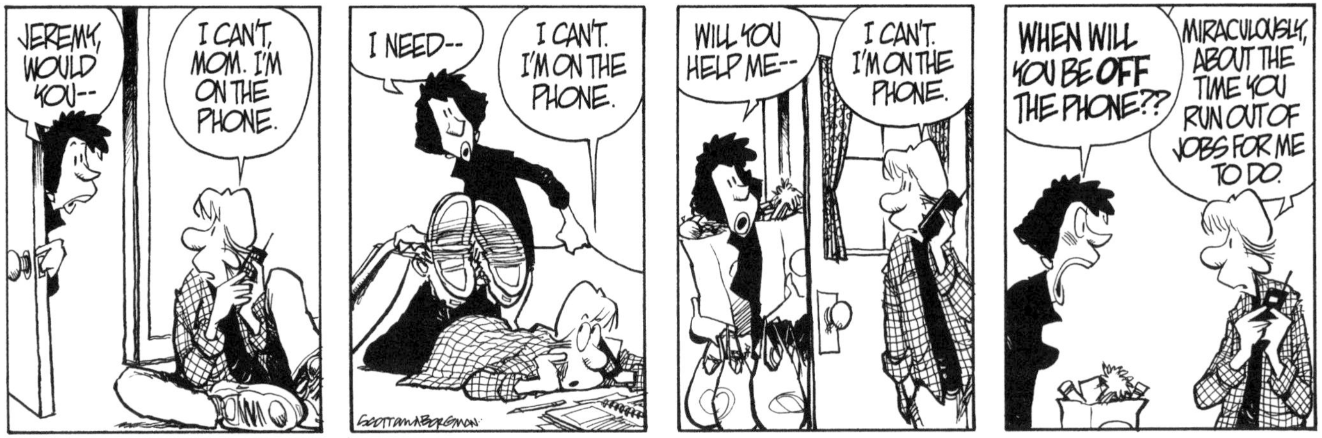
JEREMY, WOULD YOU--
I CAN'T, MOM. I'M ON THE PHONE.
I NEED--
I CAN'T. I'M ON THE PHONE.
WILL YOU HELP ME--
I CAN'T. I'M ON THE PHONE.
WHEN WILL YOU BE **OFF** THE PHONE??
MIRACULOUSLY, ABOUT THE TIME YOU RUN OUT OF JOBS FOR ME TO DO.

Zits

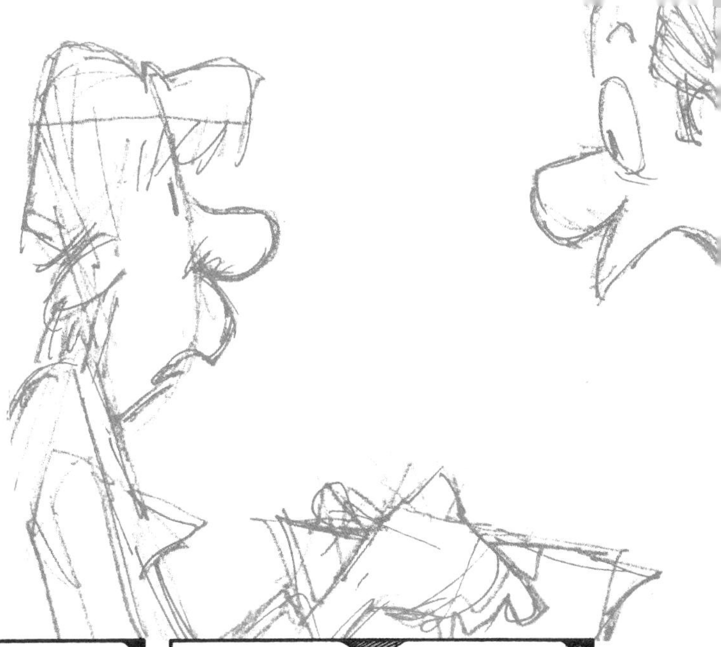

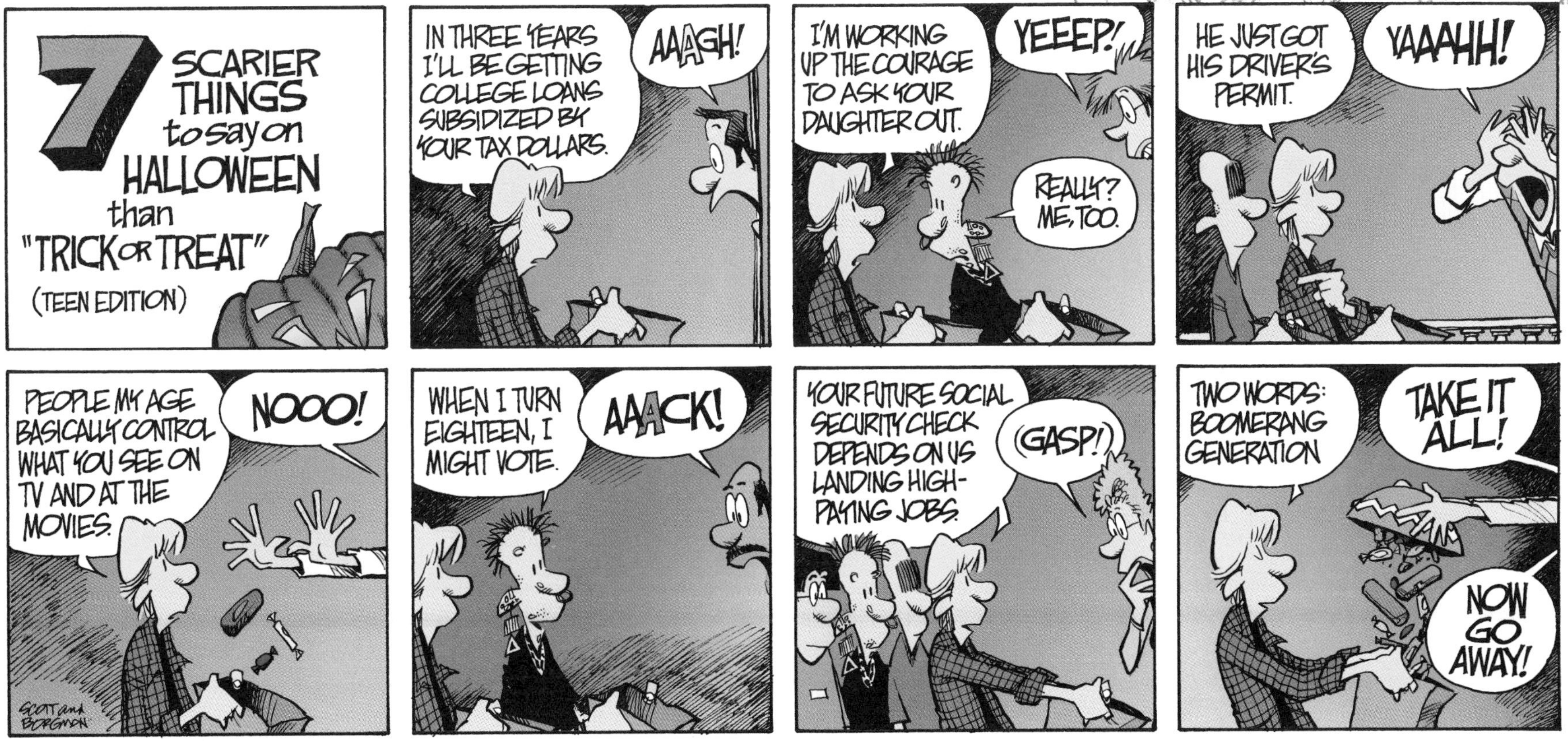
7 SCARIER THINGS to say on HALLOWEEN than "TRICK OR TREAT"
(TEEN EDITION)
IN THREE YEARS I'LL BE GETTING COLLEGE LOANS SUBSIDIZED BY YOUR TAX DOLLARS.
AAAGH!
I'M WORKING UP THE COURAGE TO ASK YOUR DAUGHTER OUT.
YEEEP!
REALLY? ME, TOO.
HE JUST GOT HIS DRIVER'S PERMIT.
YAAAHH!
PEOPLE MY AGE BASICALLY CONTROL WHAT YOU SEE ON TV AND AT THE MOVIES.
NOOO!
WHEN I TURN EIGHTEEN, I MIGHT VOTE.
AAACK!
YOUR FUTURE SOCIAL SECURITY CHECK DEPENDS ON US LANDING HIGH-PAYING JOBS.
(GASP!)
TWO WORDS: BOOMERANG GENERATION
TAKE IT ALL!
NOW GO AWAY!
SCOTT and BORGMAN

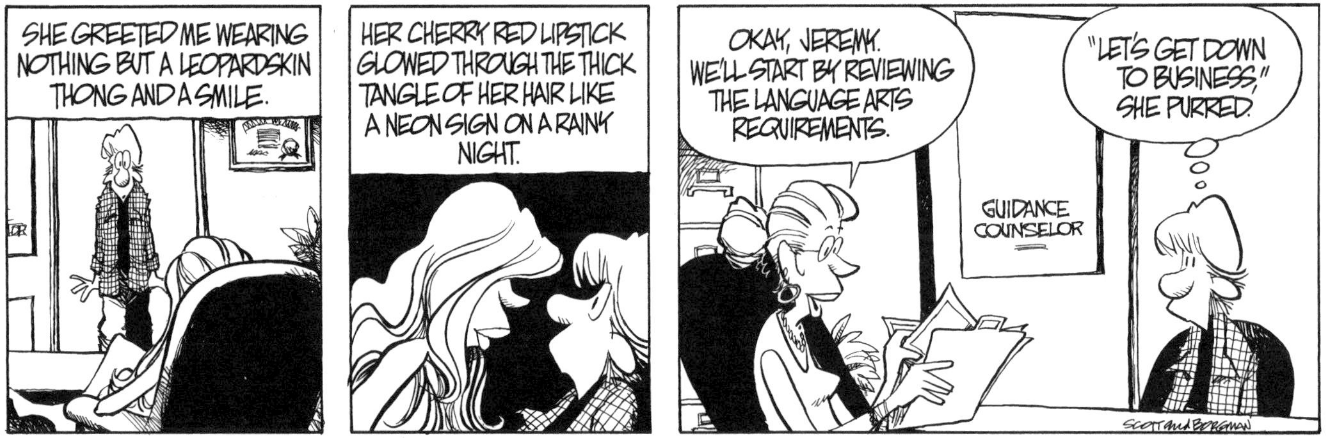
SHE GREETED ME WEARING NOTHING BUT A LEOPARDSKIN THONG AND A SMILE.
HER CHERRY RED LIPSTICK GLOWED THROUGH THE THICK TANGLE OF HER HAIR LIKE A NEON SIGN ON A RAINY NIGHT.
OKAY, JEREMY. WE'LL START BY REVIEWING THE LANGUAGE ARTS REQUIREMENTS.
GUIDANCE COUNSELOR
"LET'S GET DOWN TO BUSINESS," SHE PURRED.
SCOTT and BORGMAN

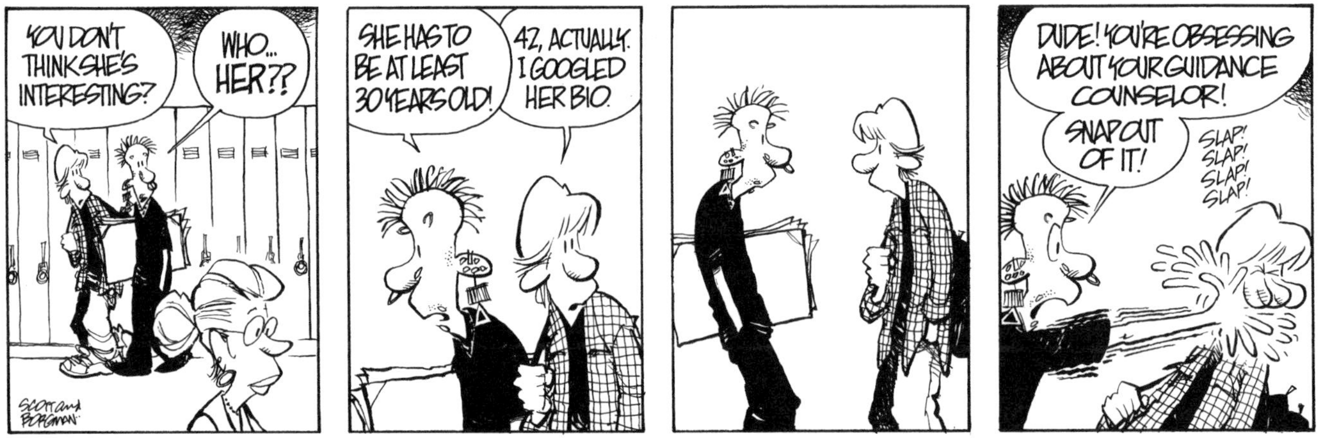
YOU DON'T THINK SHE'S INTERESTING?
WHO... HER??
SHE HAS TO BE AT LEAST 30 YEARS OLD!
42, ACTUALLY. I GOOGLED HER BIO.
DUDE! YOU'RE OBSESSING ABOUT YOUR GUIDANCE COUNSELOR!
SNAP OUT OF IT!
SLAP! SLAP! SLAP! SLAP!
SCOTT and BORGMAN

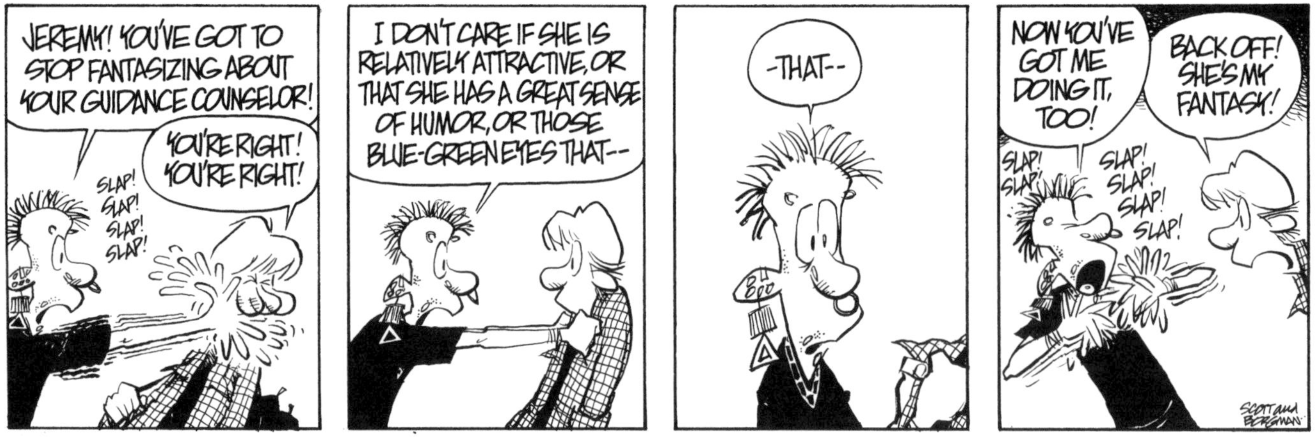
JEREMY! YOU'VE GOT TO STOP FANTASIZING ABOUT YOUR GUIDANCE COUNSELOR!
SLAP! SLAP! SLAP! SLAP!
YOU'RE RIGHT! YOU'RE RIGHT!
I DON'T CARE IF SHE IS RELATIVELY ATTRACTIVE, OR THAT SHE HAS A GREAT SENSE OF HUMOR, OR THOSE BLUE-GREEN EYES THAT--
-THAT--
NOW YOU'VE GOT ME DOING IT, TOO!
SLAP! SLAP!
SLAP! SLAP! SLAP! SLAP!
BACK OFF! SHE'S MY FANTASY!
SCOTT and BORGMAN

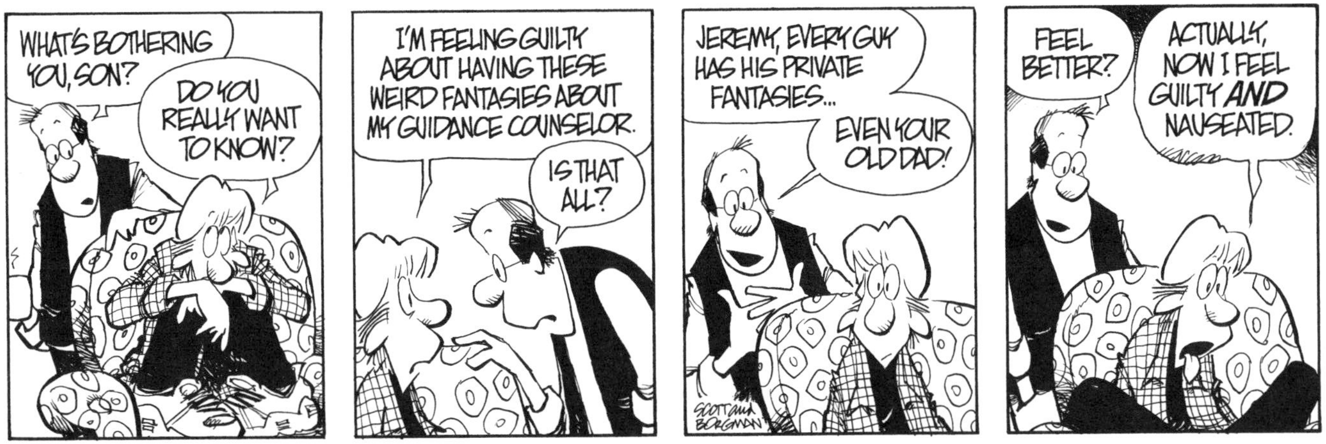
WHAT'S BOTHERING YOU, SON?
DO YOU REALLY WANT TO KNOW?
I'M FEELING GUILTY ABOUT HAVING THESE WEIRD FANTASIES ABOUT MY GUIDANCE COUNSELOR.
IS THAT ALL?
JEREMY, EVERY GUY HAS HIS PRIVATE FANTASIES...
EVEN YOUR OLD DAD!
SCOTT and BORGMAN
FEEL BETTER?
ACTUALLY, NOW I FEEL GUILTY AND NAUSEATED.

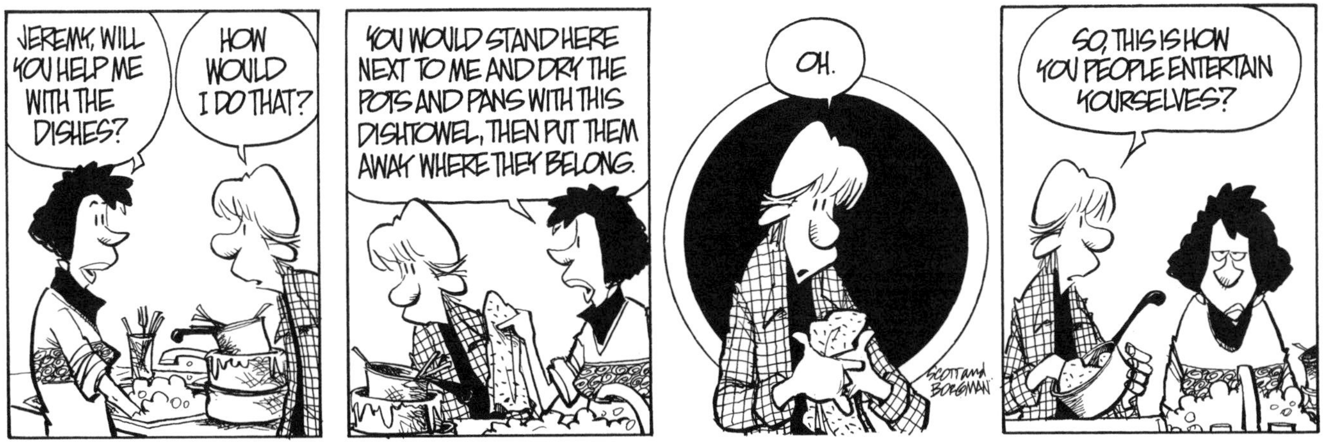
JEREMY, WILL YOU HELP ME WITH THE DISHES?
HOW WOULD I DO THAT?
YOU WOULD STAND HERE NEXT TO ME AND DRY THE POTS AND PANS WITH THIS DISHTOWEL, THEN PUT THEM AWAY WHERE THEY BELONG.
OH.
SCOTT and BORGMAN
SO, THIS IS HOW YOU PEOPLE ENTERTAIN YOURSELVES?

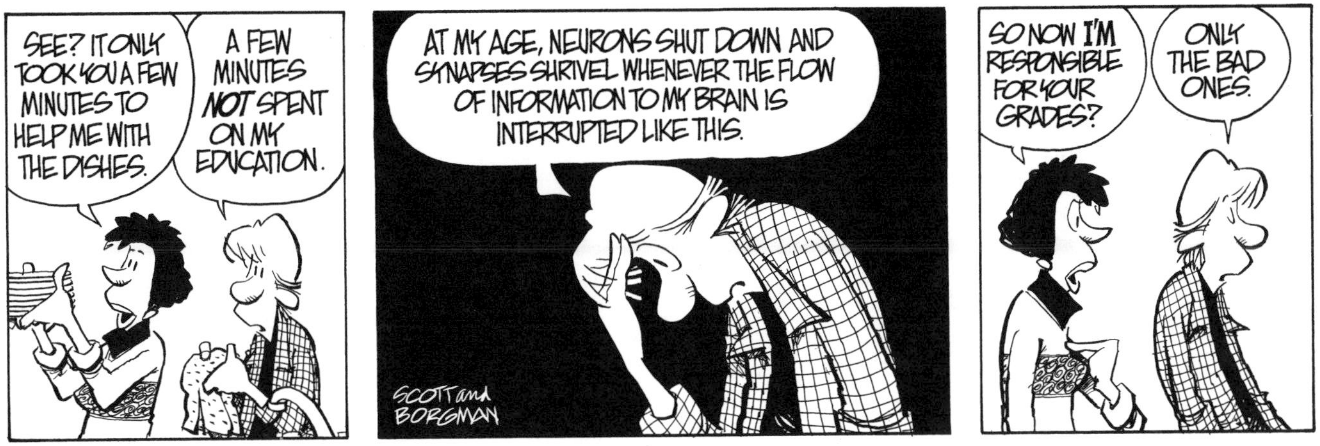
SEE? IT ONLY TOOK YOU A FEW MINUTES TO HELP ME WITH THE DISHES.
A FEW MINUTES NOT SPENT ON MY EDUCATION.
AT MY AGE, NEURONS SHUT DOWN AND SYNAPSES SHRIVEL WHENEVER THE FLOW OF INFORMATION TO MY BRAIN IS INTERRUPTED LIKE THIS.
SCOTT and BORGMAN
SO NOW I'M RESPONSIBLE FOR YOUR GRADES?
ONLY THE BAD ONES.

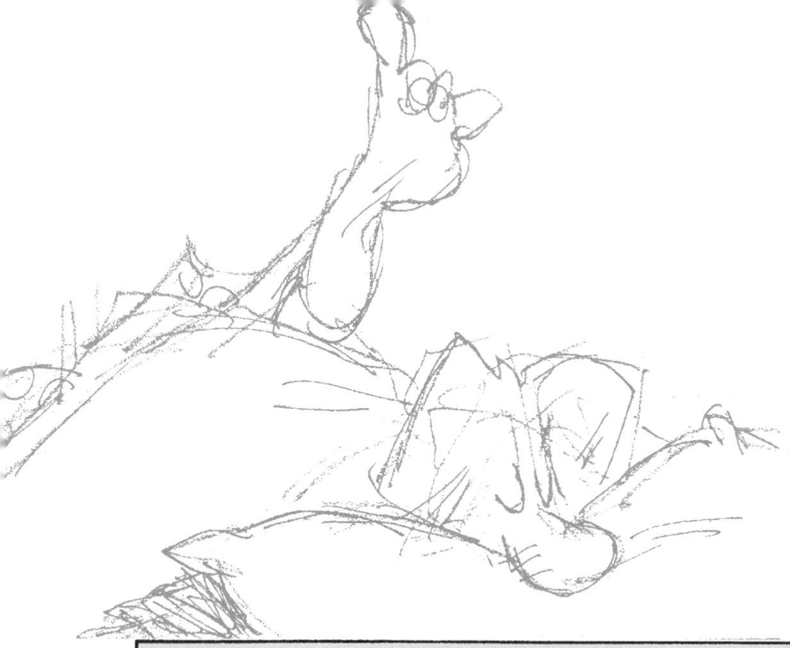

Zits

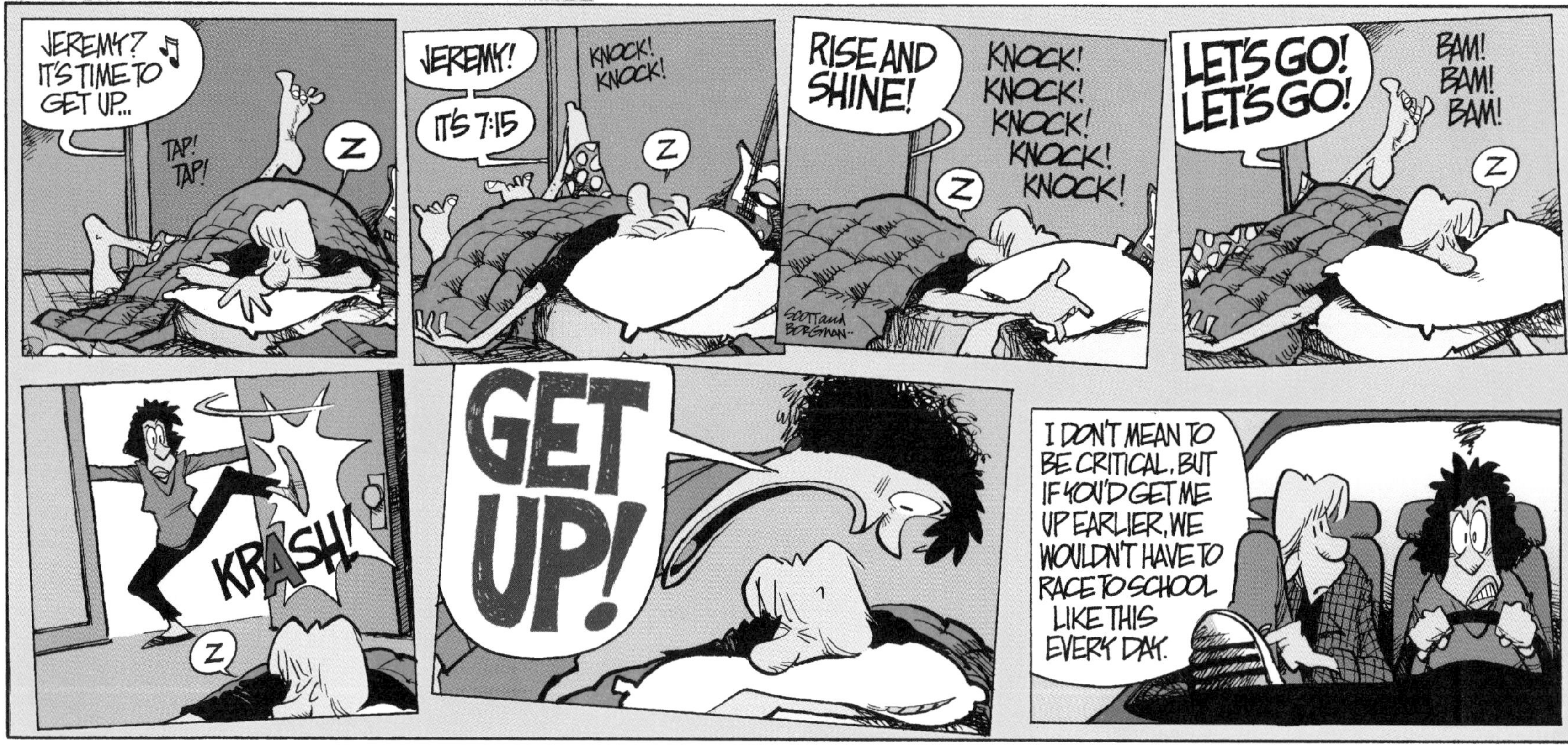

JEREMY? IT'S TIME TO GET UP...
TAP! TAP!
Z
JEREMY!
IT'S 7:15
KNOCK! KNOCK!
Z
RISE AND SHINE!
KNOCK! KNOCK! KNOCK! KNOCK! KNOCK!
Z
SCOTT and BORGMAN
LET'S GO! LET'S GO!
BAM! BAM! BAM!
Z
KRASH!
Z
GET UP!
I DON'T MEAN TO BE CRITICAL, BUT IF YOU'D GET ME UP EARLIER, WE WOULDN'T HAVE TO RACE TO SCHOOL LIKE THIS EVERY DAY.

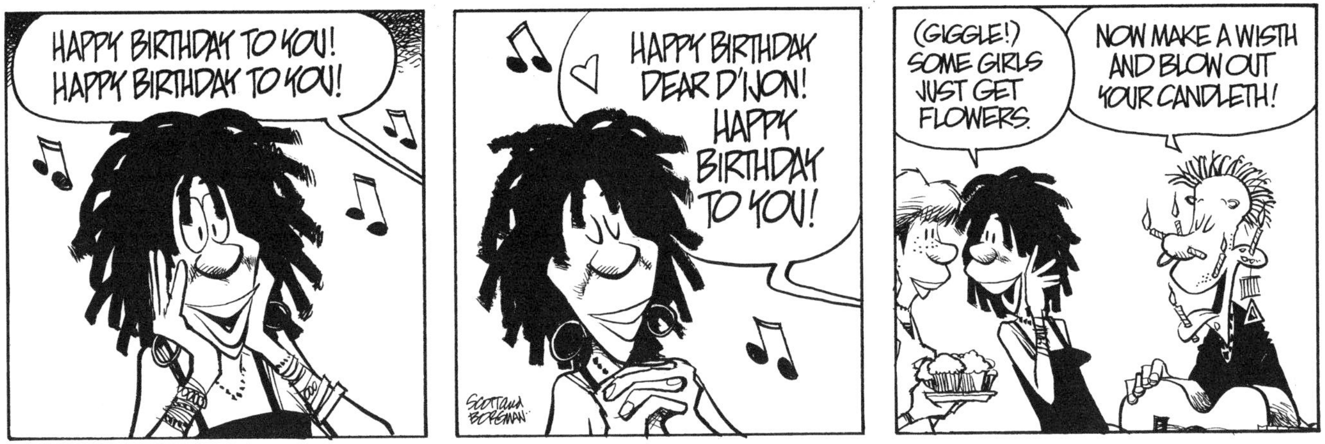
HAPPY BIRTHDAY TO YOU! HAPPY BIRTHDAY TO YOU!
HAPPY BIRTHDAY DEAR D'JON! HAPPY BIRTHDAY TO YOU!
(GIGGLE!) SOME GIRLS JUST GET FLOWERS.
NOW MAKE A WISTH AND BLOW OUT YOUR CANDLETH!

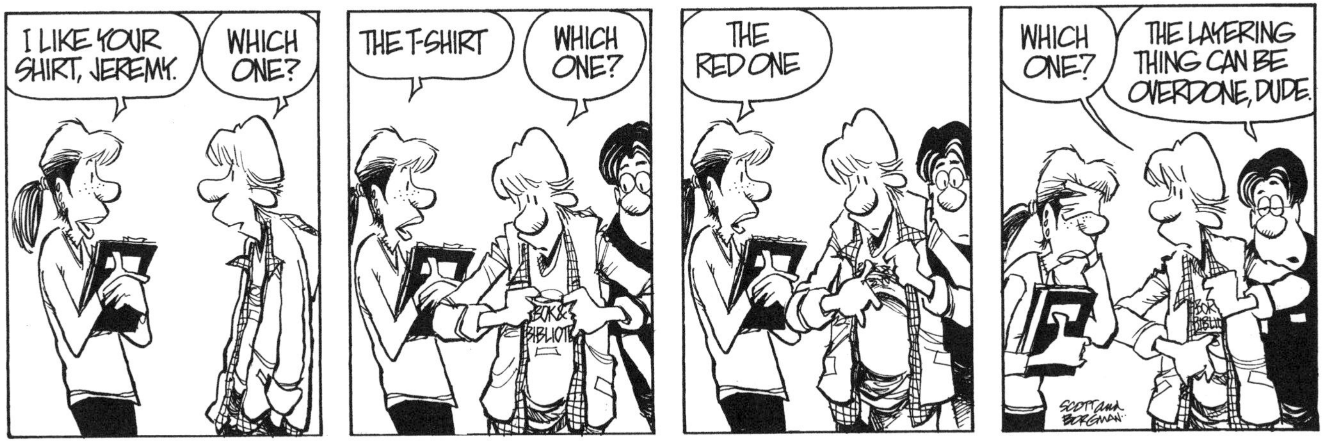
I LIKE YOUR SHIRT, JEREMY.
WHICH ONE?
THE T-SHIRT
WHICH ONE?
THE RED ONE
WHICH ONE?
THE LAYERING THING CAN BE OVERDONE, DUDE.

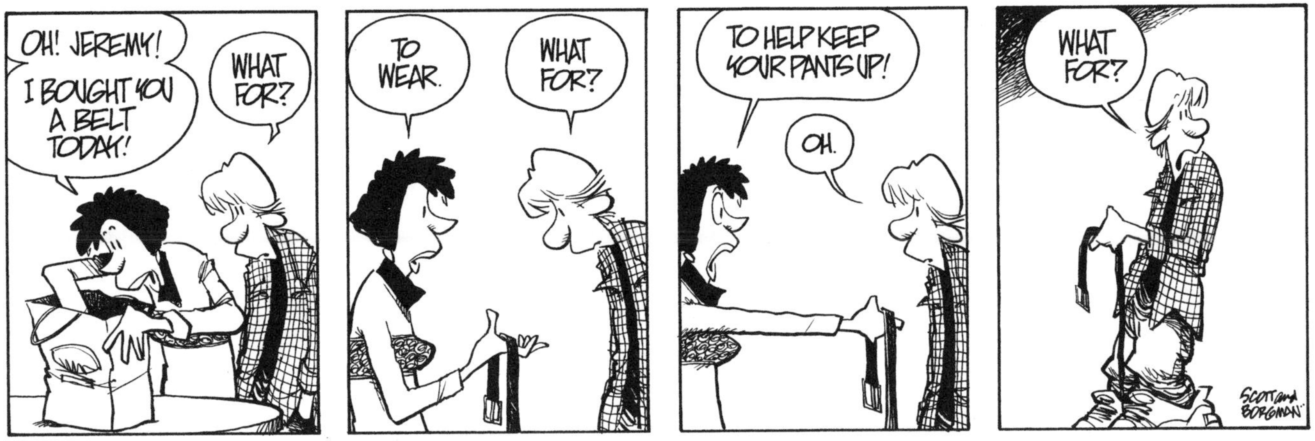
OH! JEREMY!
I BOUGHT YOU A BELT TODAY!
WHAT FOR?
TO WEAR.
WHAT FOR?
TO HELP KEEP YOUR PANTS UP!
OH.
WHAT FOR?

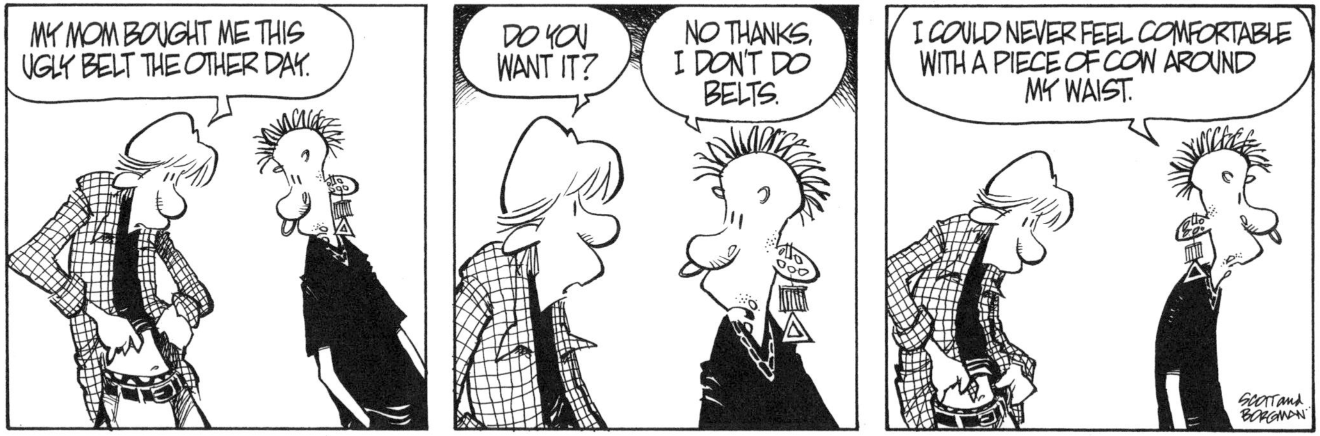
MY MOM BOUGHT ME THIS UGLY BELT THE OTHER DAY.
DO YOU WANT IT?
NO THANKS, I DON'T DO BELTS.
I COULD NEVER FEEL COMFORTABLE WITH A PIECE OF COW AROUND MY WAIST.
SCOTT AND BORGMAN

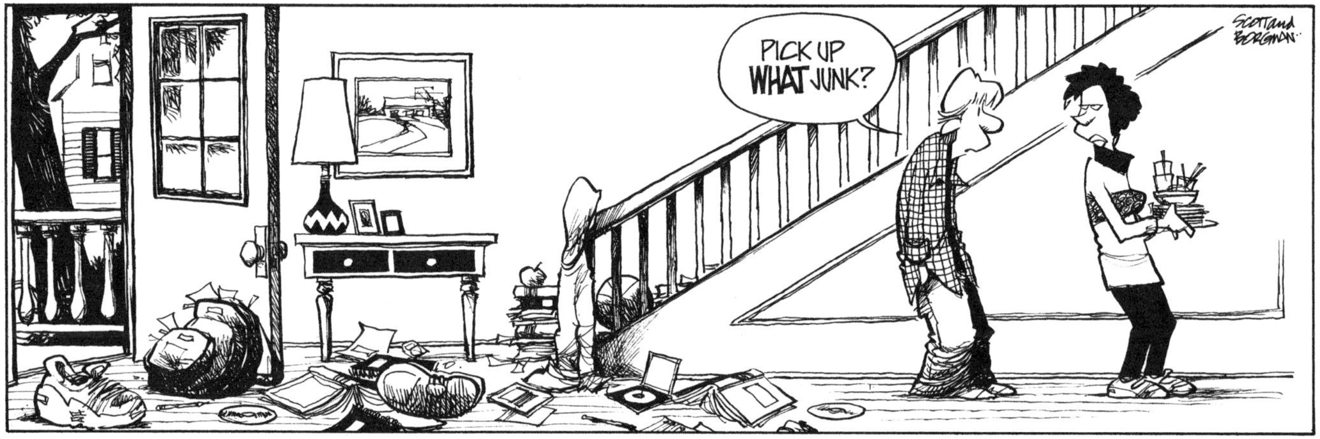
SCOTT AND BORGMAN
PICK UP WHAT JUNK?

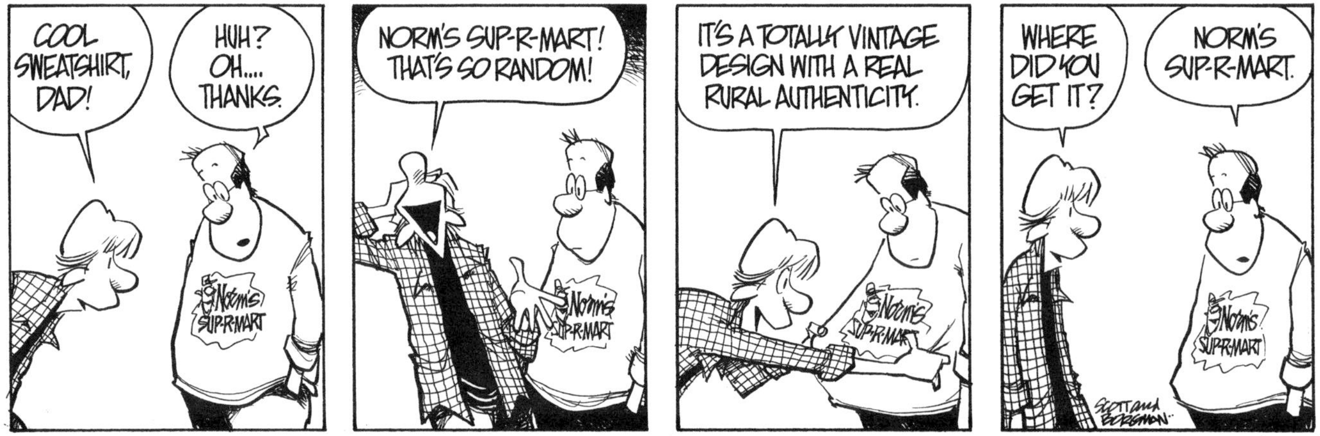
COOL SWEATSHIRT, DAD!
HUH? OH.... THANKS.
NORM'S SUP-R-MART! THAT'S SO RANDOM!
IT'S A TOTALLY VINTAGE DESIGN WITH A REAL RURAL AUTHENTICITY.
WHERE DID YOU GET IT?
NORM'S SUP-R-MART.
SCOTT AND BORGMAN

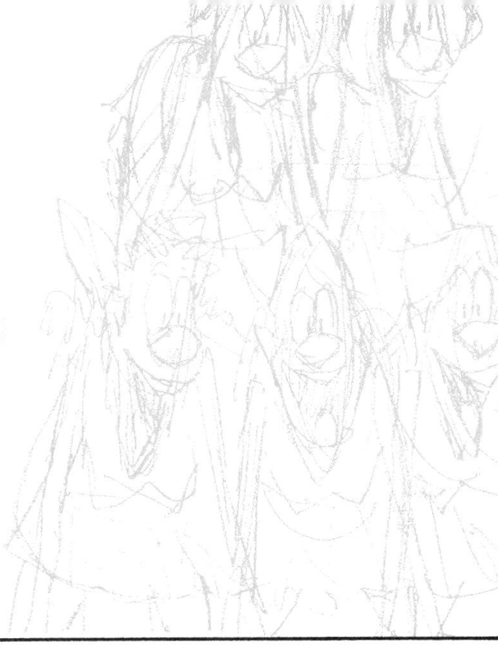

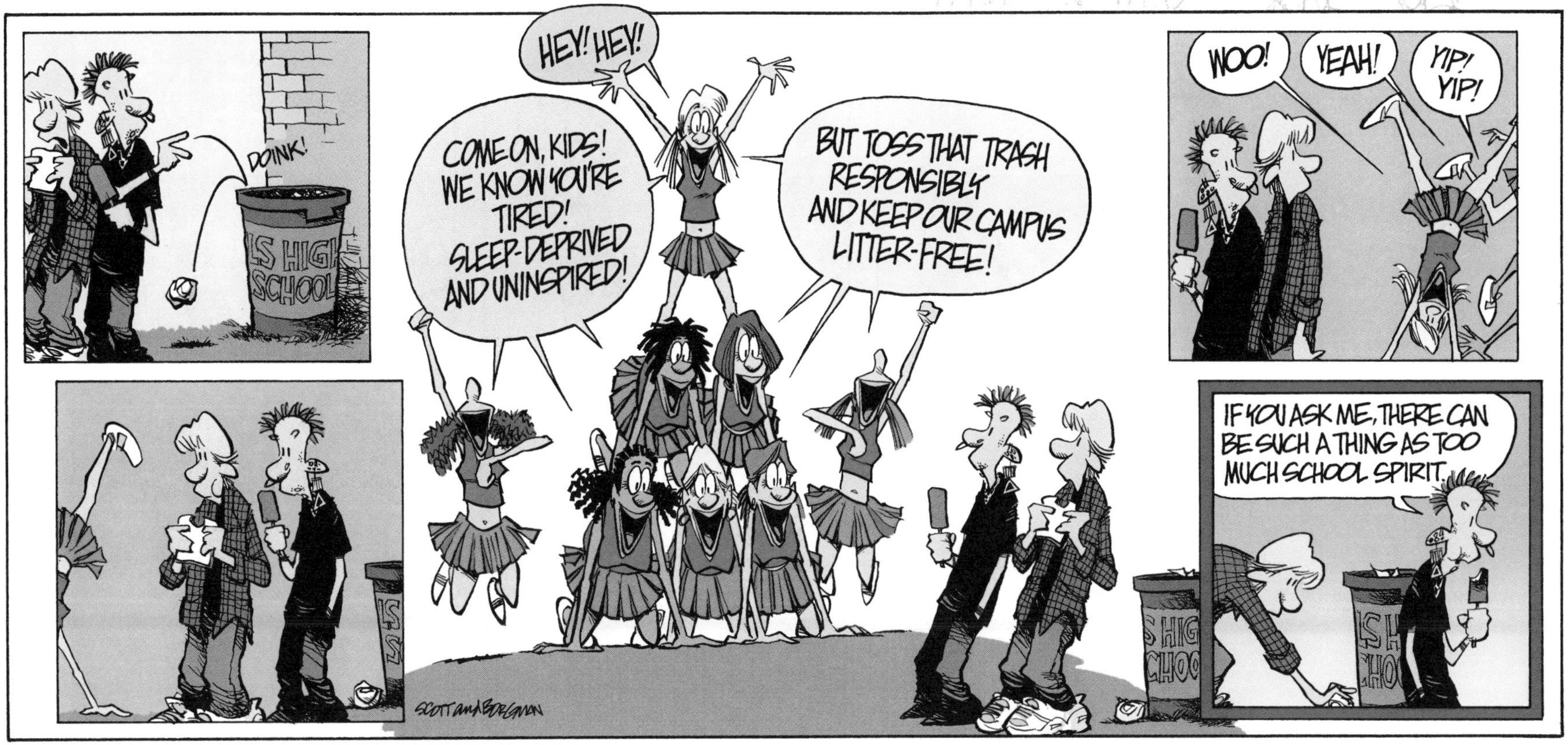
DOINK!
LS HIGH SCHOOL
HEY! HEY!
COME ON, KIDS! WE KNOW YOU'RE TIRED! SLEEP-DEPRIVED AND UNINSPIRED!
BUT TOSS THAT TRASH RESPONSIBLY AND KEEP OUR CAMPUS LITTER-FREE!
WOO!
YEAH!
YIP! YIP!
IF YOU ASK ME, THERE CAN BE SUCH A THING AS TOO MUCH SCHOOL SPIRIT.
SCOTT and BORGMAN

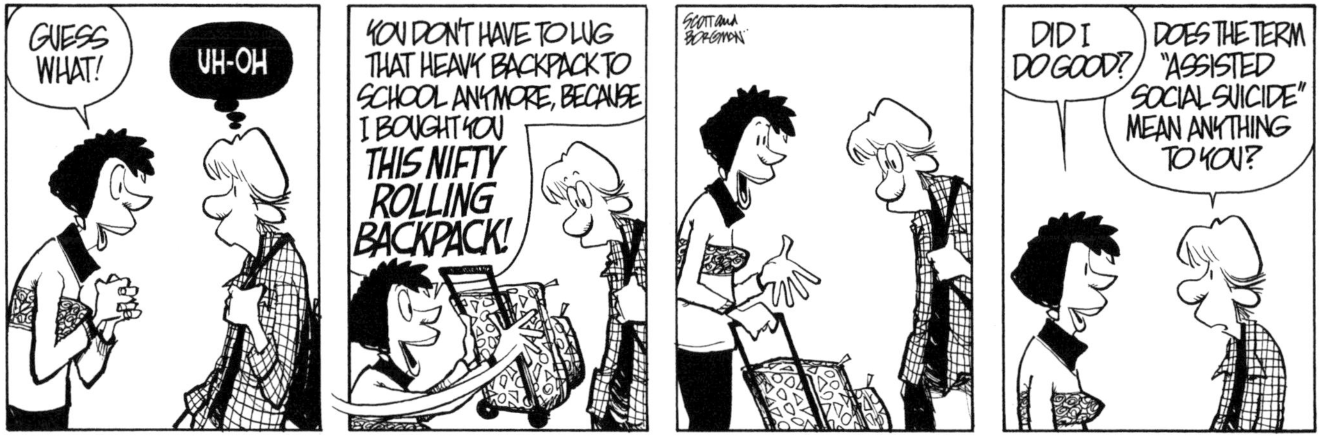
GUESS WHAT!
UH-OH
YOU DON'T HAVE TO LUG THAT HEAVY BACKPACK TO SCHOOL ANYMORE, BECAUSE I BOUGHT YOU **THIS NIFTY ROLLING BACKPACK!**
DID I DO GOOD?
DOES THE TERM "ASSISTED SOCIAL SUICIDE" MEAN ANYTHING TO YOU?

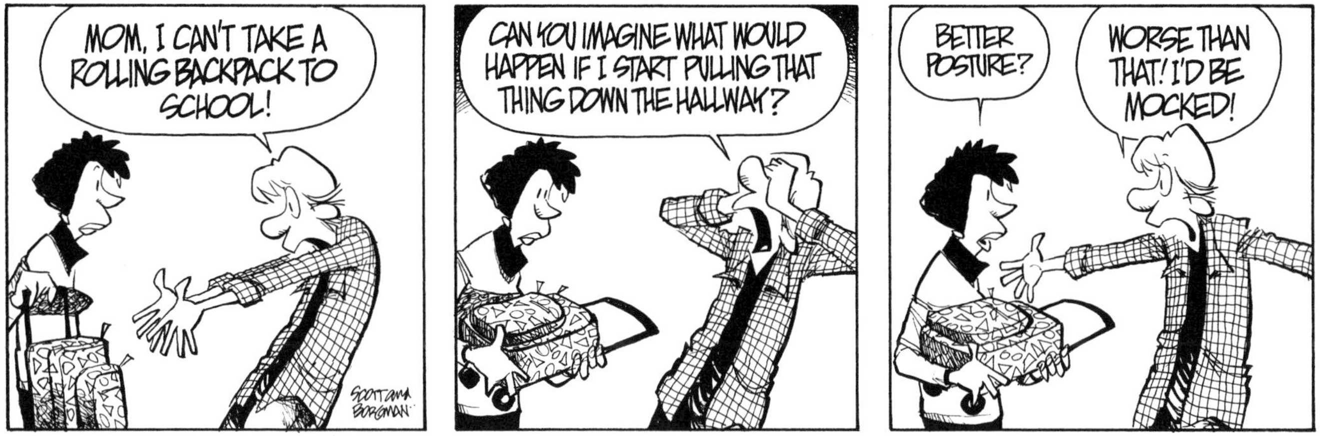
MOM, I CAN'T TAKE A ROLLING BACKPACK TO SCHOOL!
CAN YOU IMAGINE WHAT WOULD HAPPEN IF I START PULLING THAT THING DOWN THE HALLWAY?
BETTER POSTURE?
WORSE THAN THAT! I'D BE MOCKED!

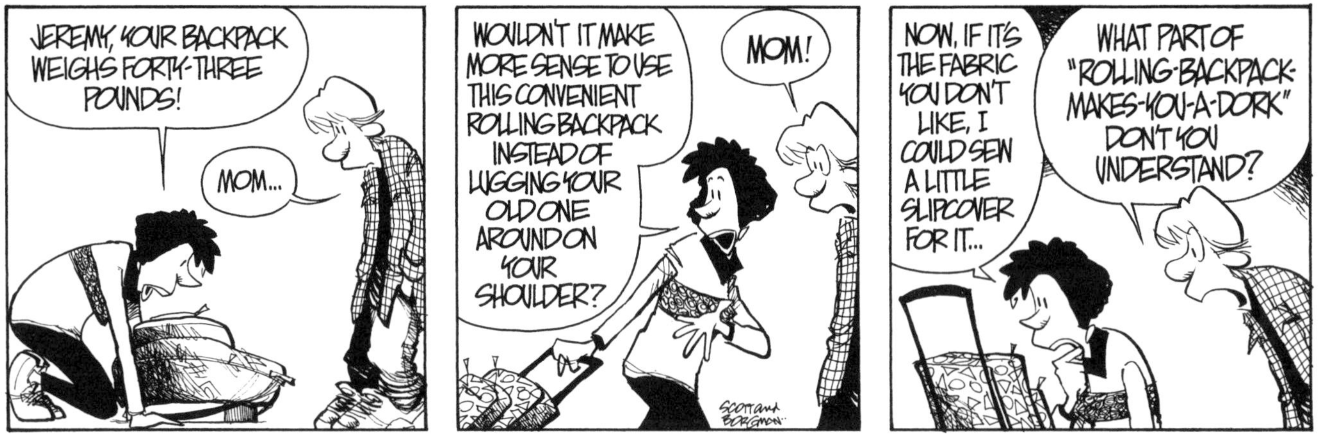
JEREMY, YOUR BACKPACK WEIGHS FORTY-THREE POUNDS!
MOM...
WOULDN'T IT MAKE MORE SENSE TO USE THIS CONVENIENT ROLLING BACKPACK INSTEAD OF LUGGING YOUR OLD ONE AROUND ON YOUR SHOULDER?
MOM!
NOW, IF IT'S THE FABRIC YOU DON'T LIKE, I COULD SEW A LITTLE SLIPCOVER FOR IT...
WHAT PART OF "ROLLING-BACKPACK-MAKES-YOU-A-DORK" DON'T YOU UNDERSTAND?

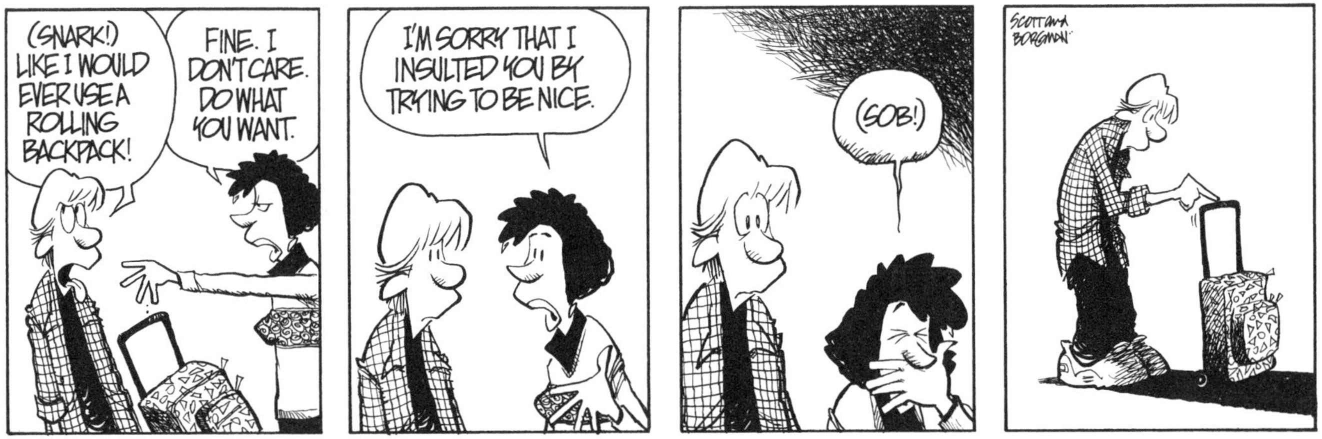
(SNARK!) LIKE I WOULD EVER USE A ROLLING BACKPACK!
FINE. I DON'T CARE. DO WHAT YOU WANT.
I'M SORRY THAT I INSULTED YOU BY TRYING TO BE NICE.
(SOB!)

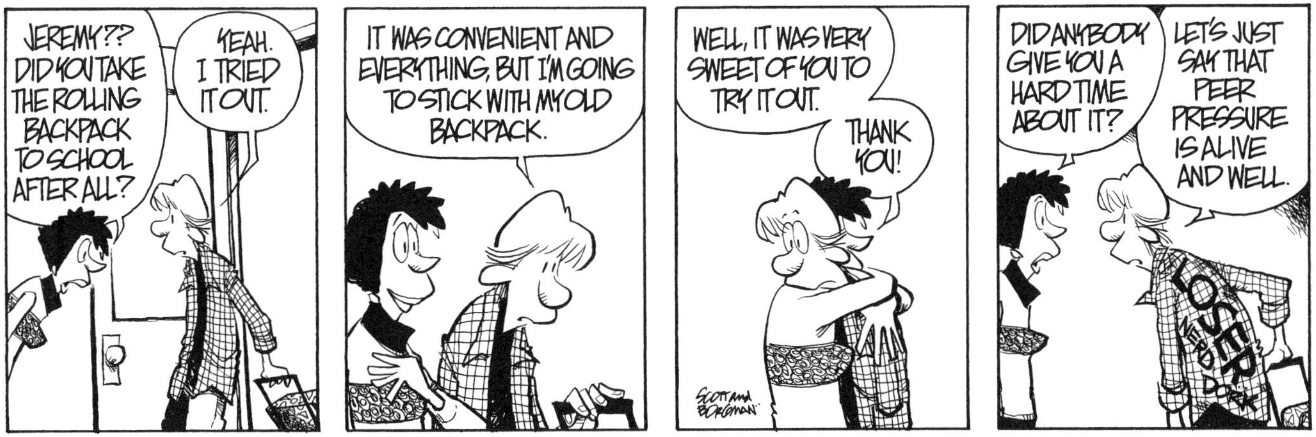
JEREMY?? DID YOU TAKE THE ROLLING BACKPACK TO SCHOOL AFTER ALL?
YEAH. I TRIED IT OUT.
IT WAS CONVENIENT AND EVERYTHING, BUT I'M GOING TO STICK WITH MY OLD BACKPACK.
WELL, IT WAS VERY SWEET OF YOU TO TRY IT OUT.
THANK YOU!
DID ANYBODY GIVE YOU A HARD TIME ABOUT IT?
LET'S JUST SAY THAT PEER PRESSURE IS ALIVE AND WELL.
LOSER

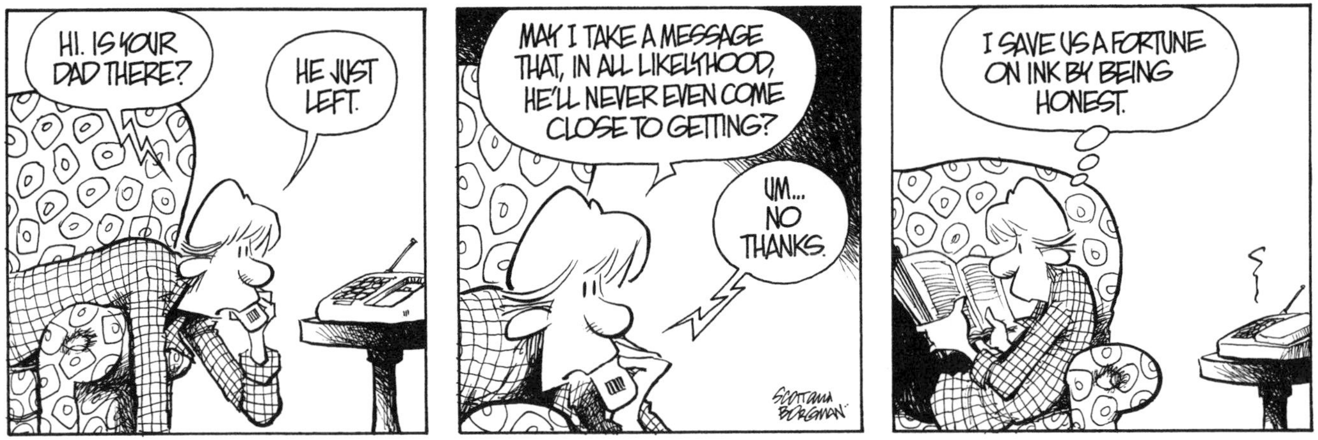
HI. IS YOUR DAD THERE?
HE JUST LEFT.
MAY I TAKE A MESSAGE THAT, IN ALL LIKELYHOOD, HE'LL NEVER EVEN COME CLOSE TO GETTING?
UM... NO THANKS.
I SAVE US A FORTUNE ON INK BY BEING HONEST.

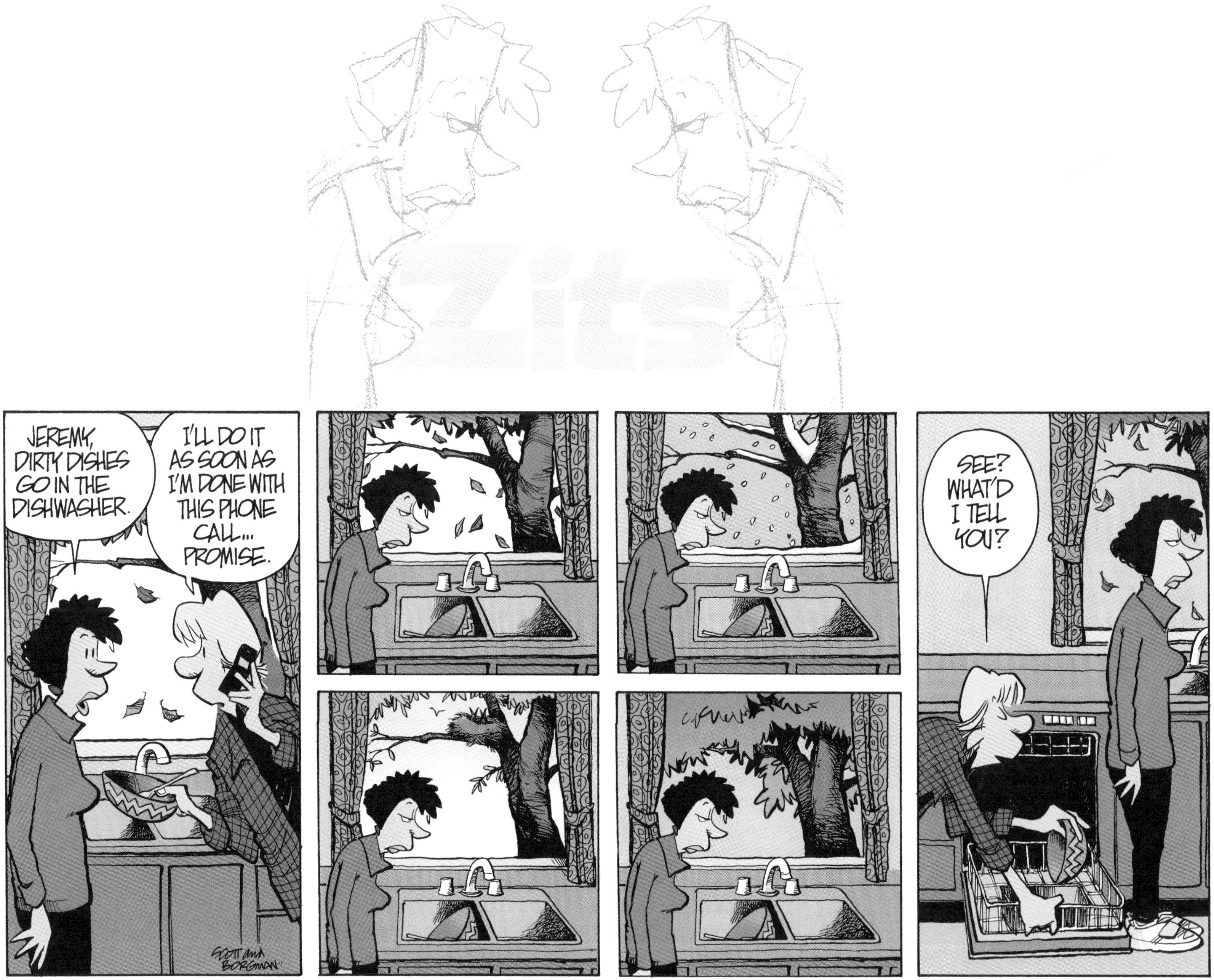
Zits
JEREMY, DIRTY DISHES GO IN THE DISHWASHER.
I'LL DO IT AS SOON AS I'M DONE WITH THIS PHONE CALL... PROMISE.
SCOTT AND BORGMAN
SEE? WHAT'D I TELL YOU?

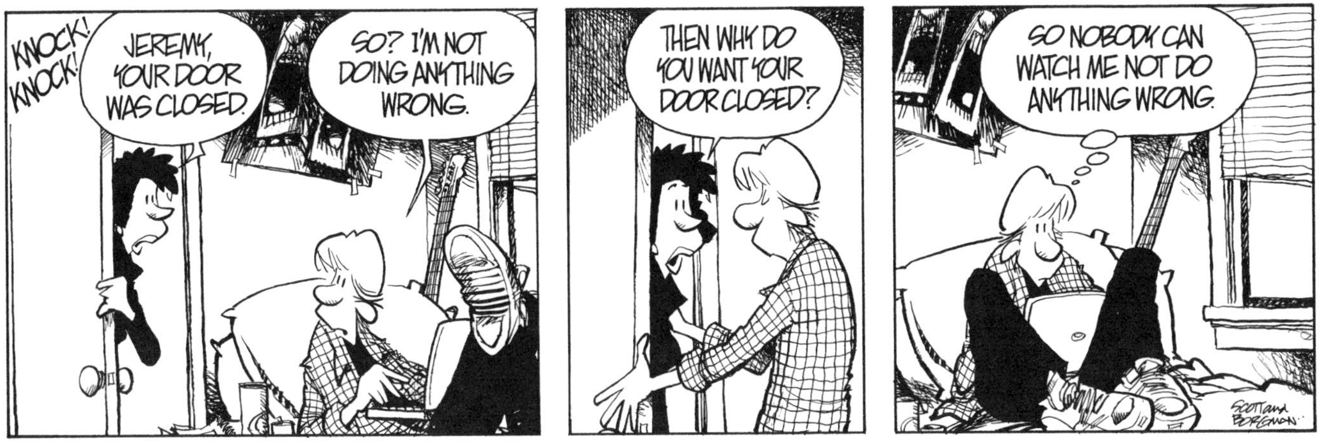
KNOCK! KNOCK!
JEREMY, YOUR DOOR WAS CLOSED.
SO? I'M NOT DOING ANYTHING WRONG.
THEN WHY DO YOU WANT YOUR DOOR CLOSED?
SO NOBODY CAN WATCH ME NOT DO ANYTHING WRONG.

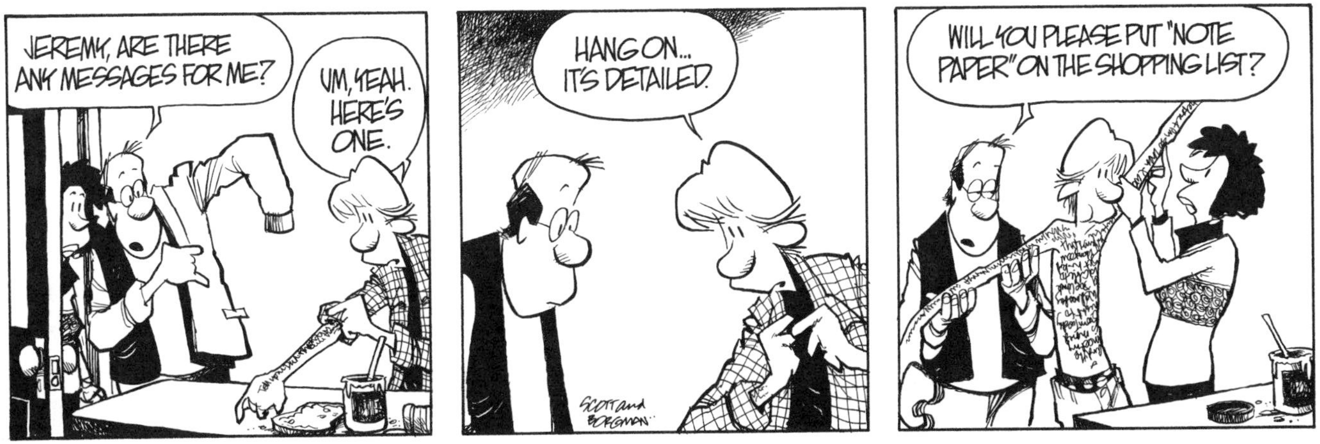
JEREMY, ARE THERE ANY MESSAGES FOR ME?
UM, YEAH. HERE'S ONE.
HANG ON... IT'S DETAILED.
WILL YOU PLEASE PUT "NOTE PAPER" ON THE SHOPPING LIST?

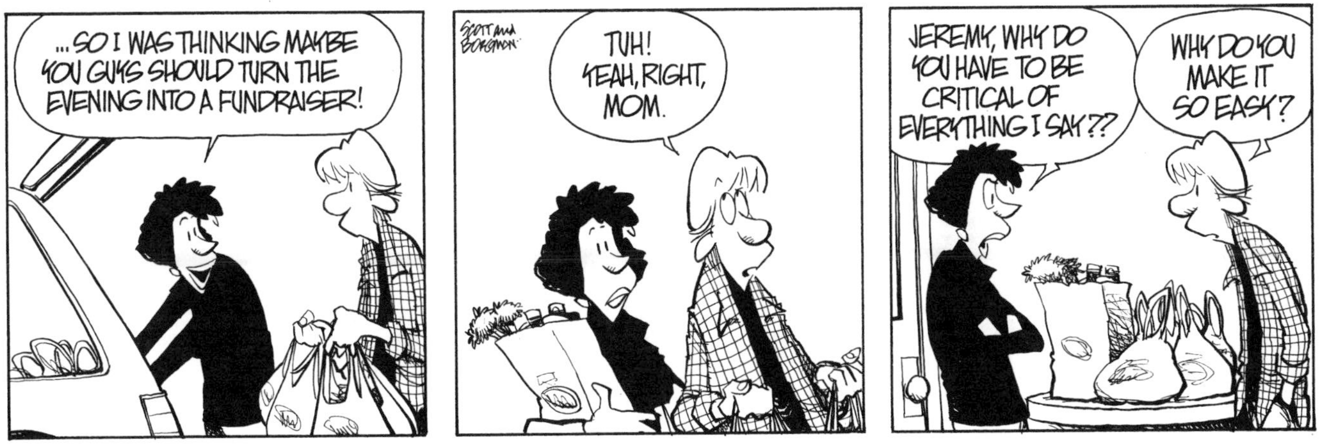
...SO I WAS THINKING MAYBE YOU GUYS SHOULD TURN THE EVENING INTO A FUNDRAISER!
TUH! YEAH, RIGHT, MOM.
JEREMY, WHY DO YOU HAVE TO BE CRITICAL OF EVERYTHING I SAY??
WHY DO YOU MAKE IT SO EASY?

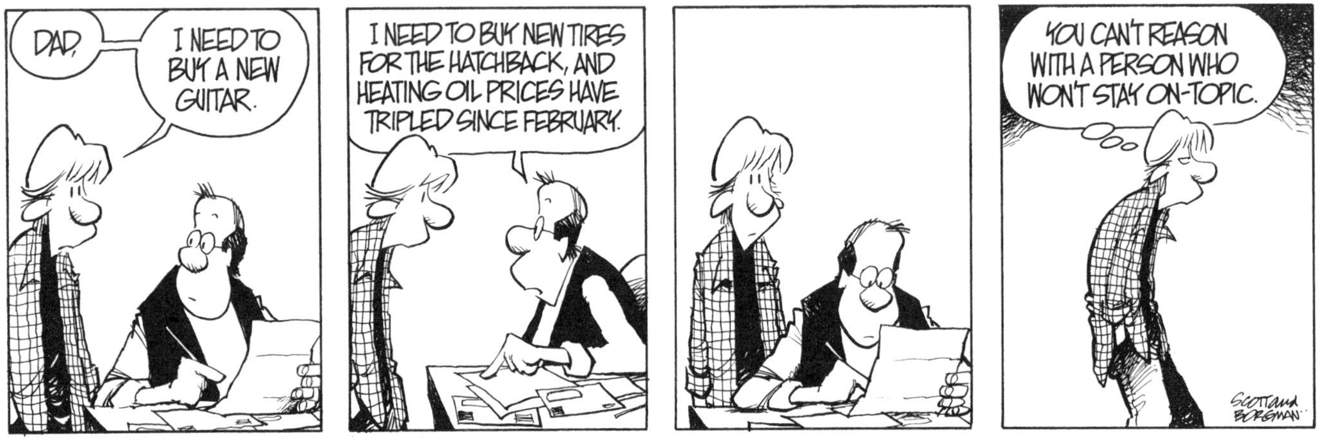
DAD,
I NEED TO BUY A NEW GUITAR.
I NEED TO BUY NEW TIRES FOR THE HATCHBACK, AND HEATING OIL PRICES HAVE TRIPLED SINCE FEBRUARY.
YOU CAN'T REASON WITH A PERSON WHO WON'T STAY ON-TOPIC.

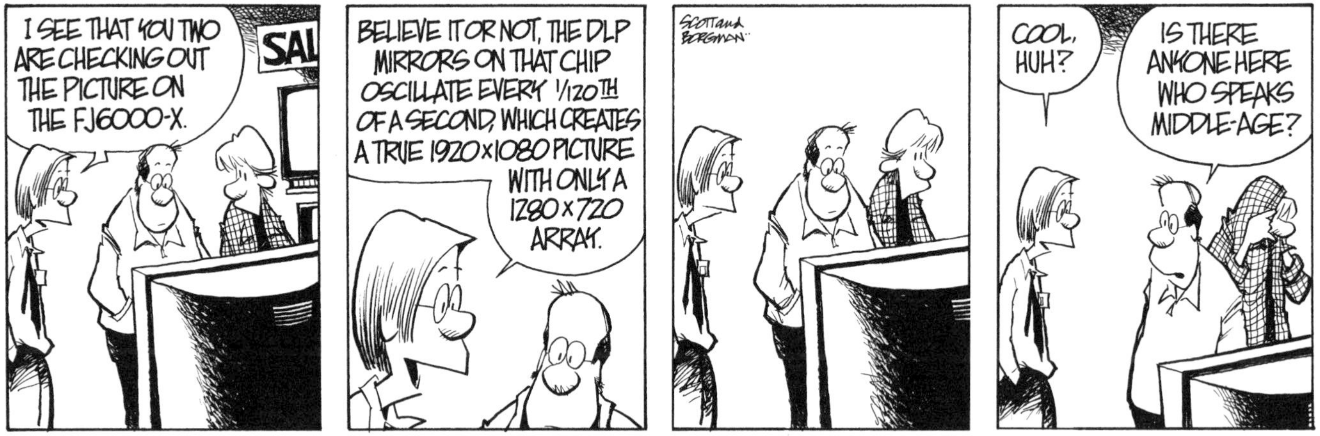
I SEE THAT YOU TWO ARE CHECKING OUT THE PICTURE ON THE FJ6000-X.
BELIEVE IT OR NOT, THE DLP MIRRORS ON THAT CHIP OSCILLATE EVERY 1/120TH OF A SECOND, WHICH CREATES A TRUE 1920×1080 PICTURE WITH ONLY A 1280×720 ARRAY.
COOL, HUH?
IS THERE ANYONE HERE WHO SPEAKS MIDDLE-AGE?

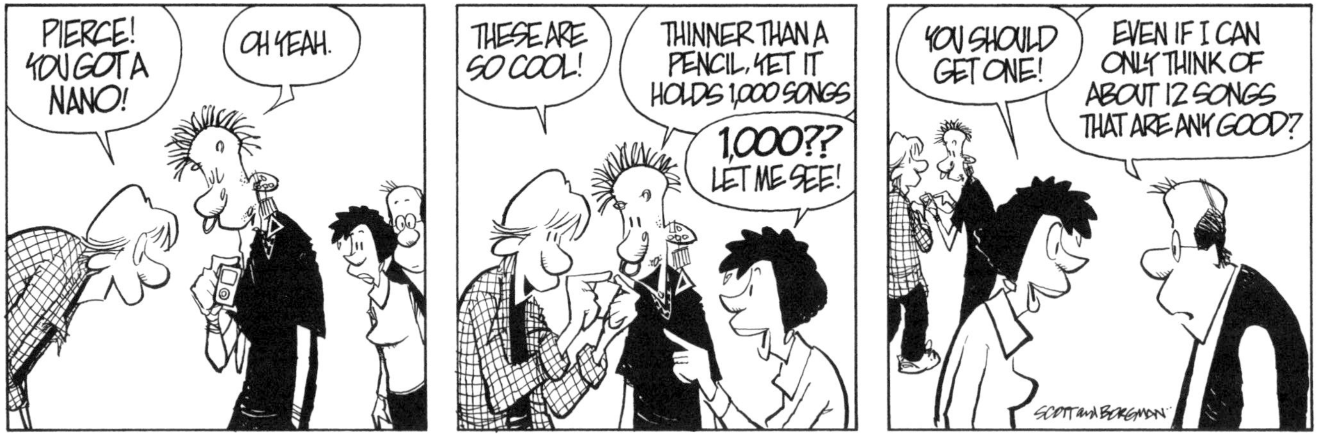
PIERCE! YOU GOT A NANO!
OH YEAH.
THESE ARE SO COOL!
THINNER THAN A PENCIL, YET IT HOLDS 1,000 SONGS
1,000?? LET ME SEE!
YOU SHOULD GET ONE!
EVEN IF I CAN ONLY THINK OF ABOUT 12 SONGS THAT ARE ANY GOOD?

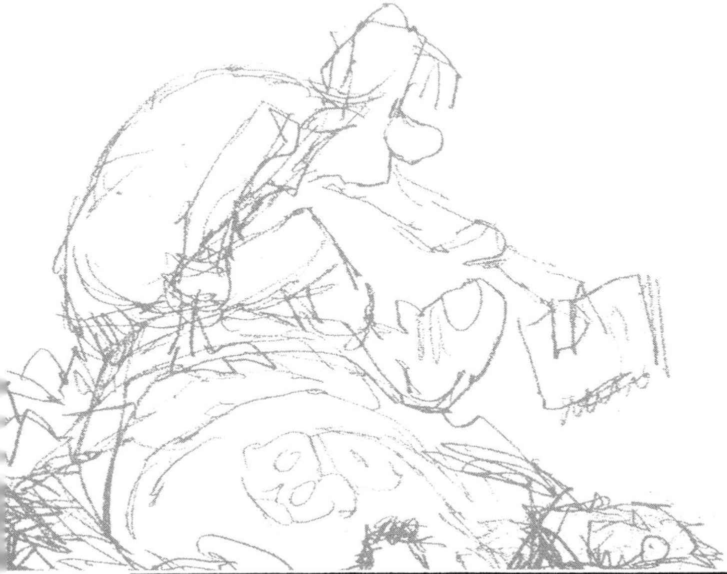

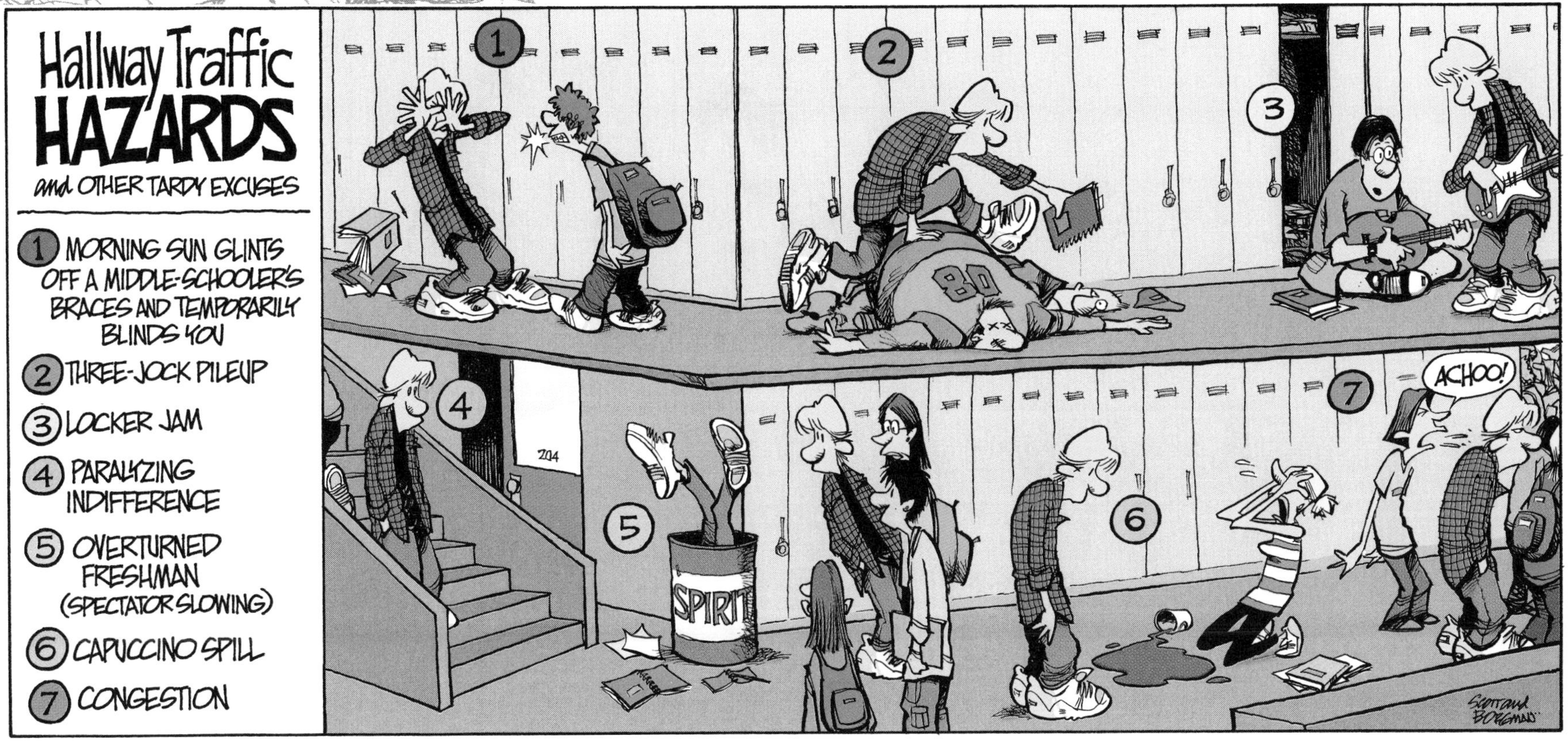

Hallway Traffic HAZARDS
and OTHER TARDY EXCUSES
1 MORNING SUN GLINTS OFF A MIDDLE-SCHOOLER'S BRACES AND TEMPORARILY BLINDS YOU
2 THREE-JOCK PILEUP
3 LOCKER JAM
4 PARALYZING INDIFFERENCE
5 OVERTURNED FRESHMAN (SPECTATOR SLOWING)
6 CAPUCCINO SPILL
7 CONGESTION
1
2
3
80
4
204
5
SPIRIT
6
7
ACHOO!

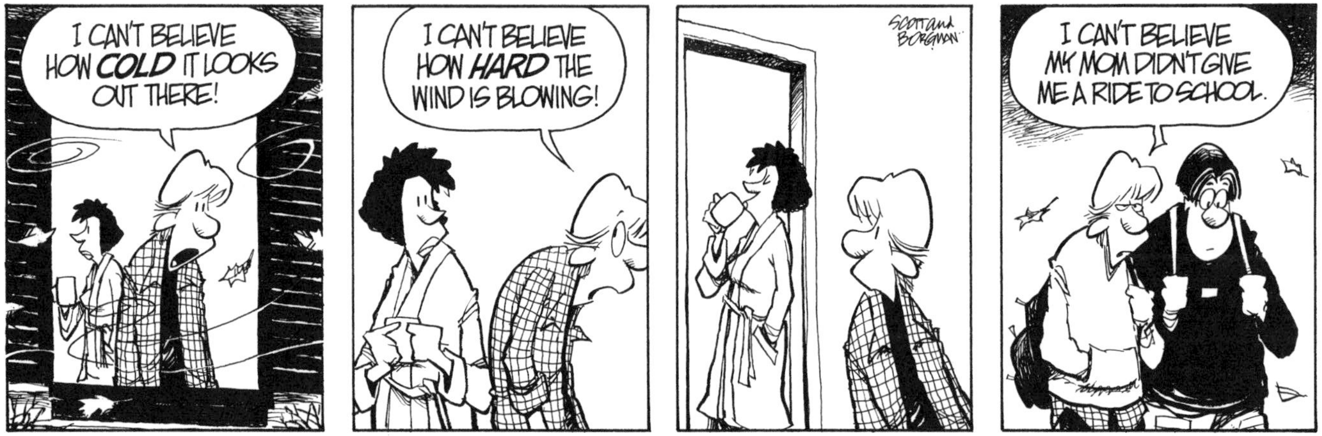
I CAN'T BELIEVE HOW **COLD** IT LOOKS OUT THERE!
I CAN'T BELIEVE HOW **HARD** THE WIND IS BLOWING!
SCOTT AND BORGMAN
I CAN'T BELIEVE MY MOM DIDN'T GIVE ME A RIDE TO SCHOOL.

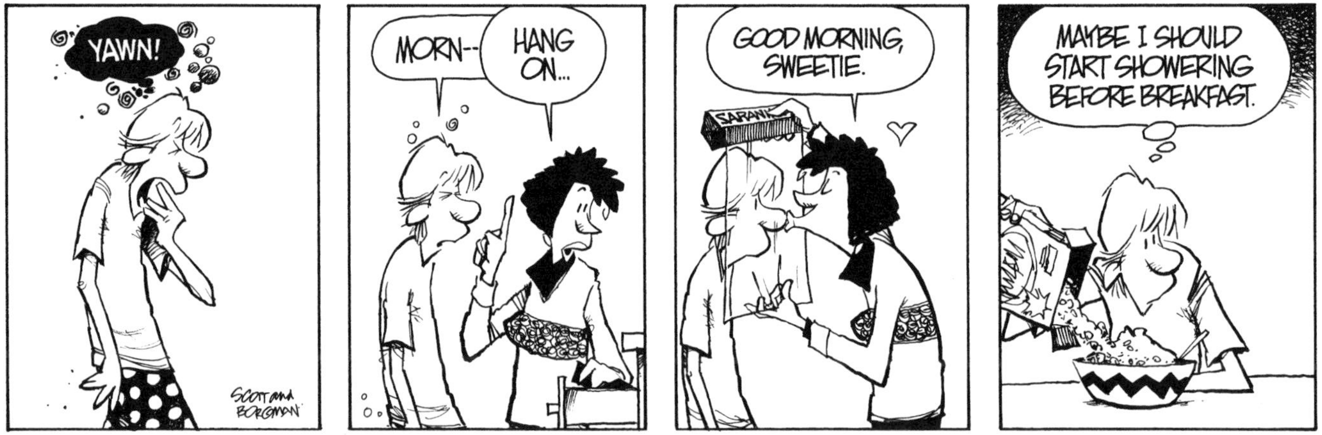
YAWN!
SCOTT AND BORGMAN
MORN--
HANG ON...
GOOD MORNING, SWEETIE.
MAYBE I SHOULD START SHOWERING BEFORE BREAKFAST.

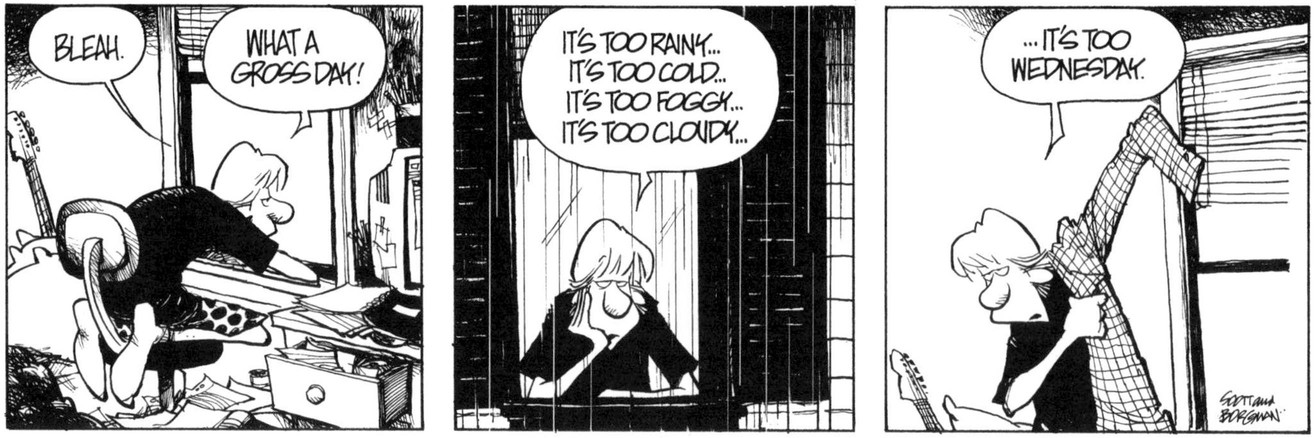
BLEAH.
WHAT A GROSS DAY!
IT'S TOO RAINY... IT'S TOO COLD... IT'S TOO FOGGY... IT'S TOO CLOUDY...
...IT'S TOO WEDNESDAY.
SCOTT AND BORGMAN

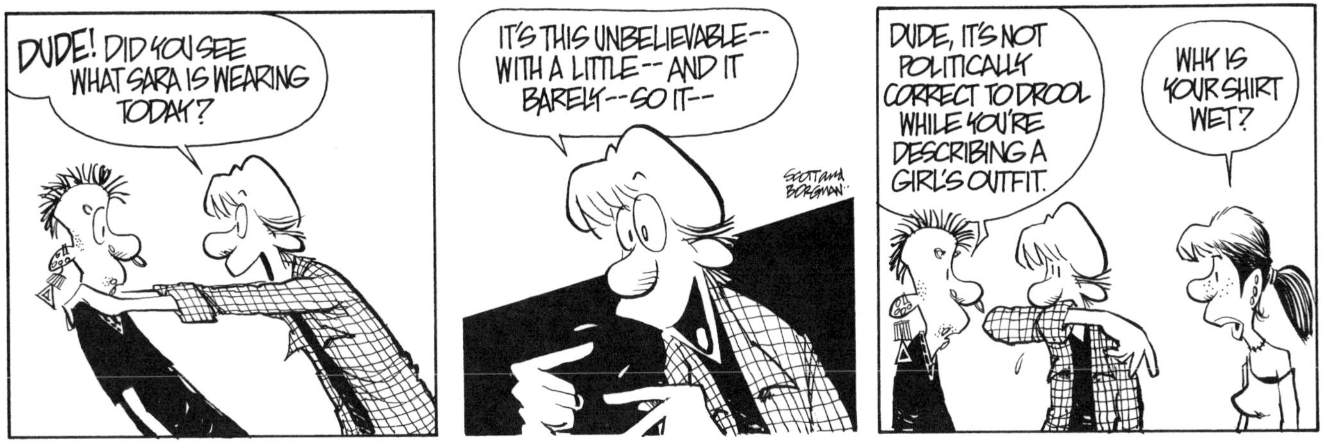
DUDE! DID YOU SEE WHAT SARA IS WEARING TODAY?
IT'S THIS UNBELIEVABLE-- WITH A LITTLE-- AND IT BARELY--SO IT--
DUDE, IT'S NOT POLITICALLY CORRECT TO DROOL WHILE YOU'RE DESCRIBING A GIRL'S OUTFIT.
WHY IS YOUR SHIRT WET?

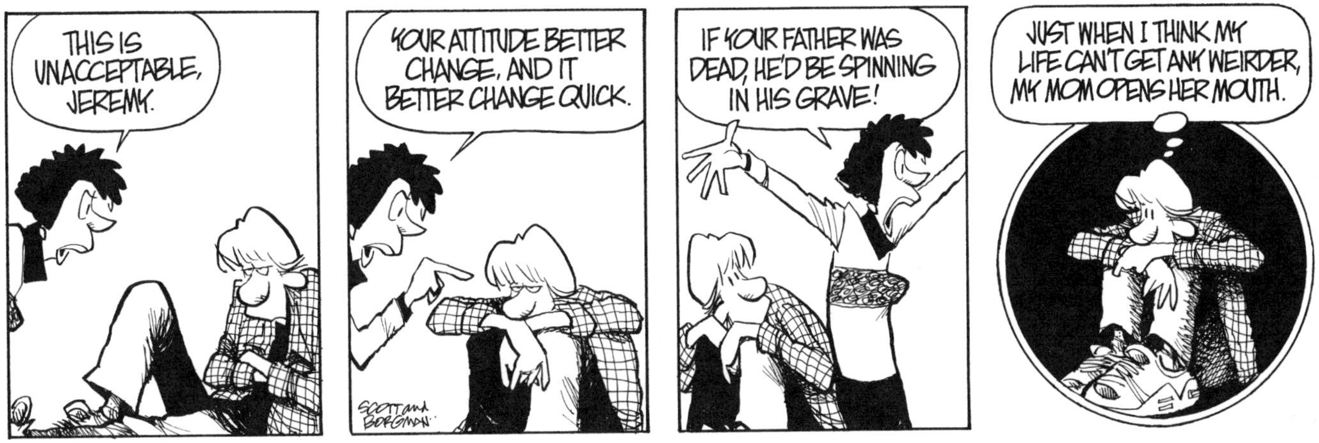
THIS IS UNACCEPTABLE, JEREMY.
YOUR ATTITUDE BETTER CHANGE, AND IT BETTER CHANGE QUICK.
IF YOUR FATHER WAS DEAD, HE'D BE SPINNING IN HIS GRAVE!
JUST WHEN I THINK MY LIFE CAN'T GET ANY WEIRDER, MY MOM OPENS HER MOUTH.

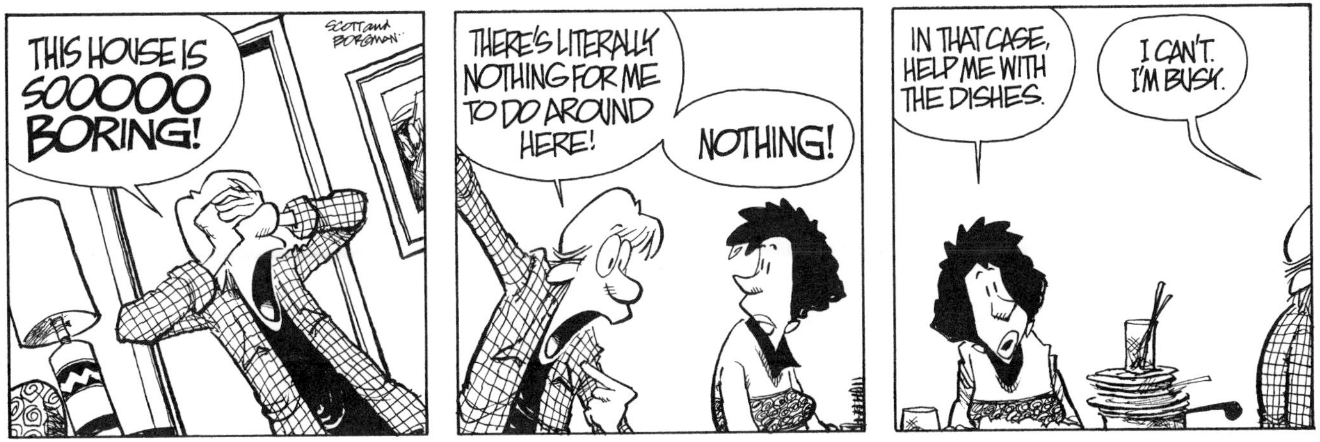
THIS HOUSE IS SOOOOO BORING!
THERE'S LITERALLY NOTHING FOR ME TO DO AROUND HERE!
NOTHING!
IN THAT CASE, HELP ME WITH THE DISHES.
I CAN'T. I'M BUSY.

Zits

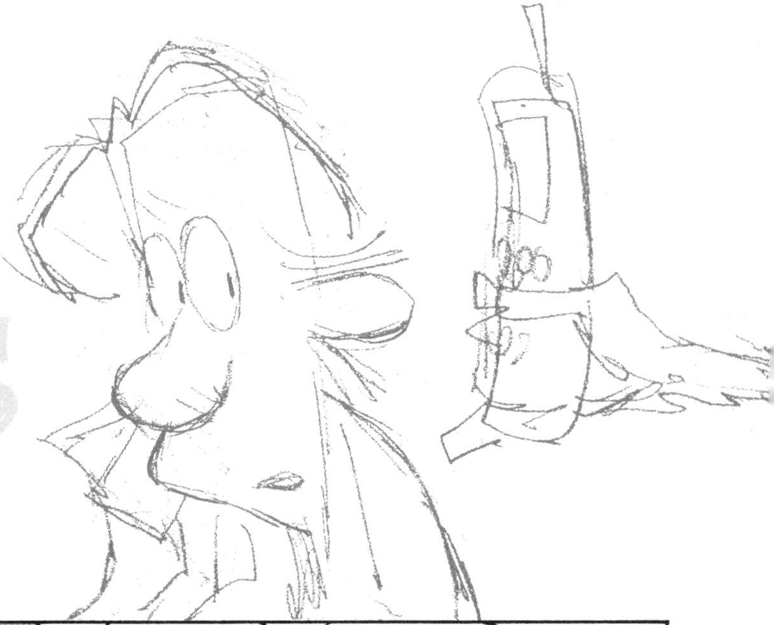

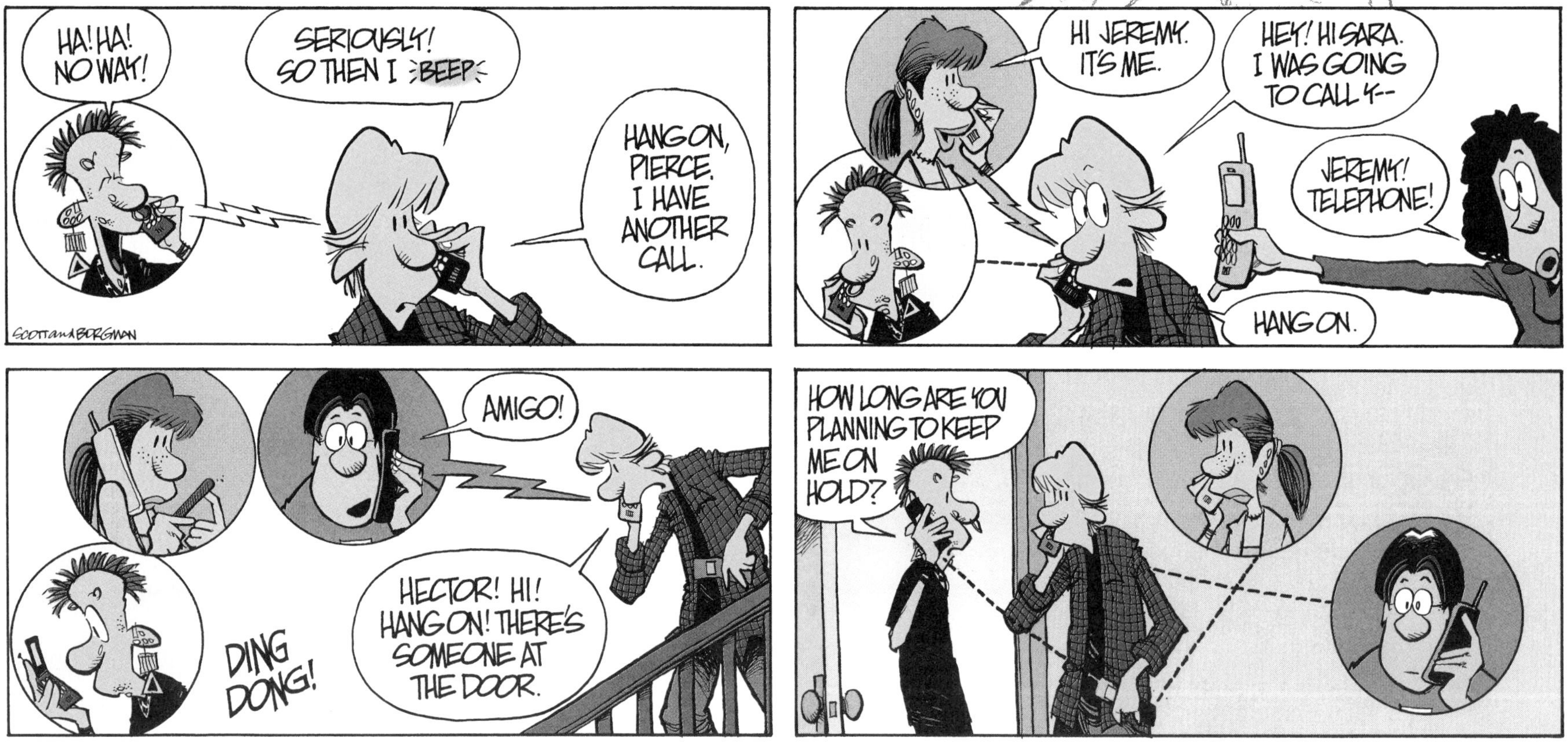
HA! HA! NO WAY!
SERIOUSLY! SO THEN I BEEP
HANG ON, PIERCE. I HAVE ANOTHER CALL.
SCOTT and BORGMAN
HI JEREMY. IT'S ME.
HEY! HI SARA. I WAS GOING TO CALL Y--
JEREMY! TELEPHONE!
HANG ON.
AMIGO!
HECTOR! HI! HANG ON! THERE'S SOMEONE AT THE DOOR.
DING DONG!
HOW LONG ARE YOU PLANNING TO KEEP ME ON HOLD?

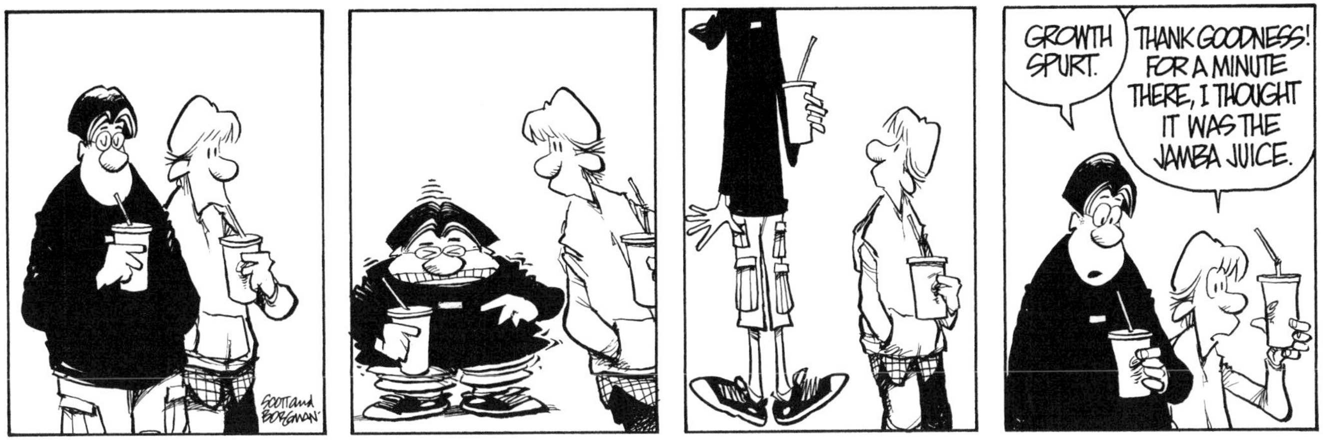
GROWTH SPURT.
THANK GOODNESS! FOR A MINUTE THERE, I THOUGHT IT WAS THE JAMBA JUICE.

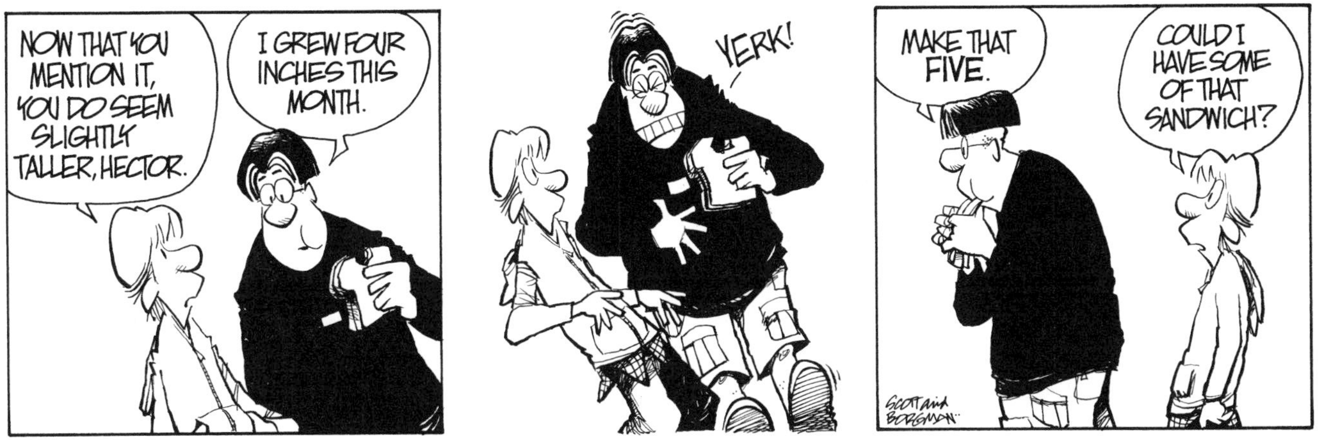
NOW THAT YOU MENTION IT, YOU DO SEEM SLIGHTLY TALLER, HECTOR.
I GREW FOUR INCHES THIS MONTH.
YERK!
MAKE THAT FIVE.
COULD I HAVE SOME OF THAT SANDWICH?

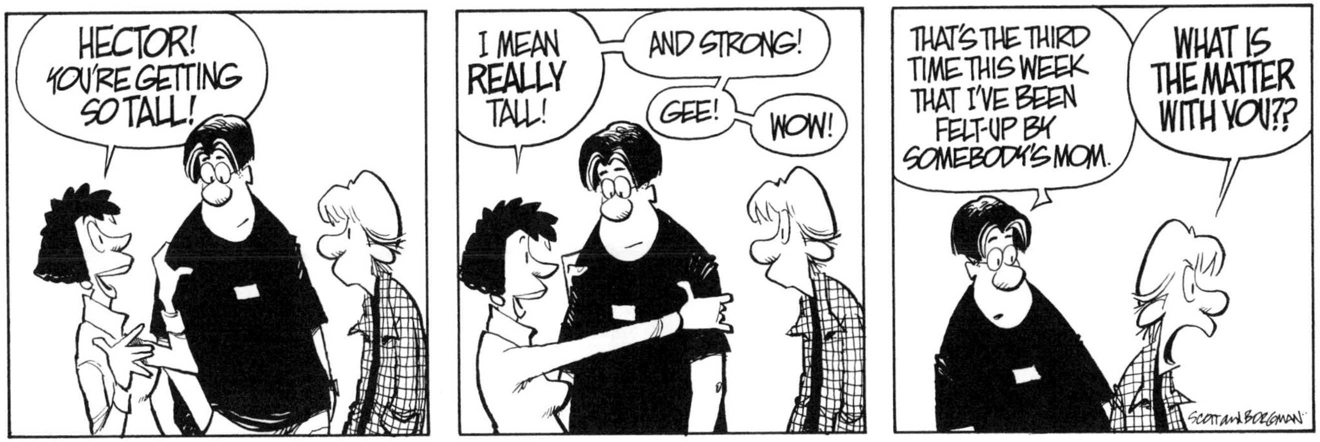
HECTOR! YOU'RE GETTING SO TALL!
I MEAN REALLY TALL!
AND STRONG!
GEE!
WOW!
THAT'S THE THIRD TIME THIS WEEK THAT I'VE BEEN FELT-UP BY SOMEBODY'S MOM.
WHAT IS THE MATTER WITH YOU??

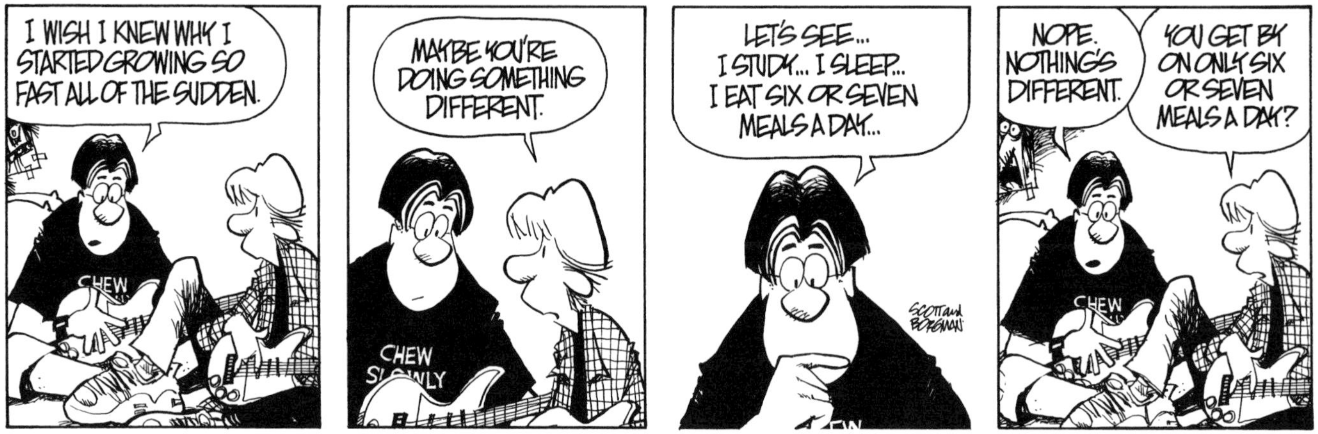
I WISH I KNEW WHY I STARTED GROWING SO FAST ALL OF THE SUDDEN.
MAYBE YOU'RE DOING SOMETHING DIFFERENT.
LET'S SEE... I STUDY... I SLEEP... I EAT SIX OR SEVEN MEALS A DAY...
NOPE. NOTHING'S DIFFERENT.
YOU GET BY ON ONLY SIX OR SEVEN MEALS A DAY?

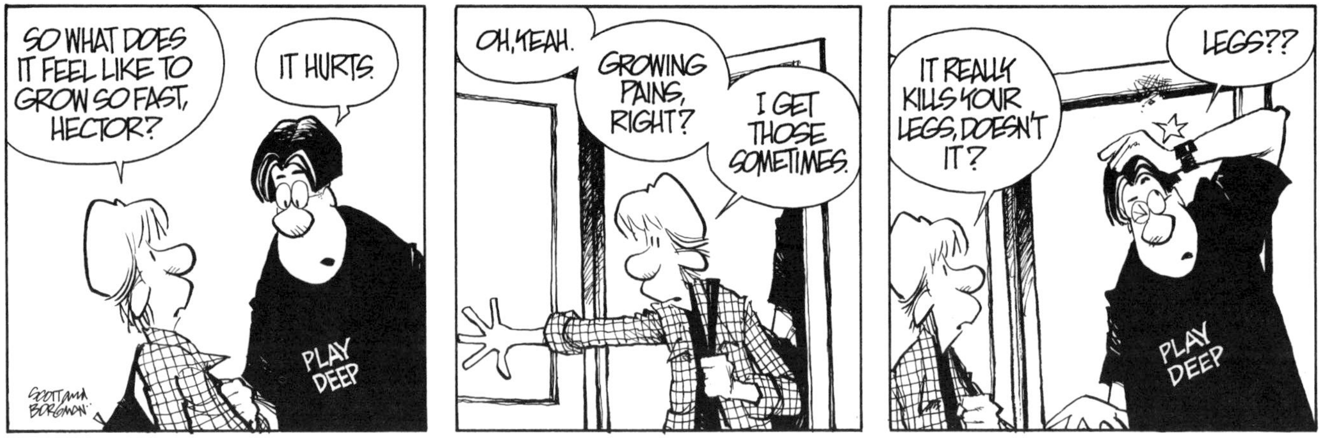
SO WHAT DOES IT FEEL LIKE TO GROW SO FAST, HECTOR?
IT HURTS.
OH, YEAH.
GROWING PAINS, RIGHT?
I GET THOSE SOMETIMES.
IT REALLY KILLS YOUR LEGS, DOESN'T IT?
LEGS??

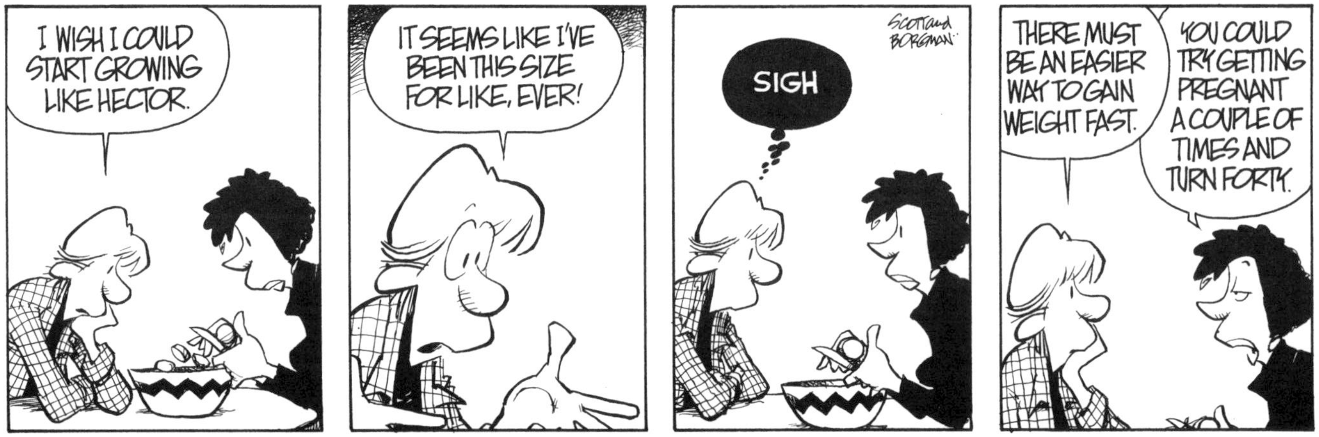
I WISH I COULD START GROWING LIKE HECTOR.
IT SEEMS LIKE I'VE BEEN THIS SIZE FOR LIKE, EVER!
SIGH
THERE MUST BE AN EASIER WAY TO GAIN WEIGHT FAST.
YOU COULD TRY GETTING PREGNANT A COUPLE OF TIMES AND TURN FORTY.

Zits

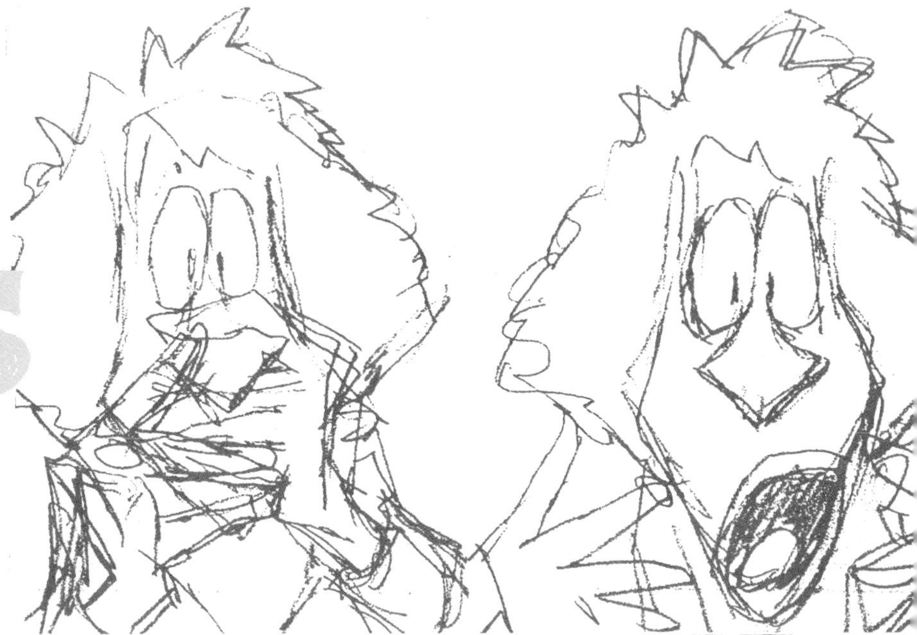

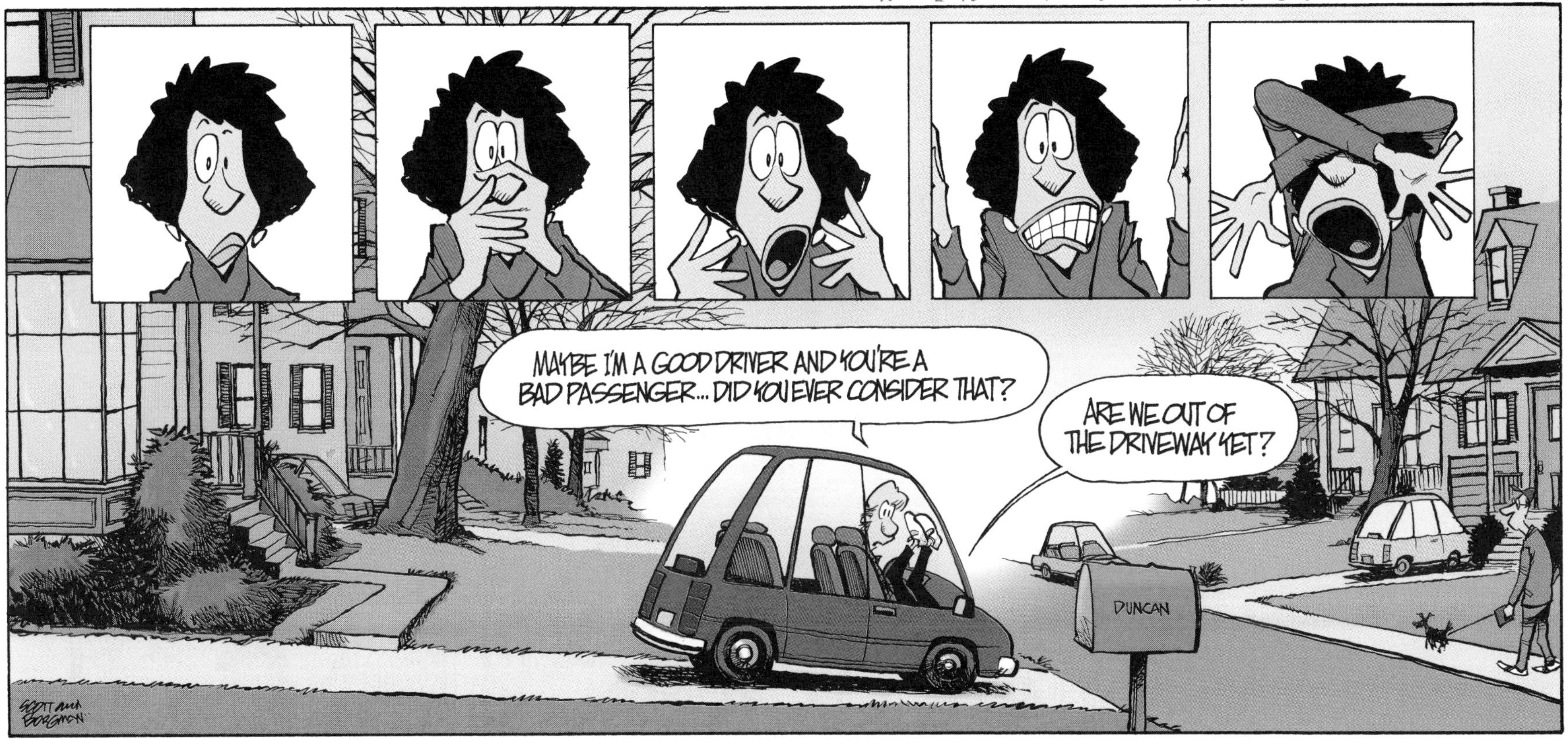

MAYBE I'M A GOOD DRIVER AND YOU'RE A BAD PASSENGER... DID YOU EVER CONSIDER THAT?
ARE WE OUT OF THE DRIVEWAY YET?
DUNCAN

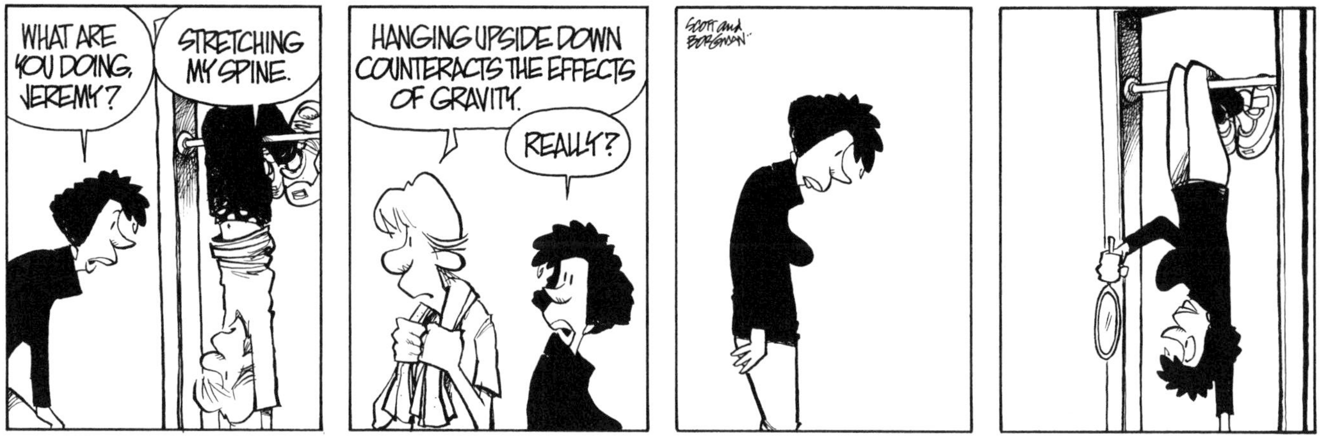
WHAT ARE YOU DOING, JEREMY?
STRETCHING MY SPINE.
HANGING UPSIDE DOWN COUNTERACTS THE EFFECTS OF GRAVITY.
REALLY?

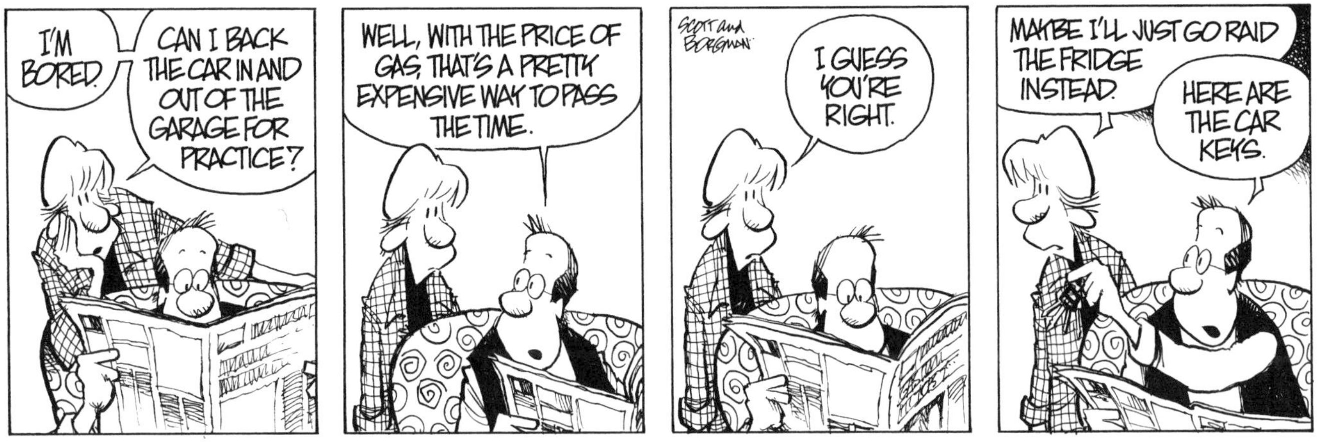
I'M BORED.
CAN I BACK THE CAR IN AND OUT OF THE GARAGE FOR PRACTICE?
WELL, WITH THE PRICE OF GAS, THAT'S A PRETTY EXPENSIVE WAY TO PASS THE TIME.
I GUESS YOU'RE RIGHT.
MAYBE I'LL JUST GO RAID THE FRIDGE INSTEAD.
HERE ARE THE CAR KEYS.

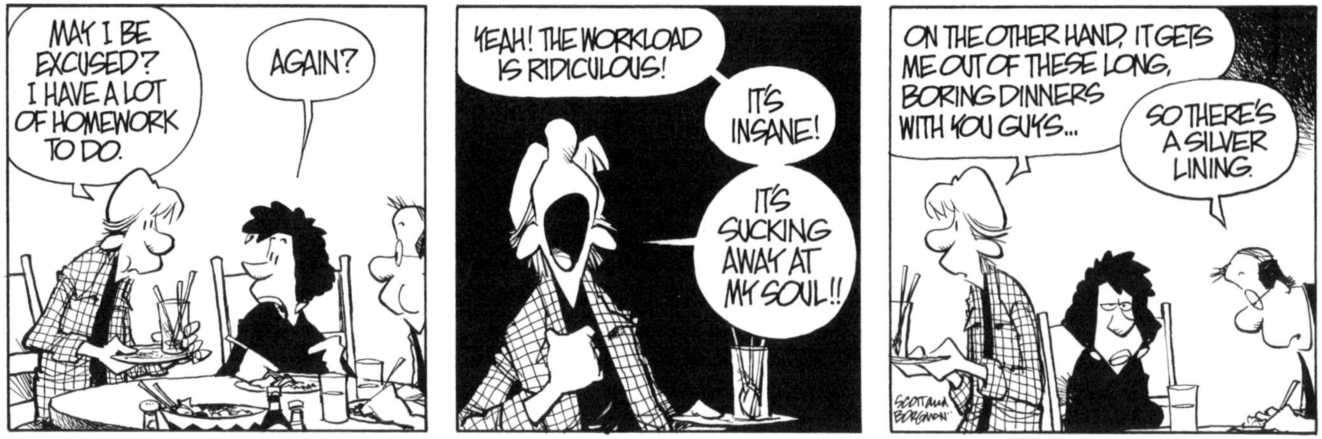
MAY I BE EXCUSED? I HAVE A LOT OF HOMEWORK TO DO.
AGAIN?
YEAH! THE WORKLOAD IS RIDICULOUS!
IT'S INSANE!
IT'S SUCKING AWAY AT MY SOUL!!
ON THE OTHER HAND, IT GETS ME OUT OF THESE LONG, BORING DINNERS WITH YOU GUYS...
SO THERE'S A SILVER LINING.

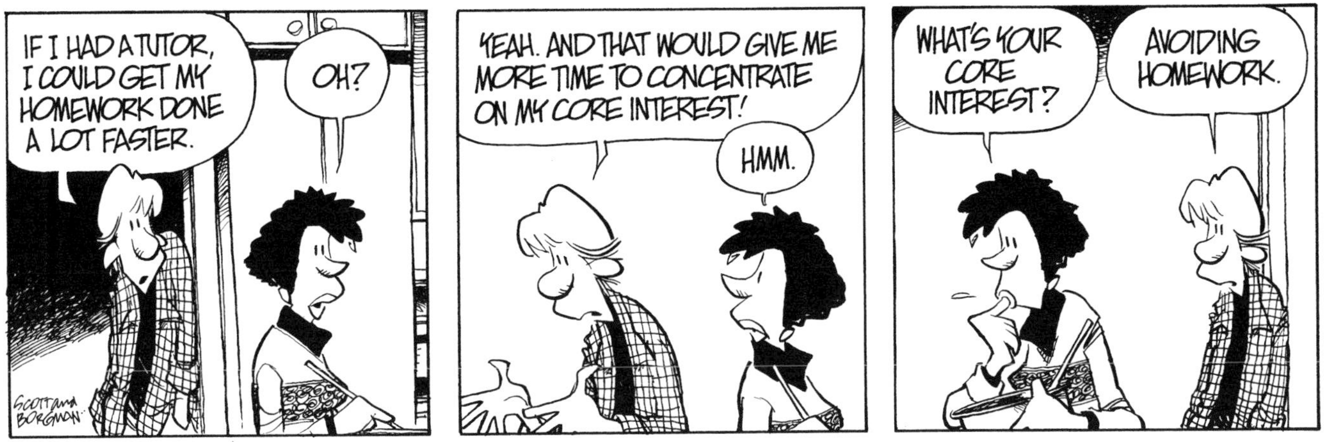
IF I HAD A TUTOR, I COULD GET MY HOMEWORK DONE A LOT FASTER.
OH?
YEAH. AND THAT WOULD GIVE ME MORE TIME TO CONCENTRATE ON MY CORE INTEREST!
HMM.
WHAT'S YOUR CORE INTEREST?
AVOIDING HOMEWORK.

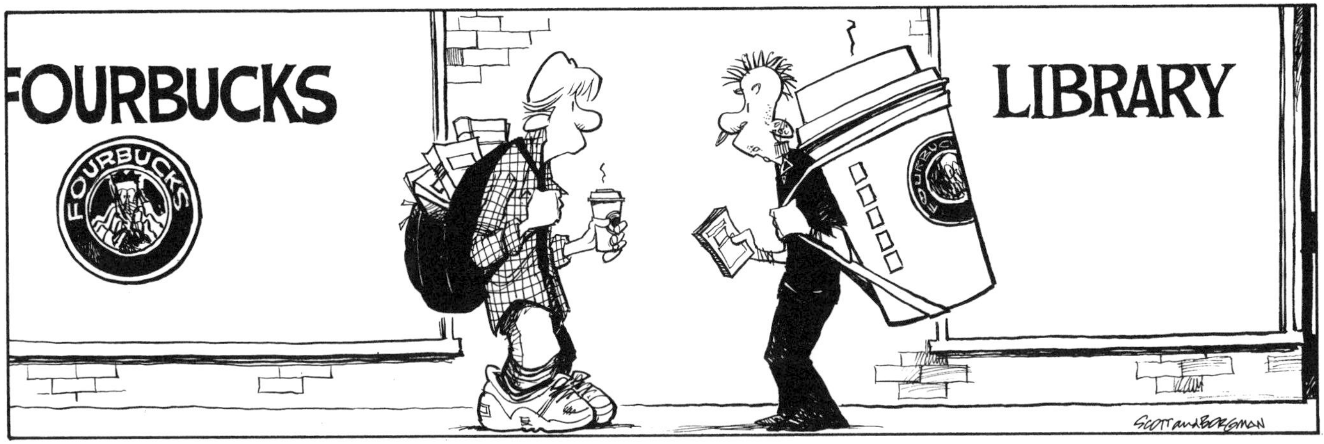
FOURBUCKS
FOURBUCKS
LIBRARY

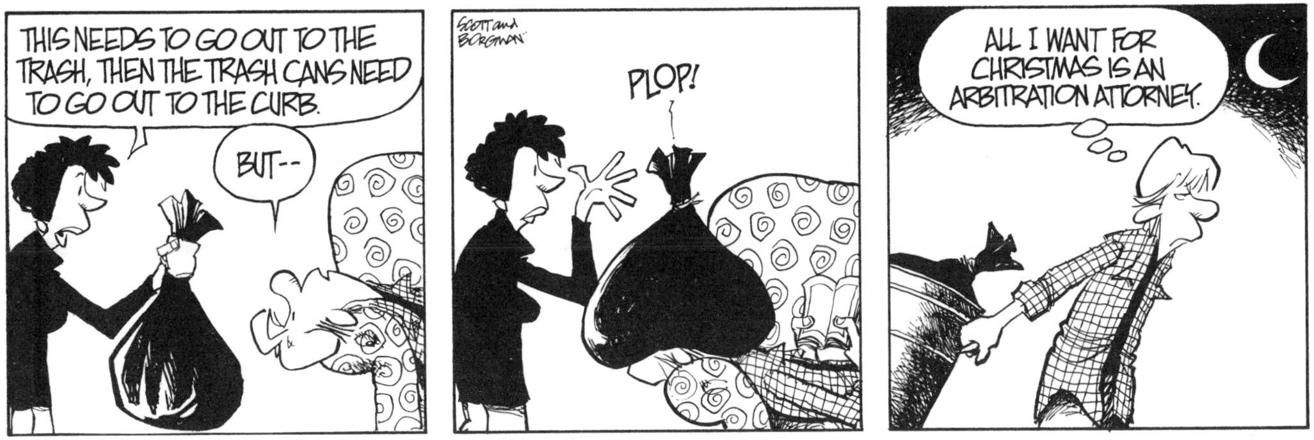
THIS NEEDS TO GO OUT TO THE TRASH, THEN THE TRASH CANS NEED TO GO OUT TO THE CURB.
BUT--
PLOP!
ALL I WANT FOR CHRISTMAS IS AN ARBITRATION ATTORNEY.

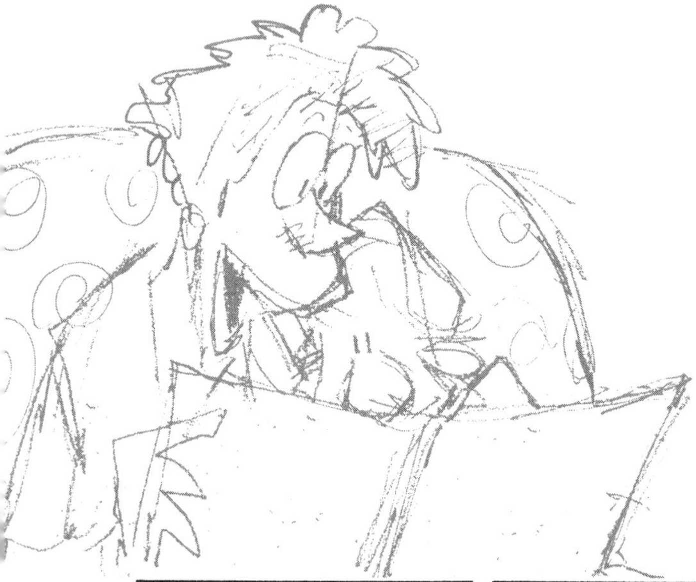

Zits

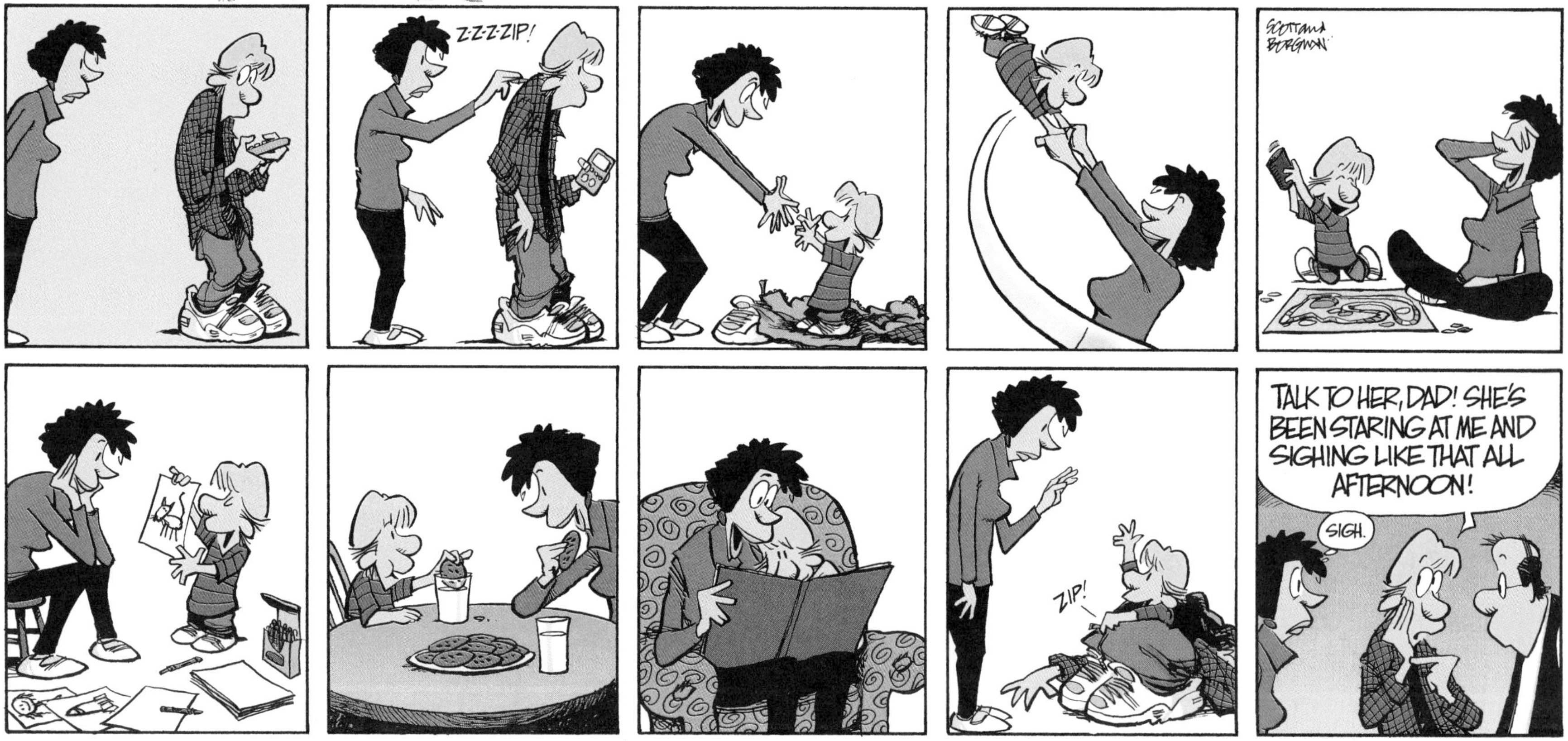
Z-Z-Z-ZIP!
ZIP!
SIGH.
TALK TO HER, DAD! SHE'S BEEN STARING AT ME AND SIGHING LIKE THAT ALL AFTERNOON!

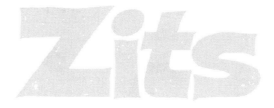

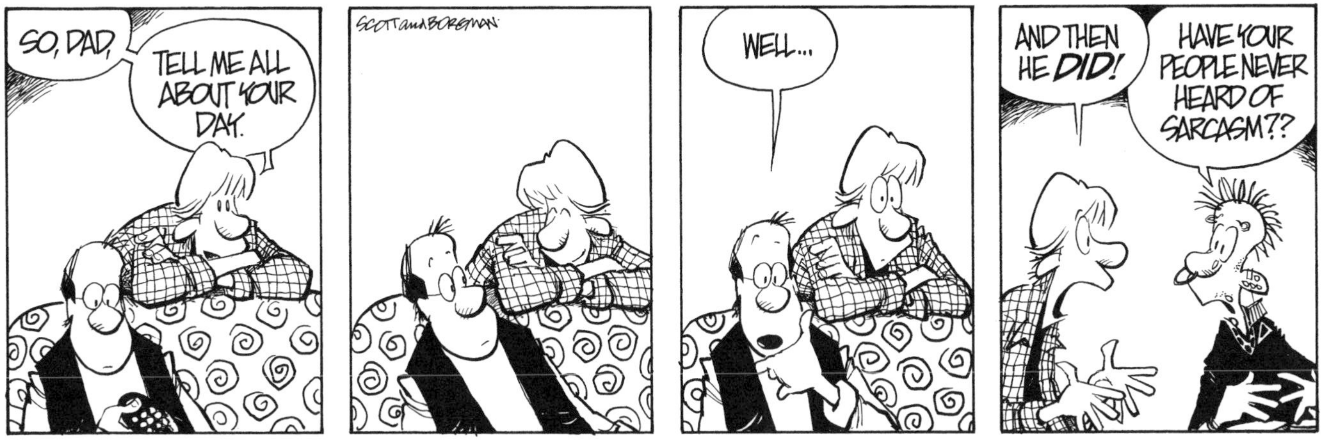
SO, DAD,
TELL ME ALL ABOUT YOUR DAY.
WELL...
AND THEN HE *DID*!
HAVE YOUR PEOPLE NEVER HEARD OF SARCASM??

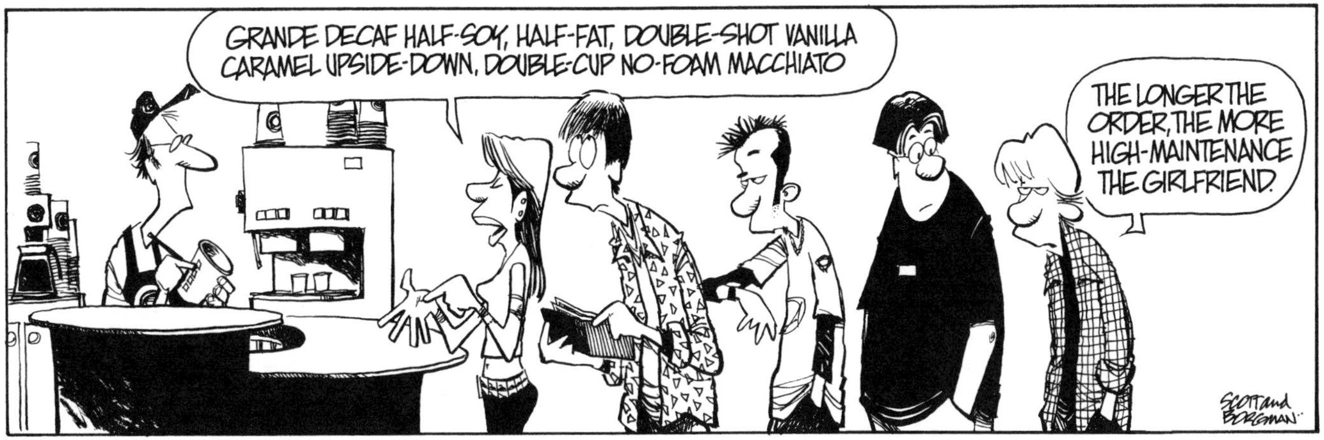
GRANDE DECAF HALF-SOY, HALF-FAT, DOUBLE-SHOT VANILLA CARAMEL UPSIDE-DOWN, DOUBLE-CUP NO-FOAM MACCHIATO
THE LONGER THE ORDER, THE MORE HIGH-MAINTENANCE THE GIRLFRIEND.

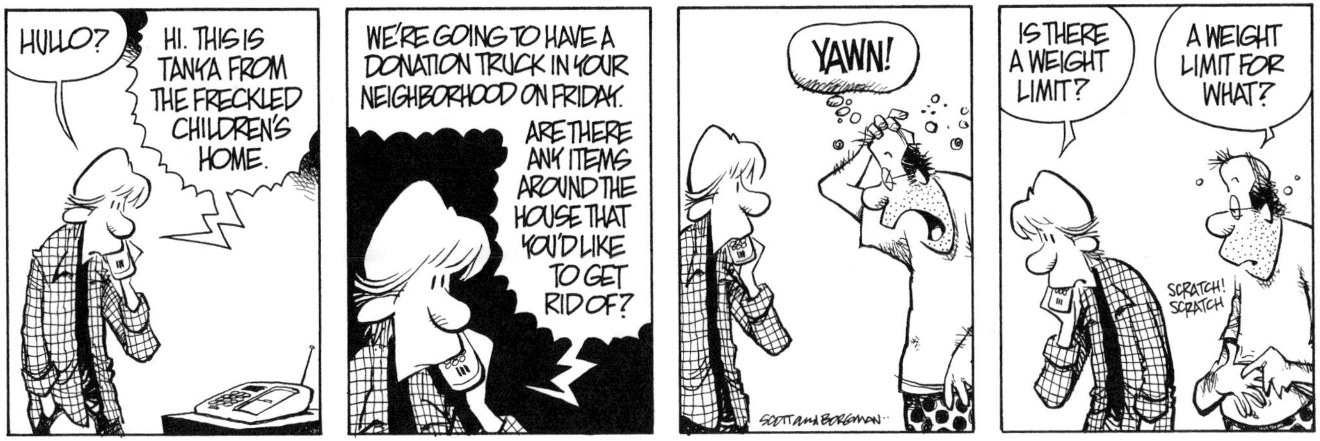
HULLO?
HI. THIS IS TANYA FROM THE FRECKLED CHILDREN'S HOME.
WE'RE GOING TO HAVE A DONATION TRUCK IN YOUR NEIGHBORHOOD ON FRIDAY.
ARE THERE ANY ITEMS AROUND THE HOUSE THAT YOU'D LIKE TO GET RID OF?
YAWN!
IS THERE A WEIGHT LIMIT?
A WEIGHT LIMIT FOR WHAT?
SCRATCH! SCRATCH

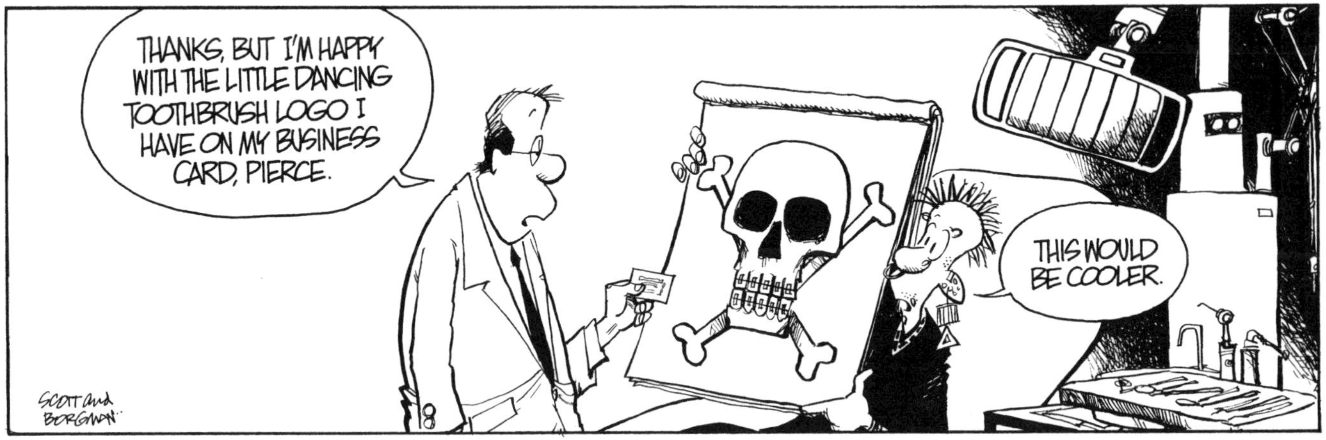
THANKS, BUT I'M HAPPY WITH THE LITTLE DANCING TOOTHBRUSH LOGO I HAVE ON MY BUSINESS CARD, PIERCE.
THIS WOULD BE COOLER.
SCOTT and BORGMAN

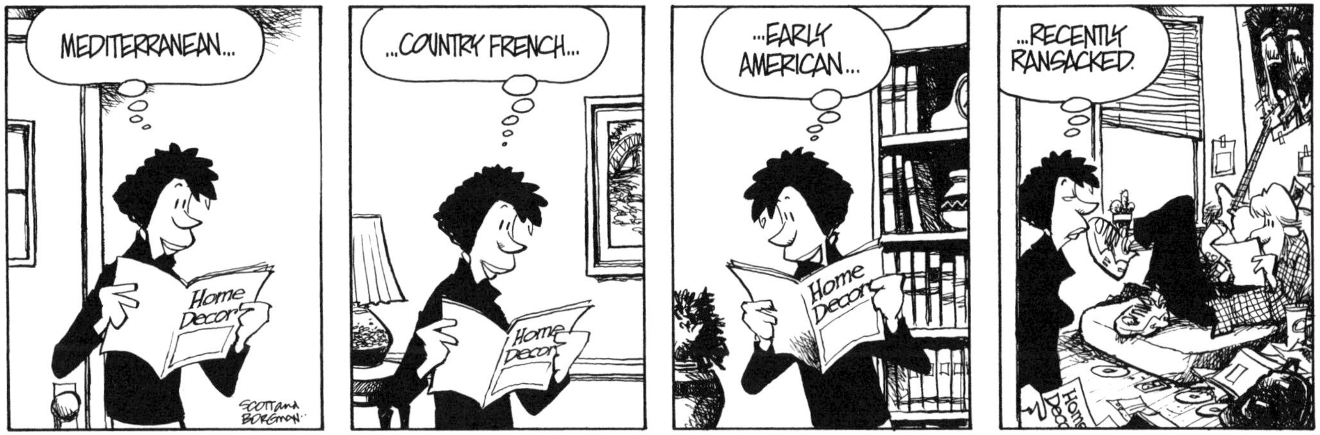
MEDITERRANEAN...
Home Decor
SCOTT and BORGMAN
...COUNTRY FRENCH...
Home Decor
...EARLY AMERICAN...
Home Decor
...RECENTLY RANSACKED.

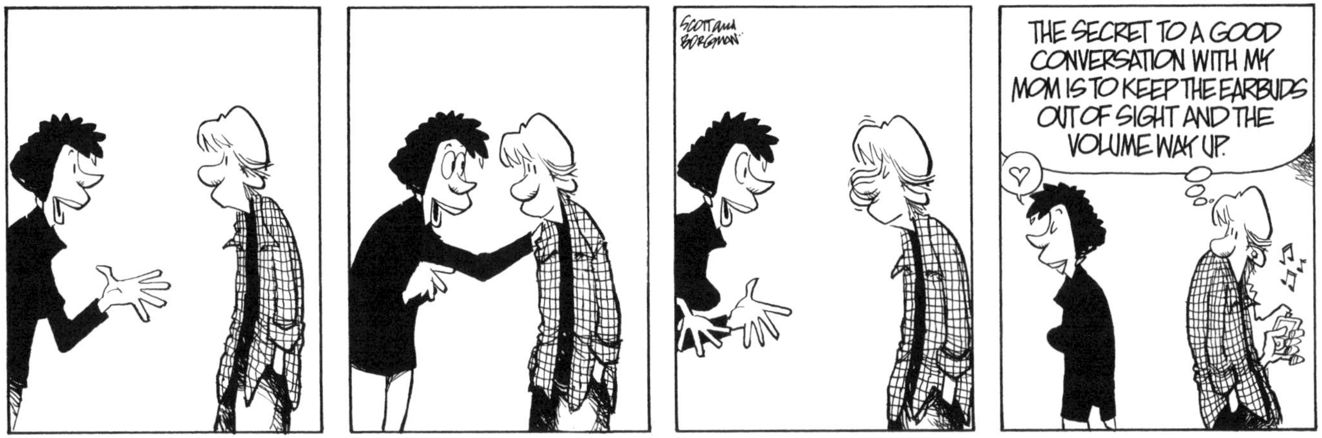
SCOTT and BORGMAN
THE SECRET TO A GOOD CONVERSATION WITH MY MOM IS TO KEEP THE EARBUDS OUT OF SIGHT AND THE VOLUME WAY UP.

Zits

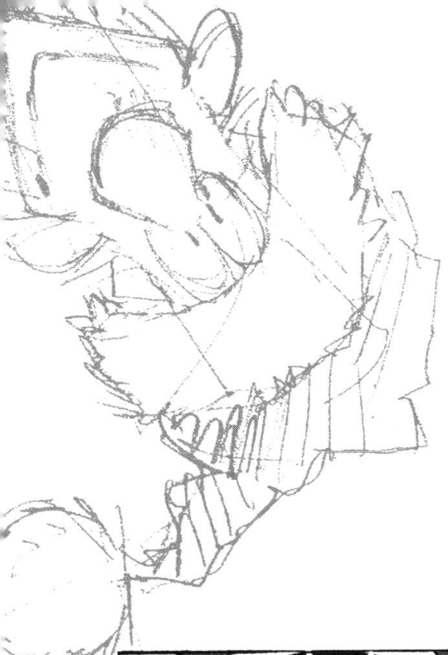

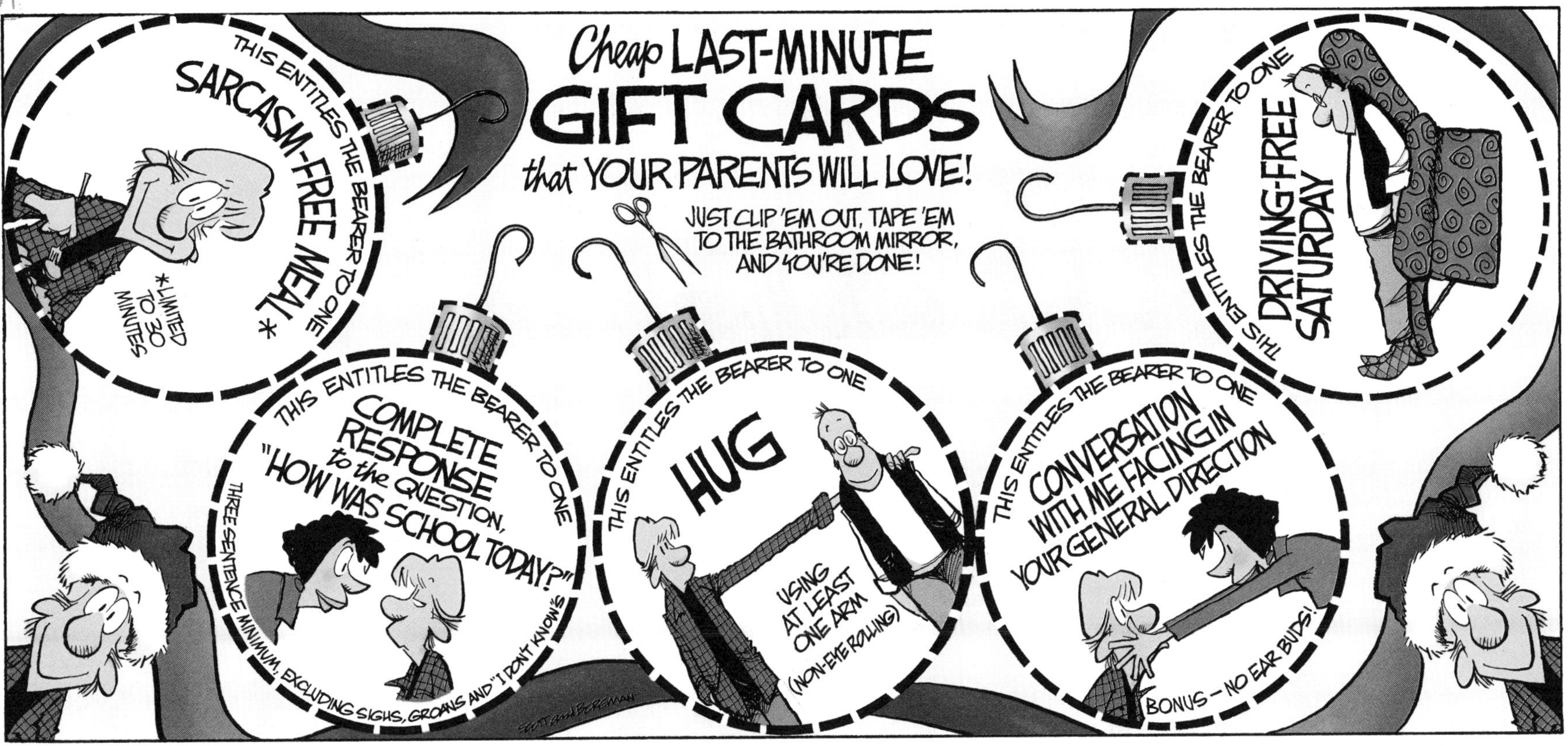

Cheap LAST-MINUTE
GIFT CARDS
that YOUR PARENTS WILL LOVE!
JUST CLIP 'EM OUT, TAPE 'EM TO THE BATHROOM MIRROR, AND YOU'RE DONE!
THIS ENTITLES THE BEARER TO ONE
SARCASM-FREE MEAL*
*LIMITED TO 30 MINUTES
THIS ENTITLES THE BEARER TO ONE
COMPLETE RESPONSE to the QUESTION, "HOW WAS SCHOOL TODAY?"
THREE-SENTENCE MINIMUM, EXCLUDING SIGHS, GROANS AND "I DON'T KNOW"S
THIS ENTITLES THE BEARER TO ONE
HUG
USING AT LEAST ONE ARM
(NON-EYE ROLLING)
THIS ENTITLES THE BEARER TO ONE
CONVERSATION WITH ME FACING IN YOUR GENERAL DIRECTION
BONUS – NO EAR BUDS!
THIS ENTITLES THE BEARER TO ONE
DRIVING-FREE SATURDAY

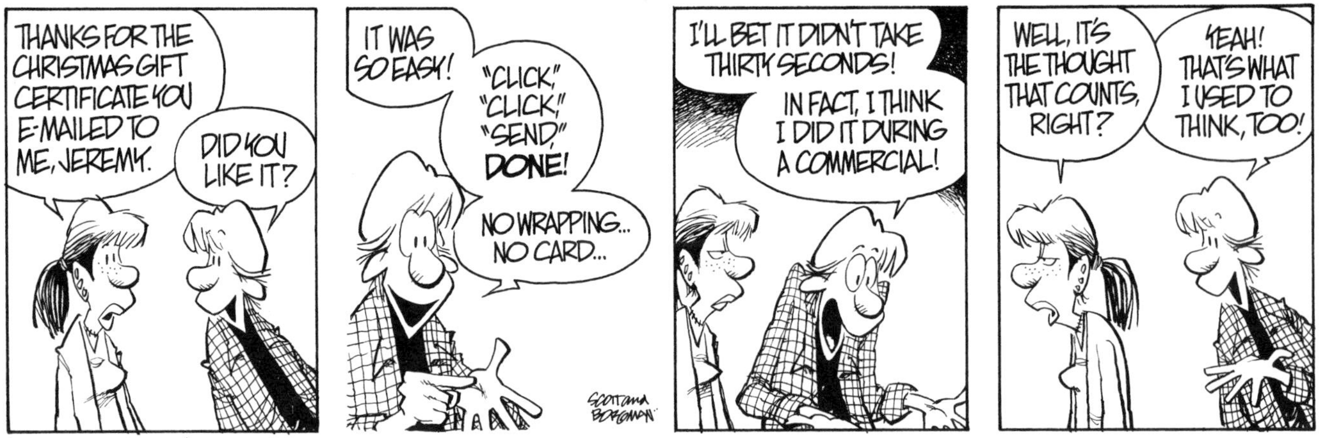
THANKS FOR THE CHRISTMAS GIFT CERTIFICATE YOU E-MAILED TO ME, JEREMY.
DID YOU LIKE IT?
IT WAS SO EASY!
"CLICK," "CLICK," "SEND," DONE!
NO WRAPPING... NO CARD...
I'LL BET IT DIDN'T TAKE THIRTY SECONDS!
IN FACT, I THINK I DID IT DURING A COMMERCIAL!
WELL, IT'S THE THOUGHT THAT COUNTS, RIGHT?
YEAH! THAT'S WHAT I USED TO THINK, TOO!

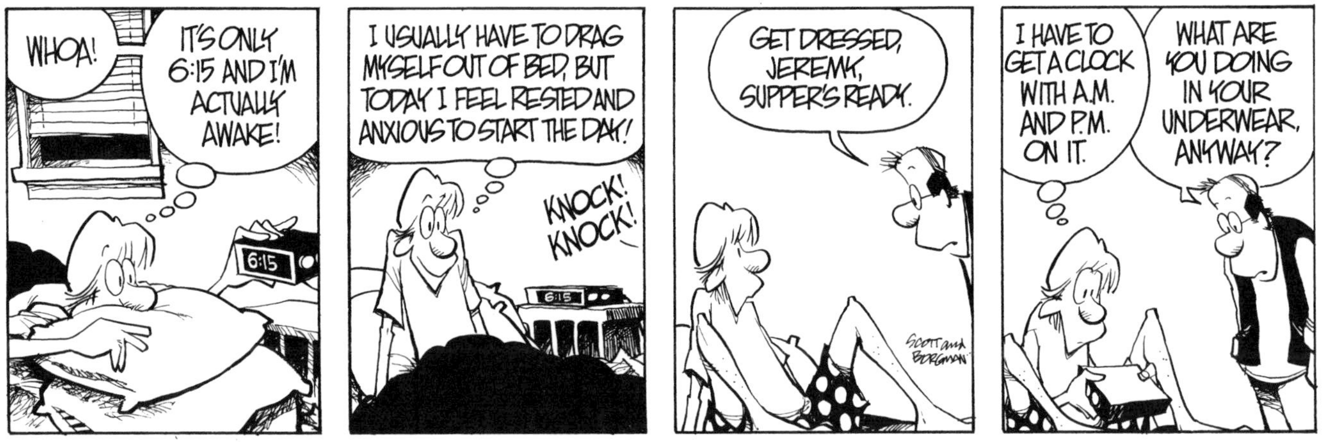
WHOA!
IT'S ONLY 6:15 AND I'M ACTUALLY AWAKE!
6:15
I USUALLY HAVE TO DRAG MYSELF OUT OF BED, BUT TODAY I FEEL RESTED AND ANXIOUS TO START THE DAY!
KNOCK! KNOCK!
6:15
GET DRESSED, JEREMY, SUPPER'S READY.
I HAVE TO GET A CLOCK WITH A.M. AND P.M. ON IT.
WHAT ARE YOU DOING IN YOUR UNDERWEAR, ANYWAY?

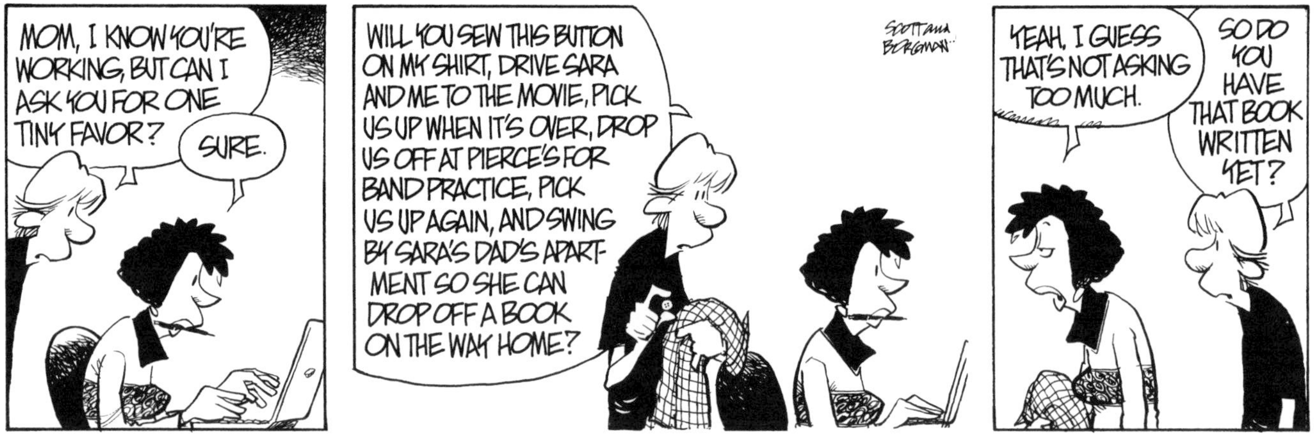
MOM, I KNOW YOU'RE WORKING, BUT CAN I ASK YOU FOR ONE TINY FAVOR?
SURE.
WILL YOU SEW THIS BUTTON ON MY SHIRT, DRIVE SARA AND ME TO THE MOVIE, PICK US UP WHEN IT'S OVER, DROP US OFF AT PIERCE'S FOR BAND PRACTICE, PICK US UP AGAIN, AND SWING BY SARA'S DAD'S APARTMENT SO SHE CAN DROP OFF A BOOK ON THE WAY HOME?
YEAH, I GUESS THAT'S NOT ASKING TOO MUCH.
SO DO YOU HAVE THAT BOOK WRITTEN YET?

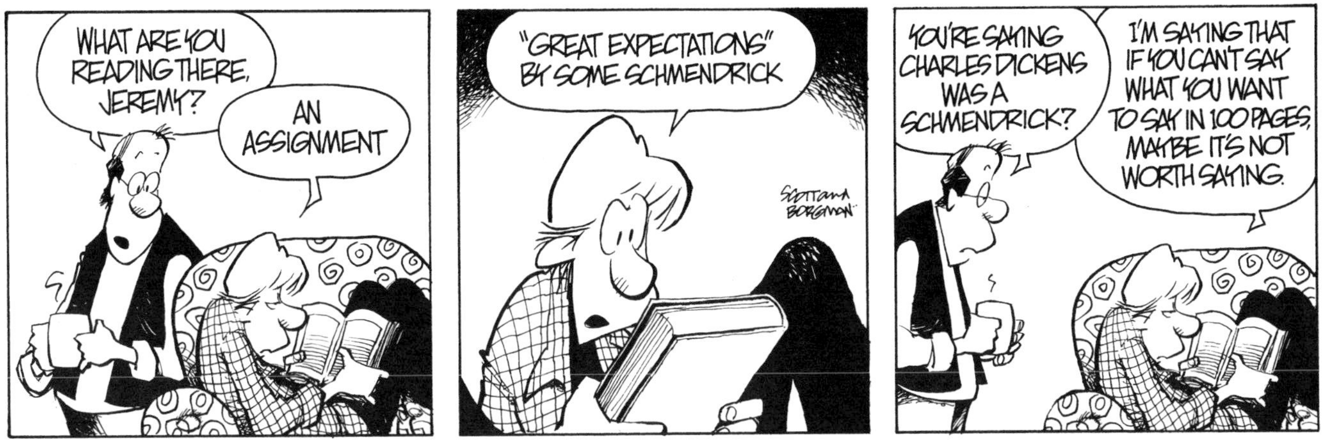
WHAT ARE YOU READING THERE, JEREMY?
AN ASSIGNMENT
"GREAT EXPECTATIONS" BY SOME SCHMENDRICK
SCOTT and BORGMAN
YOU'RE SAYING CHARLES DICKENS WAS A SCHMENDRICK?
I'M SAYING THAT IF YOU CAN'T SAY WHAT YOU WANT TO SAY IN 100 PAGES, MAYBE IT'S NOT WORTH SAYING.

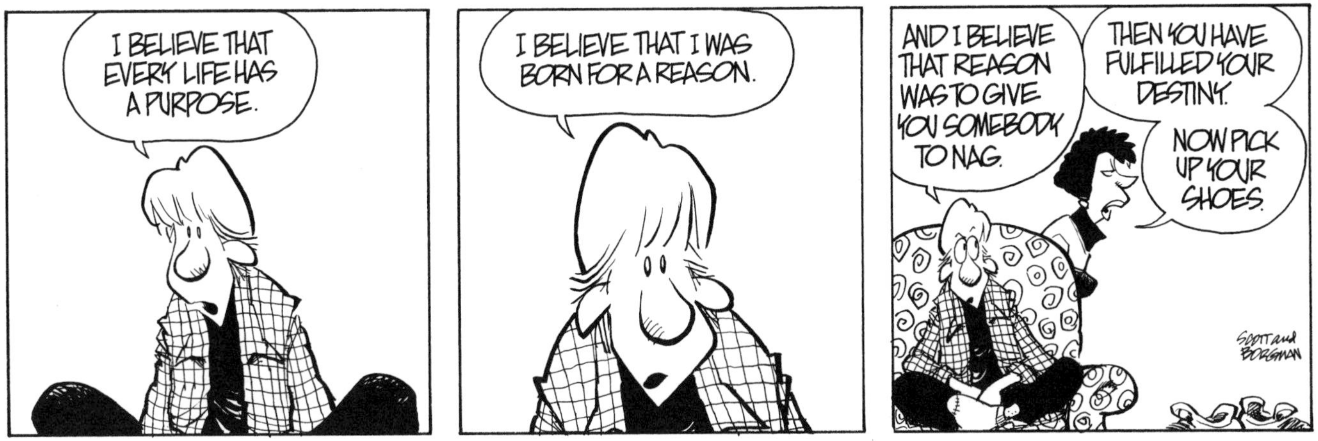
I BELIEVE THAT EVERY LIFE HAS A PURPOSE.
I BELIEVE THAT I WAS BORN FOR A REASON.
AND I BELIEVE THAT REASON WAS TO GIVE YOU SOMEBODY TO NAG.
THEN YOU HAVE FULFILLED YOUR DESTINY.
NOW PICK UP YOUR SHOES.
SCOTT and BORGMAN

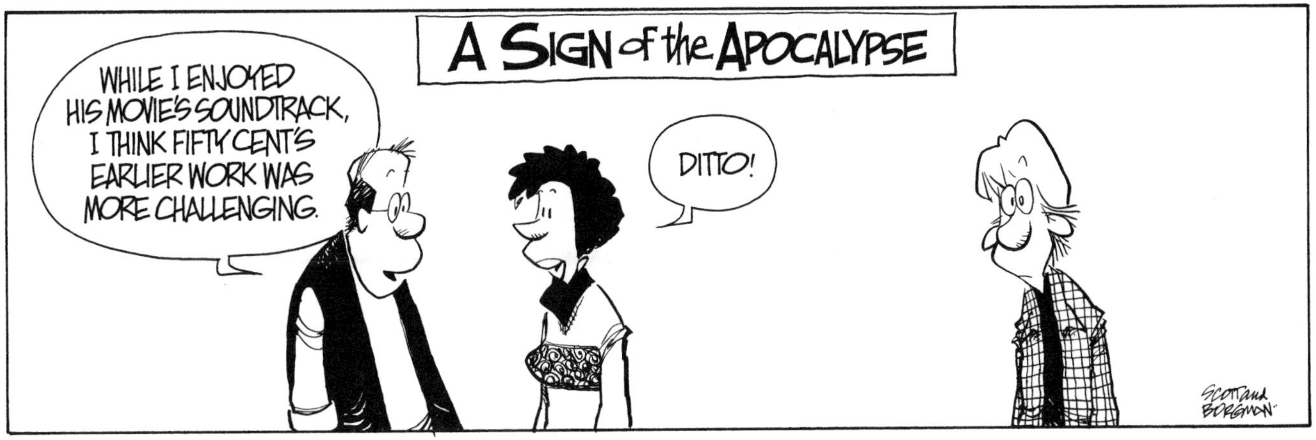
A SIGN of the APOCALYPSE
WHILE I ENJOYED HIS MOVIE'S SOUNDTRACK, I THINK FIFTY CENT'S EARLIER WORK WAS MORE CHALLENGING.
DITTO!
SCOTT and BORGMAN

Zits

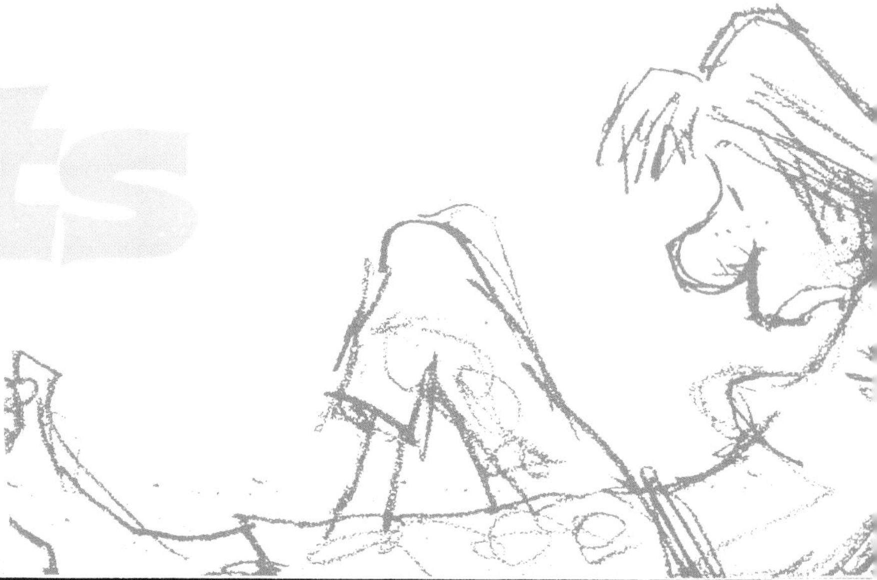

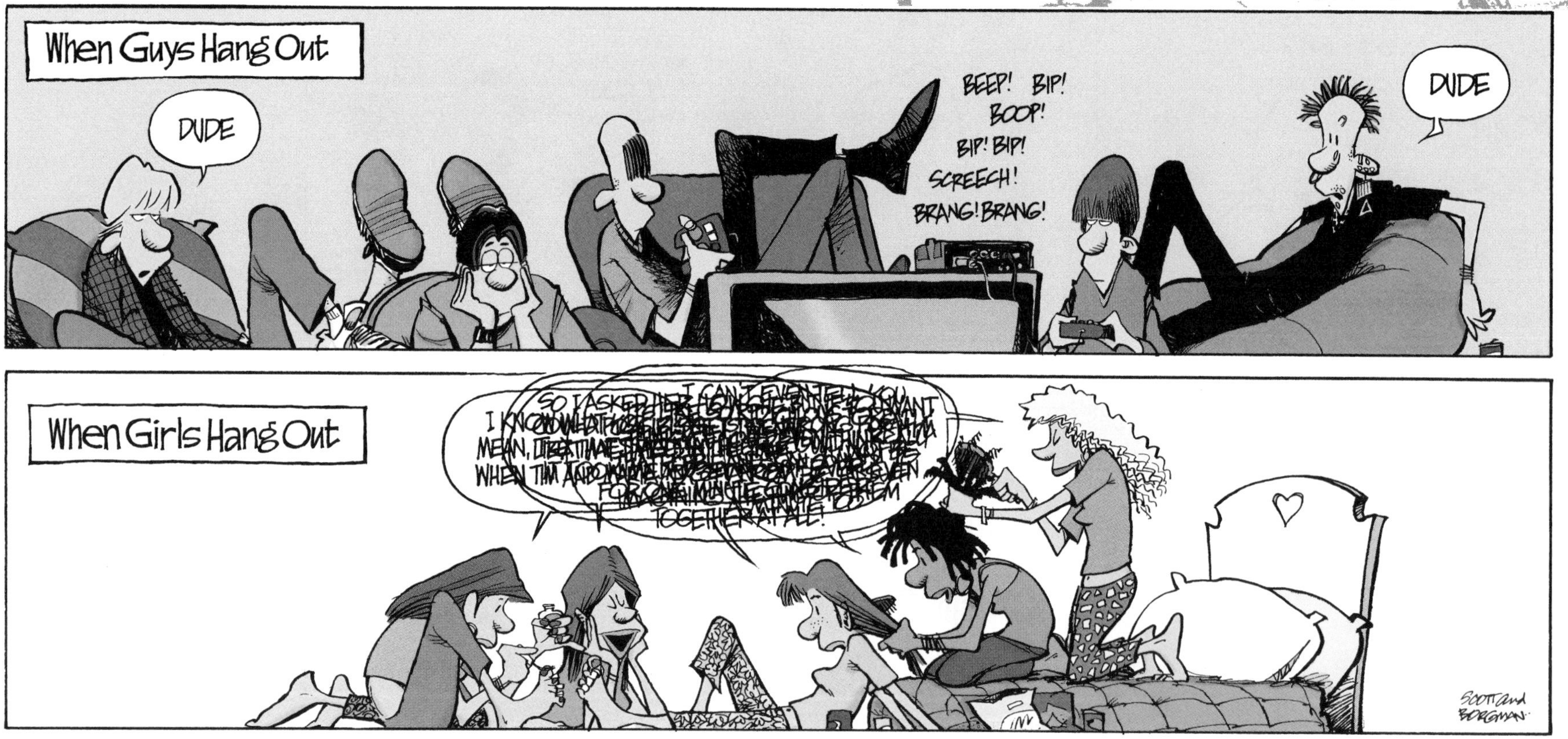

When Guys Hang Out
DUDE
BEEP! BIP! BOOP! BIP! BIP! SCREECH! BRANG! BRANG!
DUDE
When Girls Hang Out
SCOTT and BORGMAN

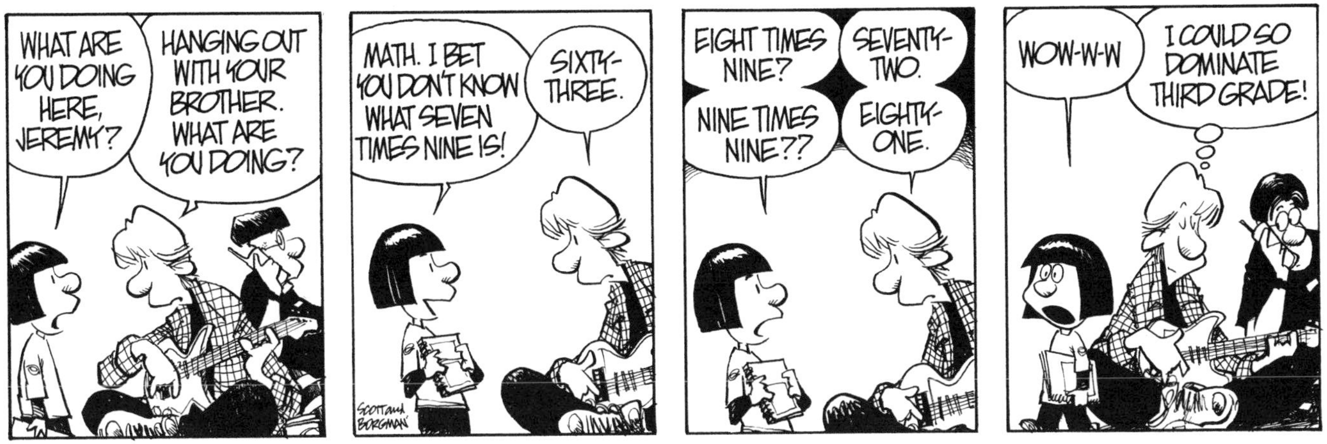
WHAT ARE YOU DOING HERE, JEREMY?
HANGING OUT WITH YOUR BROTHER. WHAT ARE YOU DOING?
MATH. I BET YOU DON'T KNOW WHAT SEVEN TIMES NINE IS!
SIXTY-THREE.
EIGHT TIMES NINE?
SEVENTY-TWO.
NINE TIMES NINE??
EIGHTY-ONE.
WOW-W-W
I COULD SO DOMINATE THIRD GRADE!

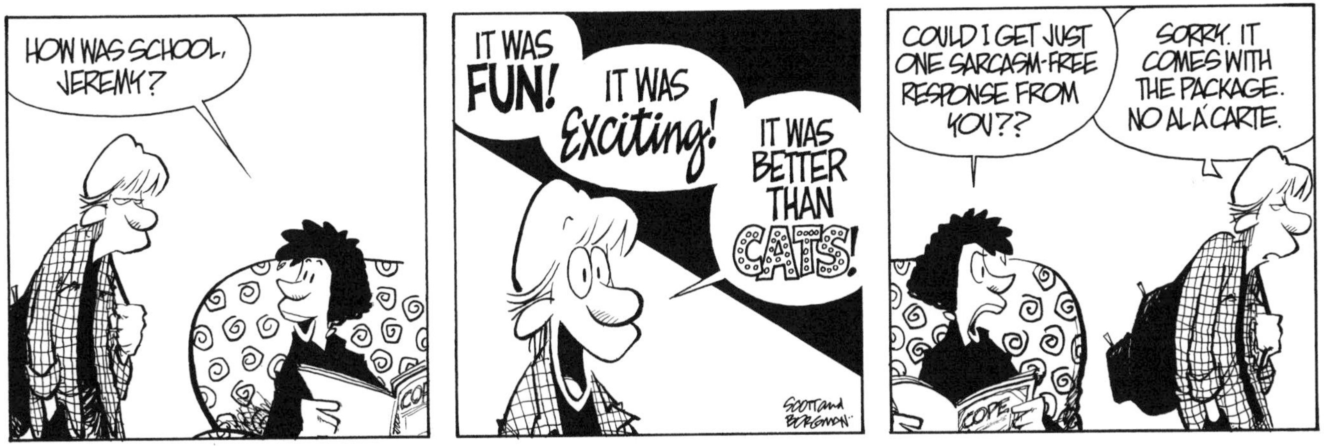
HOW WAS SCHOOL, JEREMY?
IT WAS FUN!
IT WAS Exciting!
IT WAS BETTER THAN CATS!
COULD I GET JUST ONE SARCASM-FREE RESPONSE FROM YOU??
SORRY. IT COMES WITH THE PACKAGE. NO A LA CARTE.

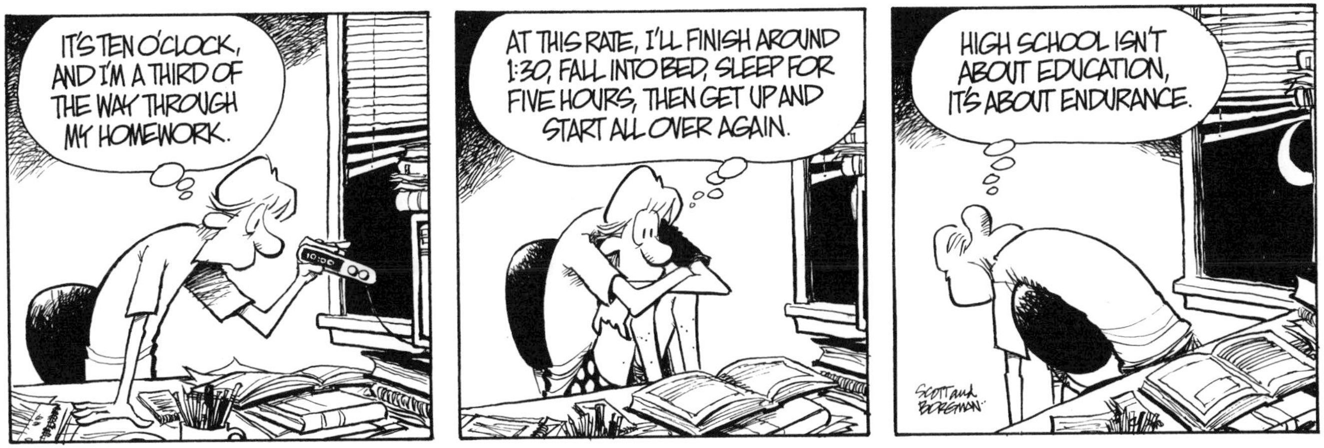
IT'S TEN O'CLOCK, AND I'M A THIRD OF THE WAY THROUGH MY HOMEWORK.
AT THIS RATE, I'LL FINISH AROUND 1:30, FALL INTO BED, SLEEP FOR FIVE HOURS, THEN GET UP AND START ALL OVER AGAIN.
HIGH SCHOOL ISN'T ABOUT EDUCATION, IT'S ABOUT ENDURANCE.

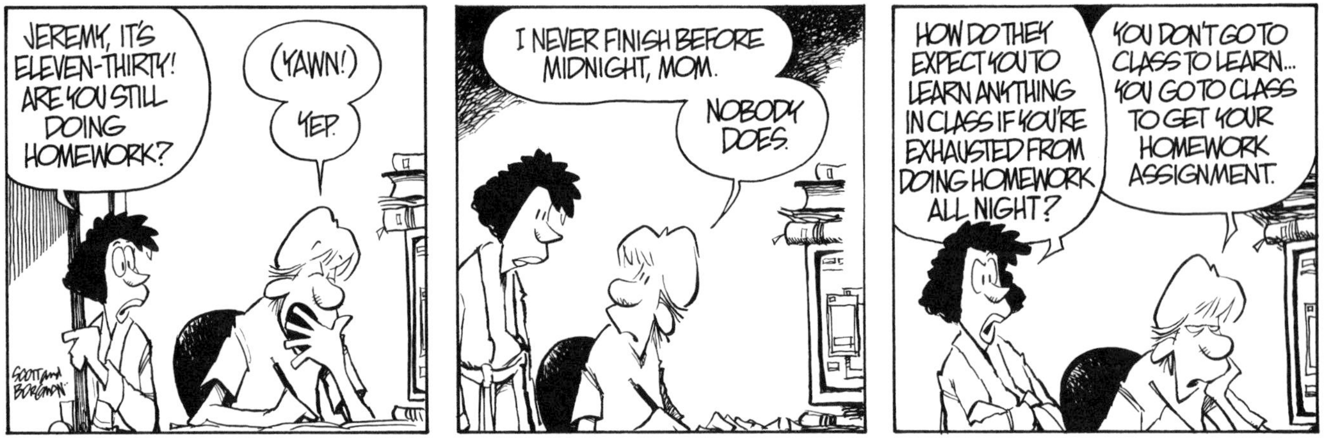
JEREMY, IT'S ELEVEN-THIRTY! ARE YOU STILL DOING HOMEWORK?
(YAWN!)
YEP.
I NEVER FINISH BEFORE MIDNIGHT, MOM.
NOBODY DOES.
HOW DO THEY EXPECT YOU TO LEARN ANYTHING IN CLASS IF YOU'RE EXHAUSTED FROM DOING HOMEWORK ALL NIGHT?
YOU DON'T GO TO CLASS TO LEARN... YOU GO TO CLASS TO GET YOUR HOMEWORK ASSIGNMENT.

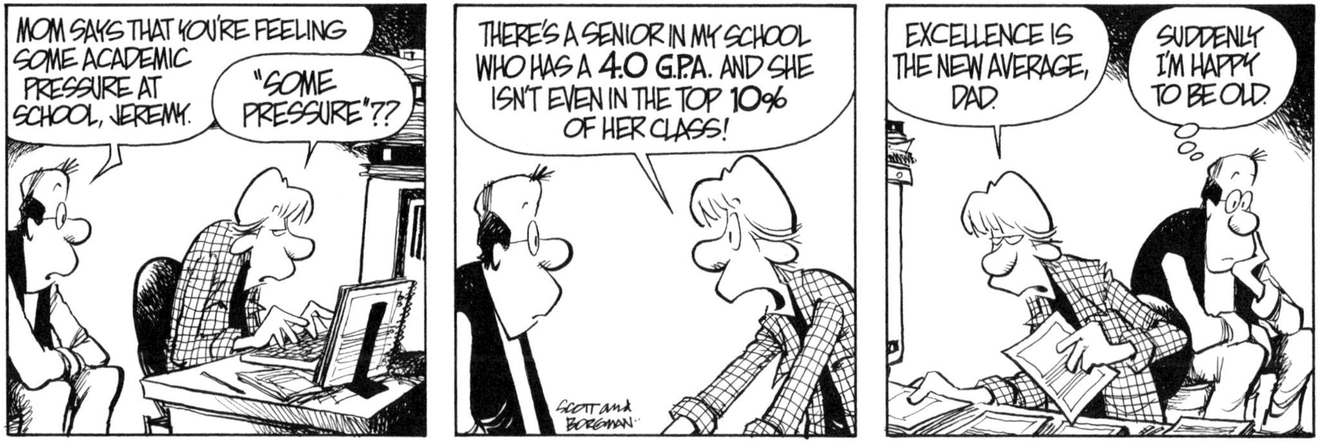
MOM SAYS THAT YOU'RE FEELING SOME ACADEMIC PRESSURE AT SCHOOL, JEREMY.
"SOME PRESSURE"??
THERE'S A SENIOR IN MY SCHOOL WHO HAS A 4.0 G.P.A. AND SHE ISN'T EVEN IN THE TOP 10% OF HER CLASS!
EXCELLENCE IS THE NEW AVERAGE, DAD.
SUDDENLY I'M HAPPY TO BE OLD.

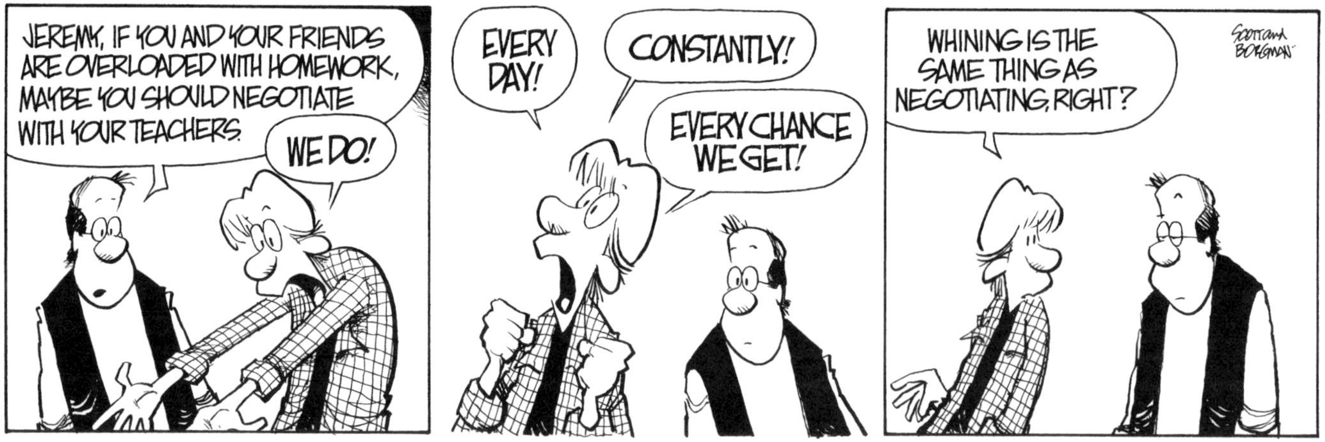
JEREMY, IF YOU AND YOUR FRIENDS ARE OVERLOADED WITH HOMEWORK, MAYBE YOU SHOULD NEGOTIATE WITH YOUR TEACHERS.
WE DO!
EVERY DAY!
CONSTANTLY!
EVERY CHANCE WE GET!
WHINING IS THE SAME THING AS NEGOTIATING, RIGHT?

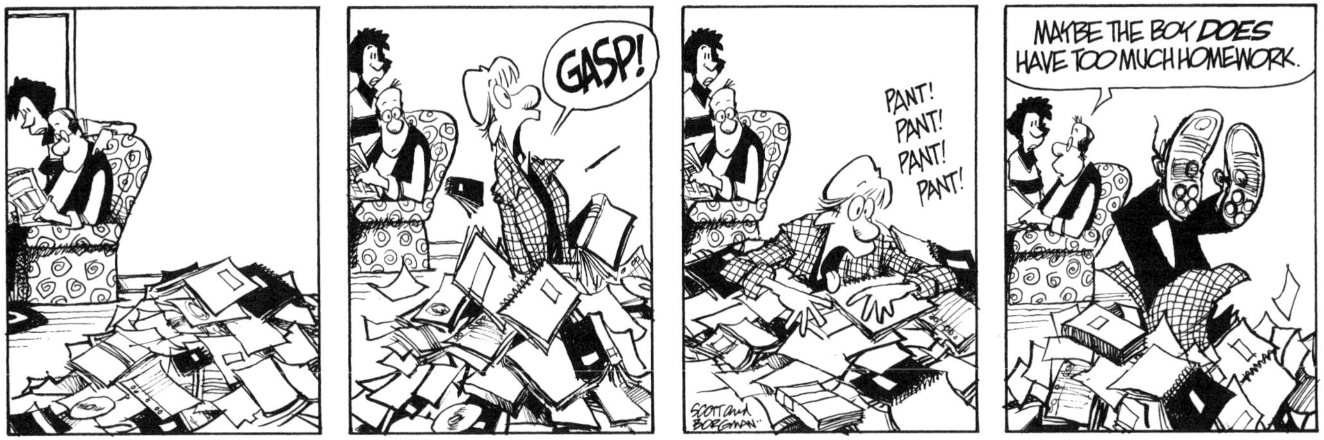
GASP!
PANT! PANT! PANT! PANT!
MAYBE THE BOY *DOES* HAVE TOO MUCH HOMEWORK.

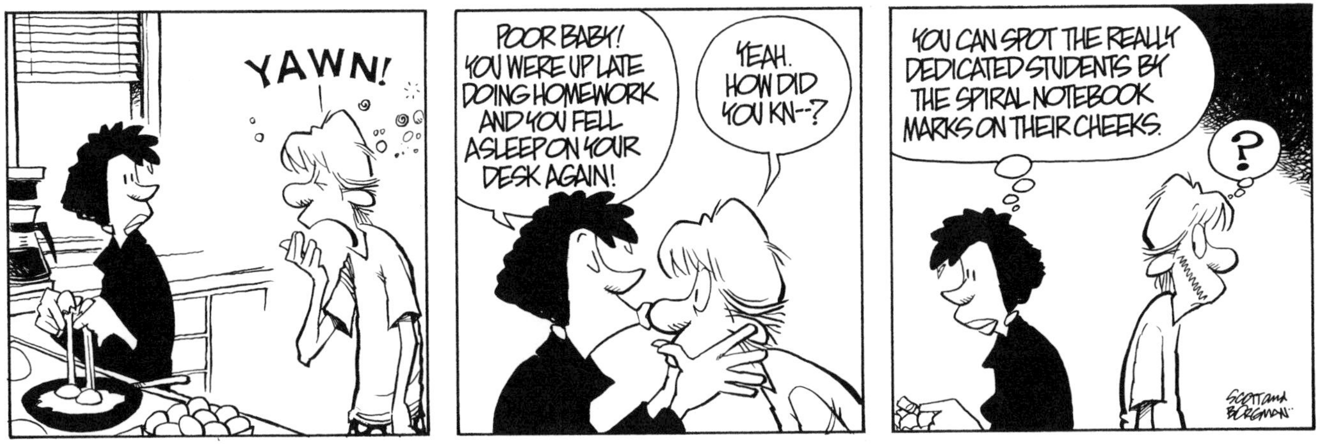
YAWN!
POOR BABY! YOU WERE UP LATE DOING HOMEWORK AND YOU FELL ASLEEP ON YOUR DESK AGAIN!
YEAH. HOW DID YOU KN--?
YOU CAN SPOT THE REALLY DEDICATED STUDENTS BY THE SPIRAL NOTEBOOK MARKS ON THEIR CHEEKS.
?

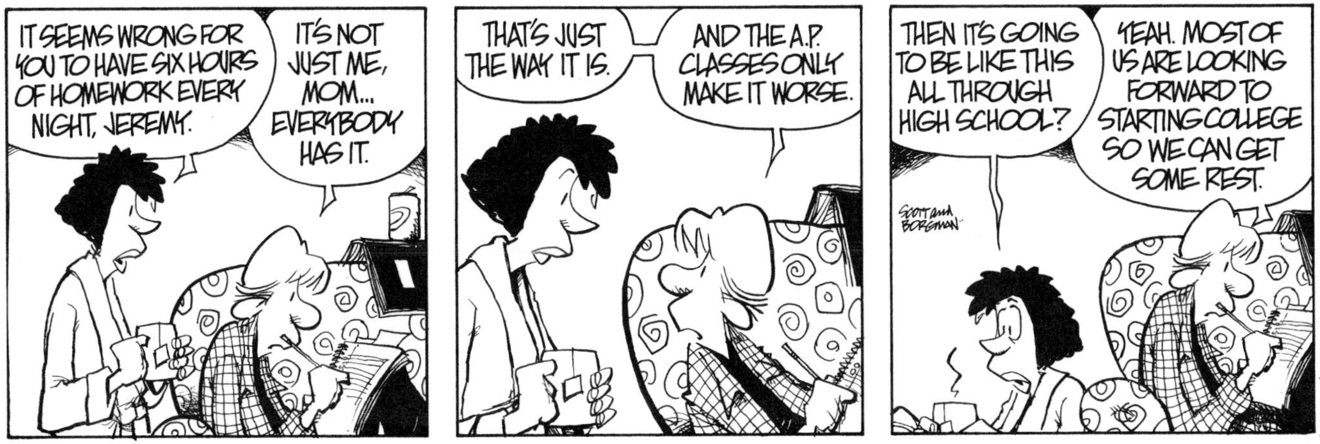
IT SEEMS WRONG FOR YOU TO HAVE SIX HOURS OF HOMEWORK EVERY NIGHT, JEREMY.
IT'S NOT JUST ME, MOM... EVERYBODY HAS IT.
THAT'S JUST THE WAY IT IS.
AND THE A.P. CLASSES ONLY MAKE IT WORSE.
THEN IT'S GOING TO BE LIKE THIS ALL THROUGH HIGH SCHOOL?
YEAH. MOST OF US ARE LOOKING FORWARD TO STARTING COLLEGE SO WE CAN GET SOME REST.

Zits

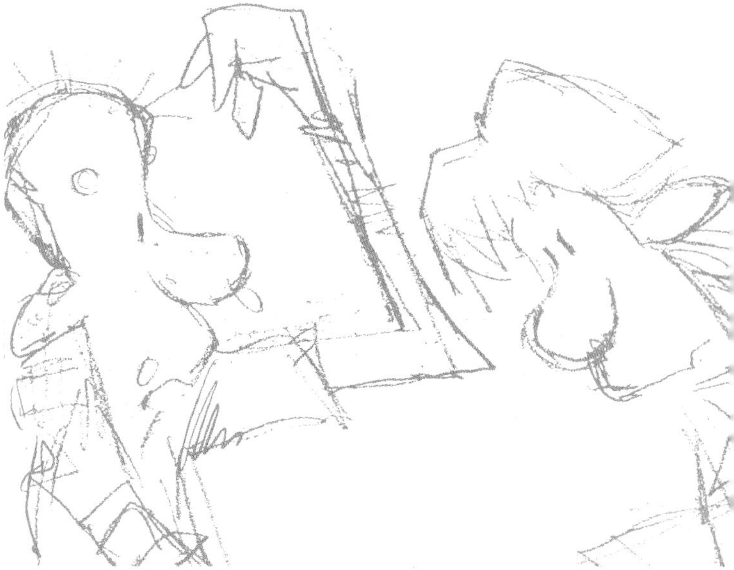

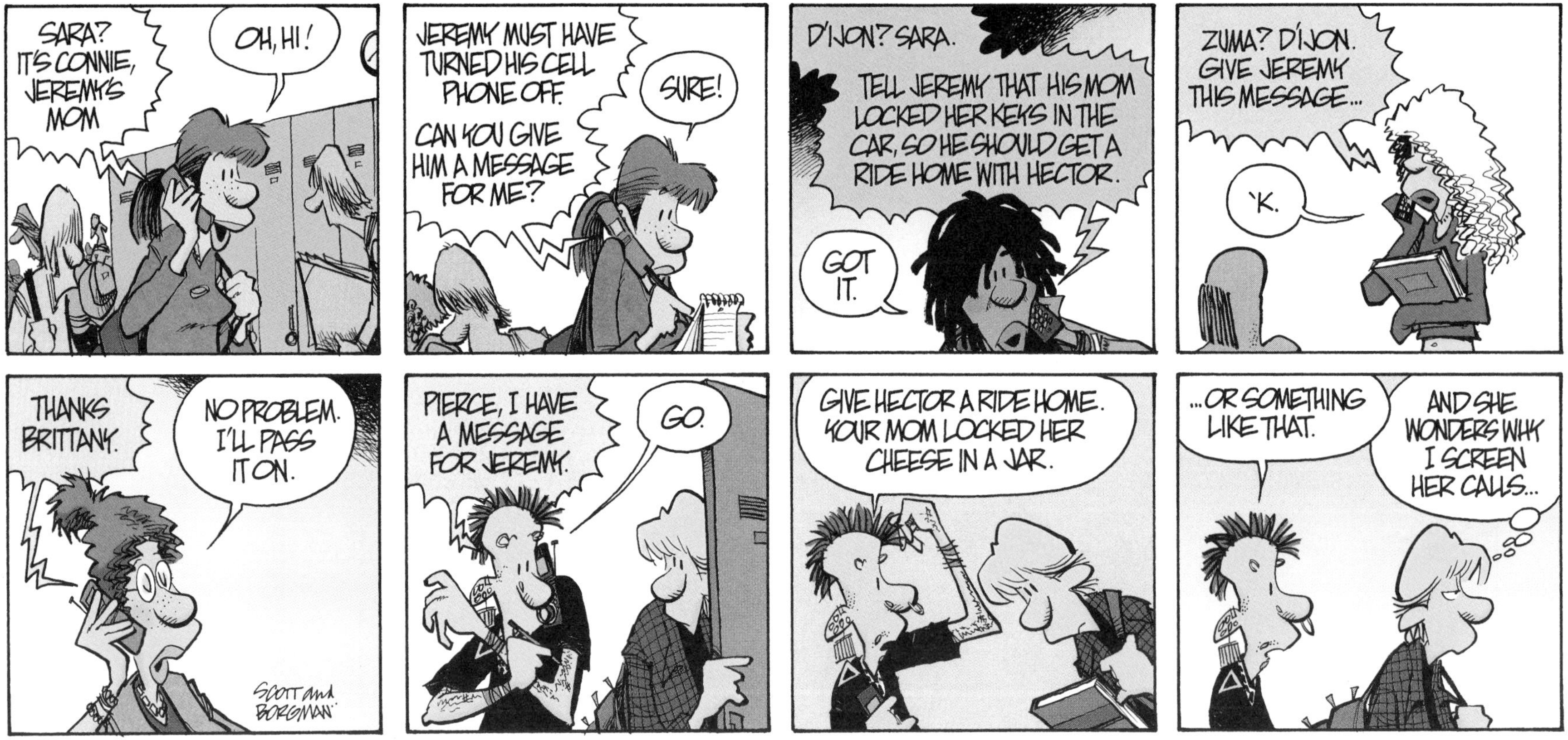

SARA? IT'S CONNIE, JEREMY'S MOM
OH, HI!
JEREMY MUST HAVE TURNED HIS CELL PHONE OFF.
CAN YOU GIVE HIM A MESSAGE FOR ME?
SURE!
D'IJON? SARA.
TELL JEREMY THAT HIS MOM LOCKED HER KEYS IN THE CAR, SO HE SHOULD GET A RIDE HOME WITH HECTOR.
GOT IT.
ZUMA? D'IJON. GIVE JEREMY THIS MESSAGE...
'K.
THANKS BRITTANY.
NO PROBLEM. I'LL PASS IT ON.
SCOTT and BORGMAN
PIERCE, I HAVE A MESSAGE FOR JEREMY.
GO.
GIVE HECTOR A RIDE HOME. YOUR MOM LOCKED HER CHEESE IN A JAR.
...OR SOMETHING LIKE THAT.
AND SHE WONDERS WHY I SCREEN HER CALLS...

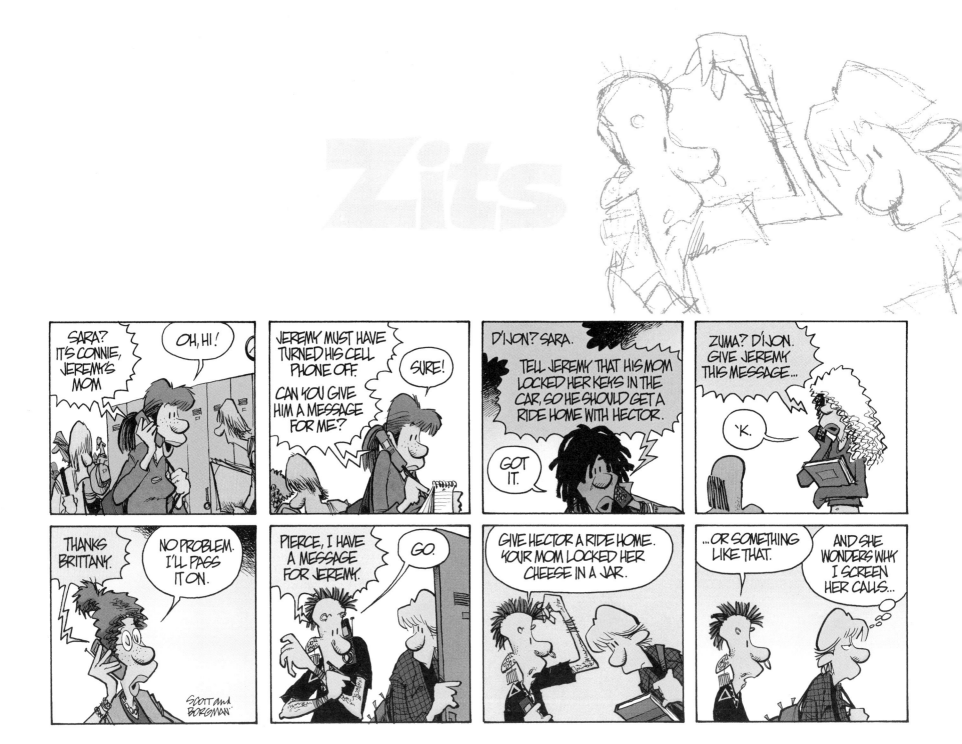

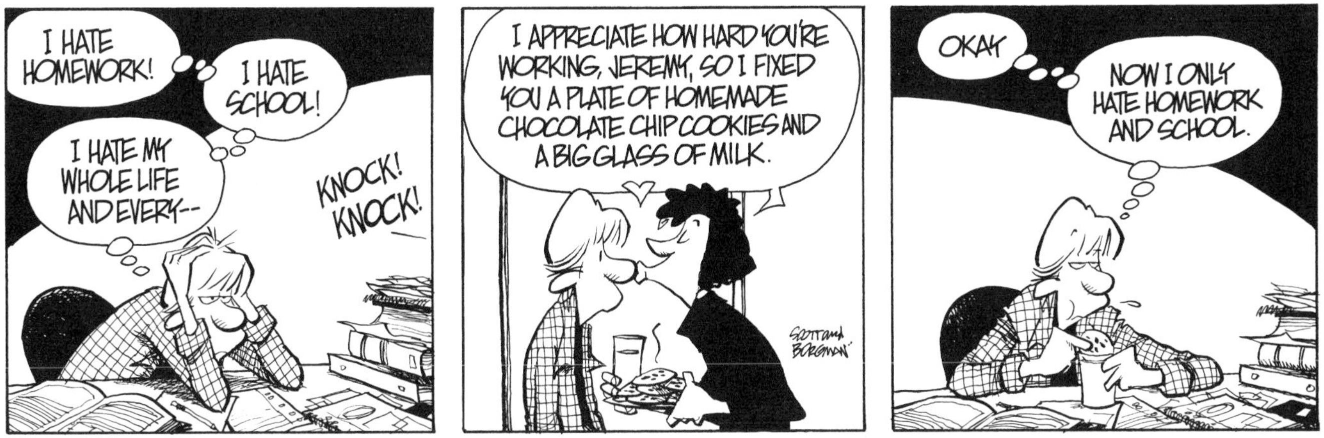
I HATE HOMEWORK!
I HATE SCHOOL!
I HATE MY WHOLE LIFE AND EVERY--
KNOCK! KNOCK!
I APPRECIATE HOW HARD YOU'RE WORKING, JEREMY, SO I FIXED YOU A PLATE OF HOMEMADE CHOCOLATE CHIP COOKIES AND A BIG GLASS OF MILK.
OKAY
NOW I ONLY HATE HOMEWORK AND SCHOOL.

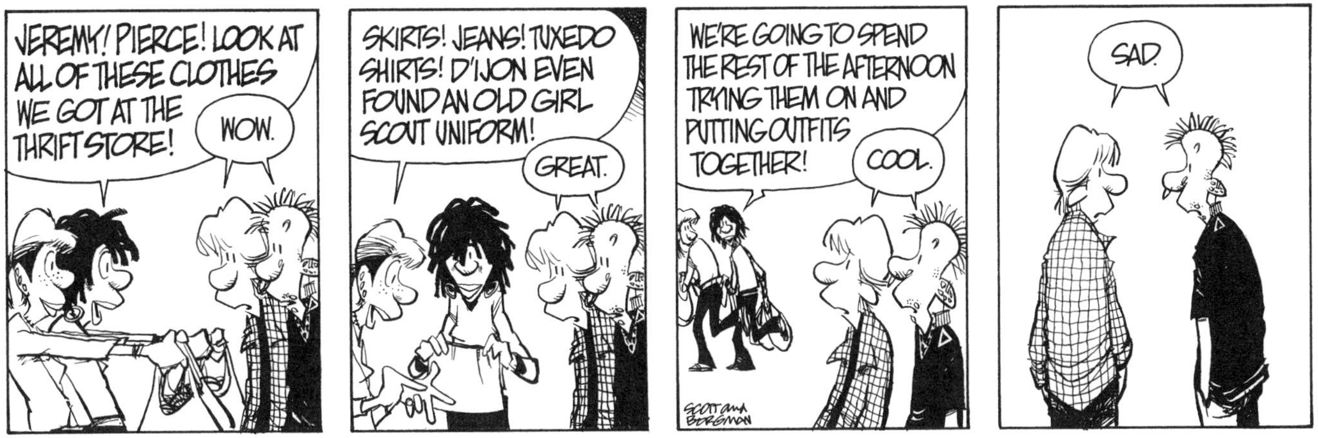
JEREMY! PIERCE! LOOK AT ALL OF THESE CLOTHES WE GOT AT THE THRIFT STORE!
WOW.
SKIRTS! JEANS! TUXEDO SHIRTS! D'IJON EVEN FOUND AN OLD GIRL SCOUT UNIFORM!
GREAT.
WE'RE GOING TO SPEND THE REST OF THE AFTERNOON TRYING THEM ON AND PUTTING OUTFITS TOGETHER!
COOL.
SAD.

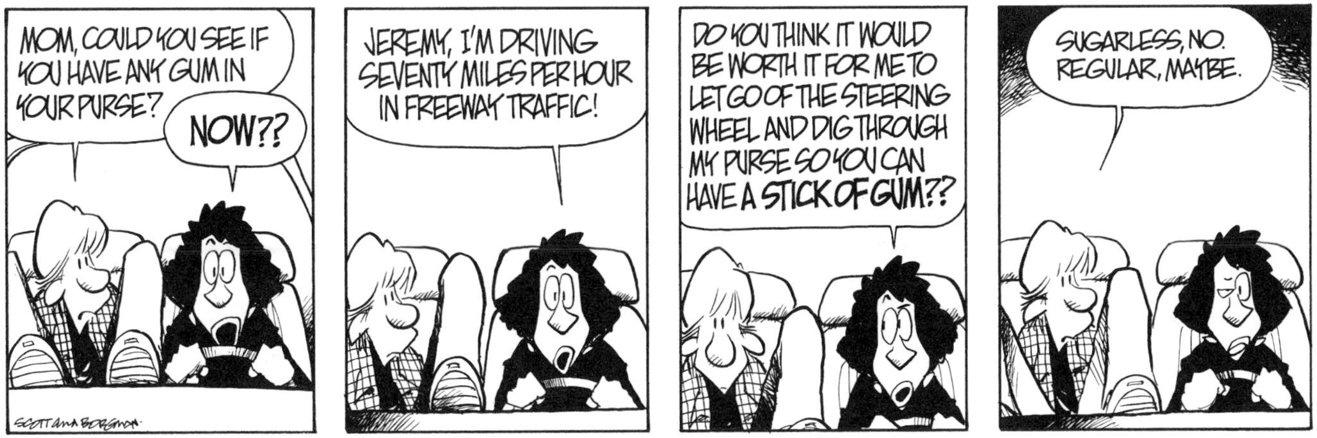
MOM, COULD YOU SEE IF YOU HAVE ANY GUM IN YOUR PURSE?
NOW??
JEREMY, I'M DRIVING SEVENTY MILES PER HOUR IN FREEWAY TRAFFIC!
DO YOU THINK IT WOULD BE WORTH IT FOR ME TO LET GO OF THE STEERING WHEEL AND DIG THROUGH MY PURSE SO YOU CAN HAVE A STICK OF GUM??
SUGARLESS, NO. REGULAR, MAYBE.

Zits

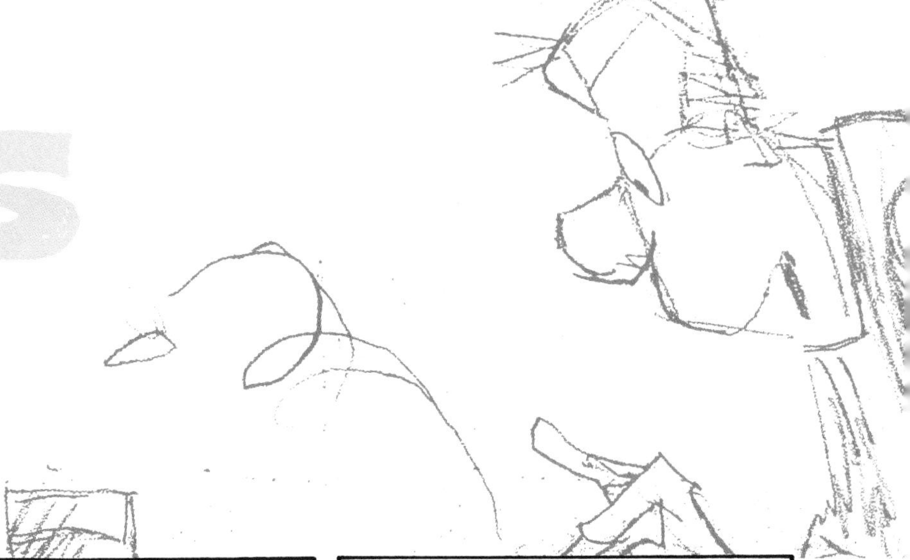

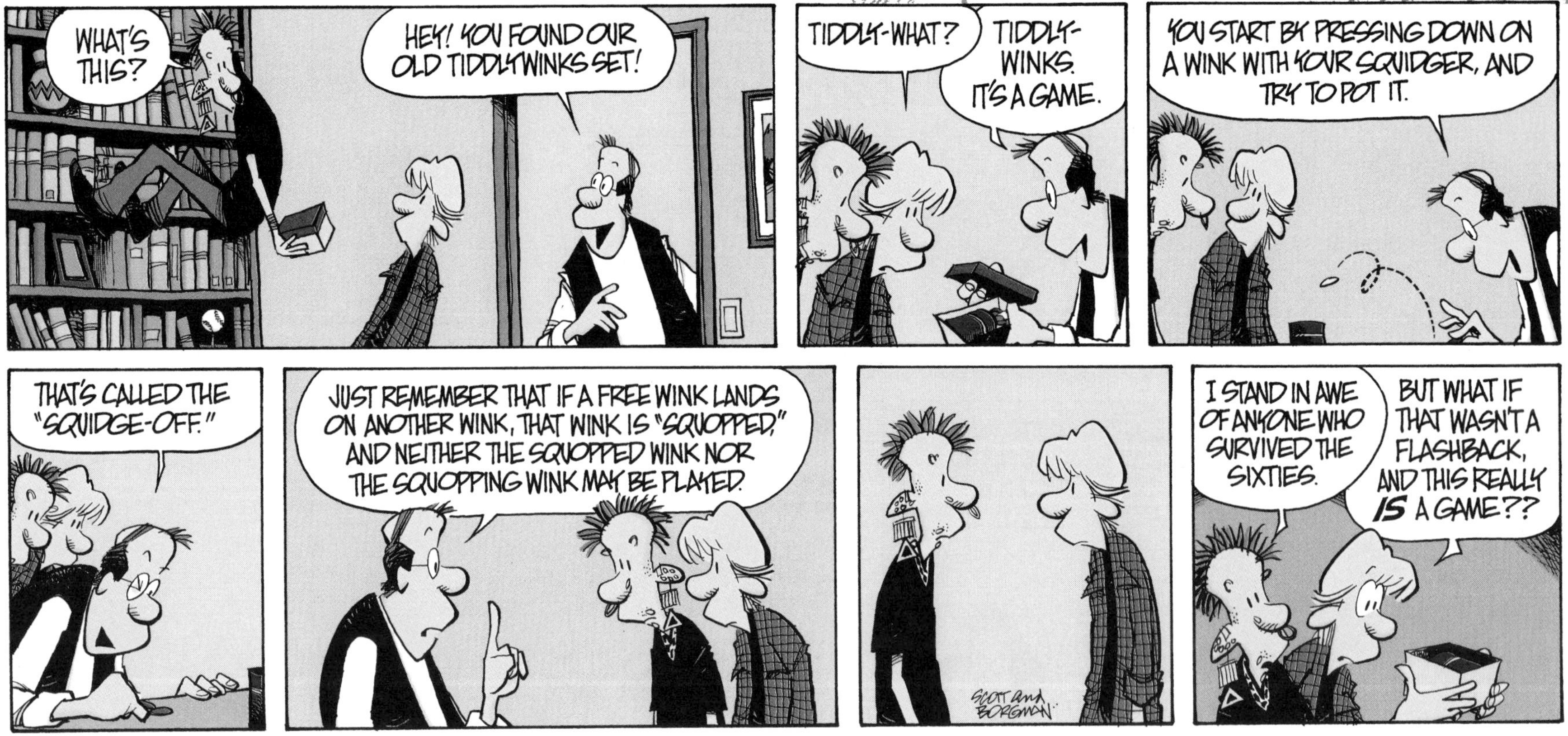

WHAT'S THIS?
HEY! YOU FOUND OUR OLD TIDDLYWINKS SET!
TIDDLY-WHAT?
TIDDLY-WINKS. IT'S A GAME.
YOU START BY PRESSING DOWN ON A WINK WITH YOUR SQUIDGER, AND TRY TO POT IT.
THAT'S CALLED THE "SQUIDGE-OFF."
JUST REMEMBER THAT IF A FREE WINK LANDS ON ANOTHER WINK, THAT WINK IS "SQUOPPED," AND NEITHER THE SQUOPPED WINK NOR THE SQUOPPING WINK MAY BE PLAYED.
SCOTT and BORGMAN
I STAND IN AWE OF ANYONE WHO SURVIVED THE SIXTIES.
BUT WHAT IF THAT WASN'T A FLASHBACK, AND THIS REALLY **IS** A GAME??

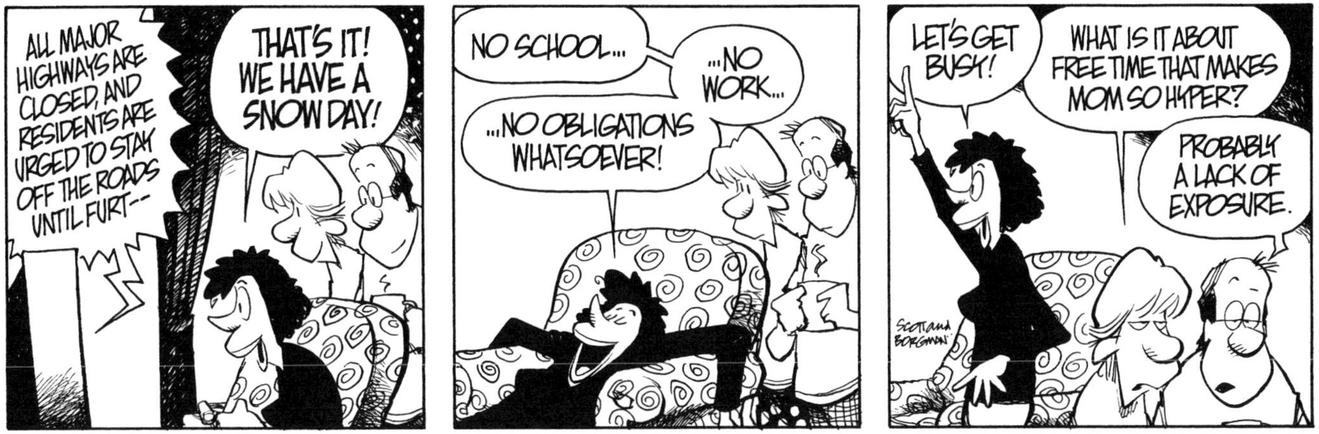
ALL MAJOR HIGHWAYS ARE CLOSED, AND RESIDENTS ARE URGED TO STAY OFF THE ROADS UNTIL FURT--
THAT'S IT! WE HAVE A SNOW DAY!
NO SCHOOL...
...NO WORK...
...NO OBLIGATIONS WHATSOEVER!
LET'S GET BUSY!
WHAT IS IT ABOUT FREE TIME THAT MAKES MOM SO HYPER?
PROBABLY A LACK OF EXPOSURE.

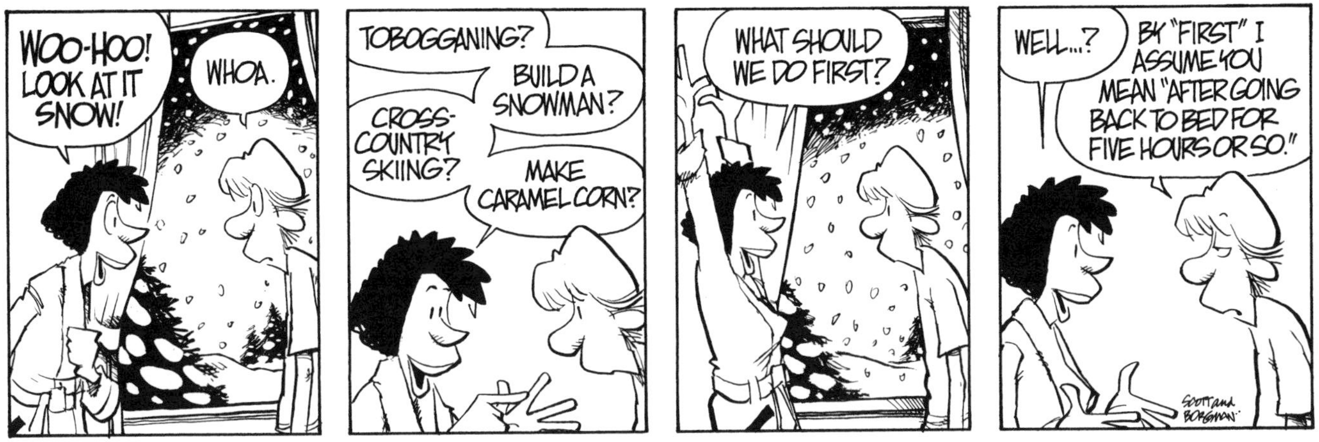
WOO-HOO! LOOK AT IT SNOW!
WHOA.
TOBOGGANING?
BUILD A SNOWMAN?
CROSS-COUNTRY SKIING?
MAKE CARAMEL CORN?
WHAT SHOULD WE DO FIRST?
WELL...?
BY "FIRST" I ASSUME YOU MEAN "AFTER GOING BACK TO BED FOR FIVE HOURS OR SO."

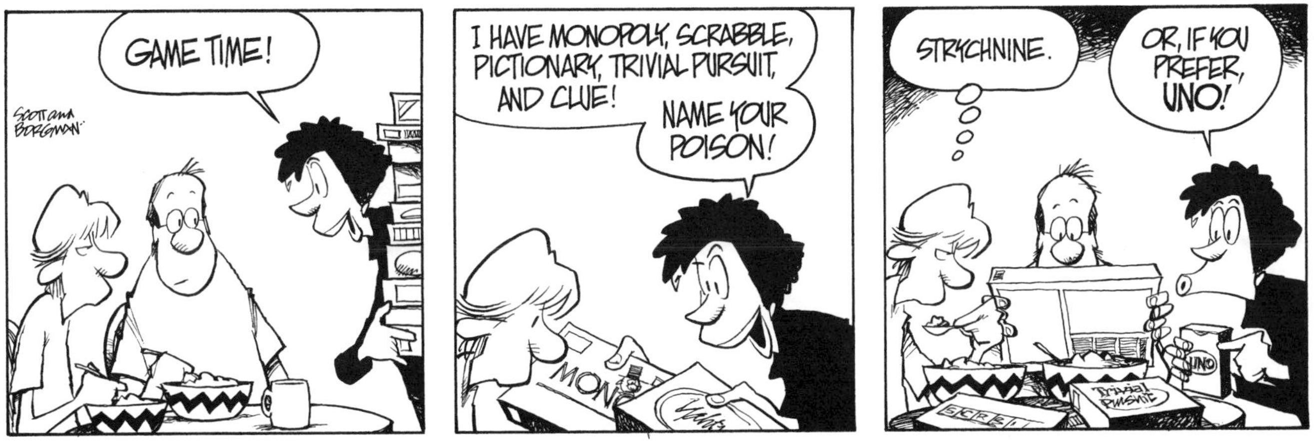
GAME TIME!
I HAVE MONOPOLY, SCRABBLE, PICTIONARY, TRIVIAL PURSUIT, AND CLUE!
NAME YOUR POISON!
STRYCHNINE.
OR, IF YOU PREFER, UNO!

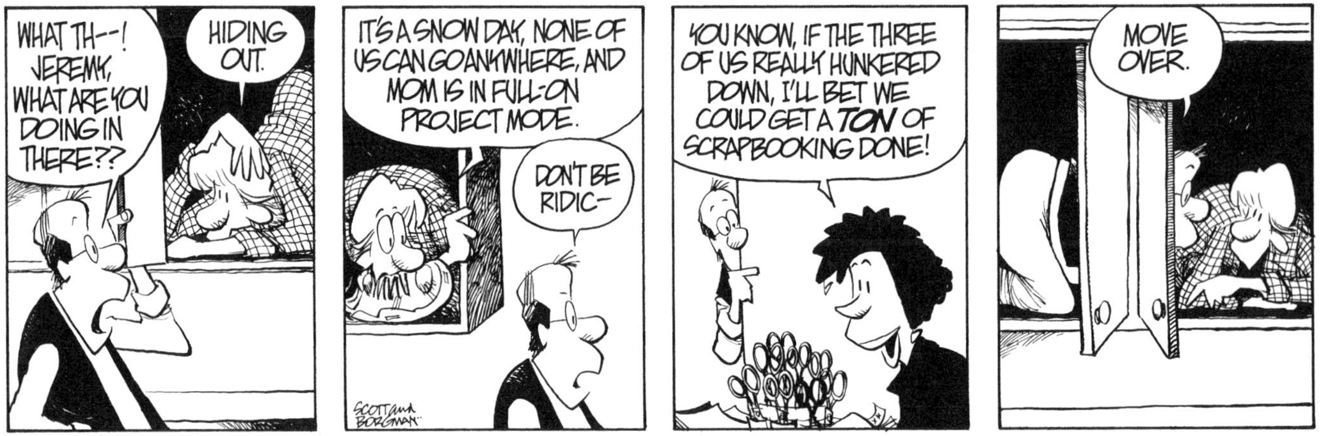
WHAT TH--! JEREMY, WHAT ARE YOU DOING IN THERE??
HIDING OUT.
IT'S A SNOW DAY, NONE OF US CAN GO ANYWHERE, AND MOM IS IN FULL-ON PROJECT MODE.
DON'T BE RIDIC-
YOU KNOW, IF THE THREE OF US REALLY HUNKERED DOWN, I'LL BET WE COULD GET A **TON** OF SCRAPBOOKING DONE!
MOVE OVER.

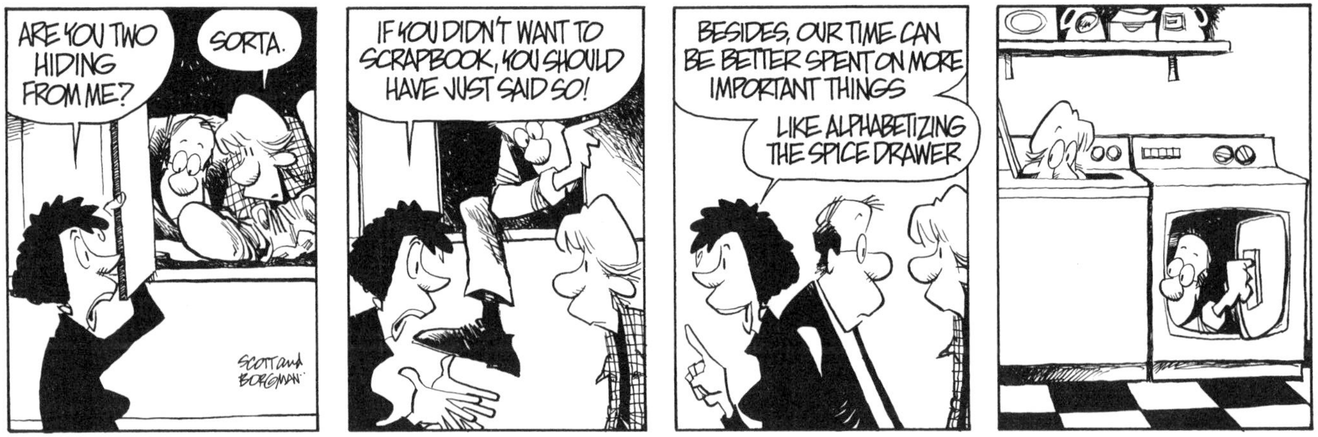
ARE YOU TWO HIDING FROM ME?
SORTA.
IF YOU DIDN'T WANT TO SCRAPBOOK, YOU SHOULD HAVE JUST SAID SO!
BESIDES, OUR TIME CAN BE BETTER SPENT ON MORE IMPORTANT THINGS
LIKE ALPHABETIZING THE SPICE DRAWER

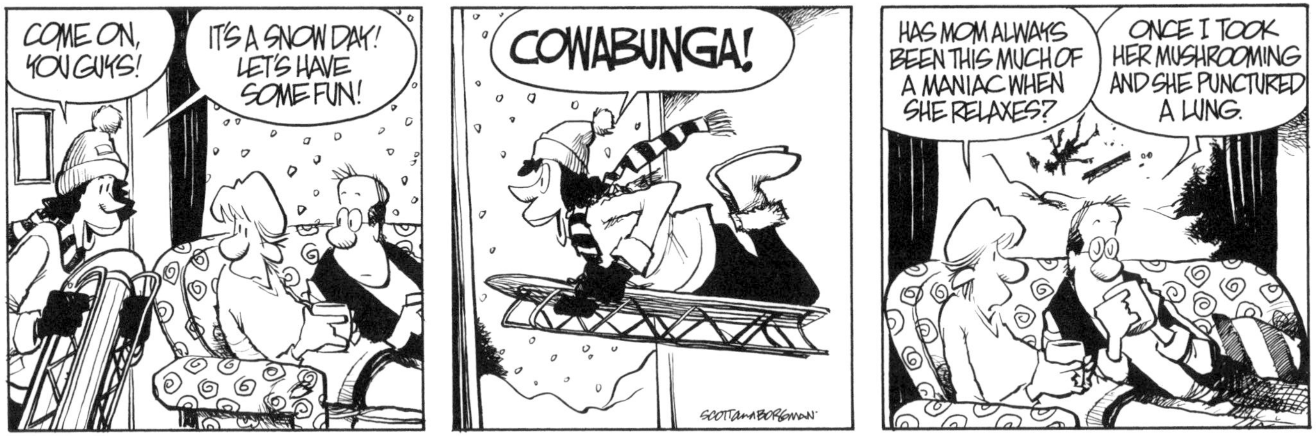
COME ON, YOU GUYS!
IT'S A SNOW DAY! LET'S HAVE SOME FUN!
COWABUNGA!
HAS MOM ALWAYS BEEN THIS MUCH OF A MANIAC WHEN SHE RELAXES?
ONCE I TOOK HER MUSHROOMING AND SHE PUNCTURED A LUNG.

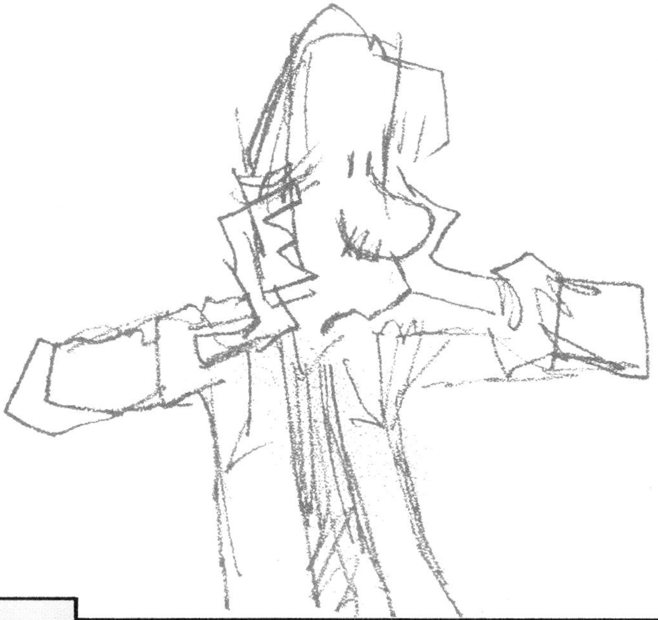

Zits

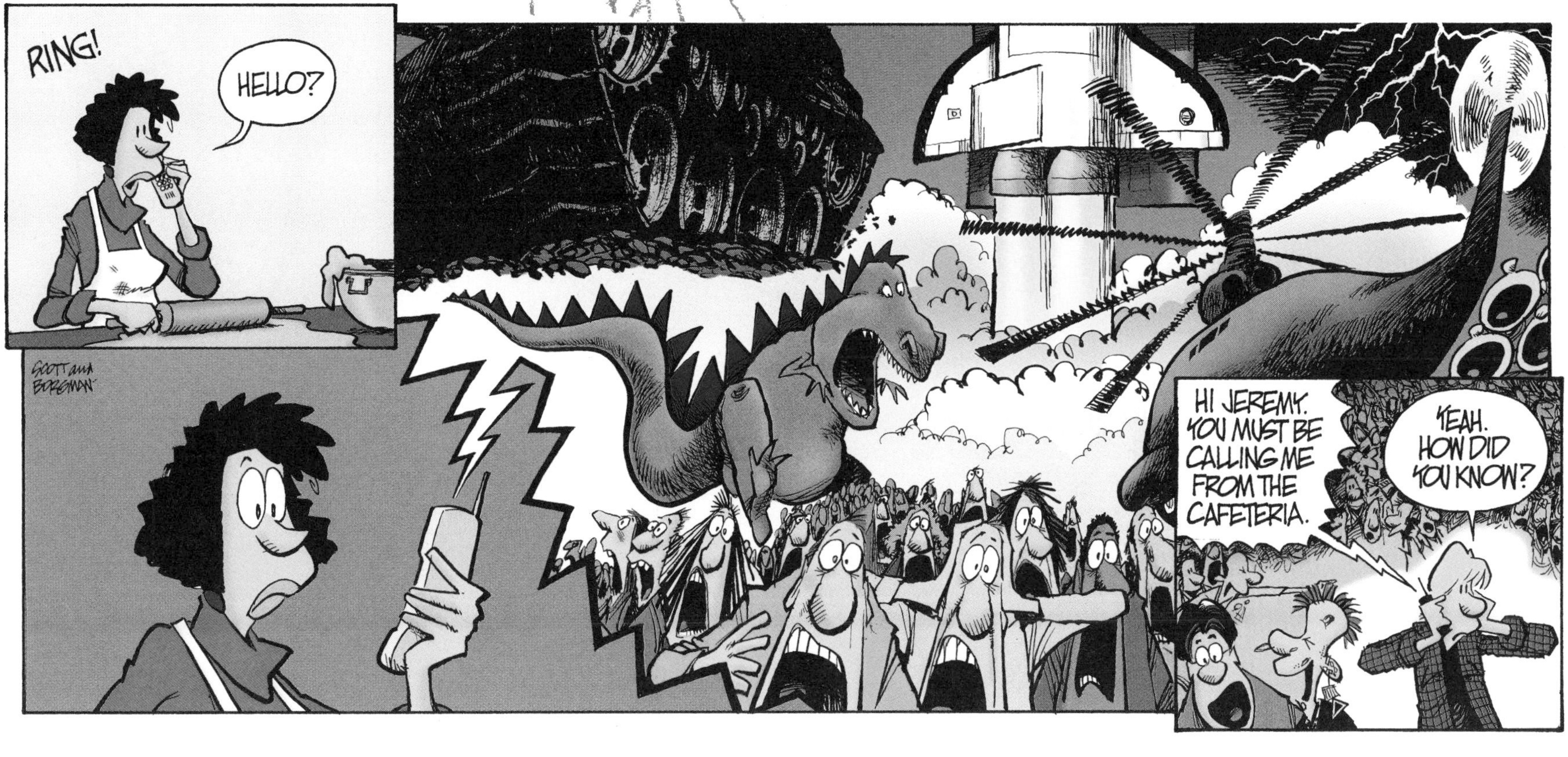
RING!
HELLO?
HI JEREMY. YOU MUST BE CALLING ME FROM THE CAFETERIA.
YEAH. HOW DID YOU KNOW?

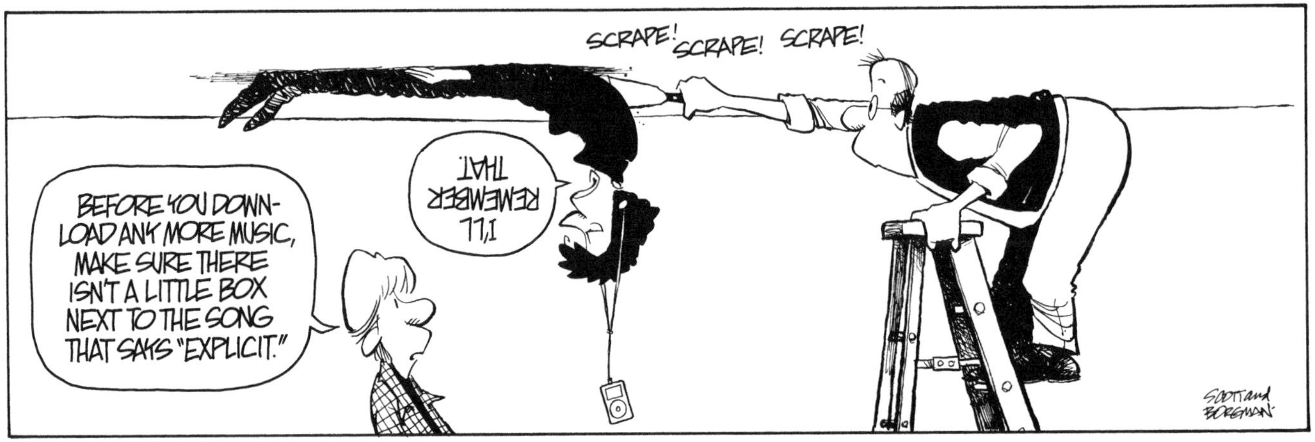
SCRAPE! SCRAPE! SCRAPE!
BEFORE YOU DOWNLOAD ANY MORE MUSIC, MAKE SURE THERE ISN'T A LITTLE BOX NEXT TO THE SONG THAT SAYS "EXPLICIT."
I'LL REMEMBER THAT.
SCOTT and BORGMAN

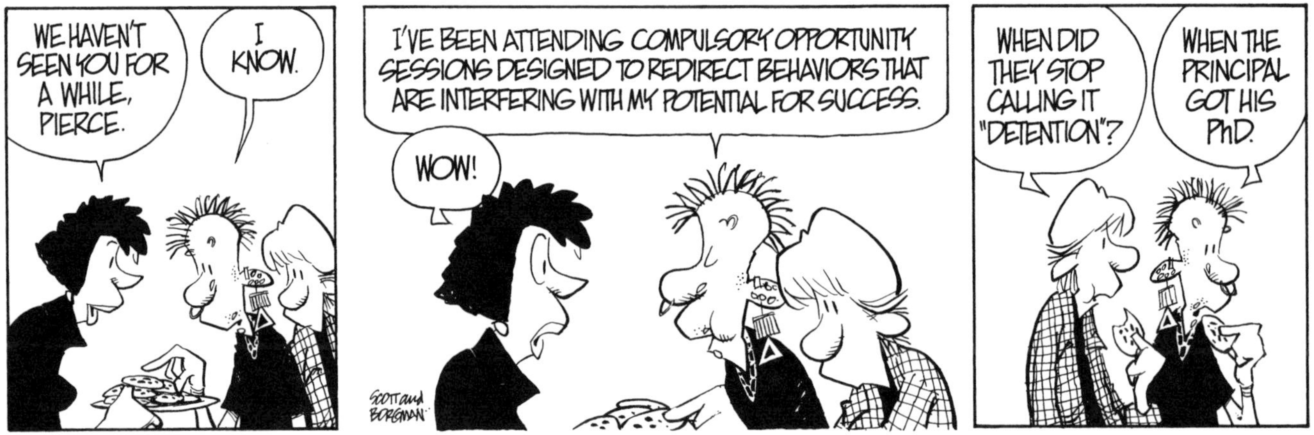
WE HAVEN'T SEEN YOU FOR A WHILE, PIERCE.
I KNOW.
I'VE BEEN ATTENDING COMPULSORY OPPORTUNITY SESSIONS DESIGNED TO REDIRECT BEHAVIORS THAT ARE INTERFERING WITH MY POTENTIAL FOR SUCCESS.
WOW!
SCOTT and BORGMAN
WHEN DID THEY STOP CALLING IT "DETENTION"?
WHEN THE PRINCIPAL GOT HIS PhD.

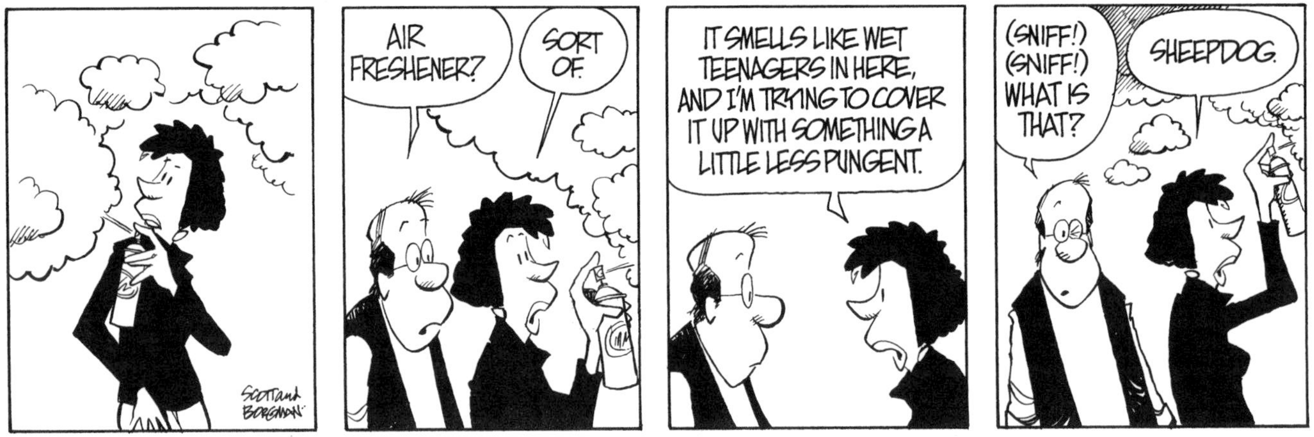
SCOTT and BORGMAN
AIR FRESHENER?
SORT OF.
IT SMELLS LIKE WET TEENAGERS IN HERE, AND I'M TRYING TO COVER IT UP WITH SOMETHING A LITTLE LESS PUNGENT.
(SNIFF!) (SNIFF!) WHAT IS THAT?
SHEEPDOG.

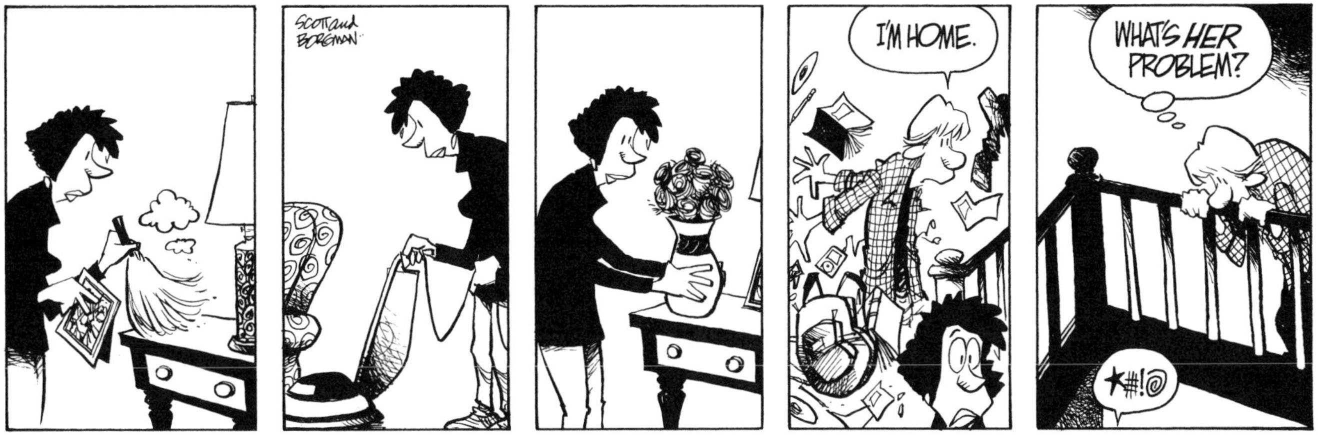
SCOTT and BORGMAN
I'M HOME.
WHAT'S HER PROBLEM?
★#!@

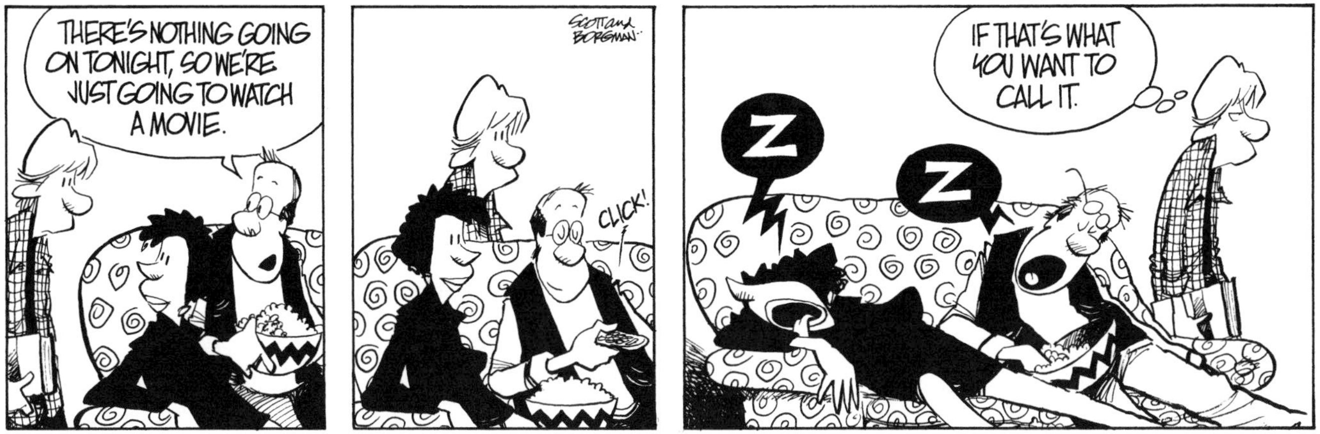
THERE'S NOTHING GOING ON TONIGHT, SO WE'RE JUST GOING TO WATCH A MOVIE.
SCOTT and BORGMAN
CLICK!
Z
Z
IF THAT'S WHAT YOU WANT TO CALL IT.

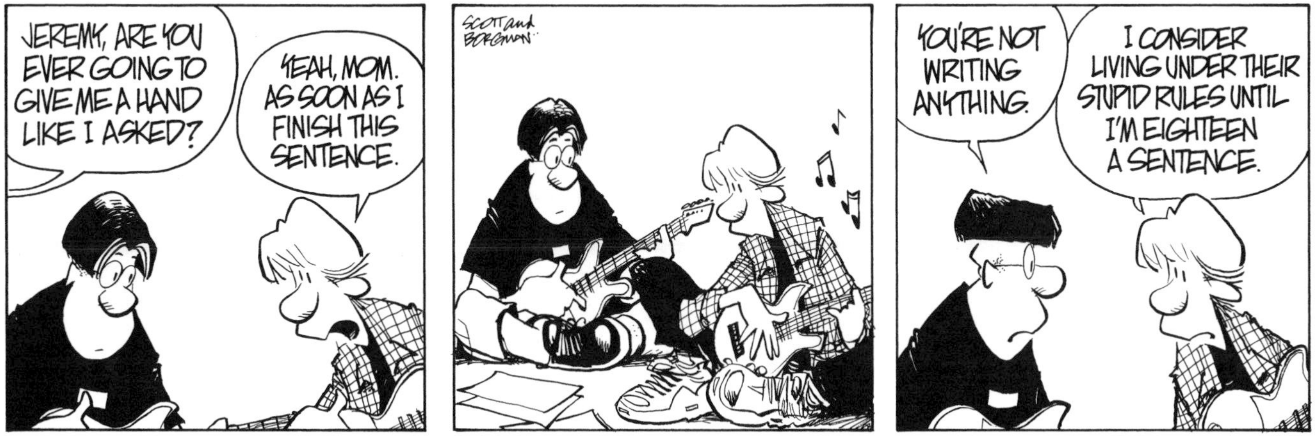
JEREMY, ARE YOU EVER GOING TO GIVE ME A HAND LIKE I ASKED?
YEAH, MOM. AS SOON AS I FINISH THIS SENTENCE.
SCOTT and BORGMAN
YOU'RE NOT WRITING ANYTHING.
I CONSIDER LIVING UNDER THEIR STUPID RULES UNTIL I'M EIGHTEEN A SENTENCE.

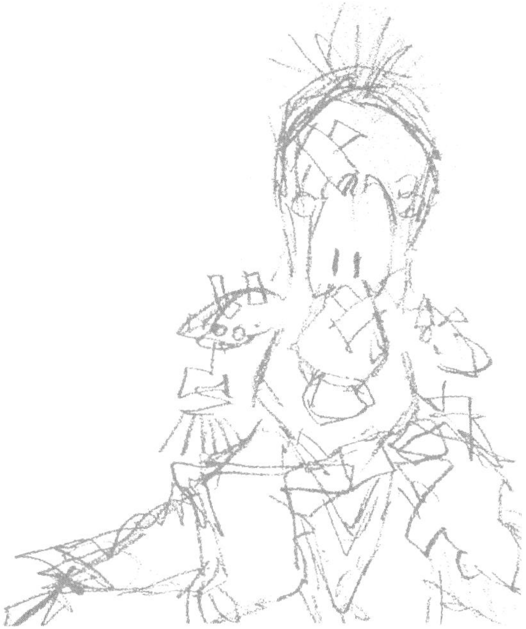

Zits

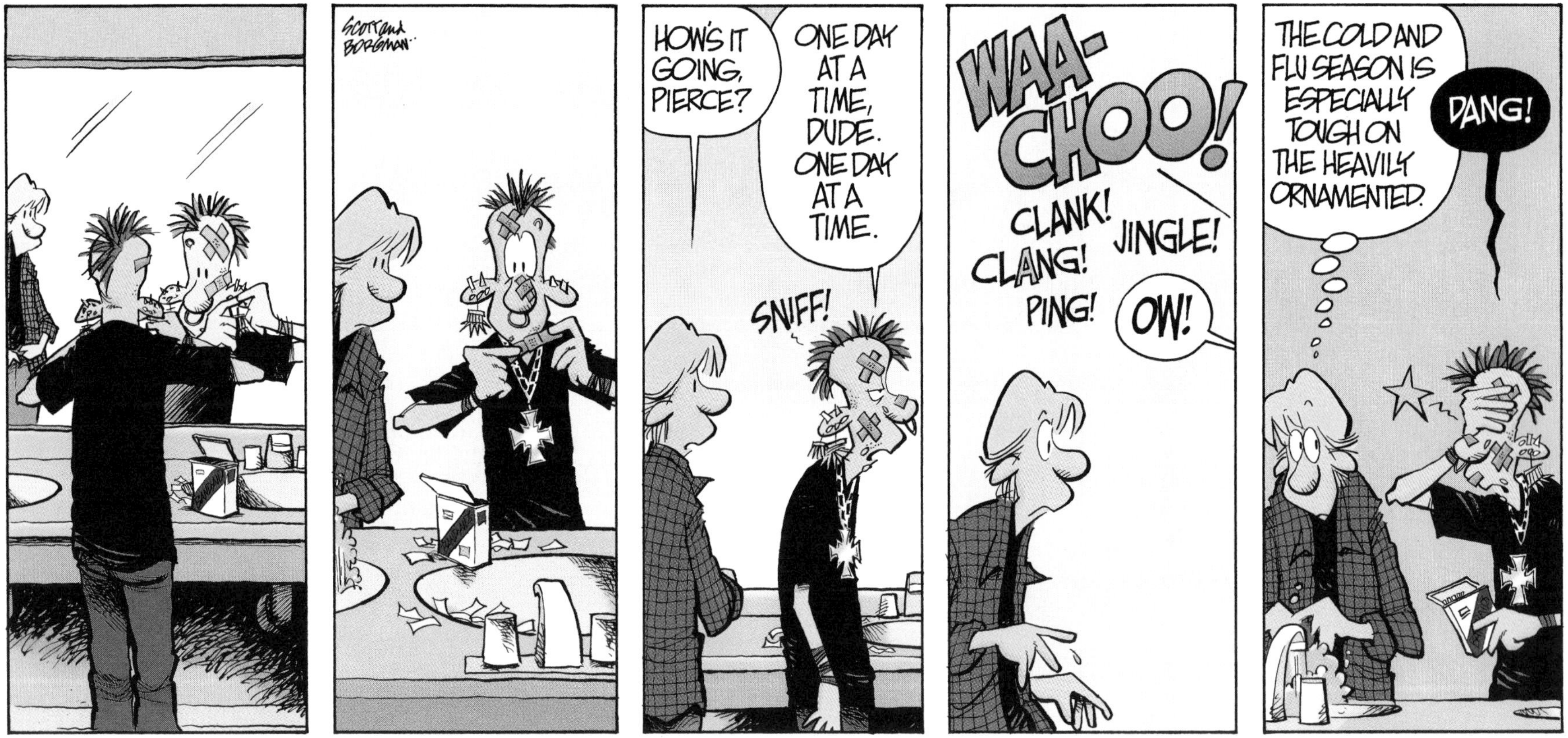

HOW'S IT GOING, PIERCE?
ONE DAY AT A TIME, DUDE. ONE DAY AT A TIME.
SNIFF!
WAA-CHOO!
CLANK!
CLANG!
JINGLE!
PING!
OW!
THE COLD AND FLU SEASON IS ESPECIALLY TOUGH ON THE HEAVILY ORNAMENTED.
DANG!

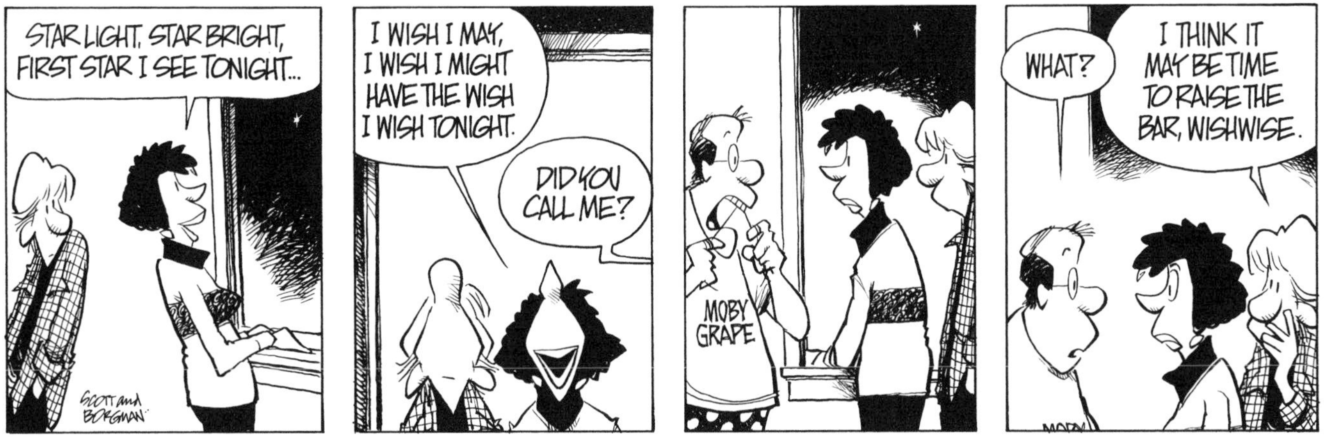
STAR LIGHT, STAR BRIGHT, FIRST STAR I SEE TONIGHT...
SCOTT and BORGMAN
I WISH I MAY, I WISH I MIGHT HAVE THE WISH I WISH TONIGHT.
DID YOU CALL ME?
MOBY GRAPE
WHAT?
I THINK IT MAY BE TIME TO RAISE THE BAR, WISHWISE.

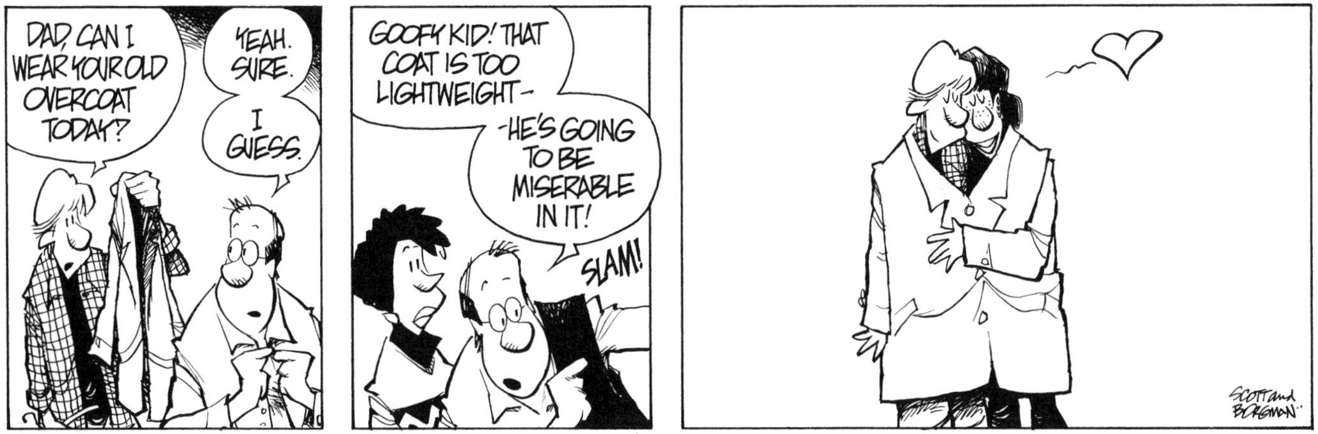
DAD, CAN I WEAR YOUR OLD OVERCOAT TODAY?
YEAH. SURE.
I GUESS.
GOOFY KID! THAT COAT IS TOO LIGHTWEIGHT–
–HE'S GOING TO BE MISERABLE IN IT!
SLAM!
SCOTT and BORGMAN

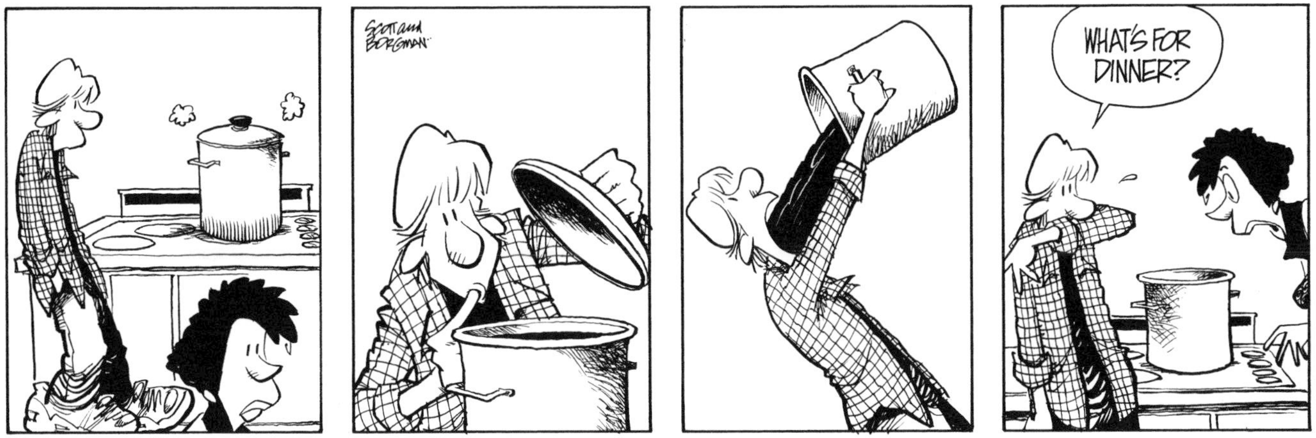
SCOTT and BORGMAN
WHAT'S FOR DINNER?

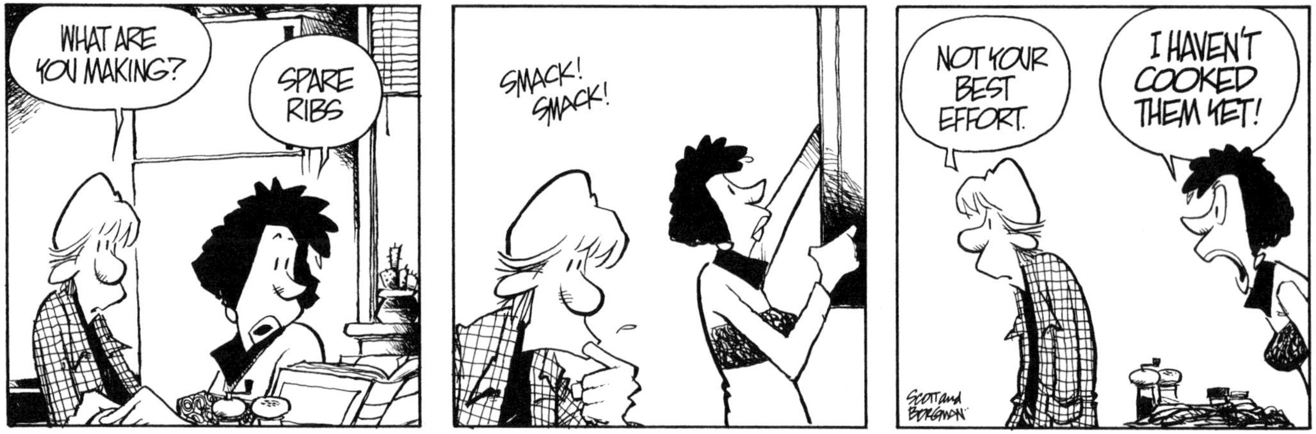
WHAT ARE YOU MAKING?
SPARE RIBS
SMACK! SMACK!
NOT YOUR BEST EFFORT.
I HAVEN'T COOKED THEM YET!
SCOTT and BORGMAN

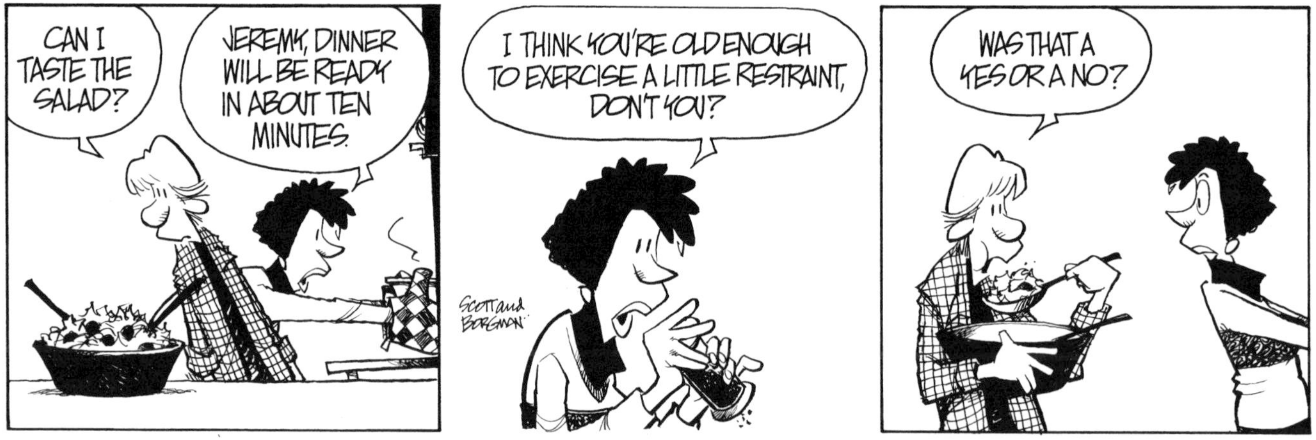
CAN I TASTE THE SALAD?
JEREMY, DINNER WILL BE READY IN ABOUT TEN MINUTES.
I THINK YOU'RE OLD ENOUGH TO EXERCISE A LITTLE RESTRAINT, DON'T YOU?
SCOTT and BORGMAN
WAS THAT A YES OR A NO?

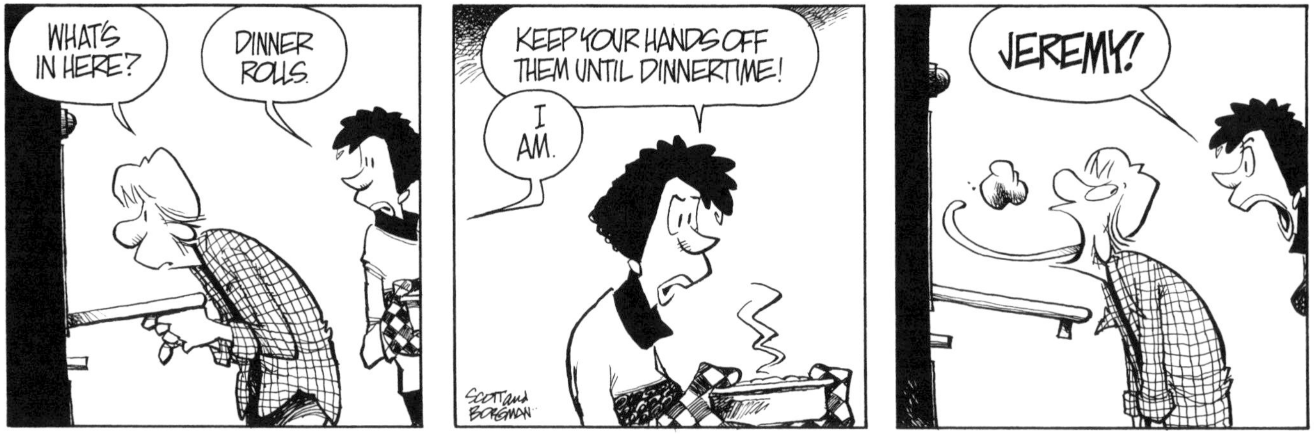
WHAT'S IN HERE?
DINNER ROLLS.
KEEP YOUR HANDS OFF THEM UNTIL DINNERTIME!
I AM.
SCOTT and BORGMAN
JEREMY!

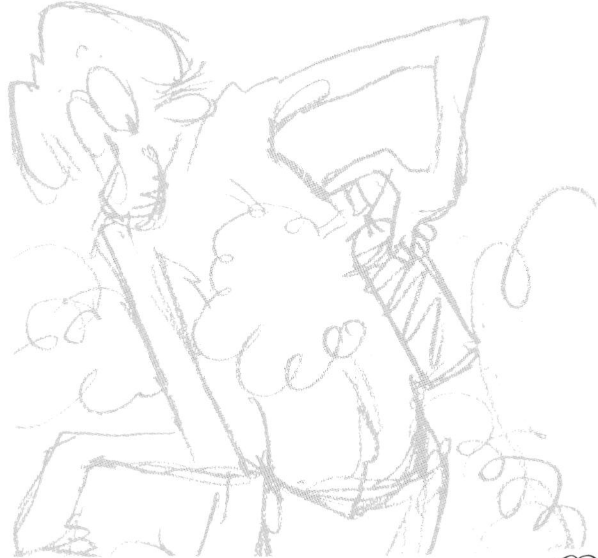

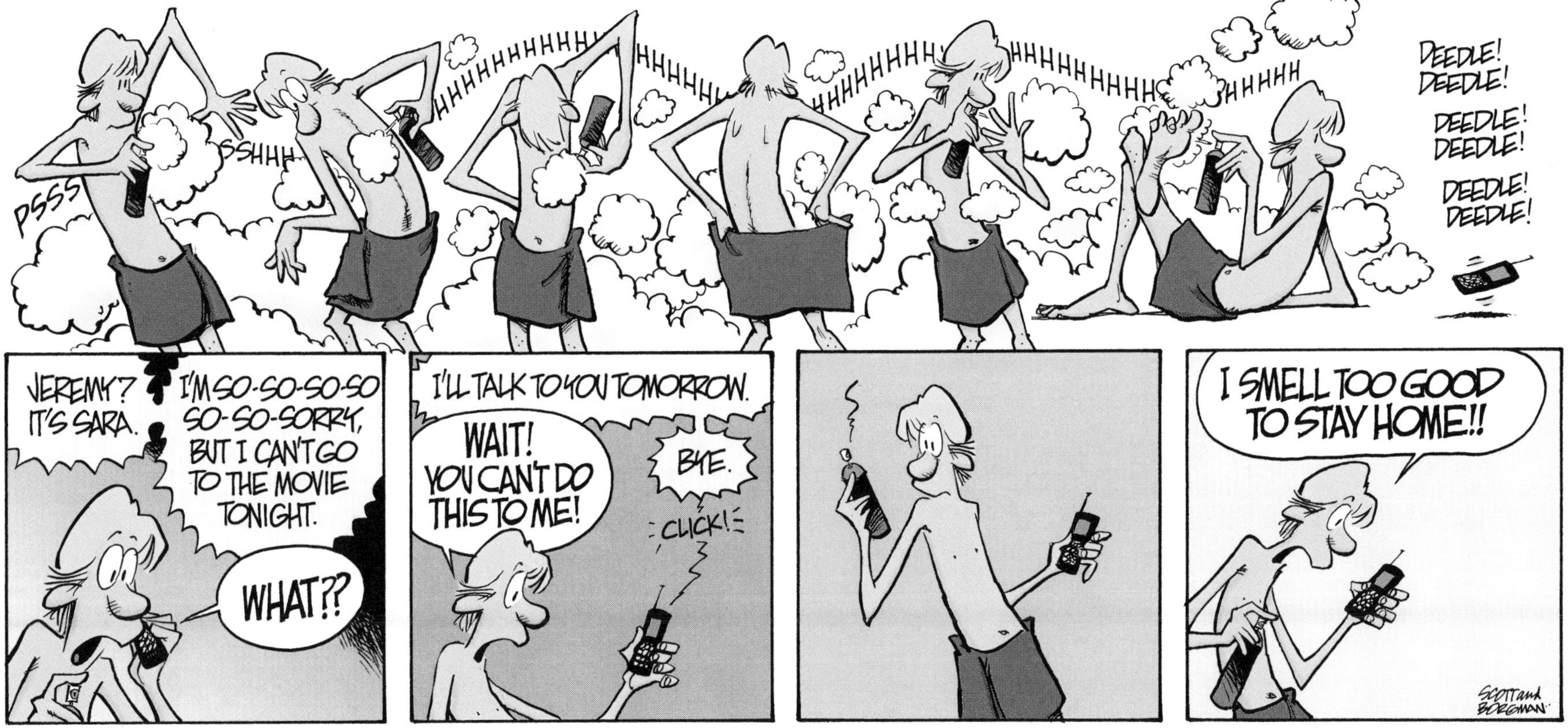
PSSS
SSHHHHHHHHHHHHHHHHHHHHHHHHHHHHHHHHHHHHHHHHHHHHHHH
DEEDLE! DEEDLE!
DEEDLE! DEEDLE!
DEEDLE! DEEDLE!
JEREMY? IT'S SARA.
I'M SO-SO-SO-SO SO-SO-SORRY, BUT I CAN'T GO TO THE MOVIE TONIGHT.
WHAT??
I'LL TALK TO YOU TOMORROW.
WAIT! YOU CAN'T DO THIS TO ME!
BYE.
CLICK!
I SMELL TOO GOOD TO STAY HOME!!
SCOTT and BORGMAN

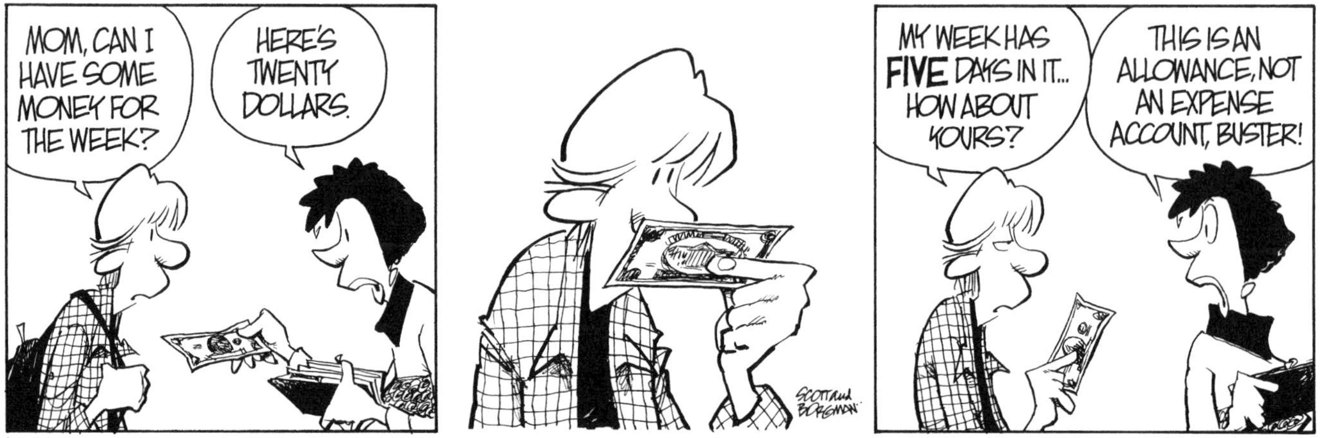
MOM, CAN I HAVE SOME MONEY FOR THE WEEK?
HERE'S TWENTY DOLLARS.
MY WEEK HAS FIVE DAYS IN IT... HOW ABOUT YOURS?
THIS IS AN ALLOWANCE, NOT AN EXPENSE ACCOUNT, BUSTER!

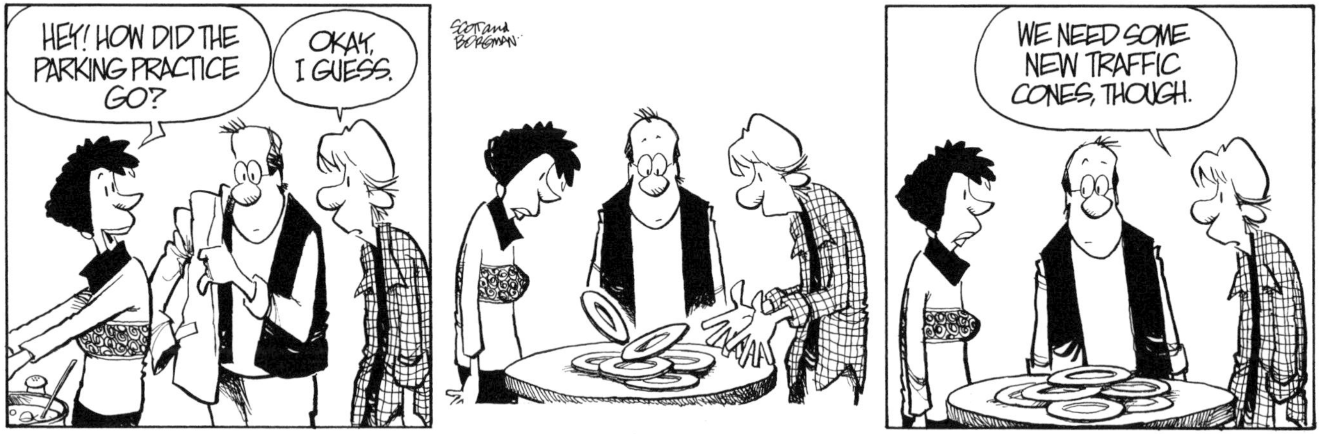
HEY! HOW DID THE PARKING PRACTICE GO?
OKAY, I GUESS.
WE NEED SOME NEW TRAFFIC CONES, THOUGH.

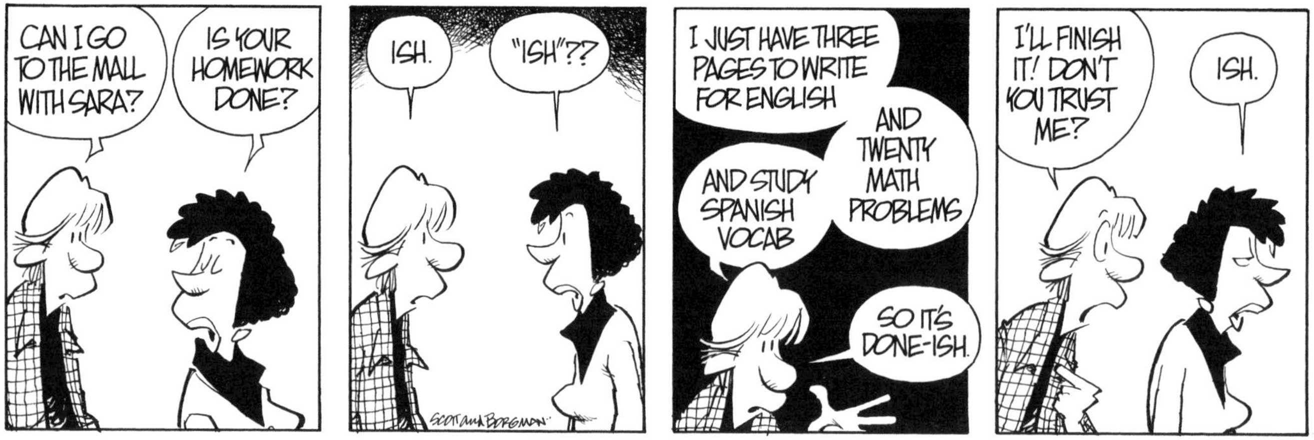
CAN I GO TO THE MALL WITH SARA?
IS YOUR HOMEWORK DONE?
ISH.
"ISH"??
I JUST HAVE THREE PAGES TO WRITE FOR ENGLISH
AND TWENTY MATH PROBLEMS
AND STUDY SPANISH VOCAB
SO IT'S DONE-ISH.
I'LL FINISH IT! DON'T YOU TRUST ME?
ISH.

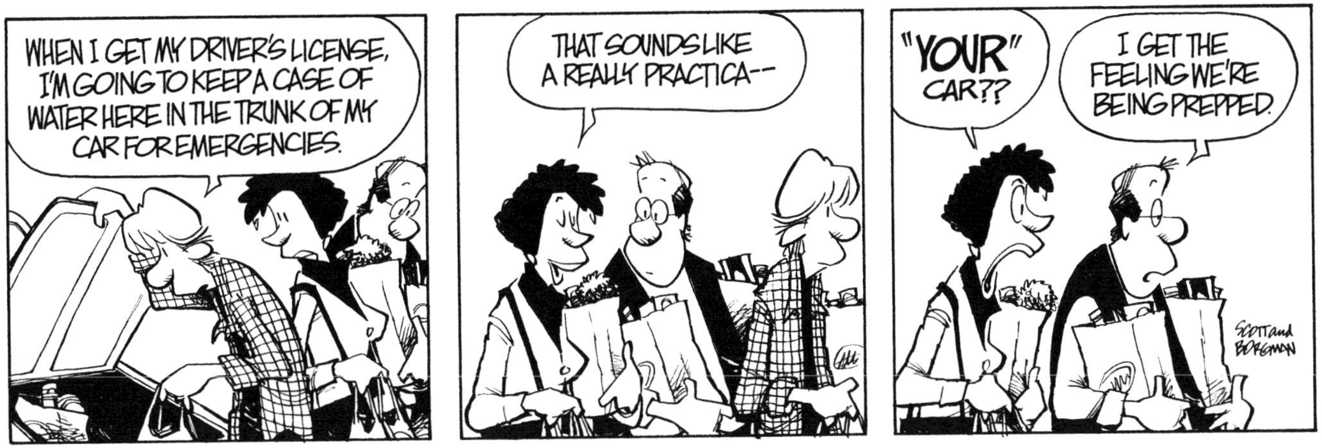
WHEN I GET MY DRIVER'S LICENSE, I'M GOING TO KEEP A CASE OF WATER HERE IN THE TRUNK OF MY CAR FOR EMERGENCIES.
THAT SOUNDS LIKE A REALLY PRACTICA--
"YOUR" CAR??
I GET THE FEELING WE'RE BEING PREPPED.

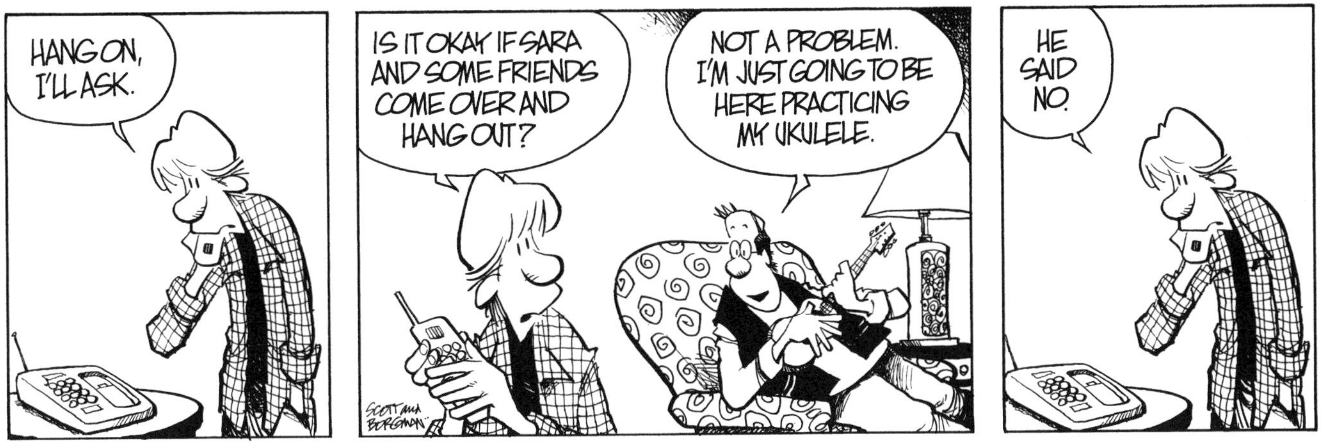
HANG ON, I'LL ASK.
IS IT OKAY IF SARA AND SOME FRIENDS COME OVER AND HANG OUT?
NOT A PROBLEM. I'M JUST GOING TO BE HERE PRACTICING MY UKULELE.
HE SAID NO.

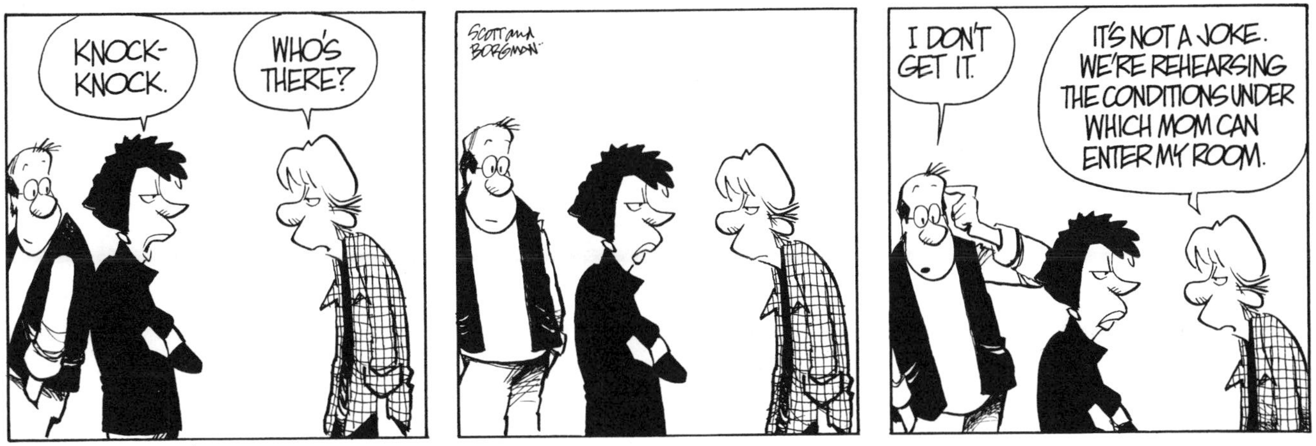
KNOCK-KNOCK.
WHO'S THERE?
I DON'T GET IT.
IT'S NOT A JOKE. WE'RE REHEARSING THE CONDITIONS UNDER WHICH MOM CAN ENTER MY ROOM.

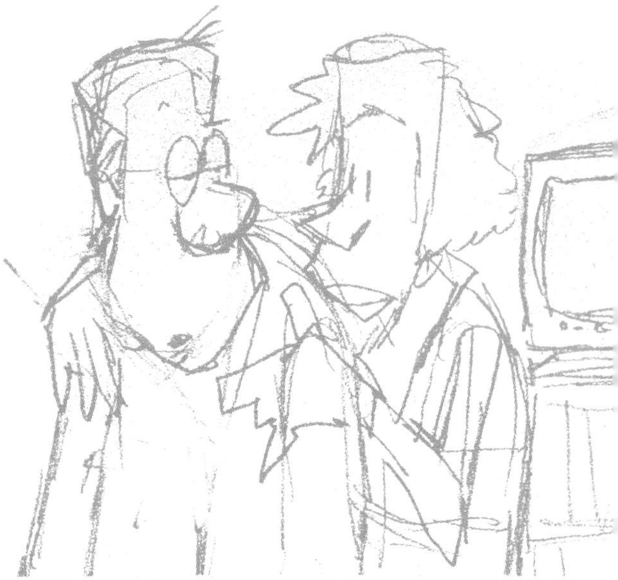

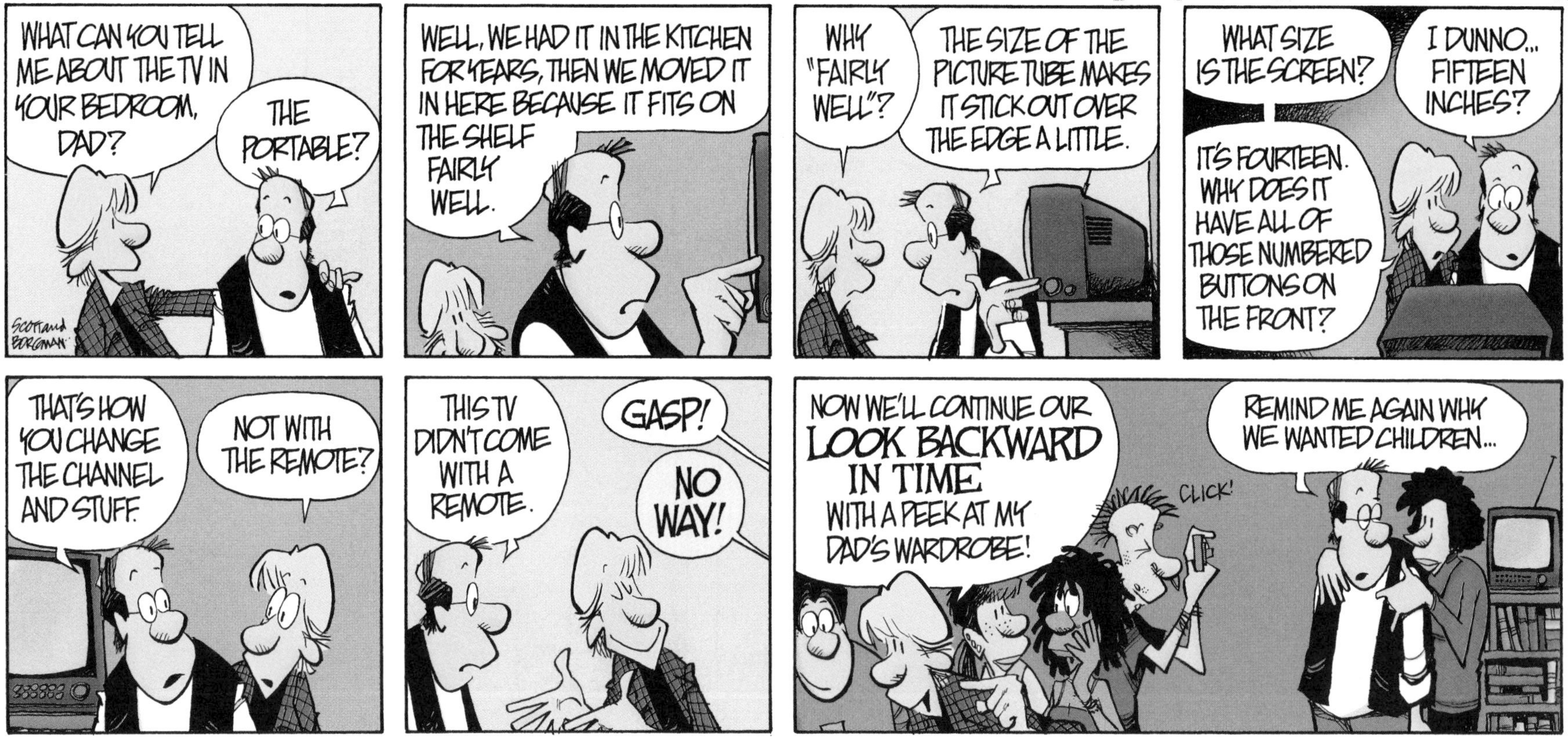

WHAT CAN YOU TELL ME ABOUT THE TV IN YOUR BEDROOM, DAD?
THE PORTABLE?
SCOTT and BORGMAN
WELL, WE HAD IT IN THE KITCHEN FOR YEARS, THEN WE MOVED IT IN HERE BECAUSE IT FITS ON THE SHELF FAIRLY WELL.
WHY "FAIRLY WELL"?
THE SIZE OF THE PICTURE TUBE MAKES IT STICK OUT OVER THE EDGE A LITTLE.
WHAT SIZE IS THE SCREEN?
I DUNNO... FIFTEEN INCHES?
IT'S FOURTEEN. WHY DOES IT HAVE ALL OF THOSE NUMBERED BUTTONS ON THE FRONT?
THAT'S HOW YOU CHANGE THE CHANNEL AND STUFF.
NOT WITH THE REMOTE?
THIS TV DIDN'T COME WITH A REMOTE.
GASP!
NO WAY!
NOW WE'LL CONTINUE OUR LOOK BACKWARD IN TIME WITH A PEEK AT MY DAD'S WARDROBE!
CLICK!
REMIND ME AGAIN WHY WE WANTED CHILDREN...

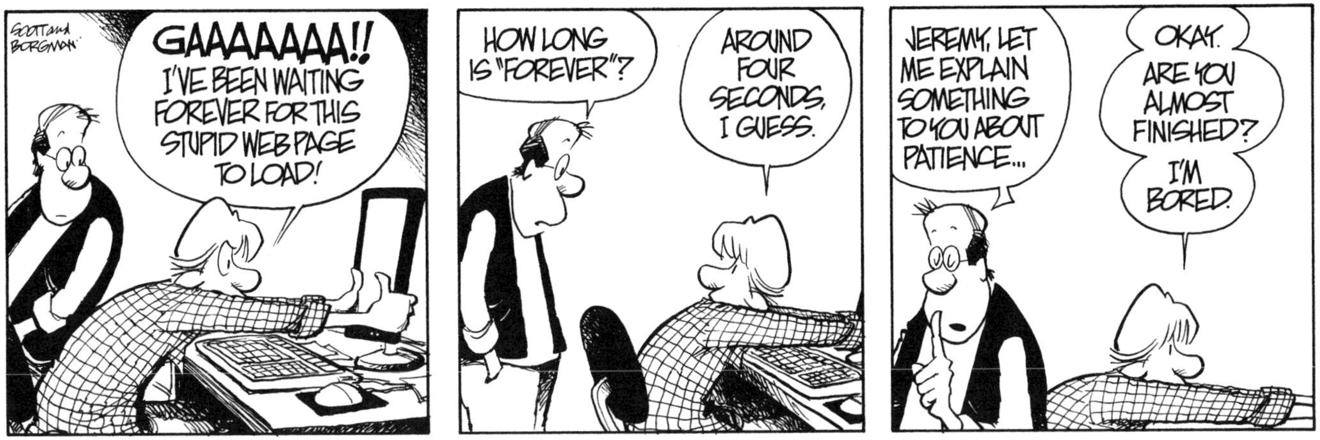
SCOTT and BORGMAN
GAAAAAAA!! I'VE BEEN WAITING FOREVER FOR THIS STUPID WEB PAGE TO LOAD!
HOW LONG IS "FOREVER"?
AROUND FOUR SECONDS, I GUESS.
JEREMY, LET ME EXPLAIN SOMETHING TO YOU ABOUT PATIENCE...
OKAY.
ARE YOU ALMOST FINISHED?
I'M BORED.

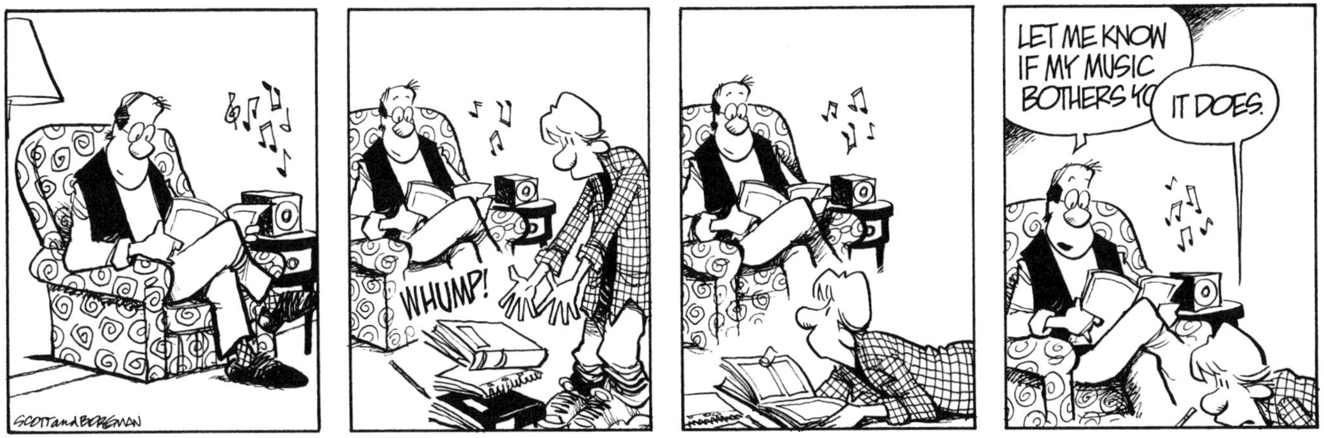
SCOTT and BORGMAN
WHUMP!
LET ME KNOW IF MY MUSIC BOTHERS YO
IT DOES.

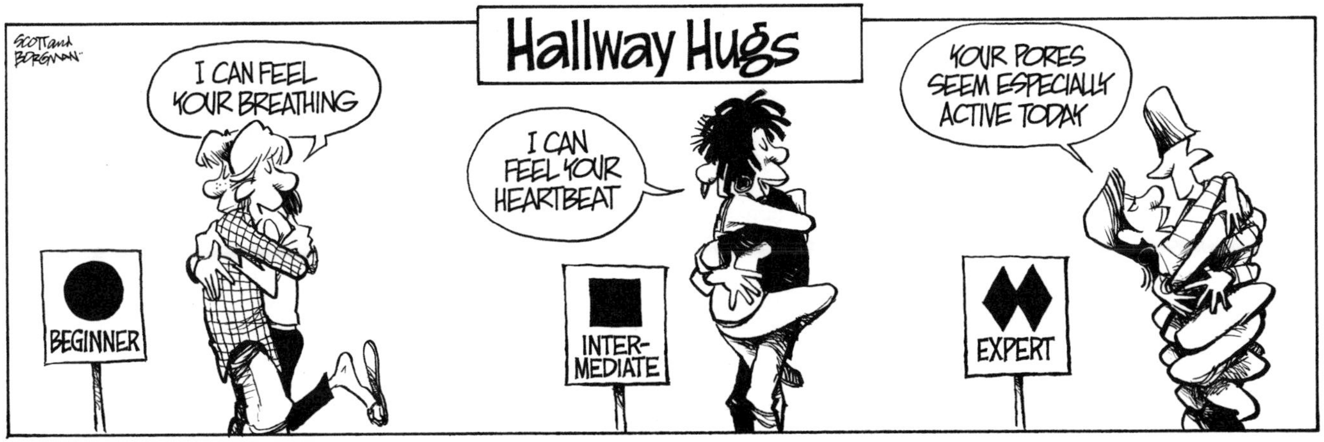
Hallway Hugs
SCOTT and BORGMAN
I CAN FEEL YOUR BREATHING
BEGINNER
I CAN FEEL YOUR HEARTBEAT
INTER-MEDIATE
YOUR PORES SEEM ESPECIALLY ACTIVE TODAY
EXPERT

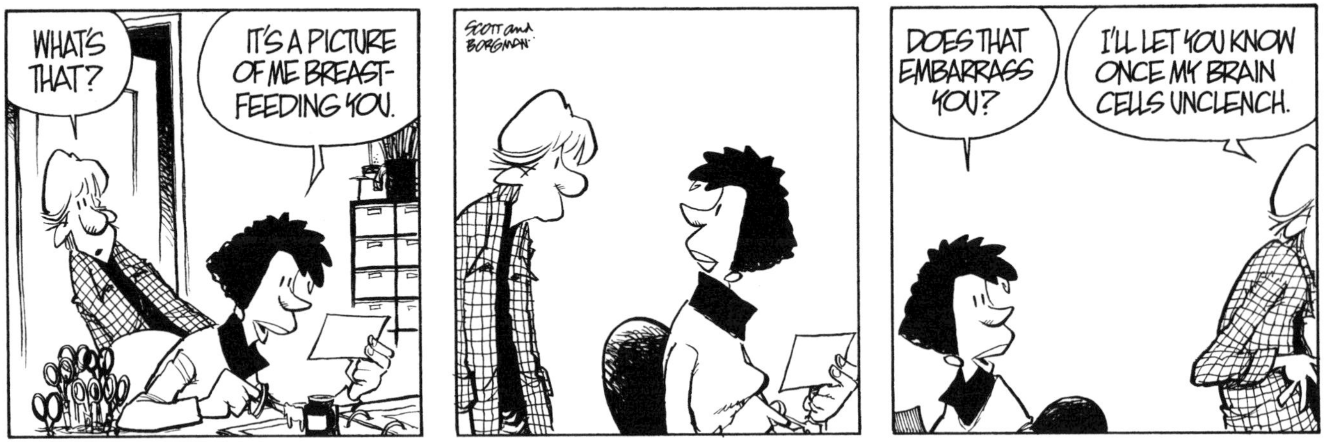
WHAT'S THAT?
IT'S A PICTURE OF ME BREAST-FEEDING YOU.
SCOTT and BORGMAN
DOES THAT EMBARRASS YOU?
I'LL LET YOU KNOW ONCE MY BRAIN CELLS UNCLENCH.

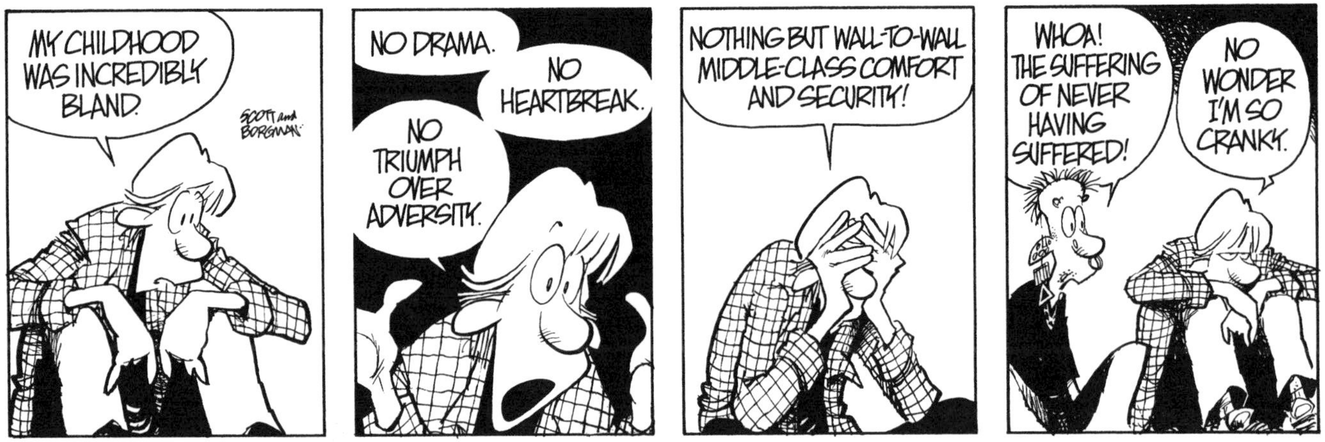
MY CHILDHOOD WAS INCREDIBLY BLAND.
SCOTT and BORGMAN
NO DRAMA.
NO HEARTBREAK.
NO TRIUMPH OVER ADVERSITY.
NOTHING BUT WALL-TO-WALL MIDDLE-CLASS COMFORT AND SECURITY!
WHOA! THE SUFFERING OF NEVER HAVING SUFFERED!
NO WONDER I'M SO CRANKY.

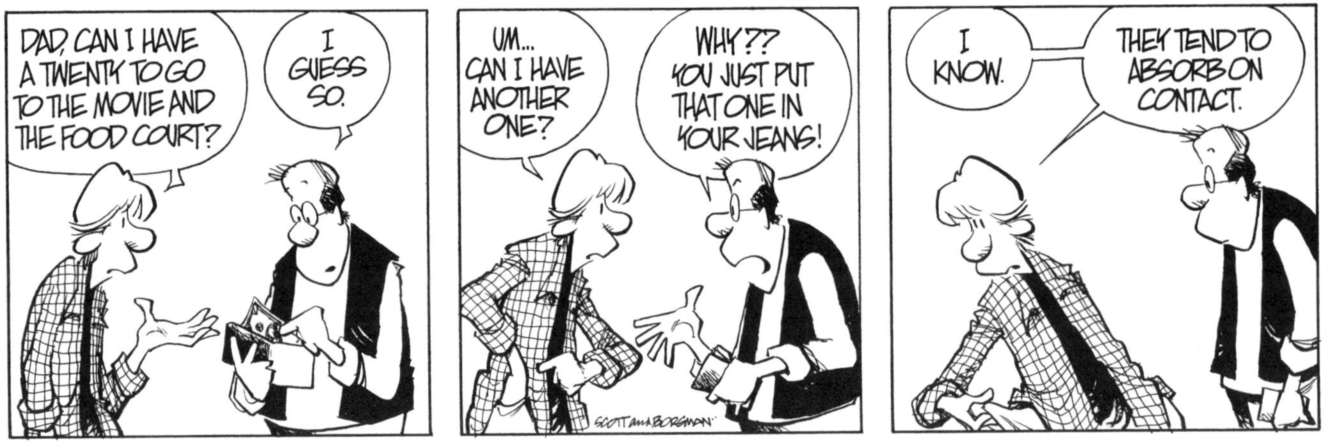
DAD, CAN I HAVE A TWENTY TO GO TO THE MOVIE AND THE FOOD COURT?
I GUESS SO.
UM... CAN I HAVE ANOTHER ONE?
WHY?? YOU JUST PUT THAT ONE IN YOUR JEANS!
SCOTT and BORGMAN
I KNOW.
THEY TEND TO ABSORB ON CONTACT.

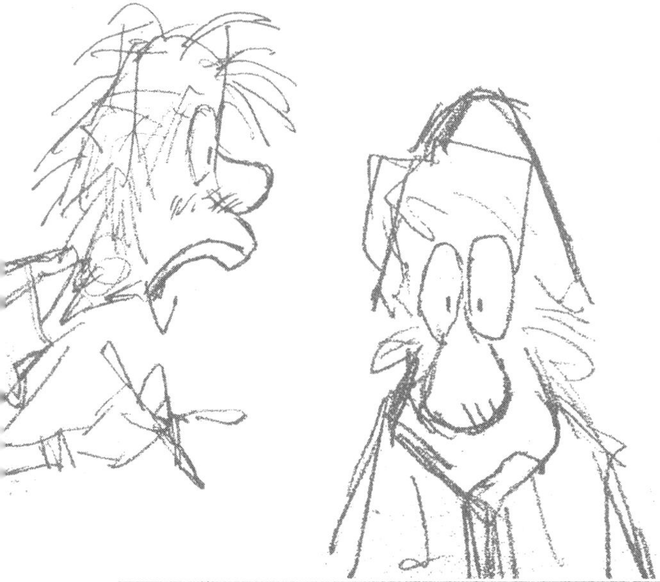

Zits

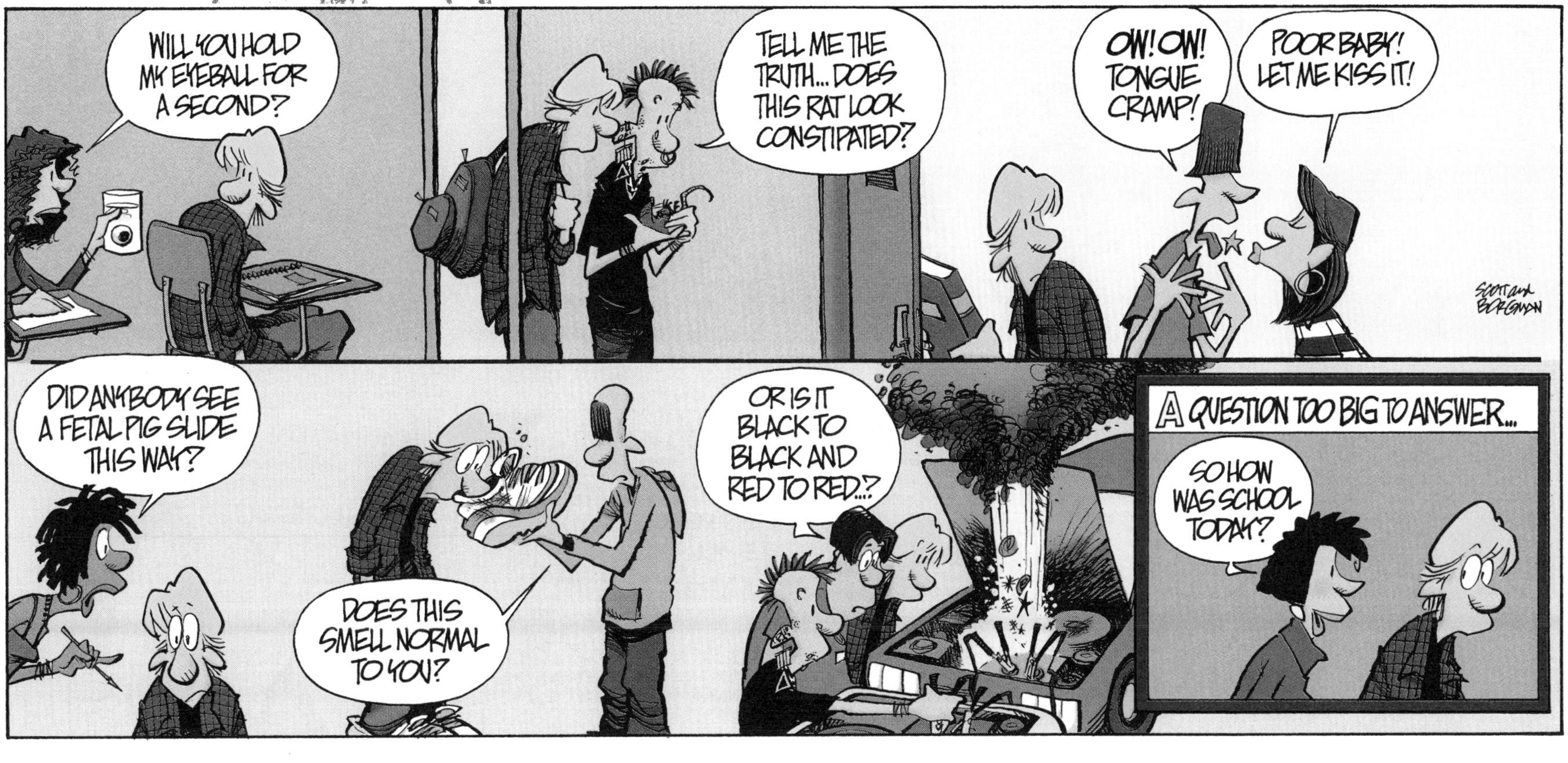
WILL YOU HOLD MY EYEBALL FOR A SECOND?
TELL ME THE TRUTH... DOES THIS RAT LOOK CONSTIPATED?
OW! OW! TONGUE CRAMP!
POOR BABY! LET ME KISS IT!
DID ANYBODY SEE A FETAL PIG SLIDE THIS WAY?
DOES THIS SMELL NORMAL TO YOU?
OR IS IT BLACK TO BLACK AND RED TO RED...?
A QUESTION TOO BIG TO ANSWER...
SO HOW WAS SCHOOL TODAY?

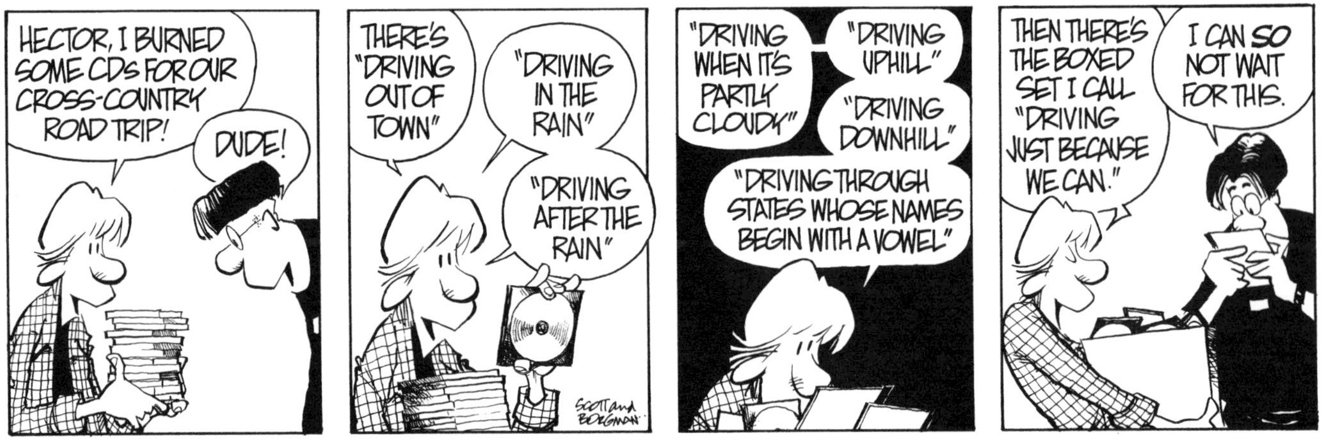
HECTOR, I BURNED SOME CDs FOR OUR CROSS-COUNTRY ROAD TRIP!
DUDE!
THERE'S "DRIVING OUT OF TOWN"
"DRIVING IN THE RAIN"
"DRIVING AFTER THE RAIN"
"DRIVING WHEN IT'S PARTLY CLOUDY"
"DRIVING UPHILL"
"DRIVING DOWNHILL"
"DRIVING THROUGH STATES WHOSE NAMES BEGIN WITH A VOWEL"
THEN THERE'S THE BOXED SET I CALL "DRIVING JUST BECAUSE WE CAN."
I CAN SO NOT WAIT FOR THIS.

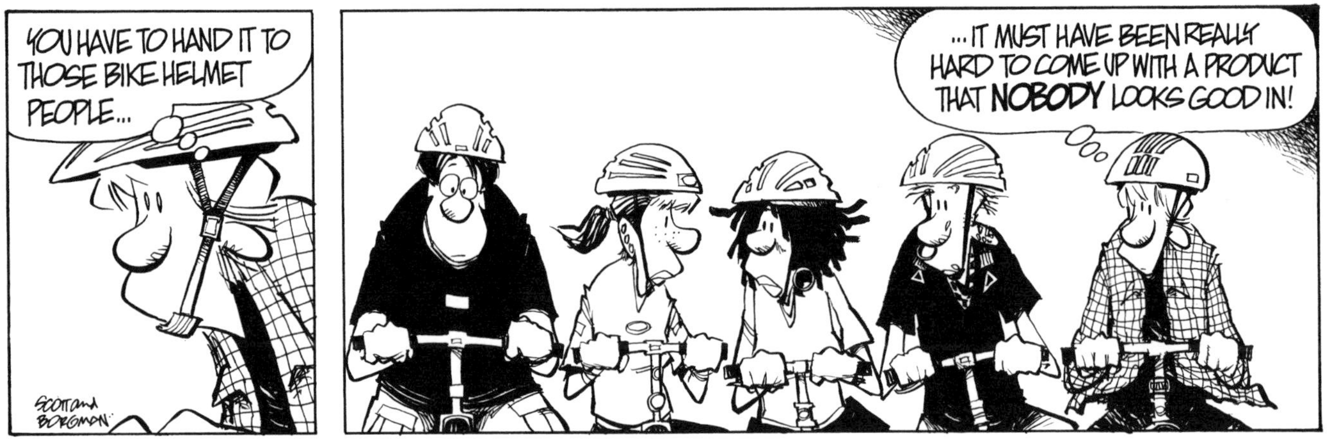
YOU HAVE TO HAND IT TO THOSE BIKE HELMET PEOPLE...
...IT MUST HAVE BEEN REALLY HARD TO COME UP WITH A PRODUCT THAT NOBODY LOOKS GOOD IN!

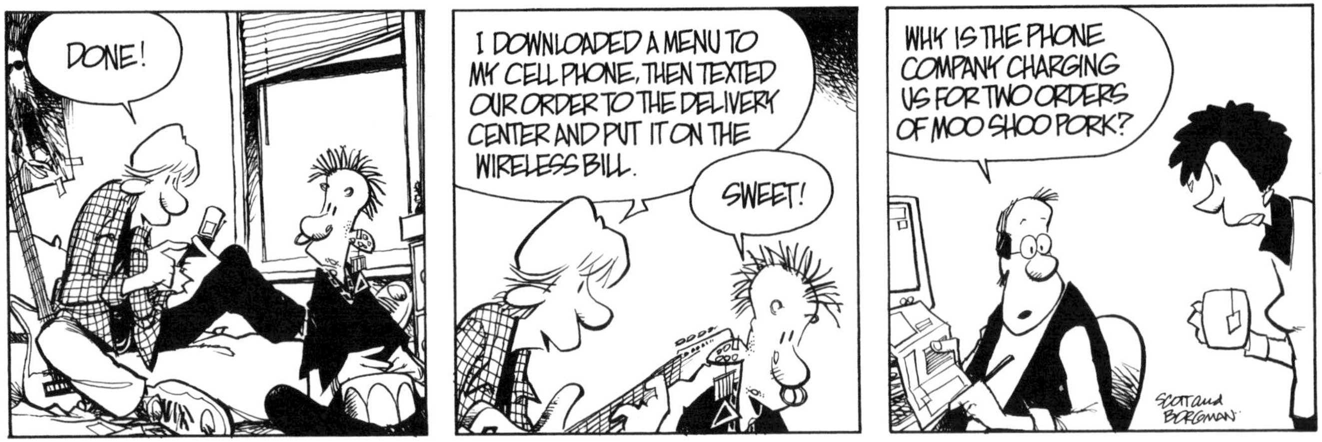
DONE!
I DOWNLOADED A MENU TO MY CELL PHONE, THEN TEXTED OUR ORDER TO THE DELIVERY CENTER AND PUT IT ON THE WIRELESS BILL.
SWEET!
WHY IS THE PHONE COMPANY CHARGING US FOR TWO ORDERS OF MOO SHOO PORK?

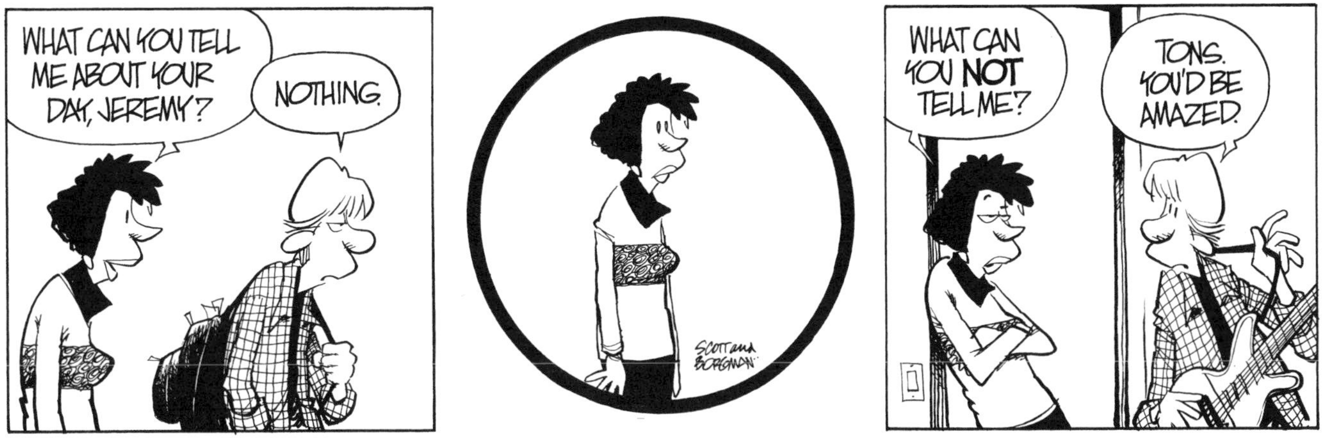
WHAT CAN YOU TELL ME ABOUT YOUR DAY, JEREMY?
NOTHING.
WHAT CAN YOU **NOT** TELL ME?
TONS. YOU'D BE AMAZED.

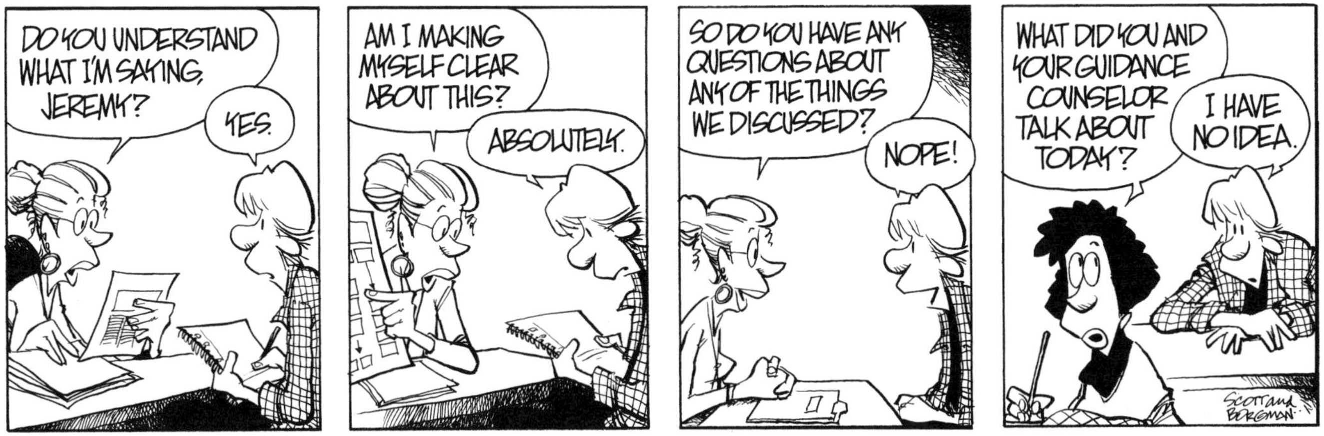
DO YOU UNDERSTAND WHAT I'M SAYING, JEREMY?
YES.
AM I MAKING MYSELF CLEAR ABOUT THIS?
ABSOLUTELY.
SO DO YOU HAVE ANY QUESTIONS ABOUT ANY OF THE THINGS WE DISCUSSED?
NOPE!
WHAT DID YOU AND YOUR GUIDANCE COUNSELOR TALK ABOUT TODAY?
I HAVE NO IDEA.

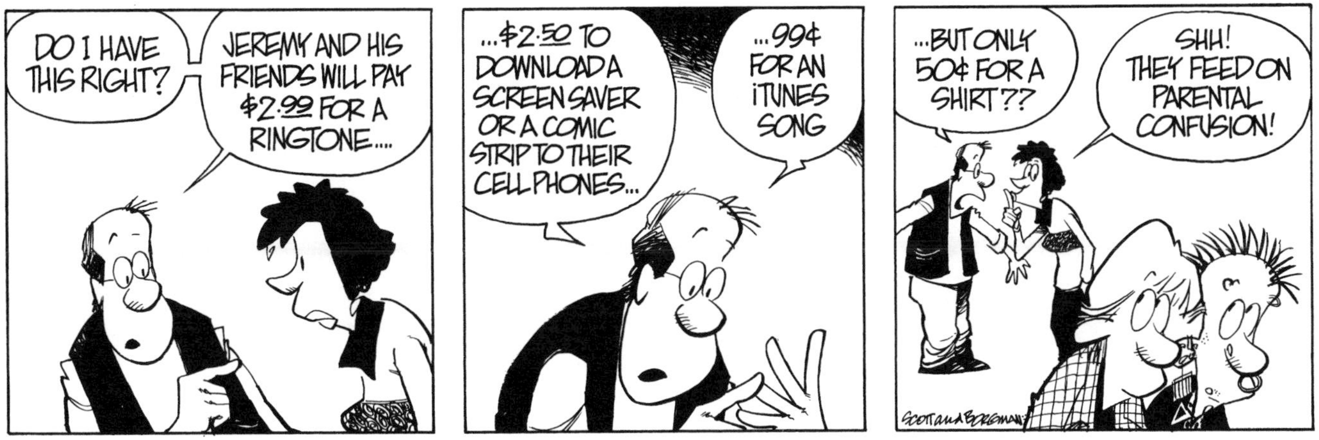
DO I HAVE THIS RIGHT?
JEREMY AND HIS FRIENDS WILL PAY $2.99 FOR A RINGTONE....
...$2.50 TO DOWNLOAD A SCREEN SAVER OR A COMIC STRIP TO THEIR CELL PHONES...
...99¢ FOR AN iTUNES SONG
...BUT ONLY 50¢ FOR A SHIRT??
SHH! THEY FEED ON PARENTAL CONFUSION!

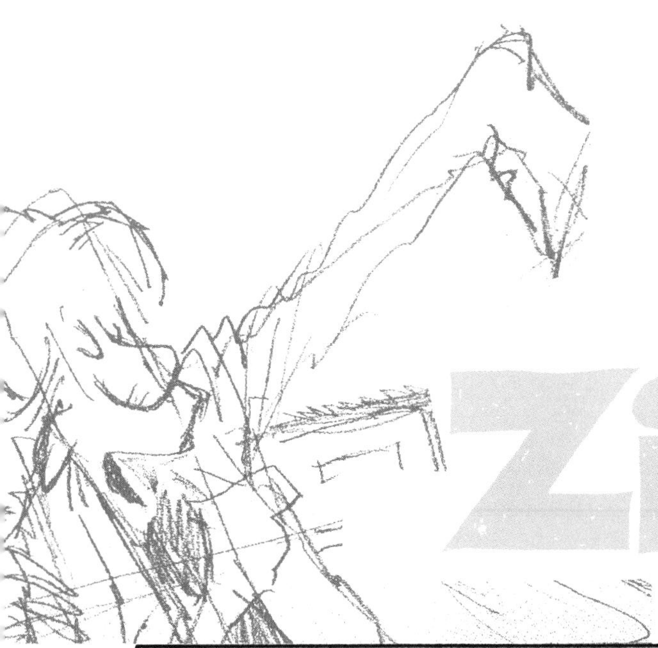

Zits

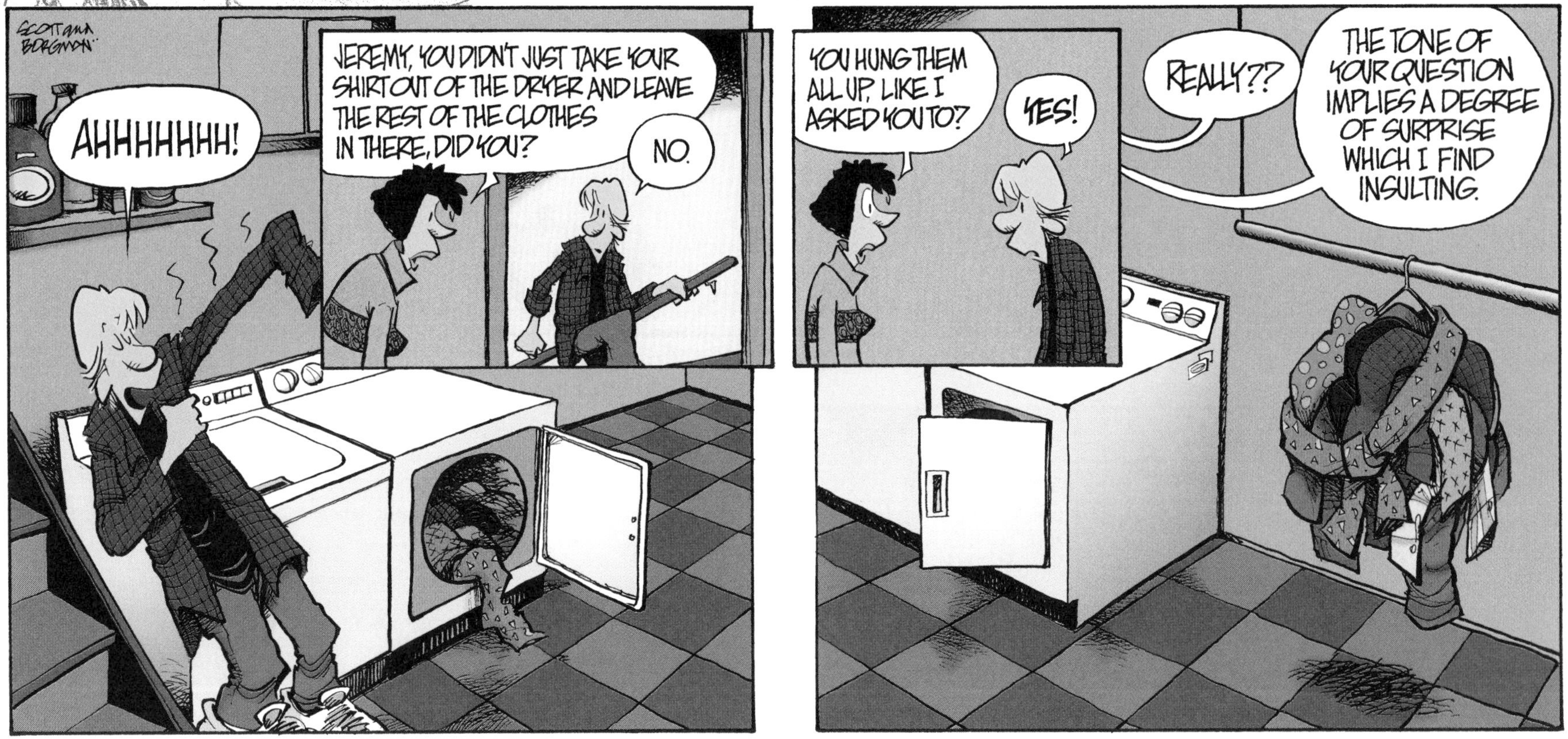

AHHHHHHH!
JEREMY, YOU DIDN'T JUST TAKE YOUR SHIRT OUT OF THE DRYER AND LEAVE THE REST OF THE CLOTHES IN THERE, DID YOU?
NO.
YOU HUNG THEM ALL UP, LIKE I ASKED YOU TO?
YES!
REALLY??
THE TONE OF YOUR QUESTION IMPLIES A DEGREE OF SURPRISE WHICH I FIND INSULTING.

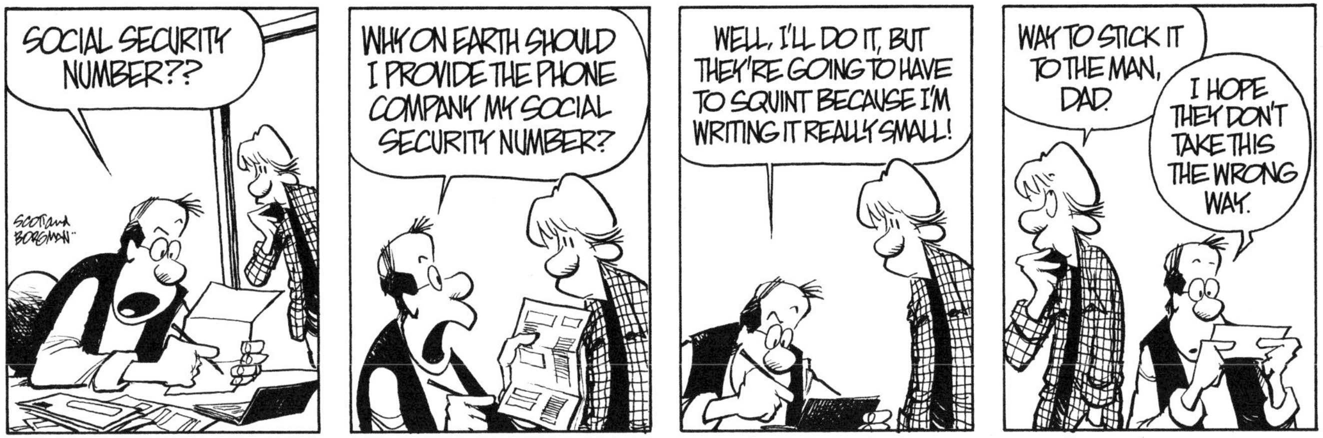
SOCIAL SECURITY NUMBER??
WHY ON EARTH SHOULD I PROVIDE THE PHONE COMPANY MY SOCIAL SECURITY NUMBER?
WELL, I'LL DO IT, BUT THEY'RE GOING TO HAVE TO SQUINT BECAUSE I'M WRITING IT REALLY SMALL!
WAY TO STICK IT TO THE MAN, DAD.
I HOPE THEY DON'T TAKE THIS THE WRONG WAY.

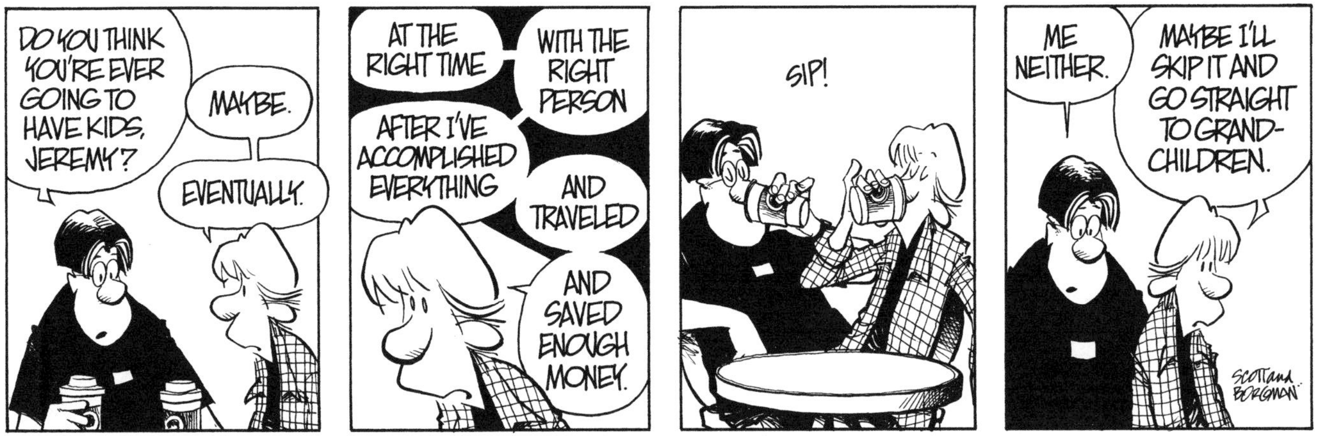
DO YOU THINK YOU'RE EVER GOING TO HAVE KIDS, JEREMY?
MAYBE.
EVENTUALLY.
AT THE RIGHT TIME
WITH THE RIGHT PERSON
AFTER I'VE ACCOMPLISHED EVERYTHING
AND TRAVELED
AND SAVED ENOUGH MONEY.
SIP!
ME NEITHER.
MAYBE I'LL SKIP IT AND GO STRAIGHT TO GRAND-CHILDREN.

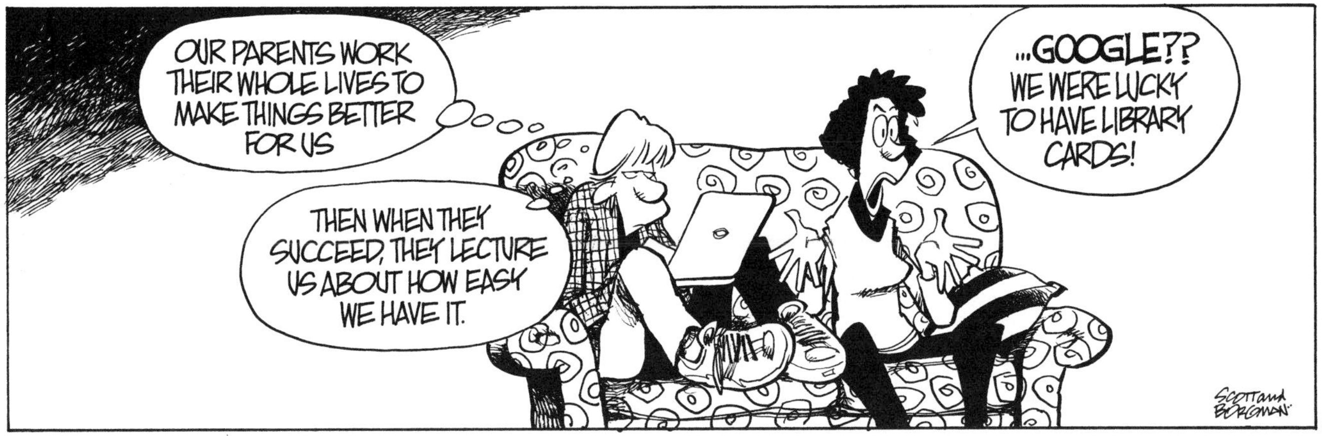
OUR PARENTS WORK THEIR WHOLE LIVES TO MAKE THINGS BETTER FOR US
THEN WHEN THEY SUCCEED, THEY LECTURE US ABOUT HOW EASY WE HAVE IT.
...GOOGLE?? WE WERE LUCKY TO HAVE LIBRARY CARDS!

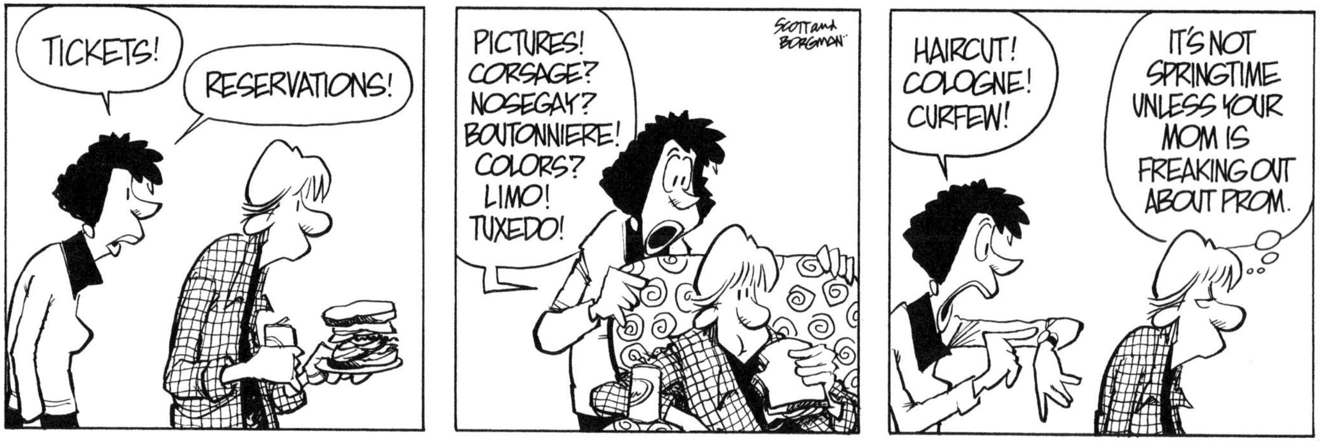
TICKETS!
RESERVATIONS!
PICTURES! CORSAGE? NOSEGAY? BOUTONNIERE! COLORS? LIMO! TUXEDO!
HAIRCUT! COLOGNE! CURFEW!
IT'S NOT SPRINGTIME UNLESS YOUR MOM IS FREAKING OUT ABOUT PROM.

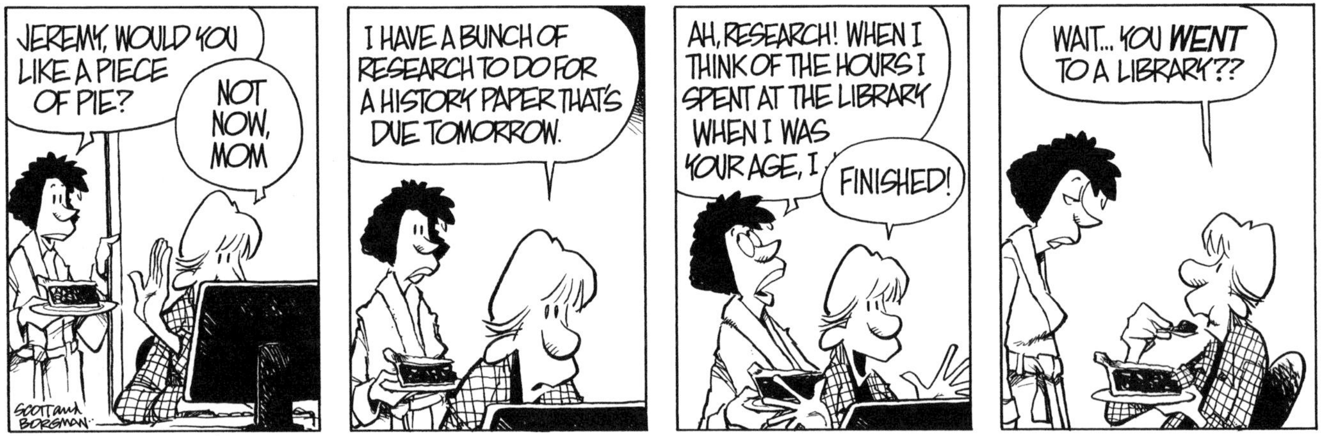
JEREMY, WOULD YOU LIKE A PIECE OF PIE?
NOT NOW, MOM
I HAVE A BUNCH OF RESEARCH TO DO FOR A HISTORY PAPER THAT'S DUE TOMORROW.
AH, RESEARCH! WHEN I THINK OF THE HOURS I SPENT AT THE LIBRARY WHEN I WAS YOUR AGE, I
FINISHED!
WAIT... YOU **WENT** TO A LIBRARY??

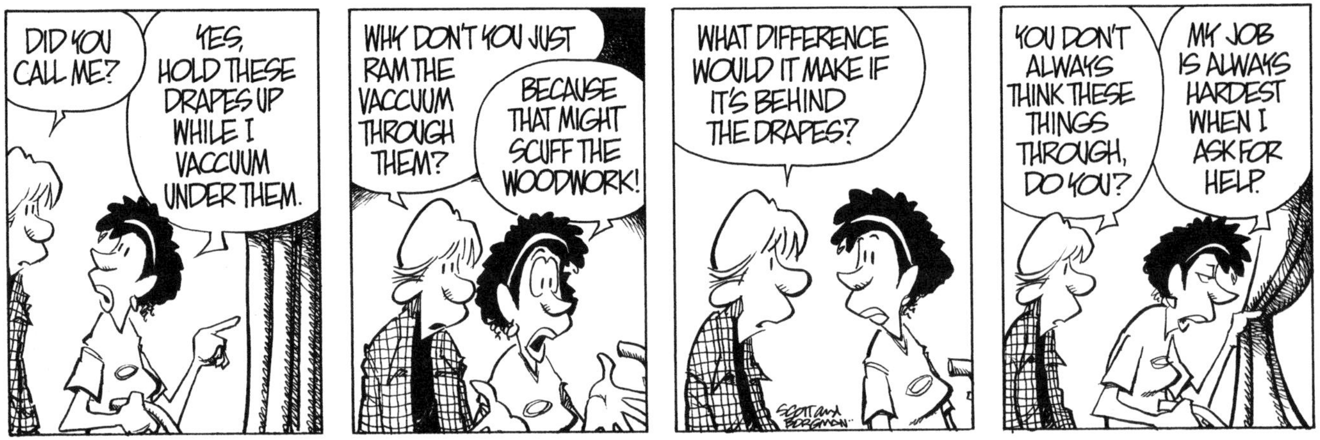
DID YOU CALL ME?
YES, HOLD THESE DRAPES UP WHILE I VACCUUM UNDER THEM.
WHY DON'T YOU JUST RAM THE VACCUUM THROUGH THEM?
BECAUSE THAT MIGHT SCUFF THE WOODWORK!
WHAT DIFFERENCE WOULD IT MAKE IF IT'S BEHIND THE DRAPES?
YOU DON'T ALWAYS THINK THESE THINGS THROUGH, DO YOU?
MY JOB IS ALWAYS HARDEST WHEN I ASK FOR HELP.

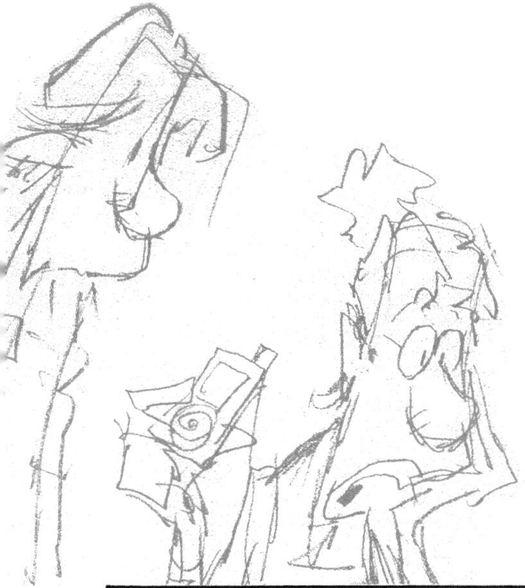

Zits

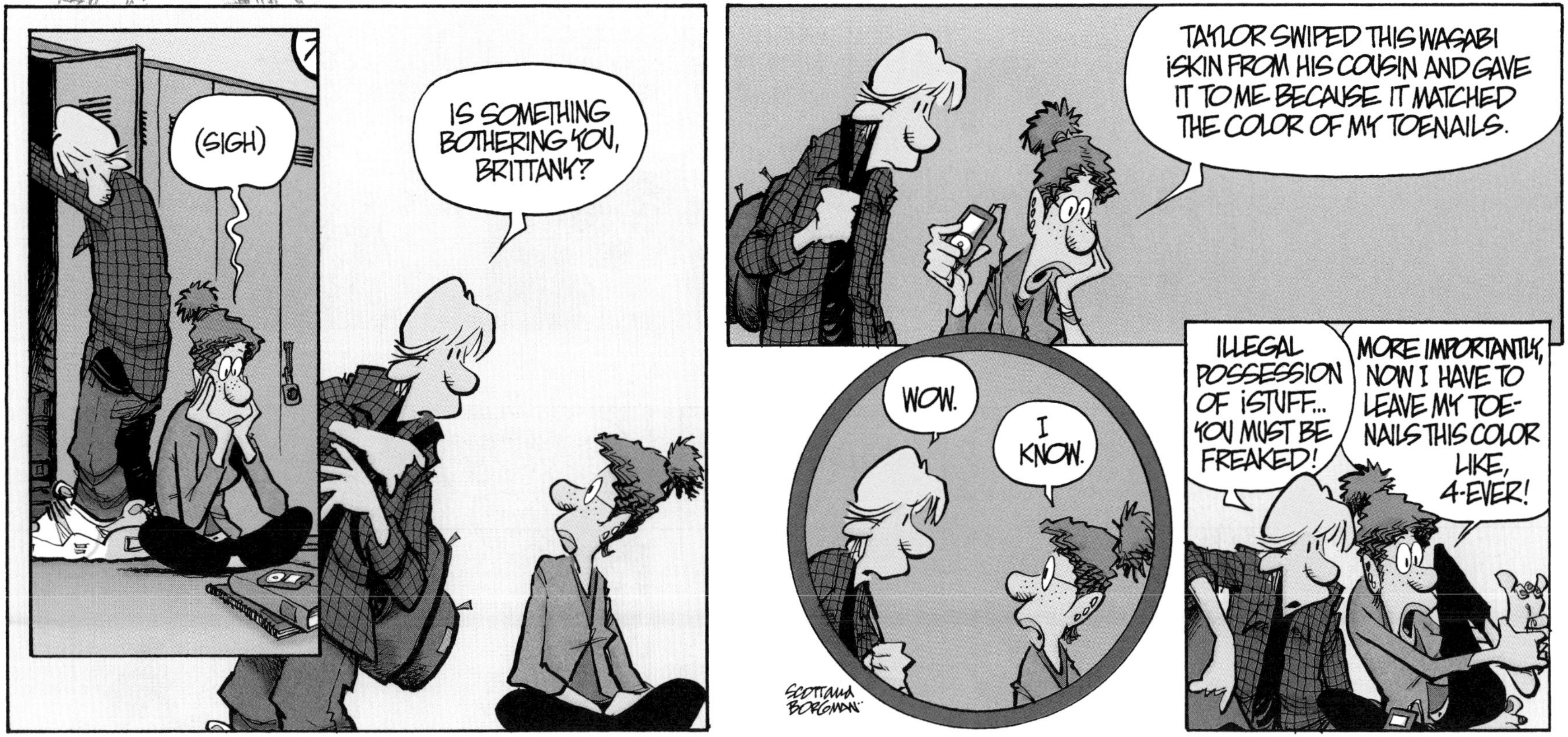

(SIGH)
IS SOMETHING BOTHERING YOU, BRITTANY?
TAYLOR SWIPED THIS WASABI iSKIN FROM HIS COUSIN AND GAVE IT TO ME BECAUSE IT MATCHED THE COLOR OF MY TOENAILS.
WOW.
I KNOW.
ILLEGAL POSSESSION OF iSTUFF... YOU MUST BE FREAKED!
MORE IMPORTANTLY, NOW I HAVE TO LEAVE MY TOE-NAILS THIS COLOR LIKE, 4-EVER!

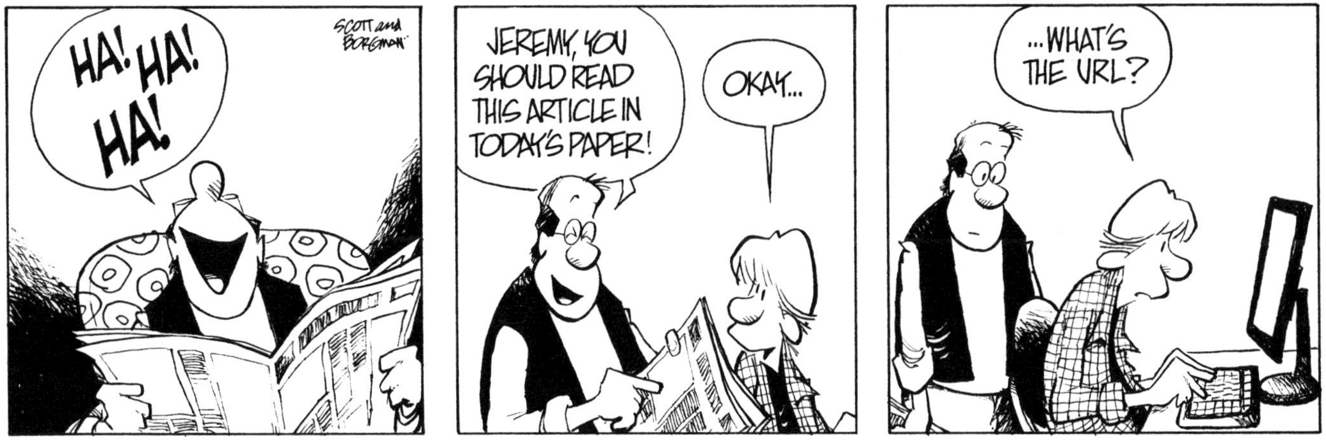
SCOTT and BORGMAN
HA! HA! HA!
JEREMY, YOU SHOULD READ THIS ARTICLE IN TODAY'S PAPER!
OKAY...
...WHAT'S THE URL?

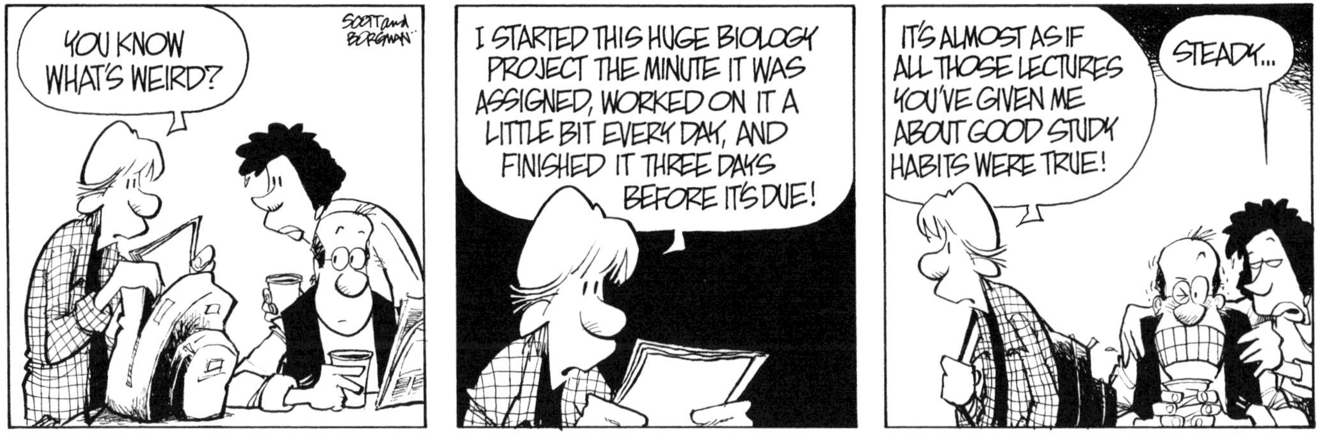
SCOTT and BORGMAN
YOU KNOW WHAT'S WEIRD?
I STARTED THIS HUGE BIOLOGY PROJECT THE MINUTE IT WAS ASSIGNED, WORKED ON IT A LITTLE BIT EVERY DAY, AND FINISHED IT THREE DAYS BEFORE IT'S DUE!
IT'S ALMOST AS IF ALL THOSE LECTURES YOU'VE GIVEN ME ABOUT GOOD STUDY HABITS WERE TRUE!
STEADY...

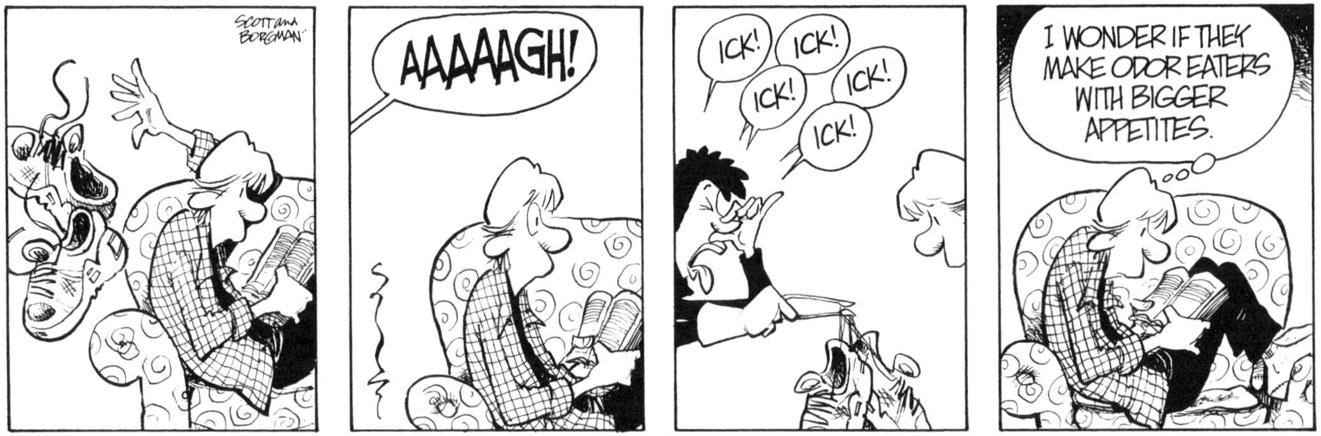
SCOTT and BORGMAN
AAAAAGH!
ICK!
ICK!
ICK!
ICK!
ICK!
I WONDER IF THEY MAKE ODOR EATERS WITH BIGGER APPETITES.

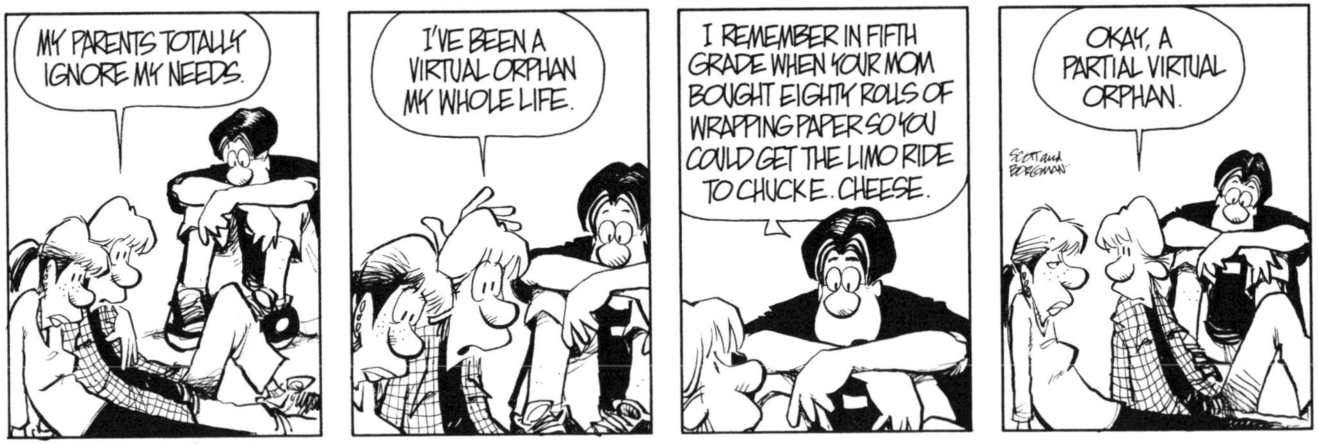
MY PARENTS TOTALLY IGNORE MY NEEDS.
I'VE BEEN A VIRTUAL ORPHAN MY WHOLE LIFE.
I REMEMBER IN FIFTH GRADE WHEN YOUR MOM BOUGHT EIGHTY ROLLS OF WRAPPING PAPER SO YOU COULD GET THE LIMO RIDE TO CHUCK E. CHEESE.
OKAY, A PARTIAL VIRTUAL ORPHAN.
SCOTT AND BORGMAN

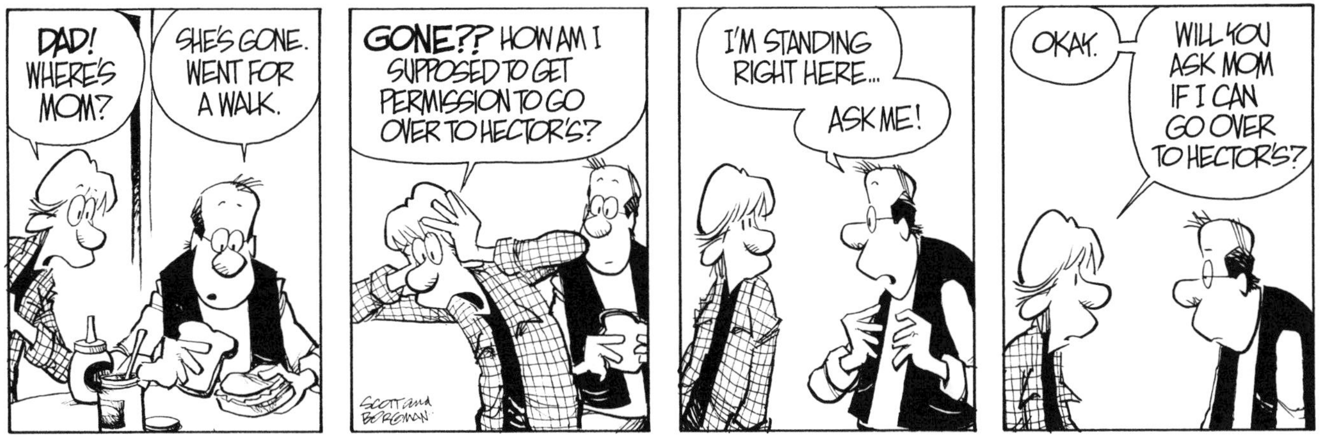
DAD! WHERE'S MOM?
SHE'S GONE. WENT FOR A WALK.
GONE?? HOW AM I SUPPOSED TO GET PERMISSION TO GO OVER TO HECTOR'S?
SCOTT AND BORGMAN
I'M STANDING RIGHT HERE...
ASK ME!
OKAY.
WILL YOU ASK MOM IF I CAN GO OVER TO HECTOR'S?

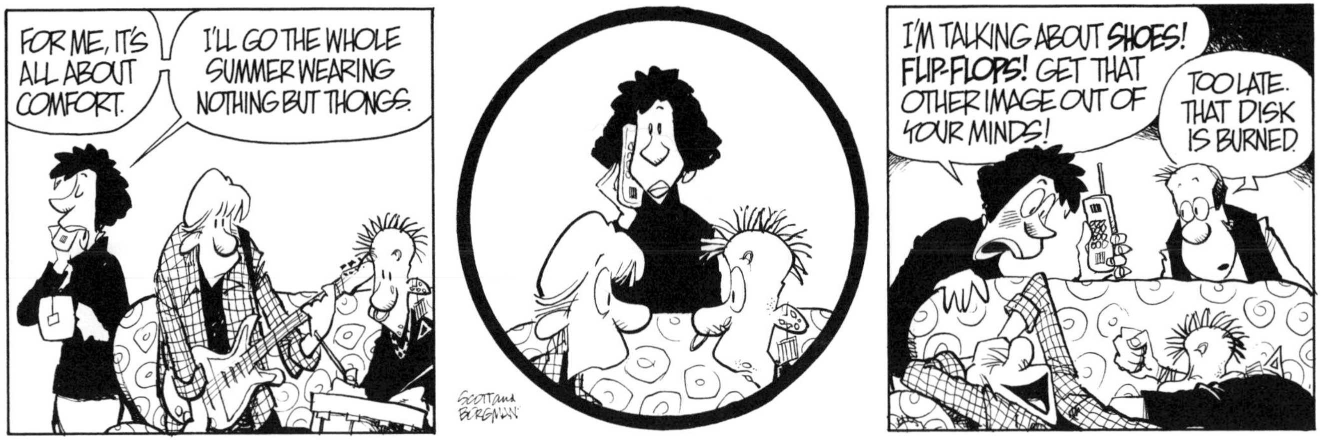
FOR ME, IT'S ALL ABOUT COMFORT.
I'LL GO THE WHOLE SUMMER WEARING NOTHING BUT THONGS.
SCOTT AND BORGMAN
I'M TALKING ABOUT SHOES! FLIP-FLOPS! GET THAT OTHER IMAGE OUT OF YOUR MINDS!
TOO LATE. THAT DISK IS BURNED.

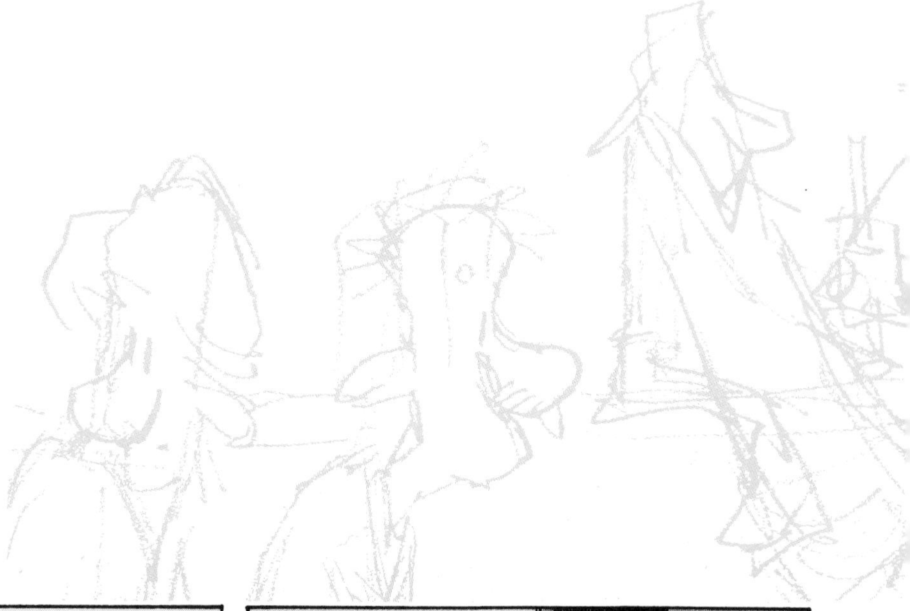

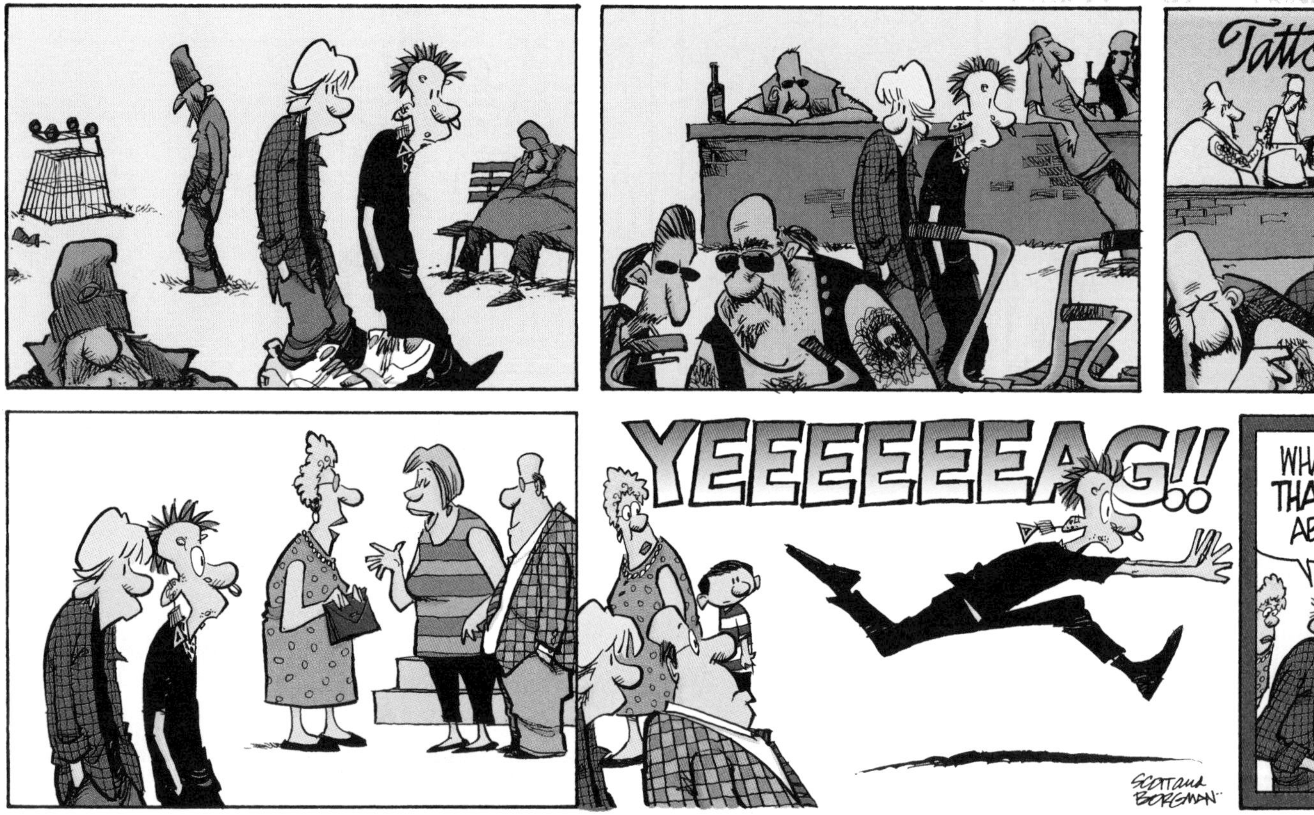
Tattoos
YEEEEEEEAG!!
WHAT WAS THAT ALL ABOUT?
BORING PEOPLE SCARE ME.

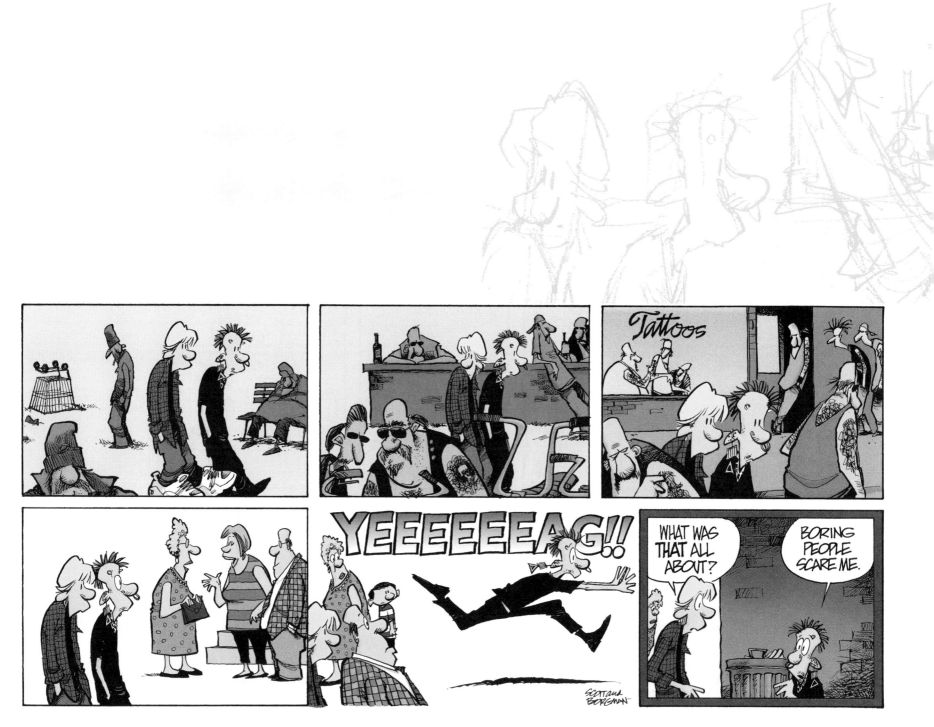

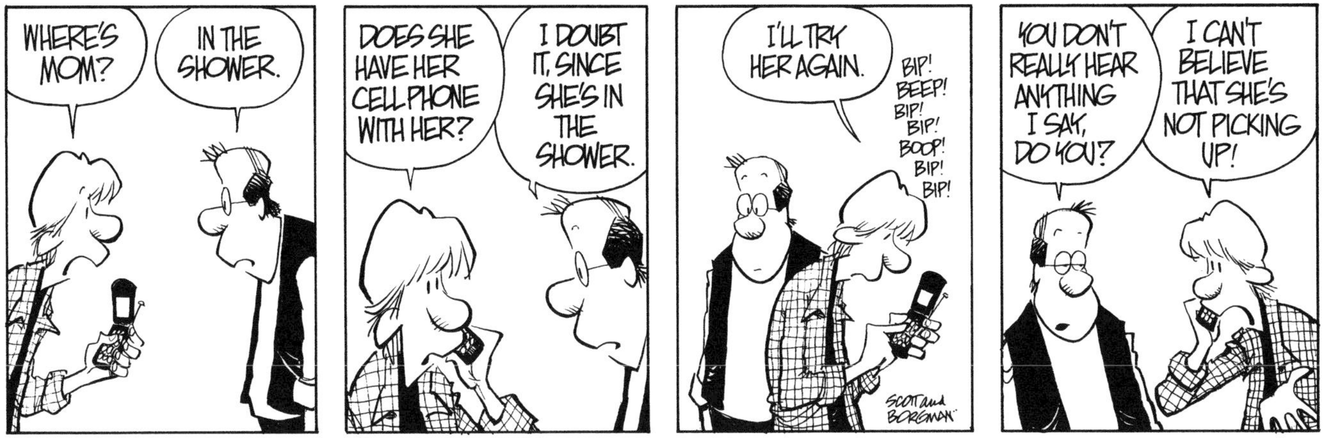
WHERE'S MOM?
IN THE SHOWER.
DOES SHE HAVE HER CELL PHONE WITH HER?
I DOUBT IT, SINCE SHE'S IN THE SHOWER.
I'LL TRY HER AGAIN.
BIP! BEEP! BIP! BIP! BOOP! BIP! BIP!
SCOTT and BORGMAN
YOU DON'T REALLY HEAR ANYTHING I SAY, DO YOU?
I CAN'T BELIEVE THAT SHE'S NOT PICKING UP!

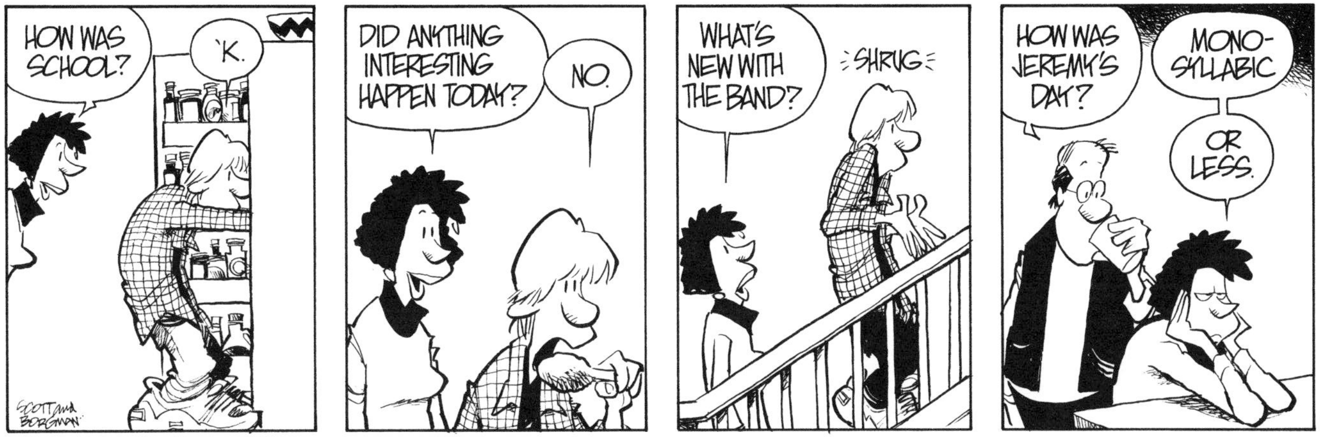
HOW WAS SCHOOL?
'K.
SCOTT and BORGMAN
DID ANYTHING INTERESTING HAPPEN TODAY?
NO.
WHAT'S NEW WITH THE BAND?
SHRUG
HOW WAS JEREMY'S DAY?
MONO-SYLLABIC
OR LESS.

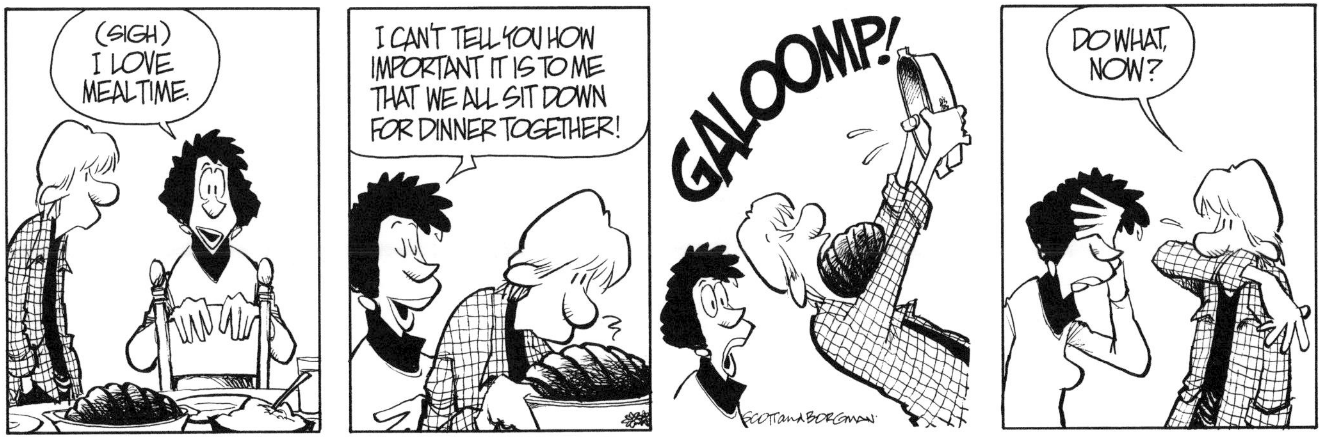
(SIGH) I LOVE MEALTIME.
I CAN'T TELL YOU HOW IMPORTANT IT IS TO ME THAT WE ALL SIT DOWN FOR DINNER TOGETHER!
GALOOMP!
SCOTT and BORGMAN
DO WHAT, NOW?

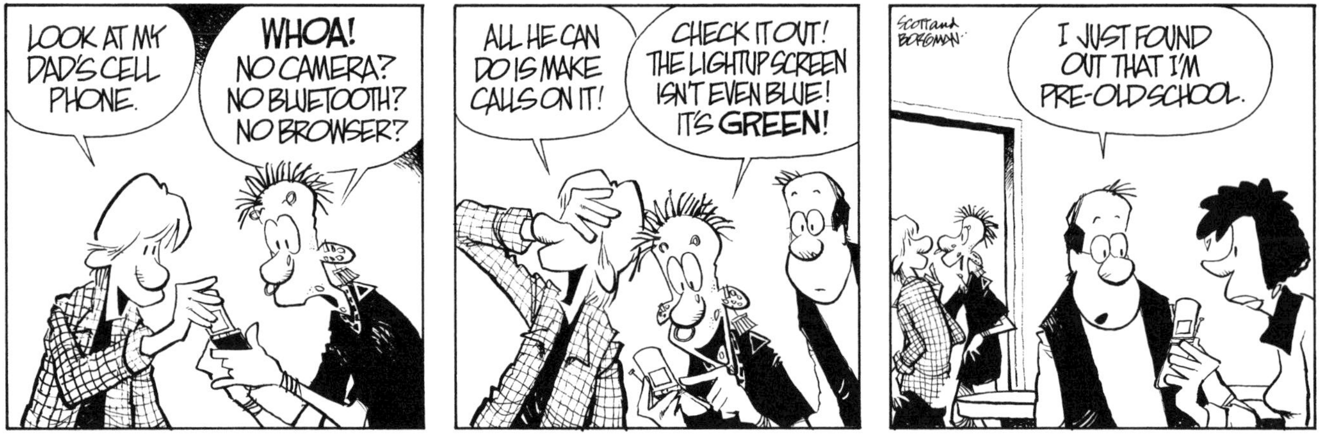
LOOK AT MY DAD'S CELL PHONE.
WHOA! NO CAMERA? NO BLUETOOTH? NO BROWSER?
ALL HE CAN DO IS MAKE CALLS ON IT!
CHECK IT OUT! THE LIGHTUP SCREEN ISN'T EVEN BLUE! IT'S GREEN!
I JUST FOUND OUT THAT I'M PRE-OLD SCHOOL.

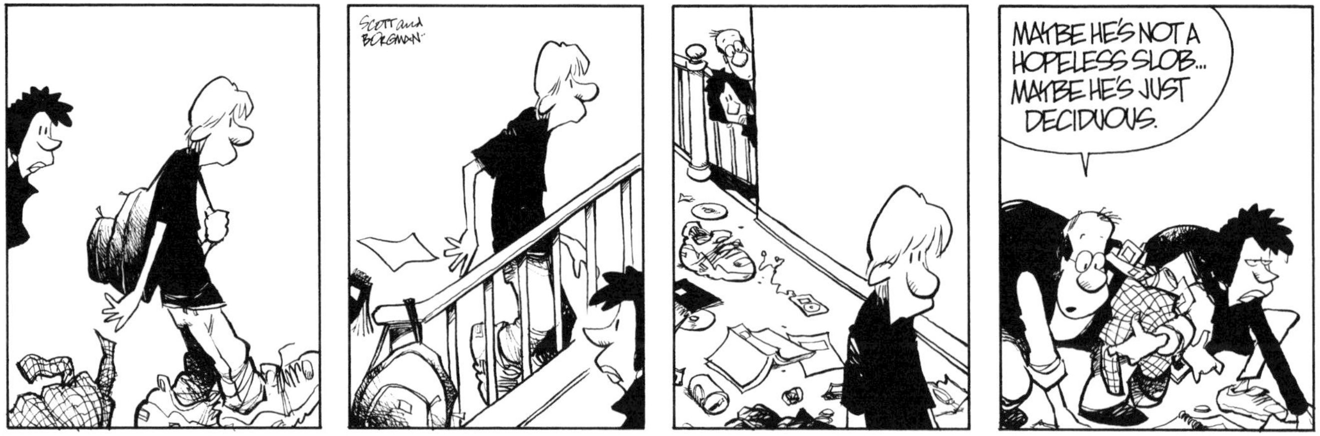
MAYBE HE'S NOT A HOPELESS SLOB... MAYBE HE'S JUST DECIDUOUS.

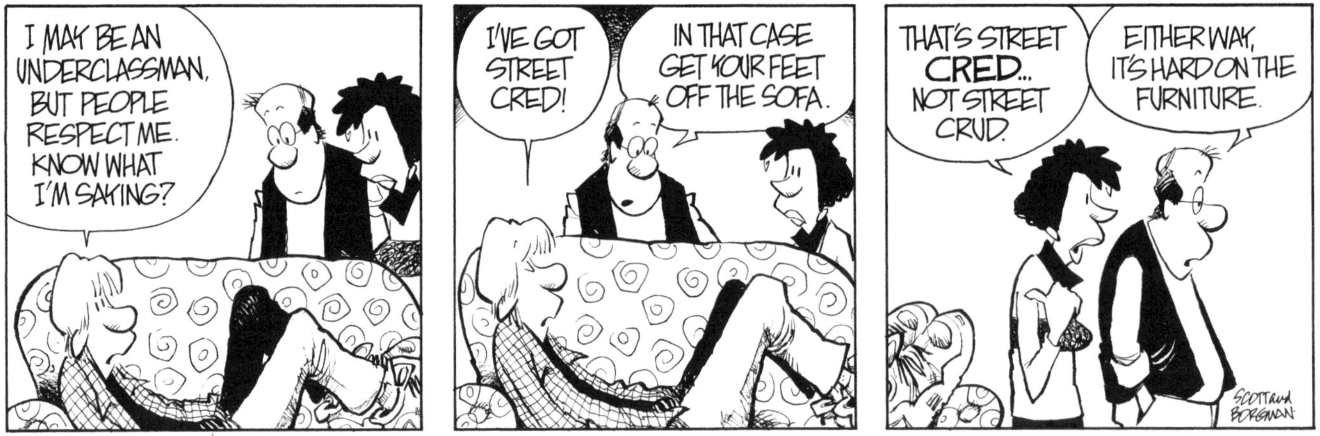
I MAY BE AN UNDERCLASSMAN, BUT PEOPLE RESPECT ME. KNOW WHAT I'M SAYING?
I'VE GOT STREET CRED!
IN THAT CASE GET YOUR FEET OFF THE SOFA.
THAT'S STREET CRED... NOT STREET CRUD.
EITHER WAY, IT'S HARD ON THE FURNITURE.

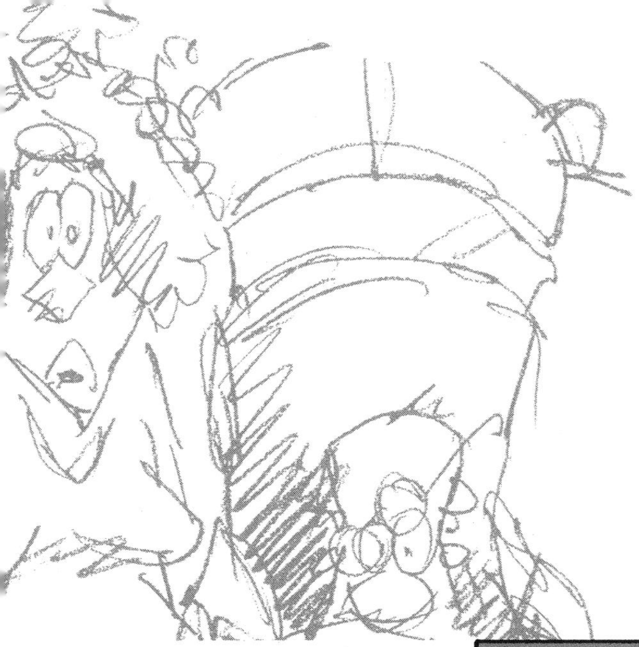

Zits

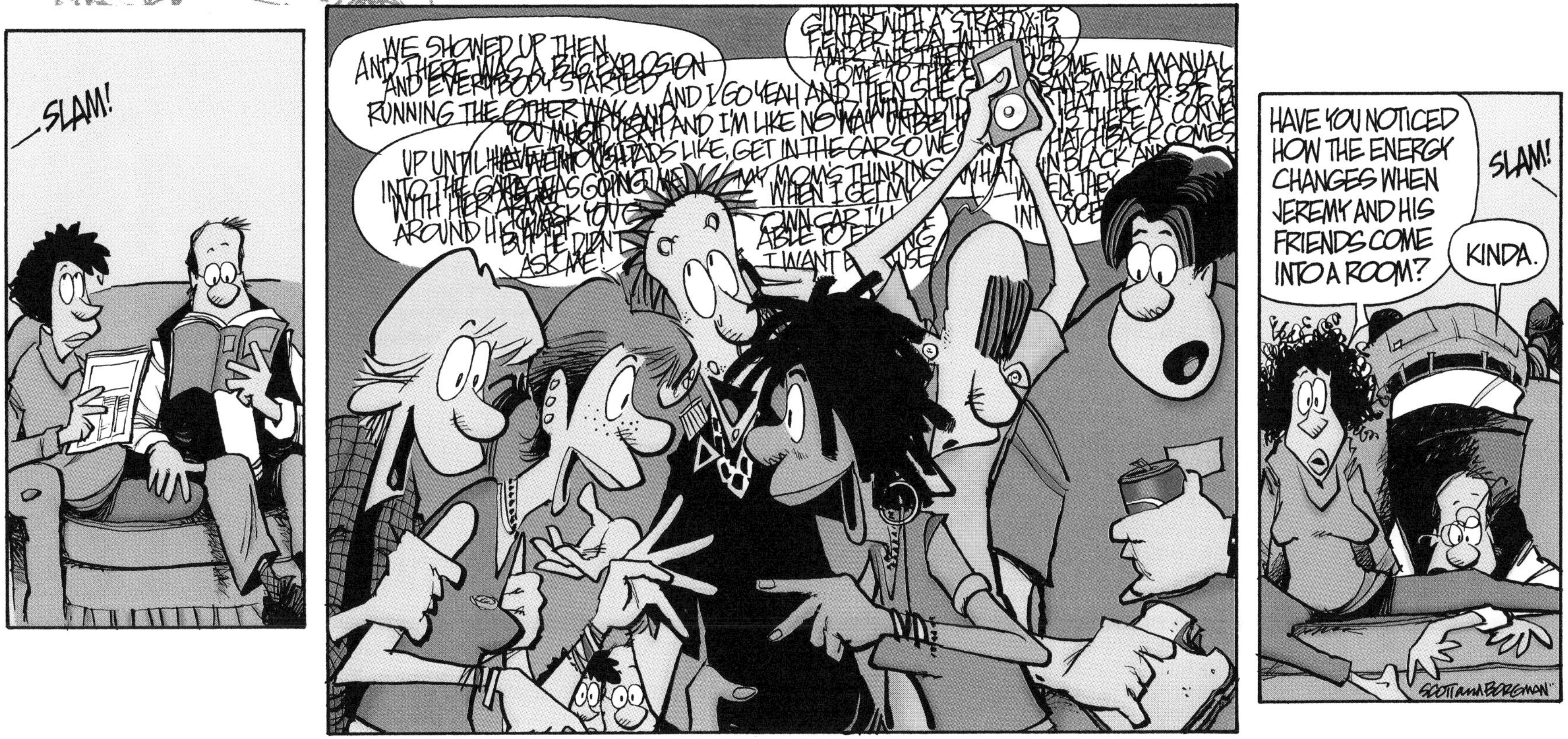

SLAM!
WE SHOWED UP THEN
AND THERE WAS A BIG EXPLOSION
AND EVERYBODY STARTED
RUNNING THE OTHER WAY AND
AND I GO YEAH AND THEN SHE
YEAH AND I'M LIKE NO WAY
LIKE, GET IN THE CAR
MY MOM'S THINKING
WHEN I GET MY
OWN CAR I'LL
ASK ME!
HAVE YOU NOTICED HOW THE ENERGY CHANGES WHEN JEREMY AND HIS FRIENDS COME INTO A ROOM?
SLAM!
KINDA.
SCOTT and BORGMAN

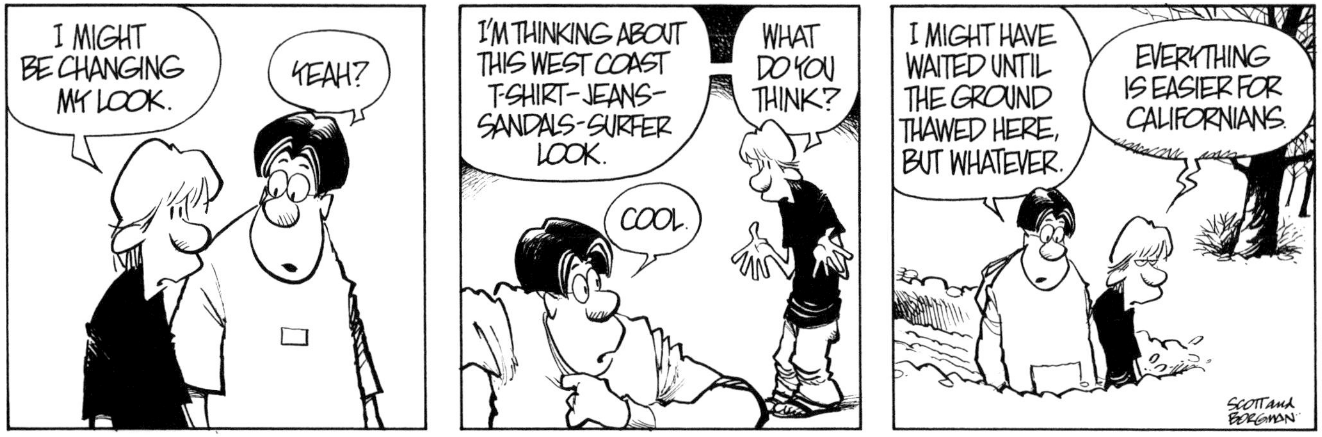
I MIGHT BE CHANGING MY LOOK.
YEAH?
I'M THINKING ABOUT THIS WEST COAST T-SHIRT-JEANS-SANDALS-SURFER LOOK.
WHAT DO YOU THINK?
COOL.
I MIGHT HAVE WAITED UNTIL THE GROUND THAWED HERE, BUT WHATEVER.
EVERYTHING IS EASIER FOR CALIFORNIANS.

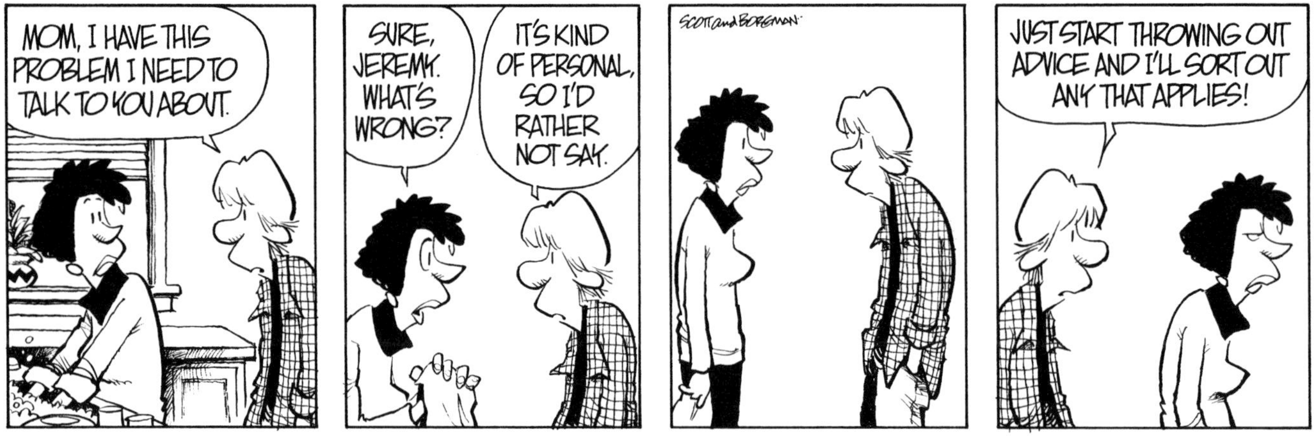
MOM, I HAVE THIS PROBLEM I NEED TO TALK TO YOU ABOUT.
SURE, JEREMY. WHAT'S WRONG?
IT'S KIND OF PERSONAL, SO I'D RATHER NOT SAY.
JUST START THROWING OUT ADVICE AND I'LL SORT OUT ANY THAT APPLIES!

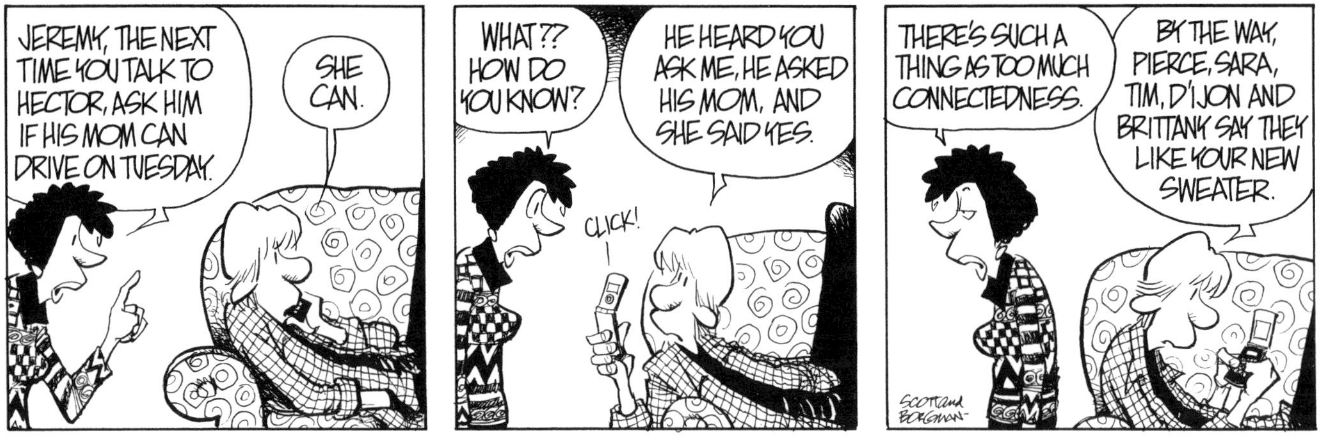
JEREMY, THE NEXT TIME YOU TALK TO HECTOR, ASK HIM IF HIS MOM CAN DRIVE ON TUESDAY.
SHE CAN.
WHAT?? HOW DO YOU KNOW?
CLICK!
HE HEARD YOU ASK ME, HE ASKED HIS MOM, AND SHE SAID YES.
THERE'S SUCH A THING AS TOO MUCH CONNECTEDNESS.
BY THE WAY, PIERCE, SARA, TIM, D'JON AND BRITTANY SAY THEY LIKE YOUR NEW SWEATER.

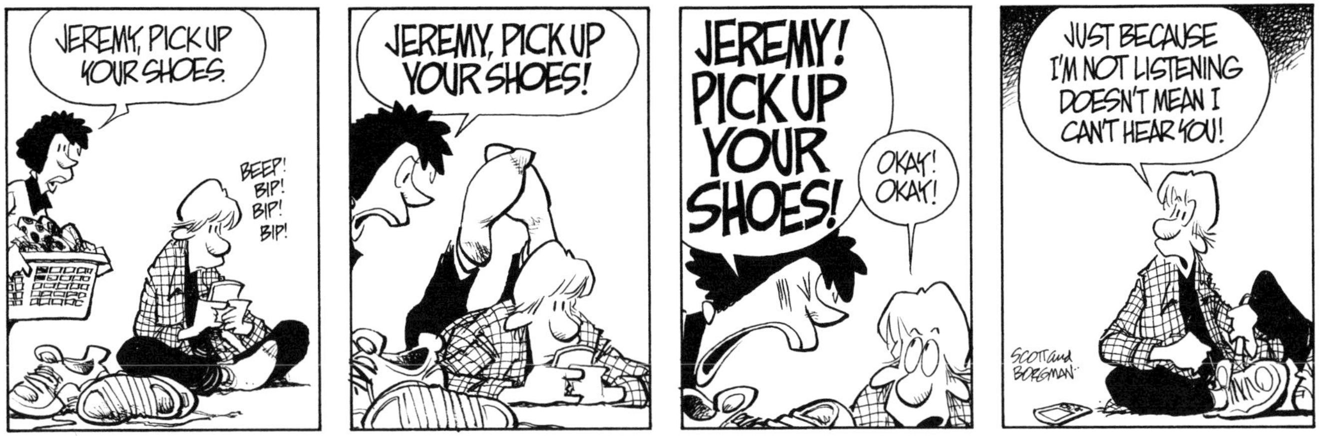
JEREMY, PICK UP YOUR SHOES.
BEEP! BIP! BIP! BIP!
JEREMY, PICK UP YOUR SHOES!
JEREMY! PICK UP YOUR SHOES!
OKAY! OKAY!
JUST BECAUSE I'M NOT LISTENING DOESN'T MEAN I CAN'T HEAR YOU!
SCOTT and BORGMAN

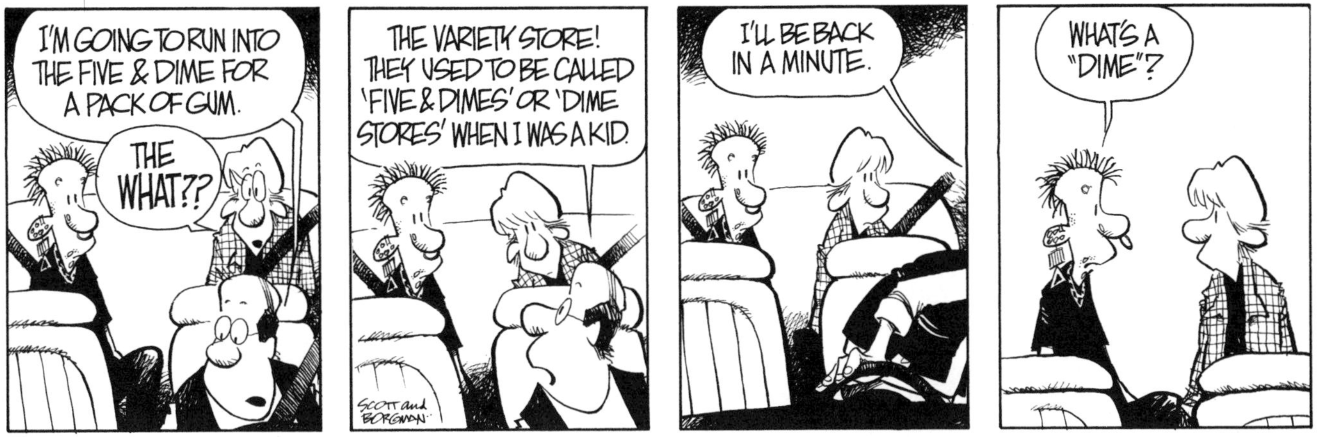
I'M GOING TO RUN INTO THE FIVE & DIME FOR A PACK OF GUM.
THE WHAT??
THE VARIETY STORE! THEY USED TO BE CALLED 'FIVE & DIMES' OR 'DIME STORES' WHEN I WAS A KID.
SCOTT and BORGMAN
I'LL BE BACK IN A MINUTE.
WHAT'S A "DIME"?

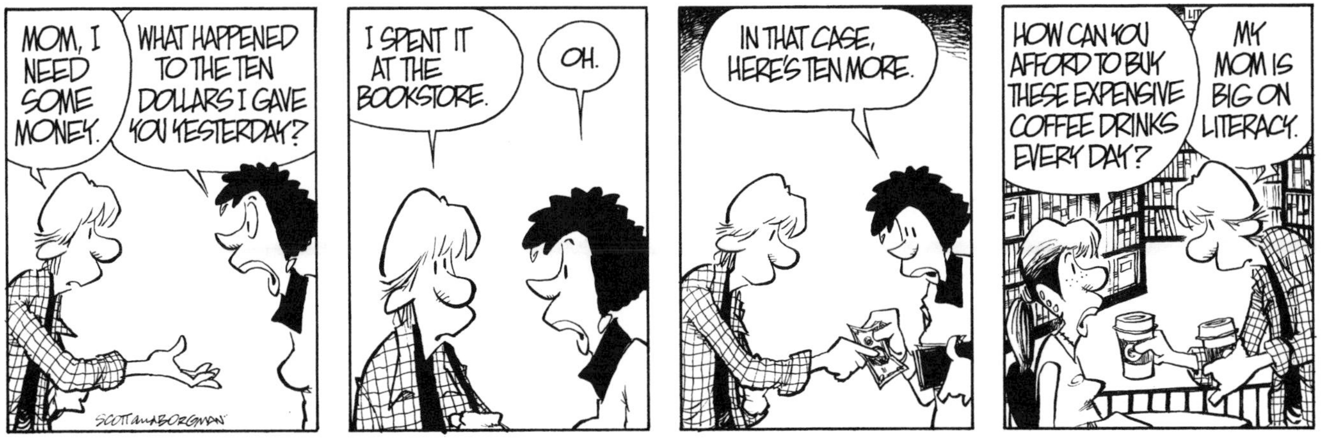
MOM, I NEED SOME MONEY.
WHAT HAPPENED TO THE TEN DOLLARS I GAVE YOU YESTERDAY?
SCOTT and BORGMAN
I SPENT IT AT THE BOOKSTORE.
OH.
IN THAT CASE, HERE'S TEN MORE.
HOW CAN YOU AFFORD TO BUY THESE EXPENSIVE COFFEE DRINKS EVERY DAY?
MY MOM IS BIG ON LITERACY.

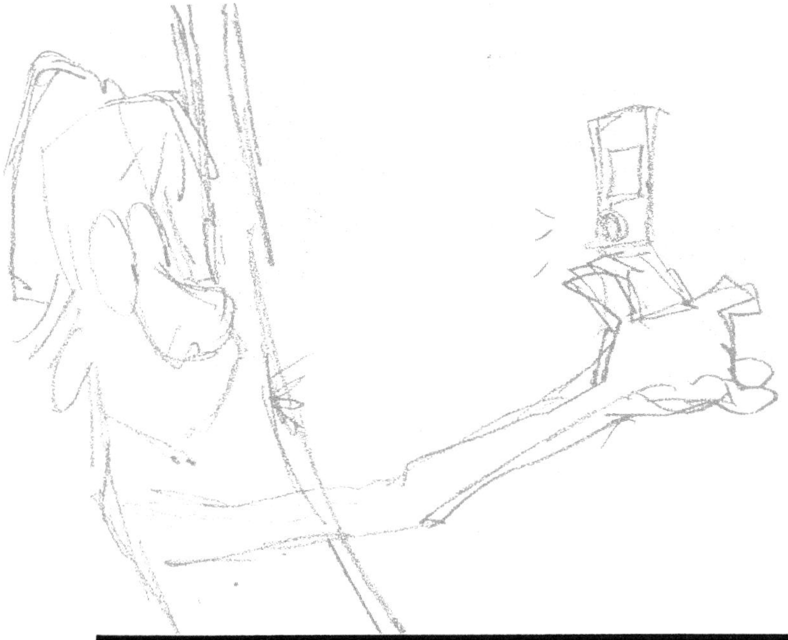

Zits

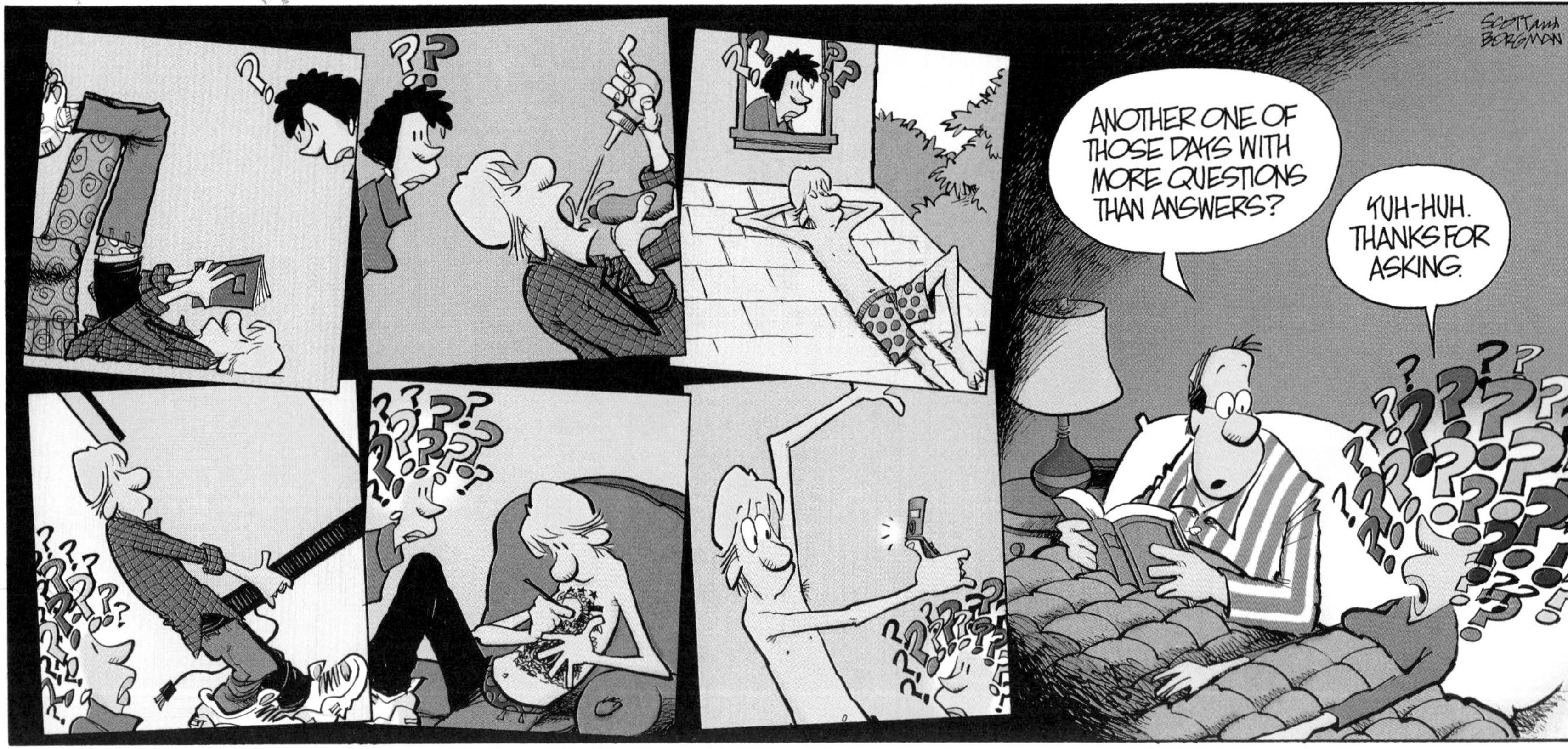

ANOTHER ONE OF THOSE DAYS WITH MORE QUESTIONS THAN ANSWERS?
YUH-HUH. THANKS FOR ASKING.

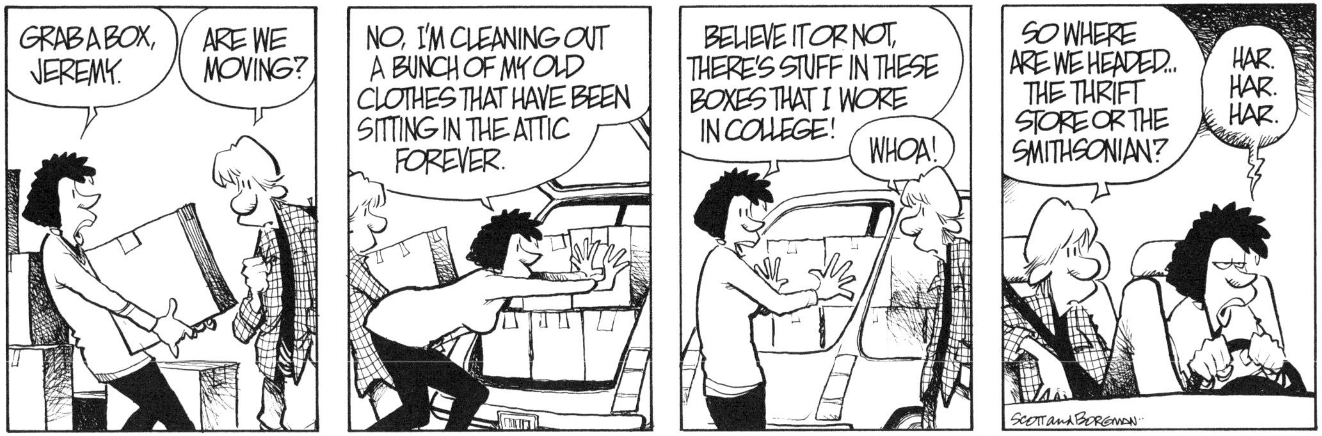
GRAB A BOX, JEREMY.
ARE WE MOVING?
NO, I'M CLEANING OUT A BUNCH OF MY OLD CLOTHES THAT HAVE BEEN SITTING IN THE ATTIC FOREVER.
BELIEVE IT OR NOT, THERE'S STUFF IN THESE BOXES THAT I WORE IN COLLEGE!
WHOA!
SO WHERE ARE WE HEADED... THE THRIFT STORE OR THE SMITHSONIAN?
HAR. HAR. HAR.

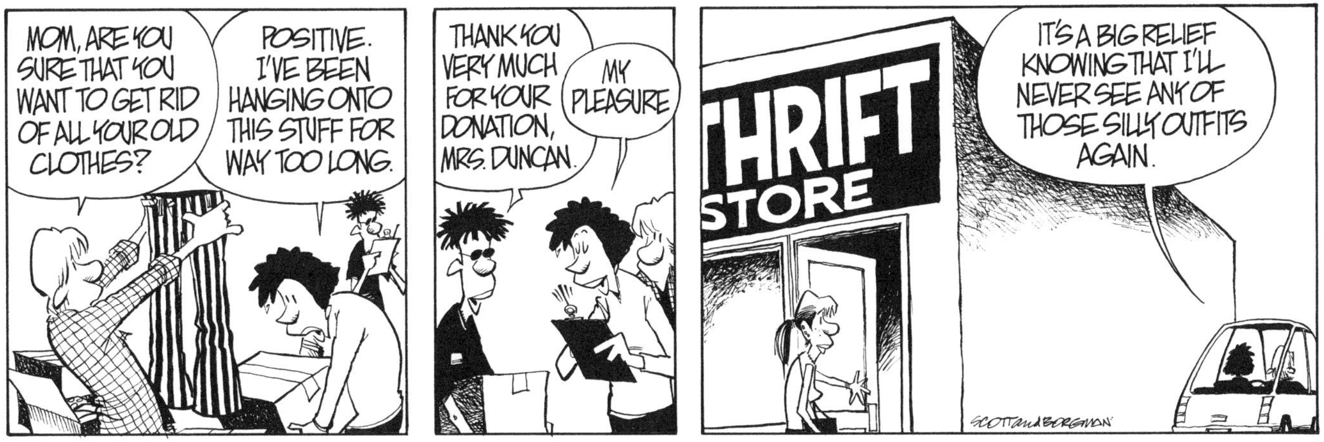
MOM, ARE YOU SURE THAT YOU WANT TO GET RID OF ALL YOUR OLD CLOTHES?
POSITIVE. I'VE BEEN HANGING ONTO THIS STUFF FOR WAY TOO LONG.
THANK YOU VERY MUCH FOR YOUR DONATION, MRS. DUNCAN.
MY PLEASURE
THRIFT STORE
IT'S A BIG RELIEF KNOWING THAT I'LL NEVER SEE ANY OF THOSE SILLY OUTFITS AGAIN.

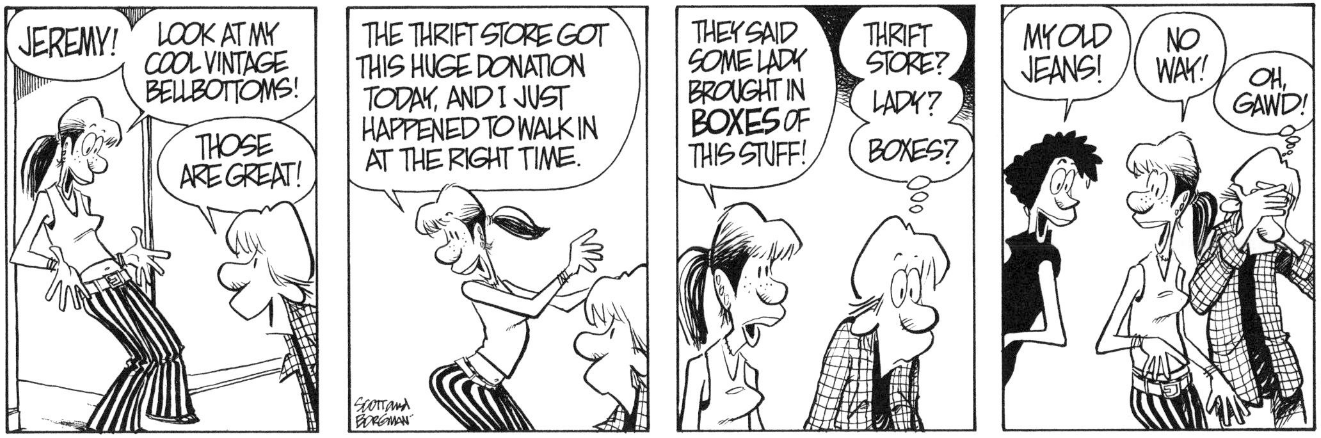
JEREMY!
LOOK AT MY COOL VINTAGE BELLBOTTOMS!
THOSE ARE GREAT!
THE THRIFT STORE GOT THIS HUGE DONATION TODAY, AND I JUST HAPPENED TO WALK IN AT THE RIGHT TIME.
THEY SAID SOME LADY BROUGHT IN **BOXES** OF THIS STUFF!
THRIFT STORE?
LADY?
BOXES?
MY OLD JEANS!
NO WAY!
OH, GAWD!

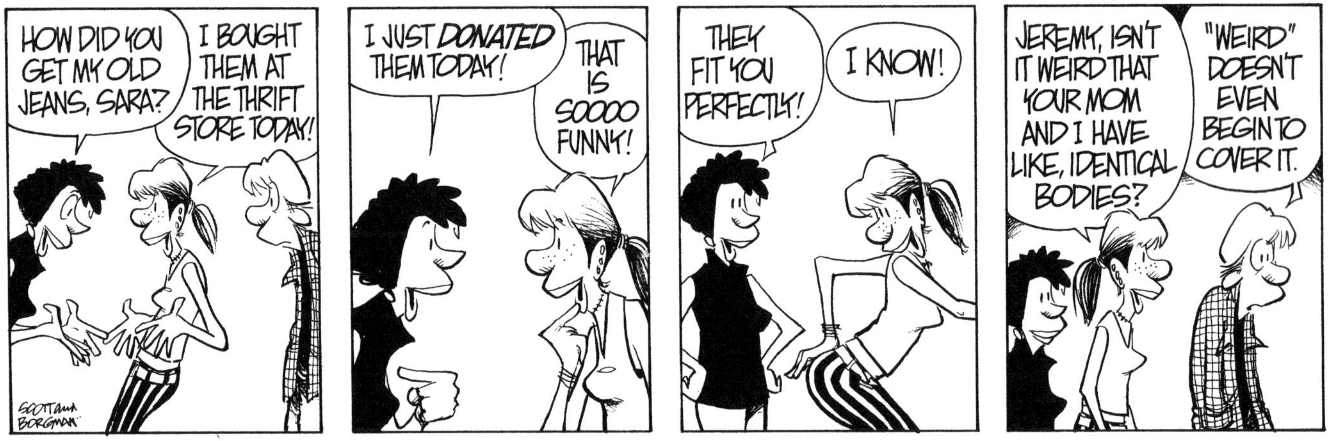
HOW DID YOU GET MY OLD JEANS, SARA?
I BOUGHT THEM AT THE THRIFT STORE TODAY!
I JUST *DONATED* THEM TODAY!
THAT IS SOOOO FUNNY!
THEY FIT YOU PERFECTLY!
I KNOW!
JEREMY, ISN'T IT WEIRD THAT YOUR MOM AND I HAVE LIKE, IDENTICAL BODIES?
"WEIRD" DOESN'T EVEN BEGIN TO COVER IT.

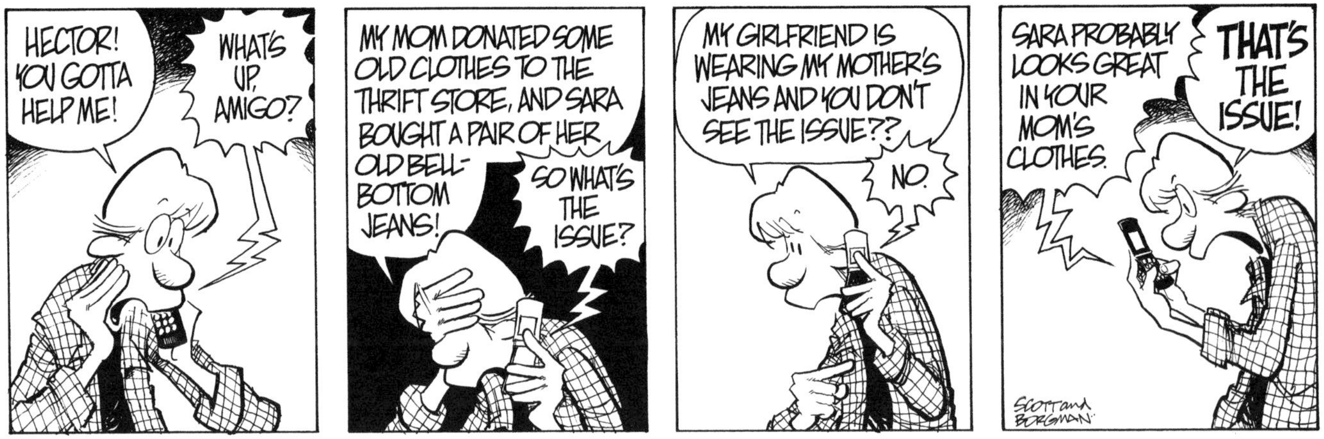
HECTOR! YOU GOTTA HELP ME!
WHAT'S UP, AMIGO?
MY MOM DONATED SOME OLD CLOTHES TO THE THRIFT STORE, AND SARA BOUGHT A PAIR OF HER OLD BELL-BOTTOM JEANS!
SO WHAT'S THE ISSUE?
MY GIRLFRIEND IS WEARING MY MOTHER'S JEANS AND YOU DON'T SEE THE ISSUE??
NO.
SARA PROBABLY LOOKS GREAT IN YOUR MOM'S CLOTHES.
THAT'S THE ISSUE!

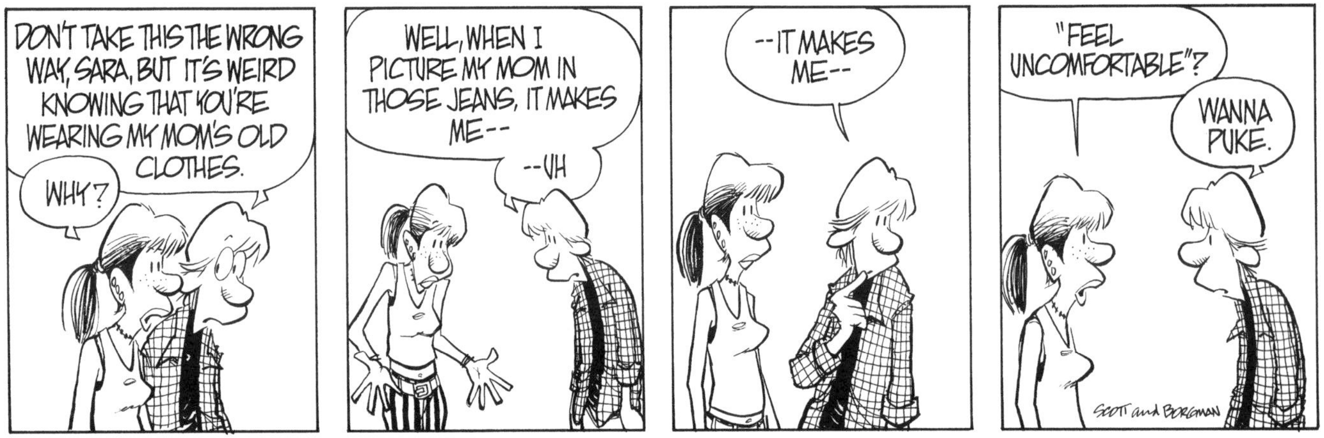
DON'T TAKE THIS THE WRONG WAY, SARA, BUT IT'S WEIRD KNOWING THAT YOU'RE WEARING MY MOM'S OLD CLOTHES.
WHY?
WELL, WHEN I PICTURE MY MOM IN THOSE JEANS, IT MAKES ME--
--UH
--IT MAKES ME--
"FEEL UNCOMFORTABLE"?
WANNA PUKE.

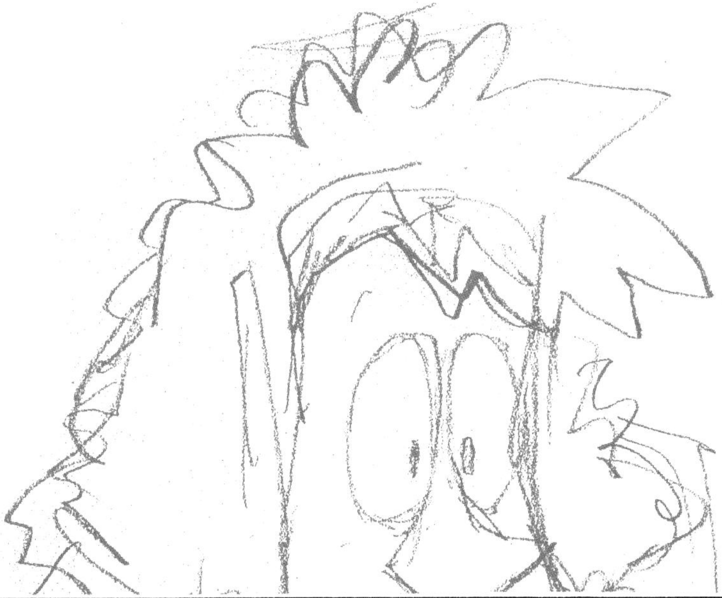

Zits

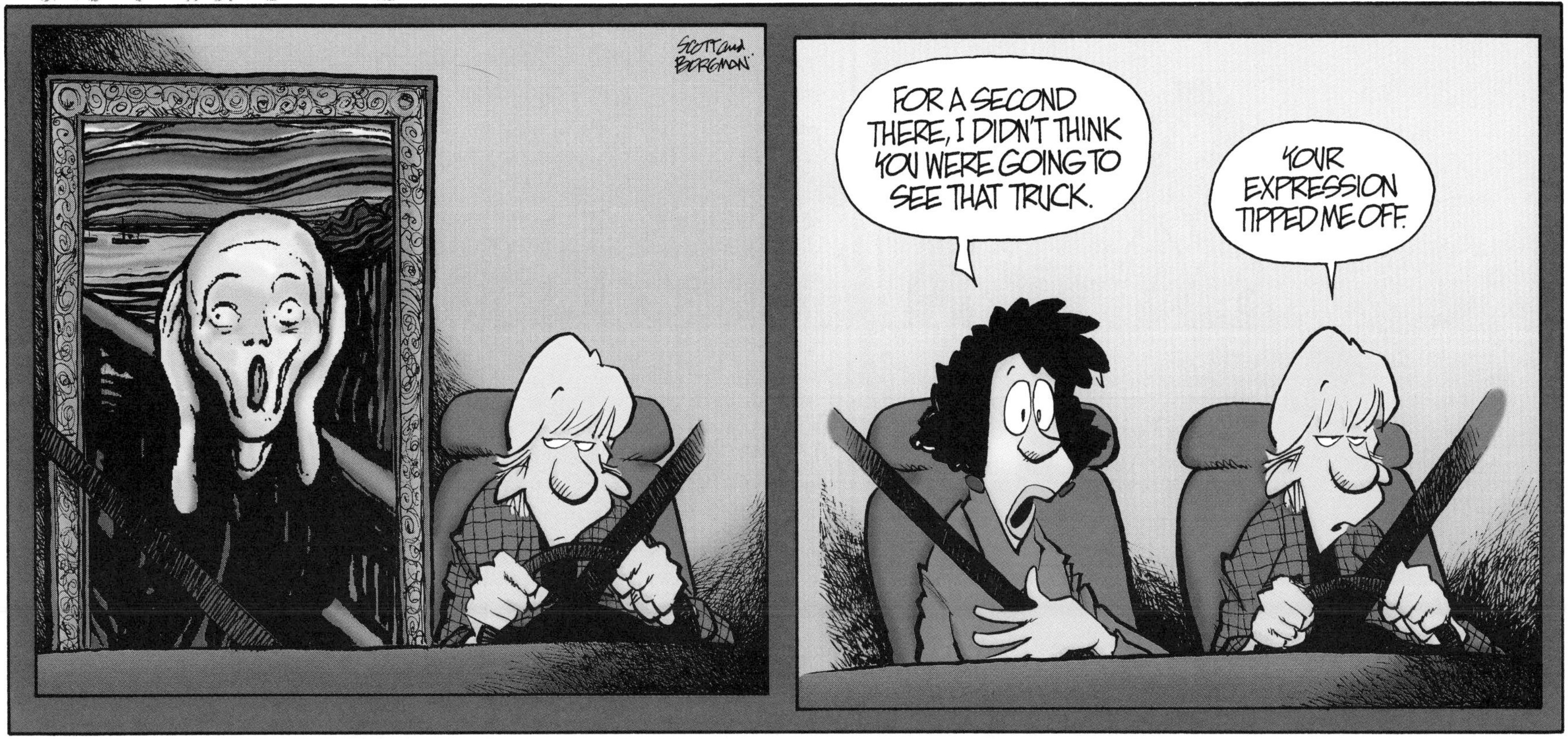
FOR A SECOND THERE, I DIDN'T THINK YOU WERE GOING TO SEE THAT TRUCK.
YOUR EXPRESSION TIPPED ME OFF.

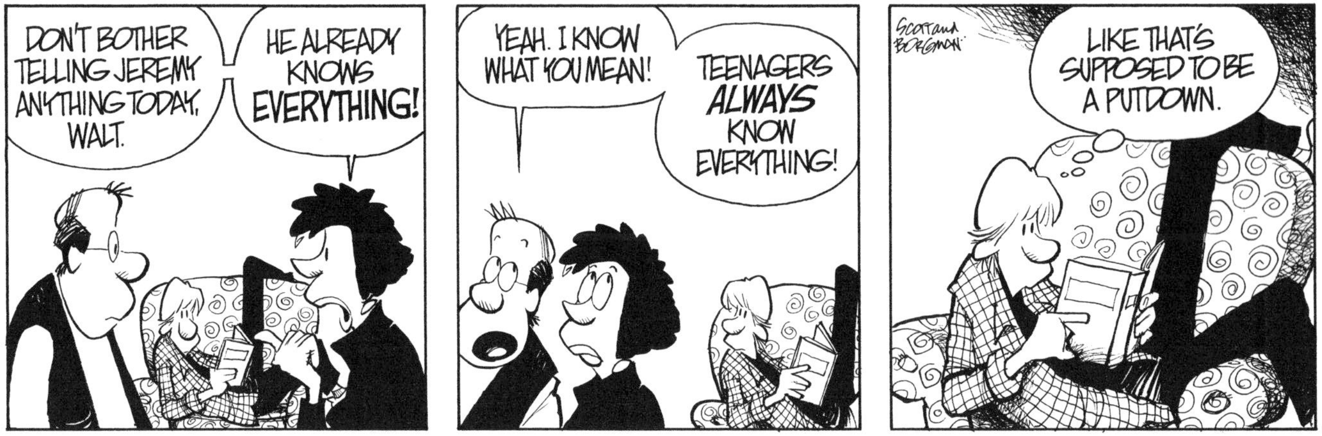
DON'T BOTHER TELLING JEREMY ANYTHING TODAY, WALT.
HE ALREADY KNOWS **EVERYTHING!**
YEAH. I KNOW WHAT YOU MEAN!
TEENAGERS ***ALWAYS*** KNOW EVERYTHING!
LIKE THAT'S SUPPOSED TO BE A PUTDOWN.

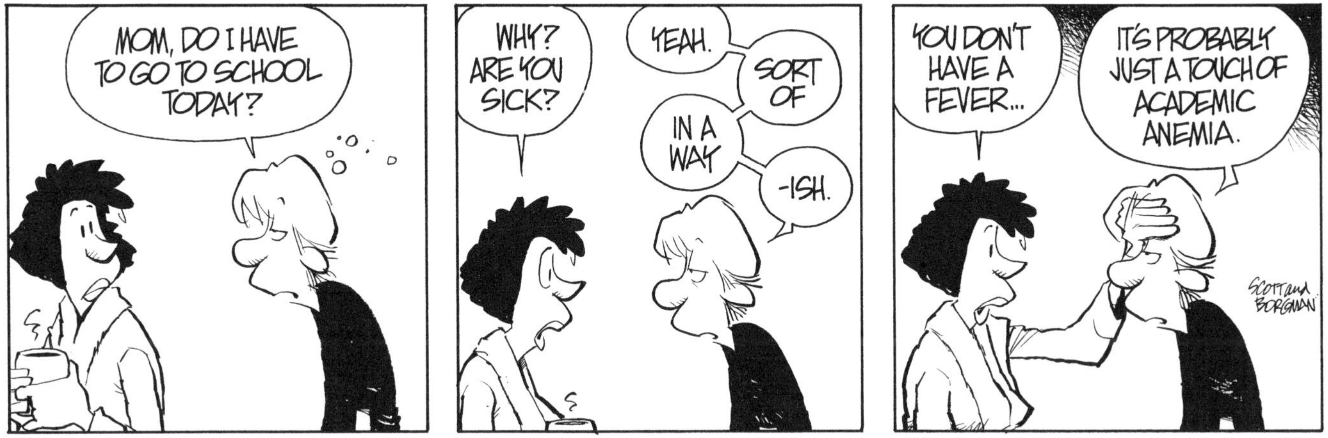
MOM, DO I HAVE TO GO TO SCHOOL TODAY?
WHY? ARE YOU SICK?
YEAH.
SORT OF
IN A WAY
-ISH.
YOU DON'T HAVE A FEVER...
IT'S PROBABLY JUST A TOUCH OF ACADEMIC ANEMIA.

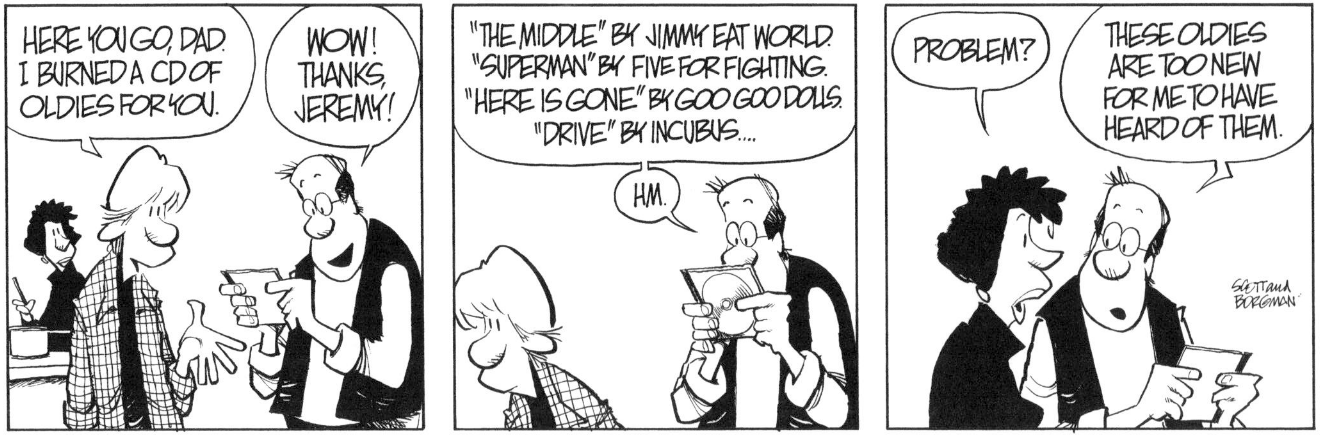
HERE YOU GO, DAD. I BURNED A CD OF OLDIES FOR YOU.
WOW! THANKS, JEREMY!
"THE MIDDLE" BY JIMMY EAT WORLD. "SUPERMAN" BY FIVE FOR FIGHTING. "HERE IS GONE" BY GOO GOO DOLLS. "DRIVE" BY INCUBUS....
HM.
PROBLEM?
THESE OLDIES ARE TOO NEW FOR ME TO HAVE HEARD OF THEM.

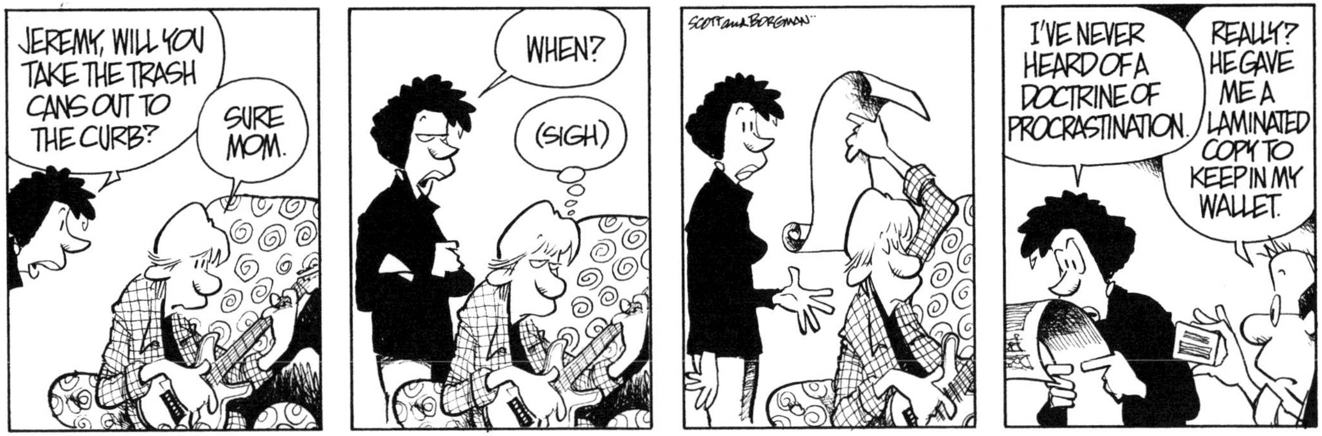
JEREMY, WILL YOU TAKE THE TRASH CANS OUT TO THE CURB?
SURE MOM.
WHEN?
(SIGH)
SCOTT and BORGMAN
I'VE NEVER HEARD OF A DOCTRINE OF PROCRASTINATION.
REALLY? HE GAVE ME A LAMINATED COPY TO KEEP IN MY WALLET.

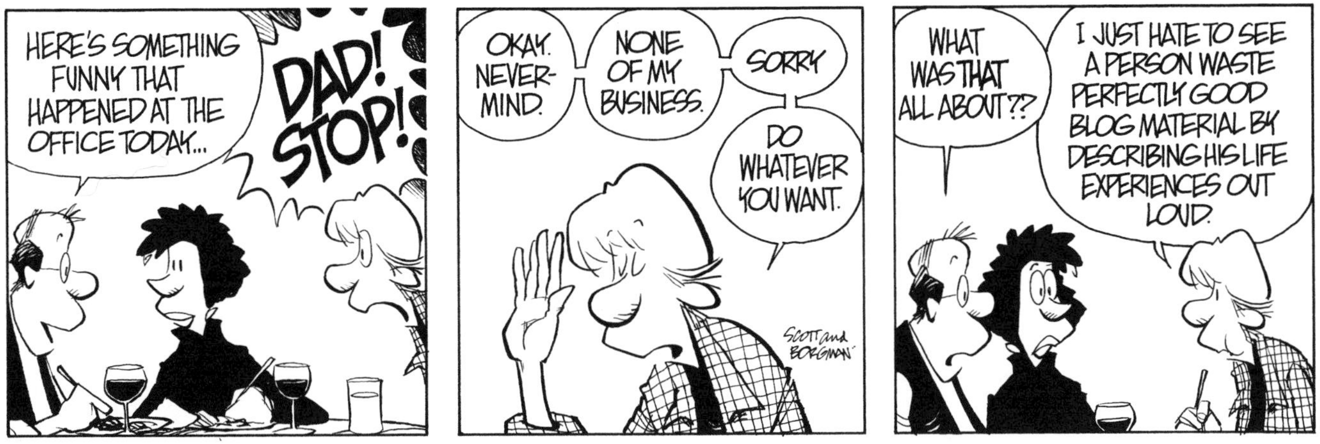
HERE'S SOMETHING FUNNY THAT HAPPENED AT THE OFFICE TODAY...
DAD! STOP!
OKAY. NEVER-MIND.
NONE OF MY BUSINESS.
SORRY
DO WHATEVER YOU WANT.
SCOTT and BORGMAN
WHAT WAS THAT ALL ABOUT??
I JUST HATE TO SEE A PERSON WASTE PERFECTLY GOOD BLOG MATERIAL BY DESCRIBING HIS LIFE EXPERIENCES OUT LOUD.

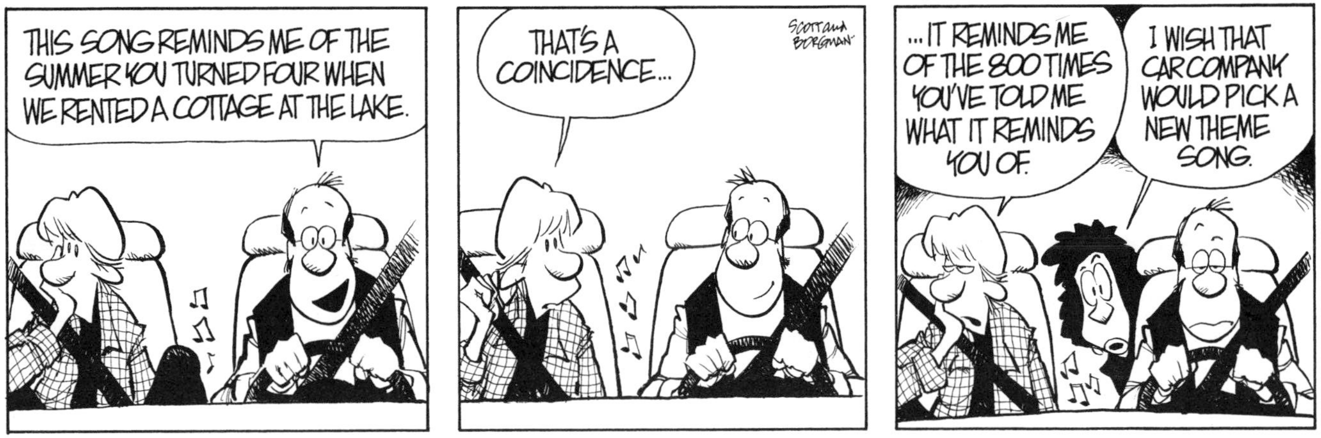
THIS SONG REMINDS ME OF THE SUMMER YOU TURNED FOUR WHEN WE RENTED A COTTAGE AT THE LAKE.
THAT'S A COINCIDENCE...
SCOTT and BORGMAN
...IT REMINDS ME OF THE 800 TIMES YOU'VE TOLD ME WHAT IT REMINDS YOU OF.
I WISH THAT CAR COMPANY WOULD PICK A NEW THEME SONG.

Zits

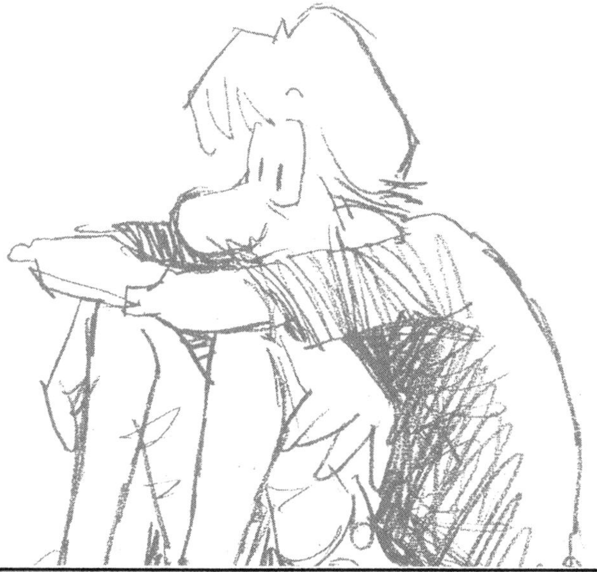

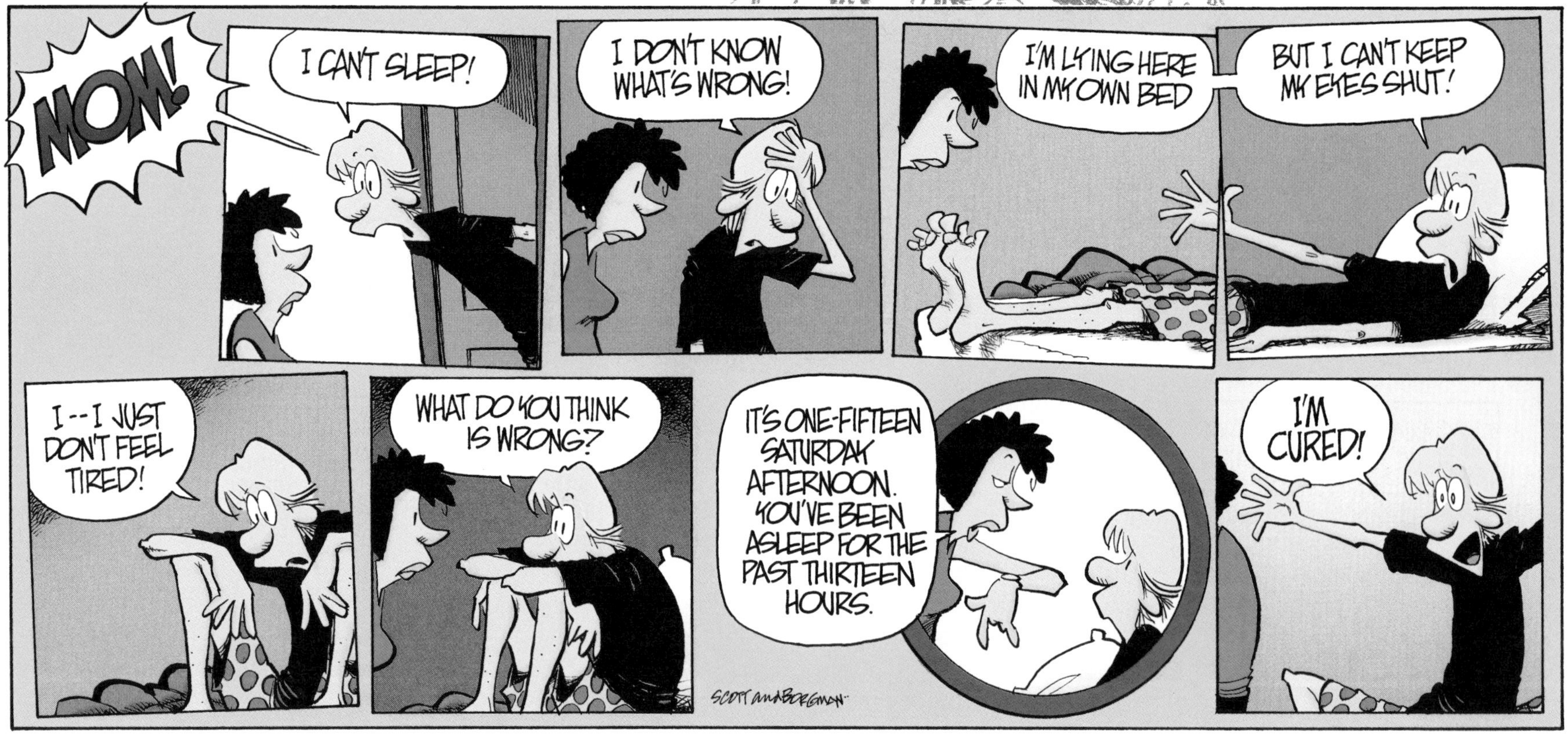

MOM!
I CAN'T SLEEP!
I DON'T KNOW WHAT'S WRONG!
I'M LYING HERE IN MY OWN BED
BUT I CAN'T KEEP MY EYES SHUT!
I -- I JUST DON'T FEEL TIRED!
WHAT DO YOU THINK IS WRONG?
IT'S ONE-FIFTEEN SATURDAY AFTERNOON. YOU'VE BEEN ASLEEP FOR THE PAST THIRTEEN HOURS.
I'M CURED!

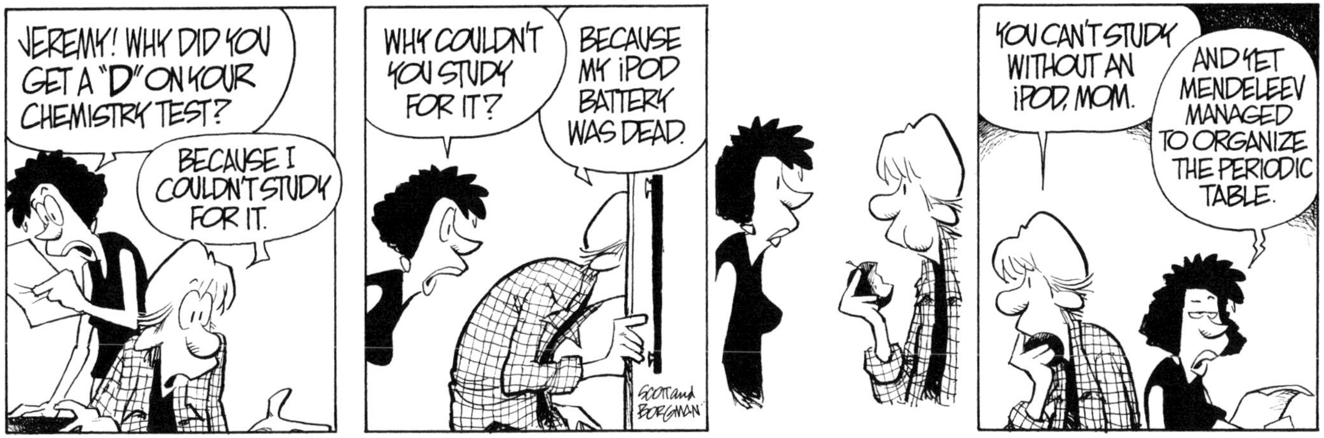
JEREMY! WHY DID YOU GET A "D" ON YOUR CHEMISTRY TEST?
BECAUSE I COULDN'T STUDY FOR IT.
WHY COULDN'T YOU STUDY FOR IT?
BECAUSE MY iPOD BATTERY WAS DEAD.
SCOTT and BORGMAN
YOU CAN'T STUDY WITHOUT AN iPOD, MOM.
AND YET MENDELEEV MANAGED TO ORGANIZE THE PERIODIC TABLE.

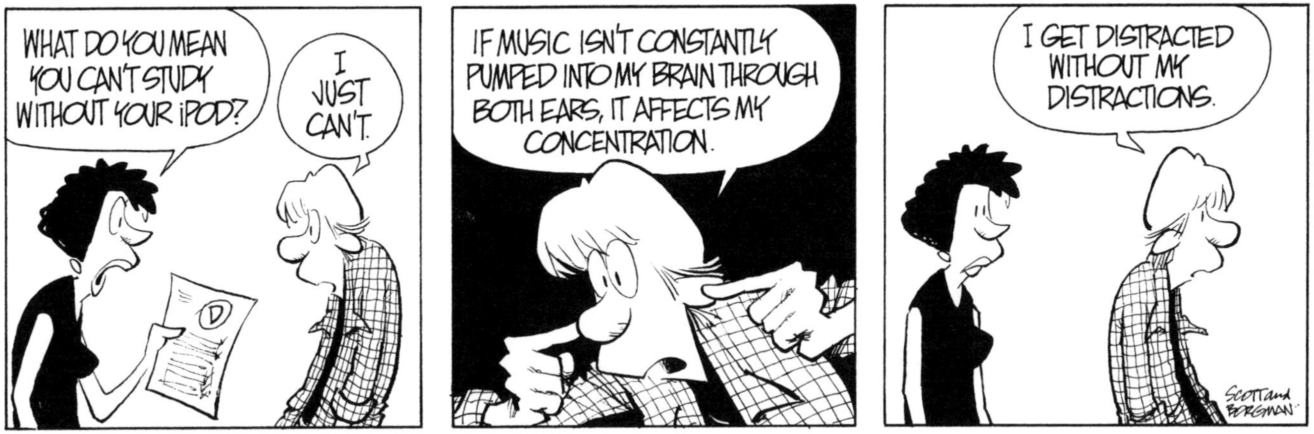
WHAT DO YOU MEAN YOU CAN'T STUDY WITHOUT YOUR iPOD?
I JUST CAN'T.
IF MUSIC ISN'T CONSTANTLY PUMPED INTO MY BRAIN THROUGH BOTH EARS, IT AFFECTS MY CONCENTRATION.
I GET DISTRACTED WITHOUT MY DISTRACTIONS.
SCOTT and BORGMAN

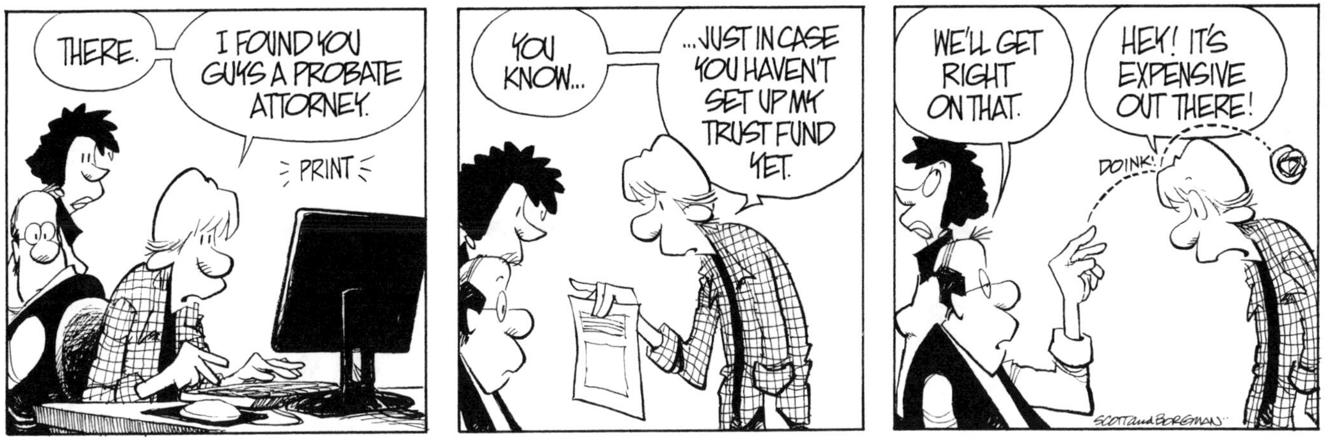
THERE.
I FOUND YOU GUYS A PROBATE ATTORNEY.
PRINT
YOU KNOW...
...JUST IN CASE YOU HAVEN'T SET UP MY TRUST FUND YET.
WE'LL GET RIGHT ON THAT.
HEY! IT'S EXPENSIVE OUT THERE!
DOINK!
SCOTT and BORGMAN

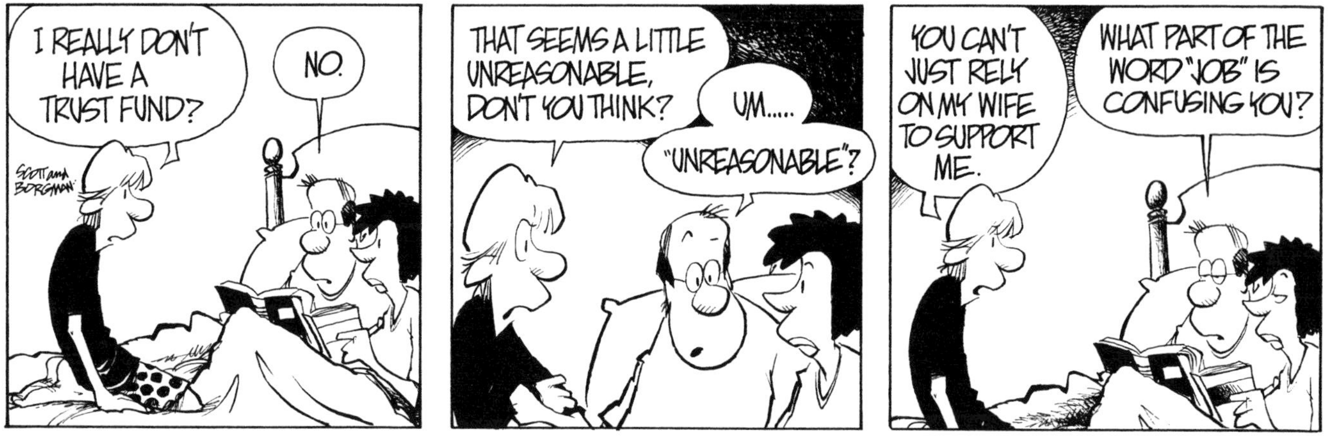
I REALLY DON'T HAVE A TRUST FUND?
NO.
THAT SEEMS A LITTLE UNREASONABLE, DON'T YOU THINK?
UM.....
"UNREASONABLE"?
YOU CAN'T JUST RELY ON MY WIFE TO SUPPORT ME.
WHAT PART OF THE WORD "JOB" IS CONFUSING YOU?

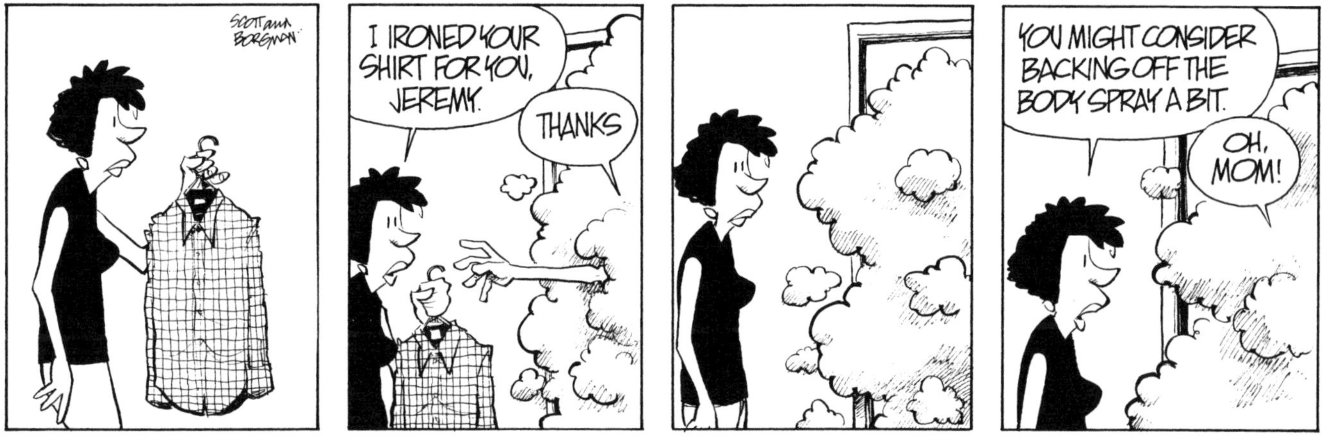
I IRONED YOUR SHIRT FOR YOU, JEREMY.
THANKS
YOU MIGHT CONSIDER BACKING OFF THE BODY SPRAY A BIT.
OH, MOM!

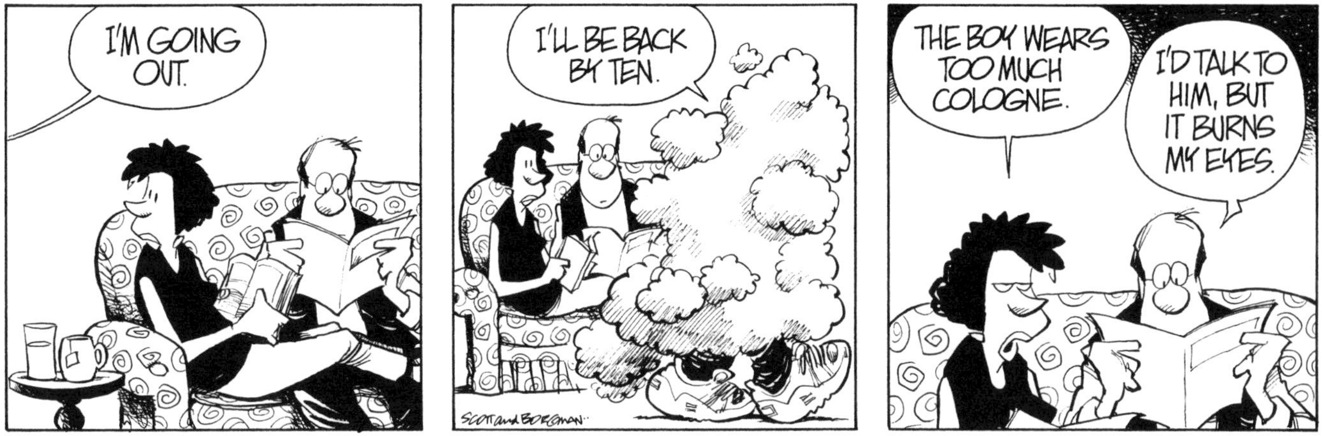
I'M GOING OUT.
I'LL BE BACK BY TEN.
THE BOY WEARS TOO MUCH COLOGNE.
I'D TALK TO HIM, BUT IT BURNS MY EYES.

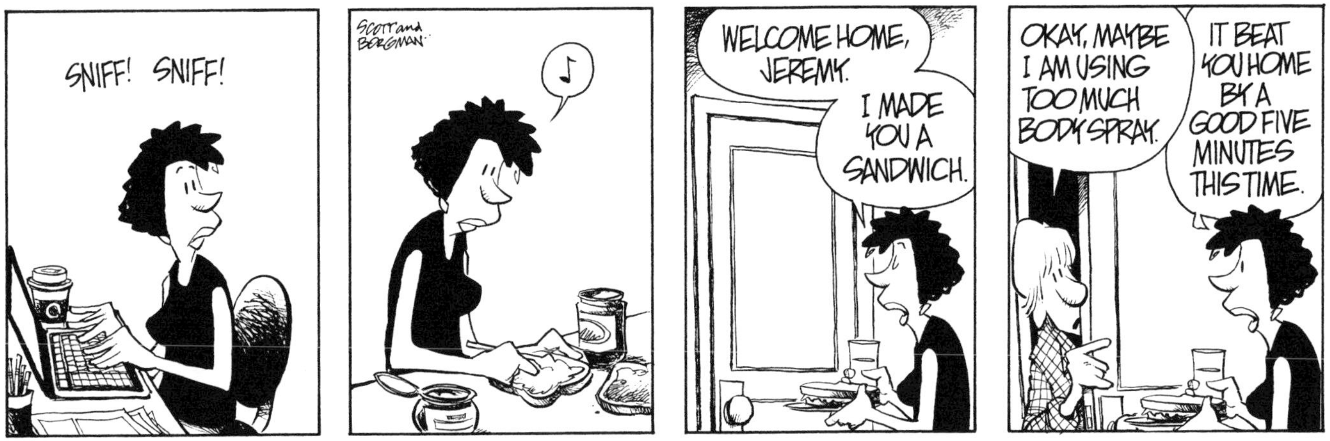
SNIFF! SNIFF!
SCOTT and BORGMAN
♪
WELCOME HOME, JEREMY.
I MADE YOU A SANDWICH.
OKAY, MAYBE I AM USING TOO MUCH BODY SPRAY.
IT BEAT YOU HOME BY A GOOD FIVE MINUTES THIS TIME.

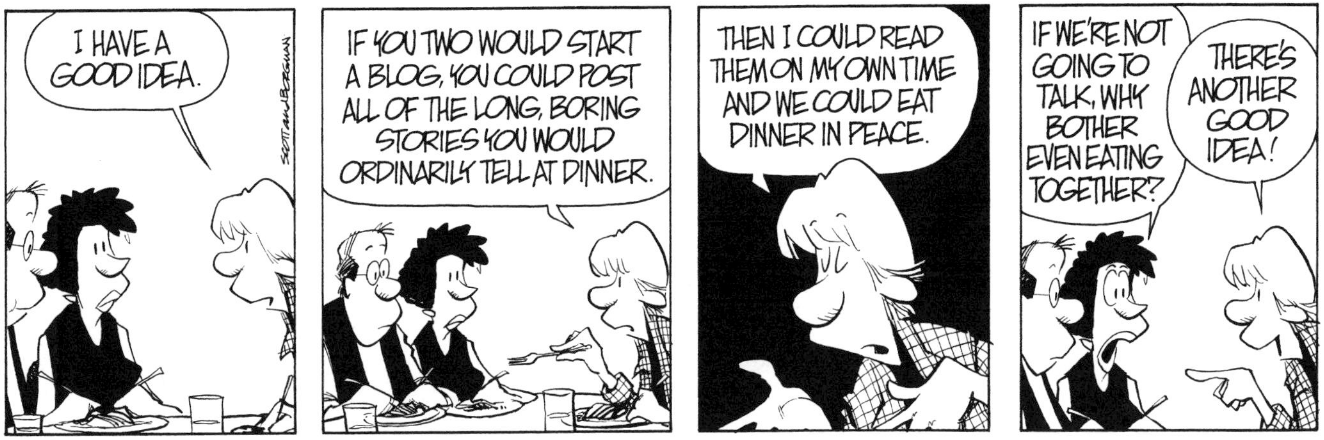
I HAVE A GOOD IDEA.
SCOTT and BORGMAN
IF YOU TWO WOULD START A BLOG, YOU COULD POST ALL OF THE LONG, BORING STORIES YOU WOULD ORDINARILY TELL AT DINNER.
THEN I COULD READ THEM ON MY OWN TIME AND WE COULD EAT DINNER IN PEACE.
IF WE'RE NOT GOING TO TALK, WHY BOTHER EVEN EATING TOGETHER?
THERE'S ANOTHER GOOD IDEA!

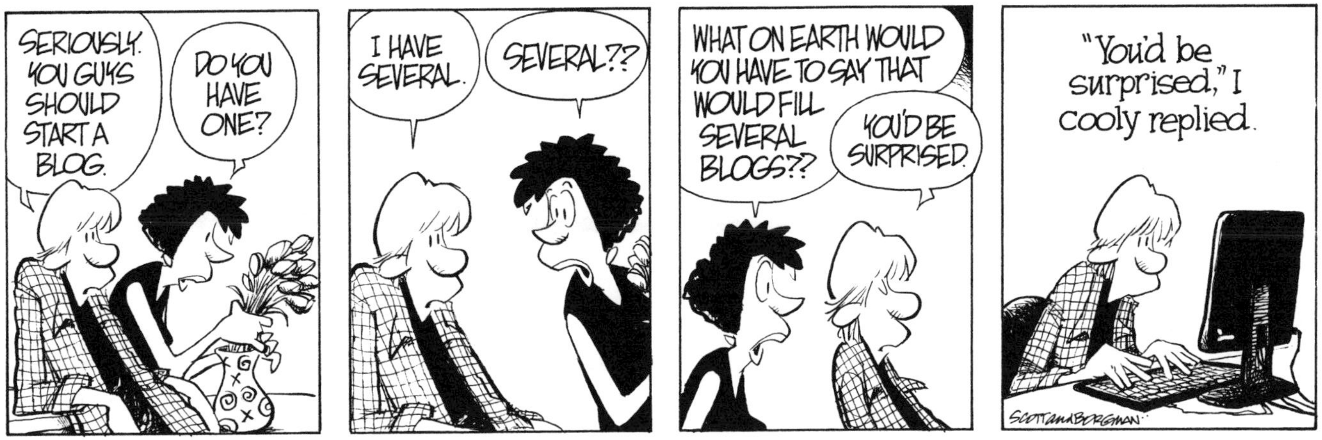
SERIOUSLY. YOU GUYS SHOULD START A BLOG.
DO YOU HAVE ONE?
I HAVE SEVERAL.
SEVERAL??
WHAT ON EARTH WOULD YOU HAVE TO SAY THAT WOULD FILL SEVERAL BLOGS??
YOU'D BE SURPRISED.
"You'd be surprised," I cooly replied.
SCOTT and BORGMAN

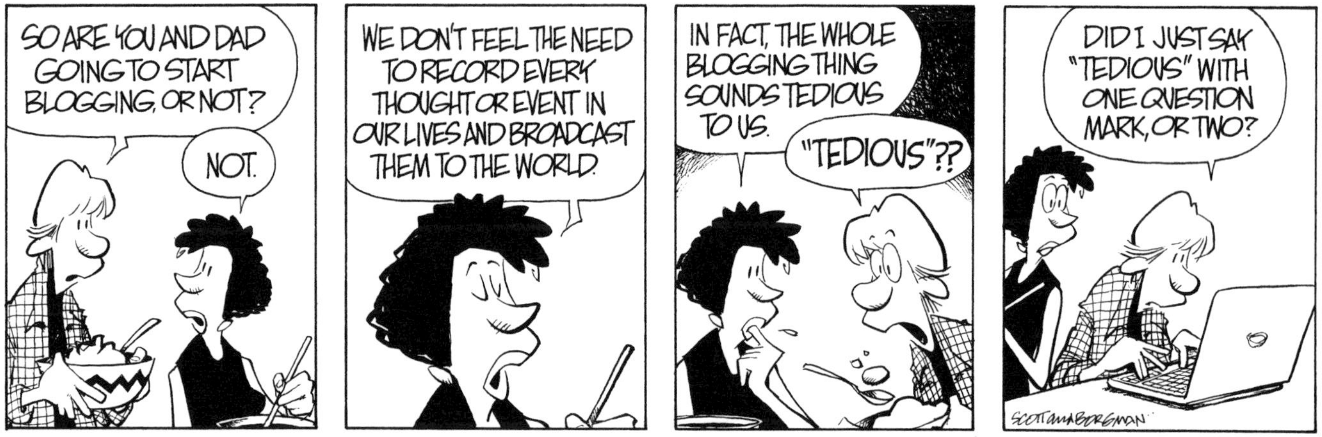
SO ARE YOU AND DAD GOING TO START BLOGGING, OR NOT?
NOT.
WE DON'T FEEL THE NEED TO RECORD EVERY THOUGHT OR EVENT IN OUR LIVES AND BROADCAST THEM TO THE WORLD.
IN FACT, THE WHOLE BLOGGING THING SOUNDS TEDIOUS TO US.
"TEDIOUS"??
DID I JUST SAY "TEDIOUS" WITH ONE QUESTION MARK, OR TWO?
SCOTT and BORGMAN

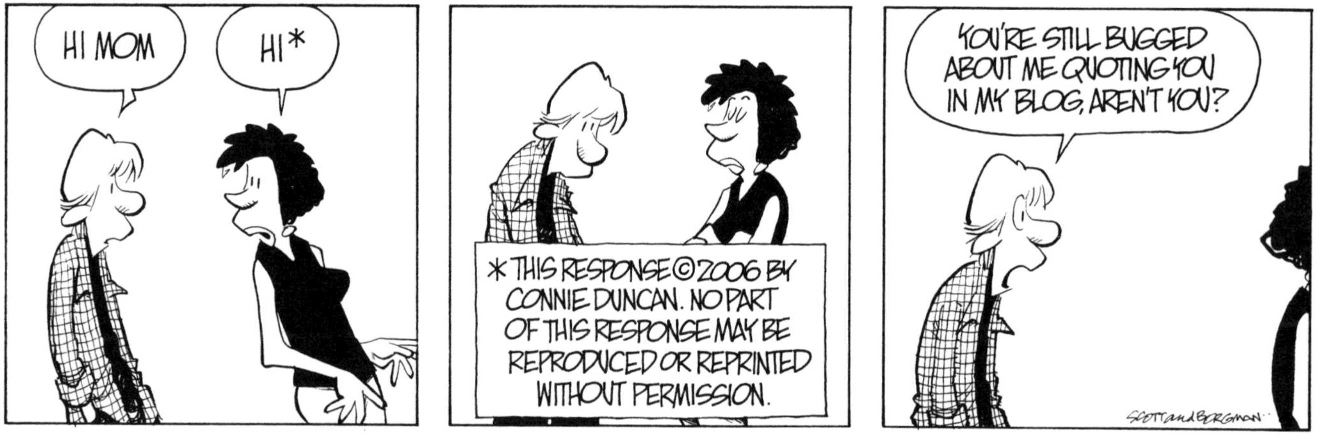
HI MOM
HI*
* THIS RESPONSE © 2006 BY CONNIE DUNCAN. NO PART OF THIS RESPONSE MAY BE REPRODUCED OR REPRINTED WITHOUT PERMISSION.
YOU'RE STILL BUGGED ABOUT ME QUOTING YOU IN MY BLOG, AREN'T YOU?
SCOTT and BORGMAN

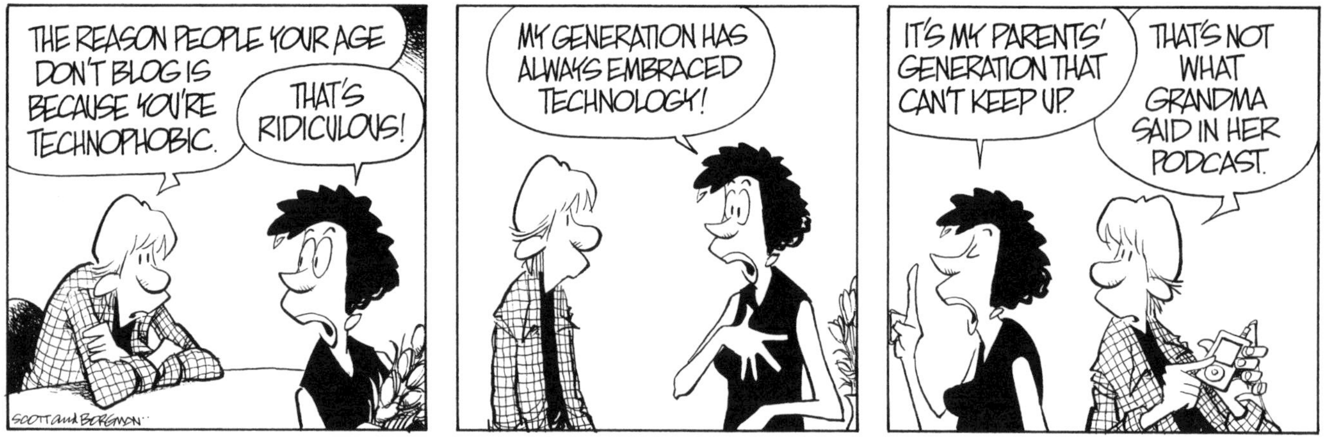
THE REASON PEOPLE YOUR AGE DON'T BLOG IS BECAUSE YOU'RE TECHNOPHOBIC.
THAT'S RIDICULOUS!
MY GENERATION HAS ALWAYS EMBRACED TECHNOLOGY!
IT'S MY PARENTS' GENERATION THAT CAN'T KEEP UP.
THAT'S NOT WHAT GRANDMA SAID IN HER PODCAST.
SCOTT and BORGMAN

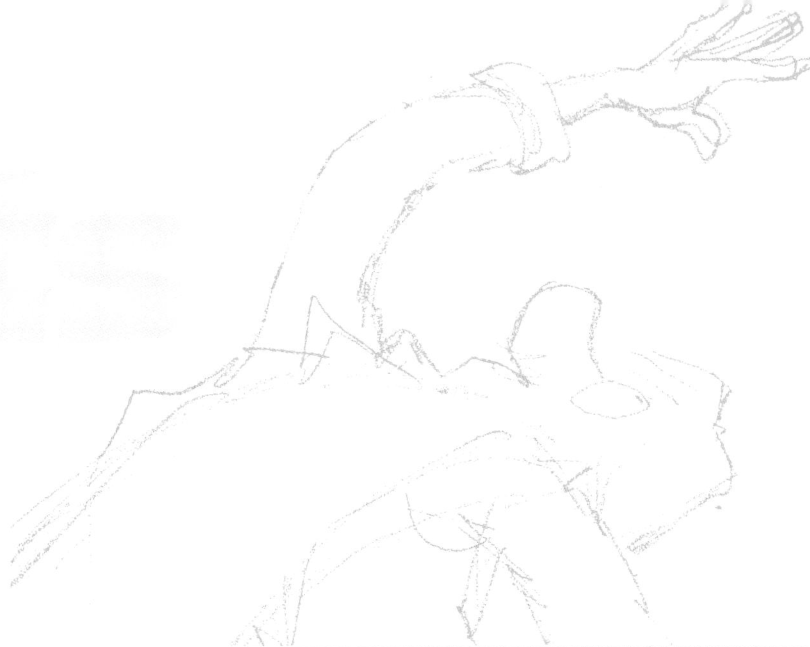

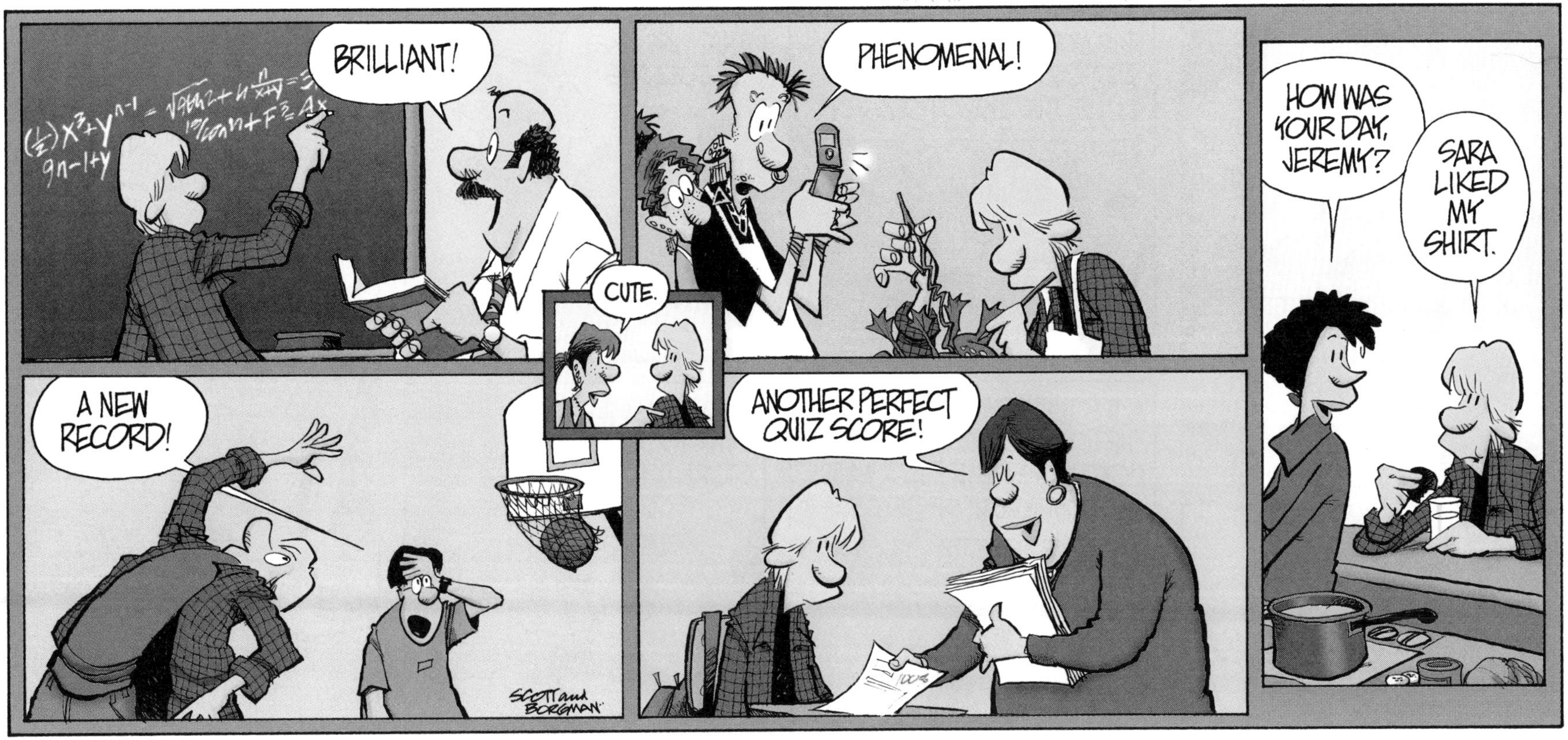
BRILLIANT!
PHENOMENAL!
CUTE.
A NEW RECORD!
ANOTHER PERFECT QUIZ SCORE!
HOW WAS YOUR DAY, JEREMY?
SARA LIKED MY SHIRT.
SCOTT and BORGMAN

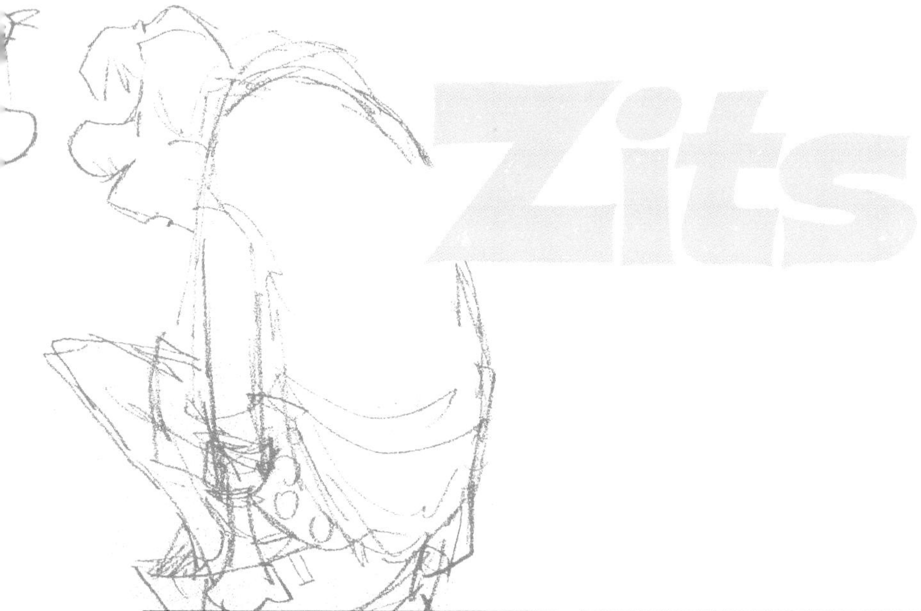
Zits

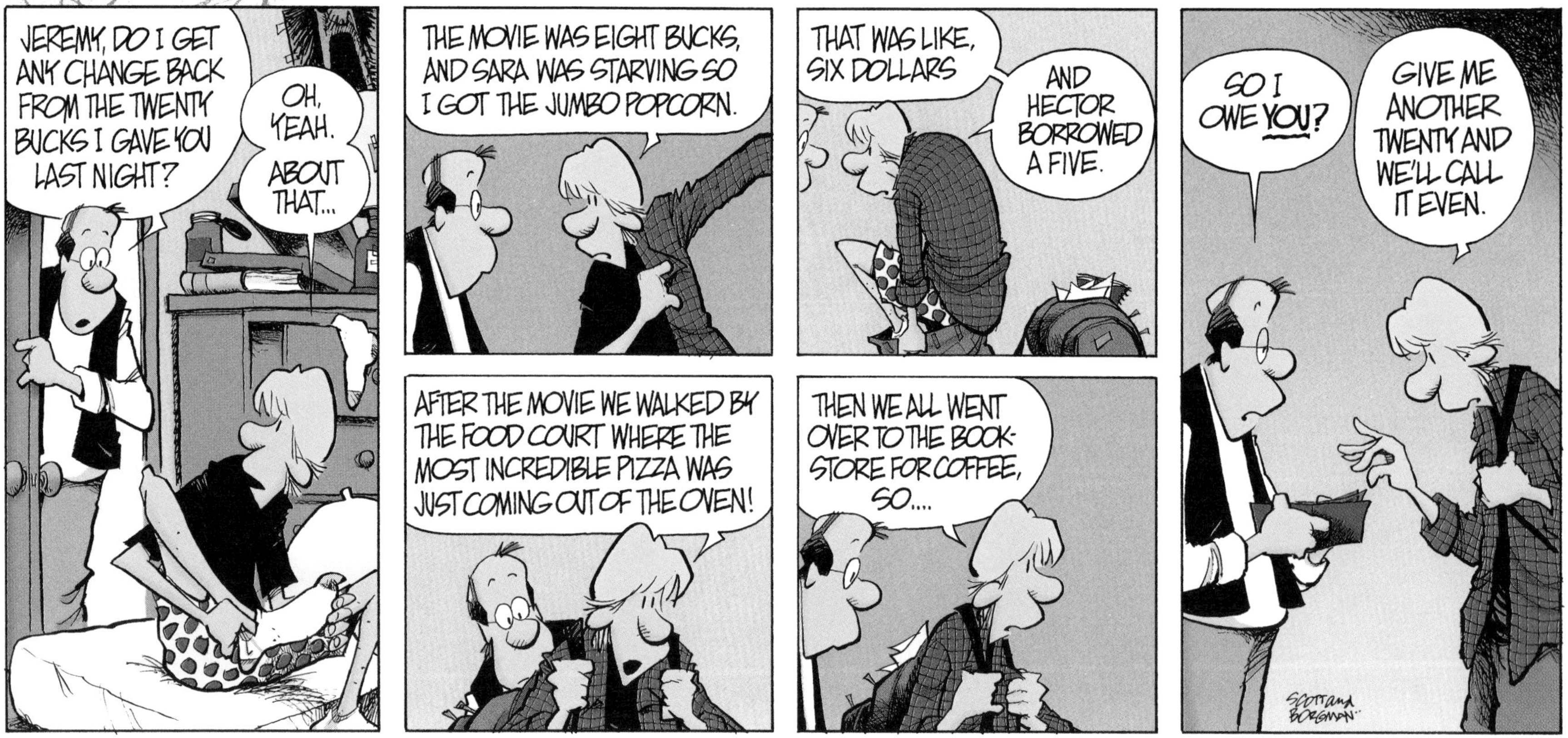
JEREMY, DO I GET ANY CHANGE BACK FROM THE TWENTY BUCKS I GAVE YOU LAST NIGHT?
OH, YEAH.
ABOUT THAT...
THE MOVIE WAS EIGHT BUCKS, AND SARA WAS STARVING SO I GOT THE JUMBO POPCORN.
AFTER THE MOVIE WE WALKED BY THE FOOD COURT WHERE THE MOST INCREDIBLE PIZZA WAS JUST COMING OUT OF THE OVEN!
THAT WAS LIKE, SIX DOLLARS
AND HECTOR BORROWED A FIVE.
THEN WE ALL WENT OVER TO THE BOOK-STORE FOR COFFEE, SO....
SO I OWE YOU?
GIVE ME ANOTHER TWENTY AND WE'LL CALL IT EVEN.
SCOTT and BORGMAN

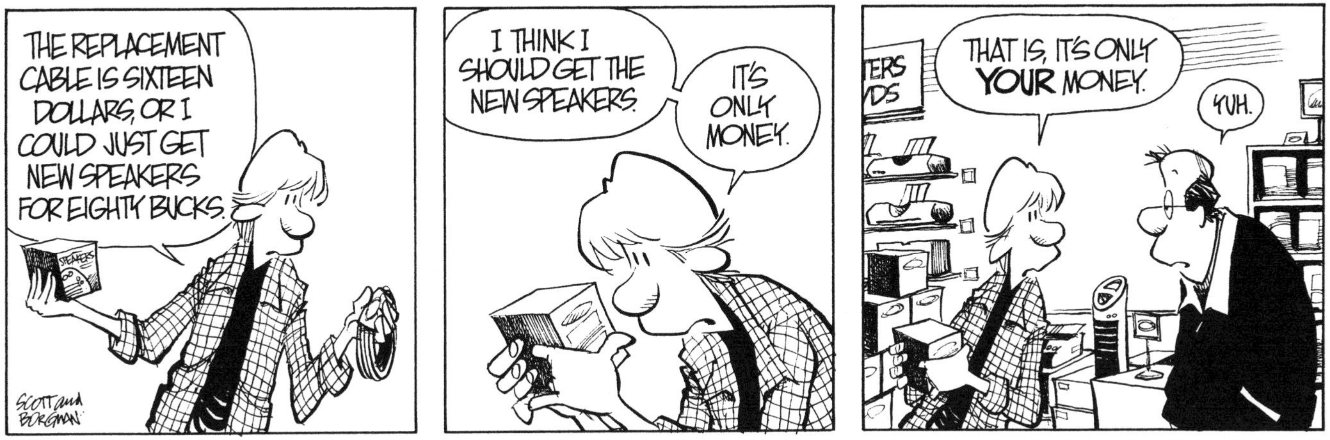
THE REPLACEMENT CABLE IS SIXTEEN DOLLARS, OR I COULD JUST GET NEW SPEAKERS FOR EIGHTY BUCKS.
SPEAKERS
SCOTT and BORGMAN
I THINK I SHOULD GET THE NEW SPEAKERS.
IT'S ONLY MONEY.
THAT IS, IT'S ONLY **YOUR** MONEY.
YUH.

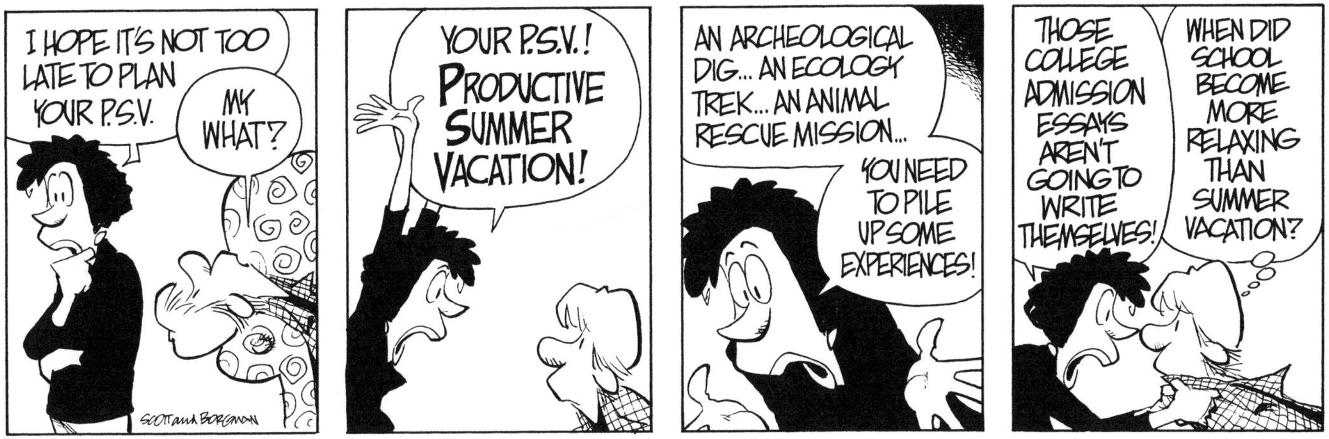
I HOPE IT'S NOT TOO LATE TO PLAN YOUR P.S.V.
MY WHAT?
SCOTT and BORGMAN
YOUR P.S.V.! PRODUCTIVE SUMMER VACATION!
AN ARCHEOLOGICAL DIG... AN ECOLOGY TREK... AN ANIMAL RESCUE MISSION...
YOU NEED TO PILE UP SOME EXPERIENCES!
THOSE COLLEGE ADMISSION ESSAYS AREN'T GOING TO WRITE THEMSELVES!
WHEN DID SCHOOL BECOME MORE RELAXING THAN SUMMER VACATION?

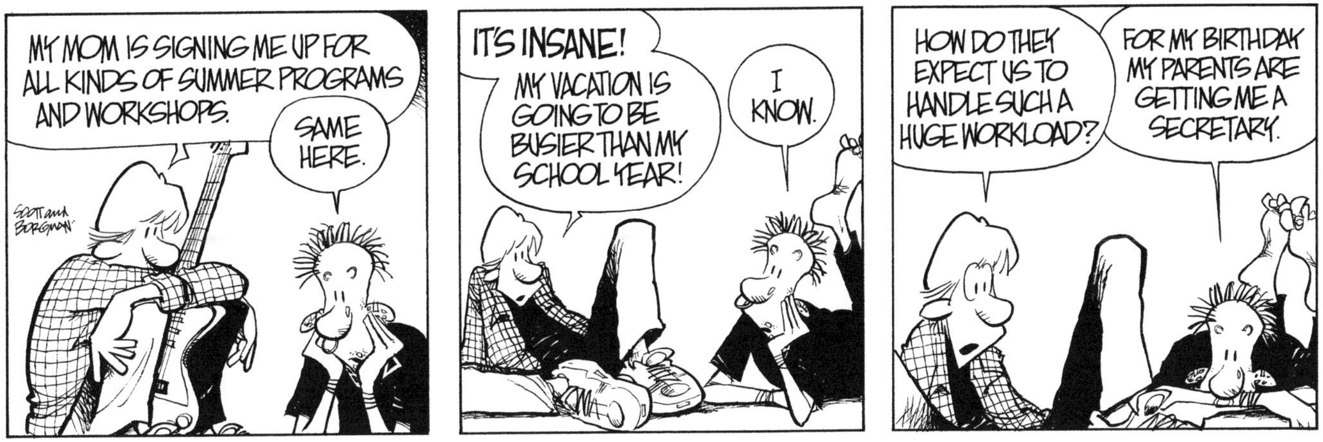
MY MOM IS SIGNING ME UP FOR ALL KINDS OF SUMMER PROGRAMS AND WORKSHOPS.
SAME HERE.
SCOTT and BORGMAN
IT'S **INSANE**!
MY VACATION IS GOING TO BE BUSIER THAN MY SCHOOL YEAR!
I KNOW.
HOW DO THEY EXPECT US TO HANDLE SUCH A HUGE WORKLOAD?
FOR MY BIRTHDAY MY PARENTS ARE GETTING ME A SECRETARY.

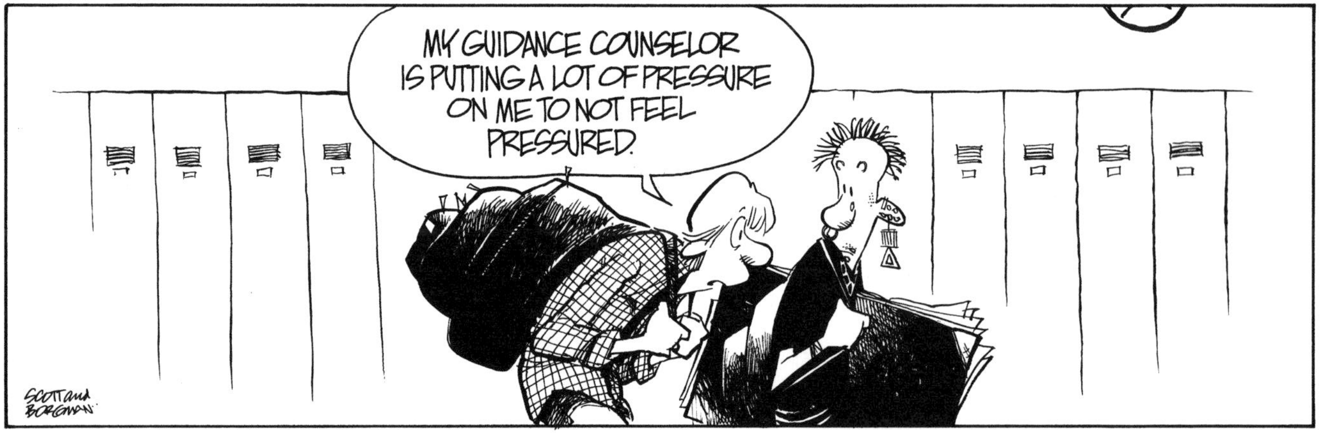
MY GUIDANCE COUNSELOR IS PUTTING A LOT OF PRESSURE ON ME TO NOT FEEL PRESSURED.

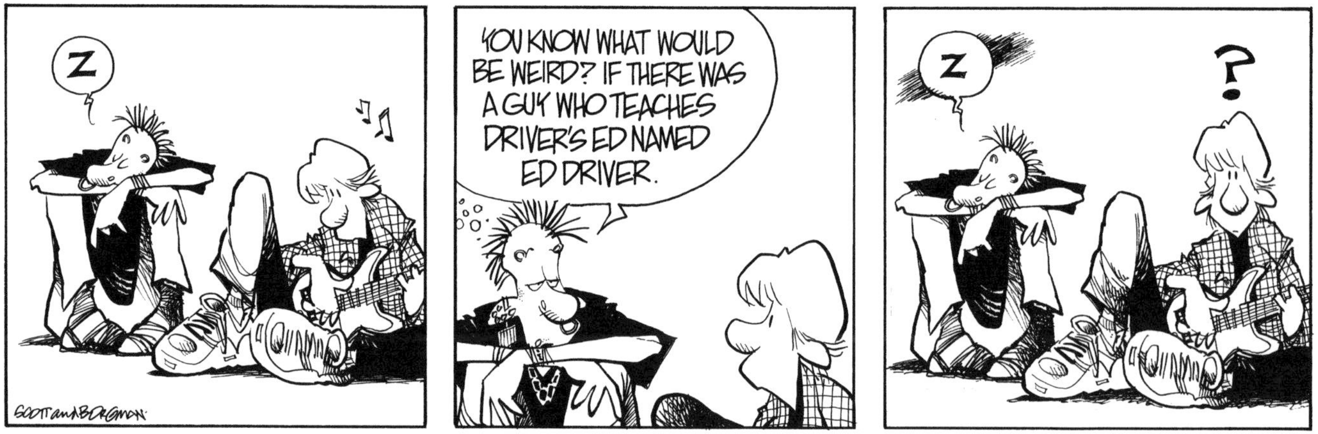
Z
YOU KNOW WHAT WOULD BE WEIRD? IF THERE WAS A GUY WHO TEACHES DRIVER'S ED NAMED ED DRIVER.
Z
?

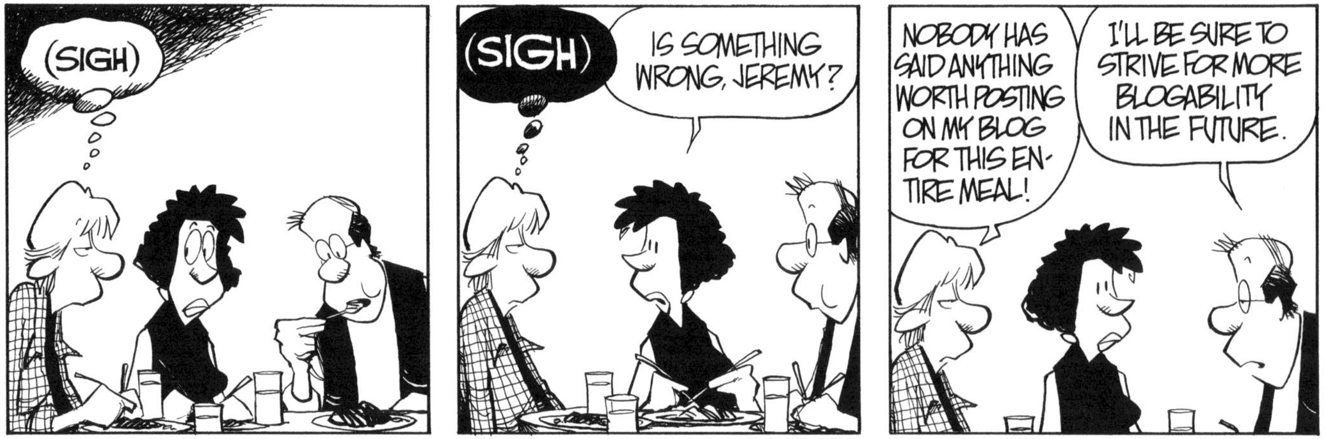
(SIGH)
(SIGH)
IS SOMETHING WRONG, JEREMY?
NOBODY HAS SAID ANYTHING WORTH POSTING ON MY BLOG FOR THIS EN-TIRE MEAL!
I'LL BE SURE TO STRIVE FOR MORE BLOGABILITY IN THE FUTURE.

Zits

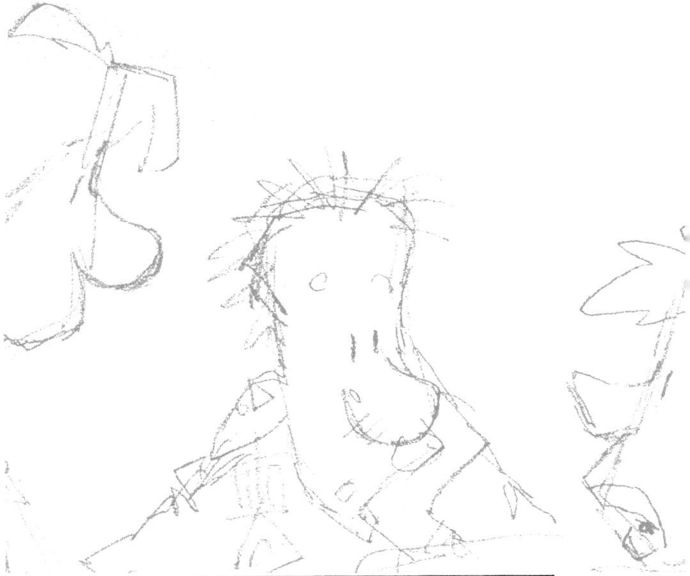

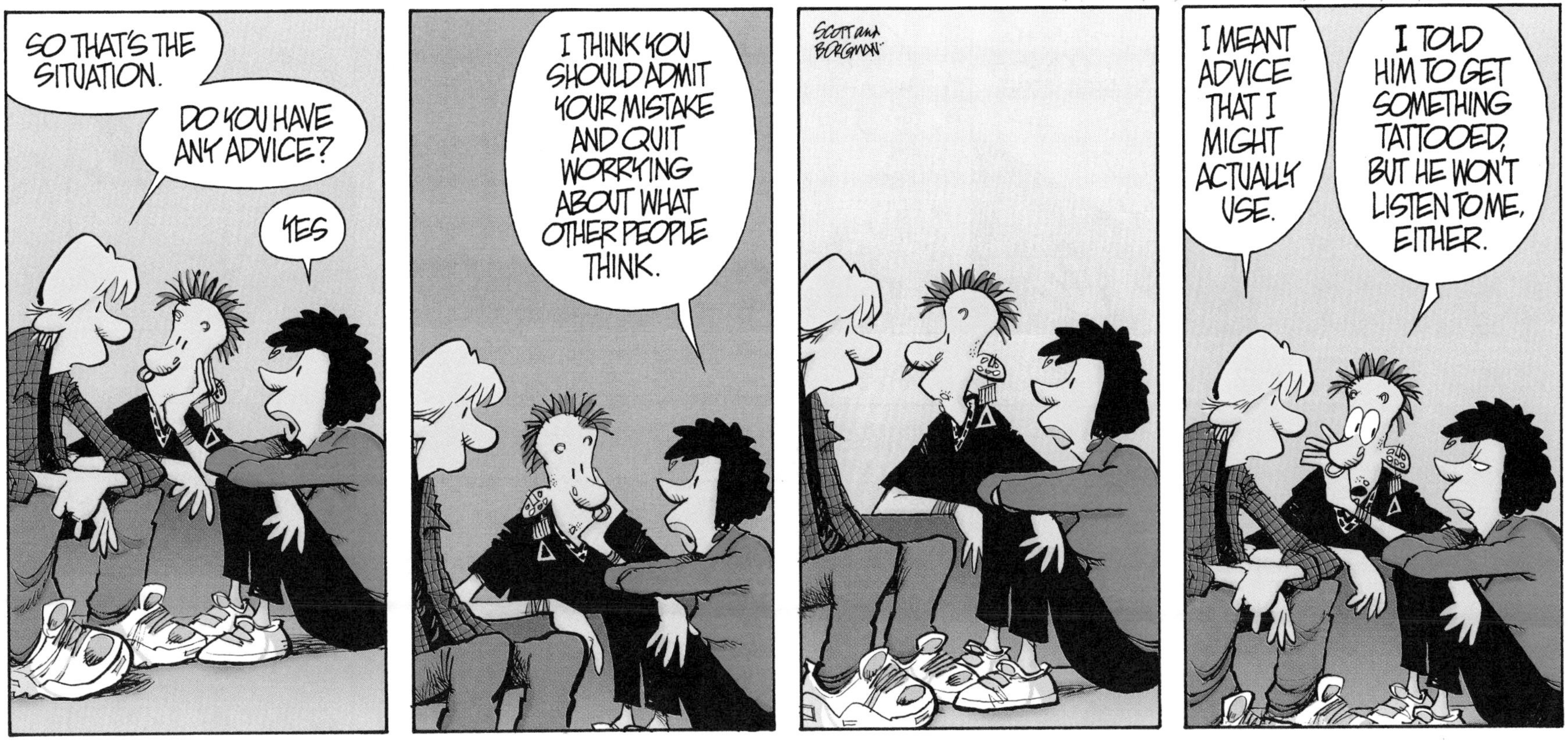
SO THAT'S THE SITUATION.
DO YOU HAVE ANY ADVICE?
YES
I THINK YOU SHOULD ADMIT YOUR MISTAKE AND QUIT WORRYING ABOUT WHAT OTHER PEOPLE THINK.
I MEANT ADVICE THAT I MIGHT ACTUALLY USE.
I TOLD HIM TO GET SOMETHING TATTOOED, BUT HE WON'T LISTEN TO ME, EITHER.

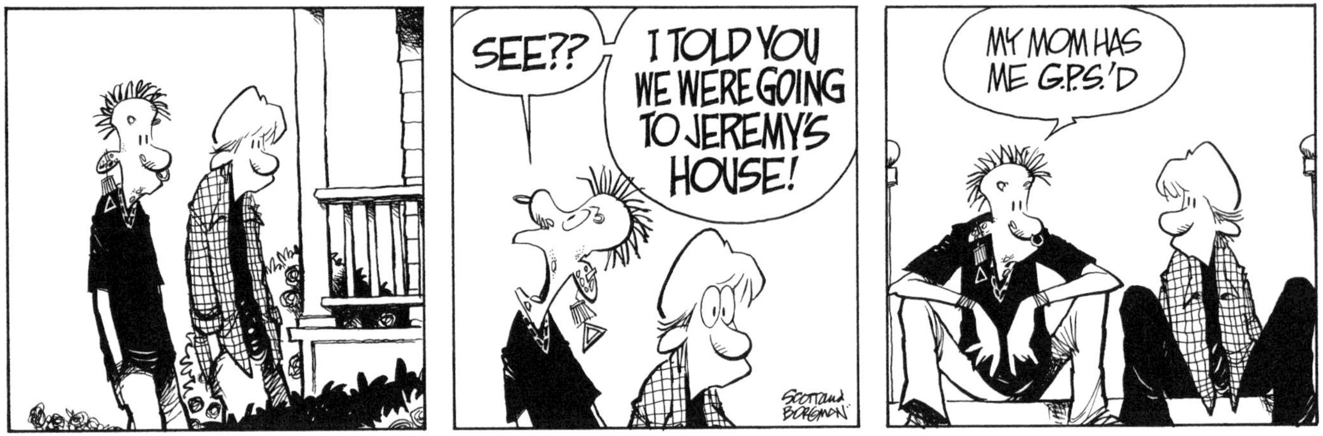
SEE??
I TOLD YOU WE WERE GOING TO JEREMY'S HOUSE!
SCOTT and BORGMAN
MY MOM HAS ME G.P.S.'D

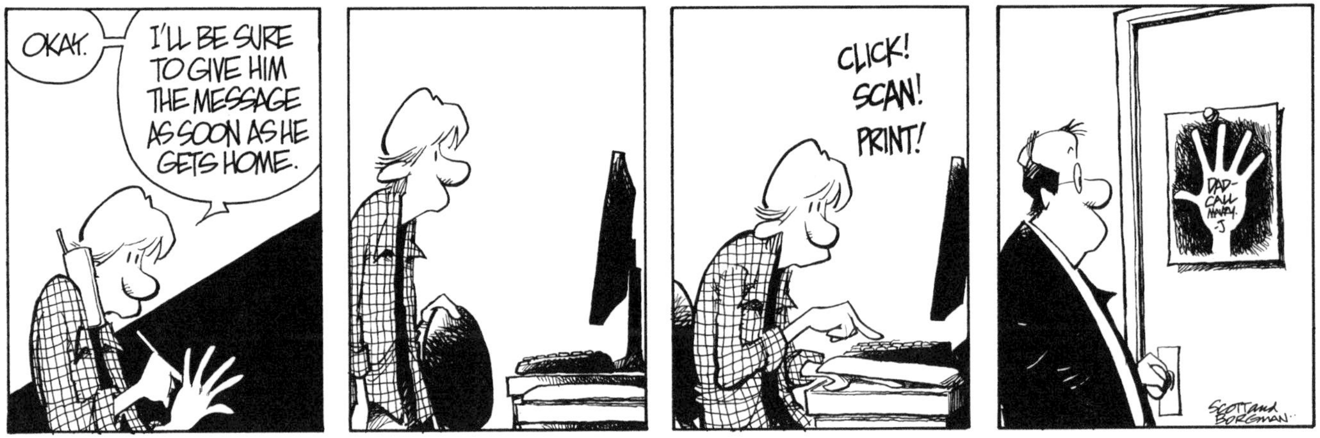
OKAY.
I'LL BE SURE TO GIVE HIM THE MESSAGE AS SOON AS HE GETS HOME.
CLICK!
SCAN!
PRINT!
DAD- CALL MARY. -J
SCOTT and BORGMAN

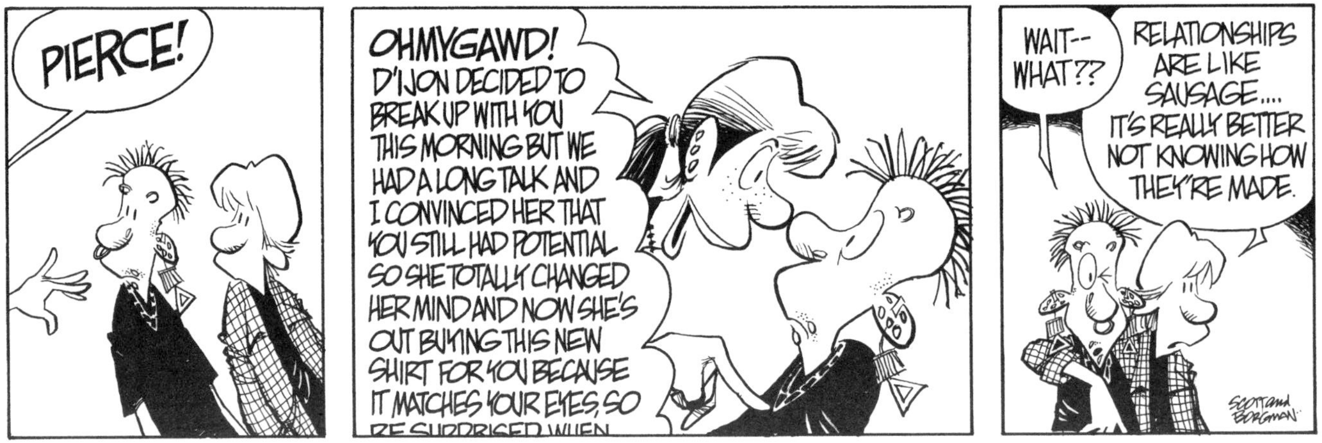
PIERCE!
OHMYGAWD! D'IJON DECIDED TO BREAK UP WITH YOU THIS MORNING BUT WE HAD A LONG TALK AND I CONVINCED HER THAT YOU STILL HAD POTENTIAL SO SHE TOTALLY CHANGED HER MIND AND NOW SHE'S OUT BUYING THIS NEW SHIRT FOR YOU BECAUSE IT MATCHES YOUR EYES, SO
WAIT-- WHAT??
RELATIONSHIPS ARE LIKE SAUSAGE.... IT'S REALLY BETTER NOT KNOWING HOW THEY'RE MADE.
SCOTT and BORGMAN

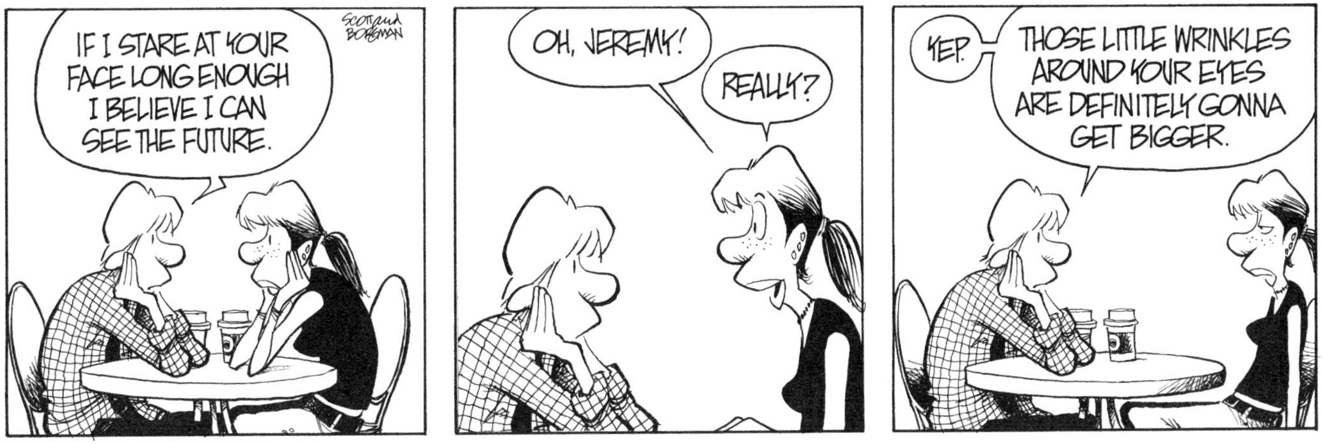
SCOTT and BORGMAN
IF I STARE AT YOUR FACE LONG ENOUGH I BELIEVE I CAN SEE THE FUTURE.
OH, JEREMY!
REALLY?
YEP.
THOSE LITTLE WRINKLES AROUND YOUR EYES ARE DEFINITELY GONNA GET BIGGER.

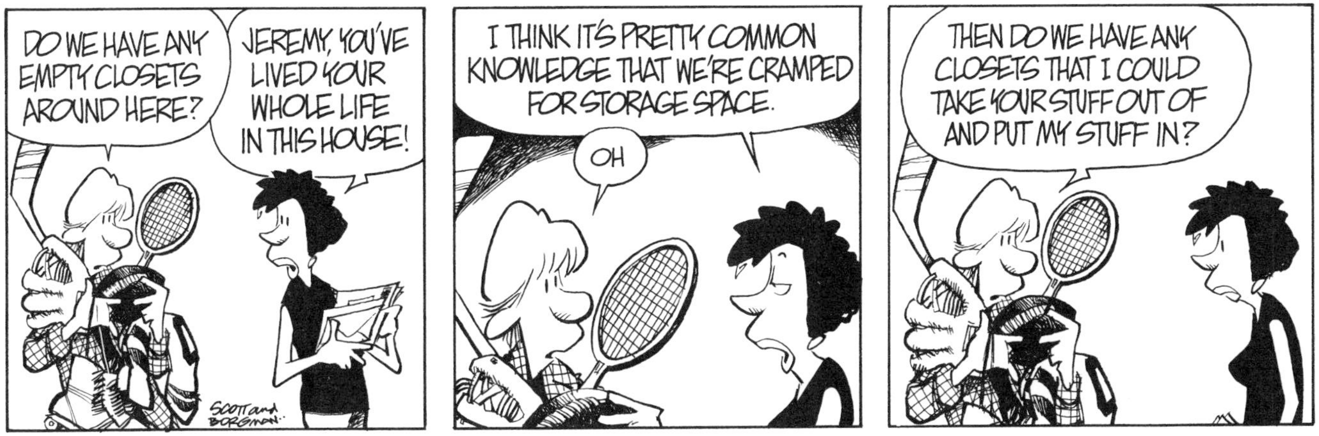
DO WE HAVE ANY EMPTY CLOSETS AROUND HERE?
JEREMY, YOU'VE LIVED YOUR WHOLE LIFE IN THIS HOUSE!
SCOTT and BORGMAN
I THINK IT'S PRETTY COMMON KNOWLEDGE THAT WE'RE CRAMPED FOR STORAGE SPACE.
OH
THEN DO WE HAVE ANY CLOSETS THAT I COULD TAKE YOUR STUFF OUT OF AND PUT MY STUFF IN?

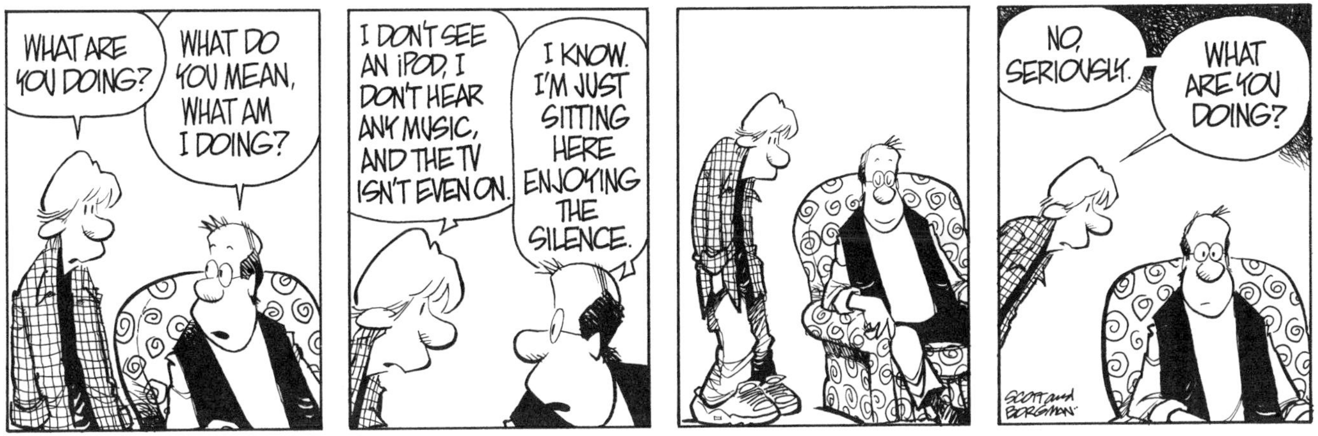
WHAT ARE YOU DOING?
WHAT DO YOU MEAN, WHAT AM I DOING?
I DON'T SEE AN iPOD, I DON'T HEAR ANY MUSIC, AND THE TV ISN'T EVEN ON.
I KNOW. I'M JUST SITTING HERE ENJOYING THE SILENCE.
NO, SERIOUSLY.
WHAT ARE YOU DOING?
SCOTT and BORGMAN

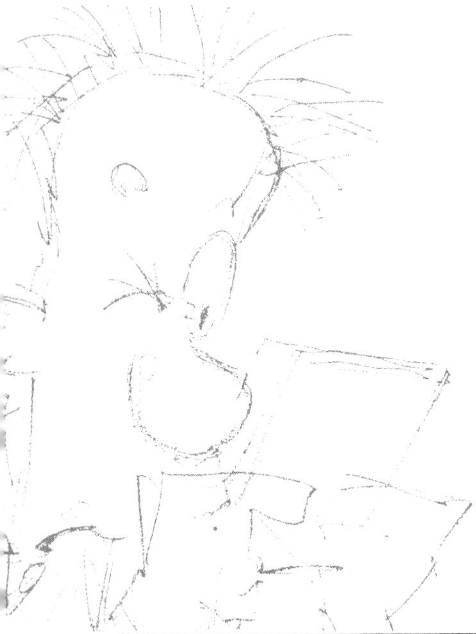

Zits

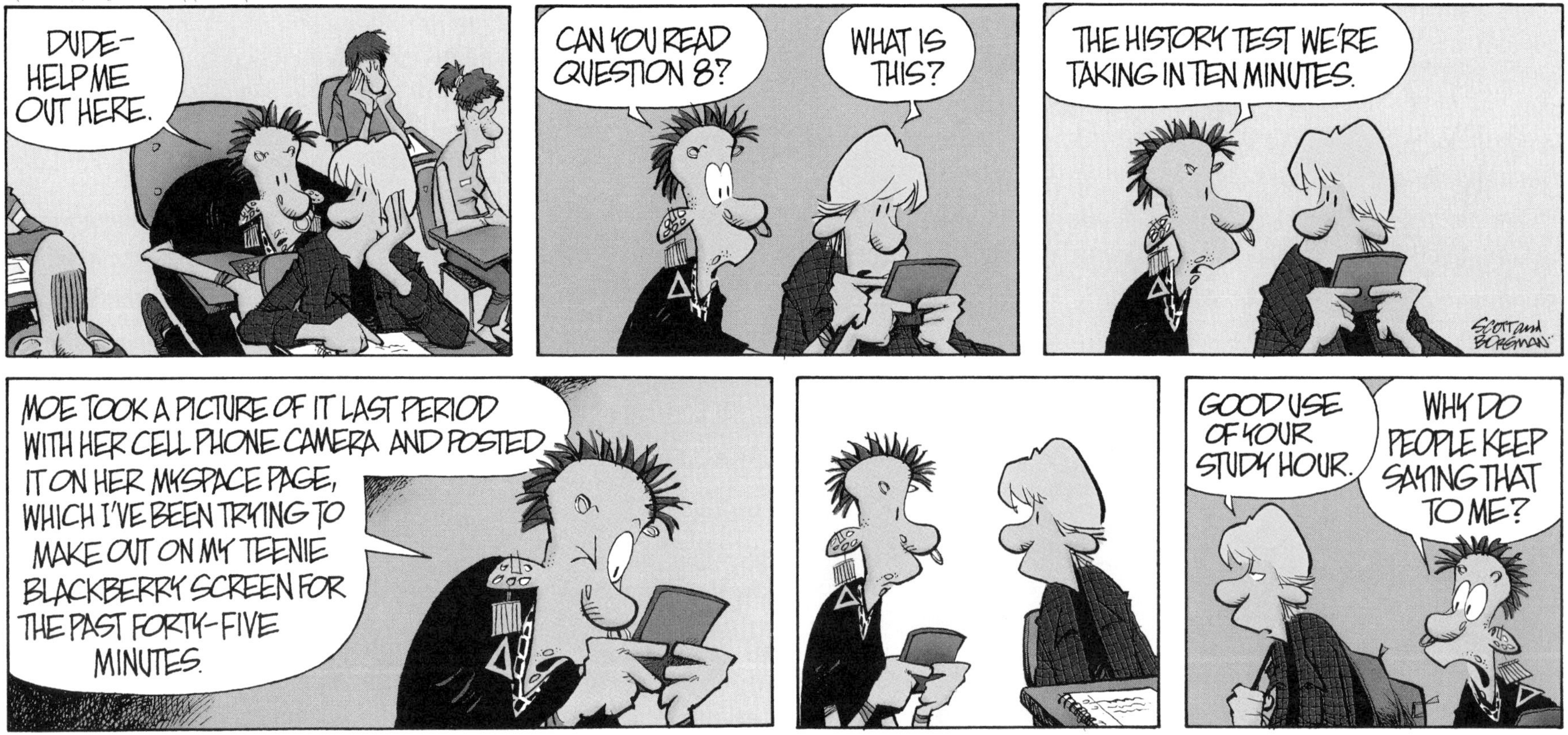
DUDE- HELP ME OUT HERE.
CAN YOU READ QUESTION 8?
WHAT IS THIS?
THE HISTORY TEST WE'RE TAKING IN TEN MINUTES.
MOE TOOK A PICTURE OF IT LAST PERIOD WITH HER CELL PHONE CAMERA AND POSTED IT ON HER MYSPACE PAGE, WHICH I'VE BEEN TRYING TO MAKE OUT ON MY TEENIE BLACKBERRY SCREEN FOR THE PAST FORTY-FIVE MINUTES.
GOOD USE OF YOUR STUDY HOUR.
WHY DO PEOPLE KEEP SAYING THAT TO ME?

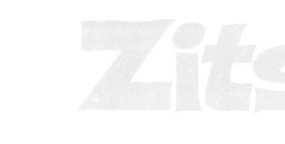

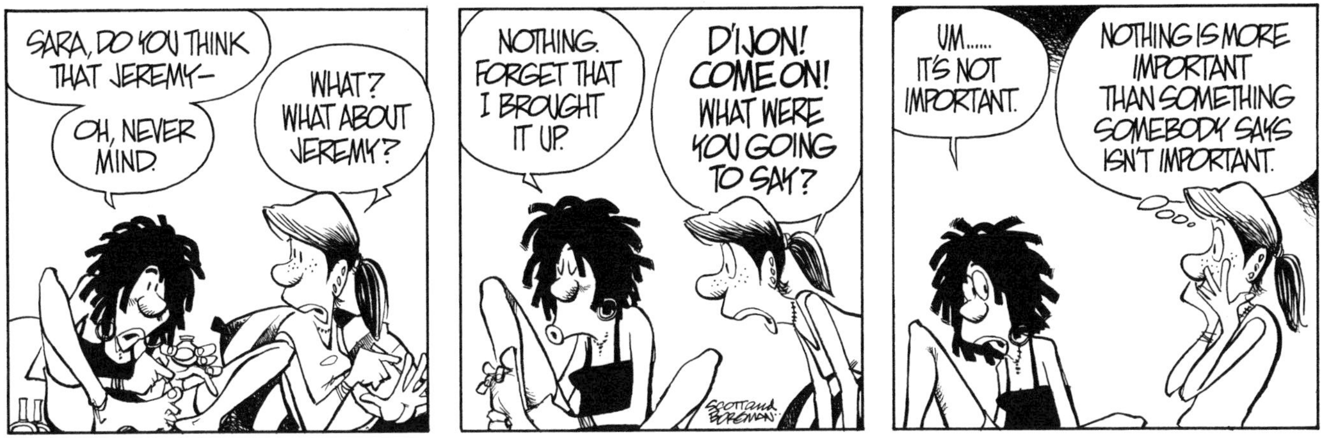
SARA, DO YOU THINK THAT JEREMY–
OH, NEVER MIND.
WHAT? WHAT ABOUT JEREMY?
NOTHING. FORGET THAT I BROUGHT IT UP.
D'IJON! COME ON! WHAT WERE YOU GOING TO SAY?
SCOTT and BORGMAN
UM...... IT'S NOT IMPORTANT.
NOTHING IS MORE IMPORTANT THAN SOMETHING SOMEBODY SAYS ISN'T IMPORTANT.

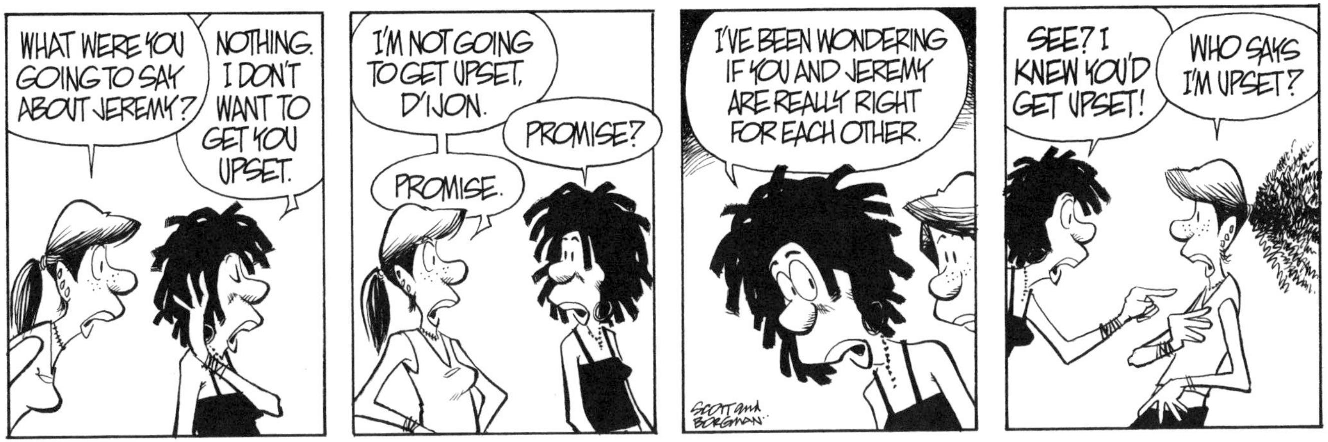
WHAT WERE YOU GOING TO SAY ABOUT JEREMY?
NOTHING. I DON'T WANT TO GET YOU UPSET.
I'M NOT GOING TO GET UPSET, D'IJON.
PROMISE?
PROMISE.
I'VE BEEN WONDERING IF YOU AND JEREMY ARE REALLY RIGHT FOR EACH OTHER.
SCOTT and BORGMAN
SEE? I KNEW YOU'D GET UPSET!
WHO SAYS I'M UPSET?

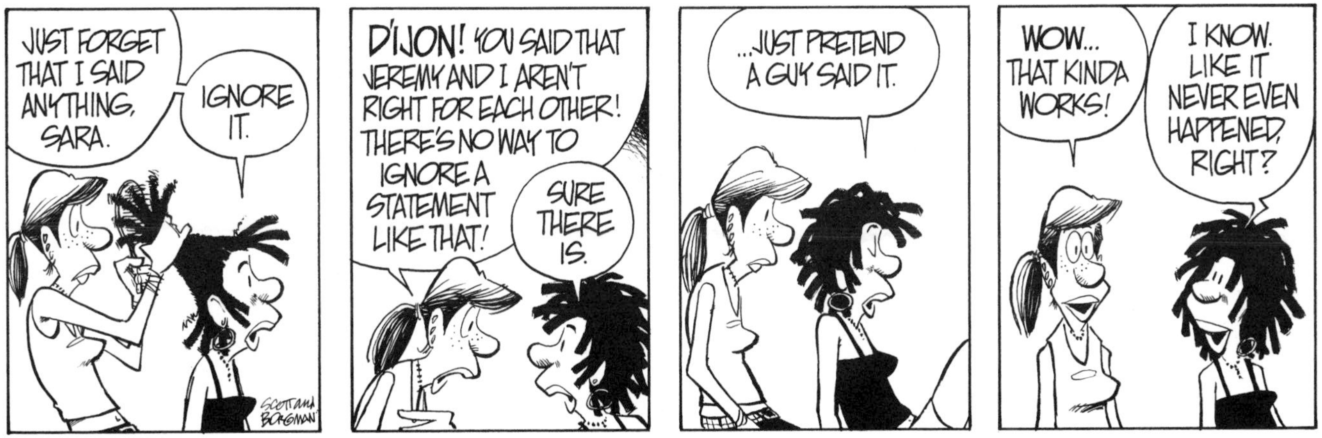
JUST FORGET THAT I SAID ANYTHING, SARA.
IGNORE IT.
SCOTT and BORGMAN
D'IJON! YOU SAID THAT JEREMY AND I AREN'T RIGHT FOR EACH OTHER! THERE'S NO WAY TO IGNORE A STATEMENT LIKE THAT!
SURE THERE IS.
...JUST PRETEND A GUY SAID IT.
WOW... THAT KINDA WORKS!
I KNOW. LIKE IT NEVER EVEN HAPPENED, RIGHT?

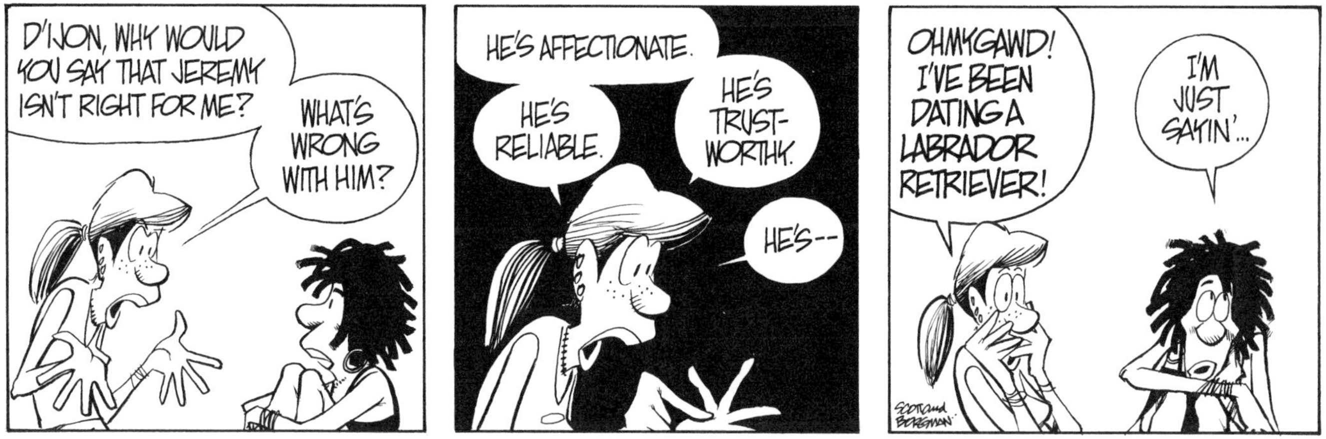
D'IJON, WHY WOULD YOU SAY THAT JEREMY ISN'T RIGHT FOR ME?
WHAT'S WRONG WITH HIM?
HE'S AFFECTIONATE.
HE'S RELIABLE.
HE'S TRUST-WORTHY.
HE'S--
OHMYGAWD! I'VE BEEN DATING A LABRADOR RETRIEVER!
I'M JUST SAYIN'...

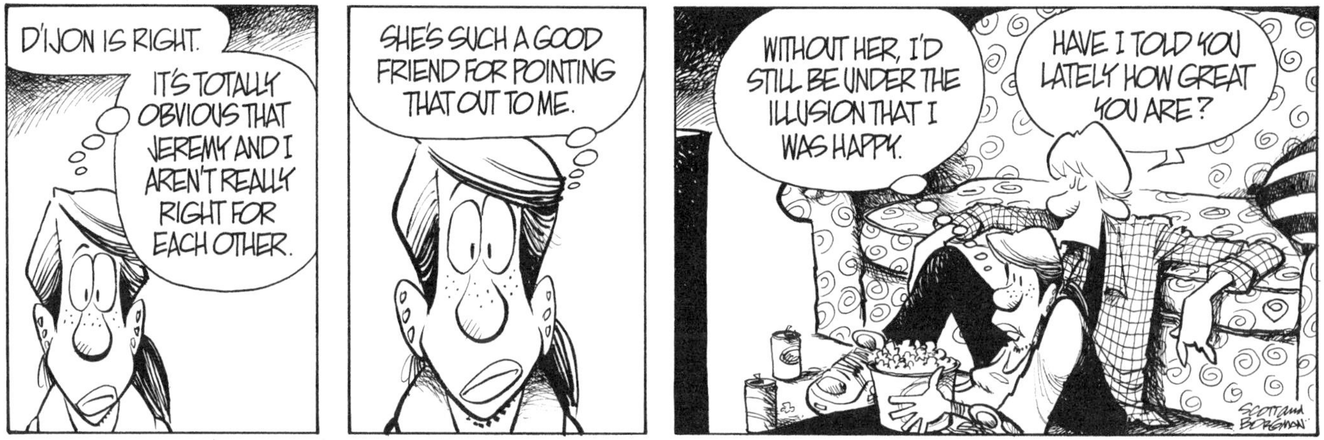
D'IJON IS RIGHT.
IT'S TOTALLY OBVIOUS THAT JEREMY AND I AREN'T REALLY RIGHT FOR EACH OTHER.
SHE'S SUCH A GOOD FRIEND FOR POINTING THAT OUT TO ME.
WITHOUT HER, I'D STILL BE UNDER THE ILLUSION THAT I WAS HAPPY.
HAVE I TOLD YOU LATELY HOW GREAT YOU ARE?

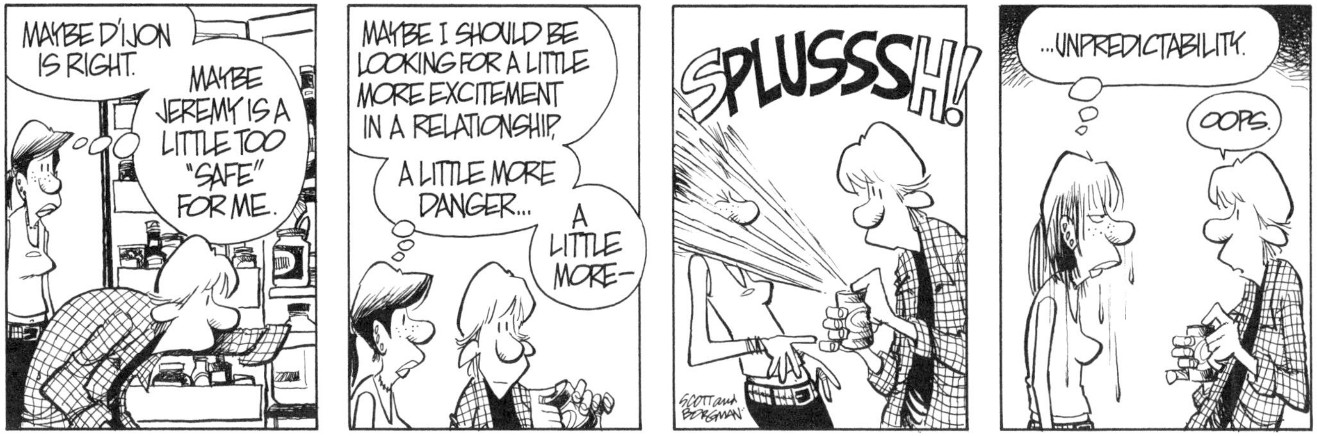
MAYBE D'IJON IS RIGHT.
MAYBE JEREMY IS A LITTLE TOO "SAFE" FOR ME.
MAYBE I SHOULD BE LOOKING FOR A LITTLE MORE EXCITEMENT IN A RELATIONSHIP,
A LITTLE MORE DANGER...
A LITTLE MORE-
SPLUSSSH!
...UNPREDICTABILITY.
OOPS.

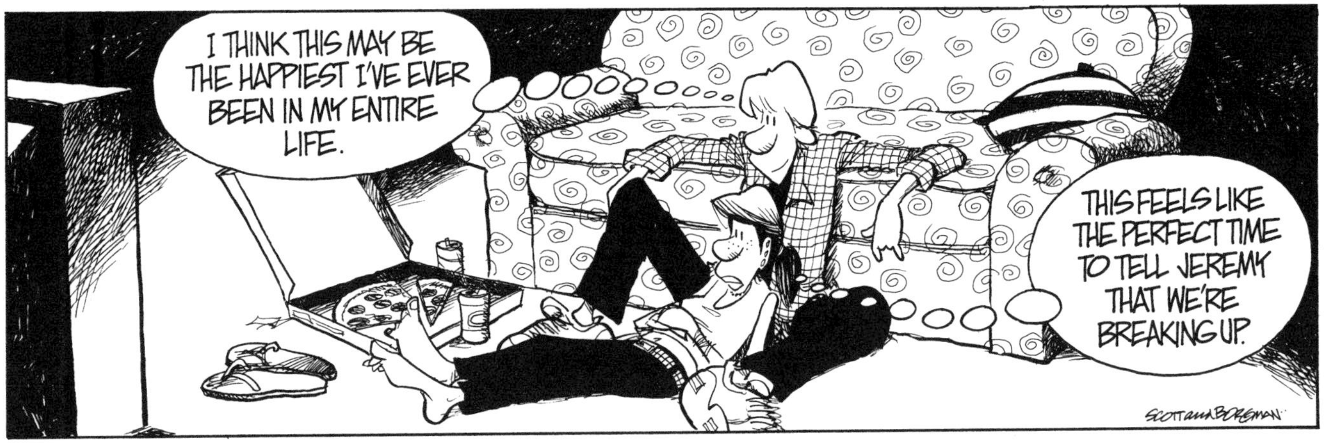
I THINK THIS MAY BE THE HAPPIEST I'VE EVER BEEN IN MY ENTIRE LIFE.
THIS FEELS LIKE THE PERFECT TIME TO TELL JEREMY THAT WE'RE BREAKING UP.
SCOTT and BORGMAN

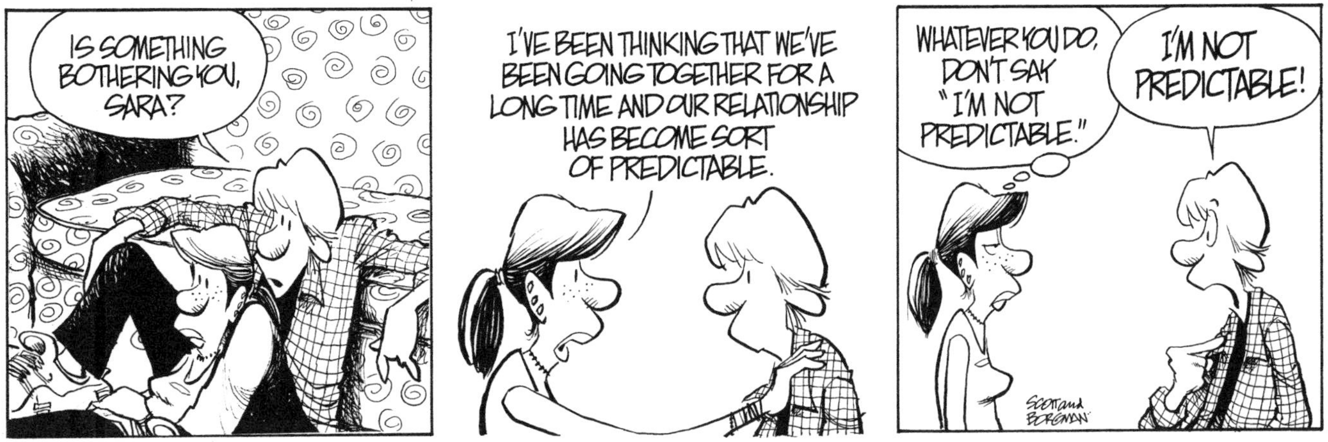
IS SOMETHING BOTHERING YOU, SARA?
I'VE BEEN THINKING THAT WE'VE BEEN GOING TOGETHER FOR A LONG TIME AND OUR RELATIONSHIP HAS BECOME SORT OF PREDICTABLE.
WHATEVER YOU DO, DON'T SAY "I'M NOT PREDICTABLE."
I'M NOT PREDICTABLE!
SCOTT and BORGMAN

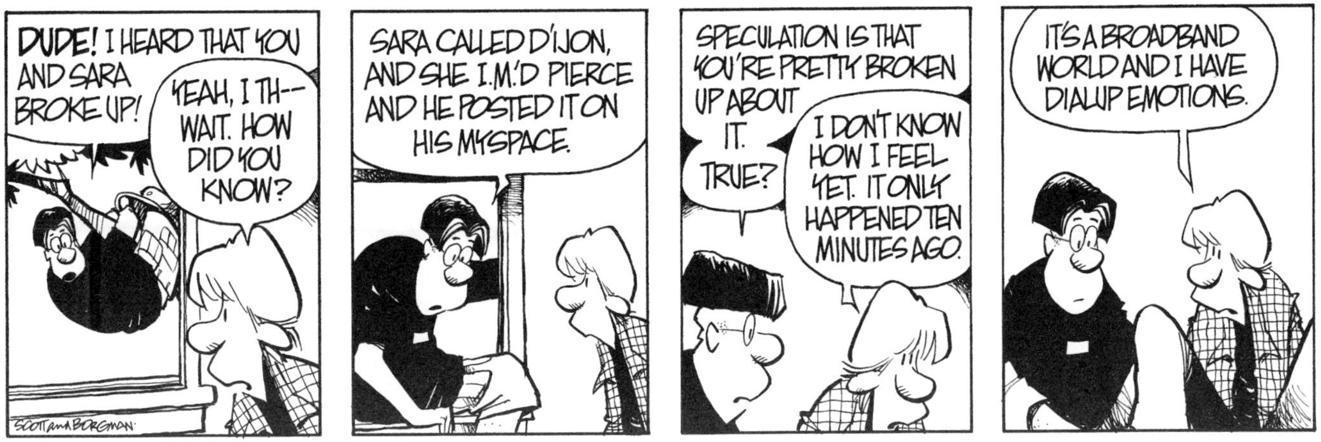
DUDE! I HEARD THAT YOU AND SARA BROKE UP!
YEAH, I TH-- WAIT. HOW DID YOU KNOW?
SARA CALLED D'IJON, AND SHE I.M.'D PIERCE AND HE POSTED IT ON HIS MYSPACE.
SPECULATION IS THAT YOU'RE PRETTY BROKEN UP ABOUT IT. TRUE?
I DON'T KNOW HOW I FEEL YET. IT ONLY HAPPENED TEN MINUTES AGO.
IT'S A BROADBAND WORLD AND I HAVE DIALUP EMOTIONS.
SCOTT and BORGMAN

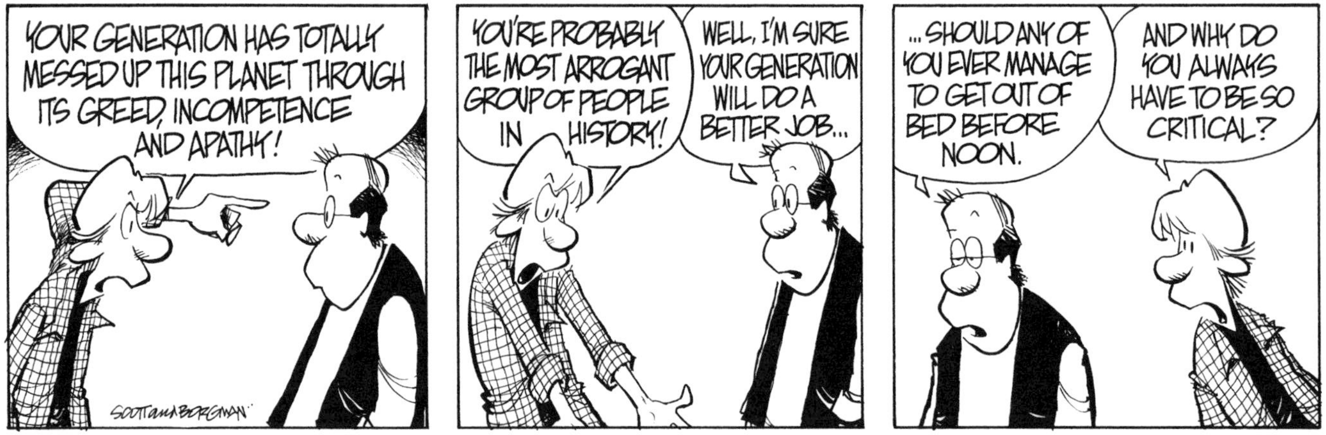
YOUR GENERATION HAS TOTALLY MESSED UP THIS PLANET THROUGH ITS GREED, INCOMPETENCE AND APATHY!
YOU'RE PROBABLY THE MOST ARROGANT GROUP OF PEOPLE IN HISTORY!
WELL, I'M SURE YOUR GENERATION WILL DO A BETTER JOB...
...SHOULD ANY OF YOU EVER MANAGE TO GET OUT OF BED BEFORE NOON.
AND WHY DO YOU ALWAYS HAVE TO BE SO CRITICAL?

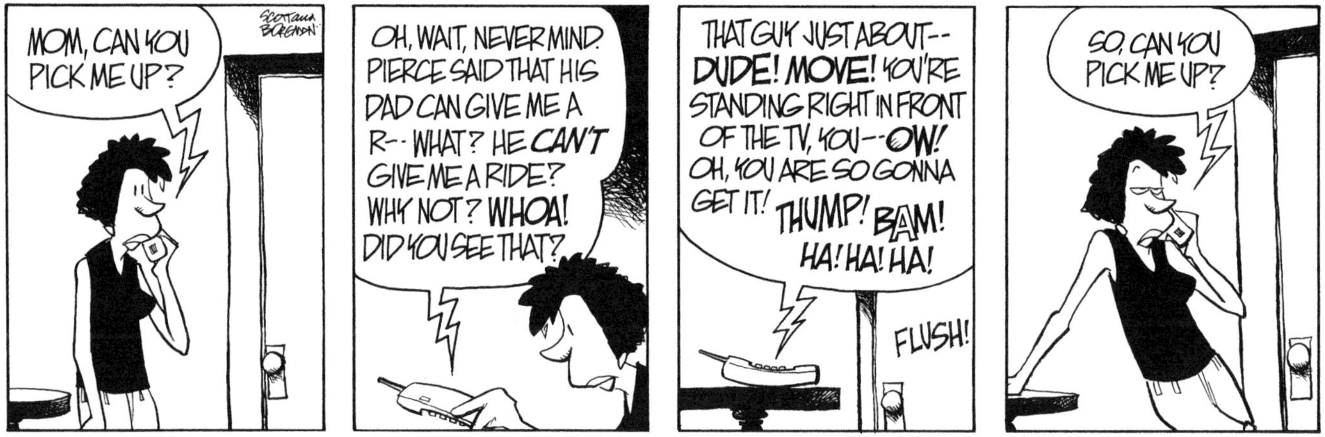
MOM, CAN YOU PICK ME UP?
OH, WAIT, NEVER MIND. PIERCE SAID THAT HIS DAD CAN GIVE ME A R-- WHAT? HE CAN'T GIVE ME A RIDE? WHY NOT? WHOA! DID YOU SEE THAT?
THAT GUY JUST ABOUT-- DUDE! MOVE! YOU'RE STANDING RIGHT IN FRONT OF THE TV, YOU--OW! OH, YOU ARE SO GONNA GET IT!
THUMP! BAM! HA! HA! HA!
FLUSH!
SO, CAN YOU PICK ME UP?

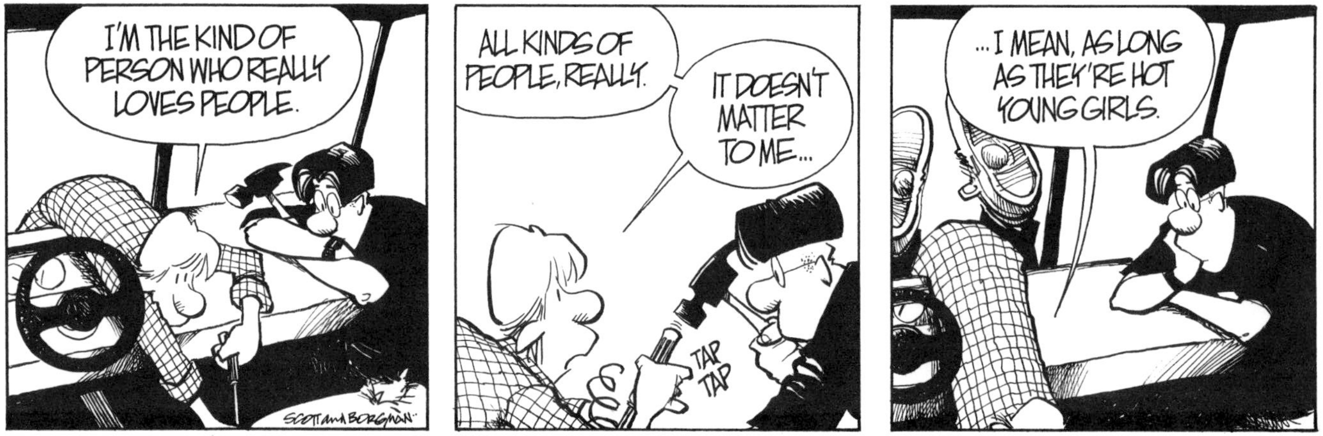
I'M THE KIND OF PERSON WHO REALLY LOVES PEOPLE.
ALL KINDS OF PEOPLE, REALLY.
IT DOESN'T MATTER TO ME...
TAP TAP
...I MEAN, AS LONG AS THEY'RE HOT YOUNG GIRLS.

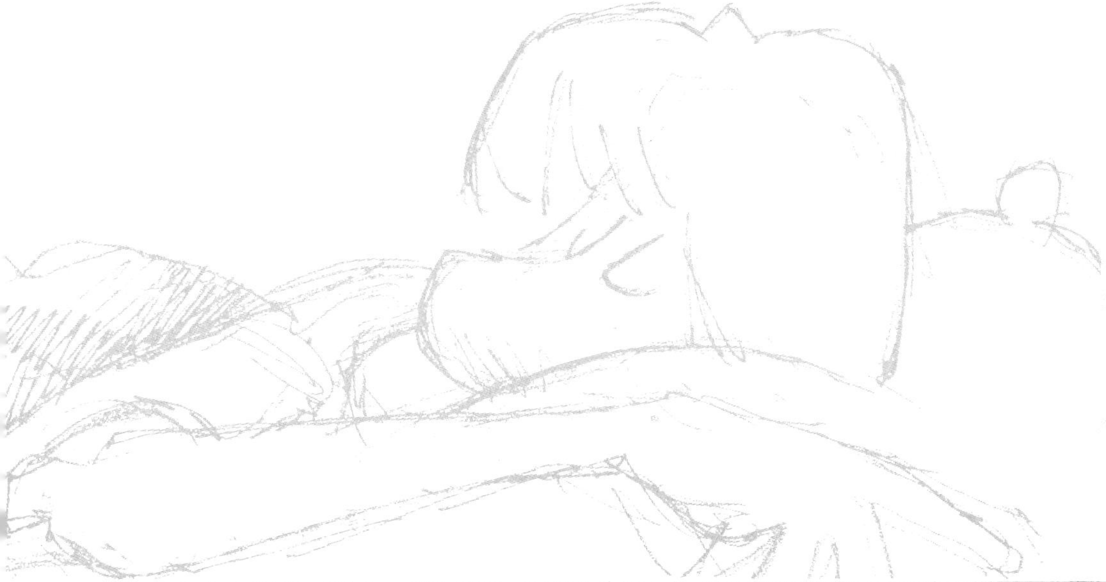

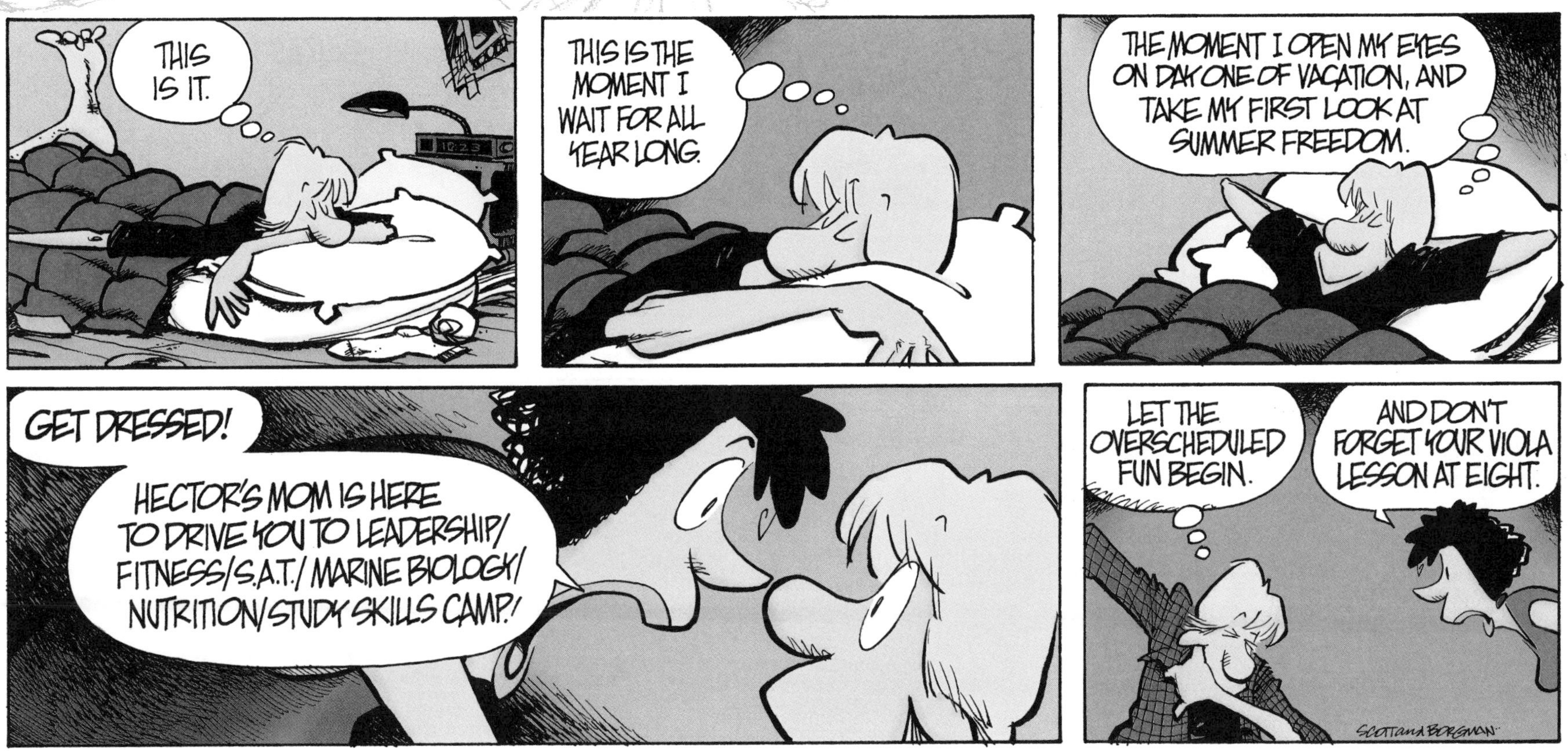
THIS IS IT.
THIS IS THE MOMENT I WAIT FOR ALL YEAR LONG.
THE MOMENT I OPEN MY EYES ON DAY ONE OF VACATION, AND TAKE MY FIRST LOOK AT SUMMER FREEDOM.
GET DRESSED!
HECTOR'S MOM IS HERE TO DRIVE YOU TO LEADERSHIP/ FITNESS/S.A.T./ MARINE BIOLOGY/ NUTRITION/STUDY SKILLS CAMP!
LET THE OVERSCHEDULED FUN BEGIN.
AND DON'T FORGET YOUR VIOLA LESSON AT EIGHT.
SCOTT and BORGMAN

Zits

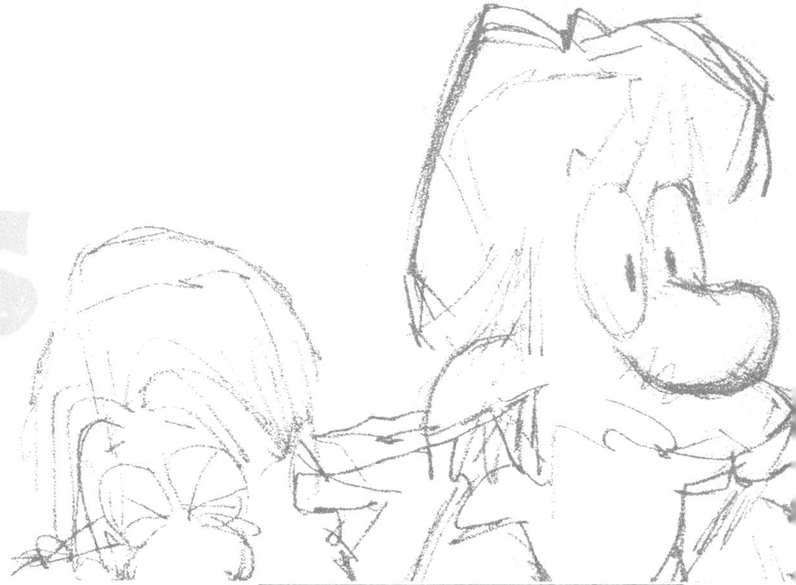

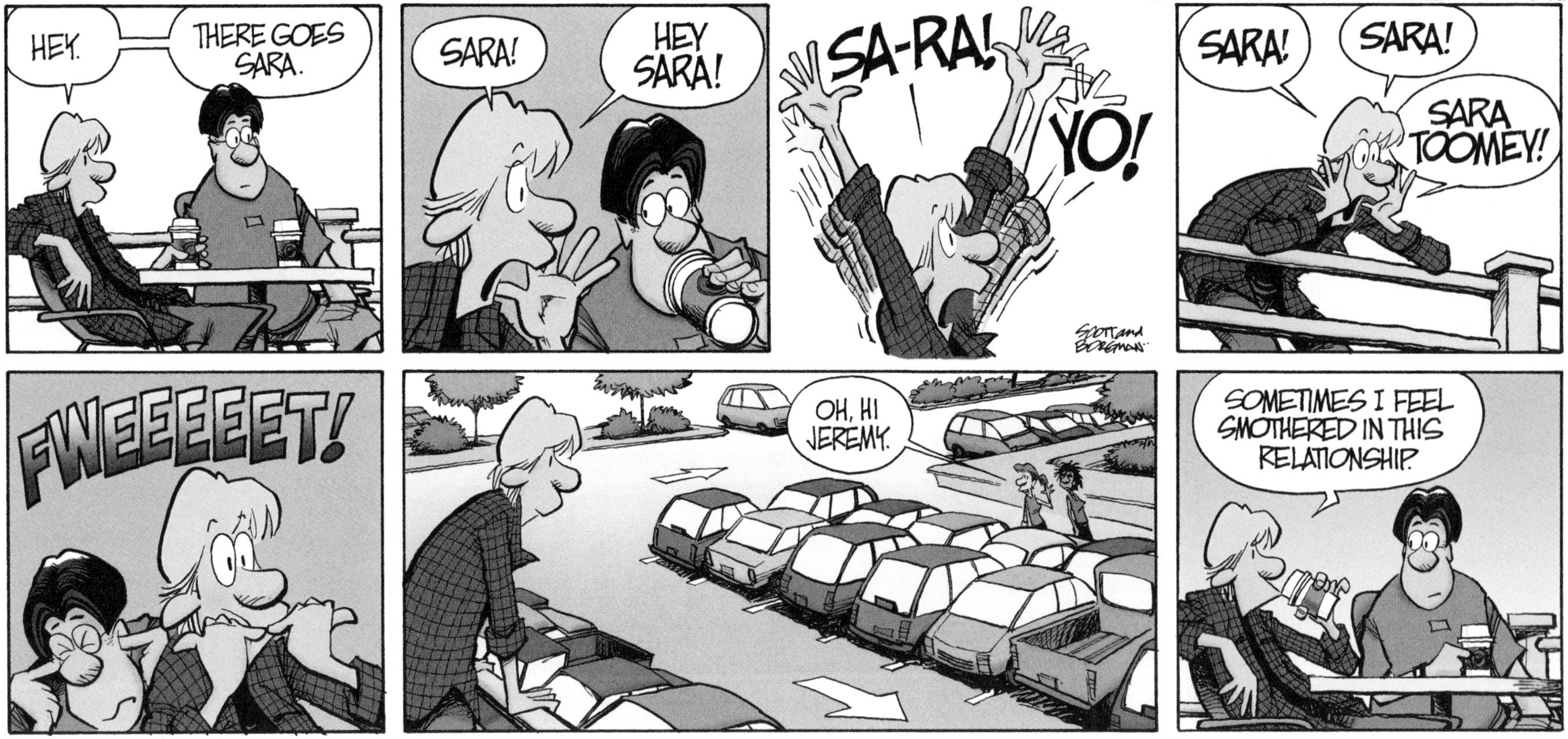

HEY.
THERE GOES SARA.
SARA!
HEY SARA!
SA-RA!
YO!
SARA!
SARA!
SARA TOOMEY!
FWEEEEEET!
OH, HI JEREMY.
SOMETIMES I FEEL SMOTHERED IN THIS RELATIONSHIP.

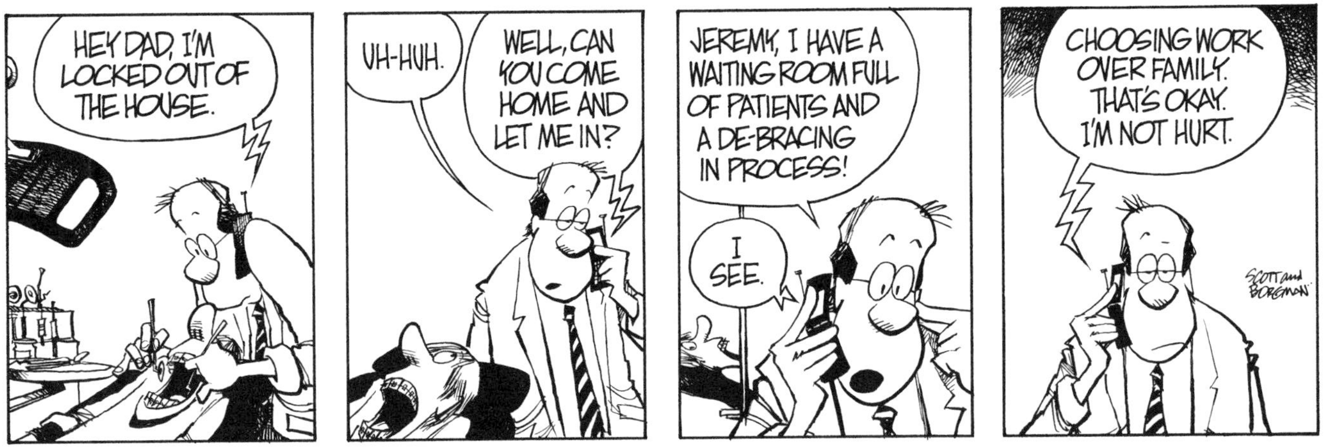
HEY DAD, I'M LOCKED OUT OF THE HOUSE.
UH-HUH.
WELL, CAN YOU COME HOME AND LET ME IN?
JEREMY, I HAVE A WAITING ROOM FULL OF PATIENTS AND A DE-BRACING IN PROCESS!
I SEE.
CHOOSING WORK OVER FAMILY. THAT'S OKAY. I'M NOT HURT.
SCOTT AND BORGMAN

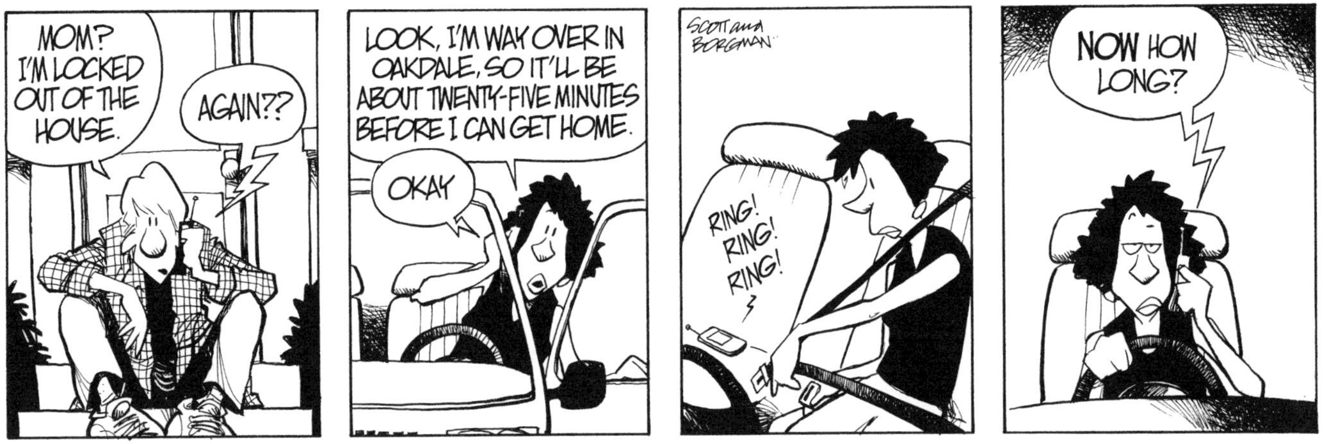
MOM? I'M LOCKED OUT OF THE HOUSE.
AGAIN??
LOOK, I'M WAY OVER IN OAKDALE, SO IT'LL BE ABOUT TWENTY-FIVE MINUTES BEFORE I CAN GET HOME.
OKAY
SCOTT AND BORGMAN
RING! RING! RING!
NOW HOW LONG?

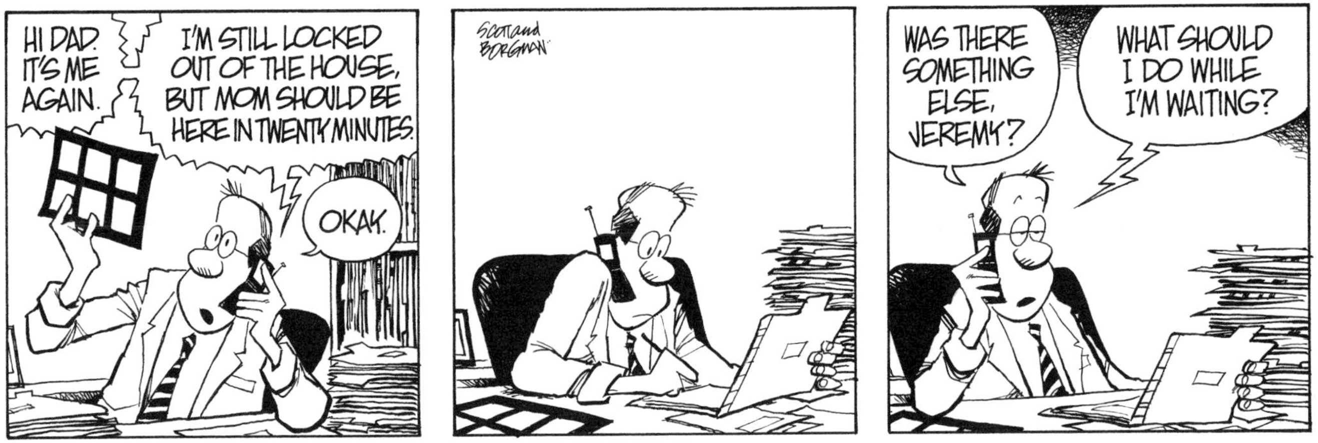
HI DAD. IT'S ME AGAIN.
I'M STILL LOCKED OUT OF THE HOUSE, BUT MOM SHOULD BE HERE IN TWENTY MINUTES.
OKAY.
SCOTT AND BORGMAN
WAS THERE SOMETHING ELSE, JEREMY?
WHAT SHOULD I DO WHILE I'M WAITING?

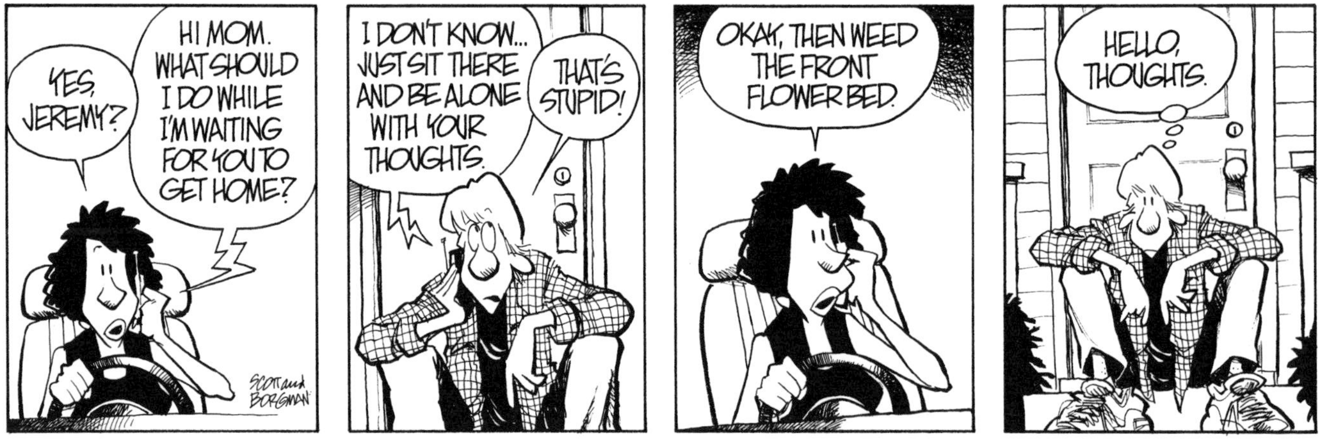
HI MOM. WHAT SHOULD I DO WHILE I'M WAITING FOR YOU TO GET HOME?
YES, JEREMY?
I DON'T KNOW... JUST SIT THERE AND BE ALONE WITH YOUR THOUGHTS.
THAT'S STUPID!
OKAY, THEN WEED THE FRONT FLOWER BED.
HELLO, THOUGHTS.
SCOTT and BORGMAN

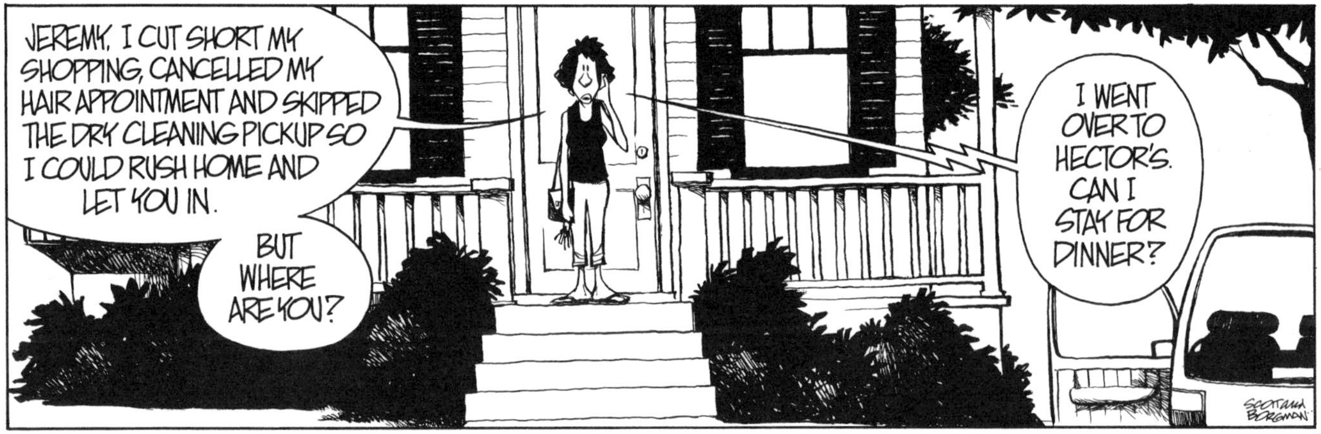
JEREMY, I CUT SHORT MY SHOPPING, CANCELLED MY HAIR APPOINTMENT AND SKIPPED THE DRY CLEANING PICKUP SO I COULD RUSH HOME AND LET YOU IN.
BUT WHERE ARE YOU?
I WENT OVER TO HECTOR'S. CAN I STAY FOR DINNER?
SCOTT and BORGMAN

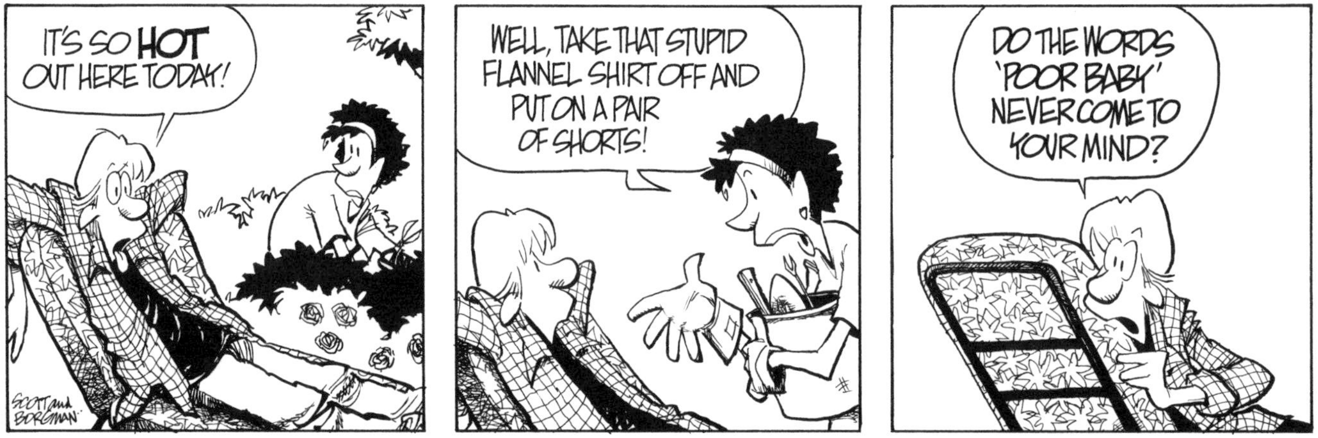
IT'S SO **HOT** OUT HERE TODAY!
WELL, TAKE THAT STUPID FLANNEL SHIRT OFF AND PUT ON A PAIR OF SHORTS!
DO THE WORDS 'POOR BABY' NEVER COME TO YOUR MIND?
SCOTT and BORGMAN

Zits

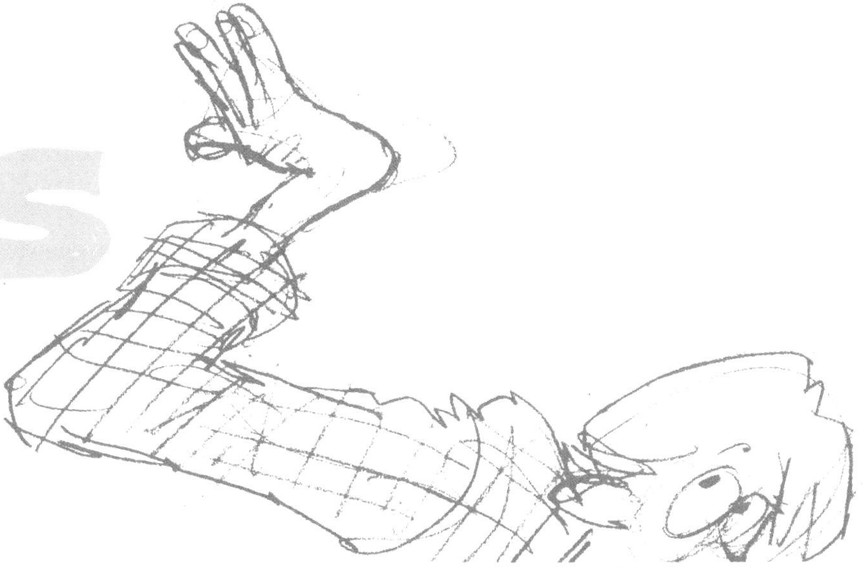

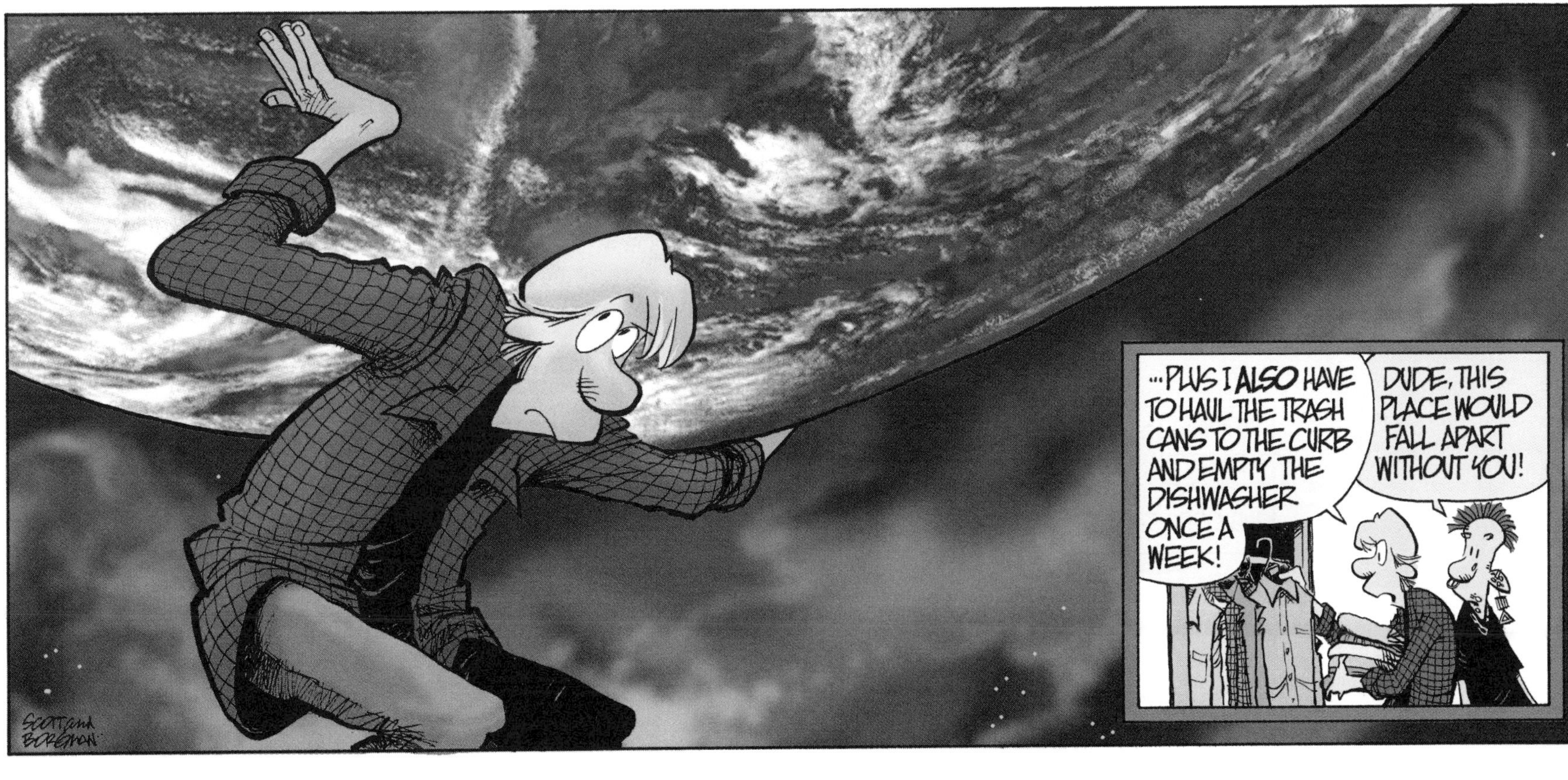
...PLUS I **ALSO** HAVE TO HAUL THE TRASH CANS TO THE CURB AND EMPTY THE DISHWASHER ONCE A WEEK!
DUDE, THIS PLACE WOULD FALL APART WITHOUT YOU!

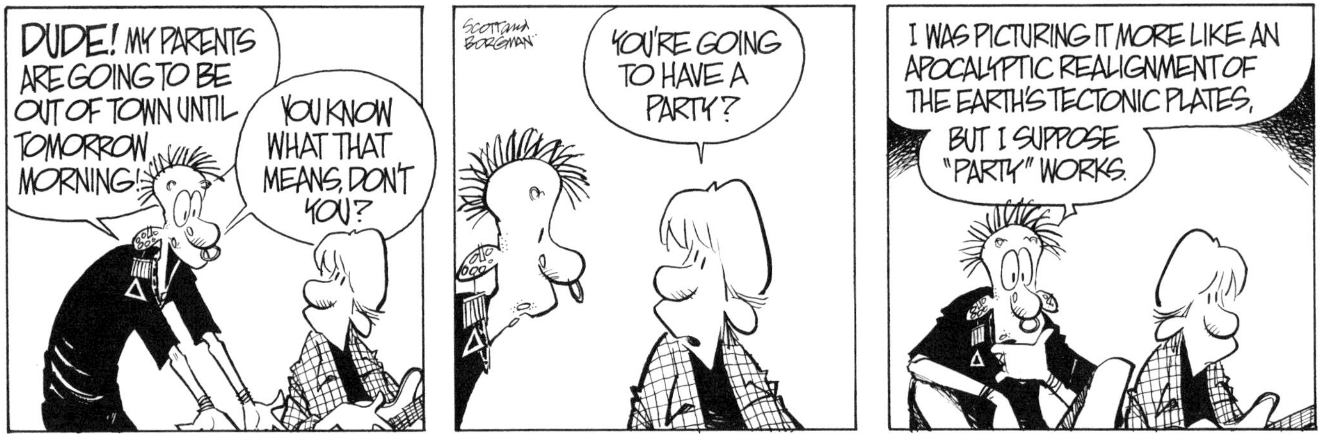
DUDE! MY PARENTS ARE GOING TO BE OUT OF TOWN UNTIL TOMORROW MORNING!
YOU KNOW WHAT THAT MEANS, DON'T YOU?
YOU'RE GOING TO HAVE A PARTY?
I WAS PICTURING IT MORE LIKE AN APOCALYPTIC REALIGNMENT OF THE EARTH'S TECTONIC PLATES,
BUT I SUPPOSE "PARTY" WORKS.

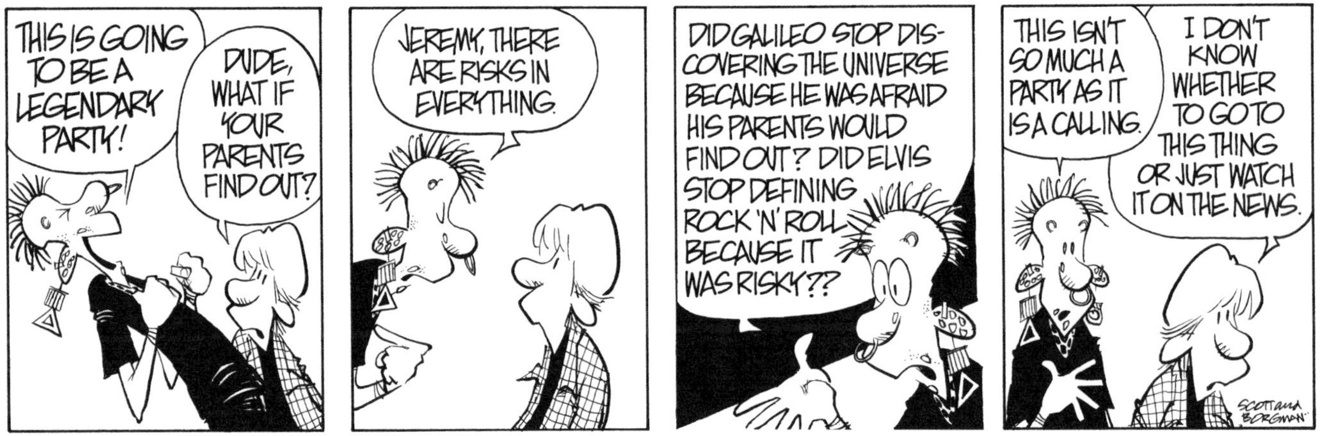
THIS IS GOING TO BE A LEGENDARY PARTY!
DUDE, WHAT IF YOUR PARENTS FIND OUT?
JEREMY, THERE ARE RISKS IN EVERYTHING.
DID GALILEO STOP DISCOVERING THE UNIVERSE BECAUSE HE WAS AFRAID HIS PARENTS WOULD FIND OUT? DID ELVIS STOP DEFINING ROCK 'N' ROLL BECAUSE IT WAS RISKY??
THIS ISN'T SO MUCH A PARTY AS IT IS A CALLING.
I DON'T KNOW WHETHER TO GO TO THIS THING OR JUST WATCH IT ON THE NEWS.

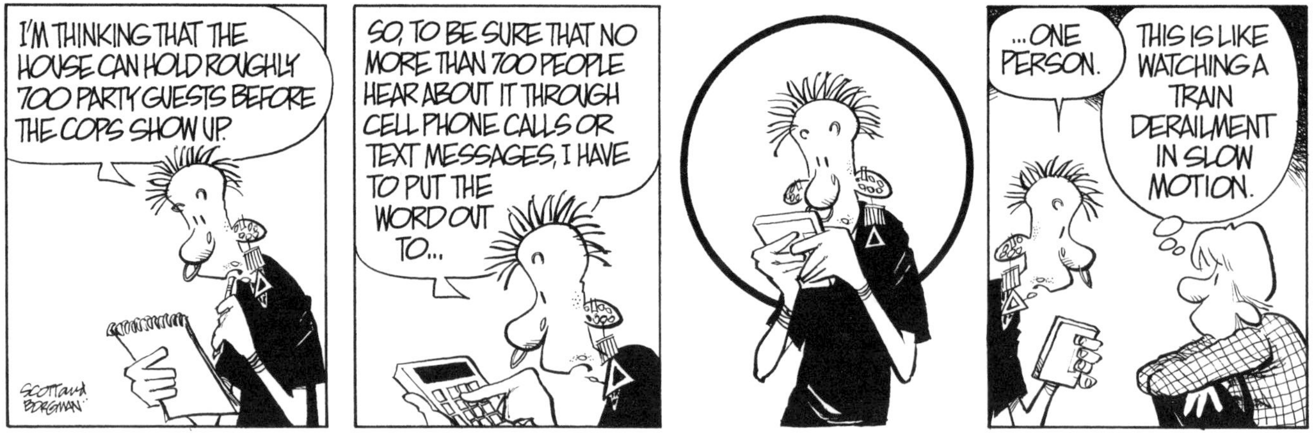
I'M THINKING THAT THE HOUSE CAN HOLD ROUGHLY 700 PARTY GUESTS BEFORE THE COPS SHOW UP.
SO, TO BE SURE THAT NO MORE THAN 700 PEOPLE HEAR ABOUT IT THROUGH CELL PHONE CALLS OR TEXT MESSAGES, I HAVE TO PUT THE WORD OUT TO...
...ONE PERSON.
THIS IS LIKE WATCHING A TRAIN DERAILMENT IN SLOW MOTION.

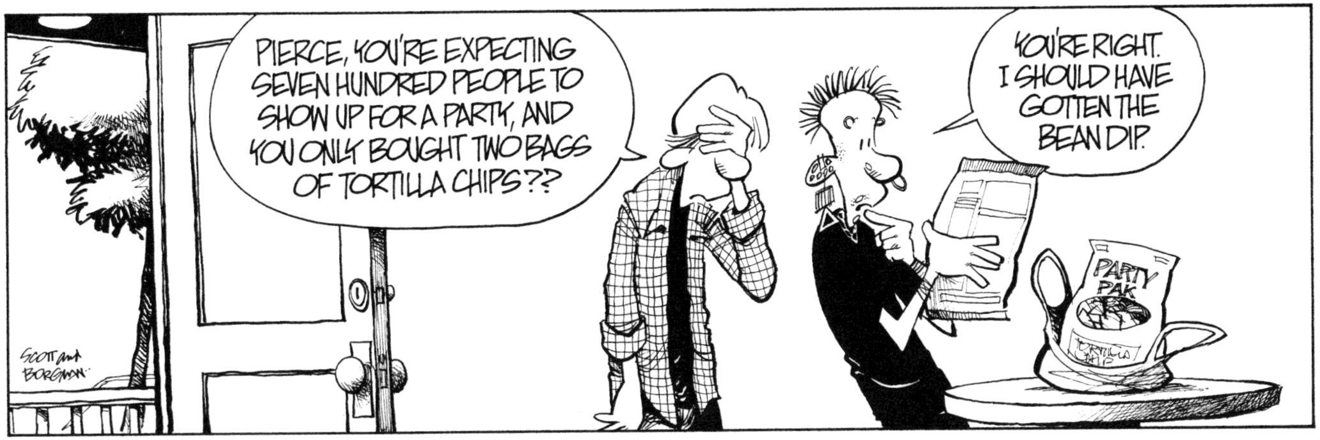
PIERCE, YOU'RE EXPECTING SEVEN HUNDRED PEOPLE TO SHOW UP FOR A PARTY, AND YOU ONLY BOUGHT TWO BAGS OF TORTILLA CHIPS??
YOU'RE RIGHT. I SHOULD HAVE GOTTEN THE BEAN DIP.
PARTY PAK
SCOTT and BORGMAN

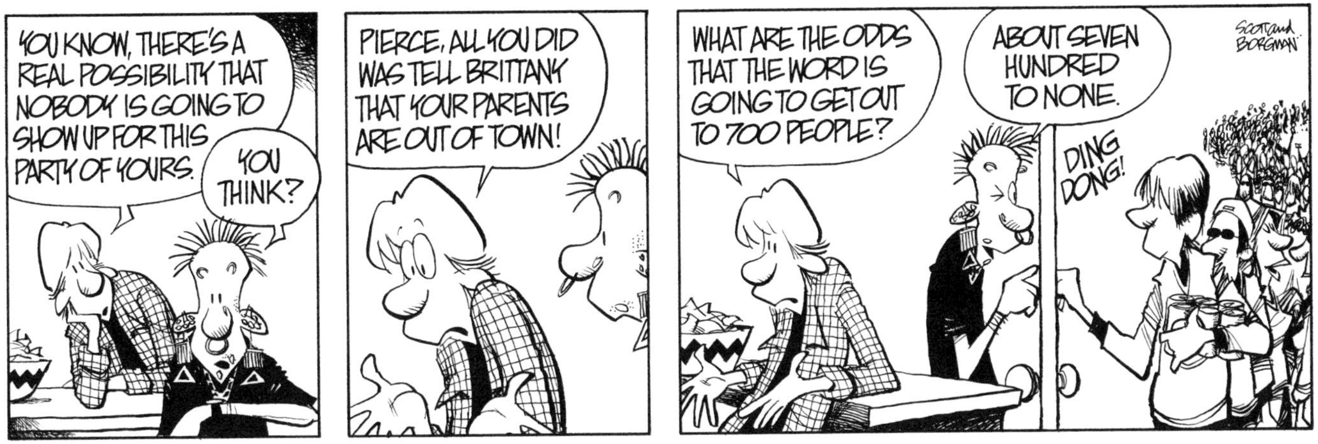
YOU KNOW, THERE'S A REAL POSSIBILITY THAT NOBODY IS GOING TO SHOW UP FOR THIS PARTY OF YOURS.
YOU THINK?
PIERCE, ALL YOU DID WAS TELL BRITTANY THAT YOUR PARENTS ARE OUT OF TOWN!
WHAT ARE THE ODDS THAT THE WORD IS GOING TO GET OUT TO 700 PEOPLE?
ABOUT SEVEN HUNDRED TO NONE.
DING DONG!
SCOTT and BORGMAN

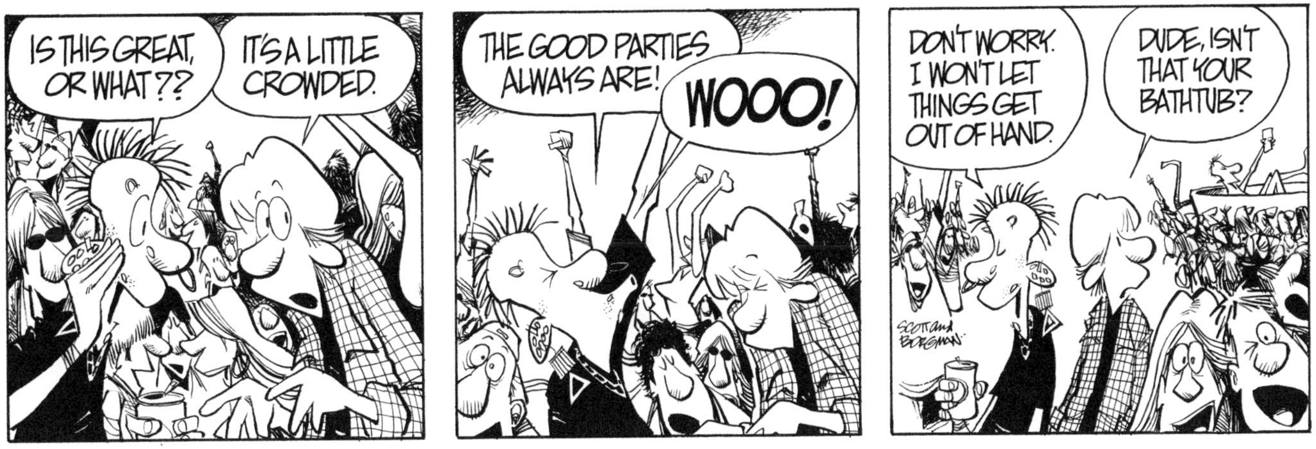
IS THIS GREAT, OR WHAT??
IT'S A LITTLE CROWDED.
THE GOOD PARTIES ALWAYS ARE!
WOOO!
DON'T WORRY. I WON'T LET THINGS GET OUT OF HAND.
DUDE, ISN'T THAT YOUR BATHTUB?
SCOTT and BORGMAN

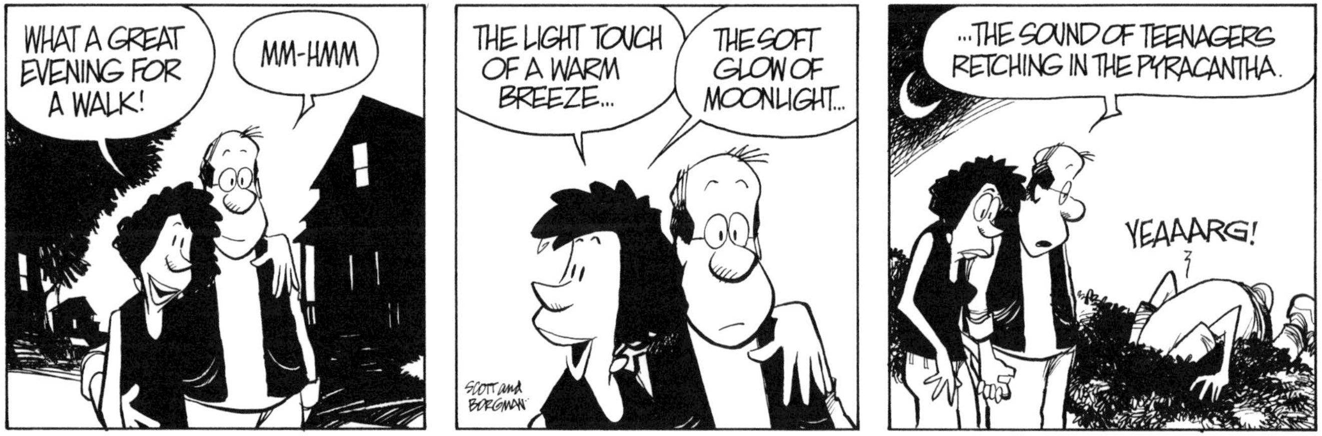
WHAT A GREAT EVENING FOR A WALK!
MM-HMM
THE LIGHT TOUCH OF A WARM BREEZE...
THE SOFT GLOW OF MOONLIGHT...
...THE SOUND OF TEENAGERS RETCHING IN THE PYRACANTHA.
YEAAARG!
SCOTT and BORGMAN

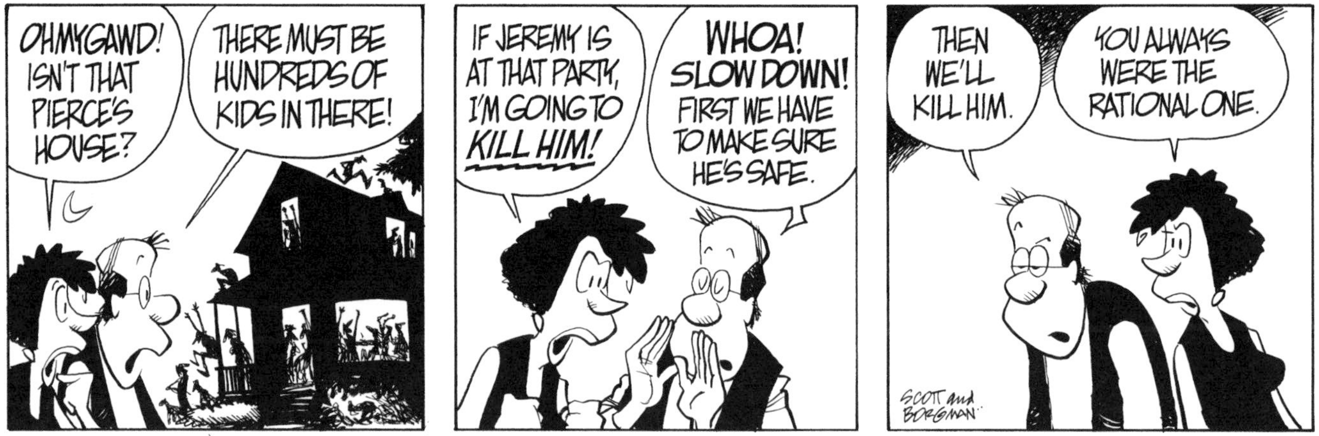
OHMYGAWD! ISN'T THAT PIERCE'S HOUSE?
THERE MUST BE HUNDREDS OF KIDS IN THERE!
IF JEREMY IS AT THAT PARTY, I'M GOING TO KILL HIM!
WHOA! SLOW DOWN! FIRST WE HAVE TO MAKE SURE HE'S SAFE.
THEN WE'LL KILL HIM.
YOU ALWAYS WERE THE RATIONAL ONE.
SCOTT and BORGMAN

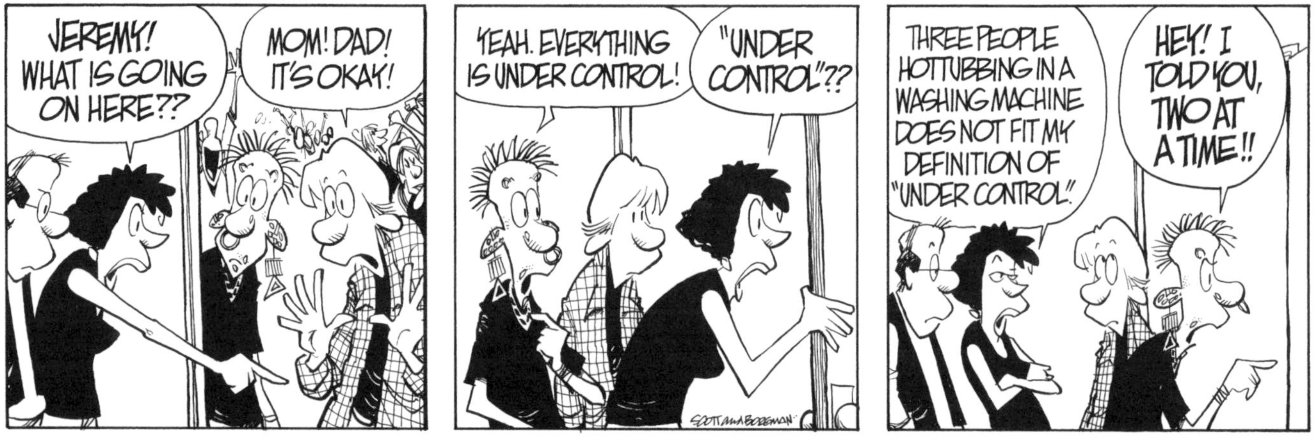
JEREMY! WHAT IS GOING ON HERE??
MOM! DAD! IT'S OKAY!
YEAH. EVERYTHING IS UNDER CONTROL!
"UNDER CONTROL"??
THREE PEOPLE HOTTUBBING IN A WASHING MACHINE DOES NOT FIT MY DEFINITION OF "UNDER CONTROL."
HEY! I TOLD YOU, TWO AT A TIME!!
SCOTT and BORGMAN

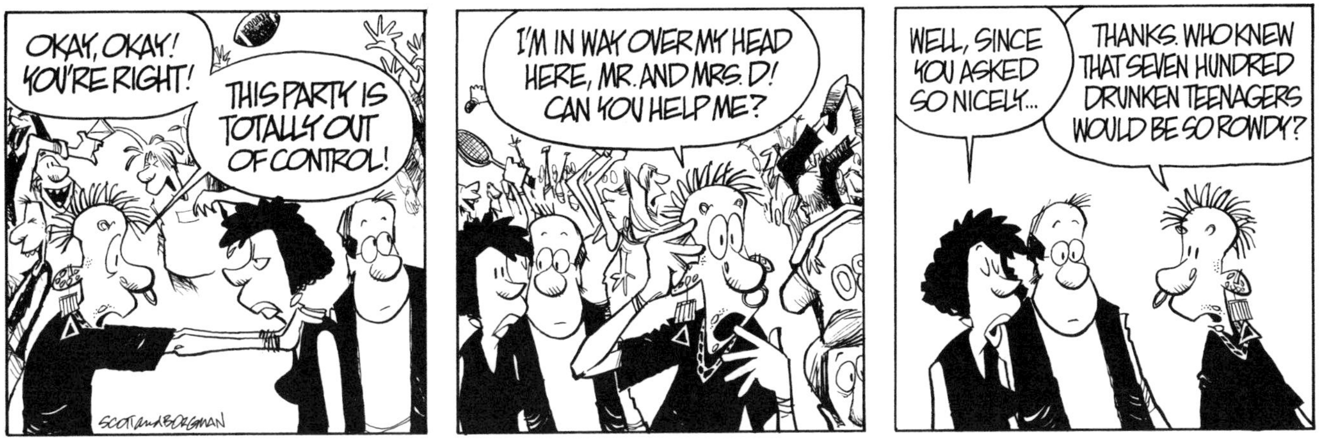
OKAY, OKAY! YOU'RE RIGHT!
THIS PARTY IS TOTALLY OUT OF CONTROL!
SCOTT and BORGMAN
I'M IN WAY OVER MY HEAD HERE, MR. AND MRS. D! CAN YOU HELP ME?
WELL, SINCE YOU ASKED SO NICELY...
THANKS. WHO KNEW THAT SEVEN HUNDRED DRUNKEN TEENAGERS WOULD BE SO ROWDY?

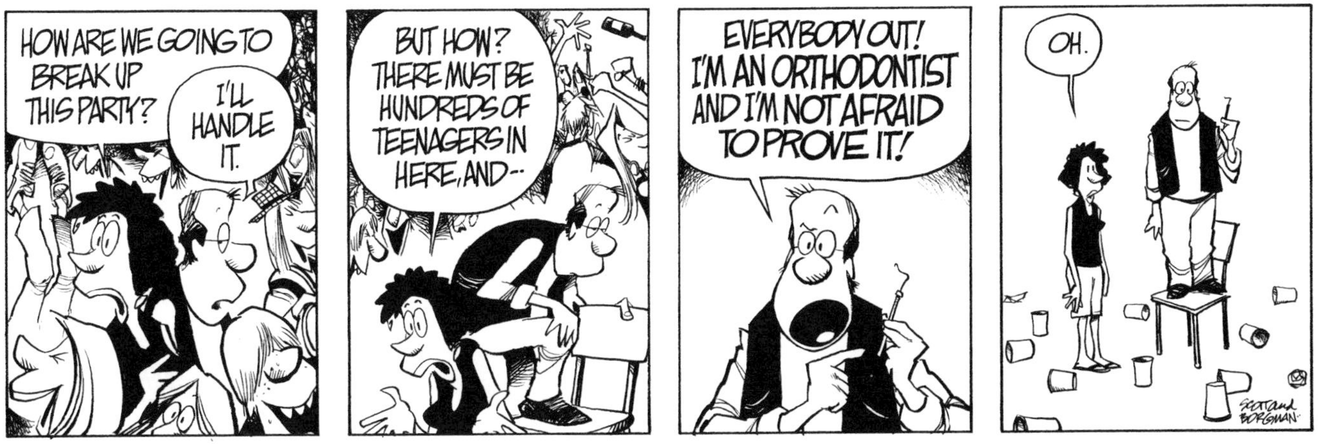
HOW ARE WE GOING TO BREAK UP THIS PARTY?
I'LL HANDLE IT.
BUT HOW? THERE MUST BE HUNDREDS OF TEENAGERS IN HERE, AND--
EVERYBODY OUT! I'M AN ORTHODONTIST AND I'M NOT AFRAID TO PROVE IT!
OH.
SCOTT and BORGMAN

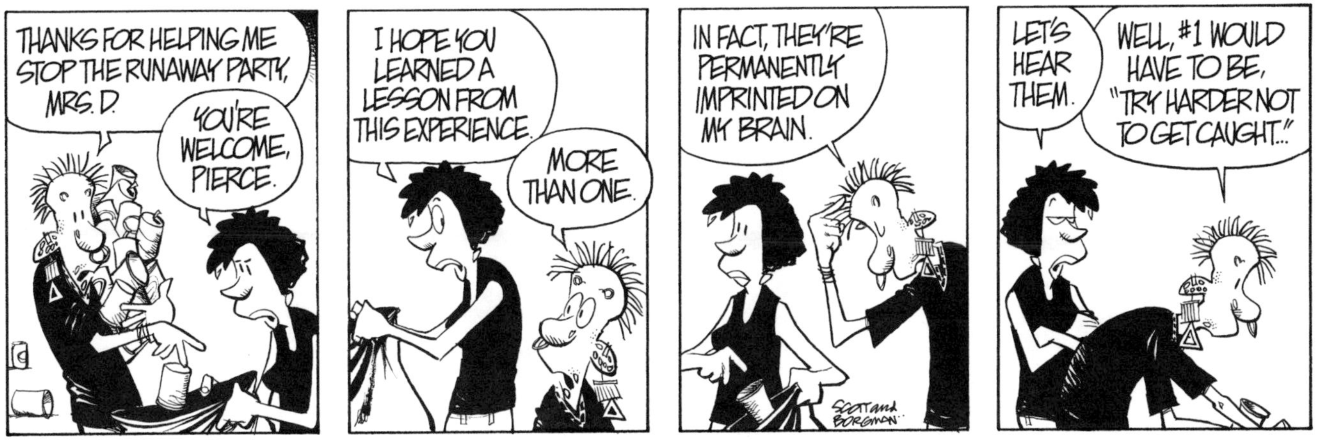
THANKS FOR HELPING ME STOP THE RUNAWAY PARTY, MRS. D.
YOU'RE WELCOME, PIERCE.
I HOPE YOU LEARNED A LESSON FROM THIS EXPERIENCE.
MORE THAN ONE.
IN FACT, THEY'RE PERMANENTLY IMPRINTED ON MY BRAIN.
SCOTT and BORGMAN
LET'S HEAR THEM.
WELL, #1 WOULD HAVE TO BE, "TRY HARDER NOT TO GET CAUGHT..."

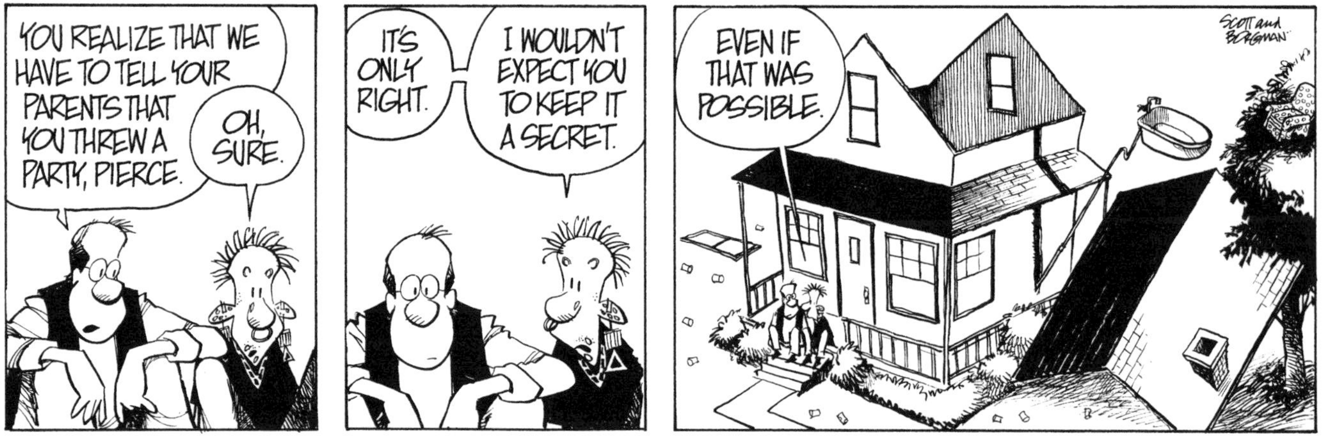
YOU REALIZE THAT WE HAVE TO TELL YOUR PARENTS THAT YOU THREW A PARTY, PIERCE.
OH, SURE.
IT'S ONLY RIGHT.
I WOULDN'T EXPECT YOU TO KEEP IT A SECRET.
EVEN IF THAT WAS POSSIBLE.

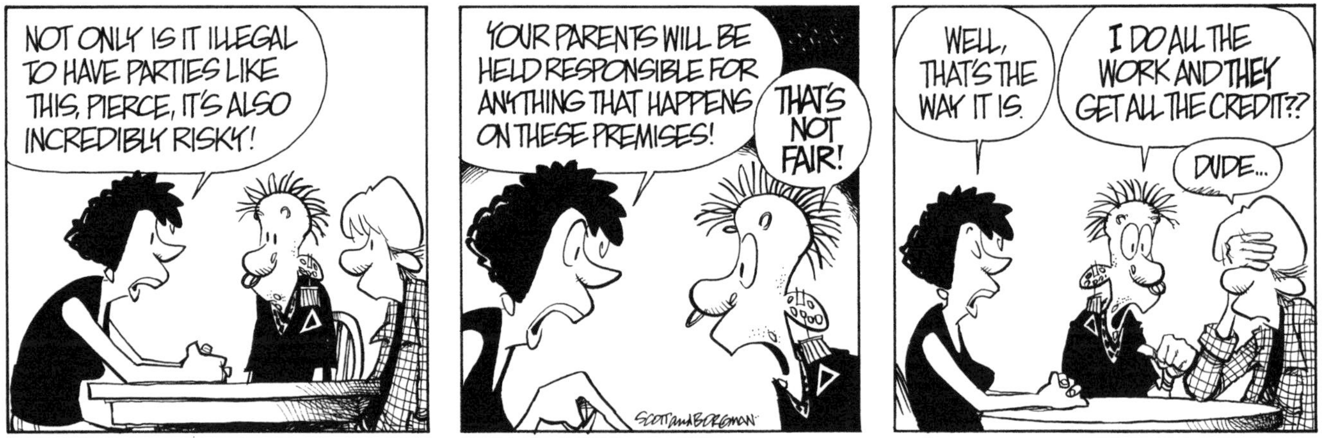
NOT ONLY IS IT ILLEGAL TO HAVE PARTIES LIKE THIS, PIERCE, IT'S ALSO INCREDIBLY RISKY!
YOUR PARENTS WILL BE HELD RESPONSIBLE FOR ANYTHING THAT HAPPENS ON THESE PREMISES!
THAT'S NOT FAIR!
WELL, THAT'S THE WAY IT IS.
I DO ALL THE WORK AND THEY GET ALL THE CREDIT??
DUDE...

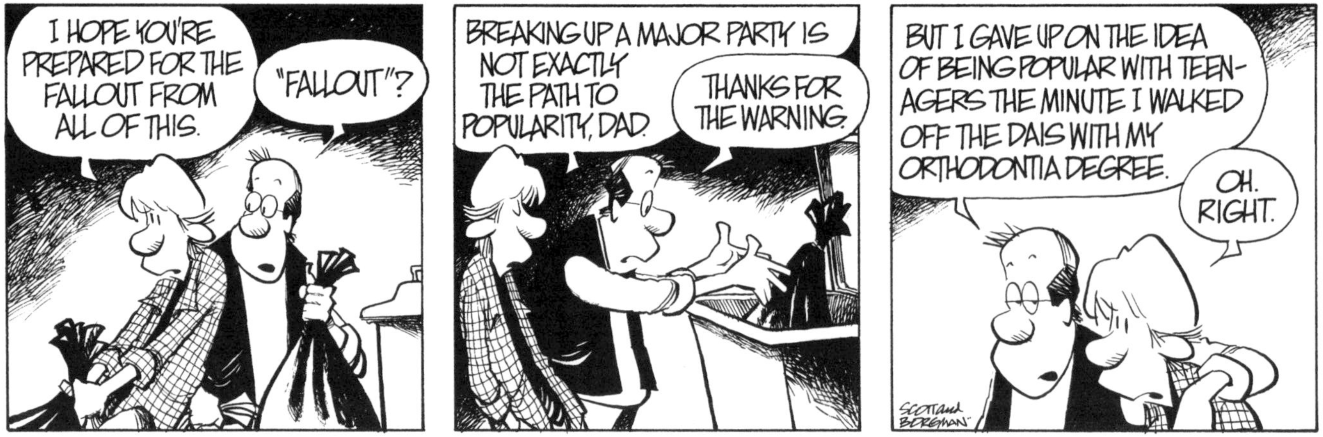
I HOPE YOU'RE PREPARED FOR THE FALLOUT FROM ALL OF THIS.
"FALLOUT"?
BREAKING UP A MAJOR PARTY IS NOT EXACTLY THE PATH TO POPULARITY, DAD.
THANKS FOR THE WARNING.
BUT I GAVE UP ON THE IDEA OF BEING POPULAR WITH TEEN-AGERS THE MINUTE I WALKED OFF THE DAIS WITH MY ORTHODONTIA DEGREE.
OH. RIGHT.

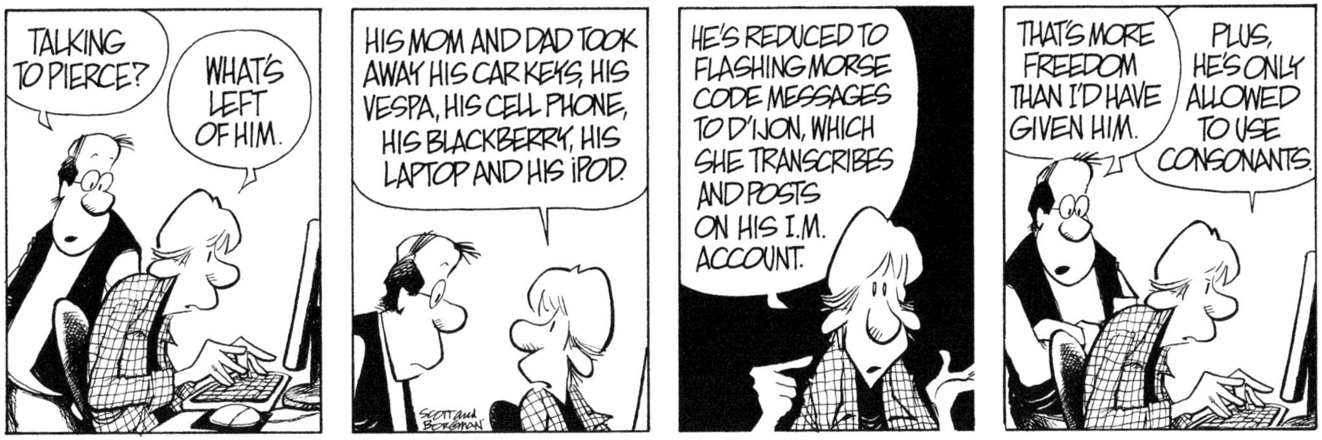
TALKING TO PIERCE?
WHAT'S LEFT OF HIM.
HIS MOM AND DAD TOOK AWAY HIS CAR KEYS, HIS VESPA, HIS CELL PHONE, HIS BLACKBERRY, HIS LAPTOP AND HIS iPOD.
SCOTT and BORGMAN
HE'S REDUCED TO FLASHING MORSE CODE MESSAGES TO D'IJON, WHICH SHE TRANSCRIBES AND POSTS ON HIS I.M. ACCOUNT.
THAT'S MORE FREEDOM THAN I'D HAVE GIVEN HIM.
PLUS, HE'S ONLY ALLOWED TO USE CONSONANTS.

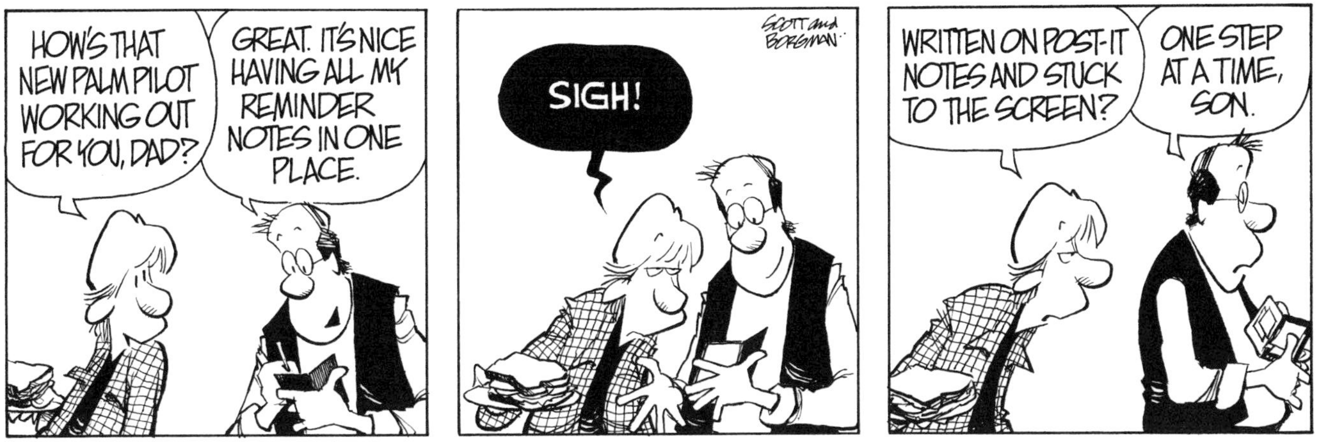
HOW'S THAT NEW PALM PILOT WORKING OUT FOR YOU, DAD?
GREAT. IT'S NICE HAVING ALL MY REMINDER NOTES IN ONE PLACE.
SCOTT and BORGMAN
SIGH!
WRITTEN ON POST-IT NOTES AND STUCK TO THE SCREEN?
ONE STEP AT A TIME, SON.

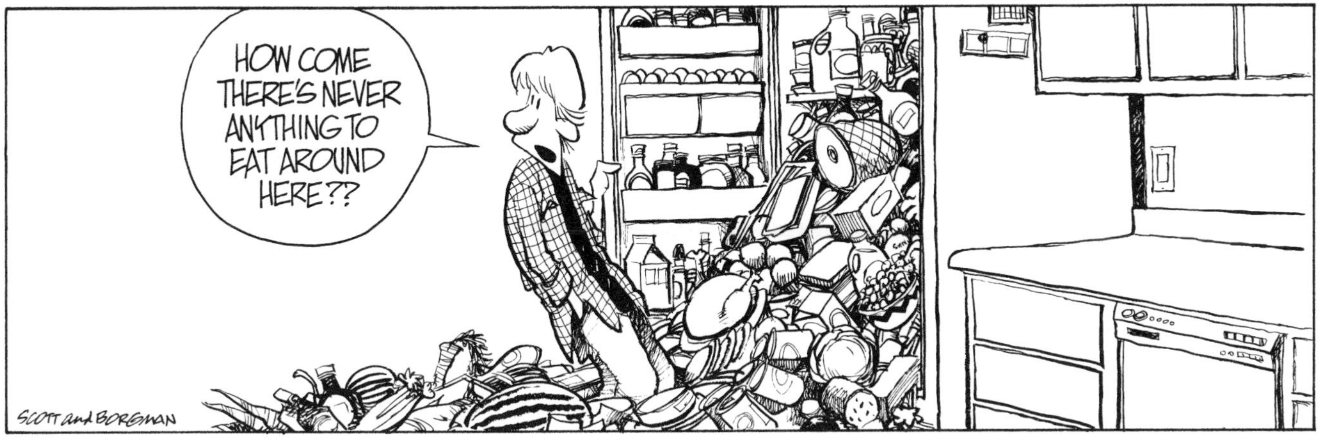
HOW COME THERE'S NEVER ANYTHING TO EAT AROUND HERE??
SCOTT and BORGMAN

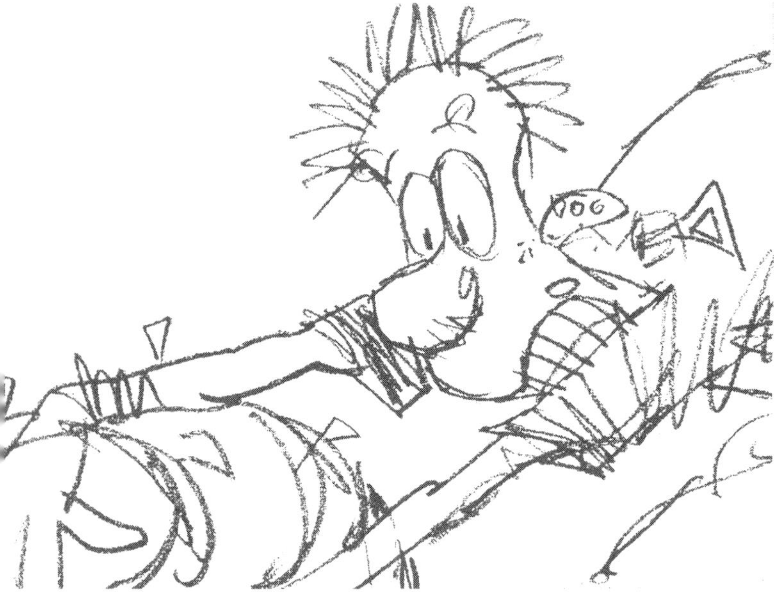

Zits

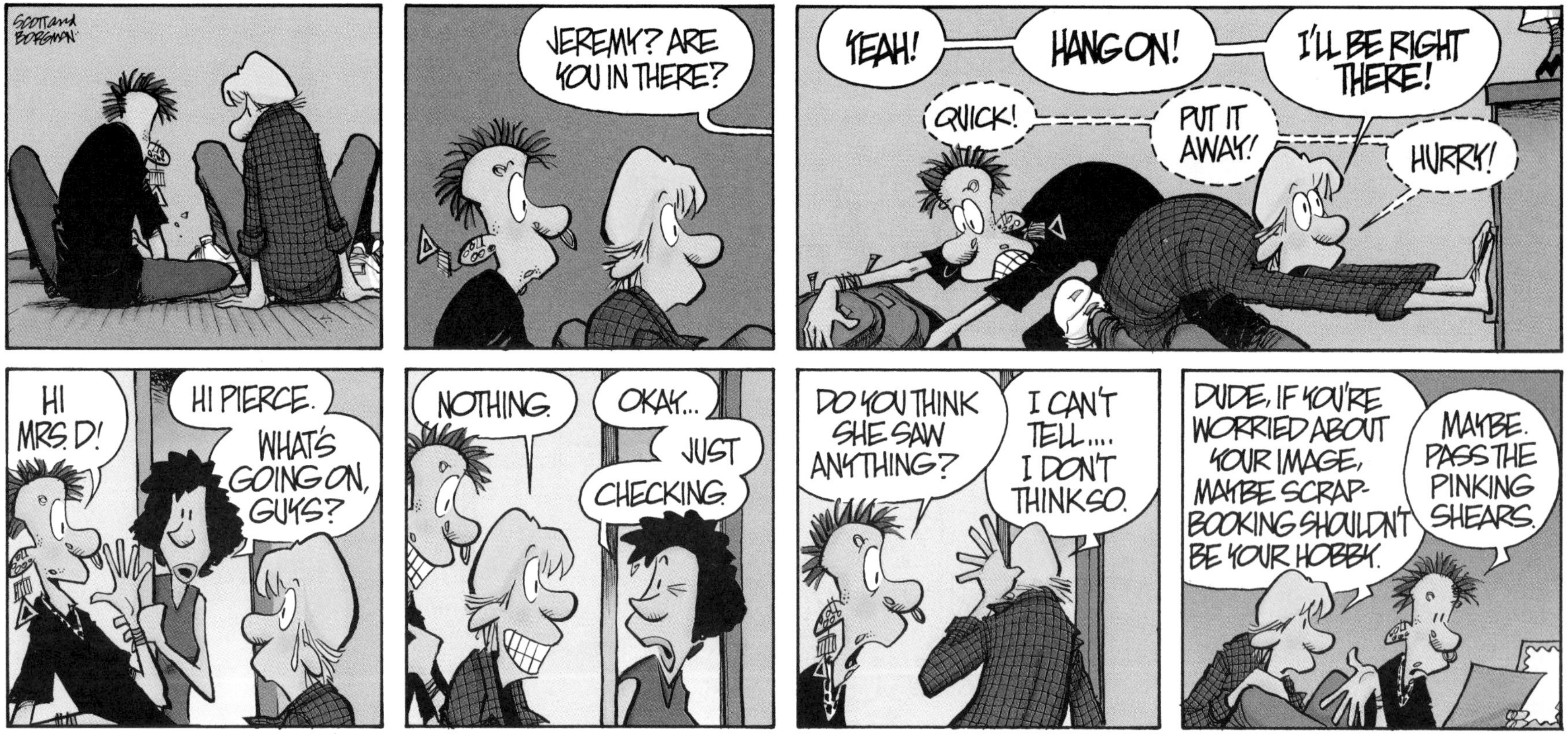
SCOTT and BORGMAN
JEREMY? ARE YOU IN THERE?
YEAH!
HANG ON!
I'LL BE RIGHT THERE!
QUICK!
PUT IT AWAY!
HURRY!
HI MRS. D!
HI PIERCE.
WHAT'S GOING ON, GUYS?
NOTHING.
OKAY...
JUST CHECKING.
DO YOU THINK SHE SAW ANYTHING?
I CAN'T TELL.... I DON'T THINK SO.
DUDE, IF YOU'RE WORRIED ABOUT YOUR IMAGE, MAYBE SCRAP-BOOKING SHOULDN'T BE YOUR HOBBY.
MAYBE. PASS THE PINKING SHEARS.

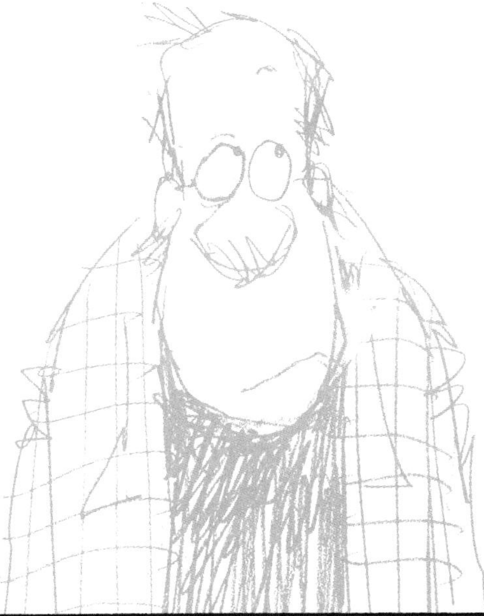

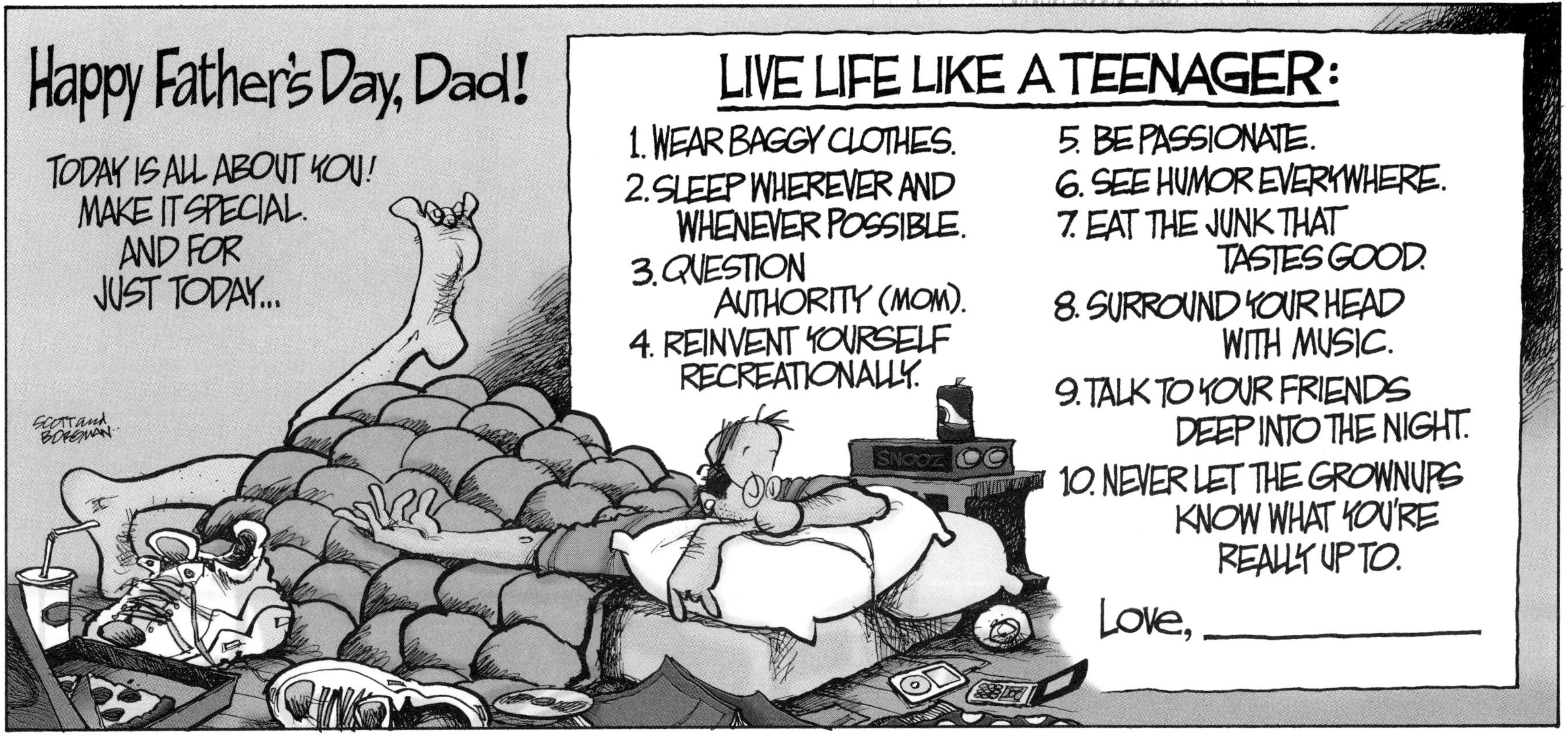
Happy Father's Day, Dad!
TODAY IS ALL ABOUT YOU! MAKE IT SPECIAL. AND FOR JUST TODAY...
LIVE LIFE LIKE A TEENAGER:
1. WEAR BAGGY CLOTHES.
2. SLEEP WHEREVER AND WHENEVER POSSIBLE.
3. QUESTION AUTHORITY (MOM).
4. REINVENT YOURSELF RECREATIONALLY.
5. BE PASSIONATE.
6. SEE HUMOR EVERYWHERE.
7. EAT THE JUNK THAT TASTES GOOD.
8. SURROUND YOUR HEAD WITH MUSIC.
9. TALK TO YOUR FRIENDS DEEP INTO THE NIGHT.
10. NEVER LET THE GROWNUPS KNOW WHAT YOU'RE REALLY UP TO.
Love, ____________
SNOOZ
SCOTT and BORGMAN

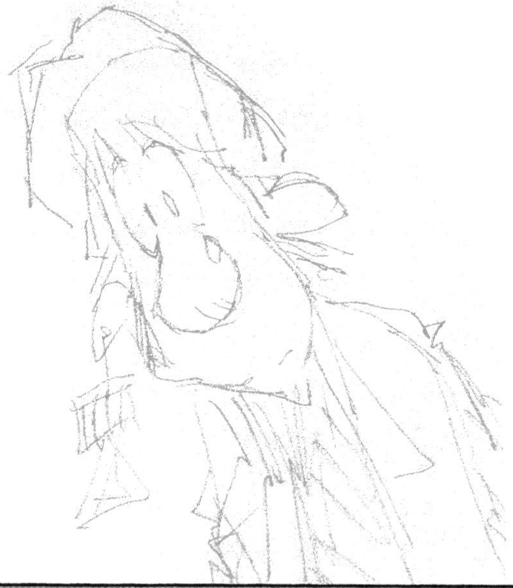

Zits

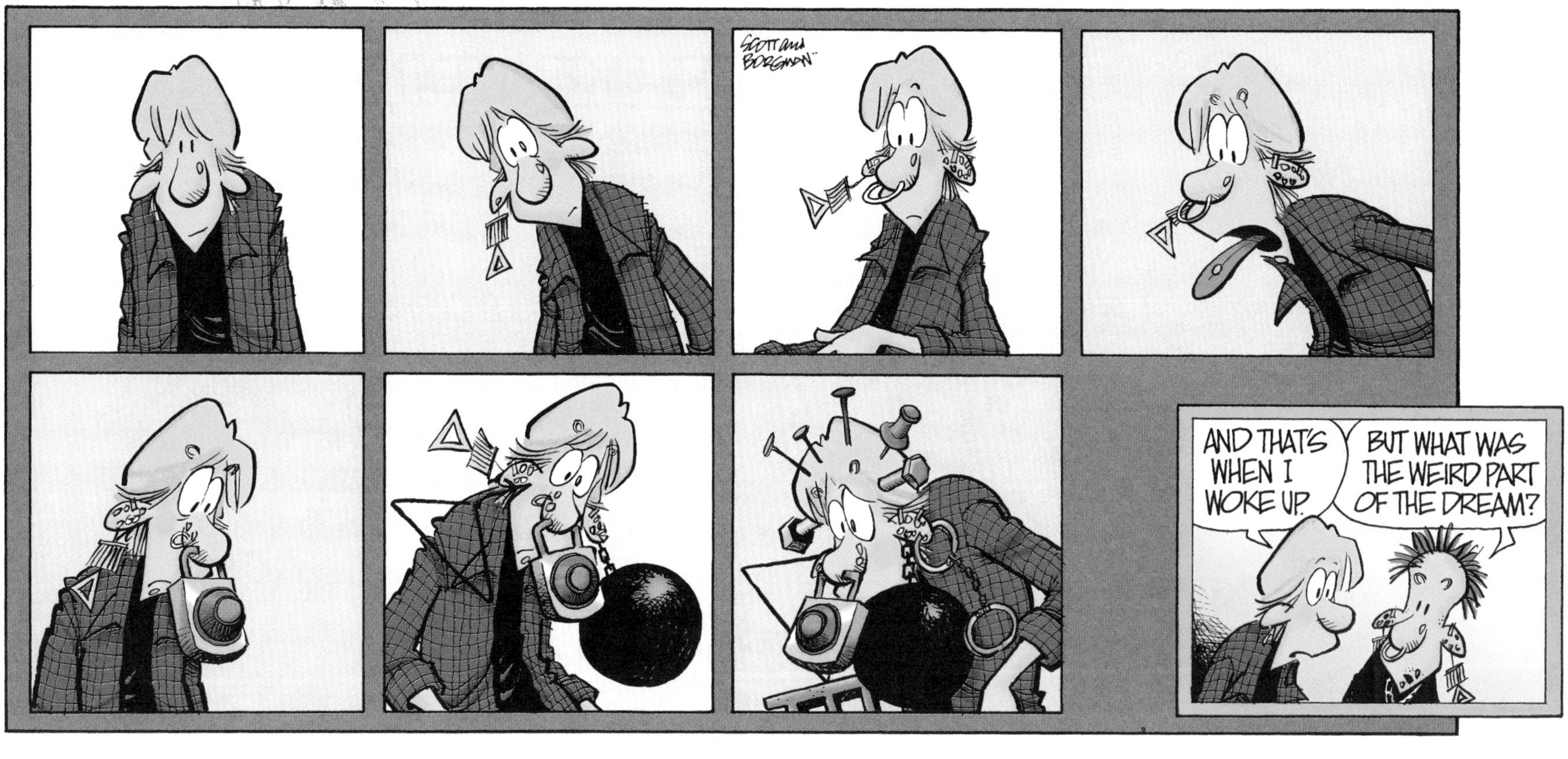
AND THAT'S WHEN I WOKE UP.
BUT WHAT WAS THE WEIRD PART OF THE DREAM?

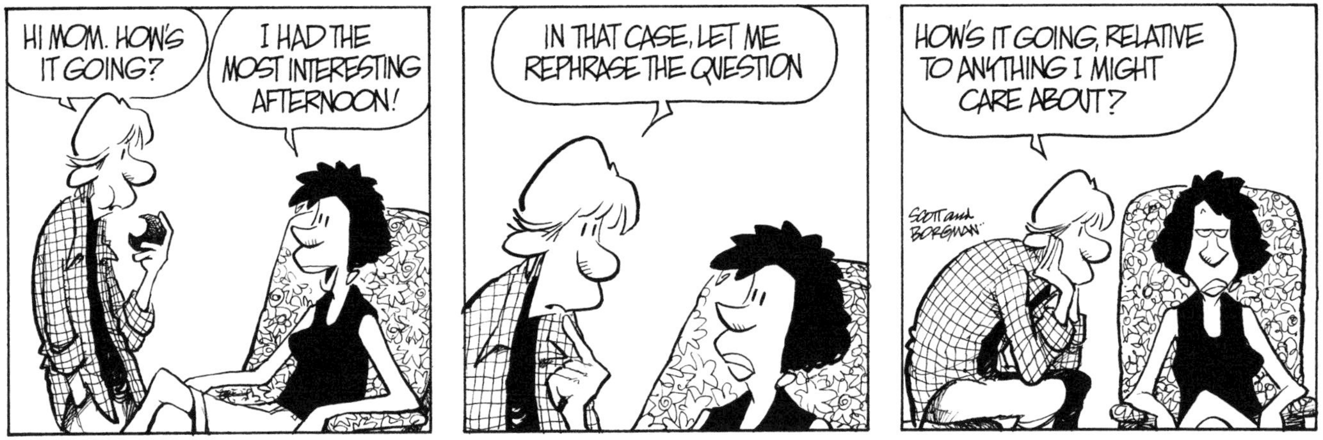
HI MOM. HOW'S IT GOING?
I HAD THE MOST INTERESTING AFTERNOON!
IN THAT CASE, LET ME REPHRASE THE QUESTION
HOW'S IT GOING, RELATIVE TO ANYTHING I MIGHT CARE ABOUT?
SCOTT and BORGMAN

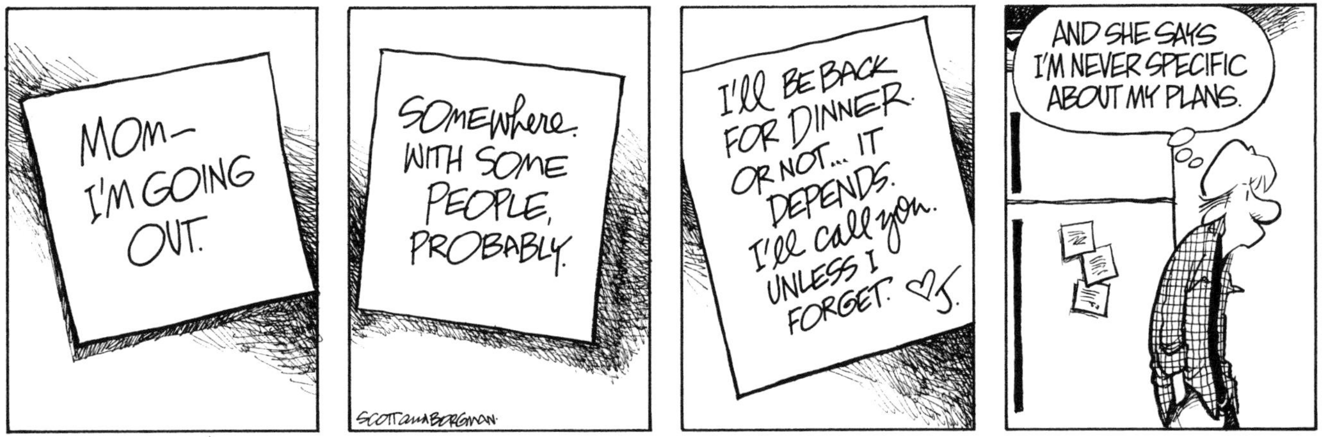
MOM– I'M GOING OUT.
SOMEWHERE. WITH SOME PEOPLE, PROBABLY.
SCOTT and BORGMAN
I'LL BE BACK FOR DINNER. OR NOT... IT DEPENDS. I'LL CALL YOU. UNLESS I FORGET. ♡ J.
AND SHE SAYS I'M NEVER SPECIFIC ABOUT MY PLANS.

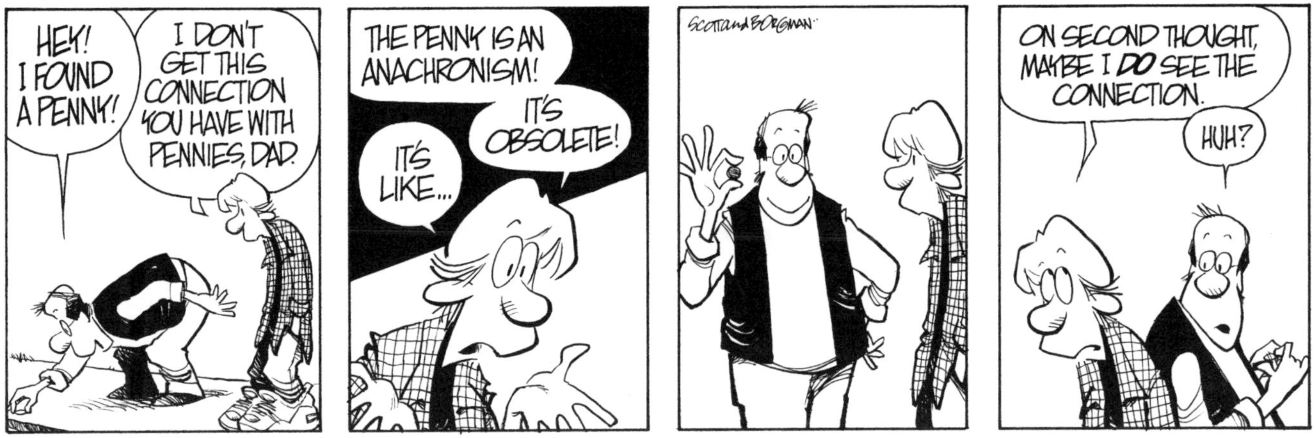
HEY! I FOUND A PENNY!
I DON'T GET THIS CONNECTION YOU HAVE WITH PENNIES, DAD.
THE PENNY IS AN ANACHRONISM!
IT'S OBSOLETE!
IT'S LIKE...
SCOTT and BORGMAN
ON SECOND THOUGHT, MAYBE I DO SEE THE CONNECTION.
HUH?

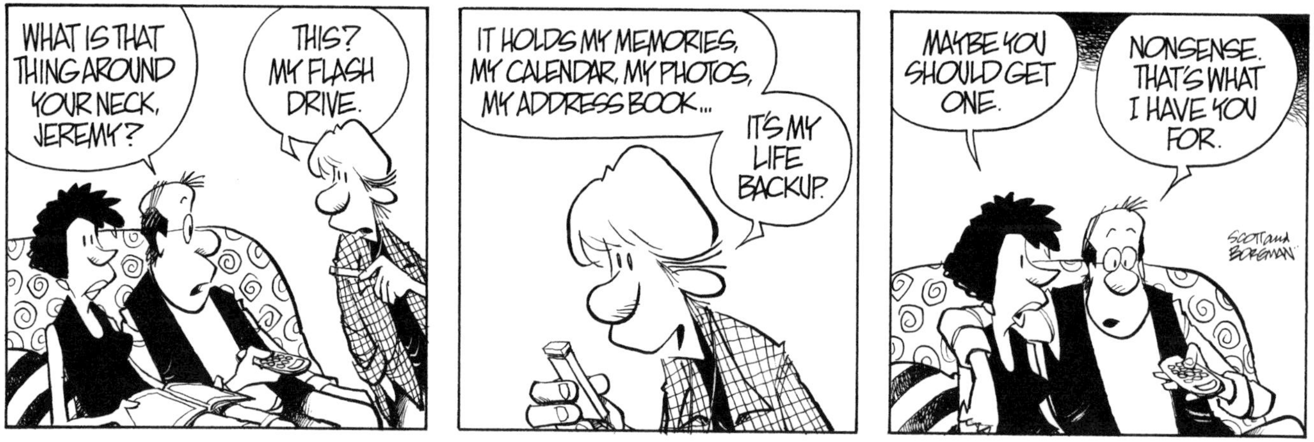
WHAT IS THAT THING AROUND YOUR NECK, JEREMY?
THIS? MY FLASH DRIVE.
IT HOLDS MY MEMORIES, MY CALENDAR, MY PHOTOS, MY ADDRESS BOOK...
IT'S MY LIFE BACKUP.
MAYBE YOU SHOULD GET ONE.
NONSENSE. THAT'S WHAT I HAVE YOU FOR.

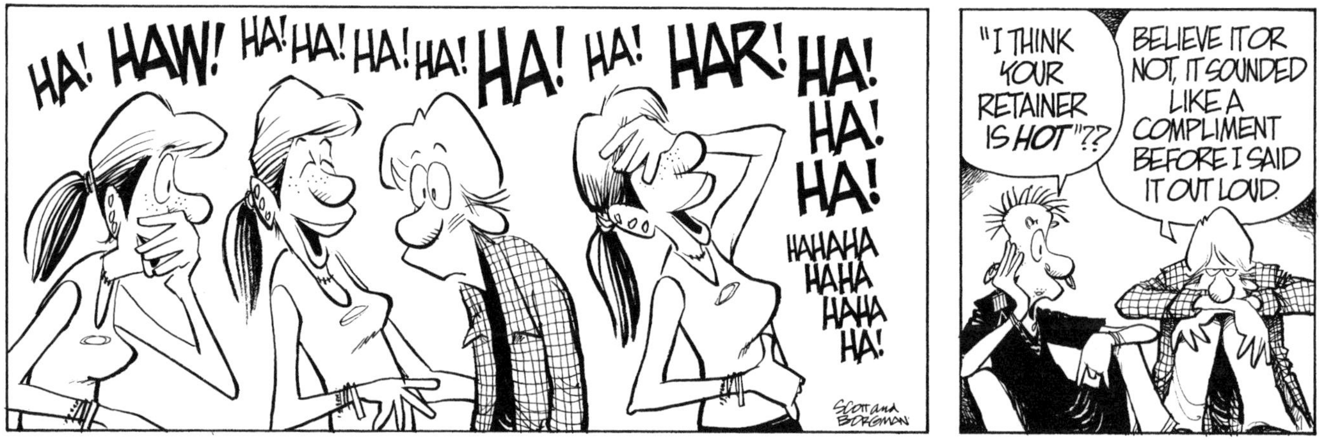
HA! HAW! HA! HA! HA! HA! HA! HA! HAR! HA! HA! HA!
HAHAHA HAHA HAHA HA!
"I THINK YOUR RETAINER IS *HOT*"??
BELIEVE IT OR NOT, IT SOUNDED LIKE A COMPLIMENT BEFORE I SAID IT OUT LOUD.

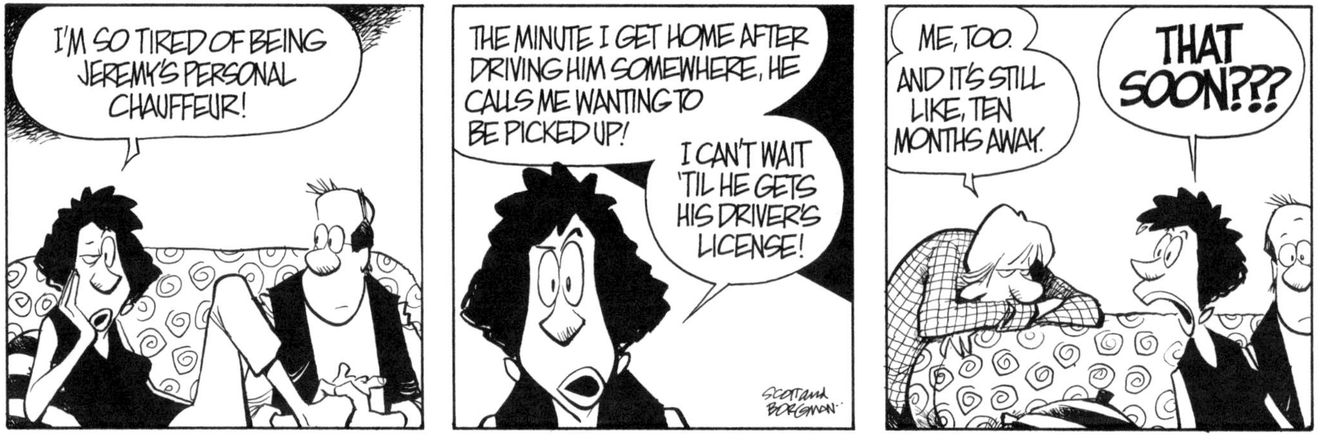
I'M SO TIRED OF BEING JEREMY'S PERSONAL CHAUFFEUR!
THE MINUTE I GET HOME AFTER DRIVING HIM SOMEWHERE, HE CALLS ME WANTING TO BE PICKED UP!
I CAN'T WAIT 'TIL HE GETS HIS DRIVER'S LICENSE!
ME, TOO.
AND IT'S STILL LIKE, TEN MONTHS AWAY.
THAT SOON???

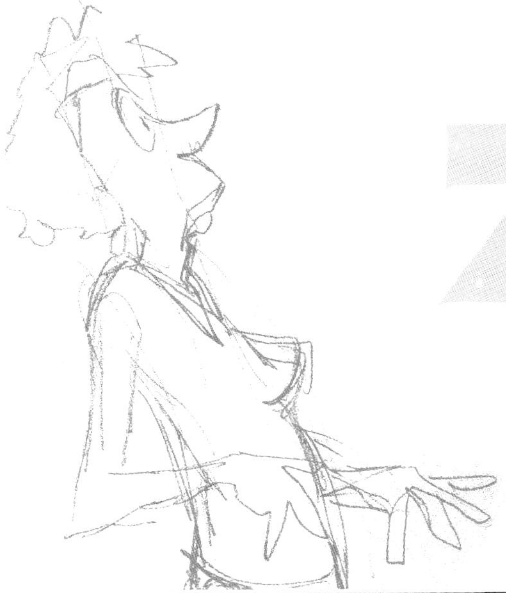

Zits

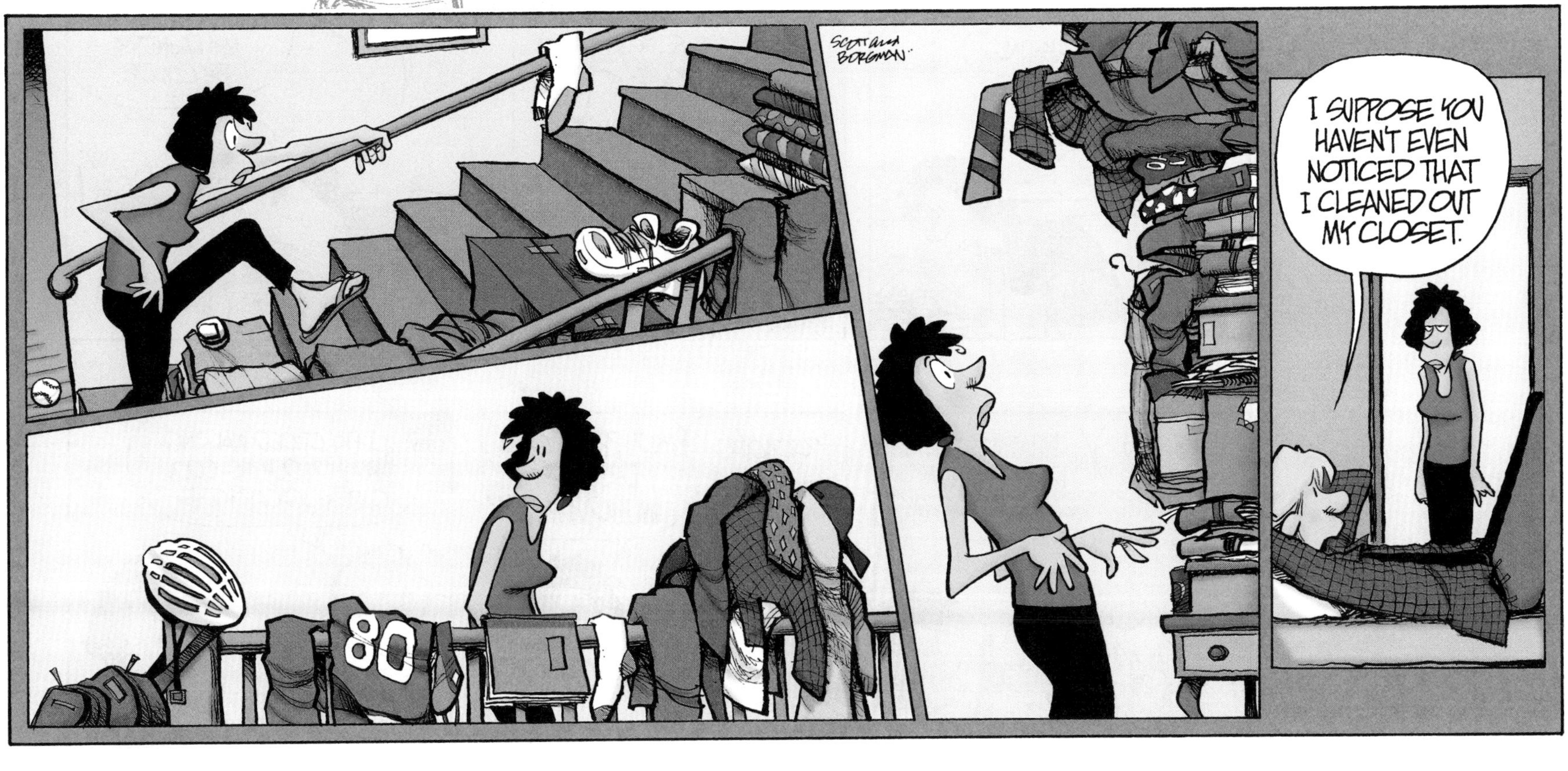
I SUPPOSE YOU HAVEN'T EVEN NOTICED THAT I CLEANED OUT MY CLOSET.

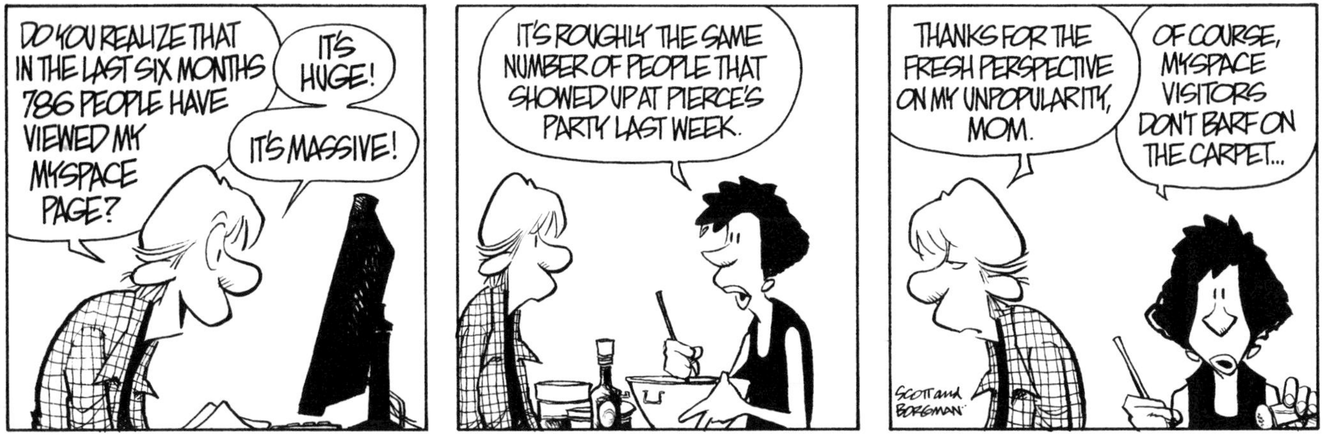
DO YOU REALIZE THAT IN THE LAST SIX MONTHS 786 PEOPLE HAVE VIEWED MY MYSPACE PAGE?
IT'S HUGE!
IT'S MASSIVE!
IT'S ROUGHLY THE SAME NUMBER OF PEOPLE THAT SHOWED UP AT PIERCE'S PARTY LAST WEEK.
THANKS FOR THE FRESH PERSPECTIVE ON MY UNPOPULARITY, MOM.
OF COURSE, MYSPACE VISITORS DON'T BARF ON THE CARPET...
SCOTT and BORGMAN

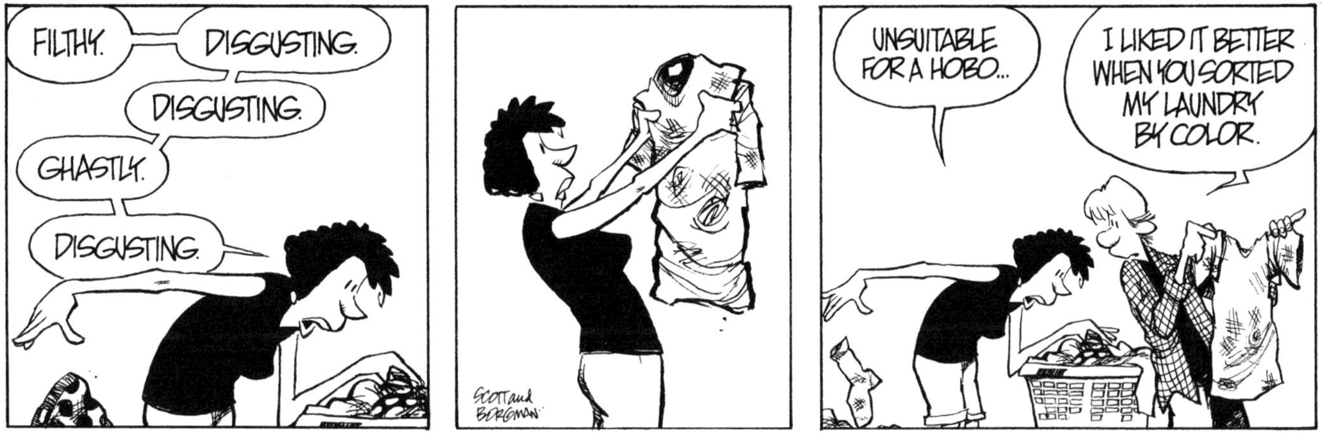
FILTHY.
DISGUSTING.
DISGUSTING.
GHASTLY.
DISGUSTING.
SCOTT and BORGMAN
UNSUITABLE FOR A HOBO...
I LIKED IT BETTER WHEN YOU SORTED MY LAUNDRY BY COLOR.

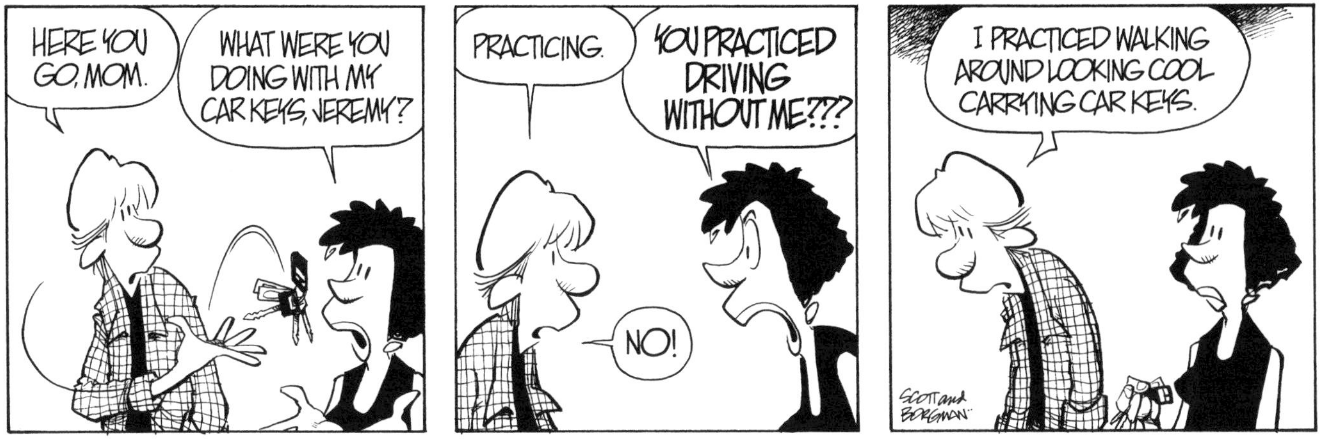
HERE YOU GO, MOM.
WHAT WERE YOU DOING WITH MY CAR KEYS, JEREMY?
PRACTICING.
YOU PRACTICED DRIVING WITHOUT ME???
NO!
I PRACTICED WALKING AROUND LOOKING COOL CARRYING CAR KEYS.
SCOTT and BORGMAN

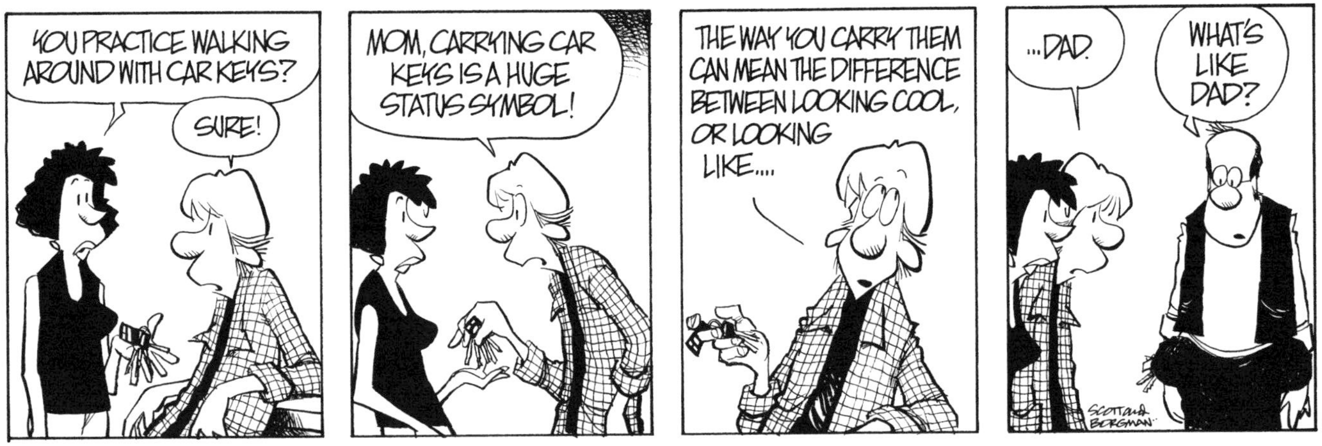
YOU PRACTICE WALKING AROUND WITH CAR KEYS?
SURE!
MOM, CARRYING CAR KEYS IS A HUGE STATUS SYMBOL!
THE WAY YOU CARRY THEM CAN MEAN THE DIFFERENCE BETWEEN LOOKING COOL, OR LOOKING LIKE....
...DAD.
WHAT'S LIKE DAD?

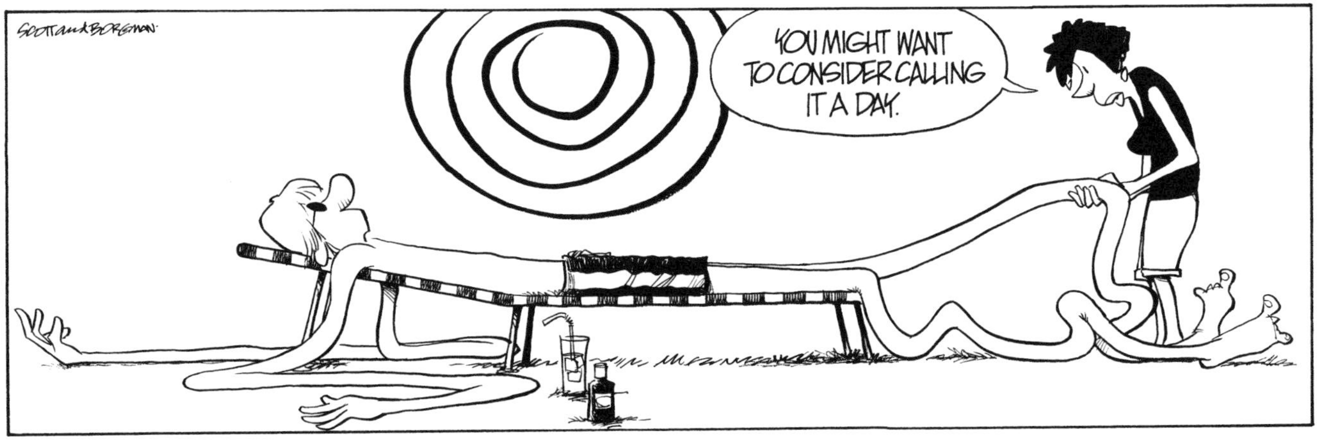
YOU MIGHT WANT TO CONSIDER CALLING IT A DAY.

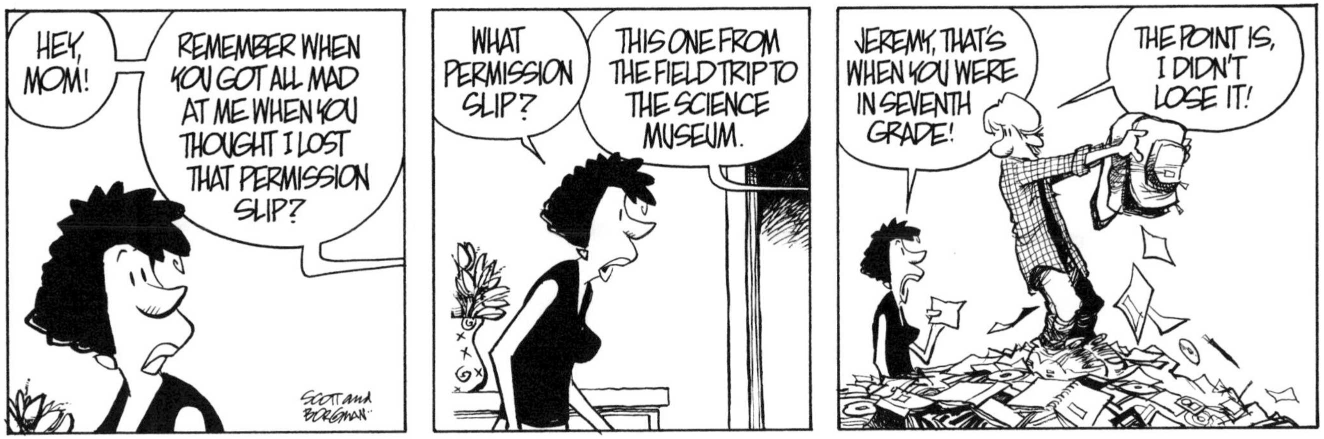
HEY, MOM!
REMEMBER WHEN YOU GOT ALL MAD AT ME WHEN YOU THOUGHT I LOST THAT PERMISSION SLIP?
WHAT PERMISSION SLIP?
THIS ONE FROM THE FIELD TRIP TO THE SCIENCE MUSEUM.
JEREMY, THAT'S WHEN YOU WERE IN SEVENTH GRADE!
THE POINT IS, I DIDN'T LOSE IT!

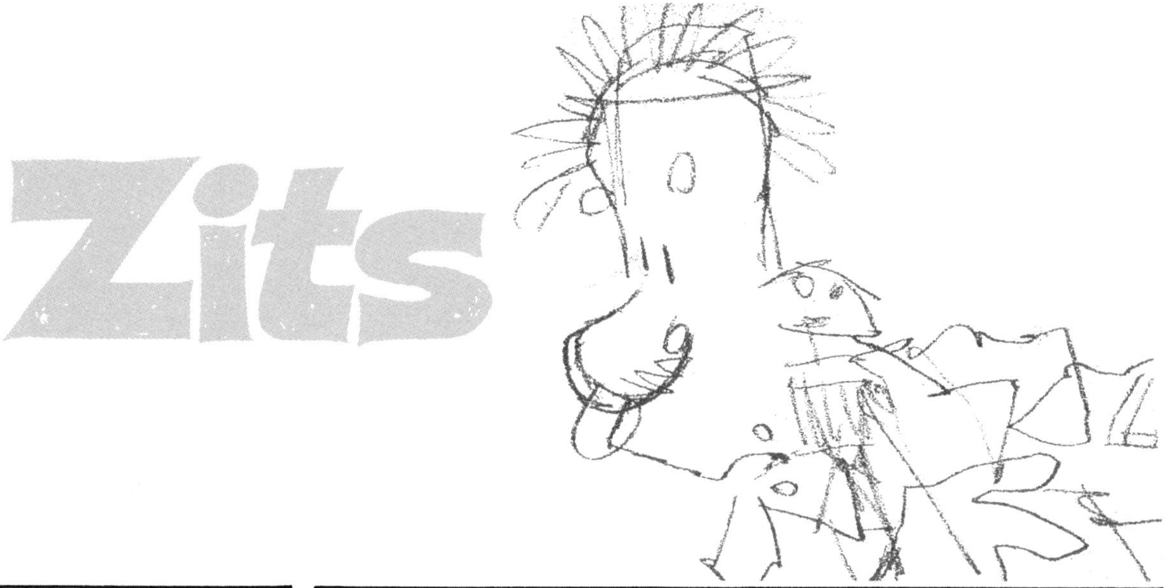
Zits

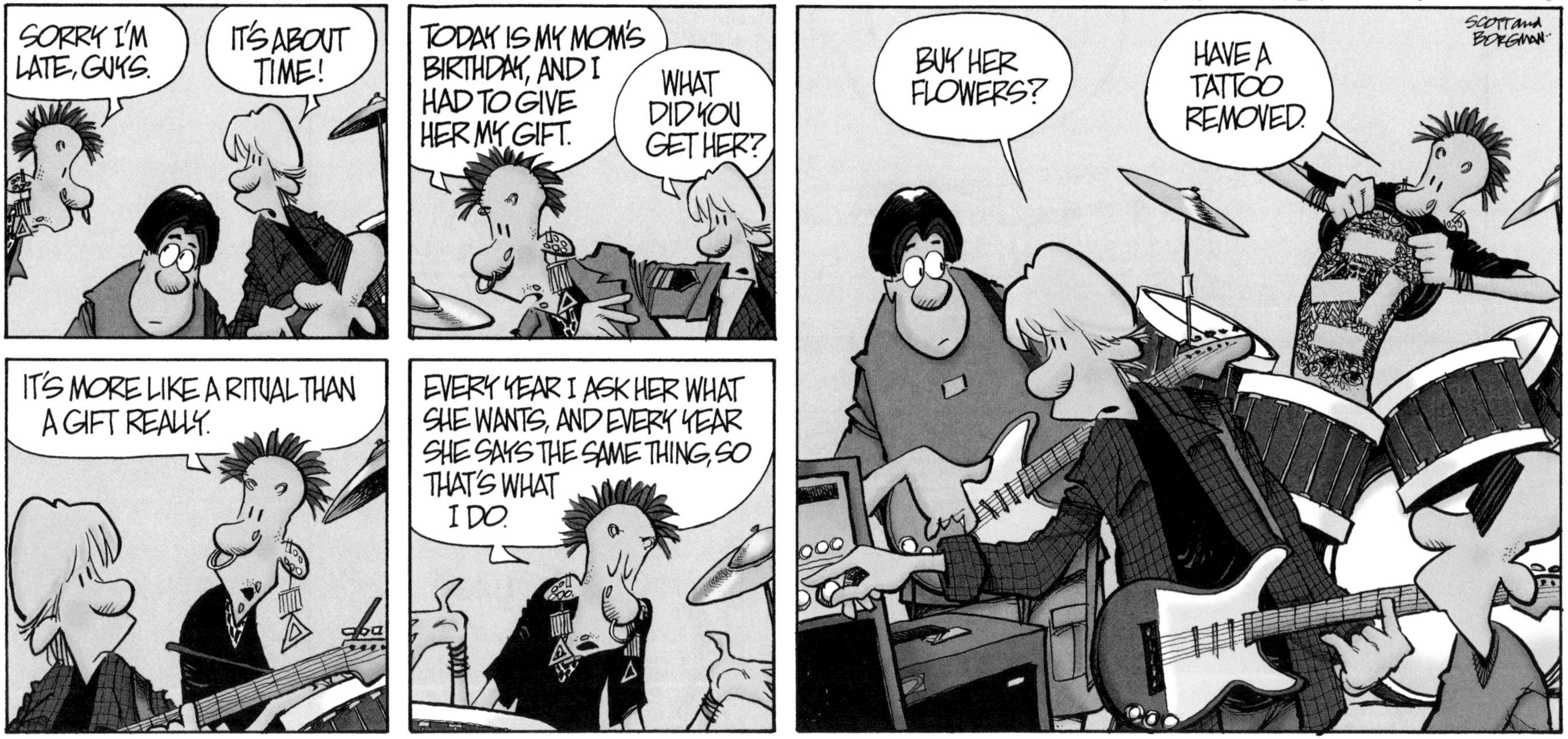
SORRY I'M LATE, GUYS.
IT'S ABOUT TIME!
TODAY IS MY MOM'S BIRTHDAY, AND I HAD TO GIVE HER MY GIFT.
WHAT DID YOU GET HER?
IT'S MORE LIKE A RITUAL THAN A GIFT REALLY.
EVERY YEAR I ASK HER WHAT SHE WANTS, AND EVERY YEAR SHE SAYS THE SAME THING, SO THAT'S WHAT I DO.
SCOTT and BORGMAN
BUY HER FLOWERS?
HAVE A TATTOO REMOVED.

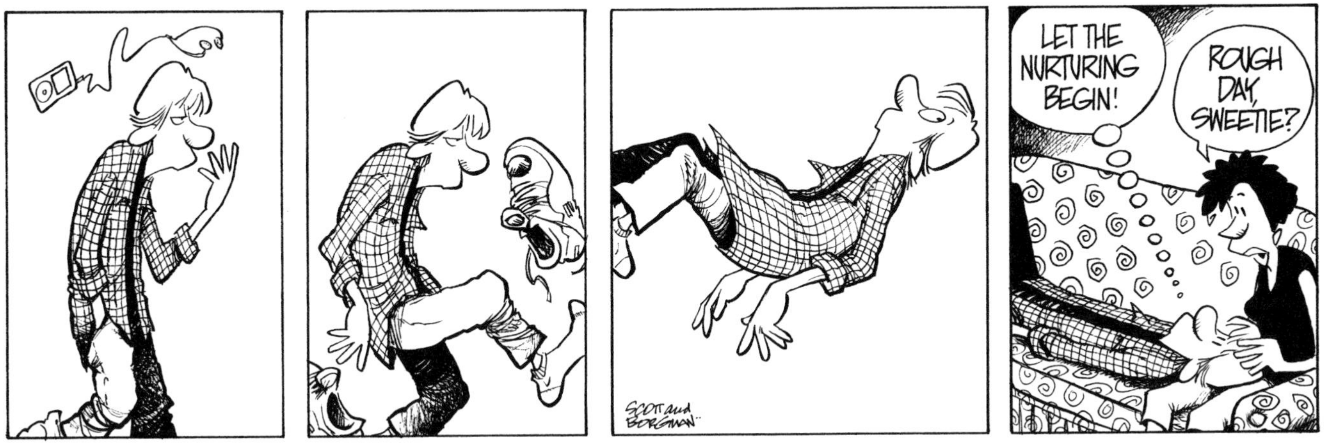
SCOTT and BORGMAN
LET THE NURTURING BEGIN!
ROUGH DAY, SWEETIE?

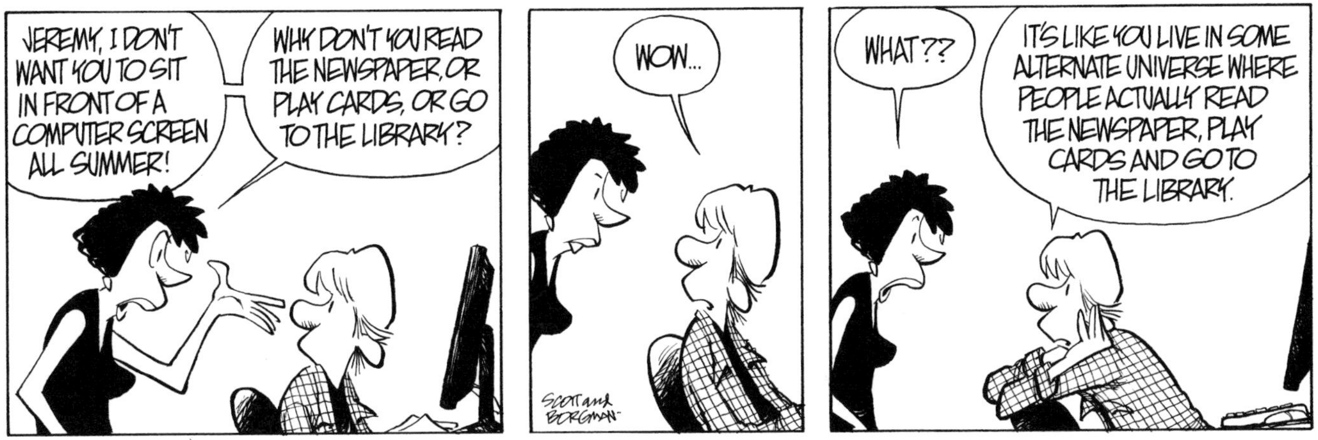
JEREMY, I DON'T WANT YOU TO SIT IN FRONT OF A COMPUTER SCREEN ALL SUMMER!
WHY DON'T YOU READ THE NEWSPAPER, OR PLAY CARDS, OR GO TO THE LIBRARY?
WOW...
SCOTT and BORGMAN
WHAT??
IT'S LIKE YOU LIVE IN SOME ALTERNATE UNIVERSE WHERE PEOPLE ACTUALLY READ THE NEWSPAPER, PLAY CARDS AND GO TO THE LIBRARY.

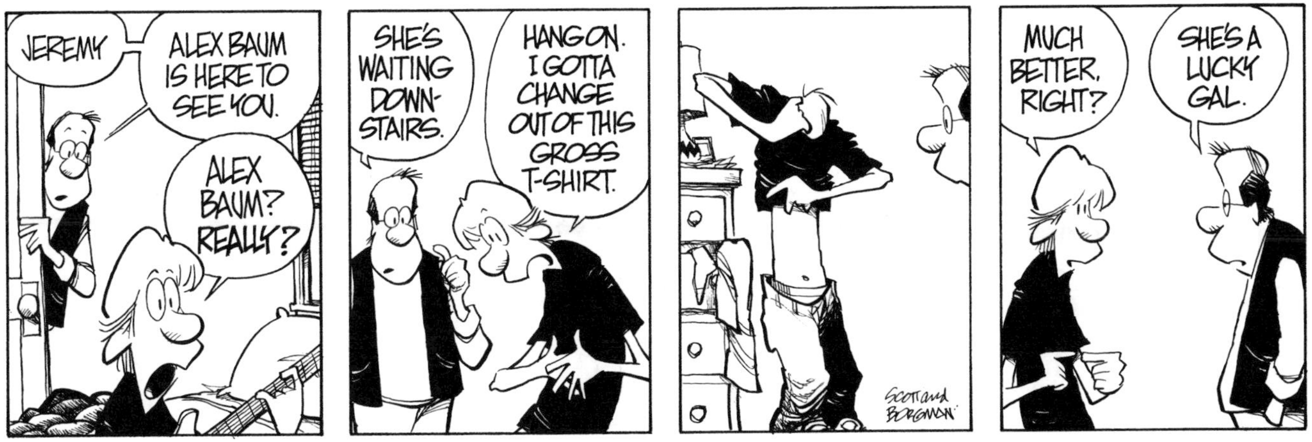
JEREMY
ALEX BAUM IS HERE TO SEE YOU.
ALEX BAUM? REALLY?
SHE'S WAITING DOWN-STAIRS.
HANG ON. I GOTTA CHANGE OUT OF THIS GROSS T-SHIRT.
SCOTT and BORGMAN
MUCH BETTER, RIGHT?
SHE'S A LUCKY GAL.

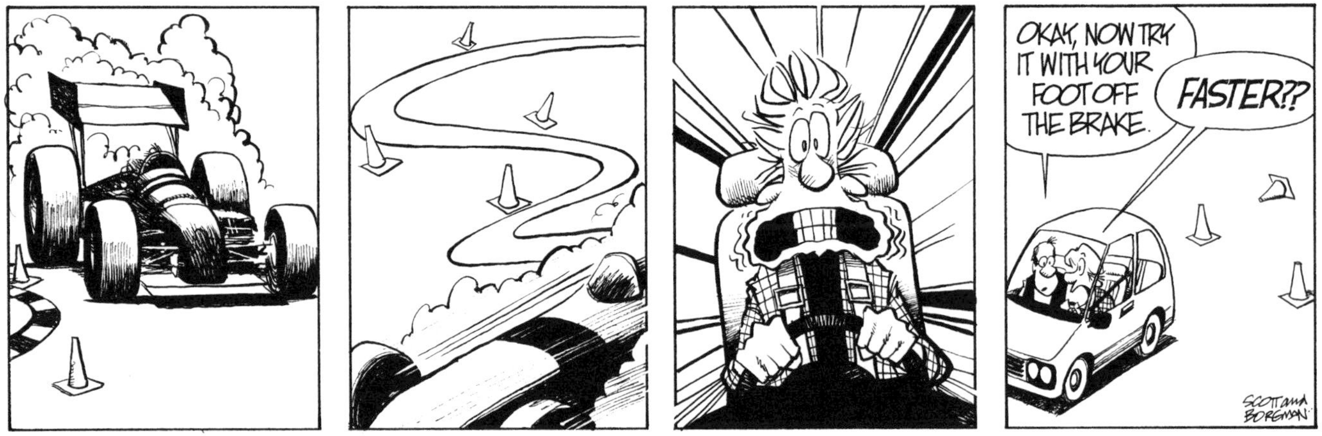
OKAY, NOW TRY IT WITH YOUR FOOT OFF THE BRAKE.
FASTER??
SCOTT and BORGMAN

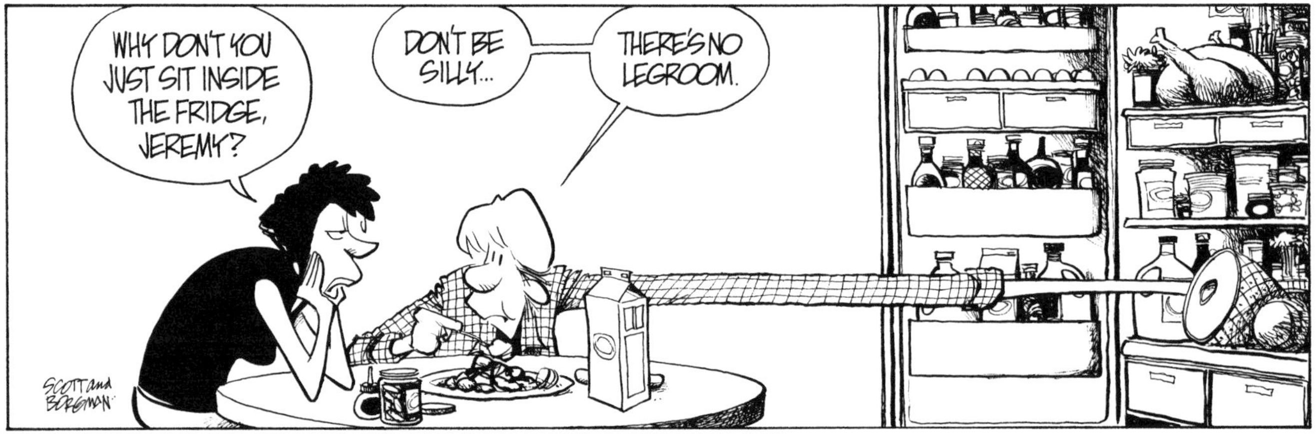
WHY DON'T YOU JUST SIT INSIDE THE FRIDGE, JEREMY?
DON'T BE SILLY...
THERE'S NO LEGROOM.
SCOTT and BORGMAN

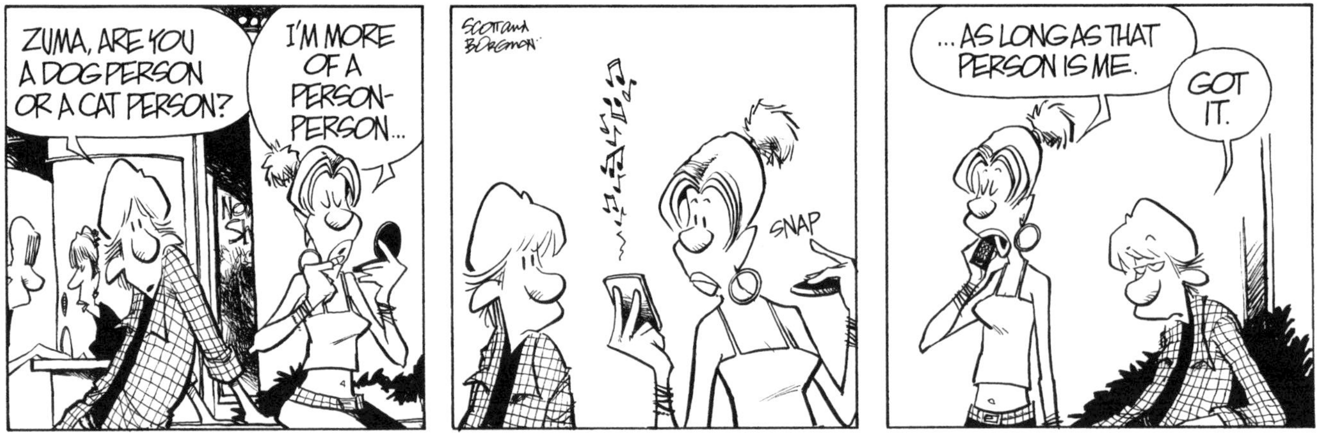
ZUMA, ARE YOU A DOG PERSON OR A CAT PERSON?
I'M MORE OF A PERSON-PERSON...
SCOTT and BORGMAN
SNAP
... AS LONG AS THAT PERSON IS ME.
GOT IT.

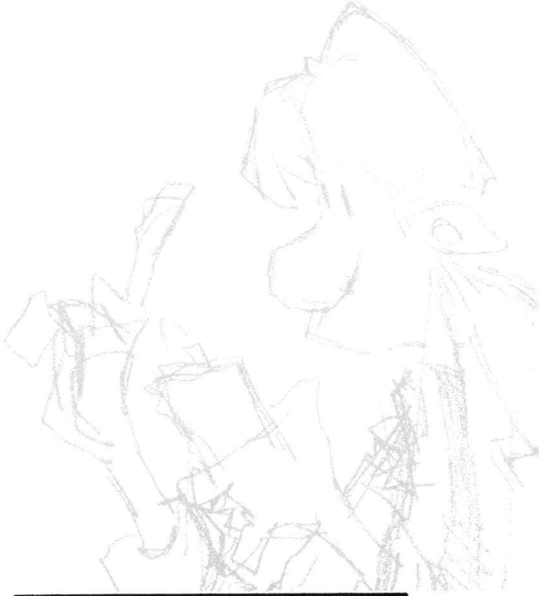

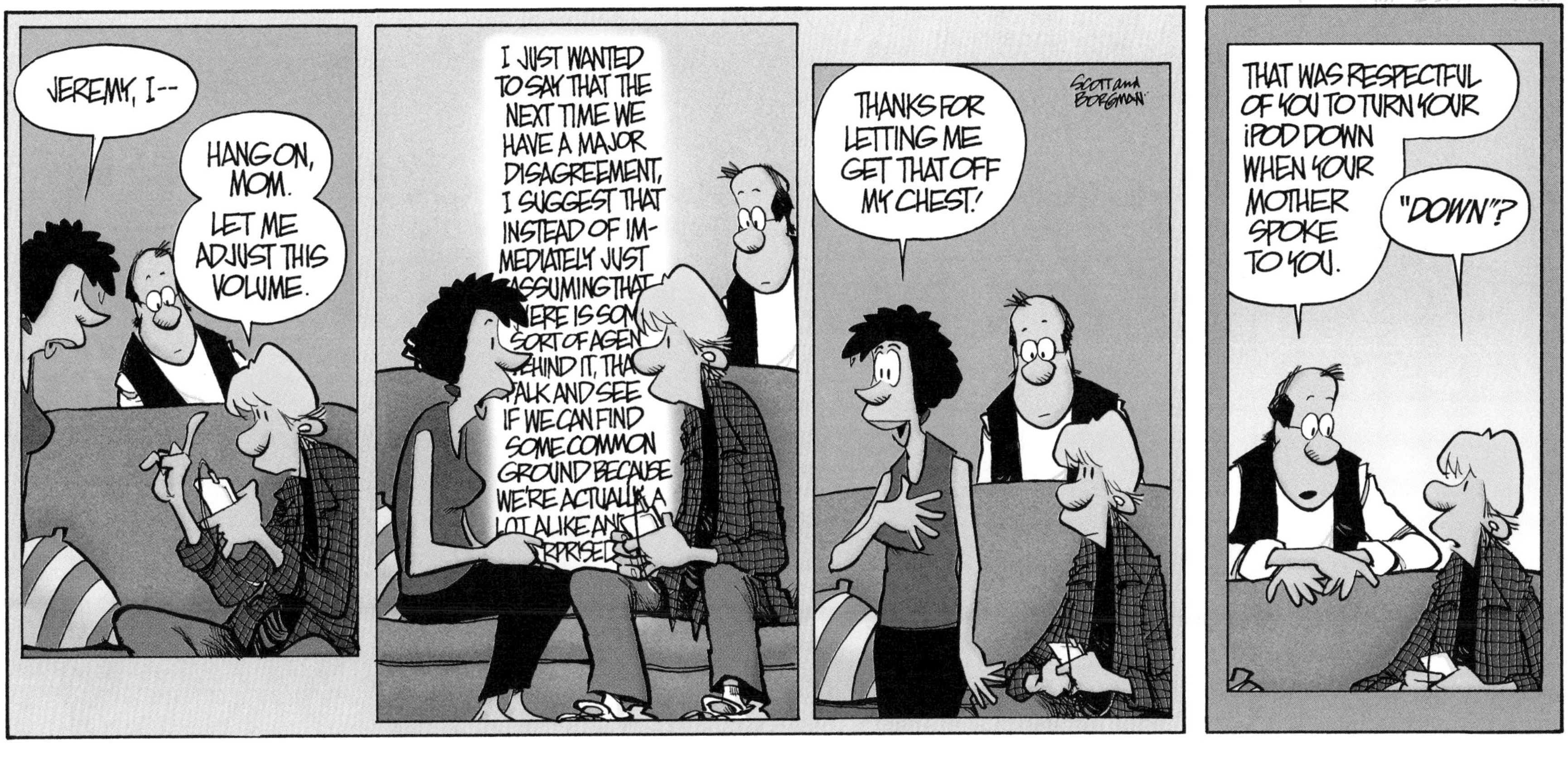
JEREMY, I--
HANG ON, MOM.
LET ME ADJUST THIS VOLUME.
I JUST WANTED TO SAY THAT THE NEXT TIME WE HAVE A MAJOR DISAGREEMENT, I SUGGEST THAT INSTEAD OF IM- MEDIATELY JUST
IF WE CAN FIND SOME COMMON GROUND BECAUSE
THANKS FOR LETTING ME GET THAT OFF MY CHEST!
SCOTT AND BORGMAN
THAT WAS RESPECTFUL OF YOU TO TURN YOUR iPOD DOWN WHEN YOUR MOTHER SPOKE TO YOU.
"DOWN"?

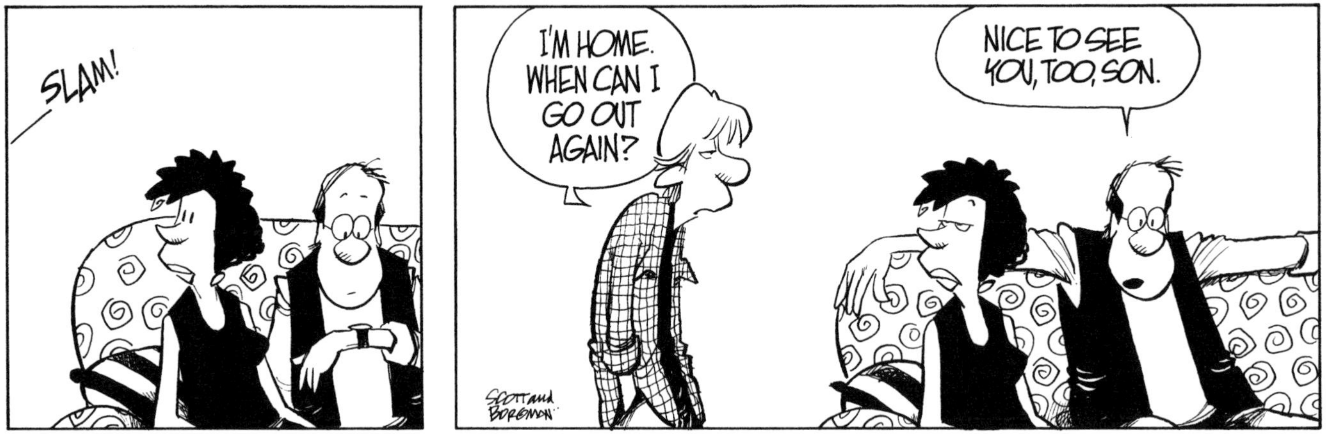
SLAM!
I'M HOME. WHEN CAN I GO OUT AGAIN?
NICE TO SEE YOU, TOO, SON.
SCOTT and BORGMAN

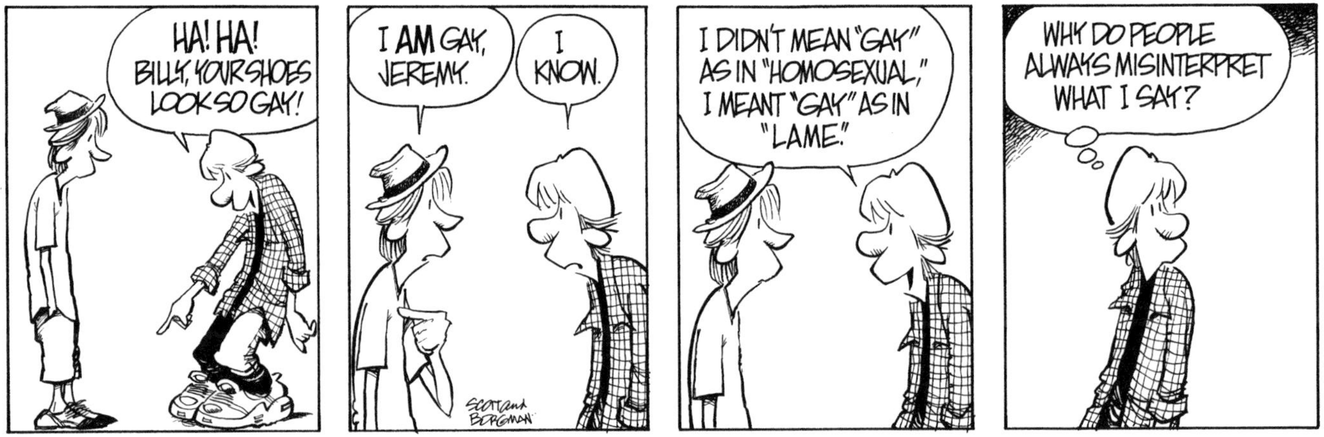
HA! HA! BILLY, YOUR SHOES LOOK SO GAY!
I **AM** GAY, JEREMY.
I KNOW.
SCOTT and BORGMAN
I DIDN'T MEAN "GAY" AS IN "HOMOSEXUAL," I MEANT "GAY" AS IN "LAME."
WHY DO PEOPLE ALWAYS MISINTERPRET WHAT I SAY?

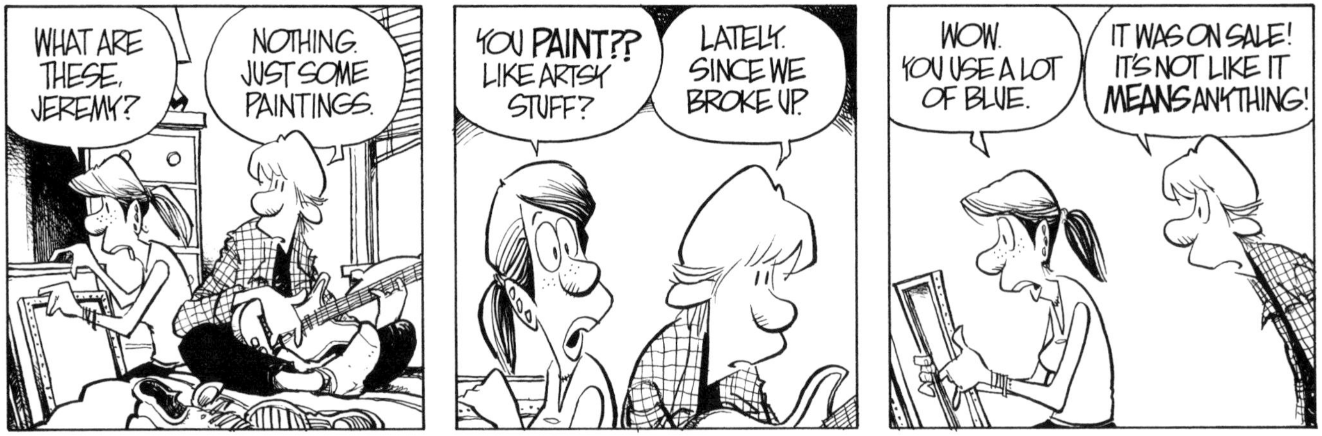
WHAT ARE THESE, JEREMY?
NOTHING. JUST SOME PAINTINGS.
YOU **PAINT??** LIKE ARTSY STUFF?
LATELY. SINCE WE BROKE UP.
WOW. YOU USE A LOT OF BLUE.
IT WAS ON SALE! IT'S NOT LIKE IT **MEANS** ANYTHING!

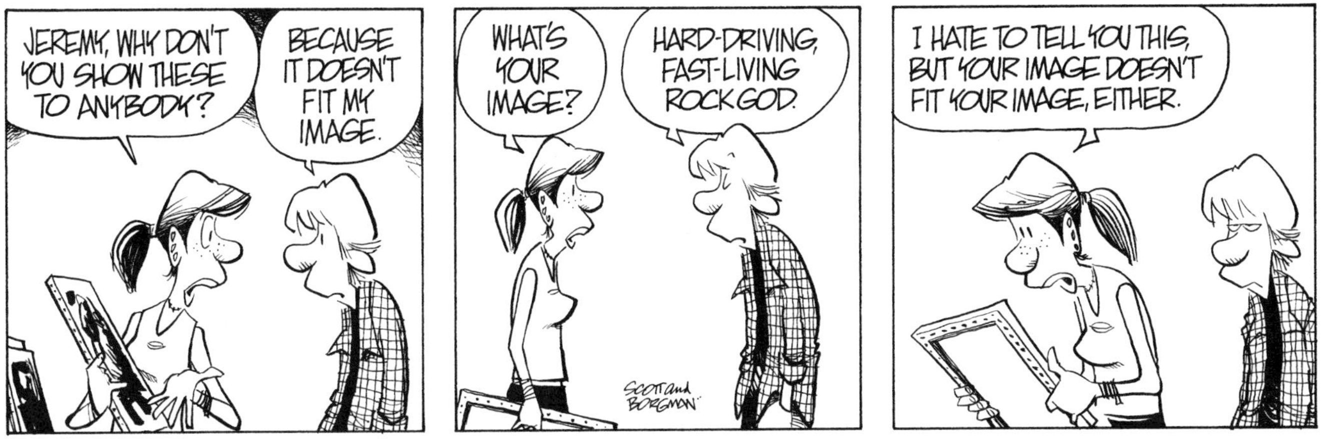
JEREMY, WHY DON'T YOU SHOW THESE TO ANYBODY?
BECAUSE IT DOESN'T FIT MY IMAGE.
WHAT'S YOUR IMAGE?
HARD-DRIVING, FAST-LIVING ROCK GOD.
SCOTT and BORGMAN
I HATE TO TELL YOU THIS, BUT YOUR IMAGE DOESN'T FIT YOUR IMAGE, EITHER.

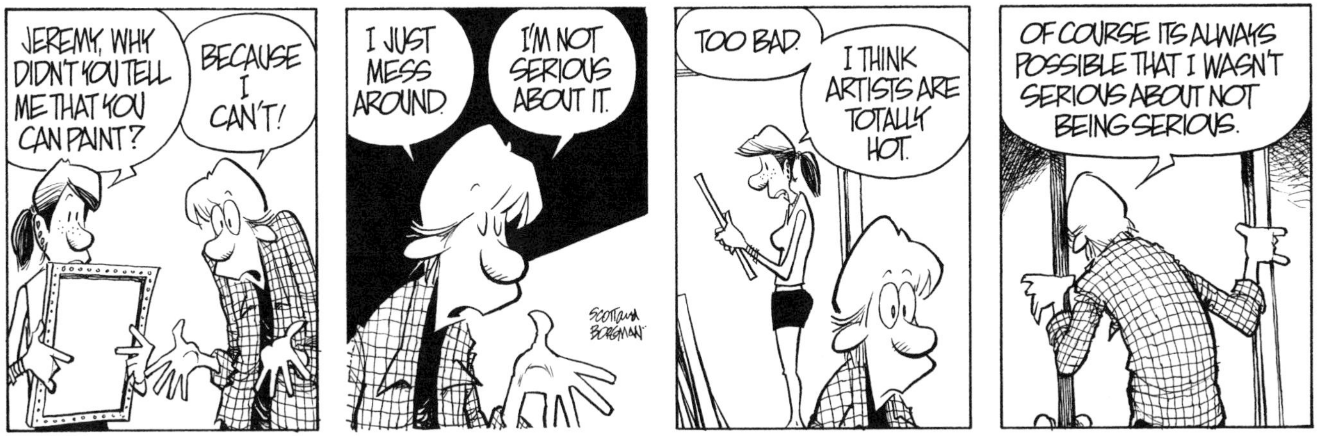
JEREMY, WHY DIDN'T YOU TELL ME THAT YOU CAN PAINT?
BECAUSE I CAN'T!
I JUST MESS AROUND.
I'M NOT SERIOUS ABOUT IT.
SCOTT and BORGMAN
TOO BAD.
I THINK ARTISTS ARE TOTALLY HOT.
OF COURSE ITS ALWAYS POSSIBLE THAT I WASN'T SERIOUS ABOUT NOT BEING SERIOUS.

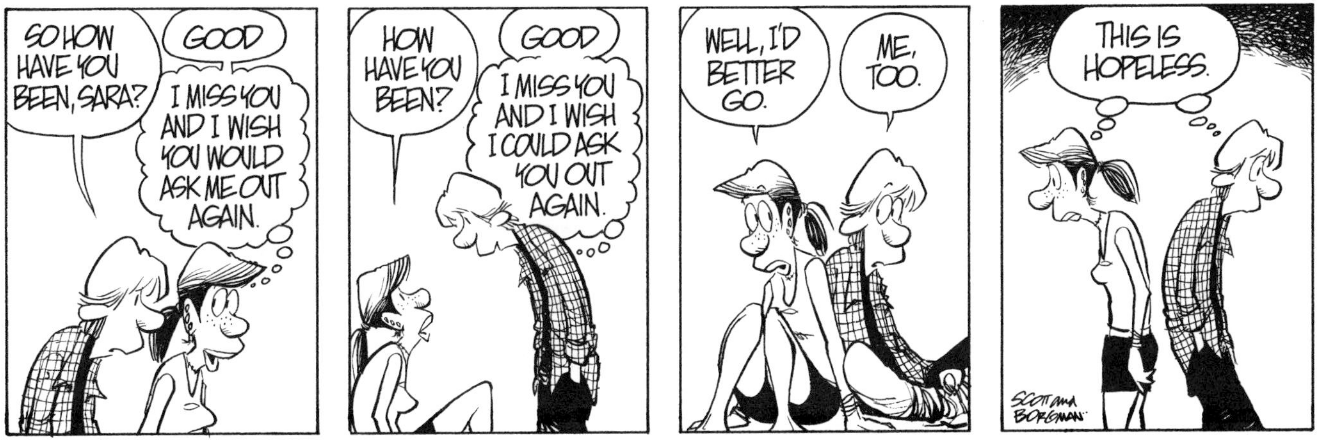
SO HOW HAVE YOU BEEN, SARA?
GOOD
I MISS YOU AND I WISH YOU WOULD ASK ME OUT AGAIN.
HOW HAVE YOU BEEN?
GOOD
I MISS YOU AND I WISH I COULD ASK YOU OUT AGAIN.
WELL, I'D BETTER GO.
ME, TOO.
THIS IS HOPELESS.
SCOTT and BORGMAN

Zits

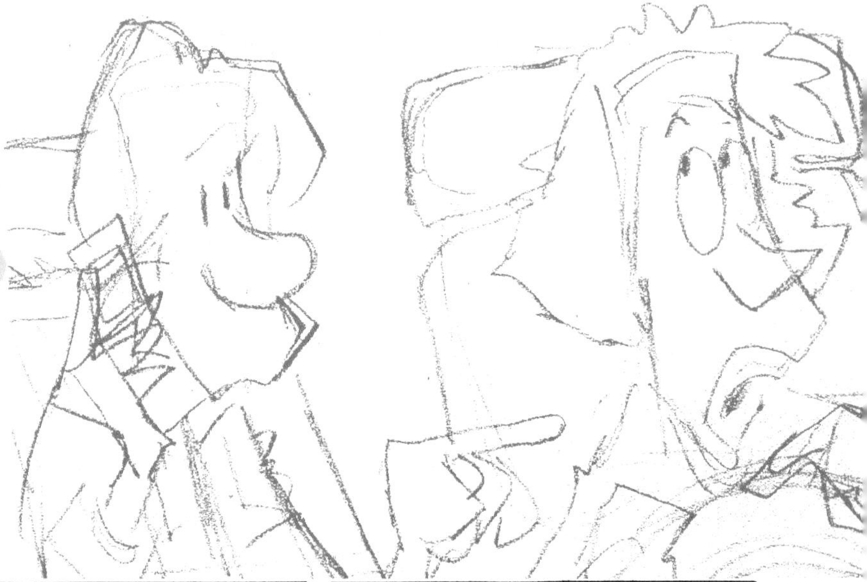

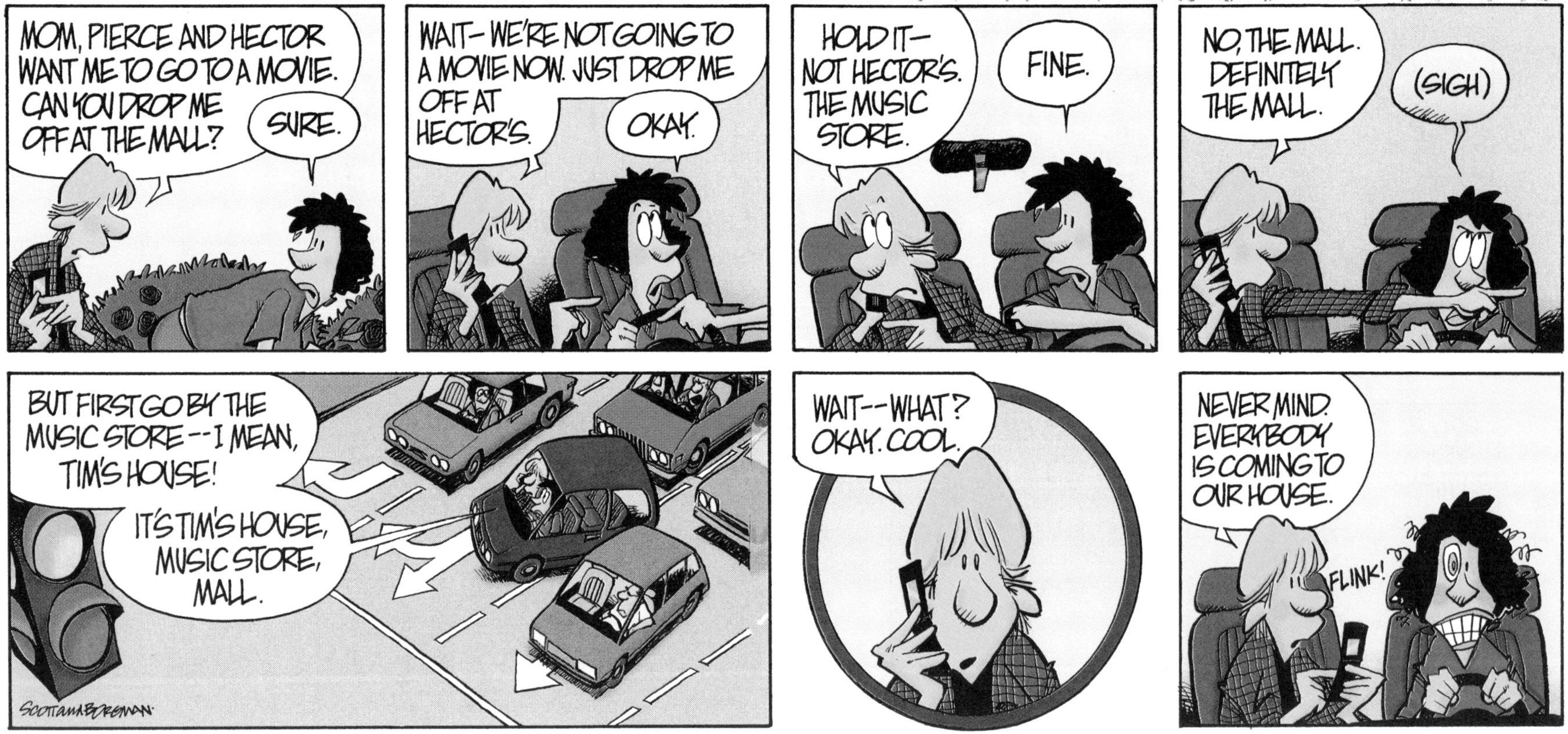

MOM, PIERCE AND HECTOR WANT ME TO GO TO A MOVIE. CAN YOU DROP ME OFF AT THE MALL?
SURE.
WAIT- WE'RE NOT GOING TO A MOVIE NOW. JUST DROP ME OFF AT HECTOR'S.
OKAY.
HOLD IT- NOT HECTOR'S. THE MUSIC STORE.
FINE.
NO, THE MALL. DEFINITELY THE MALL.
(SIGH)
BUT FIRST GO BY THE MUSIC STORE--I MEAN, TIM'S HOUSE!
IT'S TIM'S HOUSE, MUSIC STORE, MALL.
WAIT--WHAT? OKAY. COOL.
NEVER MIND. EVERYBODY IS COMING TO OUR HOUSE.
FLINK!

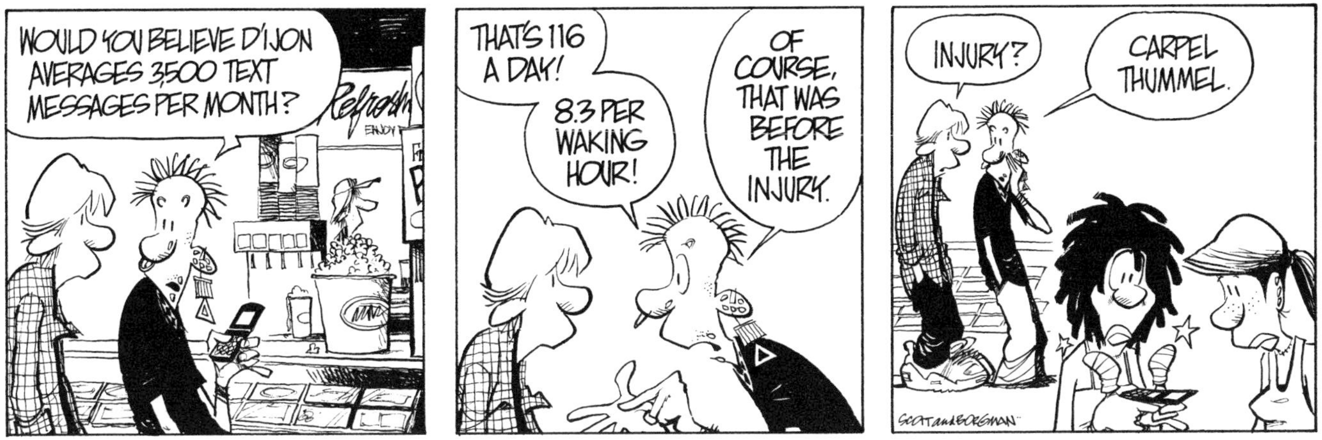
WOULD YOU BELIEVE D'IJON AVERAGES 3,500 TEXT MESSAGES PER MONTH?
THAT'S 116 A DAY!
8.3 PER WAKING HOUR!
OF COURSE, THAT WAS BEFORE THE INJURY.
INJURY?
CARPEL THUMMEL.
SCOTT and BORGMAN

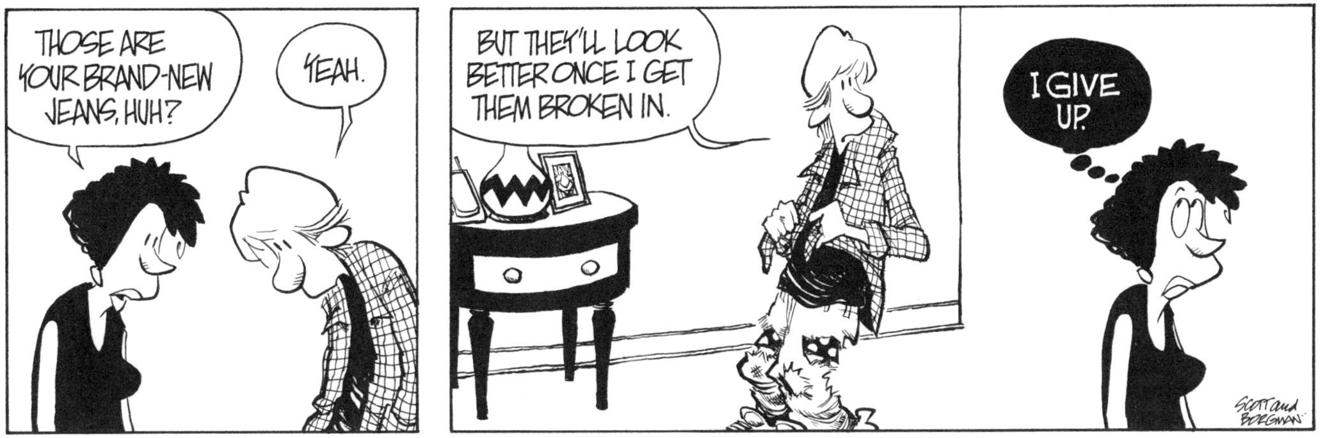
THOSE ARE YOUR BRAND-NEW JEANS, HUH?
YEAH.
BUT THEY'LL LOOK BETTER ONCE I GET THEM BROKEN IN.
I GIVE UP.
SCOTT and BORGMAN

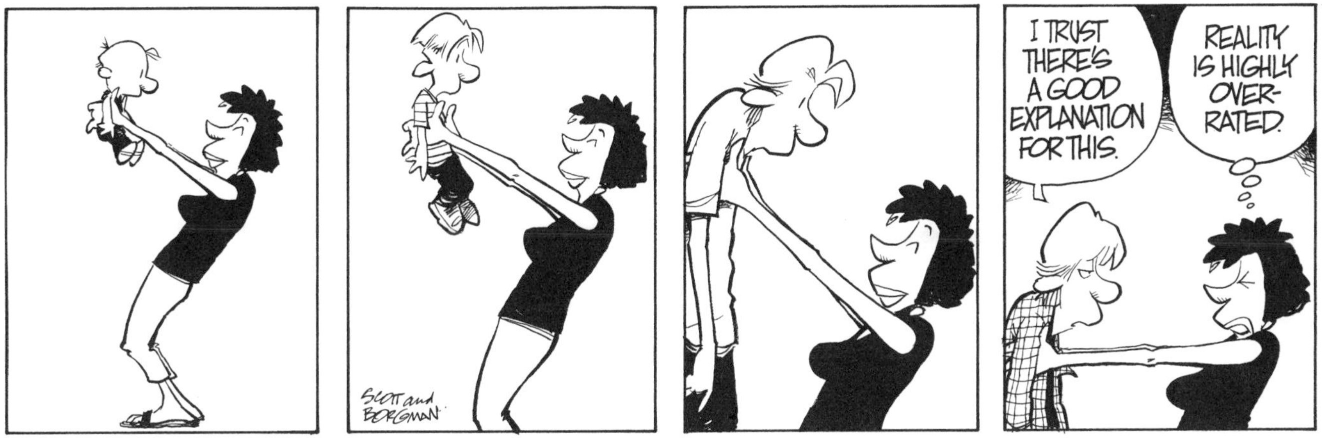
SCOTT and BORGMAN
I TRUST THERE'S A GOOD EXPLANATION FOR THIS.
REALITY IS HIGHLY OVER-RATED.

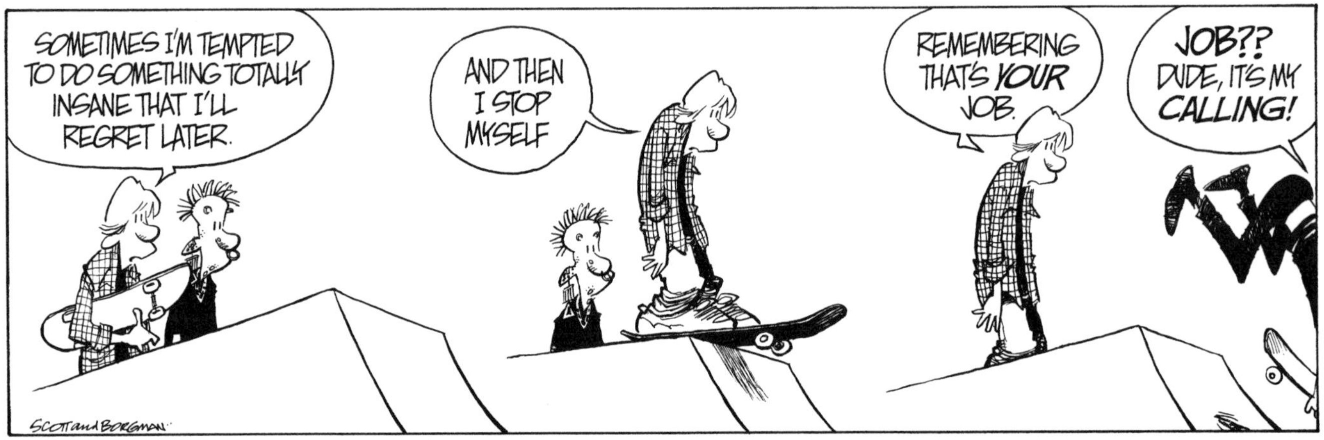
SOMETIMES I'M TEMPTED TO DO SOMETHING TOTALLY INSANE THAT I'LL REGRET LATER.
AND THEN I STOP MYSELF
REMEMBERING THAT'S **YOUR** JOB.
JOB?? DUDE, IT'S MY **CALLING!**
SCOTT and BORGMAN

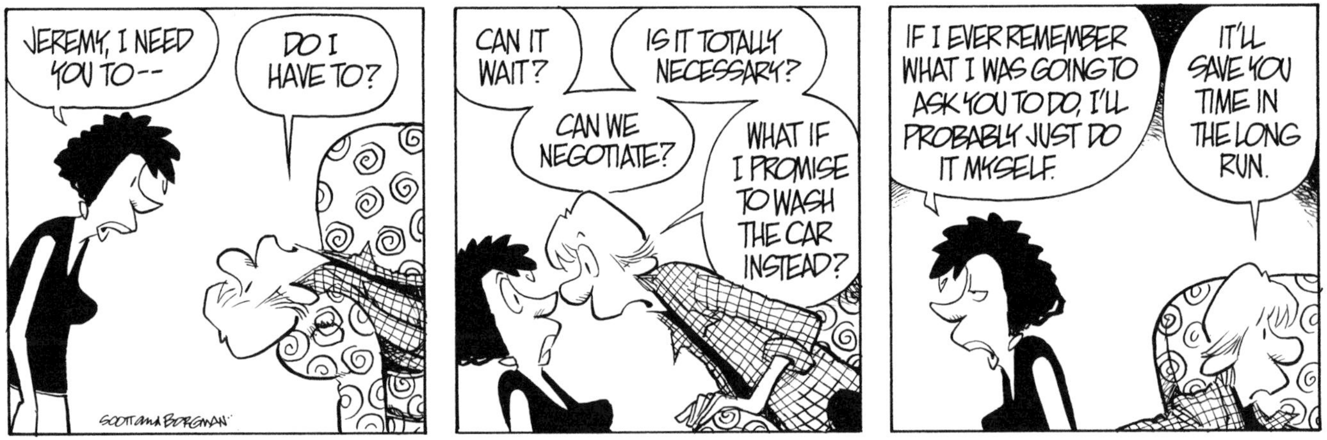
JEREMY, I NEED YOU TO--
DO I HAVE TO?
SCOTT and BORGMAN
CAN IT WAIT?
IS IT TOTALLY NECESSARY?
CAN WE NEGOTIATE?
WHAT IF I PROMISE TO WASH THE CAR INSTEAD?
IF I EVER REMEMBER WHAT I WAS GOING TO ASK YOU TO DO, I'LL PROBABLY JUST DO IT MYSELF.
IT'LL SAVE YOU TIME IN THE LONG RUN.

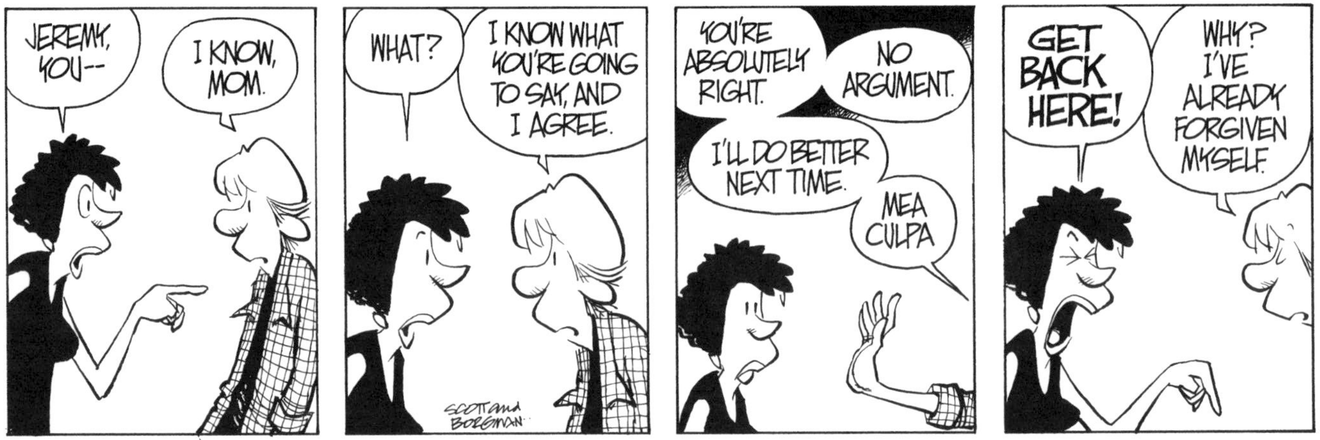
JEREMY, YOU--
I KNOW, MOM.
WHAT?
I KNOW WHAT YOU'RE GOING TO SAY, AND I AGREE.
SCOTT and BORGMAN
YOU'RE ABSOLUTELY RIGHT.
NO ARGUMENT.
I'LL DO BETTER NEXT TIME.
MEA CULPA
GET BACK HERE!
WHY? I'VE ALREADY FORGIVEN MYSELF.

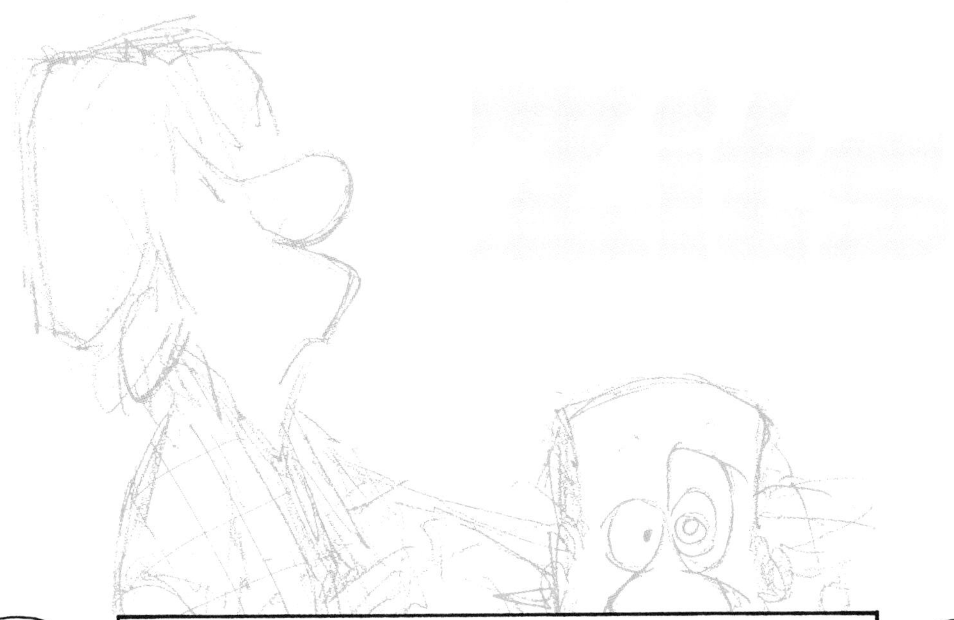

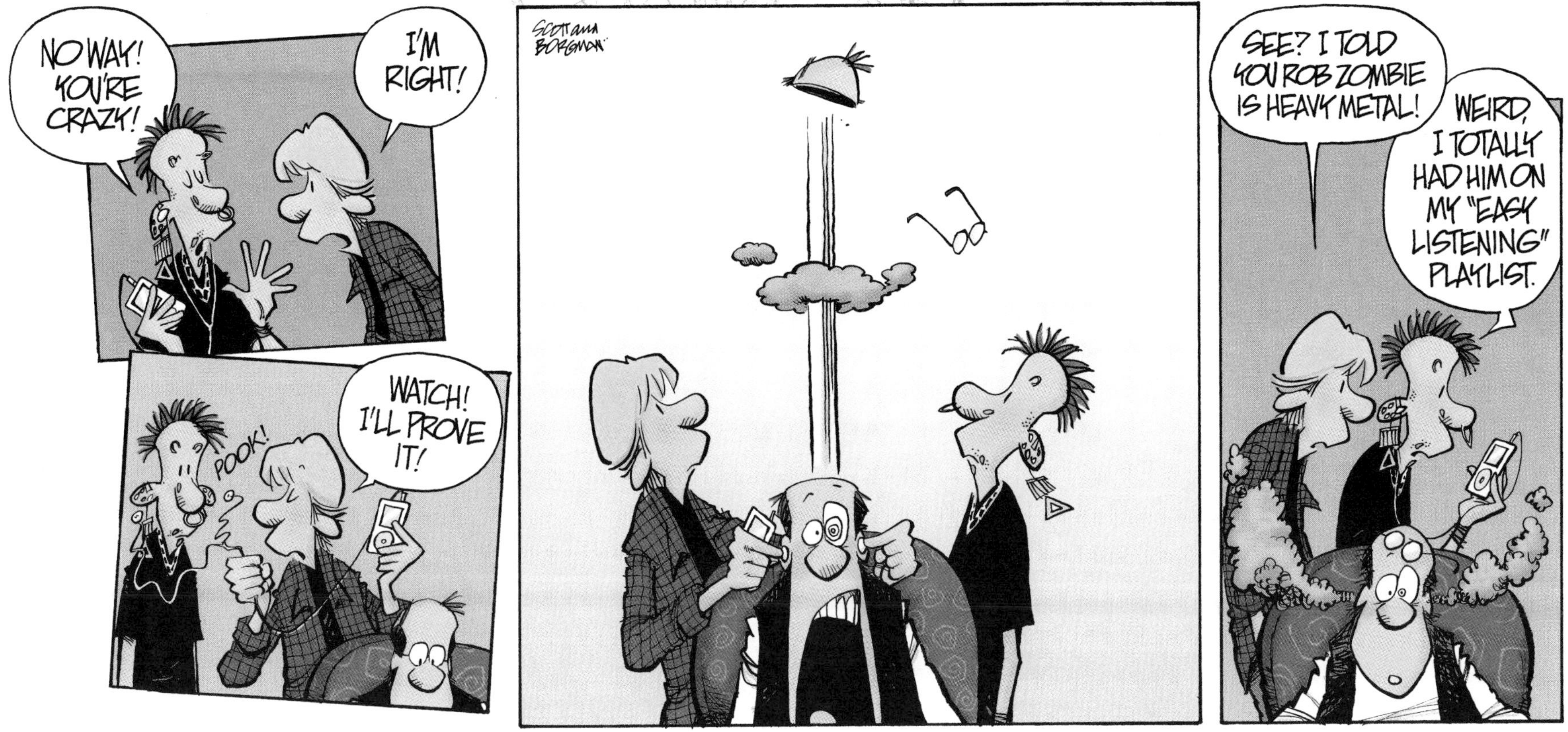

NO WAY! YOU'RE CRAZY!
I'M RIGHT!
POOK!
WATCH! I'LL PROVE IT!
SEE? I TOLD YOU ROB ZOMBIE IS HEAVY METAL!
WEIRD, I TOTALLY HAD HIM ON MY "EASY LISTENING" PLAYLIST.

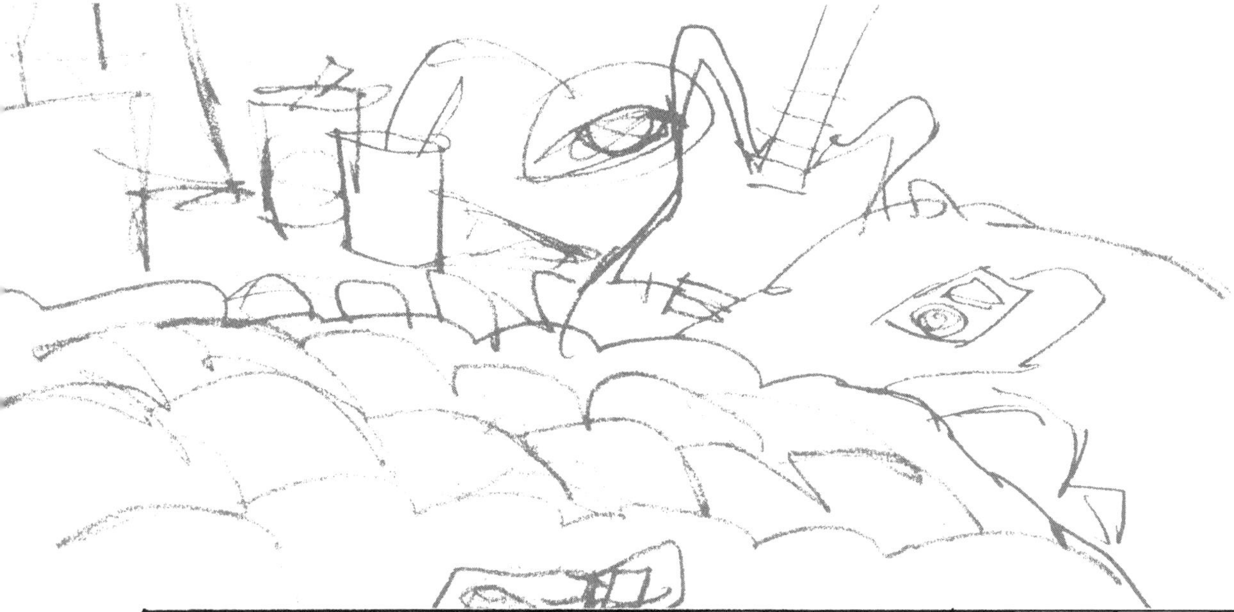

Zits

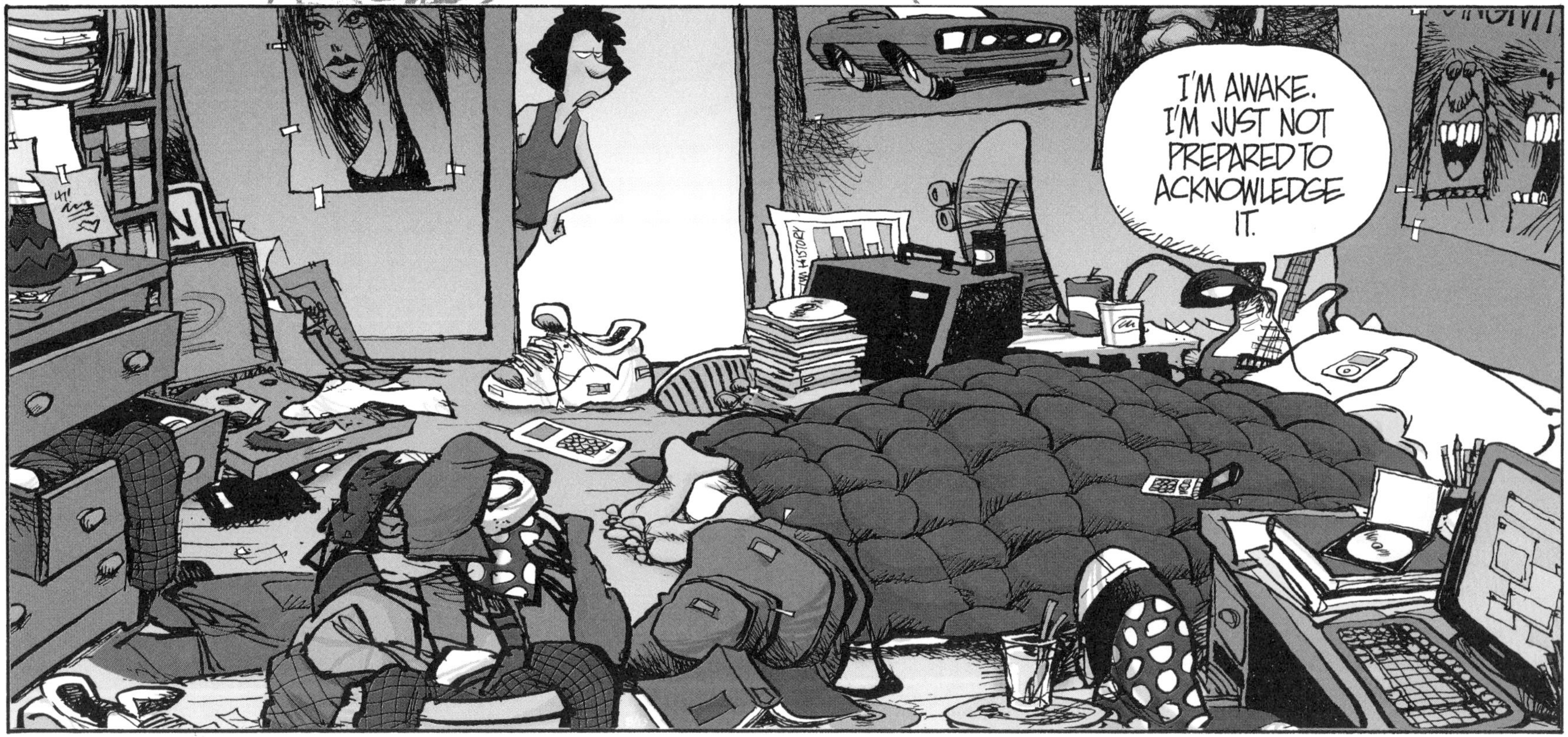
I'M AWAKE. I'M JUST NOT PREPARED TO ACKNOWLEDGE IT.

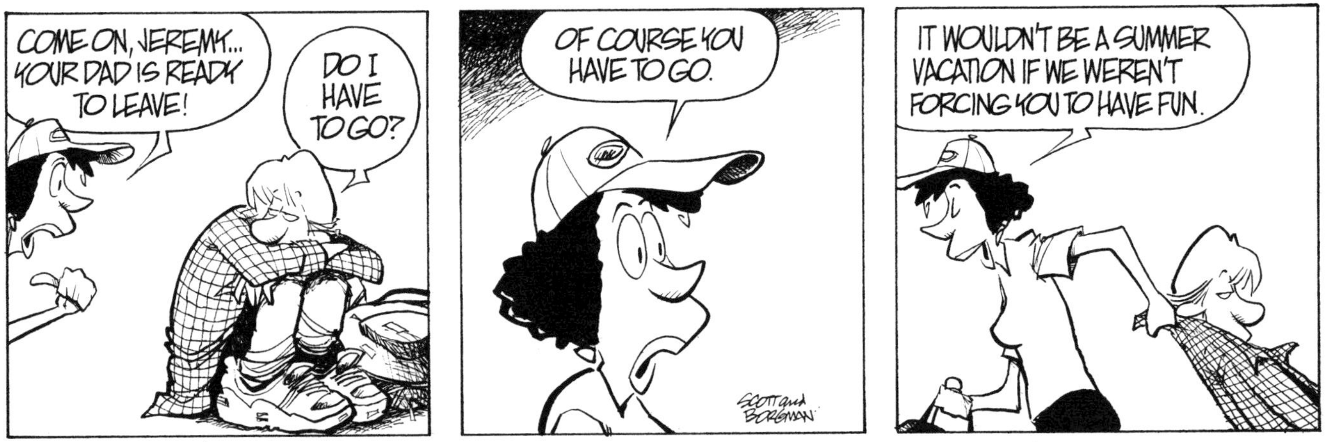
COME ON, JEREMY... YOUR DAD IS READY TO LEAVE!
DO I HAVE TO GO?
OF COURSE YOU HAVE TO GO.
IT WOULDN'T BE A SUMMER VACATION IF WE WEREN'T FORCING YOU TO HAVE FUN.

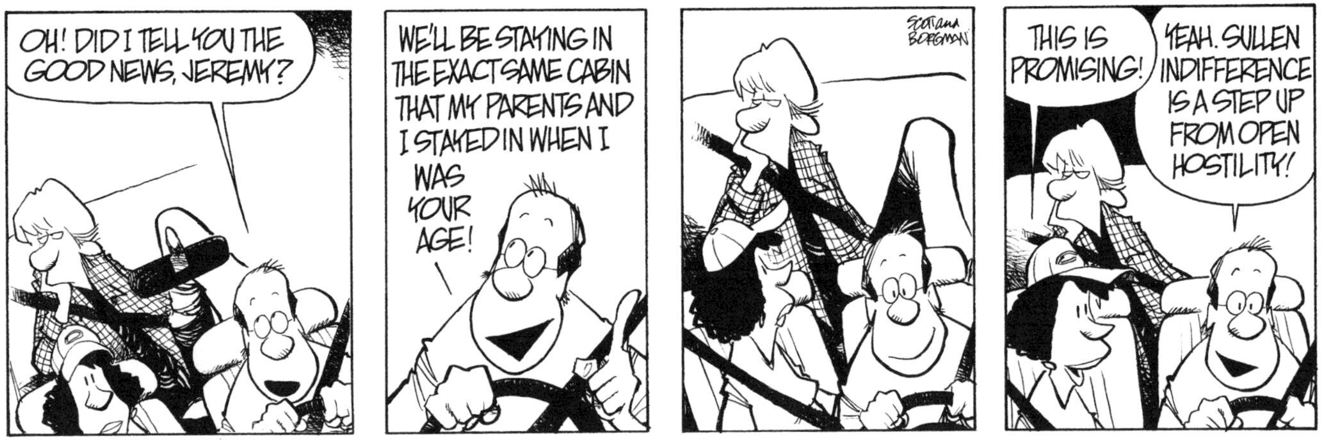
OH! DID I TELL YOU THE GOOD NEWS, JEREMY?
WE'LL BE STAYING IN THE EXACT SAME CABIN THAT MY PARENTS AND I STAYED IN WHEN I WAS YOUR AGE!
THIS IS PROMISING!
YEAH. SULLEN INDIFFERENCE IS A STEP UP FROM OPEN HOSTILITY!

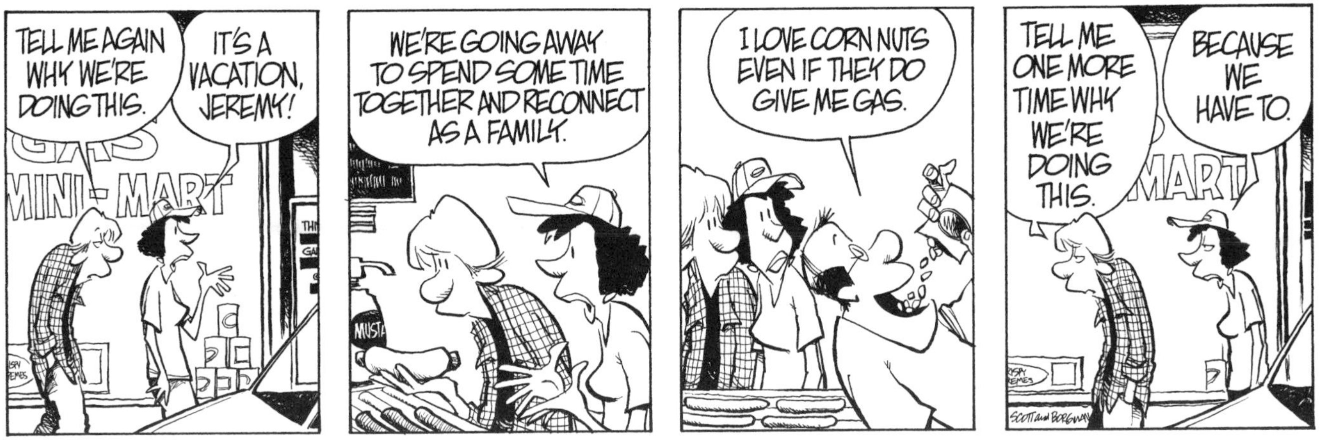
TELL ME AGAIN WHY WE'RE DOING THIS.
IT'S A VACATION, JEREMY!
GAS
MINI-MART
WE'RE GOING AWAY TO SPEND SOME TIME TOGETHER AND RECONNECT AS A FAMILY.
I LOVE CORN NUTS EVEN IF THEY DO GIVE ME GAS.
TELL ME ONE MORE TIME WHY WE'RE DOING THIS.
BECAUSE WE HAVE TO.

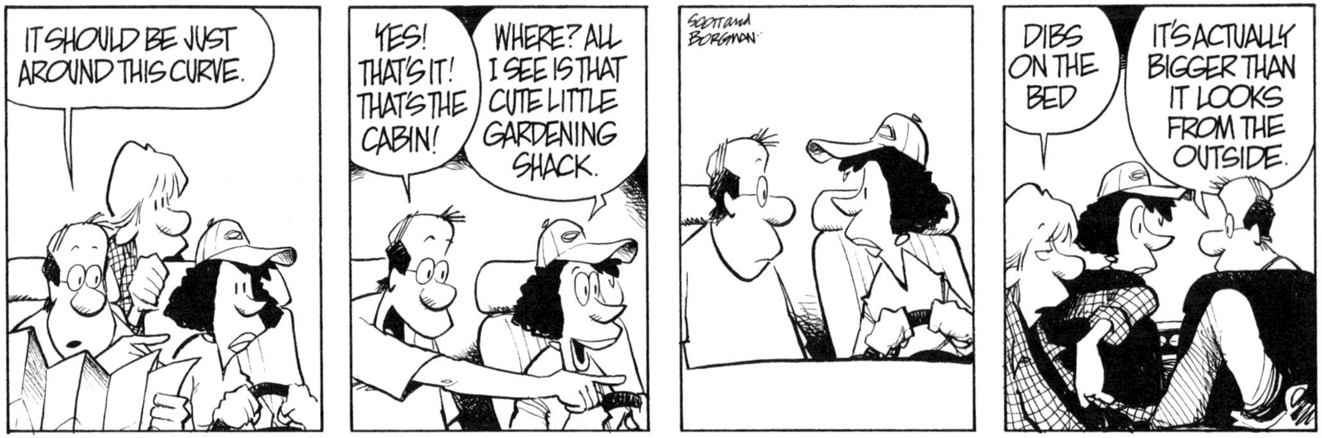
IT SHOULD BE JUST AROUND THIS CURVE.
YES! THAT'S IT! THAT'S THE CABIN!
WHERE? ALL I SEE IS THAT CUTE LITTLE GARDENING SHACK.
SCOTT and BORGMAN
DIBS ON THE BED
IT'S ACTUALLY BIGGER THAN IT LOOKS FROM THE OUTSIDE.

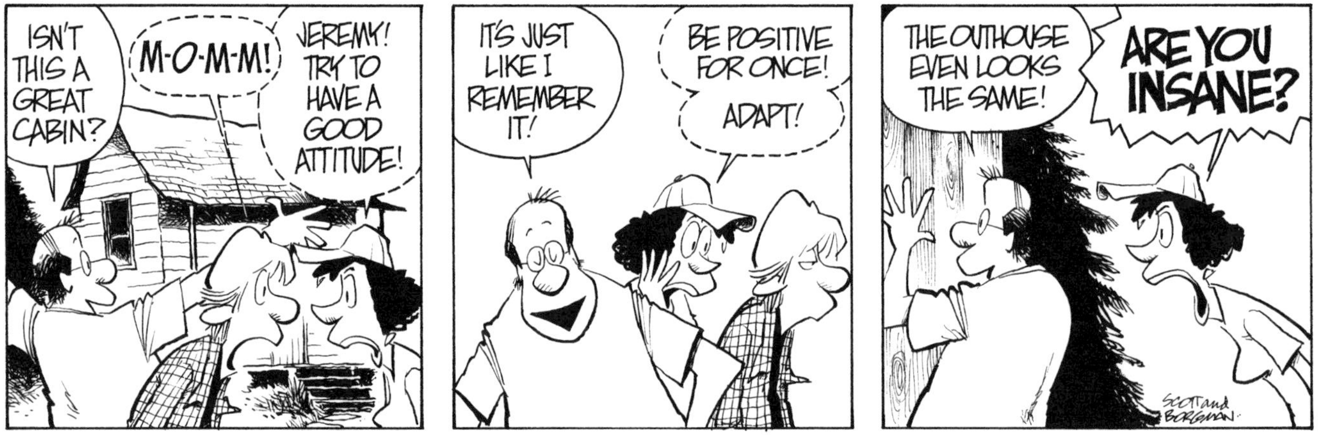
ISN'T THIS A GREAT CABIN?
M-O-M-M!
JEREMY! TRY TO HAVE A GOOD ATTITUDE!
IT'S JUST LIKE I REMEMBER IT!
BE POSITIVE FOR ONCE!
ADAPT!
THE OUTHOUSE EVEN LOOKS THE SAME!
ARE YOU INSANE?
SCOTT and BORGMAN

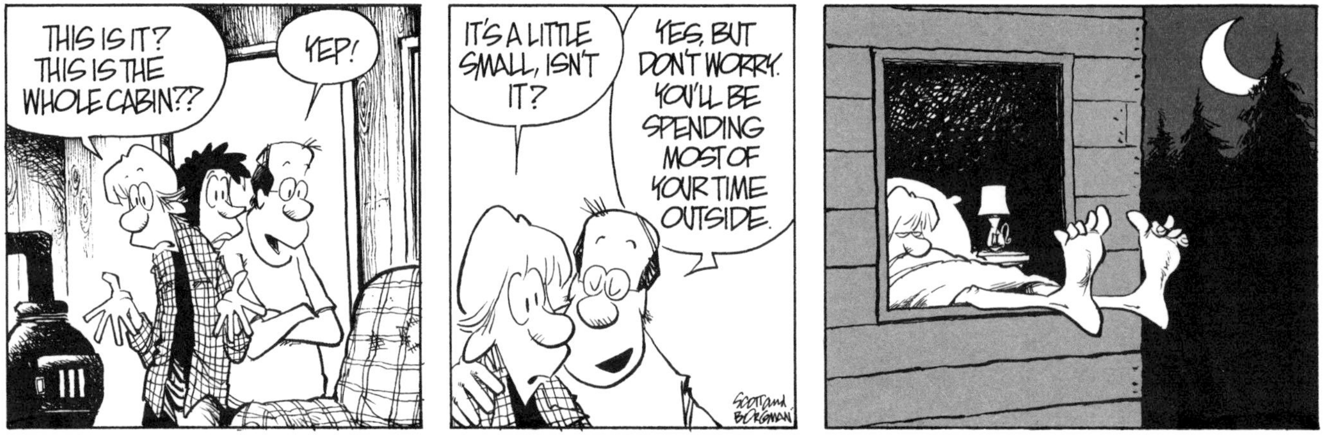
THIS IS IT? THIS IS THE WHOLE CABIN??
YEP!
IT'S A LITTLE SMALL, ISN'T IT?
YES, BUT DON'T WORRY. YOU'LL BE SPENDING MOST OF YOUR TIME OUTSIDE.
SCOTT and BORGMAN

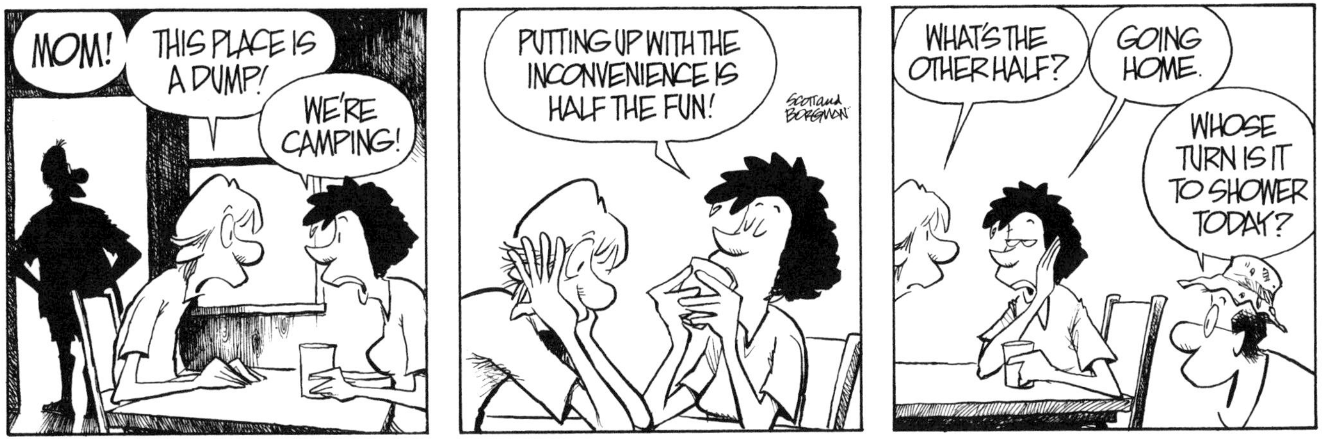
MOM!
THIS PLACE IS A DUMP!
WE'RE CAMPING!
PUTTING UP WITH THE INCONVENIENCE IS HALF THE FUN!
SCOTT and BORGMAN
WHAT'S THE OTHER HALF?
GOING HOME.
WHOSE TURN IS IT TO SHOWER TODAY?

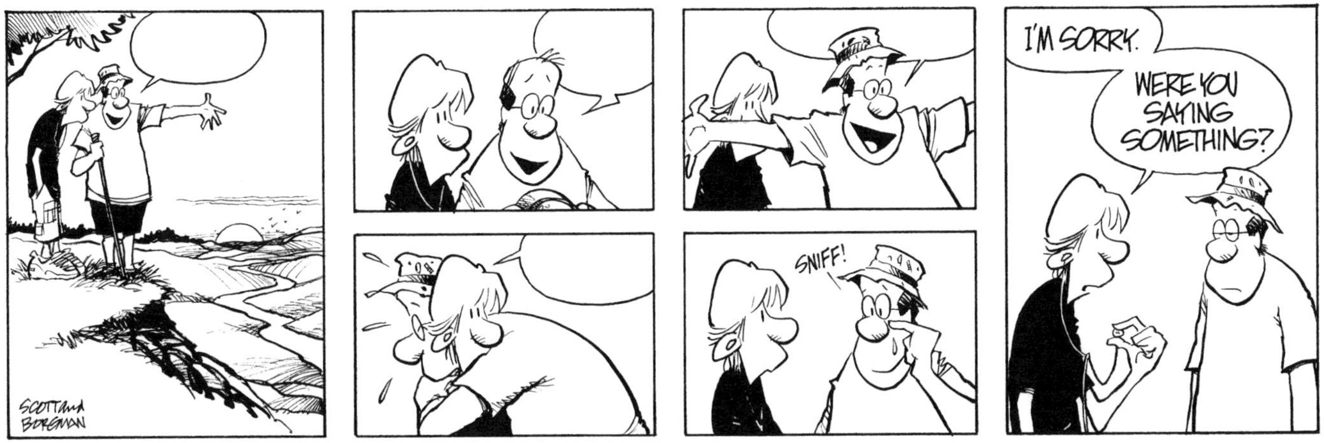
SCOTT and BORGMAN
SNIFF!
I'M SORRY.
WERE YOU SAYING SOMETHING?

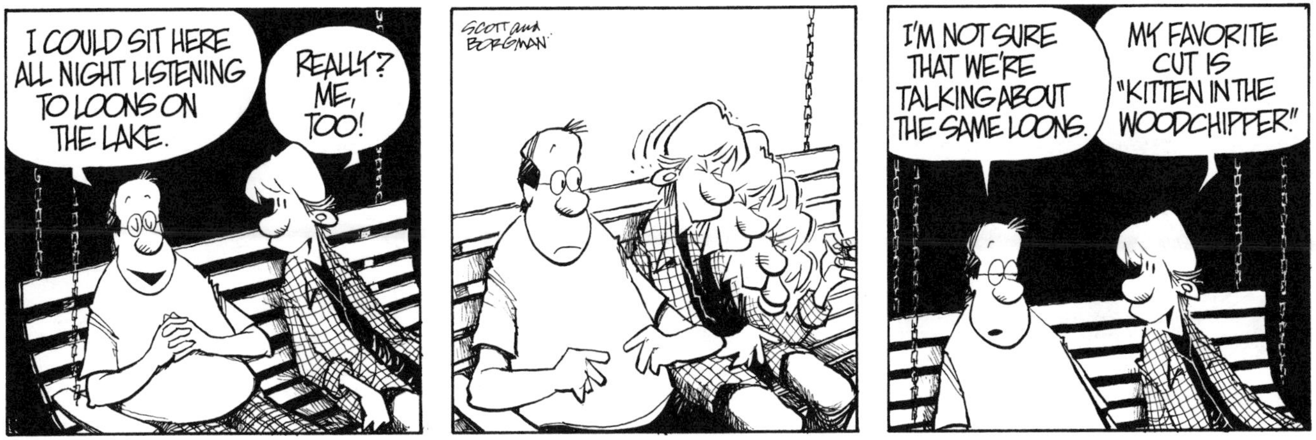
I COULD SIT HERE ALL NIGHT LISTENING TO LOONS ON THE LAKE.
REALLY? ME, TOO!
SCOTT and BORGMAN
I'M NOT SURE THAT WE'RE TALKING ABOUT THE SAME LOONS.
MY FAVORITE CUT IS "KITTEN IN THE WOODCHIPPER."

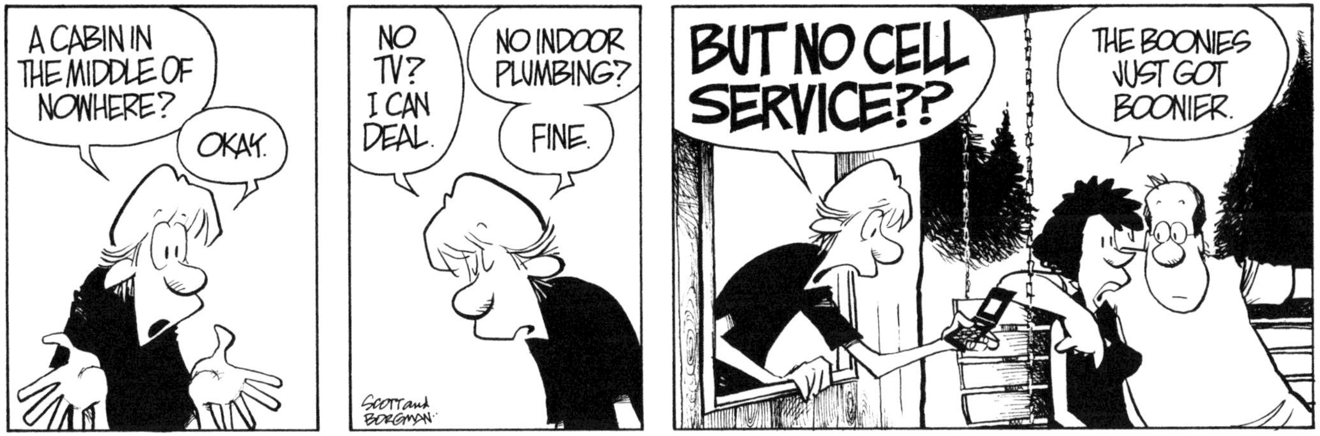
A CABIN IN THE MIDDLE OF NOWHERE?
OKAY.
NO TV? I CAN DEAL.
NO INDOOR PLUMBING?
FINE.
SCOTT and BORGMAN
BUT NO CELL SERVICE??
THE BOONIES JUST GOT BOONIER.

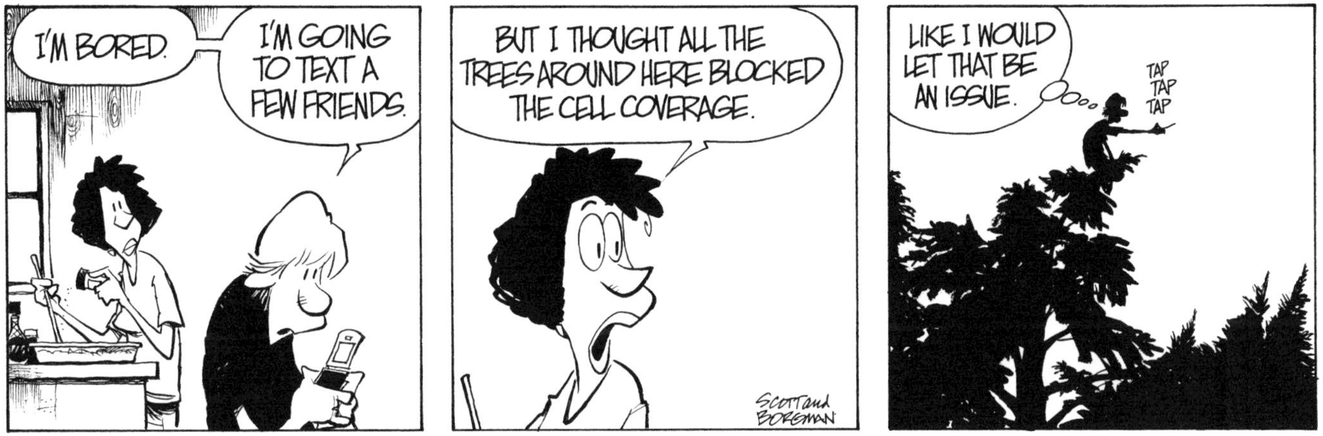
I'M BORED.
I'M GOING TO TEXT A FEW FRIENDS.
BUT I THOUGHT ALL THE TREES AROUND HERE BLOCKED THE CELL COVERAGE.
SCOTT and BORGMAN
LIKE I WOULD LET THAT BE AN ISSUE.
TAP TAP TAP

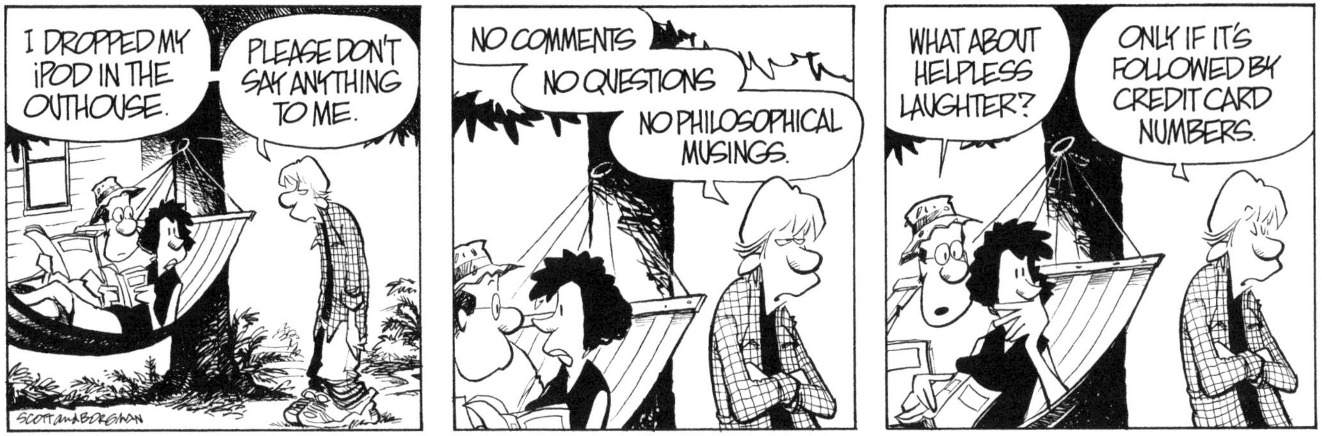
I DROPPED MY iPOD IN THE OUTHOUSE.
PLEASE DON'T SAY ANYTHING TO ME.
SCOTT and BORGMAN
NO COMMENTS
NO QUESTIONS
NO PHILOSOPHICAL MUSINGS.
WHAT ABOUT HELPLESS LAUGHTER?
ONLY IF IT'S FOLLOWED BY CREDIT CARD NUMBERS.

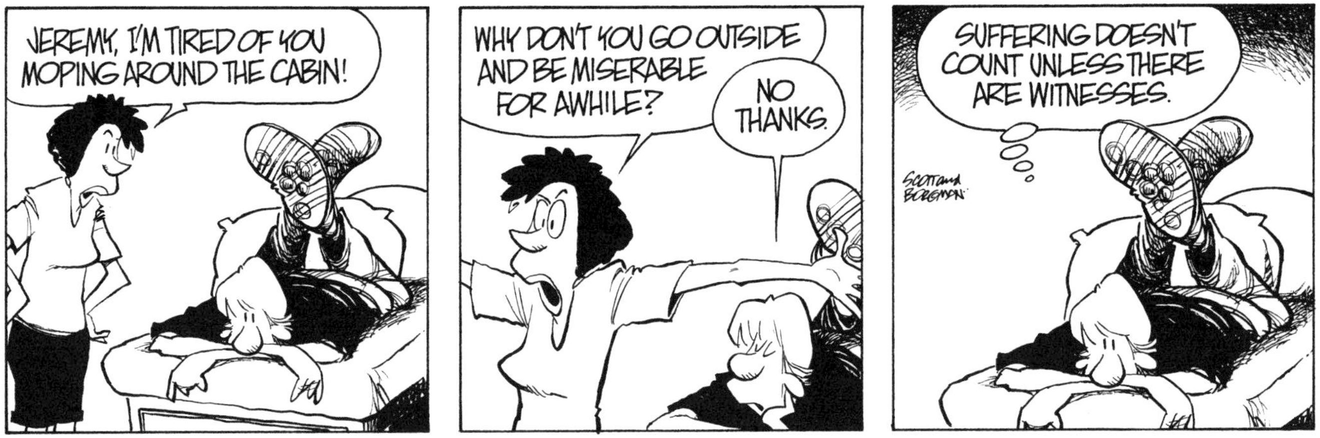
JEREMY, I'M TIRED OF YOU MOPING AROUND THE CABIN!
WHY DON'T YOU GO OUTSIDE AND BE MISERABLE FOR AWHILE?
NO THANKS.
SUFFERING DOESN'T COUNT UNLESS THERE ARE WITNESSES.
SCOTT and BORGMAN

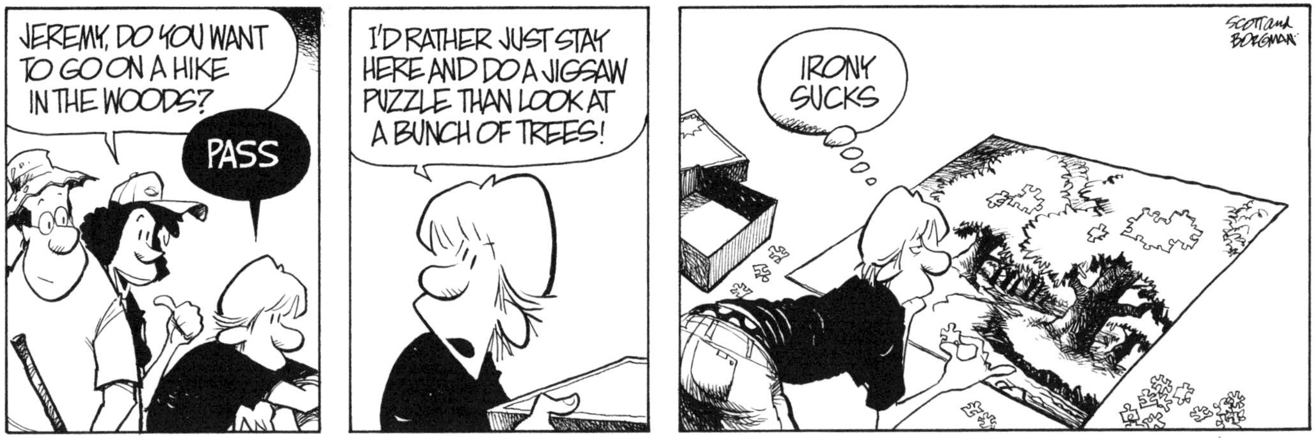
JEREMY, DO YOU WANT TO GO ON A HIKE IN THE WOODS?
PASS
I'D RATHER JUST STAY HERE AND DO A JIGSAW PUZZLE THAN LOOK AT A BUNCH OF TREES!
SCOTT and BORGMAN
IRONY SUCKS

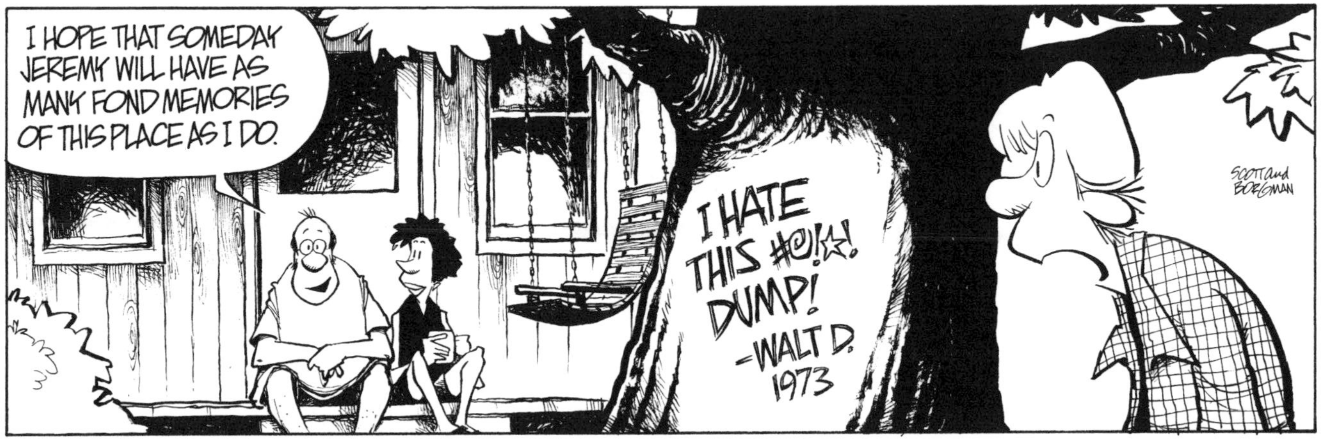
I HOPE THAT SOMEDAY JEREMY WILL HAVE AS MANY FOND MEMORIES OF THIS PLACE AS I DO.
I HATE THIS #@!☆! DUMP! -WALT D. 1973
SCOTT and BORGMAN

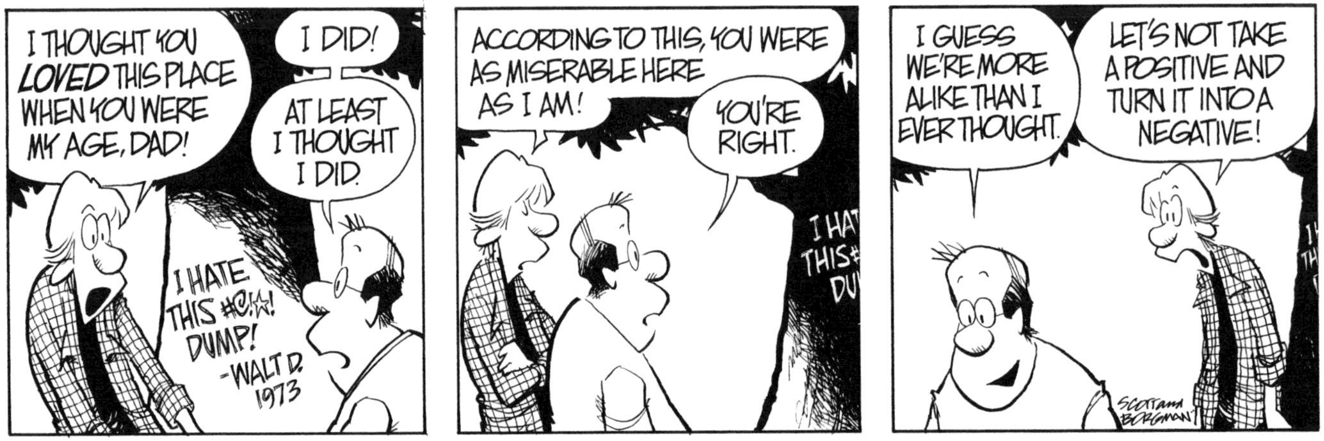
I THOUGHT YOU *LOVED* THIS PLACE WHEN YOU WERE MY AGE, DAD!
I DID!
AT LEAST I THOUGHT I DID.
I HATE THIS #@☆! DUMP! -WALT D. 1973
ACCORDING TO THIS, YOU WERE AS MISERABLE HERE AS I AM!
YOU'RE RIGHT.
I GUESS WE'RE MORE ALIKE THAN I EVER THOUGHT.
LET'S NOT TAKE A POSITIVE AND TURN IT INTO A NEGATIVE!
SCOTT and BORGMAN

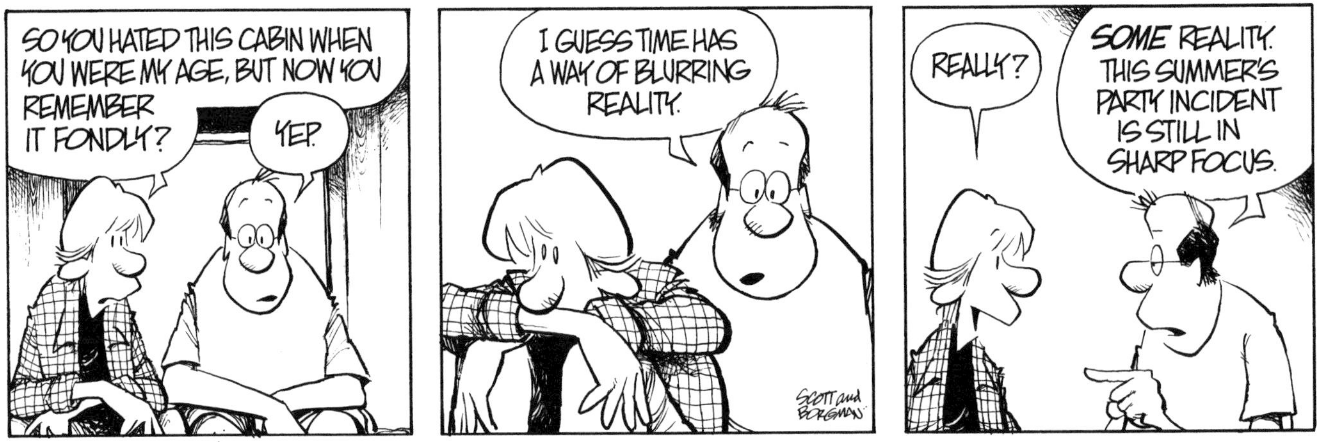
SO YOU HATED THIS CABIN WHEN YOU WERE MY AGE, BUT NOW YOU REMEMBER IT FONDLY?
YEP.
I GUESS TIME HAS A WAY OF BLURRING REALITY.
SCOTT and BORGMAN
REALLY?
SOME REALITY. THIS SUMMER'S PARTY INCIDENT IS STILL IN SHARP FOCUS.

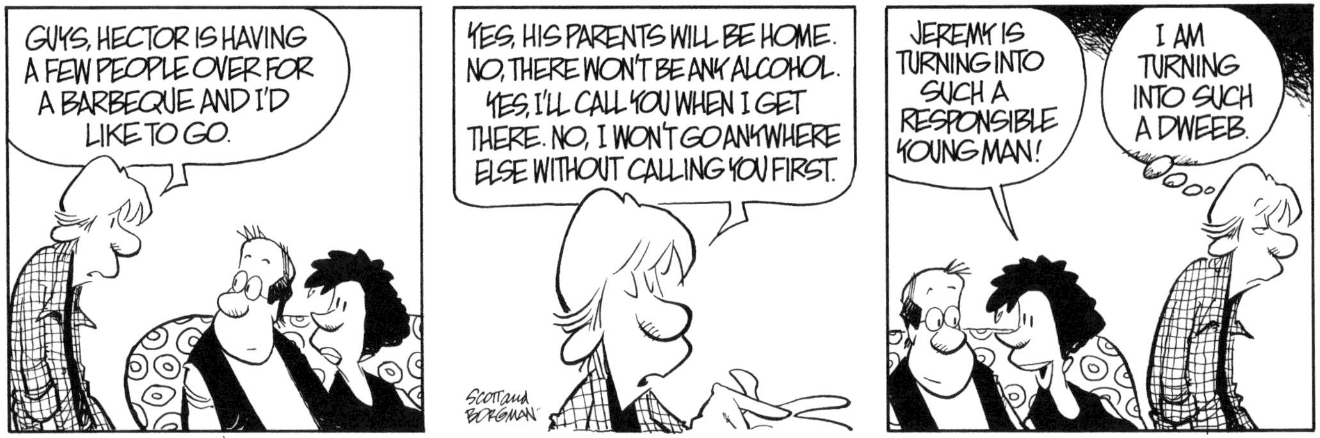
GUYS, HECTOR IS HAVING A FEW PEOPLE OVER FOR A BARBEQUE AND I'D LIKE TO GO.
YES, HIS PARENTS WILL BE HOME. NO, THERE WON'T BE ANY ALCOHOL. YES, I'LL CALL YOU WHEN I GET THERE. NO, I WON'T GO ANYWHERE ELSE WITHOUT CALLING YOU FIRST.
SCOTT and BORGMAN
JEREMY IS TURNING INTO SUCH A RESPONSIBLE YOUNG MAN!
I AM TURNING INTO SUCH A DWEEB.

Zits

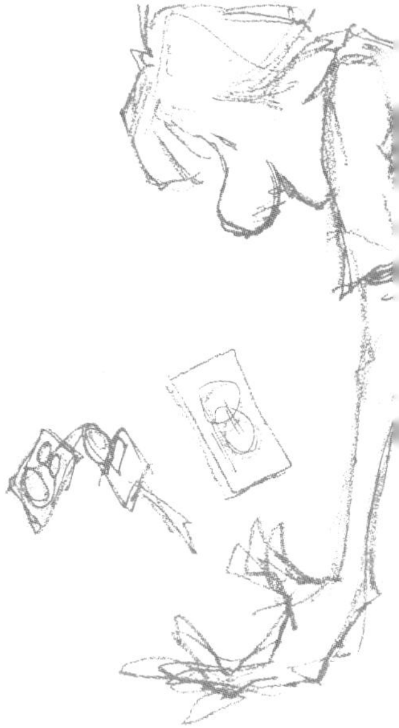

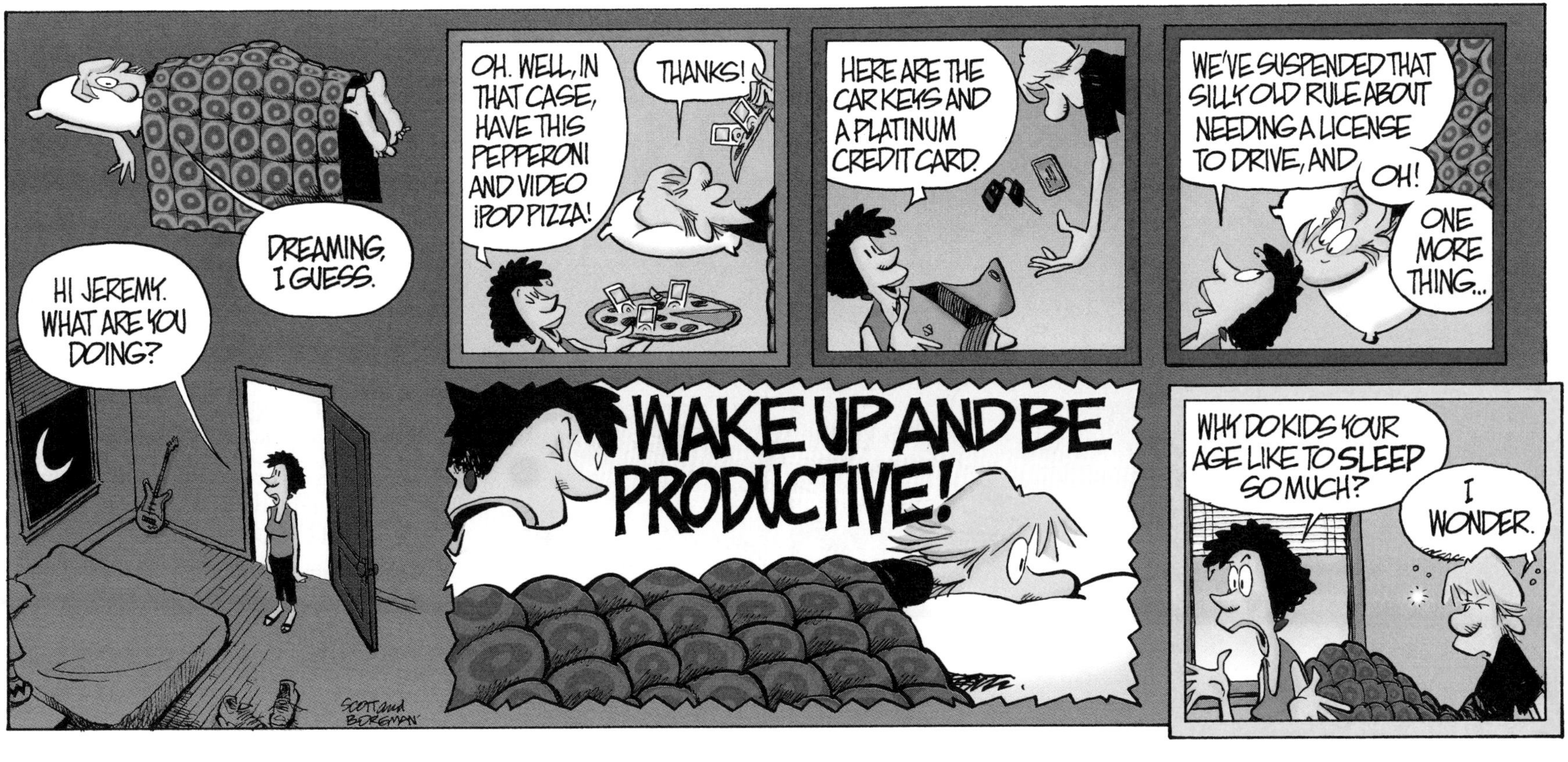
HI JEREMY. WHAT ARE YOU DOING?
DREAMING, I GUESS.
OH. WELL, IN THAT CASE, HAVE THIS PEPPERONI AND VIDEO iPOD PIZZA!
THANKS!
HERE ARE THE CAR KEYS AND A PLATINUM CREDIT CARD.
WE'VE SUSPENDED THAT SILLY OLD RULE ABOUT NEEDING A LICENSE TO DRIVE, AND
OH!
ONE MORE THING...
WAKE UP AND BE PRODUCTIVE!
WHY DO KIDS YOUR AGE LIKE TO SLEEP SO MUCH?
I WONDER.
SCOTT and BORGMAN

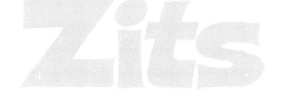

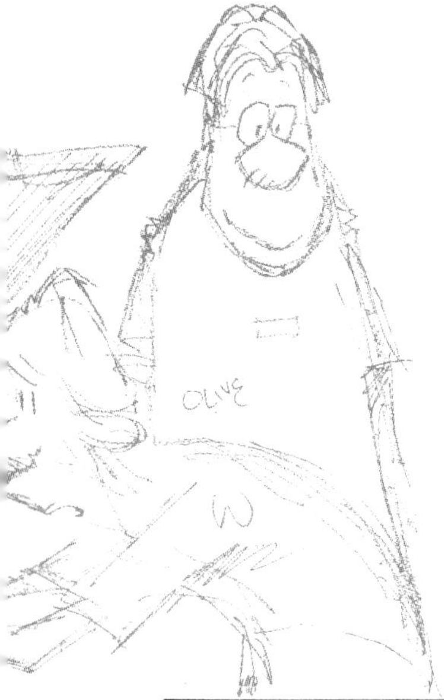

Zits

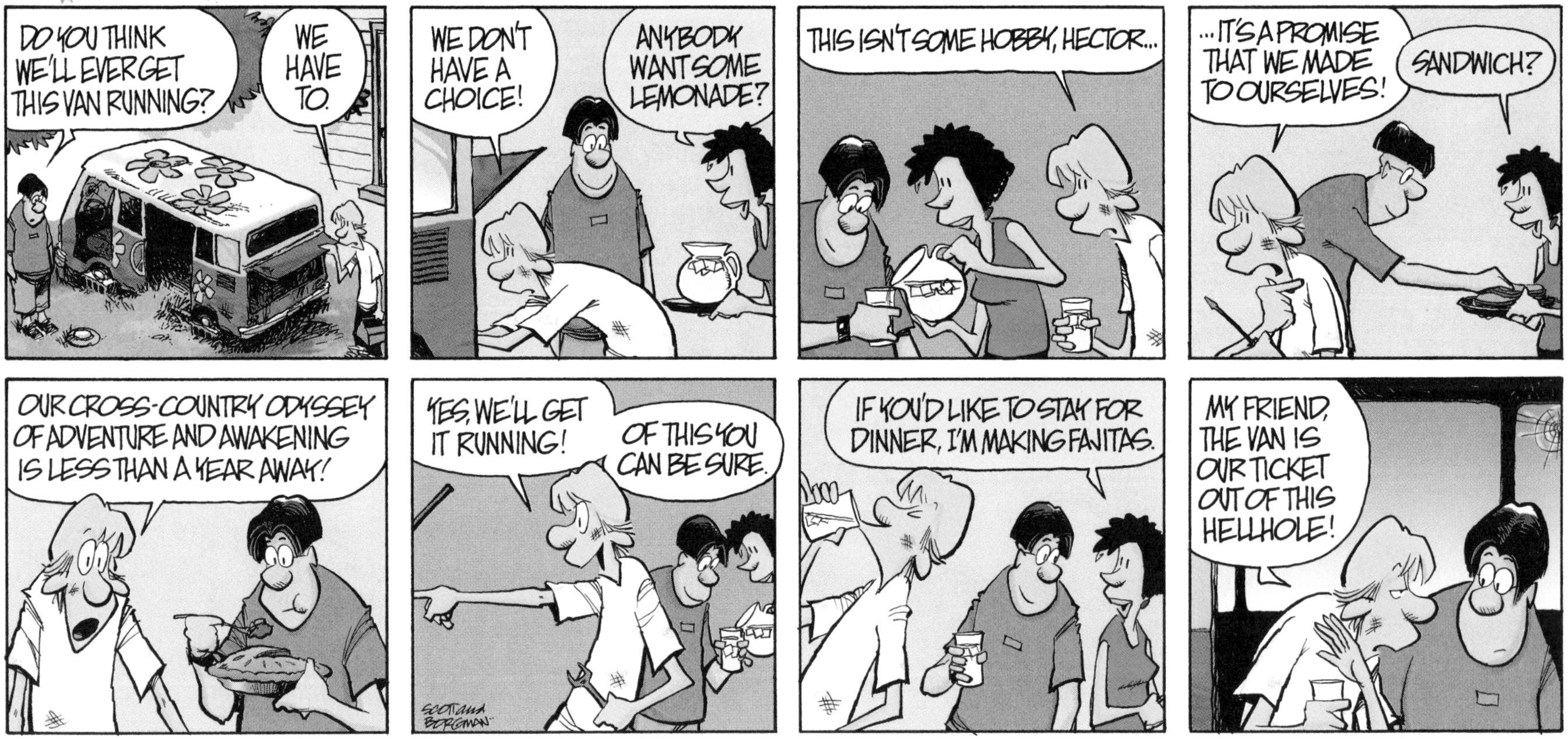

DO YOU THINK WE'LL EVER GET THIS VAN RUNNING?
WE HAVE TO.
WE DON'T HAVE A CHOICE!
ANYBODY WANT SOME LEMONADE?
THIS ISN'T SOME HOBBY, HECTOR...
...IT'S A PROMISE THAT WE MADE TO OURSELVES!
SANDWICH?
OUR CROSS-COUNTRY ODYSSEY OF ADVENTURE AND AWAKENING IS LESS THAN A YEAR AWAY!
YES, WE'LL GET IT RUNNING!
OF THIS YOU CAN BE SURE.
SCOTT AND BORGMAN
IF YOU'D LIKE TO STAY FOR DINNER, I'M MAKING FAJITAS.
MY FRIEND, THE VAN IS OUR TICKET OUT OF THIS HELLHOLE!

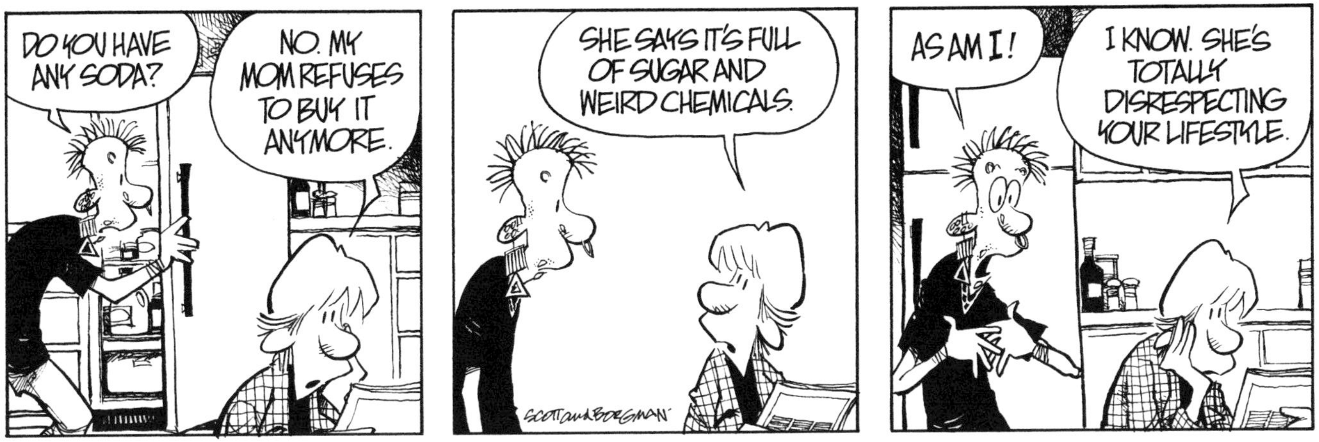
DO YOU HAVE ANY SODA?
NO. MY MOM REFUSES TO BUY IT ANYMORE.
SHE SAYS IT'S FULL OF SUGAR AND WEIRD CHEMICALS.
SCOTT and BORGMAN
AS AM I!
I KNOW. SHE'S TOTALLY DISRESPECTING YOUR LIFESTYLE.

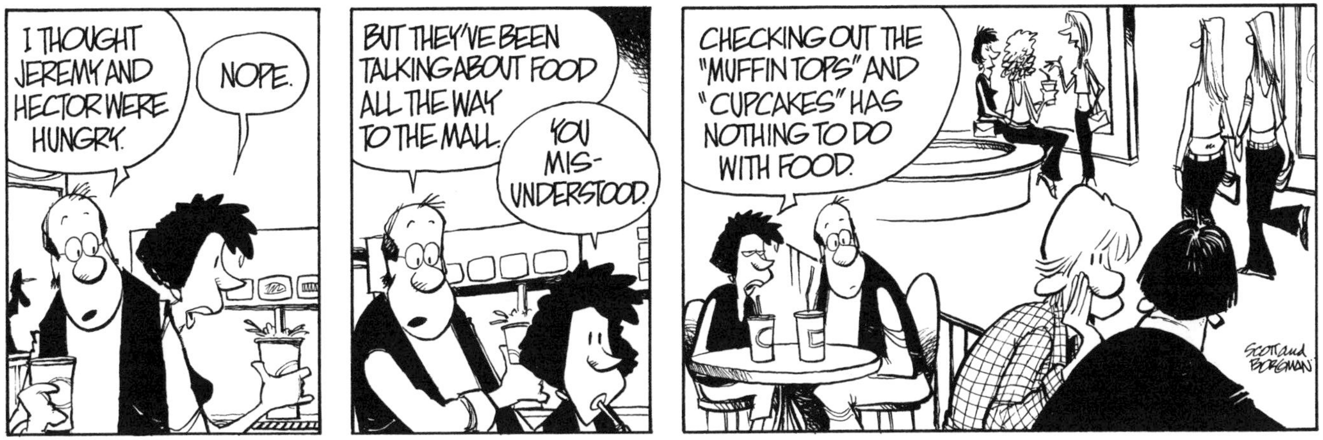
I THOUGHT JEREMY AND HECTOR WERE HUNGRY.
NOPE.
BUT THEY'VE BEEN TALKING ABOUT FOOD ALL THE WAY TO THE MALL.
YOU MIS-UNDERSTOOD.
CHECKING OUT THE "MUFFIN TOPS" AND "CUPCAKES" HAS NOTHING TO DO WITH FOOD.
SCOTT and BORGMAN

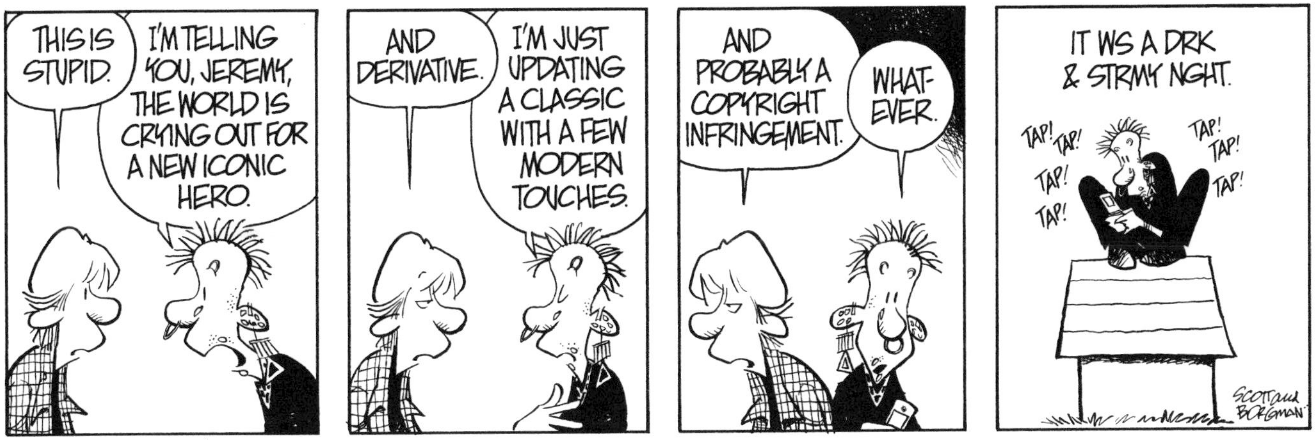
THIS IS STUPID.
I'M TELLING YOU, JEREMY, THE WORLD IS CRYING OUT FOR A NEW ICONIC HERO.
AND DERIVATIVE.
I'M JUST UPDATING A CLASSIC WITH A FEW MODERN TOUCHES.
AND PROBABLY A COPYRIGHT INFRINGEMENT.
WHAT-EVER.
IT WS A DRK & STRMY NGHT.
TAP! TAP! TAP! TAP!
TAP! TAP! TAP!
SCOTT and BORGMAN

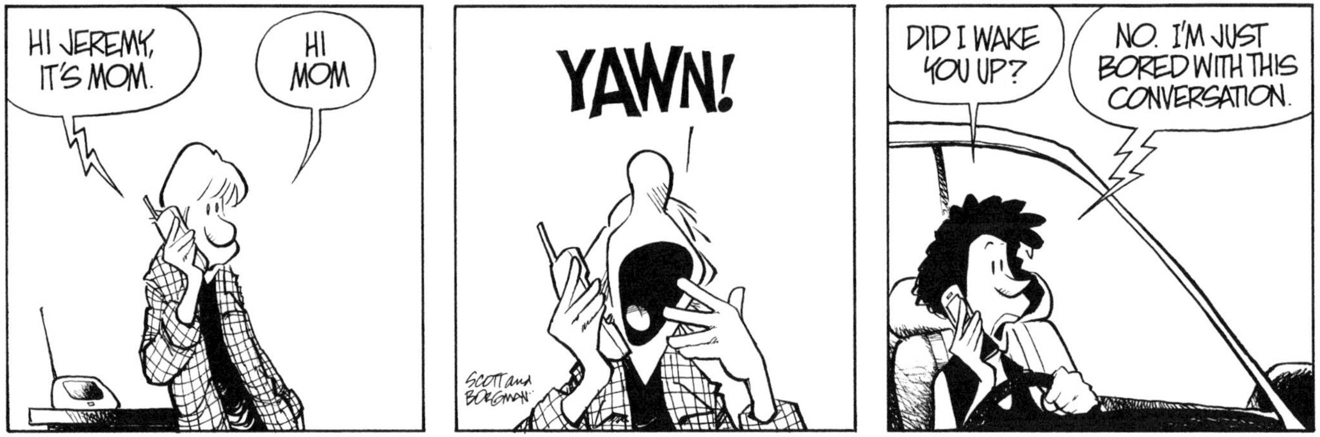
HI JEREMY, IT'S MOM.
HI MOM
YAWN!
DID I WAKE YOU UP?
NO. I'M JUST BORED WITH THIS CONVERSATION.

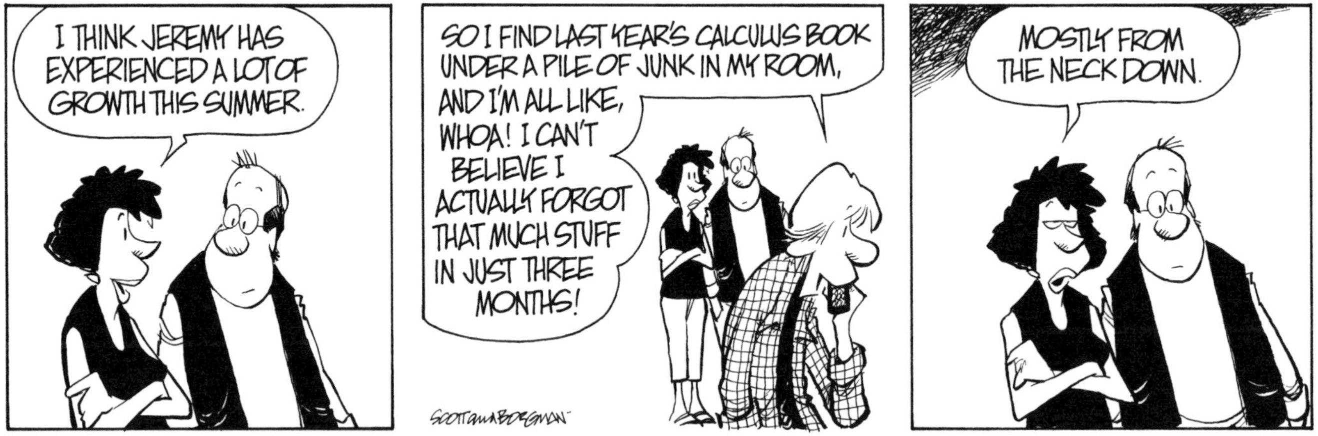
I THINK JEREMY HAS EXPERIENCED A LOT OF GROWTH THIS SUMMER.
SO I FIND LAST YEAR'S CALCULUS BOOK UNDER A PILE OF JUNK IN MY ROOM, AND I'M ALL LIKE, WHOA! I CAN'T BELIEVE I ACTUALLY FORGOT THAT MUCH STUFF IN JUST THREE MONTHS!
MOSTLY FROM THE NECK DOWN.

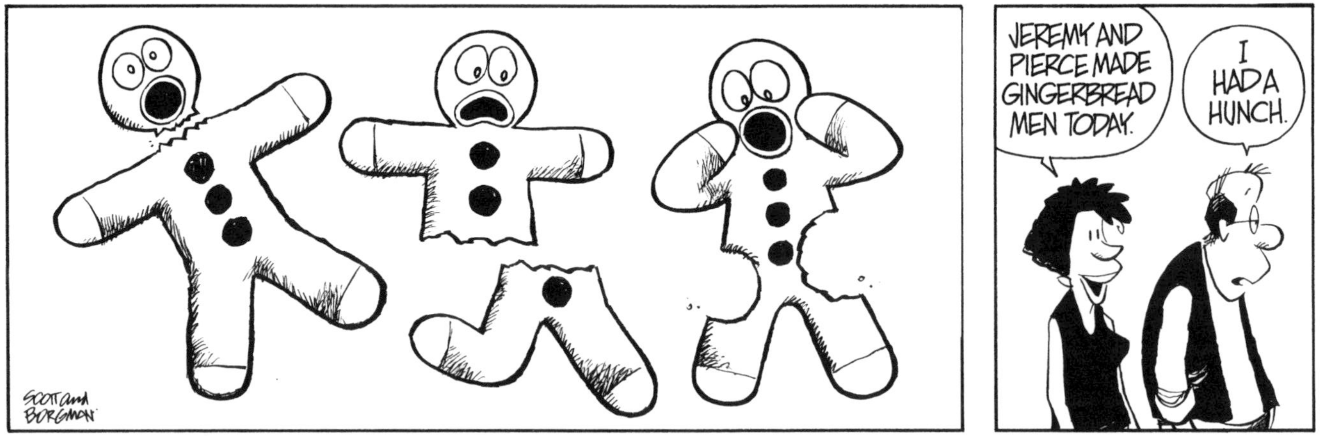
JEREMY AND PIERCE MADE GINGERBREAD MEN TODAY.
I HAD A HUNCH.

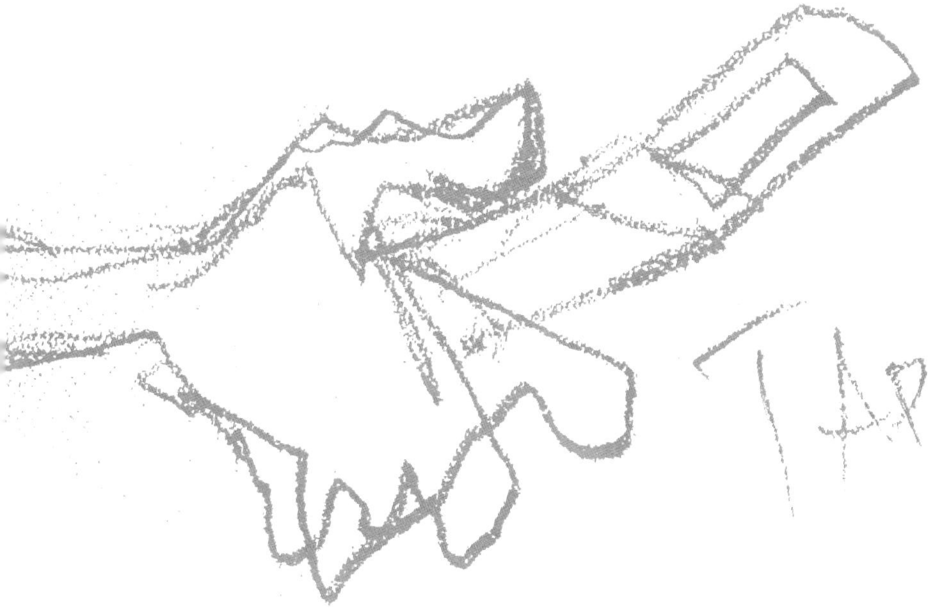
TAP

Zits

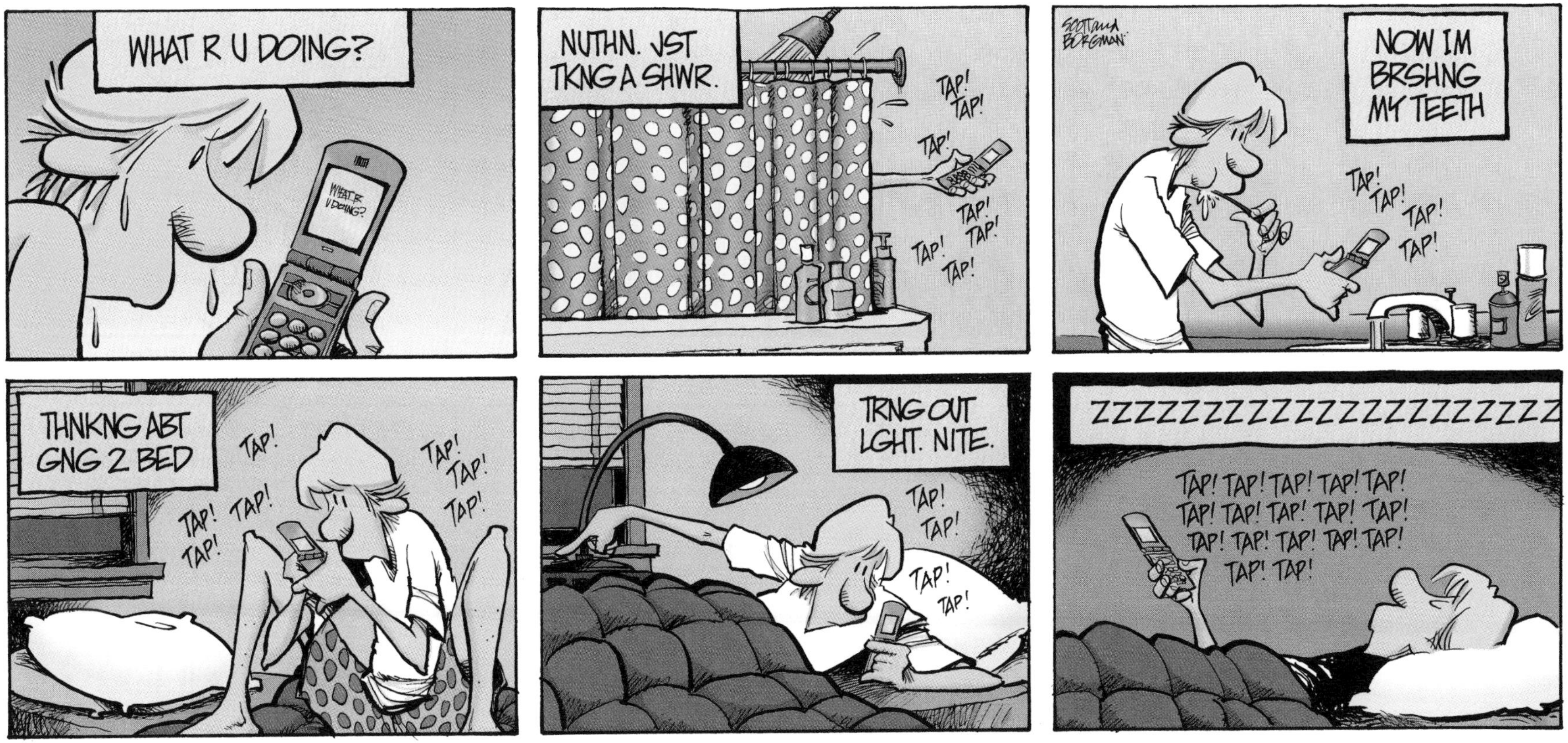
WHAT R U DOING?
WHAT R U DOING?
NUTHN. JST TKNG A SHWR.
TAP! TAP! TAP! TAP! TAP! TAP! TAP!
NOW IM BRSHNG MY TEETH
TAP! TAP! TAP! TAP!
THNKNG ABT GNG 2 BED
TAP! TAP! TAP! TAP! TAP! TAP! TAP!
TRNG OUT LGHT. NITE.
TAP! TAP! TAP! TAP!
ZZZZZZZZZZZZZZZZZZZZZZZ
TAP! TAP! TAP! TAP! TAP!
TAP! TAP! TAP! TAP! TAP!
TAP! TAP! TAP! TAP! TAP!
TAP! TAP!

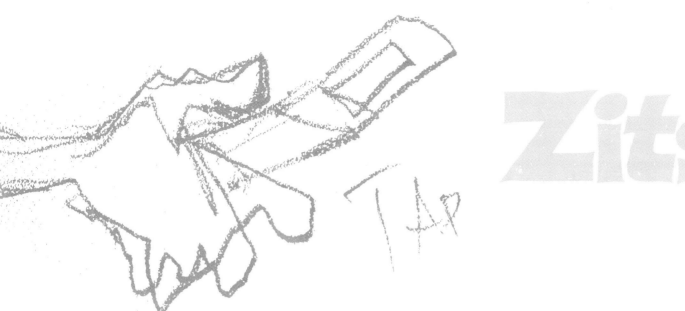

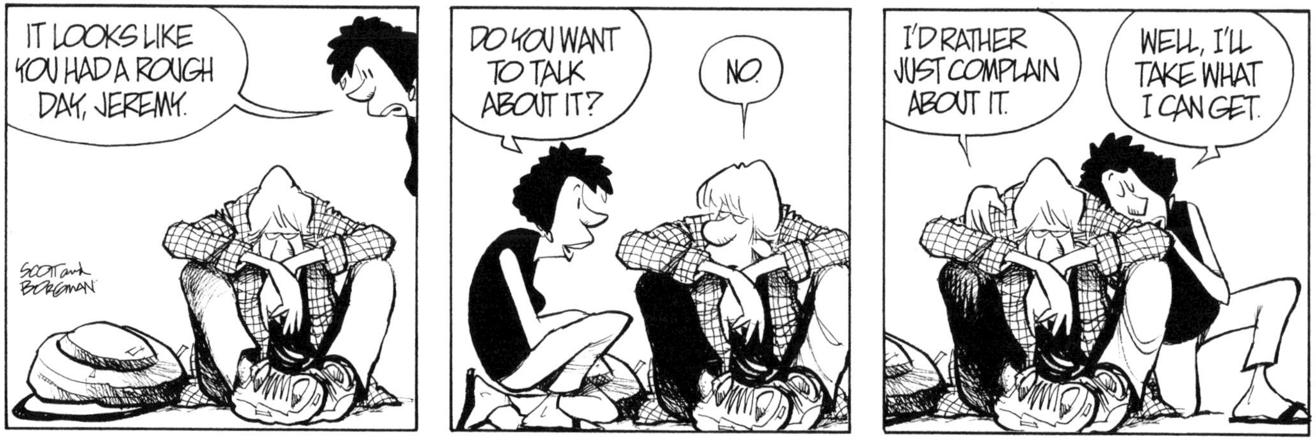
IT LOOKS LIKE YOU HAD A ROUGH DAY, JEREMY.
SCOTT and BORGMAN
DO YOU WANT TO TALK ABOUT IT?
NO.
I'D RATHER JUST COMPLAIN ABOUT IT.
WELL, I'LL TAKE WHAT I CAN GET.

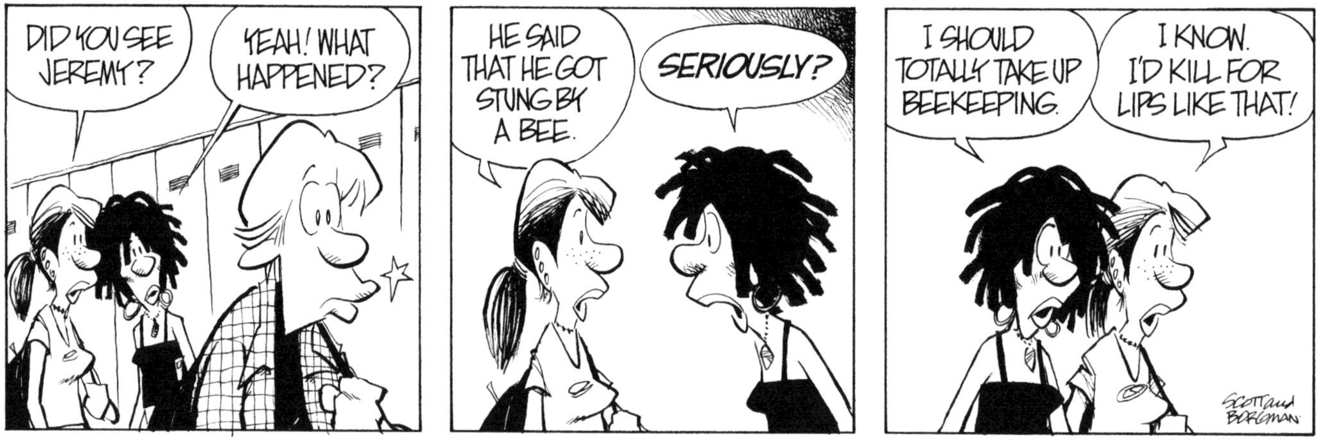
DID YOU SEE JEREMY?
YEAH! WHAT HAPPENED?
HE SAID THAT HE GOT STUNG BY A BEE.
SERIOUSLY?
I SHOULD TOTALLY TAKE UP BEEKEEPING.
I KNOW. I'D KILL FOR LIPS LIKE THAT!
SCOTT and BORGMAN

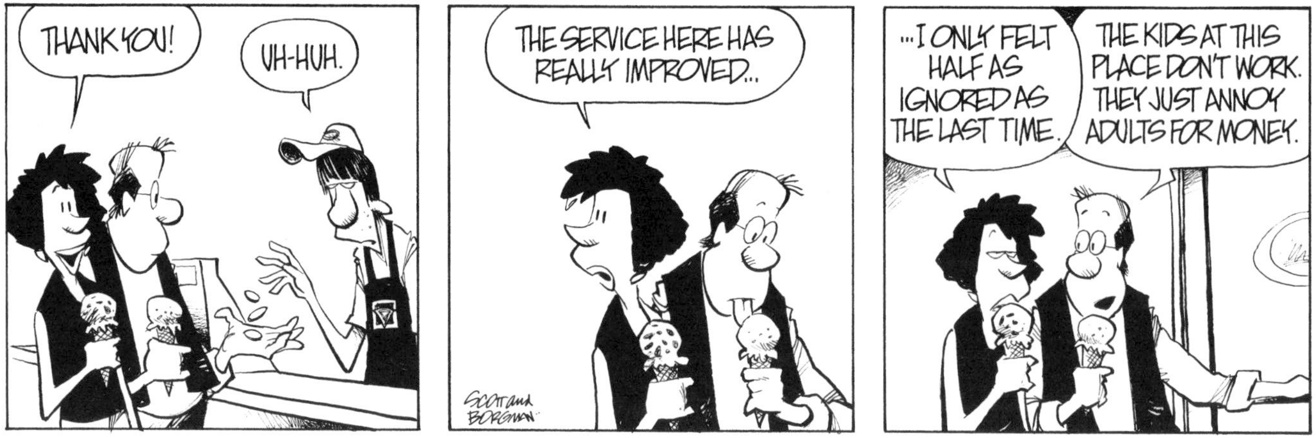
THANK YOU!
UH-HUH.
THE SERVICE HERE HAS REALLY IMPROVED...
SCOTT and BORGMAN
...I ONLY FELT HALF AS IGNORED AS THE LAST TIME.
THE KIDS AT THIS PLACE DON'T WORK. THEY JUST ANNOY ADULTS FOR MONEY.

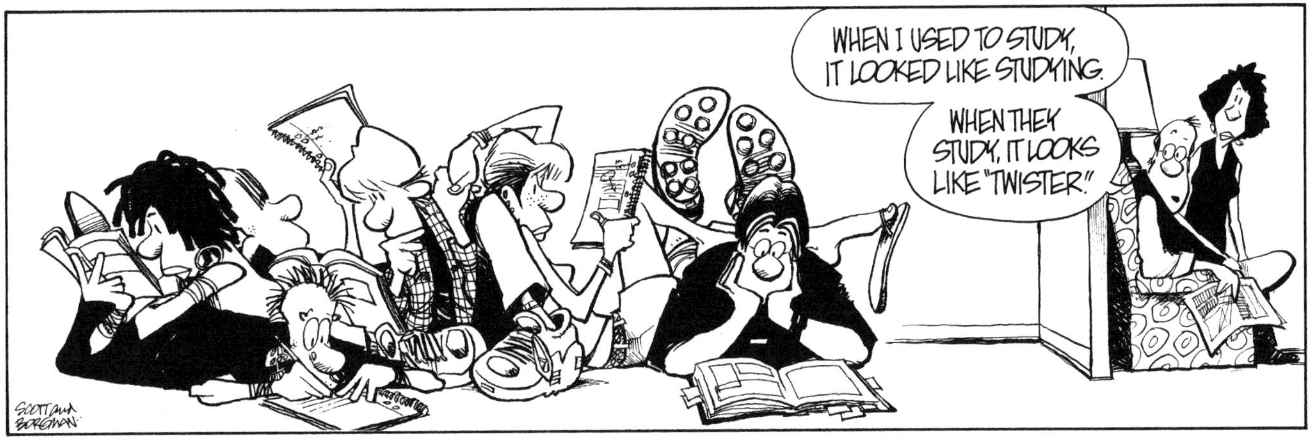
WHEN I USED TO STUDY, IT LOOKED LIKE STUDYING.
WHEN THEY STUDY, IT LOOKS LIKE "TWISTER."
SCOTT AND BORGMAN

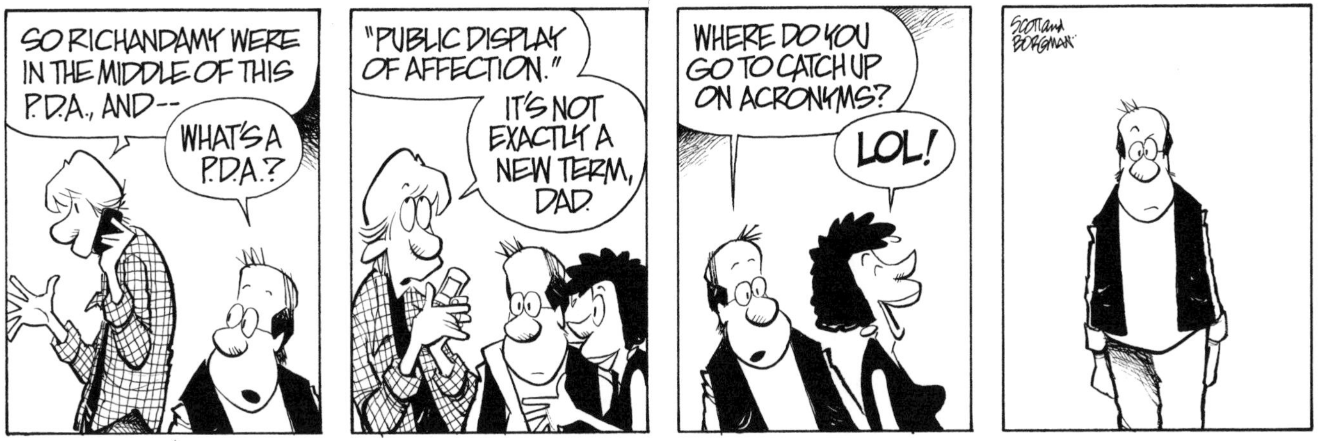
SO RICHANDAMY WERE IN THE MIDDLE OF THIS P.D.A., AND--
WHAT'S A P.D.A.?
"PUBLIC DISPLAY OF AFFECTION."
IT'S NOT EXACTLY A NEW TERM, DAD.
WHERE DO YOU GO TO CATCH UP ON ACRONYMS?
LOL!
SCOTT AND BORGMAN

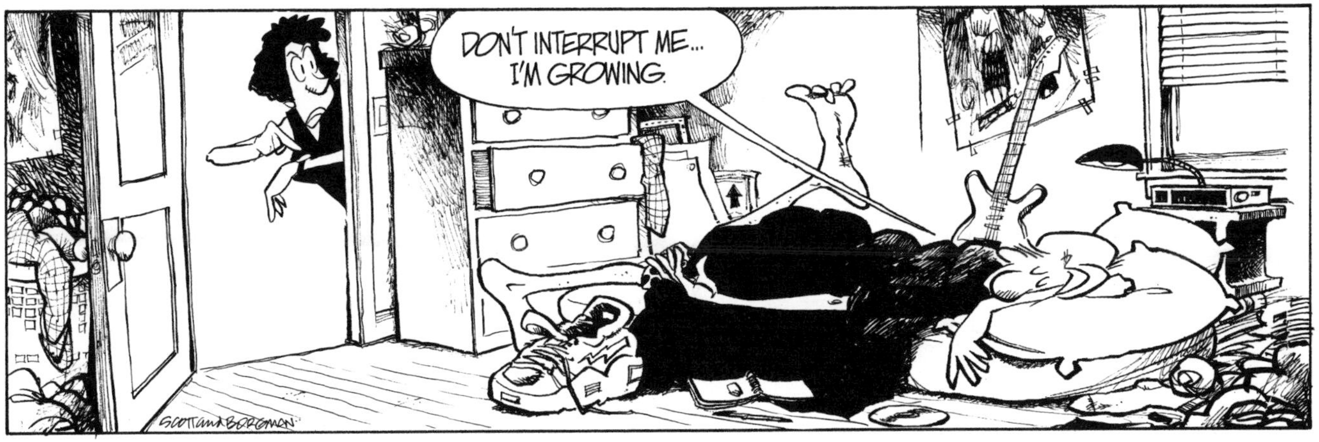
DON'T INTERRUPT ME... I'M GROWING.
SCOTT AND BORGMAN

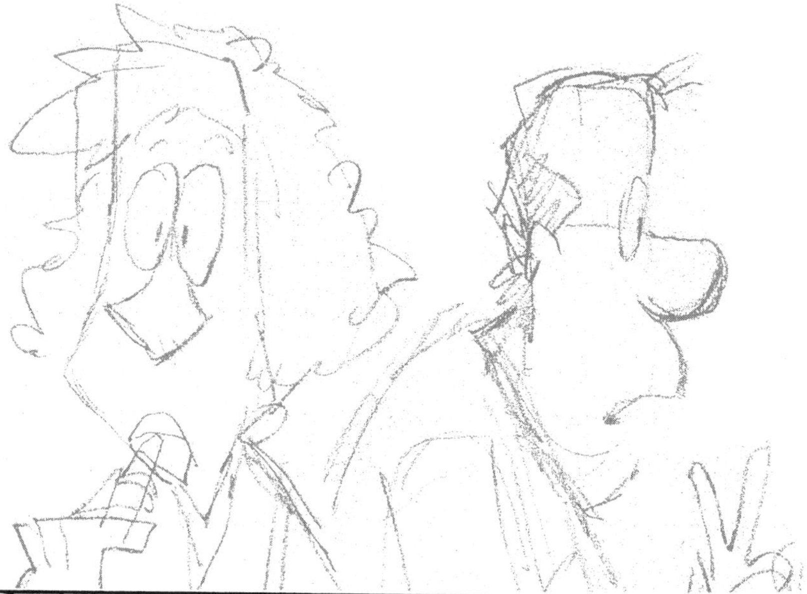

Zits

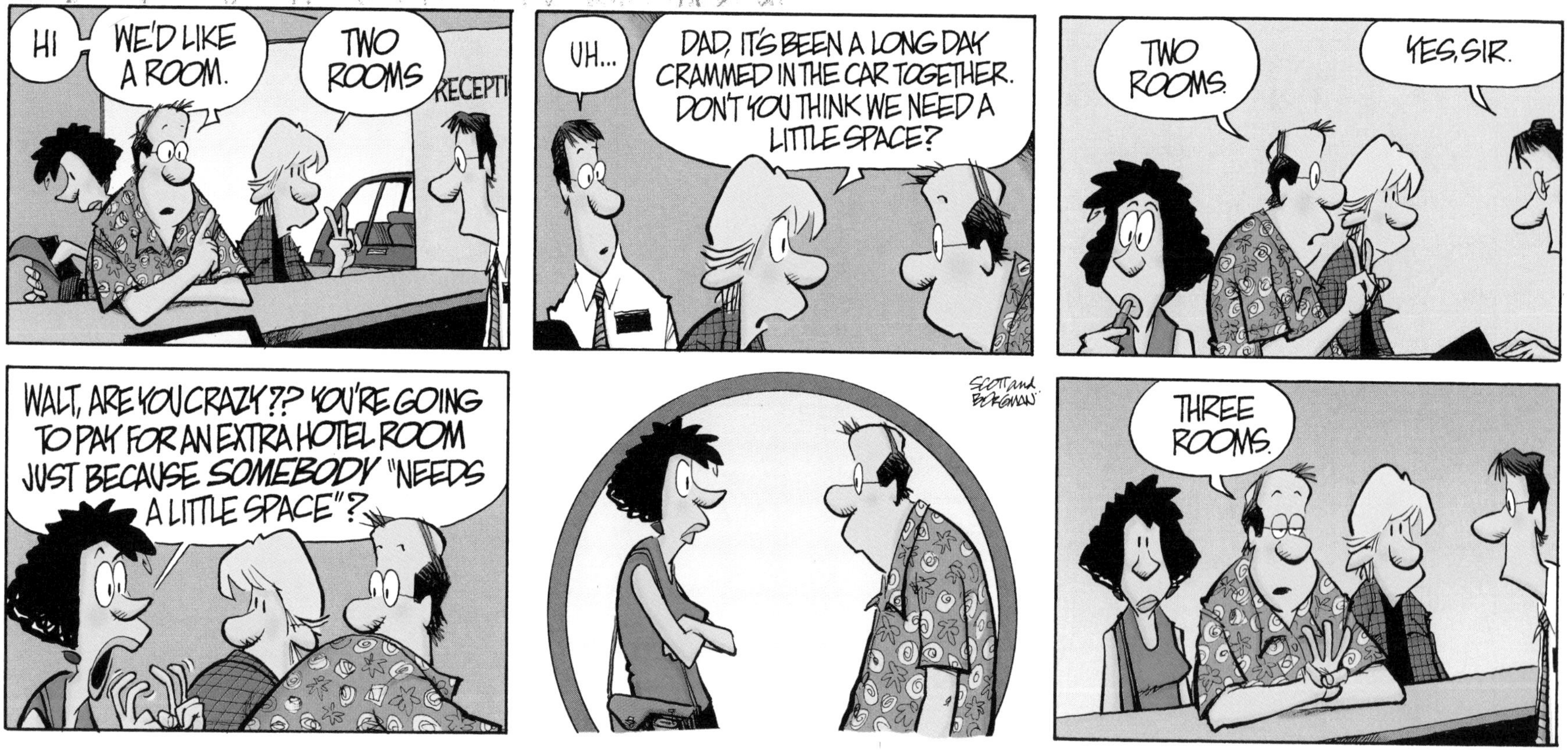

HI
WE'D LIKE A ROOM.
TWO ROOMS
RECEPTI
UH...
DAD, IT'S BEEN A LONG DAY CRAMMED IN THE CAR TOGETHER. DON'T YOU THINK WE NEED A LITTLE SPACE?
TWO ROOMS.
YES, SIR.
WALT, ARE YOU CRAZY?? YOU'RE GOING TO PAY FOR AN EXTRA HOTEL ROOM JUST BECAUSE *SOMEBODY* "NEEDS A LITTLE SPACE"?
SCOTT and BORGMAN
THREE ROOMS.

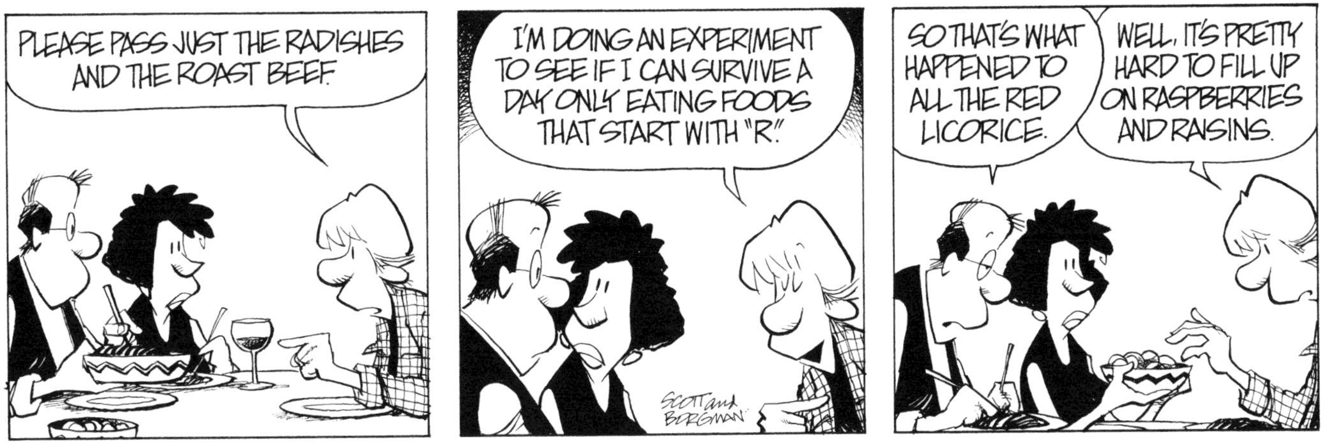
PLEASE PASS JUST THE RADISHES AND THE ROAST BEEF.
I'M DOING AN EXPERIMENT TO SEE IF I CAN SURVIVE A DAY ONLY EATING FOODS THAT START WITH "R."
SO THAT'S WHAT HAPPENED TO ALL THE RED LICORICE.
WELL, IT'S PRETTY HARD TO FILL UP ON RASPBERRIES AND RAISINS.

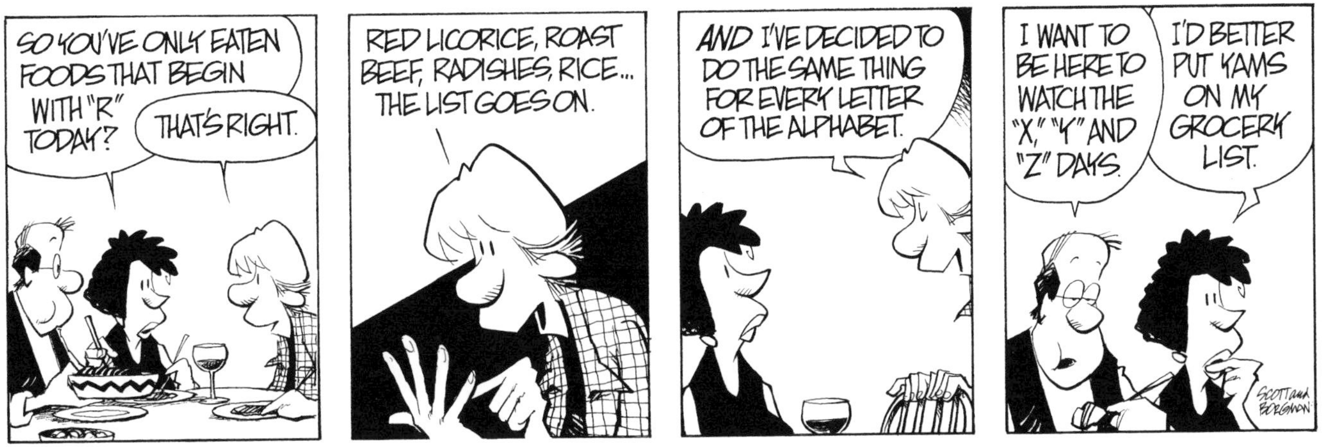
SO YOU'VE ONLY EATEN FOODS THAT BEGIN WITH "R" TODAY?
THAT'S RIGHT.
RED LICORICE, ROAST BEEF, RADISHES, RICE... THE LIST GOES ON.
AND I'VE DECIDED TO DO THE SAME THING FOR EVERY LETTER OF THE ALPHABET.
I WANT TO BE HERE TO WATCH THE "X," "Y" AND "Z" DAYS.
I'D BETTER PUT YAMS ON MY GROCERY LIST.

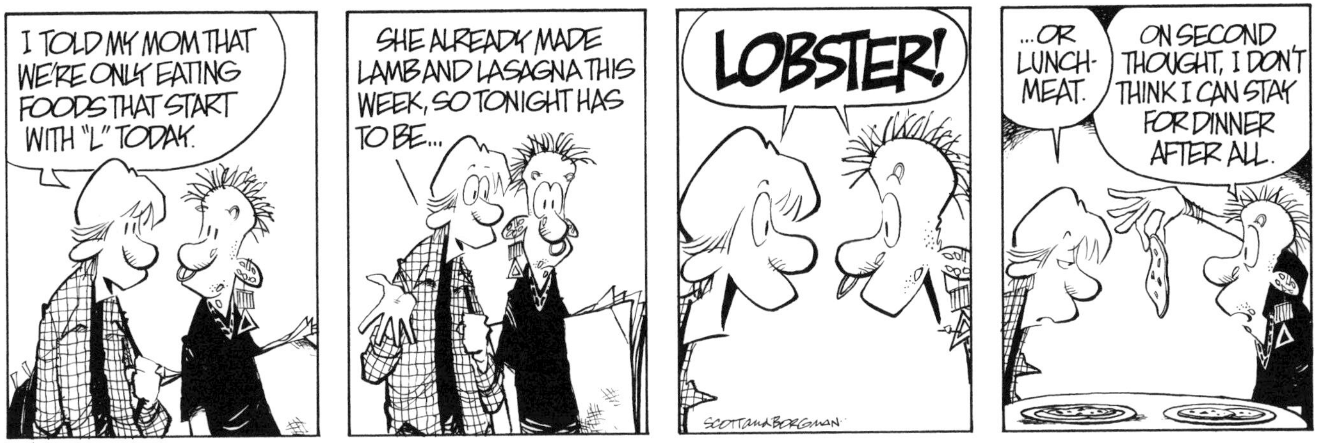
I TOLD MY MOM THAT WE'RE ONLY EATING FOODS THAT START WITH "L" TODAY.
SHE ALREADY MADE LAMB AND LASAGNA THIS WEEK, SO TONIGHT HAS TO BE...
LOBSTER!
...OR LUNCH-MEAT.
ON SECOND THOUGHT, I DON'T THINK I CAN STAY FOR DINNER AFTER ALL.

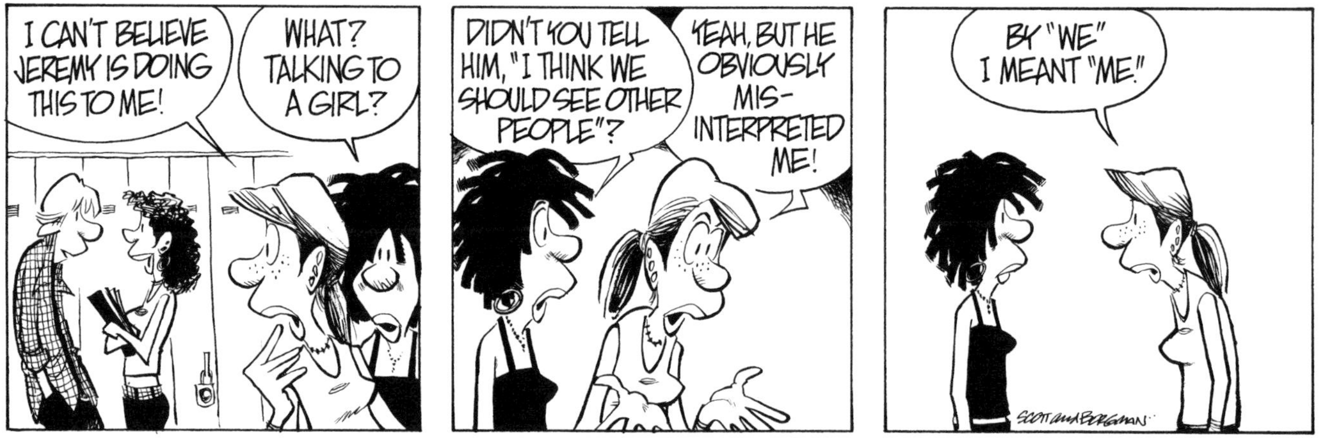
I CAN'T BELIEVE JEREMY IS DOING THIS TO ME!
WHAT? TALKING TO A GIRL?
DIDN'T YOU TELL HIM, "I THINK WE SHOULD SEE OTHER PEOPLE"?
YEAH, BUT HE OBVIOUSLY MIS-INTERPRETED ME!
BY "WE" I MEANT "ME."

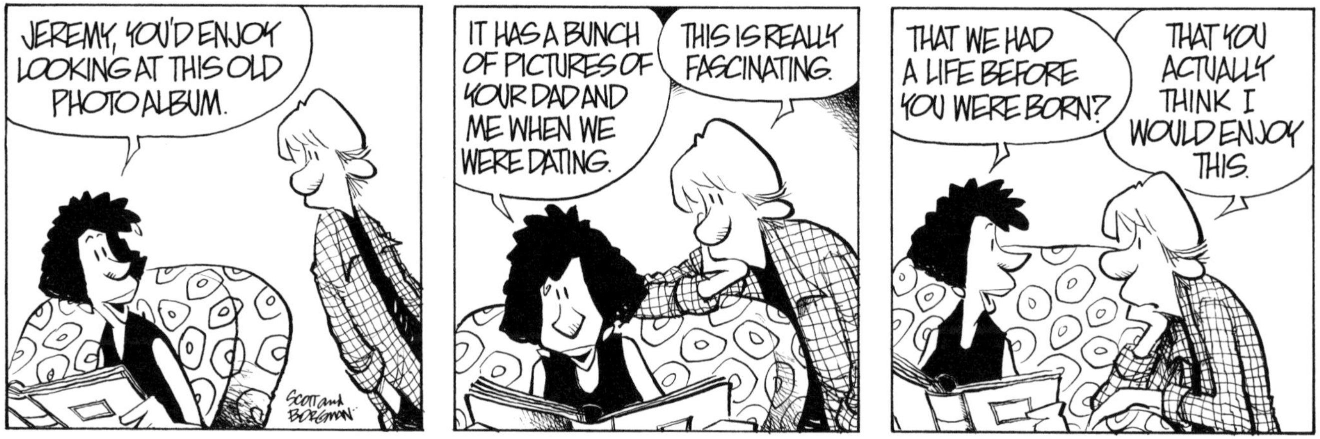
JEREMY, YOU'D ENJOY LOOKING AT THIS OLD PHOTO ALBUM.
IT HAS A BUNCH OF PICTURES OF YOUR DAD AND ME WHEN WE WERE DATING.
THIS IS REALLY FASCINATING.
THAT WE HAD A LIFE BEFORE YOU WERE BORN?
THAT YOU ACTUALLY THINK I WOULD ENJOY THIS.

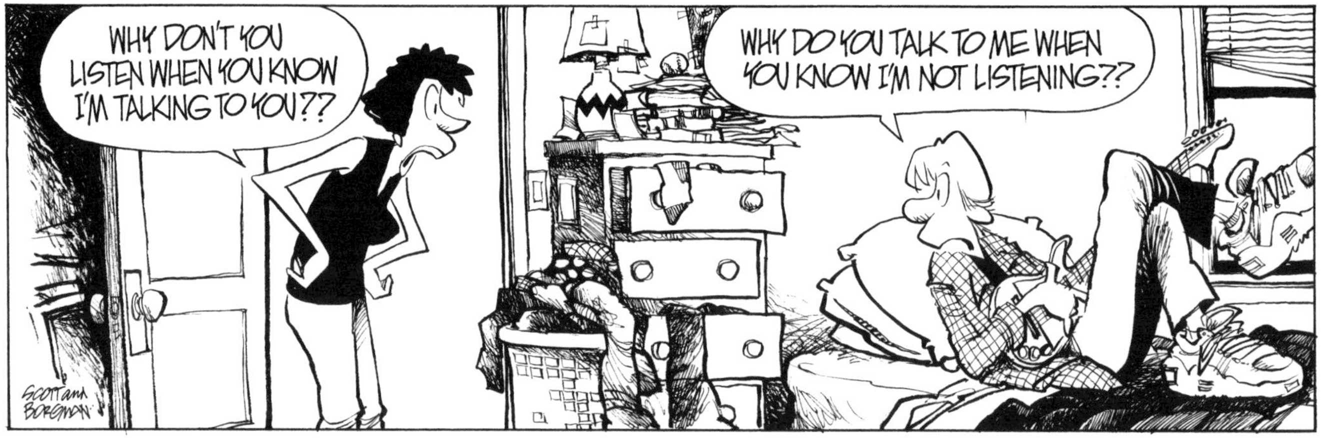
WHY DON'T YOU LISTEN WHEN YOU KNOW I'M TALKING TO YOU??
WHY DO YOU TALK TO ME WHEN YOU KNOW I'M NOT LISTENING??

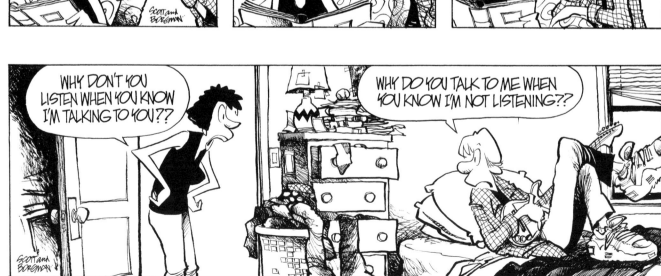

Zits

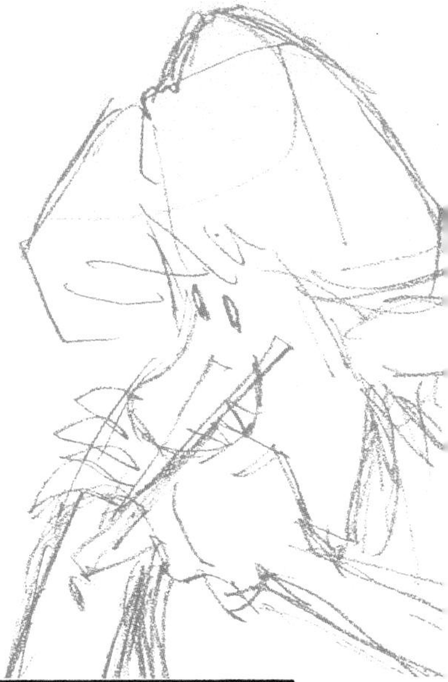

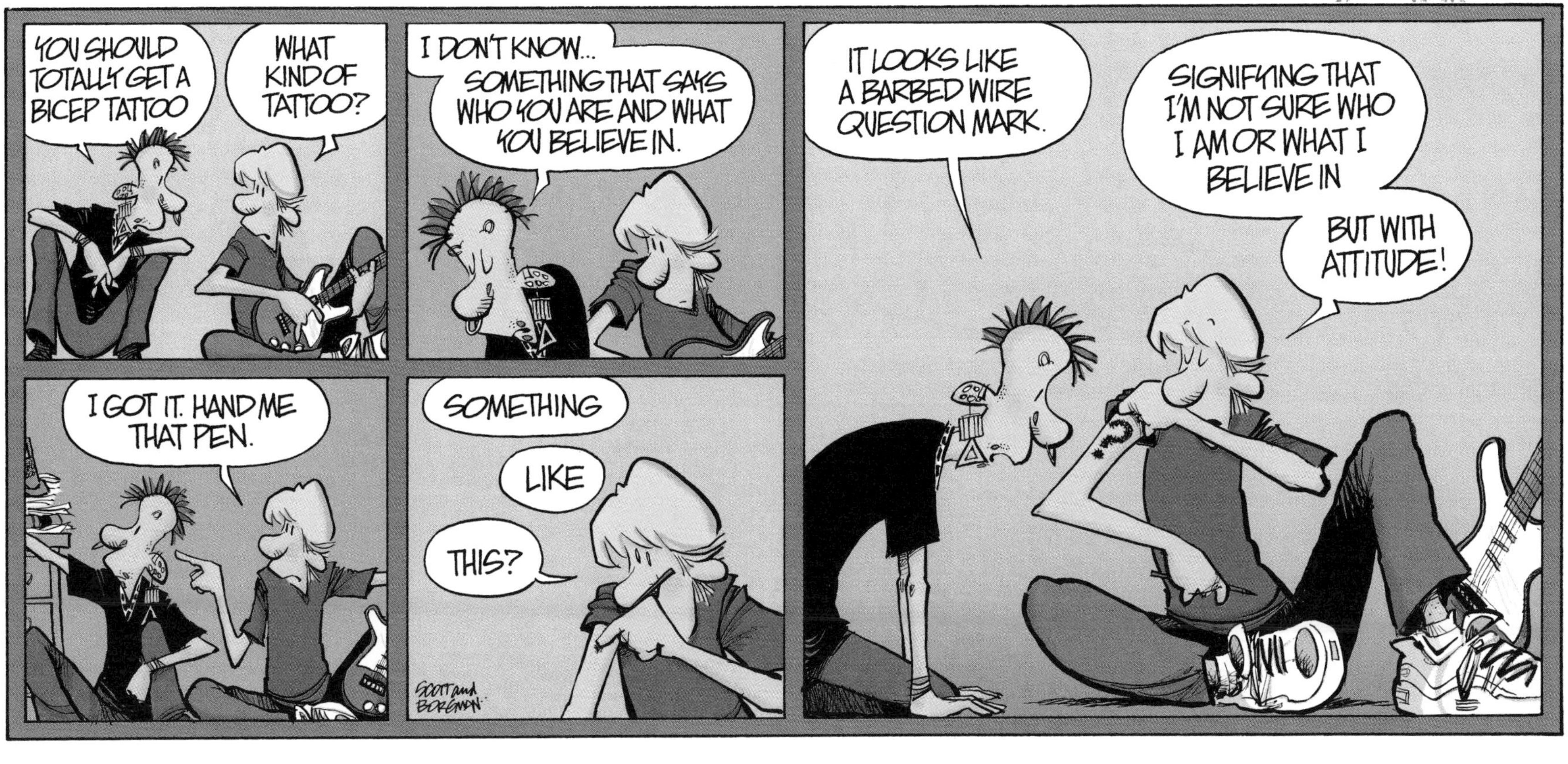
YOU SHOULD TOTALLY GET A BICEP TATTOO
WHAT KIND OF TATTOO?
I DON'T KNOW... SOMETHING THAT SAYS WHO YOU ARE AND WHAT YOU BELIEVE IN.
I GOT IT. HAND ME THAT PEN.
SOMETHING
LIKE
THIS?
IT LOOKS LIKE A BARBED WIRE QUESTION MARK.
SIGNIFYING THAT I'M NOT SURE WHO I AM OR WHAT I BELIEVE IN
BUT WITH ATTITUDE!
SCOTT and BORGMAN

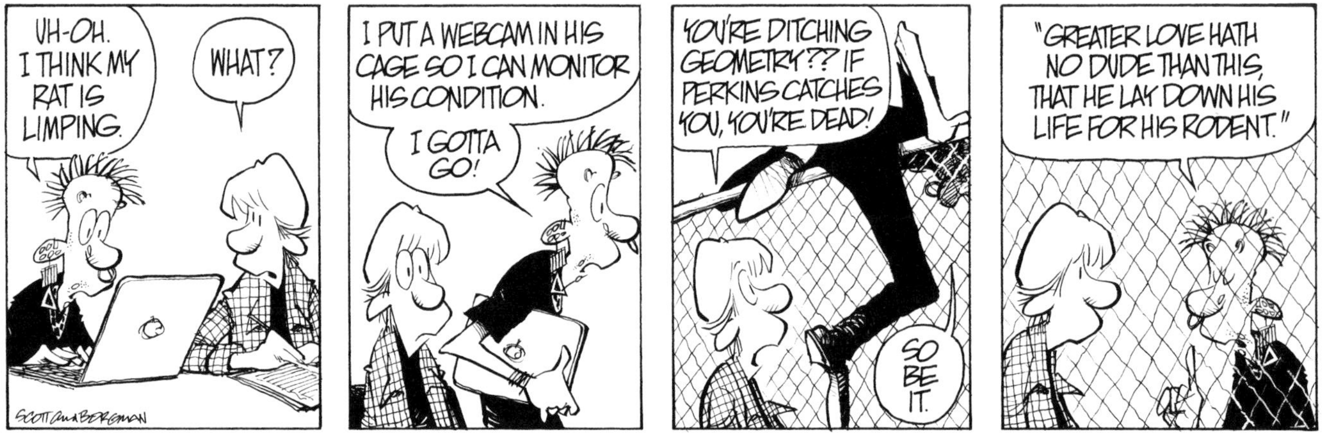
UH-OH. I THINK MY RAT IS LIMPING.
WHAT?
I PUT A WEBCAM IN HIS CAGE SO I CAN MONITOR HIS CONDITION.
I GOTTA GO!
YOU'RE DITCHING GEOMETRY?? IF PERKINS CATCHES YOU, YOU'RE DEAD!
SO BE IT.
"GREATER LOVE HATH NO DUDE THAN THIS, THAT HE LAY DOWN HIS LIFE FOR HIS RODENT."

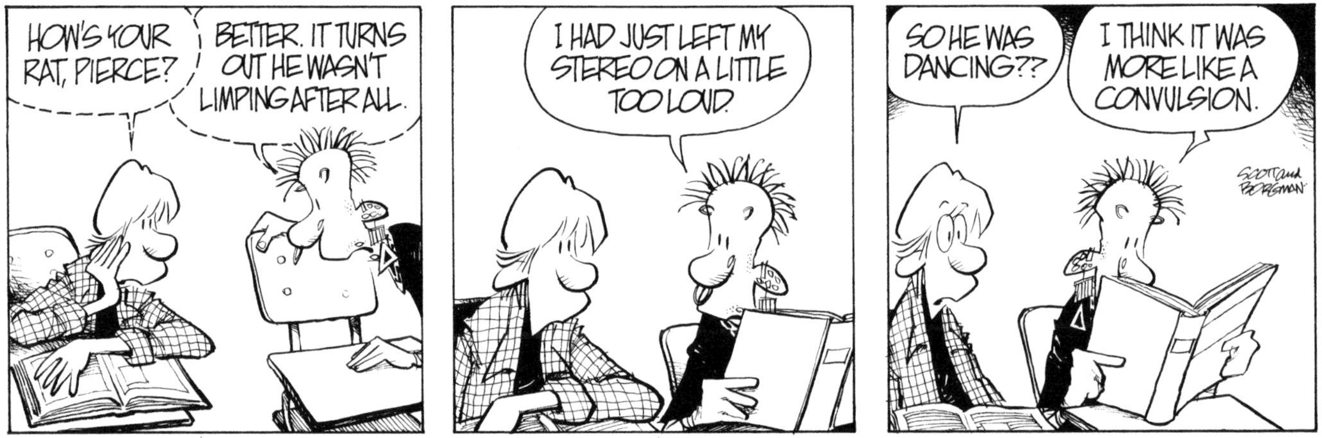
HOW'S YOUR RAT, PIERCE?
BETTER. IT TURNS OUT HE WASN'T LIMPING AFTER ALL.
I HAD JUST LEFT MY STEREO ON A LITTLE TOO LOUD.
SO HE WAS DANCING??
I THINK IT WAS MORE LIKE A CONVULSION.

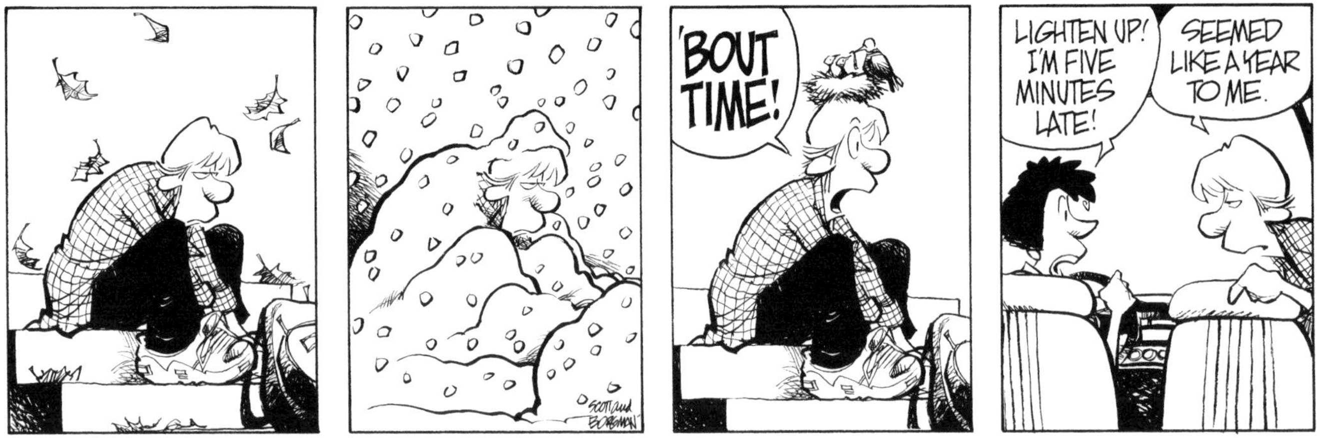
'BOUT TIME!
LIGHTEN UP! I'M FIVE MINUTES LATE!
SEEMED LIKE A YEAR TO ME.

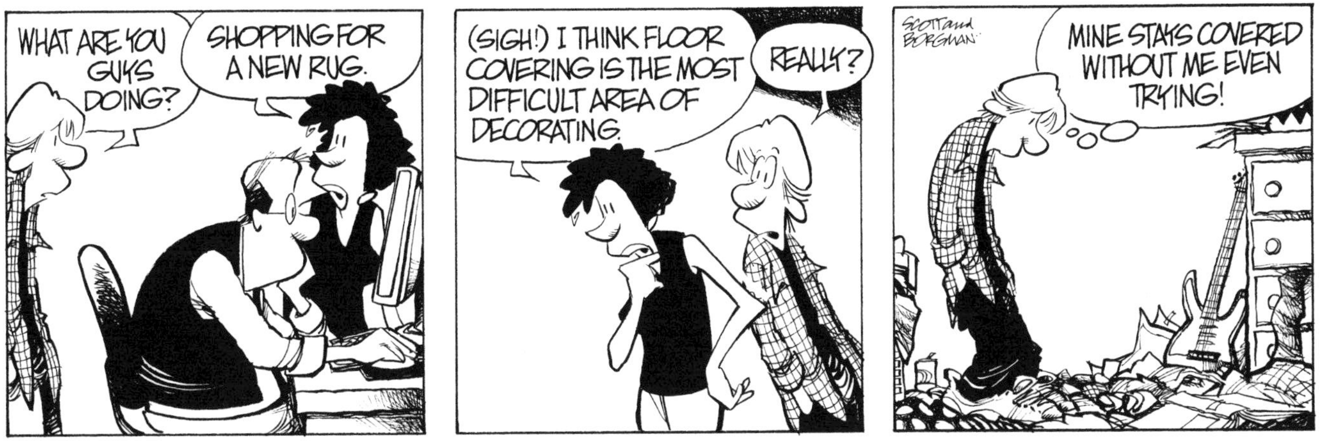
WHAT ARE YOU GUYS DOING?
SHOPPING FOR A NEW RUG.
(SIGH!) I THINK FLOOR COVERING IS THE MOST DIFFICULT AREA OF DECORATING.
REALLY?
SCOTT and BORGMAN
MINE STAYS COVERED WITHOUT ME EVEN TRYING!

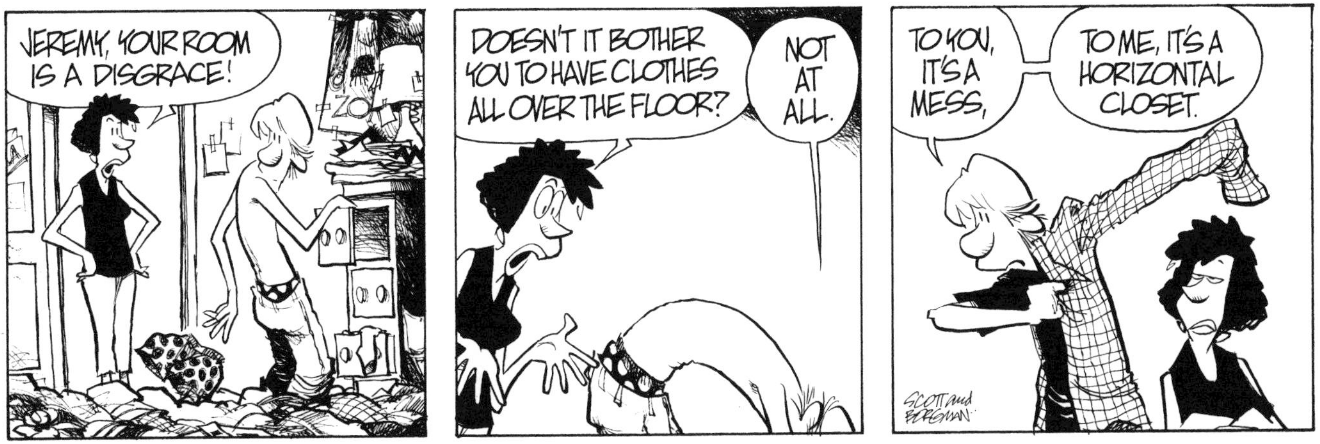
JEREMY, YOUR ROOM IS A DISGRACE!
DOESN'T IT BOTHER YOU TO HAVE CLOTHES ALL OVER THE FLOOR?
NOT AT ALL.
TO YOU, IT'S A MESS,
TO ME, IT'S A HORIZONTAL CLOSET.
SCOTT and BORGMAN

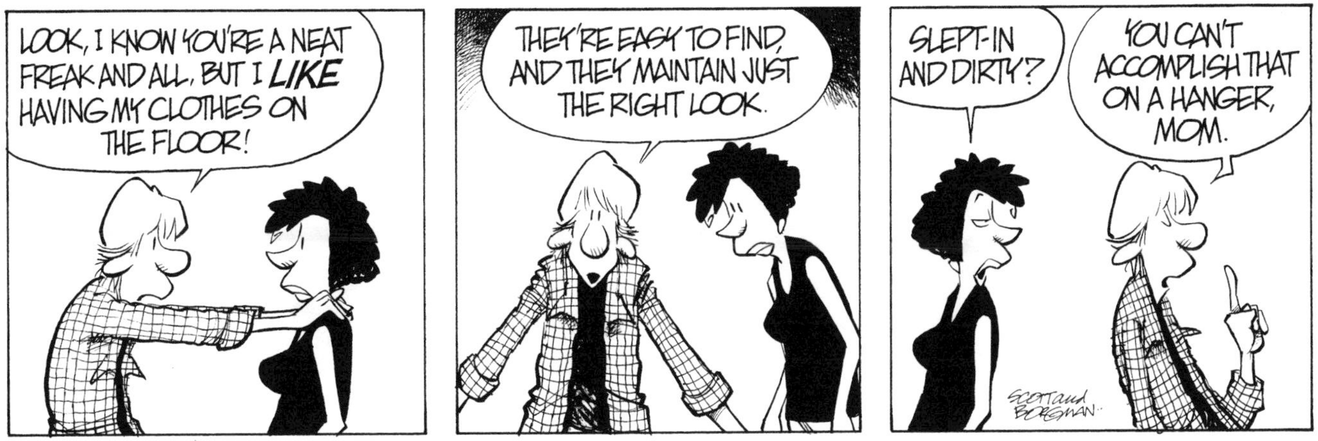
LOOK, I KNOW YOU'RE A NEAT FREAK AND ALL, BUT I LIKE HAVING MY CLOTHES ON THE FLOOR!
THEY'RE EASY TO FIND, AND THEY MAINTAIN JUST THE RIGHT LOOK.
SLEPT-IN AND DIRTY?
YOU CAN'T ACCOMPLISH THAT ON A HANGER, MOM.
SCOTT and BORGMAN

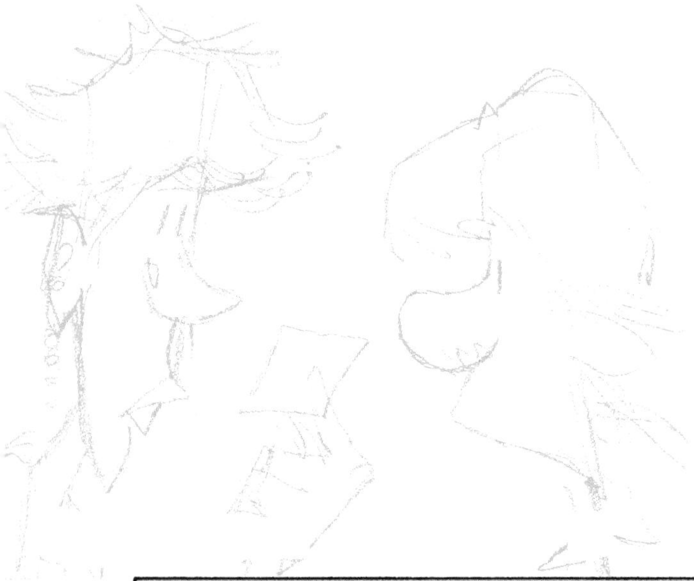

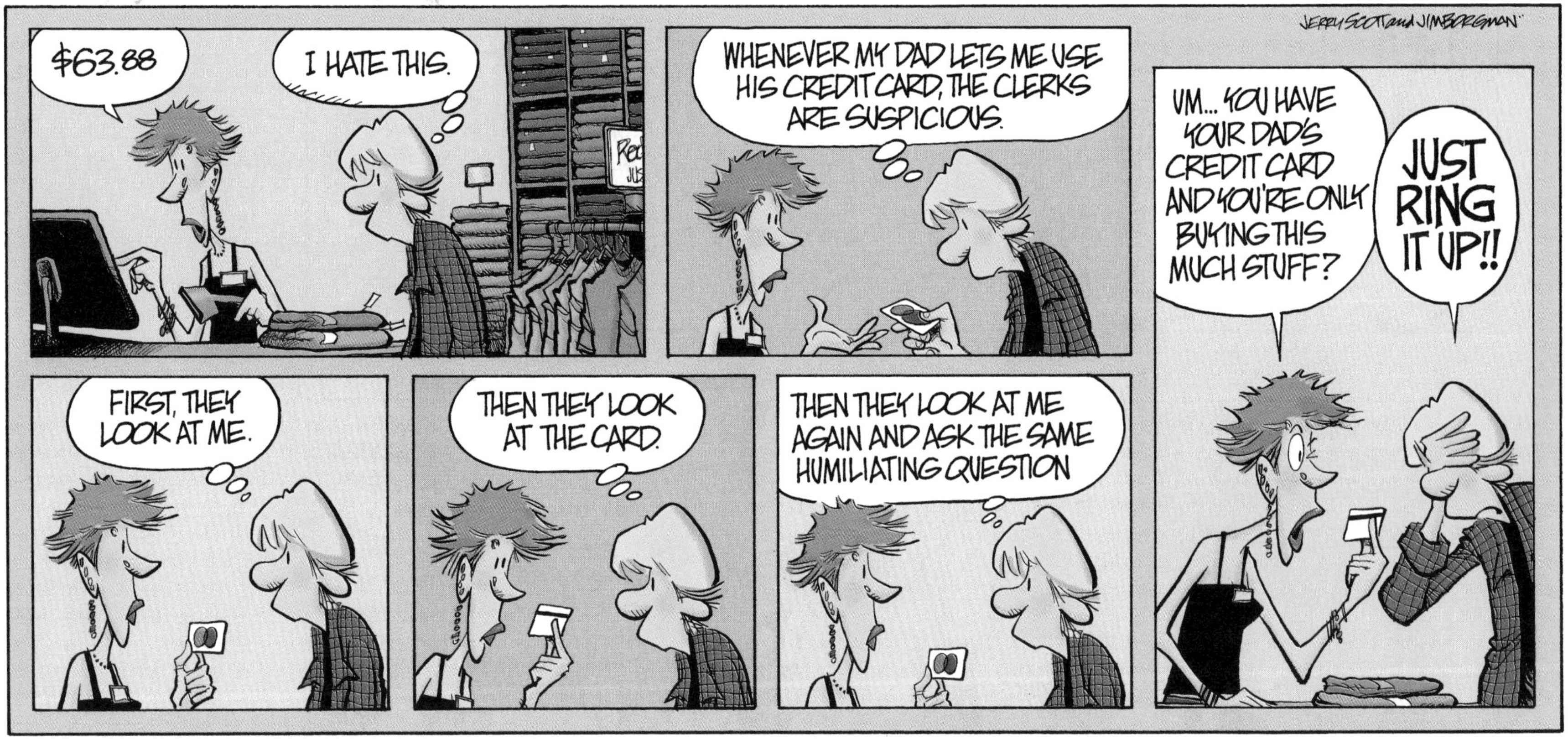

JERRY SCOTT and JIM BORGMAN
$63.88
I HATE THIS.
WHENEVER MY DAD LETS ME USE HIS CREDIT CARD, THE CLERKS ARE SUSPICIOUS.
FIRST, THEY LOOK AT ME.
THEN THEY LOOK AT THE CARD.
THEN THEY LOOK AT ME AGAIN AND ASK THE SAME HUMILIATING QUESTION
UM... YOU HAVE YOUR DAD'S CREDIT CARD AND YOU'RE ONLY BUYING THIS MUCH STUFF?
JUST RING IT UP!!

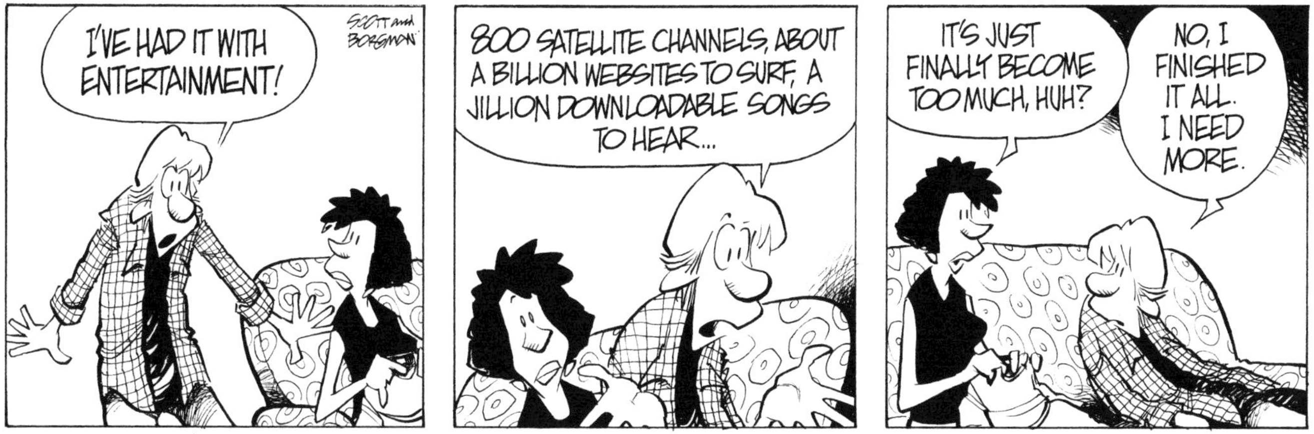
I'VE HAD IT WITH ENTERTAINMENT!
SCOTT and BORGMAN
800 SATELLITE CHANNELS, ABOUT A BILLION WEBSITES TO SURF, A JILLION DOWNLOADABLE SONGS TO HEAR...
IT'S JUST FINALLY BECOME TOO MUCH, HUH?
NO, I FINISHED IT ALL. I NEED MORE.

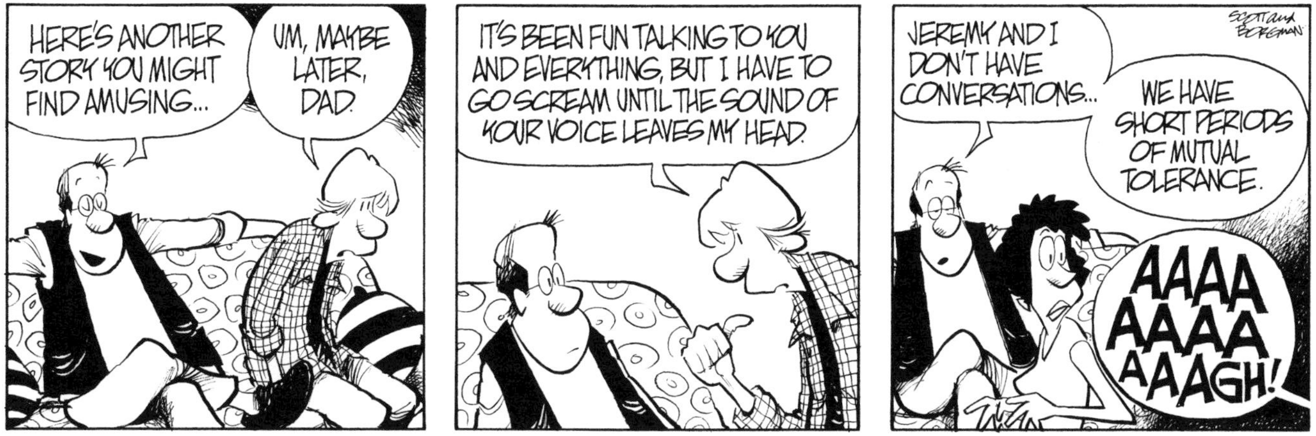
HERE'S ANOTHER STORY YOU MIGHT FIND AMUSING...
UM, MAYBE LATER, DAD.
IT'S BEEN FUN TALKING TO YOU AND EVERYTHING, BUT I HAVE TO GO SCREAM UNTIL THE SOUND OF YOUR VOICE LEAVES MY HEAD.
SCOTT and BORGMAN
JEREMY AND I DON'T HAVE CONVERSATIONS...
WE HAVE SHORT PERIODS OF MUTUAL TOLERANCE.
AAAAAAAAAAAGH!

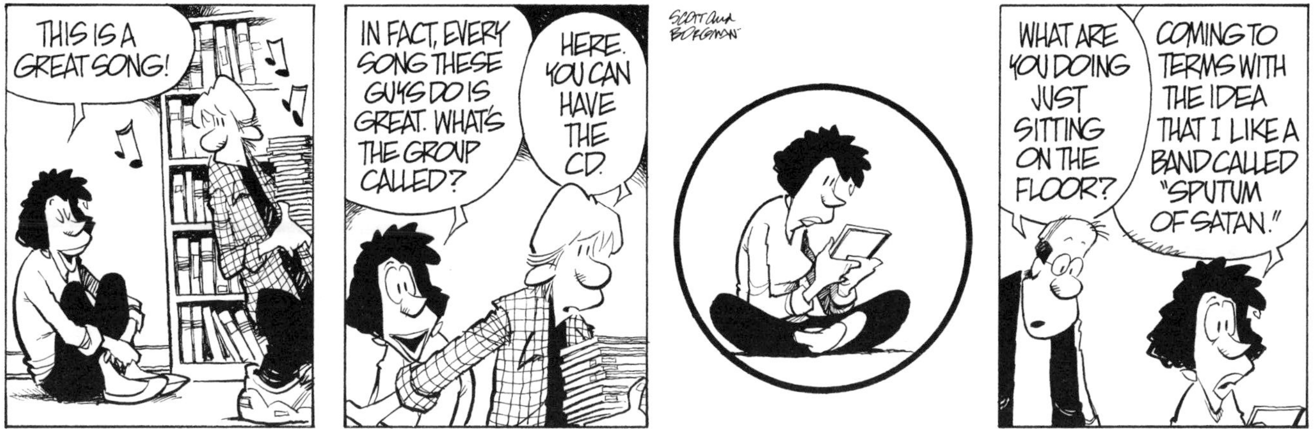
THIS IS A GREAT SONG!
IN FACT, EVERY SONG THESE GUYS DO IS GREAT. WHAT'S THE GROUP CALLED?
HERE. YOU CAN HAVE THE CD.
SCOTT and BORGMAN
WHAT ARE YOU DOING JUST SITTING ON THE FLOOR?
COMING TO TERMS WITH THE IDEA THAT I LIKE A BAND CALLED "SPUTUM OF SATAN."

Zits

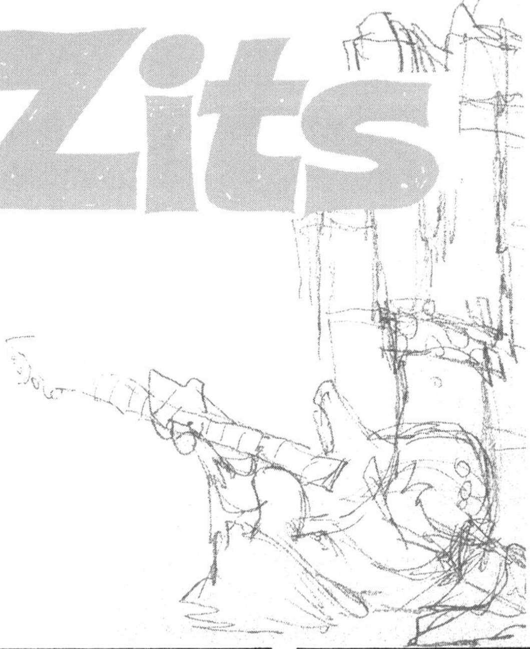

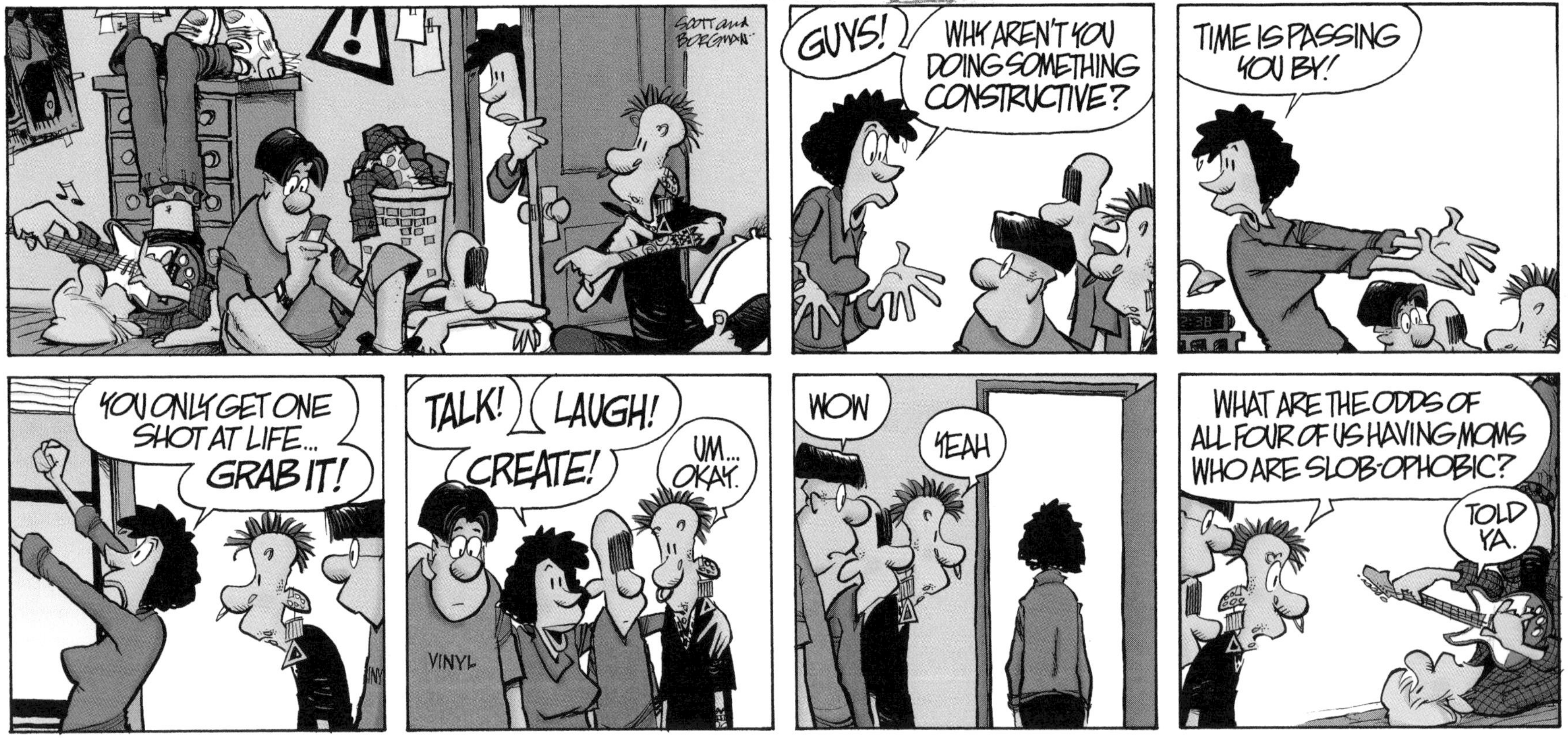
GUYS!
WHY AREN'T YOU DOING SOMETHING CONSTRUCTIVE?
TIME IS PASSING YOU BY!
YOU ONLY GET ONE SHOT AT LIFE... GRAB IT!
TALK!
LAUGH!
CREATE!
UM... OKAY.
VINYL
WOW
YEAH
WHAT ARE THE ODDS OF ALL FOUR OF US HAVING MOMS WHO ARE SLOB-OPHOBIC?
TOLD YA.

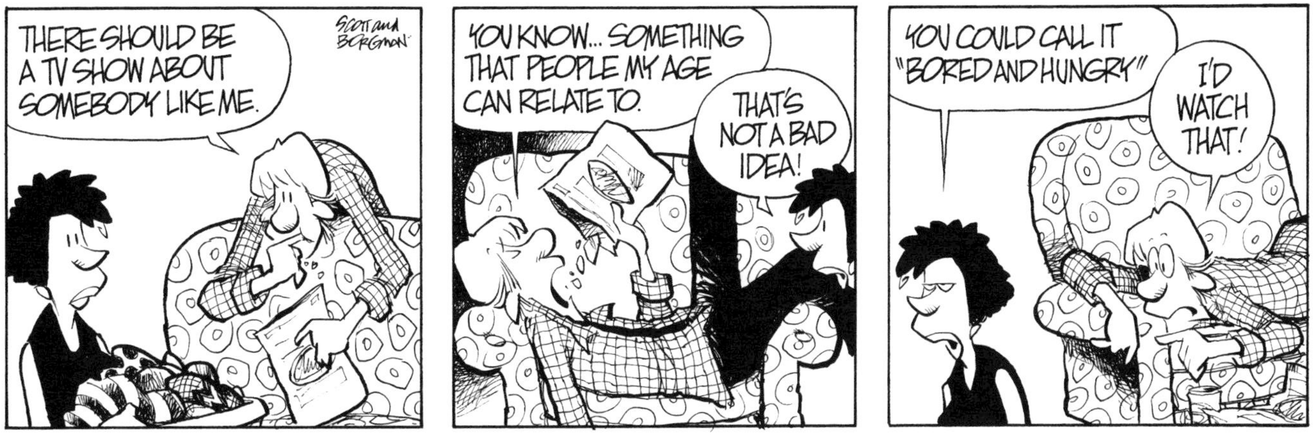
SCOTT and BORGMAN
THERE SHOULD BE A TV SHOW ABOUT SOMEBODY LIKE ME.
YOU KNOW... SOMETHING THAT PEOPLE MY AGE CAN RELATE TO.
THAT'S NOT A BAD IDEA!
YOU COULD CALL IT "BORED AND HUNGRY"
I'D WATCH THAT!

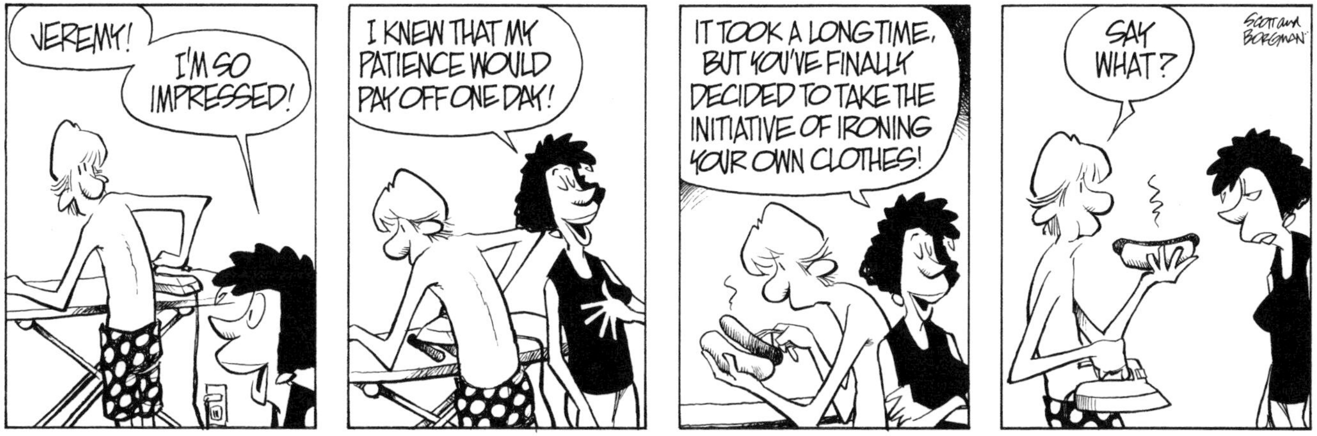
JEREMY!
I'M SO IMPRESSED!
I KNEW THAT MY PATIENCE WOULD PAY OFF ONE DAY!
IT TOOK A LONG TIME, BUT YOU'VE FINALLY DECIDED TO TAKE THE INITIATIVE OF IRONING YOUR OWN CLOTHES!
SCOTT and BORGMAN
SAY WHAT?

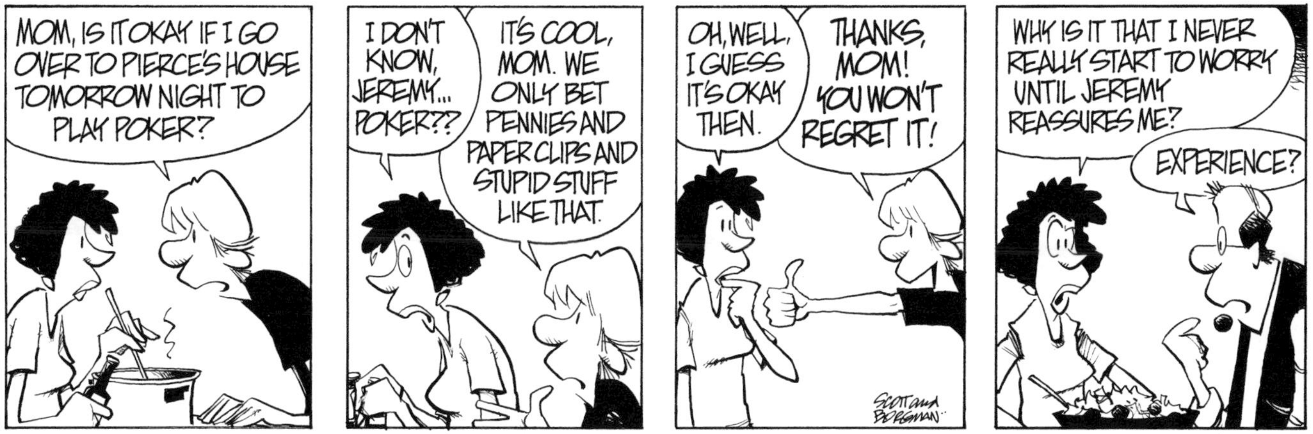
MOM, IS IT OKAY IF I GO OVER TO PIERCE'S HOUSE TOMORROW NIGHT TO PLAY POKER?
I DON'T KNOW, JEREMY... POKER??
IT'S COOL, MOM. WE ONLY BET PENNIES AND PAPER CLIPS AND STUPID STUFF LIKE THAT.
OH, WELL, I GUESS IT'S OKAY THEN.
THANKS, MOM! YOU WON'T REGRET IT!
SCOTT and BORGMAN
WHY IS IT THAT I NEVER REALLY START TO WORRY UNTIL JEREMY REASSURES ME?
EXPERIENCE?

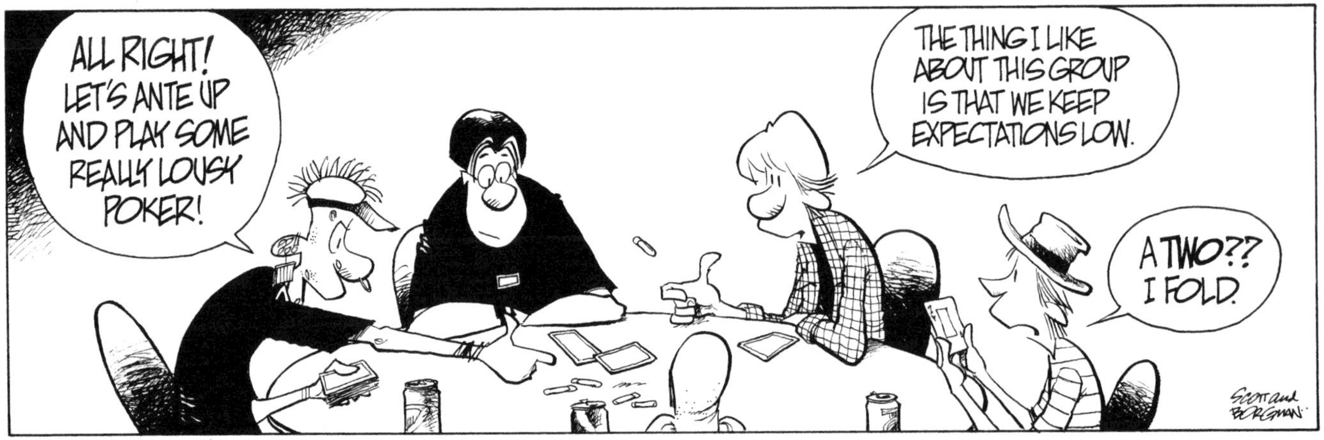
ALL RIGHT! LET'S ANTE UP AND PLAY SOME REALLY LOUSY POKER!
THE THING I LIKE ABOUT THIS GROUP IS THAT WE KEEP EXPECTATIONS LOW.
A TWO?? I FOLD.
SCOTT and BORGMAN

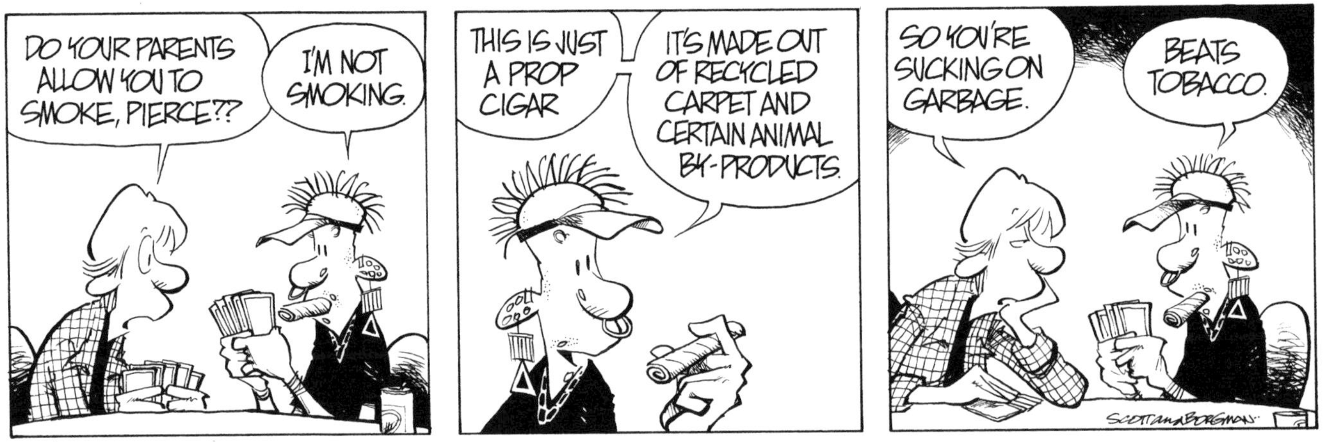
DO YOUR PARENTS ALLOW YOU TO SMOKE, PIERCE??
I'M NOT SMOKING.
THIS IS JUST A PROP CIGAR
IT'S MADE OUT OF RECYCLED CARPET AND CERTAIN ANIMAL BY-PRODUCTS.
SO YOU'RE SUCKING ON GARBAGE.
BEATS TOBACCO.
SCOTT and BORGMAN

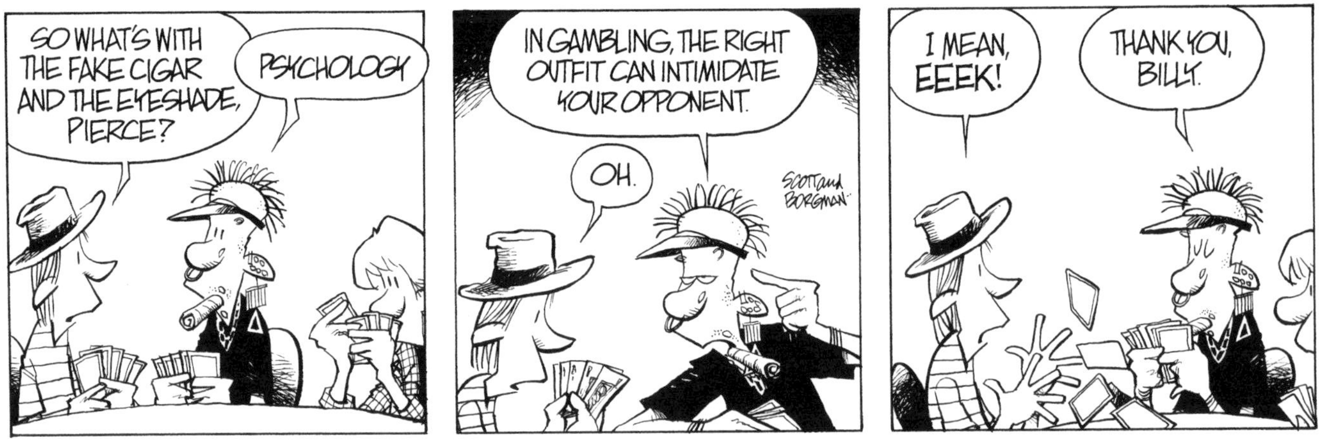
SO WHAT'S WITH THE FAKE CIGAR AND THE EYESHADE, PIERCE?
PSYCHOLOGY
IN GAMBLING, THE RIGHT OUTFIT CAN INTIMIDATE YOUR OPPONENT.
OH.
SCOTT and BORGMAN
I MEAN, EEEK!
THANK YOU, BILLY.

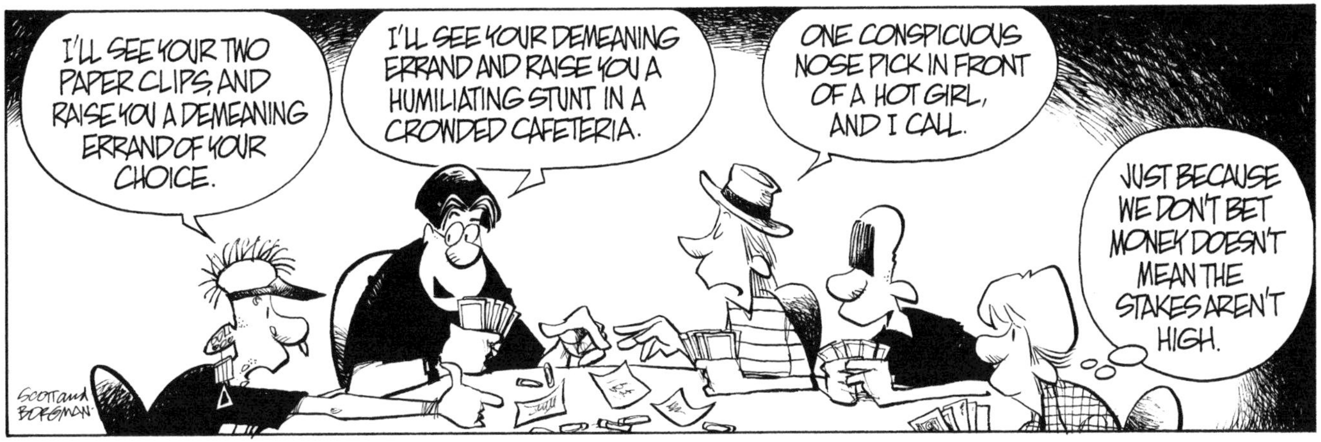
I'LL SEE YOUR TWO PAPER CLIPS, AND RAISE YOU A DEMEANING ERRAND OF YOUR CHOICE.
I'LL SEE YOUR DEMEANING ERRAND AND RAISE YOU A HUMILIATING STUNT IN A CROWDED CAFETERIA.
ONE CONSPICUOUS NOSE PICK IN FRONT OF A HOT GIRL, AND I CALL.
JUST BECAUSE WE DON'T BET MONEY DOESN'T MEAN THE STAKES AREN'T HIGH.

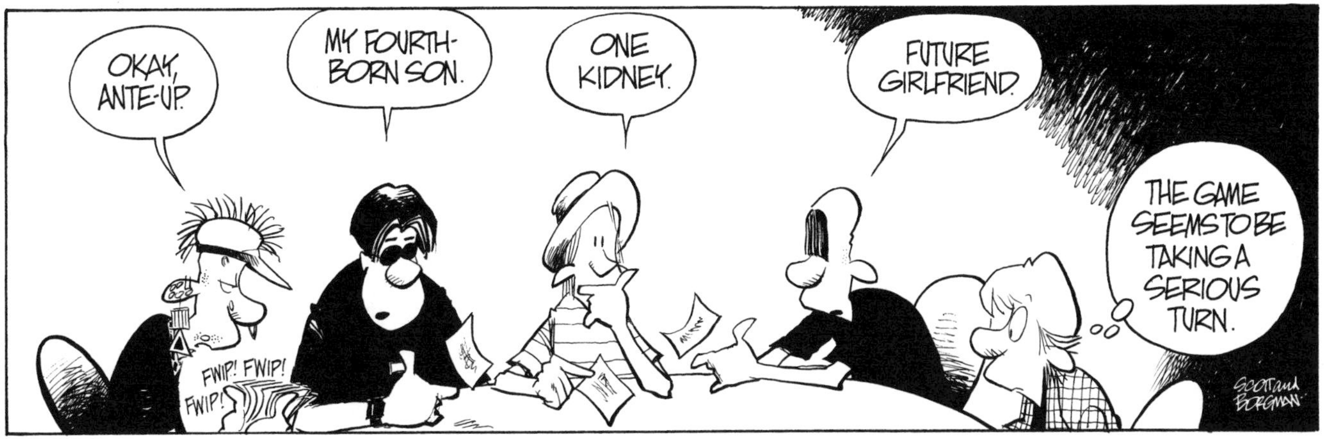
OKAY, ANTE-UP.
MY FOURTH-BORN SON.
ONE KIDNEY.
FUTURE GIRLFRIEND.
THE GAME SEEMS TO BE TAKING A SERIOUS TURN.
FWIP! FWIP! FWIP!

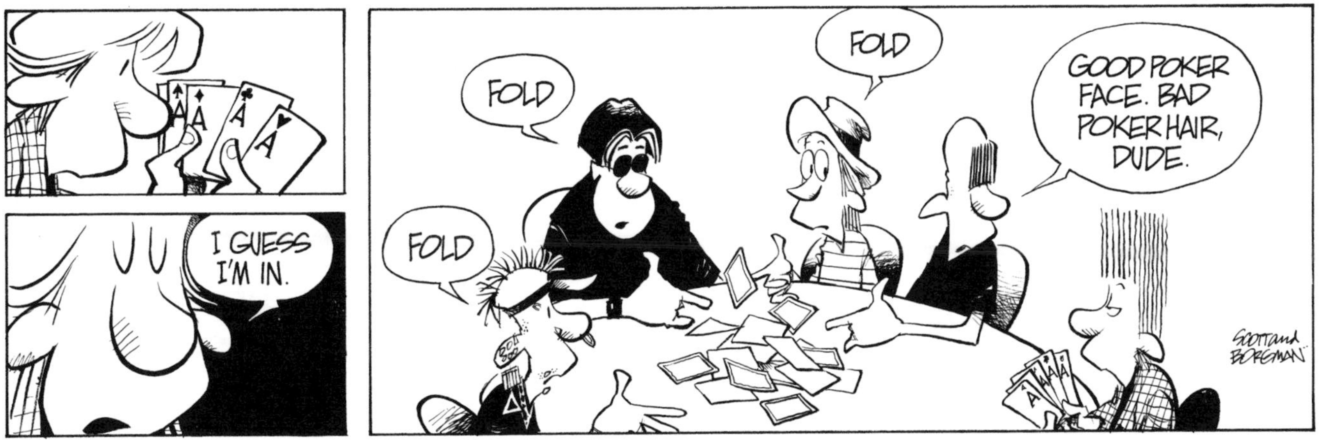
I GUESS I'M IN.
FOLD
FOLD
FOLD
GOOD POKER FACE. BAD POKER HAIR, DUDE.

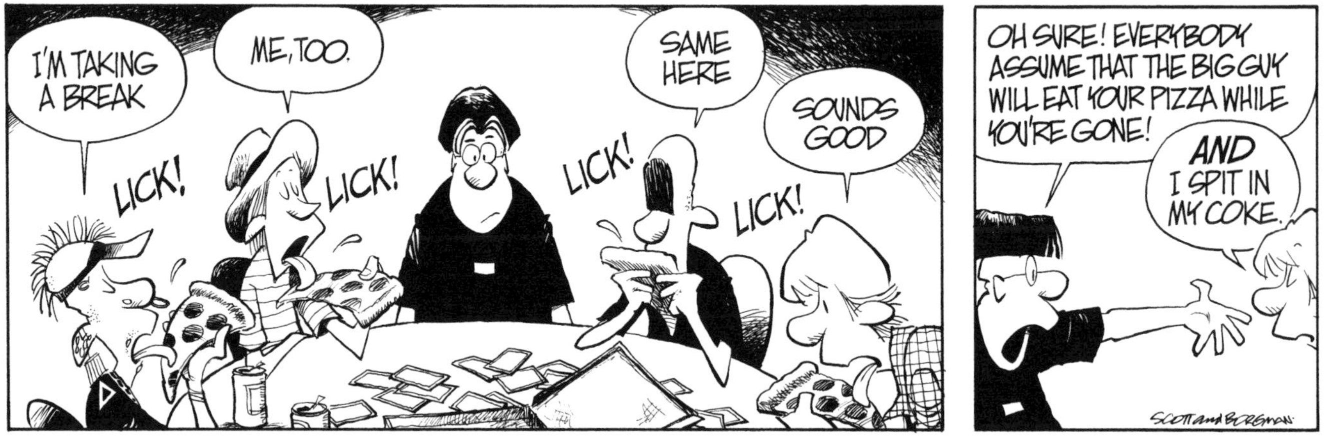
I'M TAKING A BREAK
ME, TOO.
SAME HERE
SOUNDS GOOD
LICK!
LICK!
LICK!
LICK!
OH SURE! EVERYBODY ASSUME THAT THE BIG GUY WILL EAT YOUR PIZZA WHILE YOU'RE GONE!
AND I SPIT IN MY COKE.
SCOTT and BORGMAN

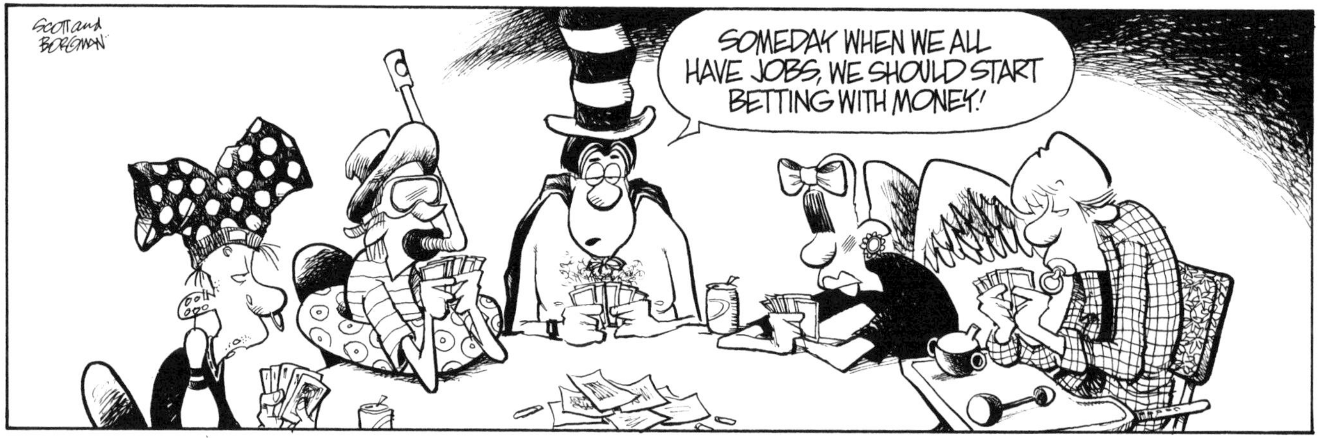
SCOTT and BORGMAN
SOMEDAY WHEN WE ALL HAVE JOBS, WE SHOULD START BETTING WITH MONEY!

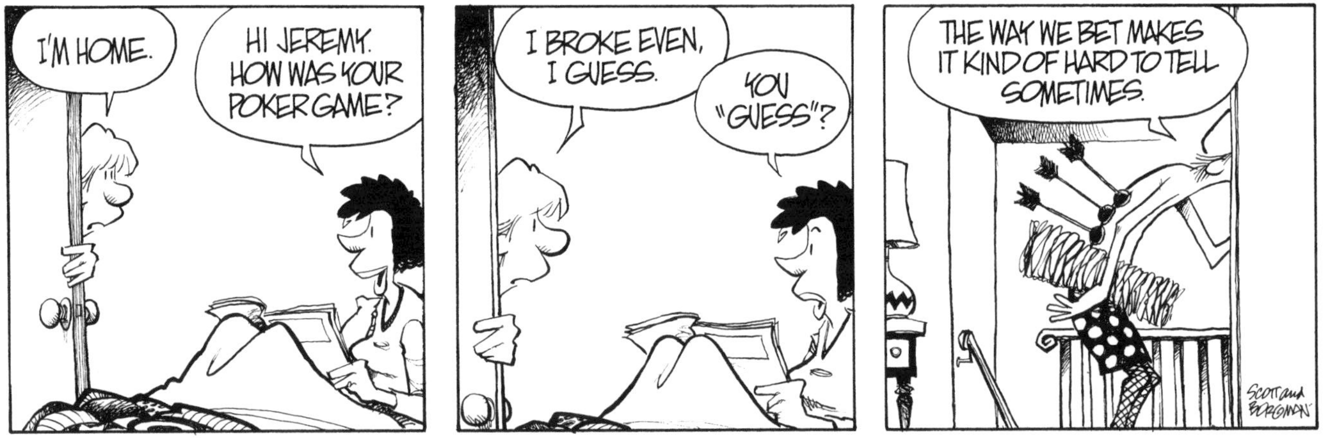
I'M HOME.
HI JEREMY. HOW WAS YOUR POKER GAME?
I BROKE EVEN, I GUESS.
YOU "GUESS"?
THE WAY WE BET MAKES IT KIND OF HARD TO TELL SOMETIMES.
SCOTT and BORGMAN

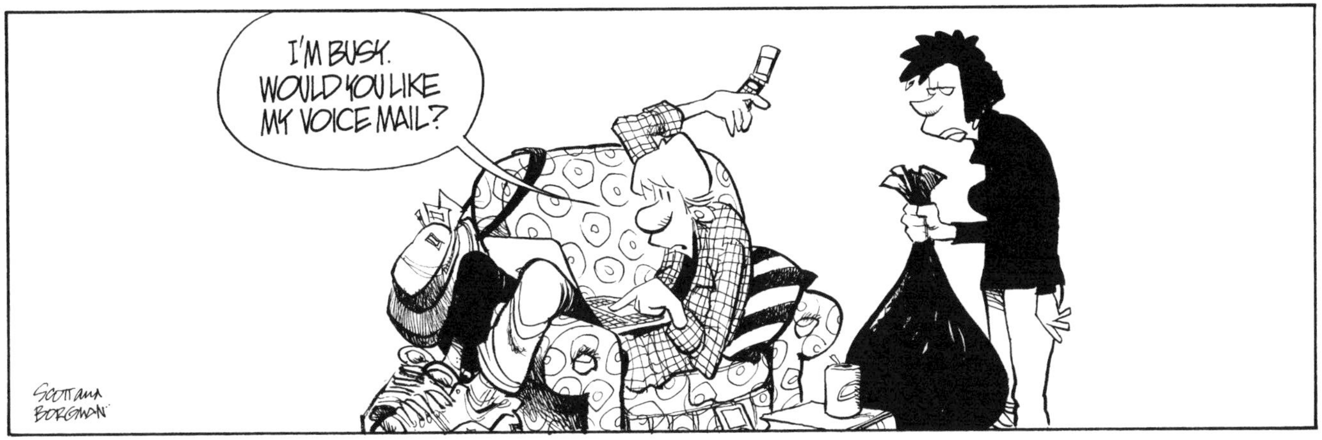
I'M BUSY. WOULD YOU LIKE MY VOICE MAIL?

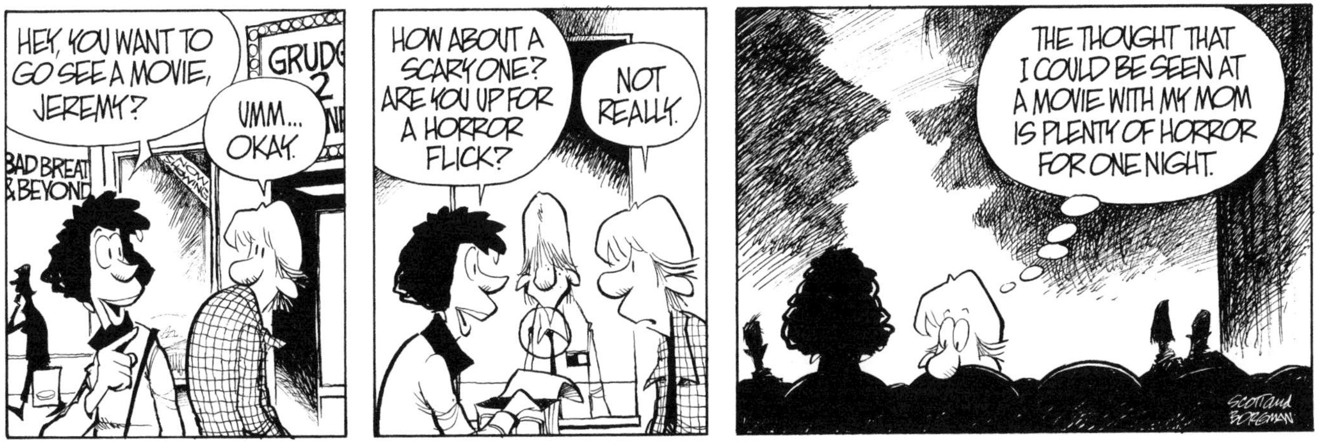
HEY, YOU WANT TO GO SEE A MOVIE, JEREMY?
UMM... OKAY.
HOW ABOUT A SCARY ONE? ARE YOU UP FOR A HORROR FLICK?
NOT REALLY.
THE THOUGHT THAT I COULD BE SEEN AT A MOVIE WITH MY MOM IS PLENTY OF HORROR FOR ONE NIGHT.

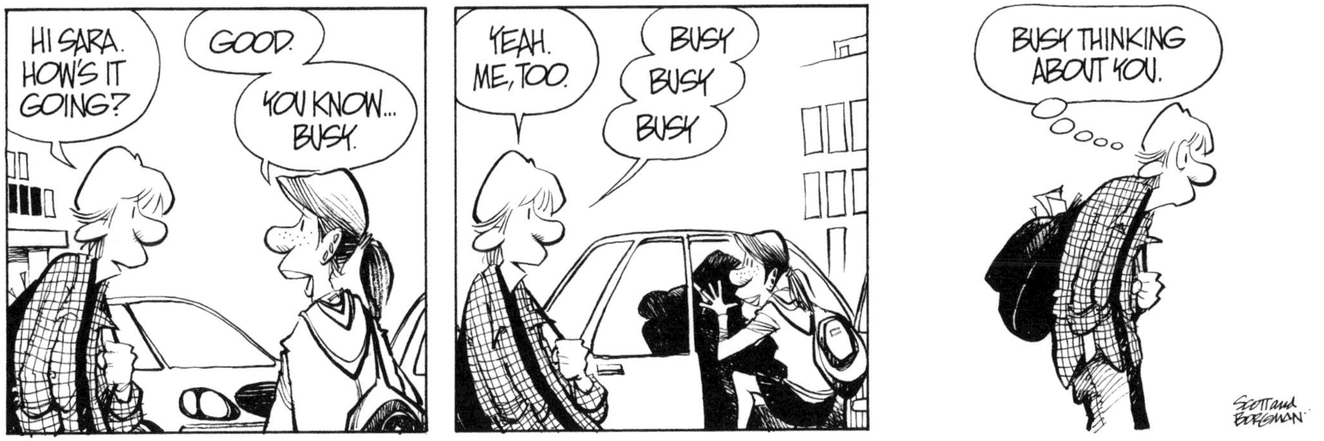
HI SARA. HOW'S IT GOING?
GOOD.
YOU KNOW... BUSY.
YEAH. ME, TOO.
BUSY
BUSY
BUSY
BUSY THINKING ABOUT YOU.

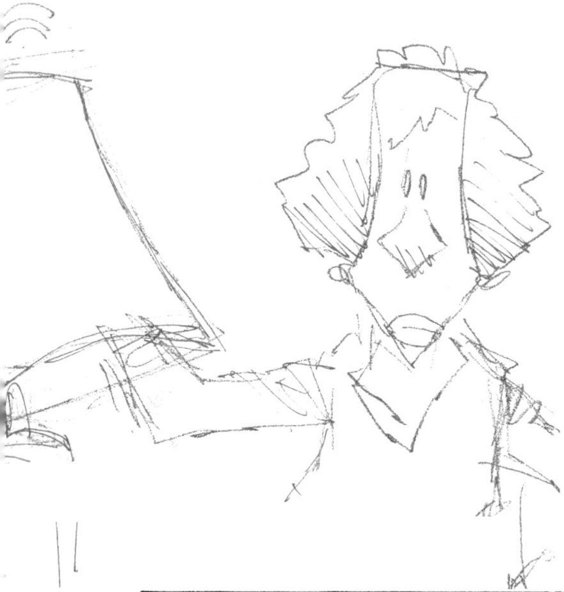

Zits

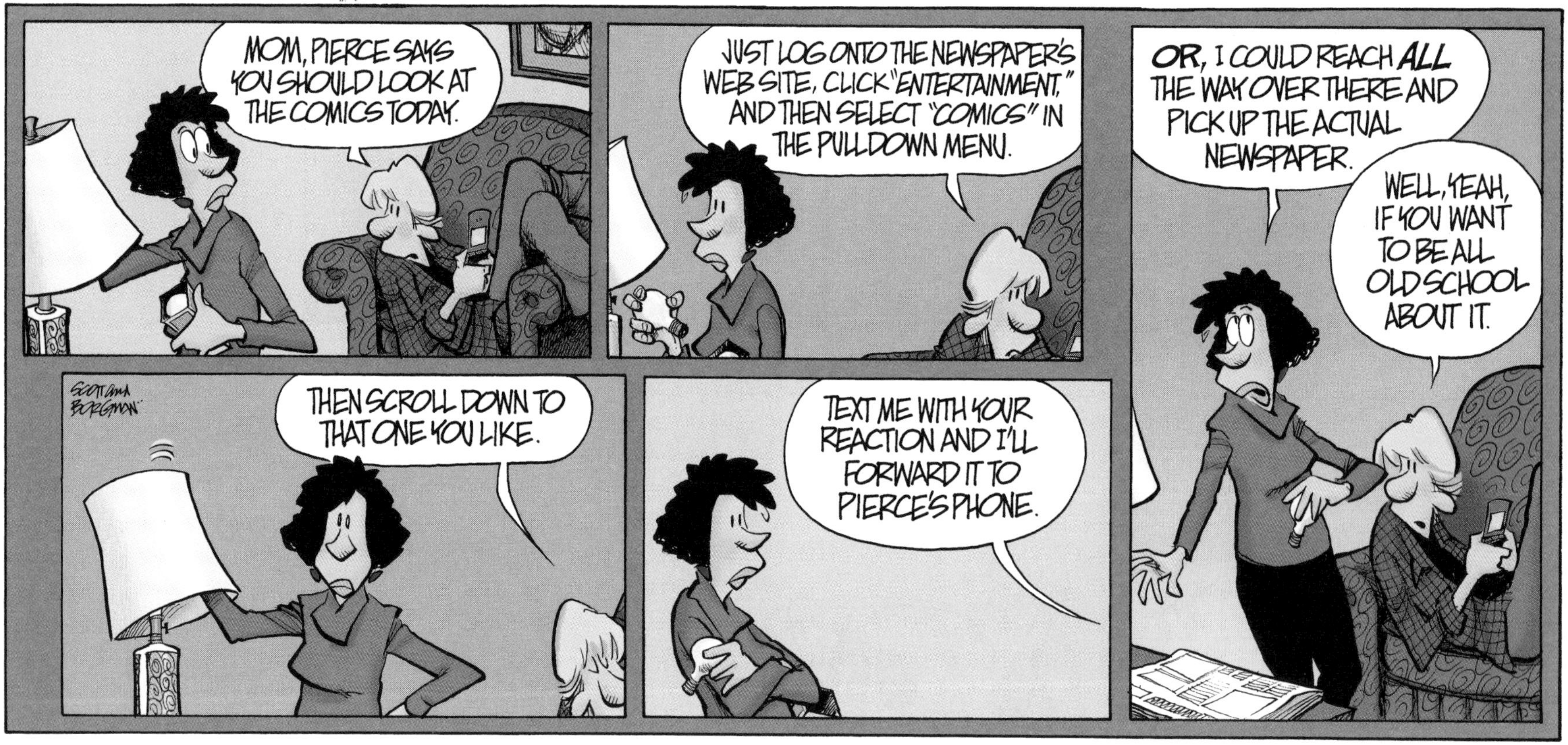
MOM, PIERCE SAYS YOU SHOULD LOOK AT THE COMICS TODAY.
JUST LOG ONTO THE NEWSPAPER'S WEB SITE, CLICK "ENTERTAINMENT," AND THEN SELECT "COMICS" IN THE PULLDOWN MENU.
THEN SCROLL DOWN TO THAT ONE YOU LIKE.
TEXT ME WITH YOUR REACTION AND I'LL FORWARD IT TO PIERCE'S PHONE.
OR, I COULD REACH ALL THE WAY OVER THERE AND PICK UP THE ACTUAL NEWSPAPER.
WELL, YEAH, IF YOU WANT TO BE ALL OLD SCHOOL ABOUT IT.

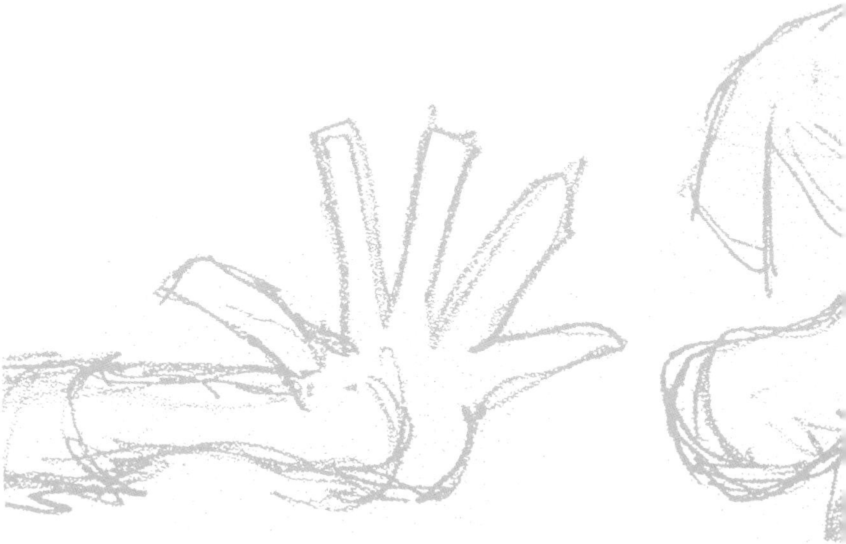

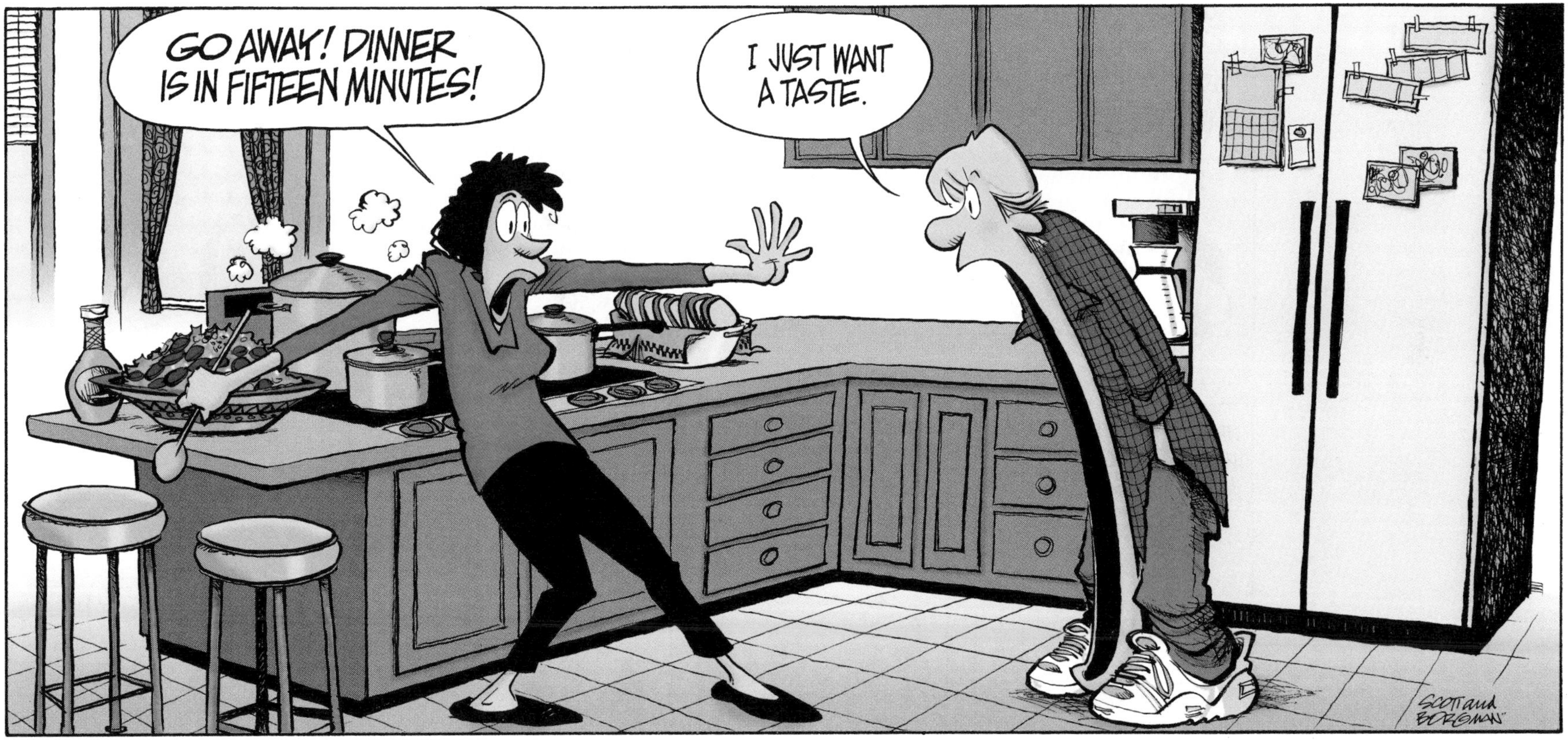
GO AWAY! DINNER IS IN FIFTEEN MINUTES!
I JUST WANT A TASTE.
SCOTT AND BORGMAN

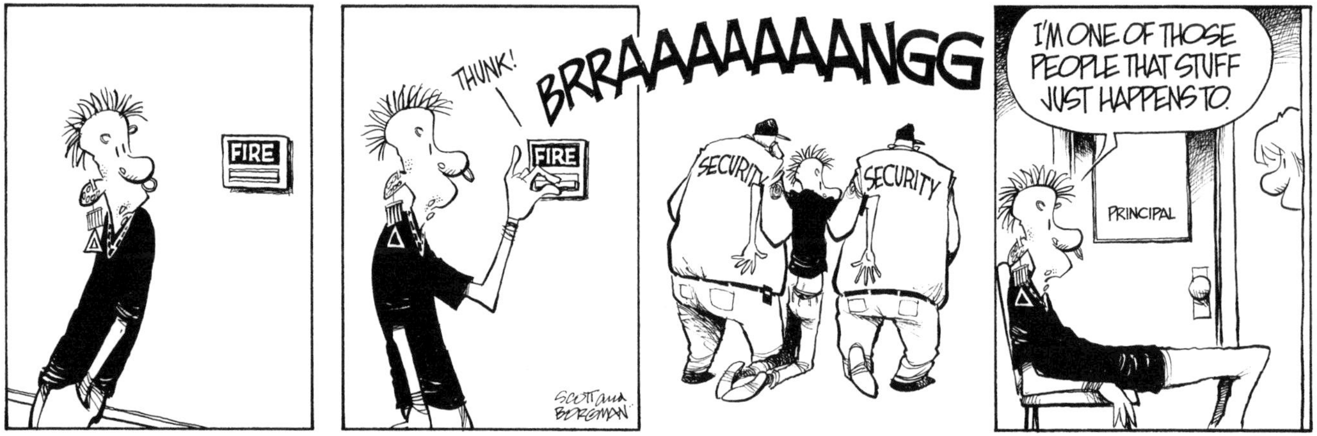
FIRE
THUNK!
FIRE
SCOTT and BORGMAN
BRRAAAAAAANGG
SECURITY
SECURITY
I'M ONE OF THOSE PEOPLE THAT STUFF JUST HAPPENS TO.
PRINCIPAL

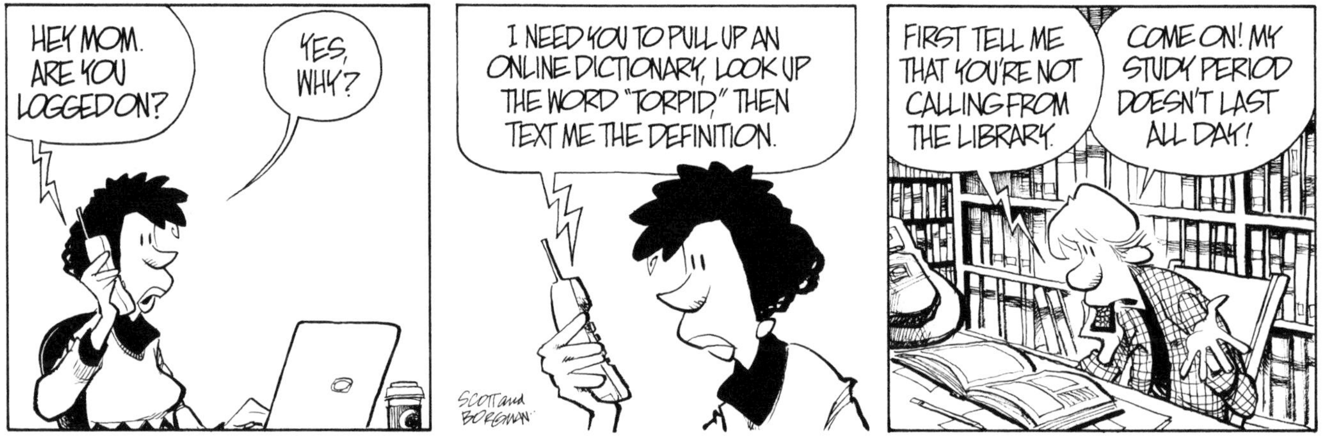
HEY MOM. ARE YOU LOGGED ON?
YES, WHY?
I NEED YOU TO PULL UP AN ONLINE DICTIONARY, LOOK UP THE WORD "TORPID," THEN TEXT ME THE DEFINITION.
SCOTT and BORGMAN
FIRST TELL ME THAT YOU'RE NOT CALLING FROM THE LIBRARY.
COME ON! MY STUDY PERIOD DOESN'T LAST ALL DAY!

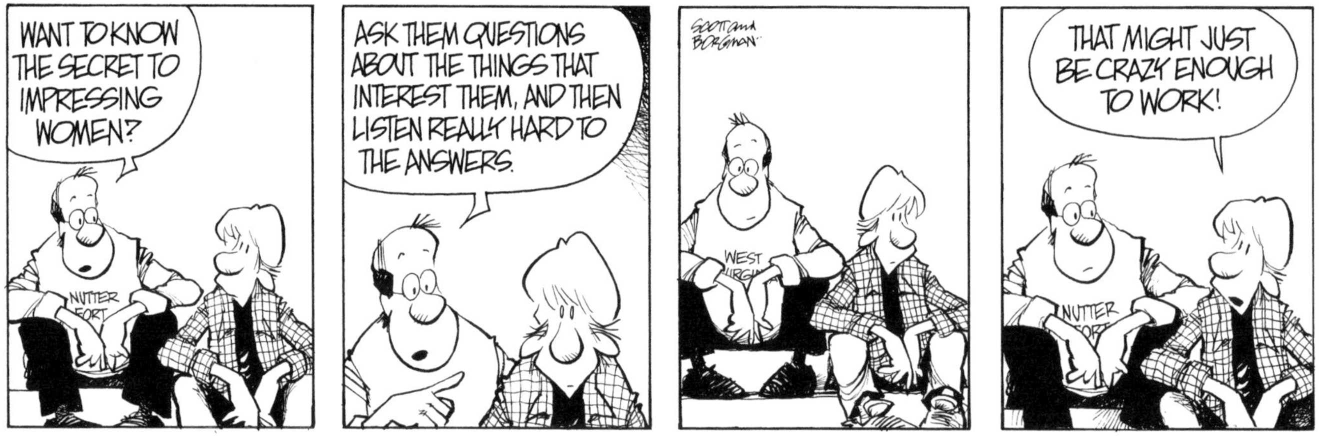
WANT TO KNOW THE SECRET TO IMPRESSING WOMEN?
NUTTER FORT
ASK THEM QUESTIONS ABOUT THE THINGS THAT INTEREST THEM, AND THEN LISTEN REALLY HARD TO THE ANSWERS.
SCOTT and BORGMAN
THAT MIGHT JUST BE CRAZY ENOUGH TO WORK!

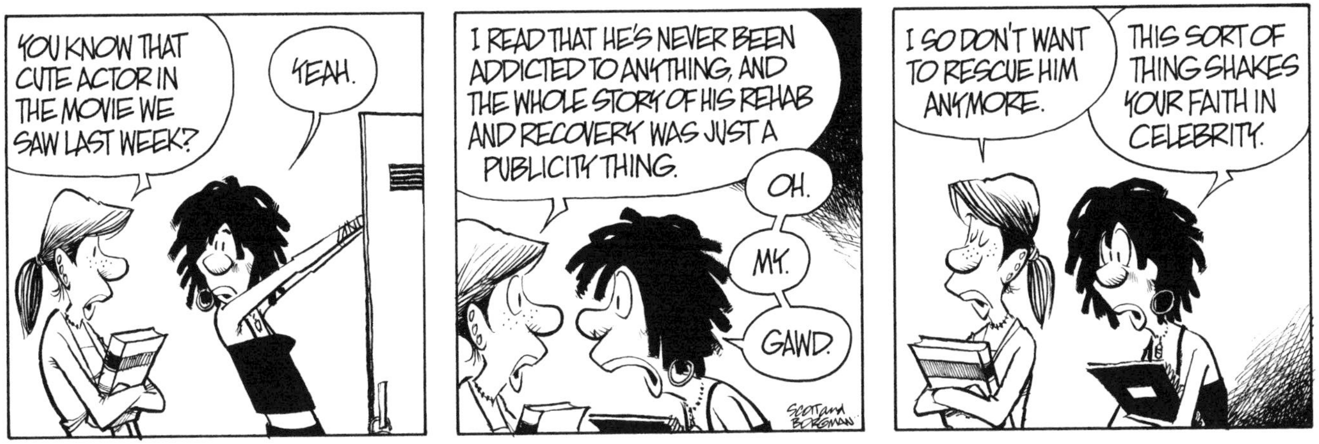
YOU KNOW THAT CUTE ACTOR IN THE MOVIE WE SAW LAST WEEK?
YEAH.
I READ THAT HE'S NEVER BEEN ADDICTED TO ANYTHING, AND THE WHOLE STORY OF HIS REHAB AND RECOVERY WAS JUST A PUBLICITY THING.
OH.
MY.
GAWD.
I SO DON'T WANT TO RESCUE HIM ANYMORE.
THIS SORT OF THING SHAKES YOUR FAITH IN CELEBRITY.

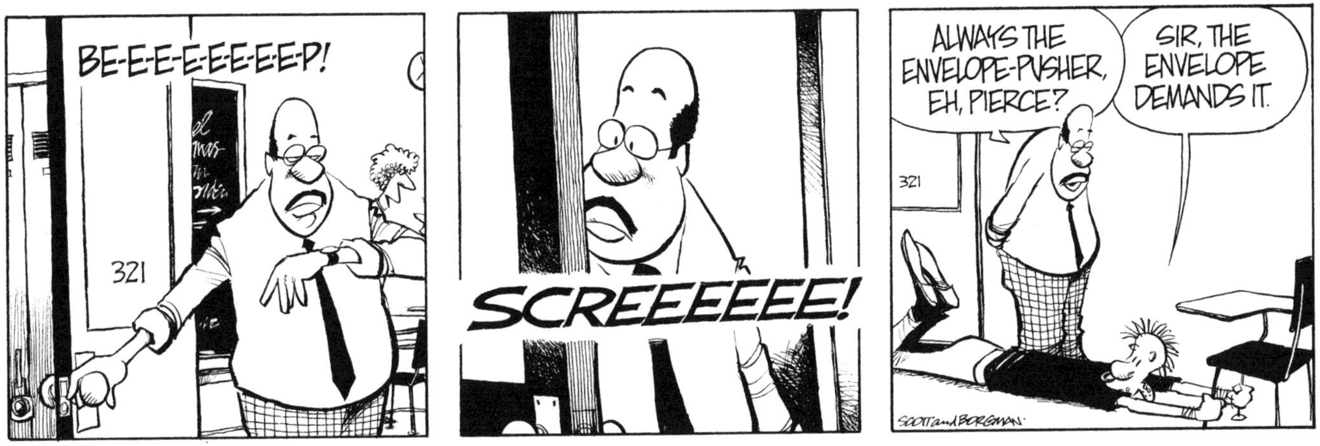
BE-E-E-E-E-E-E-E-P!
321
SCREEEEEEE!
ALWAYS THE ENVELOPE-PUSHER, EH, PIERCE?
SIR, THE ENVELOPE DEMANDS IT.
321

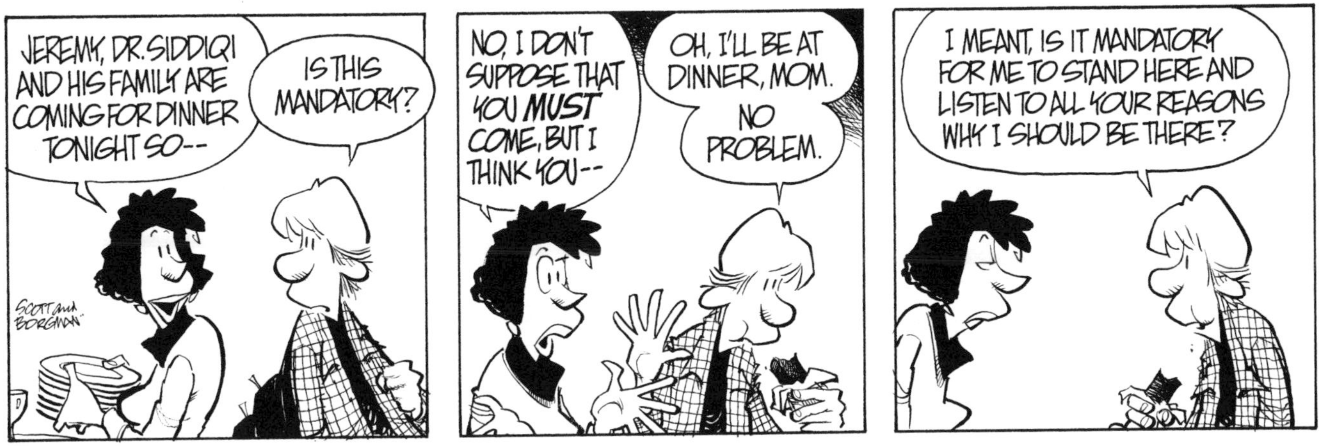
JEREMY, DR. SIDDIQI AND HIS FAMILY ARE COMING FOR DINNER TONIGHT SO--
IS THIS MANDATORY?
NO, I DON'T SUPPOSE THAT YOU **MUST** COME, BUT I THINK YOU--
OH, I'LL BE AT DINNER, MOM.
NO PROBLEM.
I MEANT, IS IT MANDATORY FOR ME TO STAND HERE AND LISTEN TO ALL YOUR REASONS WHY I SHOULD BE THERE?

Zits

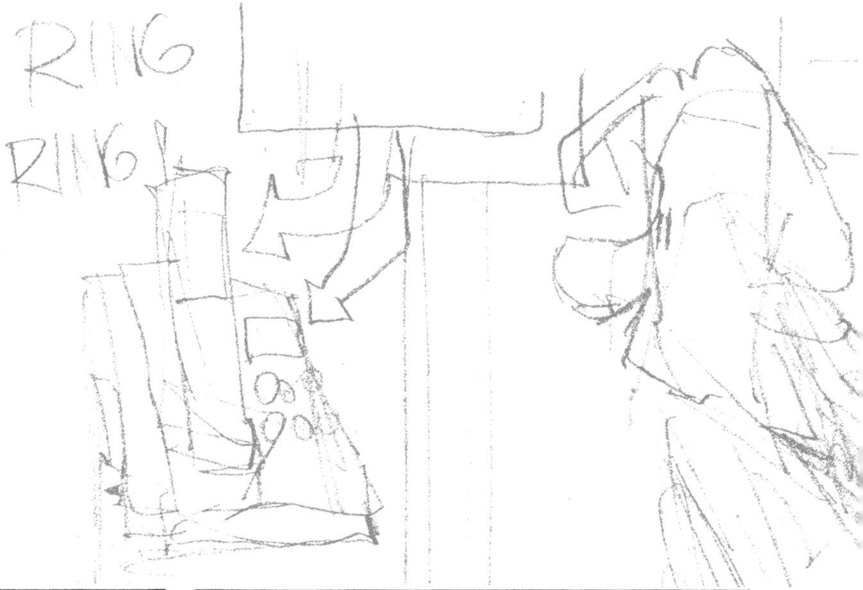

RING
RING!

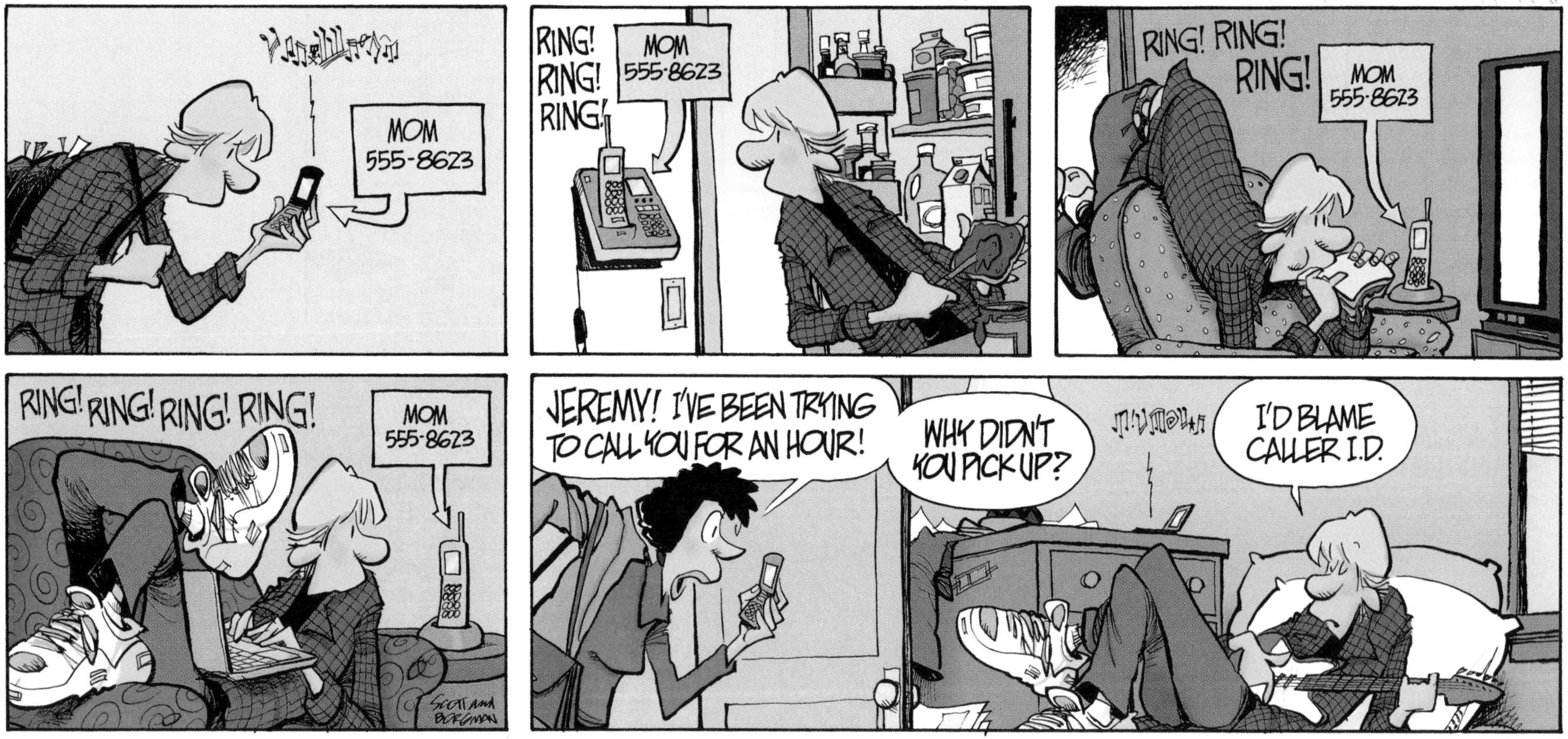

MOM
555-8623
RING!
RING!
RING!
MOM
555-8623
RING! RING!
RING!
MOM
555-8623
RING! RING! RING! RING!
MOM
555-8623
SCOTT AND BORGMAN
JEREMY! I'VE BEEN TRYING TO CALL YOU FOR AN HOUR!
WHY DIDN'T YOU PICK UP?
I'D BLAME CALLER I.D.

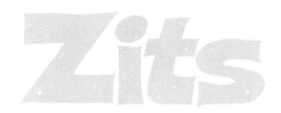

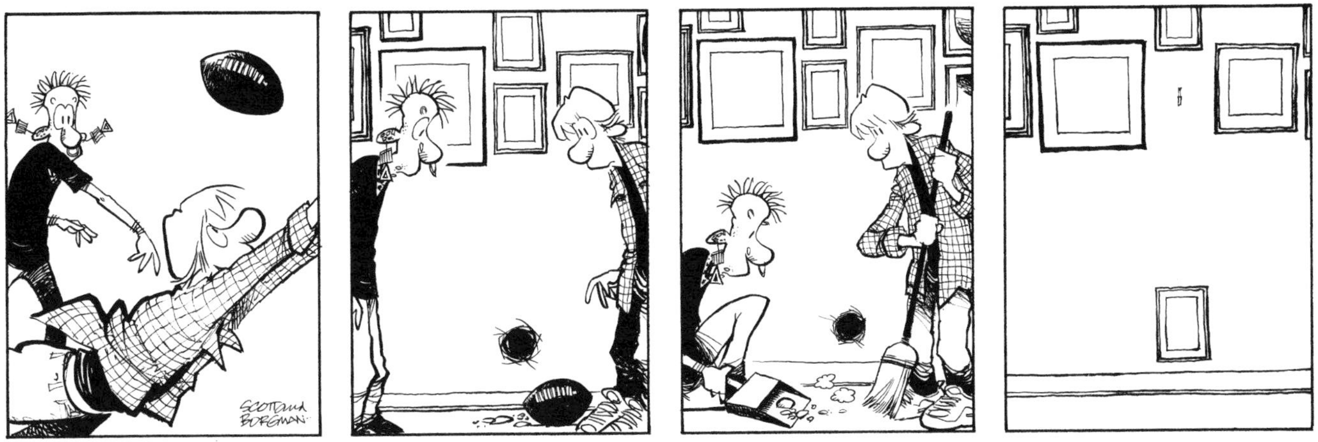

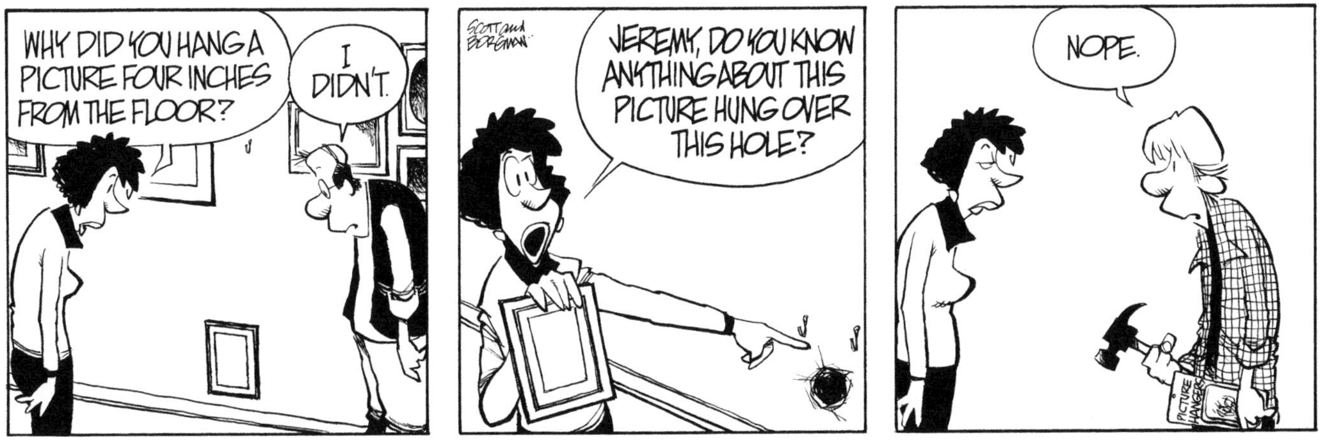
WHY DID YOU HANG A PICTURE FOUR INCHES FROM THE FLOOR?
I DIDN'T.
JEREMY, DO YOU KNOW ANYTHING ABOUT THIS PICTURE HUNG OVER THIS HOLE?
NOPE.
PICTURE HANGERS

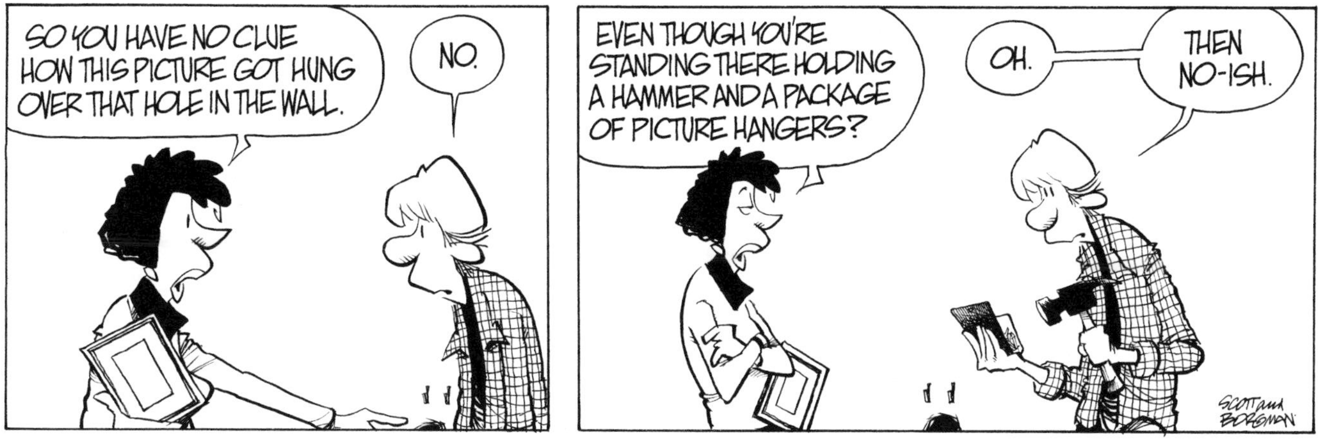
SO YOU HAVE NO CLUE HOW THIS PICTURE GOT HUNG OVER THAT HOLE IN THE WALL.
NO.
EVEN THOUGH YOU'RE STANDING THERE HOLDING A HAMMER AND A PACKAGE OF PICTURE HANGERS?
OH.
THEN NO-ISH.

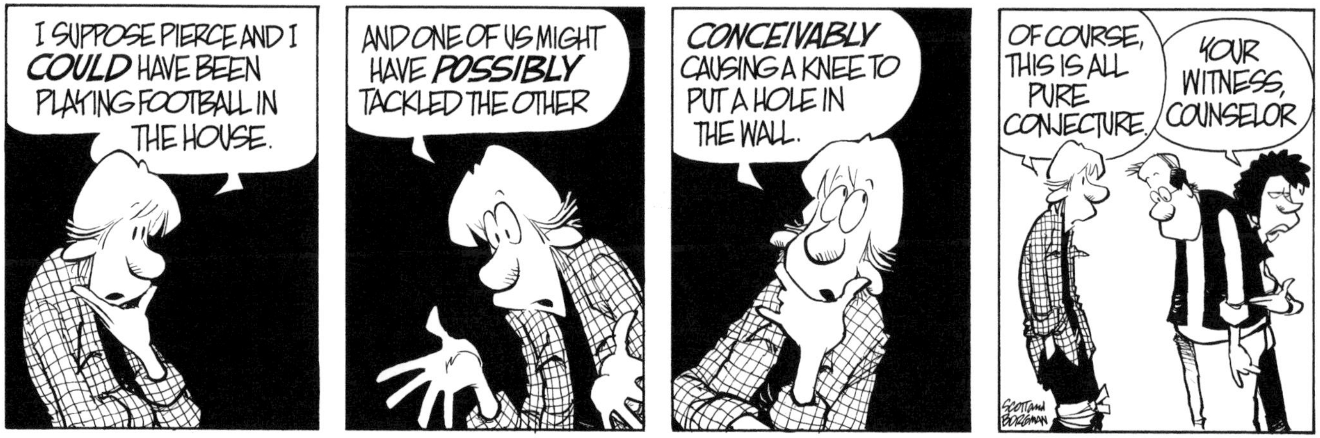
I SUPPOSE PIERCE AND I COULD HAVE BEEN PLAYING FOOTBALL IN THE HOUSE.
AND ONE OF US MIGHT HAVE POSSIBLY TACKLED THE OTHER
CONCEIVABLY CAUSING A KNEE TO PUT A HOLE IN THE WALL.
OF COURSE, THIS IS ALL PURE CONJECTURE.
YOUR WITNESS, COUNSELOR
SCOTT and BORGMAN

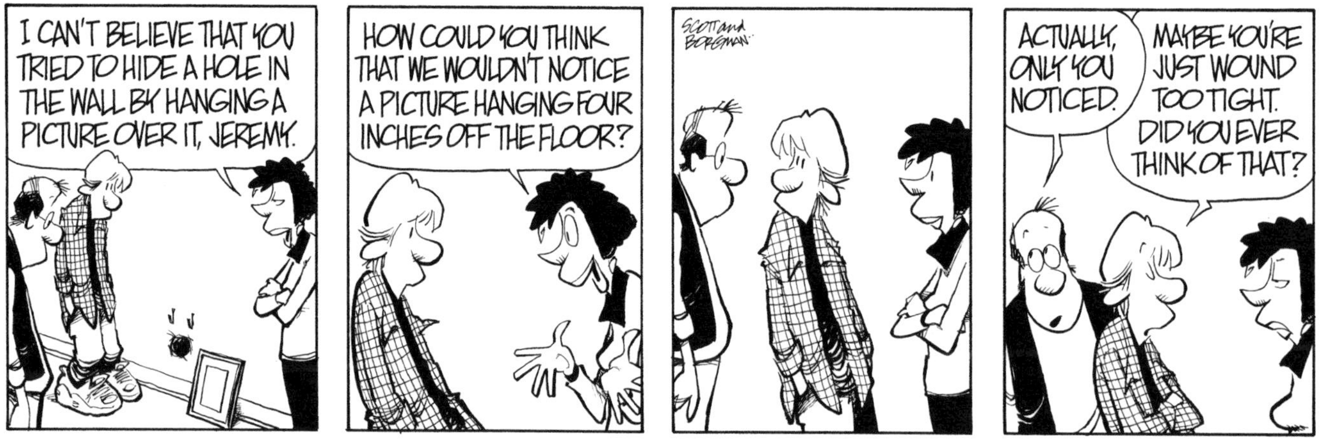
I CAN'T BELIEVE THAT YOU TRIED TO HIDE A HOLE IN THE WALL BY HANGING A PICTURE OVER IT, JEREMY.
HOW COULD YOU THINK THAT WE WOULDN'T NOTICE A PICTURE HANGING FOUR INCHES OFF THE FLOOR?
SCOTT and BORGMAN
ACTUALLY, ONLY YOU NOTICED.
MAYBE YOU'RE JUST WOUND TOO TIGHT. DID YOU EVER THINK OF THAT?

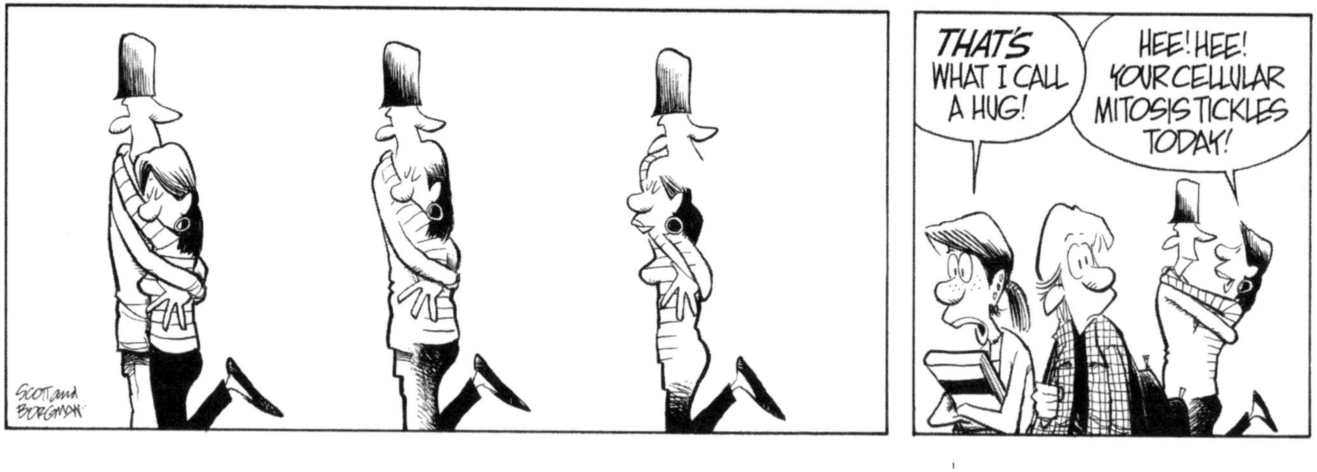
SCOTT and BORGMAN
THAT'S WHAT I CALL A HUG!
HEE! HEE! YOUR CELLULAR MITOSIS TICKLES TODAY!

Zits

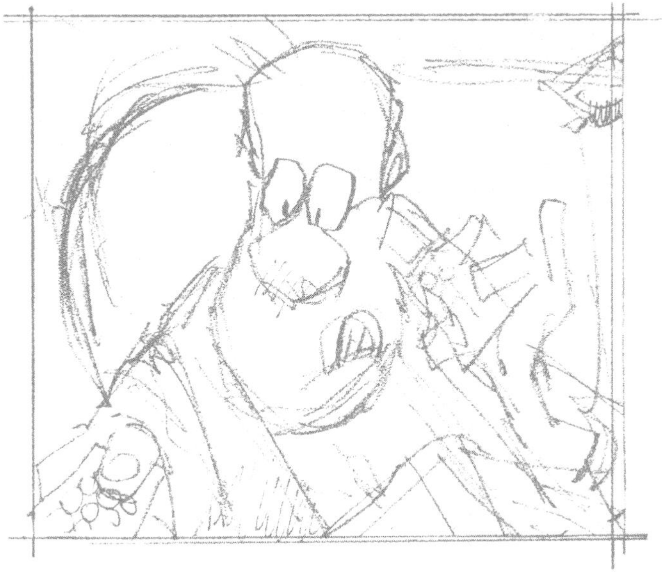

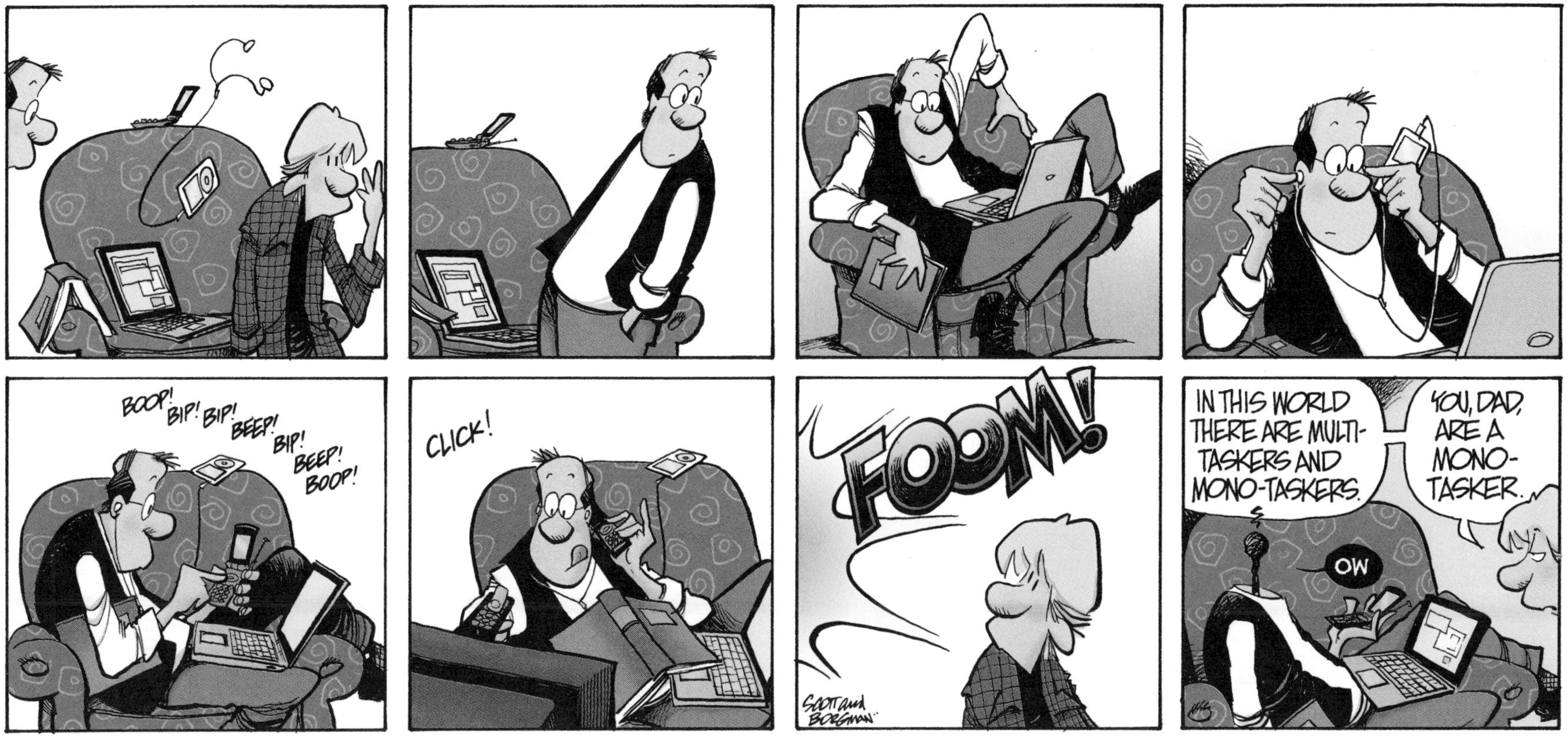
BOOP! BIP! BIP! BEEP! BIP! BEEP! BOOP!
CLICK!
FOOM!
SCOTT AND BORGMAN
IN THIS WORLD THERE ARE MULTI-TASKERS AND MONO-TASKERS.
YOU, DAD, ARE A MONO-TASKER.
OW

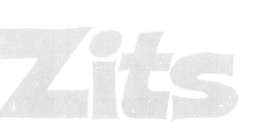

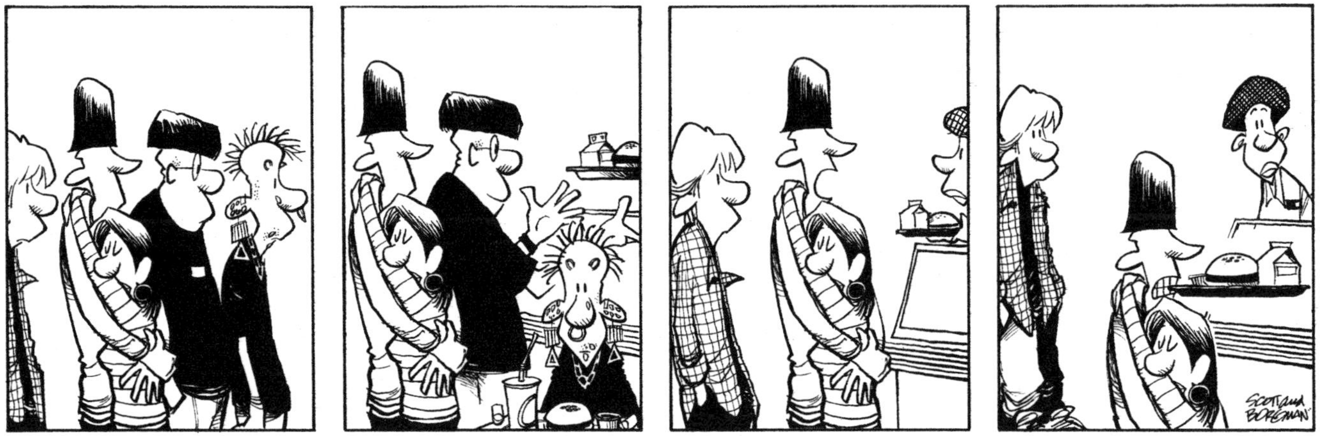

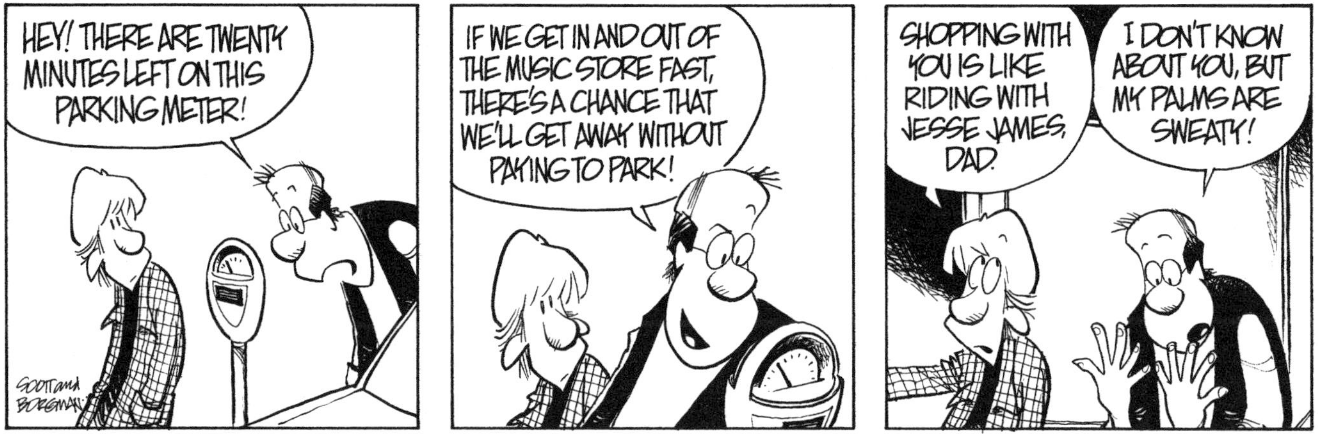
HEY! THERE ARE TWENTY MINUTES LEFT ON THIS PARKING METER!
IF WE GET IN AND OUT OF THE MUSIC STORE FAST, THERE'S A CHANCE THAT WE'LL GET AWAY WITHOUT PAYING TO PARK!
SHOPPING WITH YOU IS LIKE RIDING WITH JESSE JAMES, DAD.
I DON'T KNOW ABOUT YOU, BUT MY PALMS ARE SWEATY!

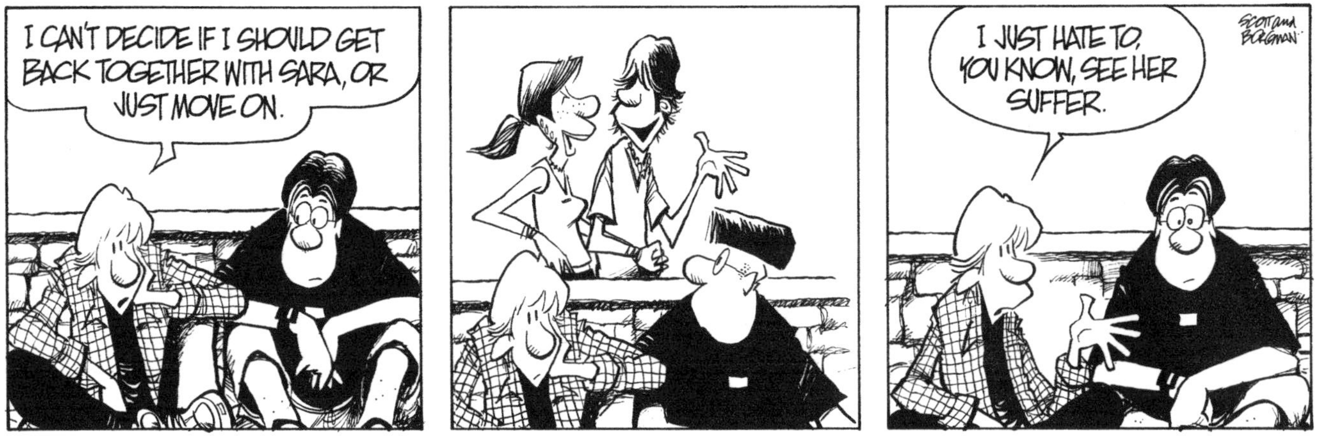
I CAN'T DECIDE IF I SHOULD GET BACK TOGETHER WITH SARA, OR JUST MOVE ON.
I JUST HATE TO, YOU KNOW, SEE HER SUFFER.

Zits

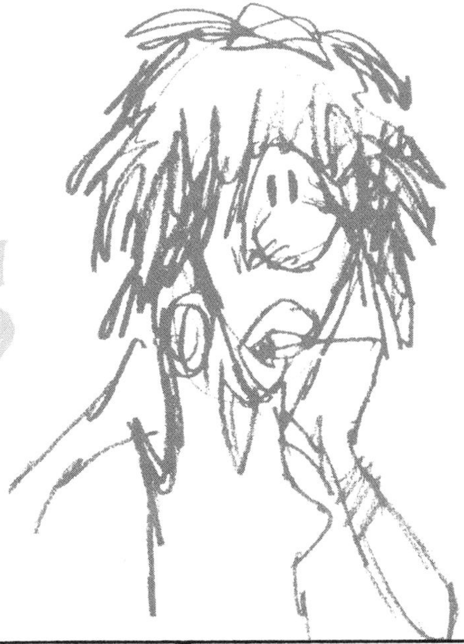

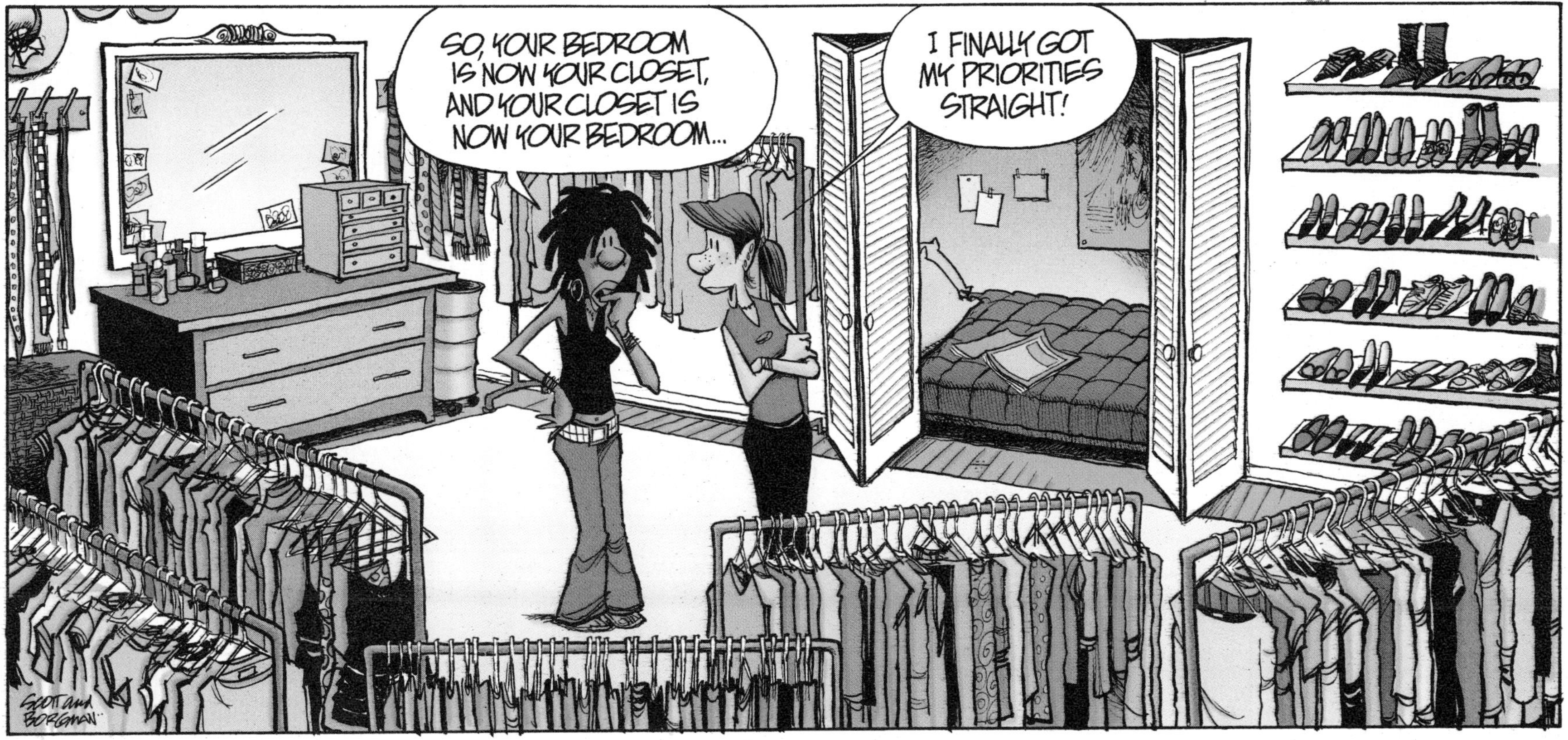
SO, YOUR BEDROOM IS NOW YOUR CLOSET, AND YOUR CLOSET IS NOW YOUR BEDROOM...
I FINALLY GOT MY PRIORITIES STRAIGHT!
SCOTT and BORGMAN

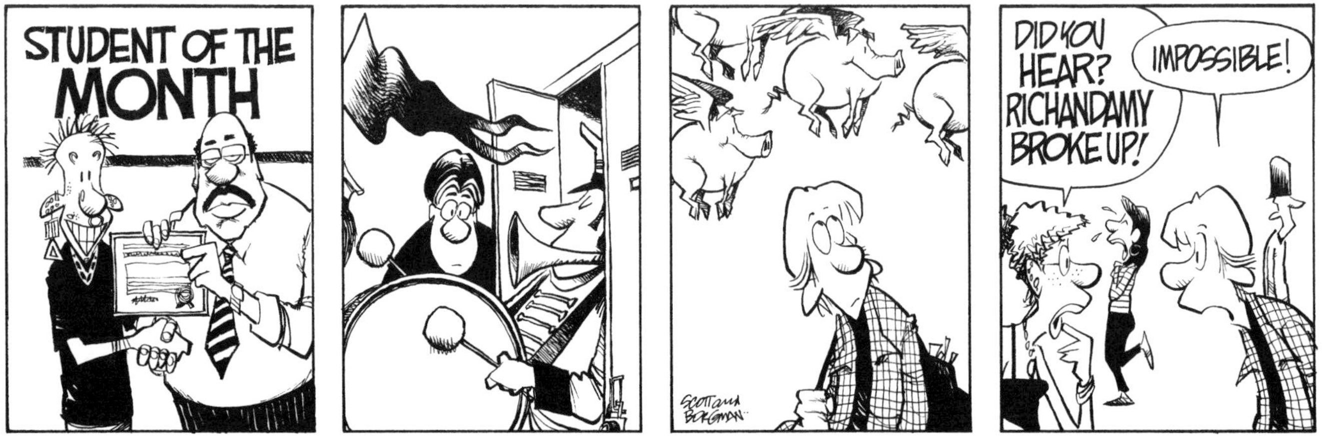
STUDENT OF THE MONTH
SCOTT and BORGMAN
DID YOU HEAR? RICHANDAMY BROKE UP!
IMPOSSIBLE!

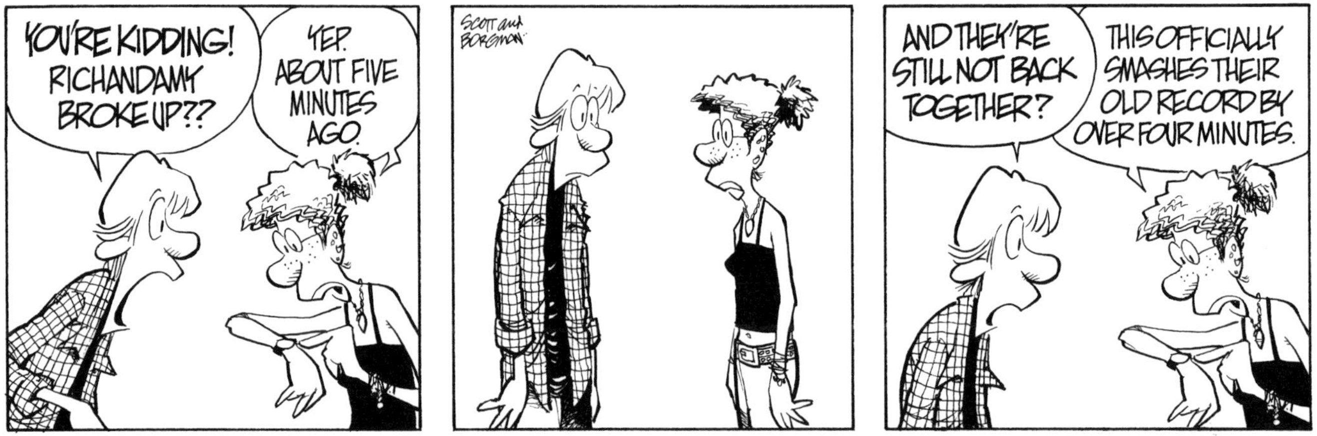
YOU'RE KIDDING! RICHANDAMY BROKE UP??
YEP. ABOUT FIVE MINUTES AGO.
SCOTT and BORGMAN
AND THEY'RE STILL NOT BACK TOGETHER?
THIS OFFICIALLY SMASHES THEIR OLD RECORD BY OVER FOUR MINUTES.

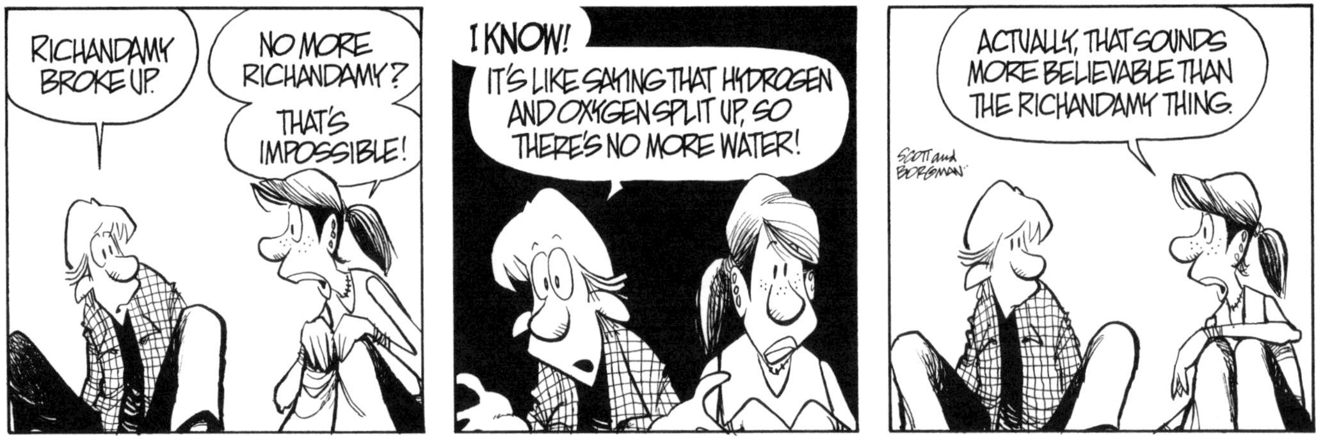
RICHANDAMY BROKE UP.
NO MORE RICHANDAMY?
THAT'S IMPOSSIBLE!
I KNOW!
IT'S LIKE SAYING THAT HYDROGEN AND OXYGEN SPLIT UP, SO THERE'S NO MORE WATER!
SCOTT and BORGMAN
ACTUALLY, THAT SOUNDS MORE BELIEVABLE THAN THE RICHANDAMY THING.

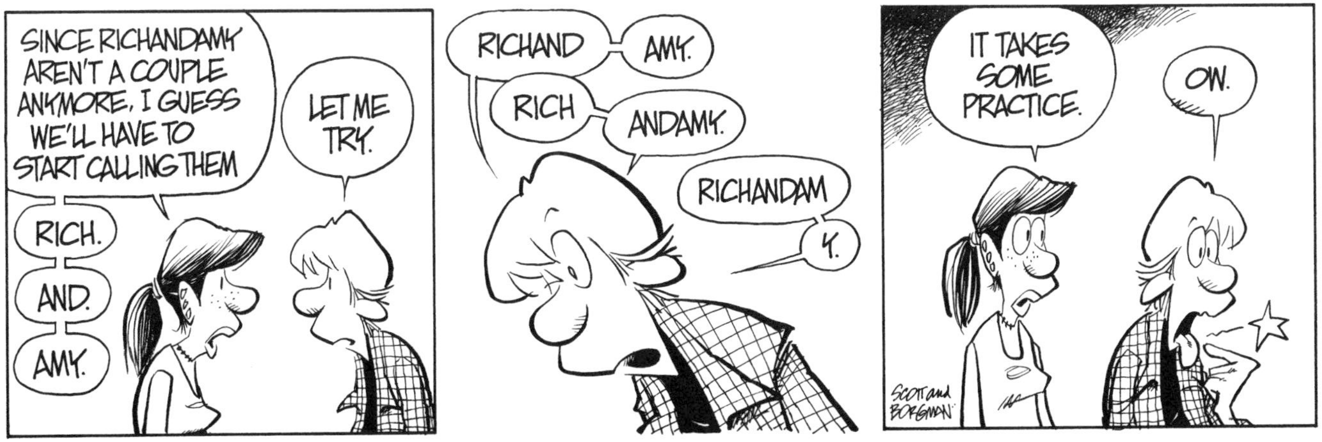
SINCE RICHANDAMY AREN'T A COUPLE ANYMORE, I GUESS WE'LL HAVE TO START CALLING THEM
RICH.
AND.
AMY.
LET ME TRY.
RICHAND
AMY.
RICH
ANDAMY.
RICHANDAM
Y.
IT TAKES SOME PRACTICE.
OW.
SCOTT and BORGMAN

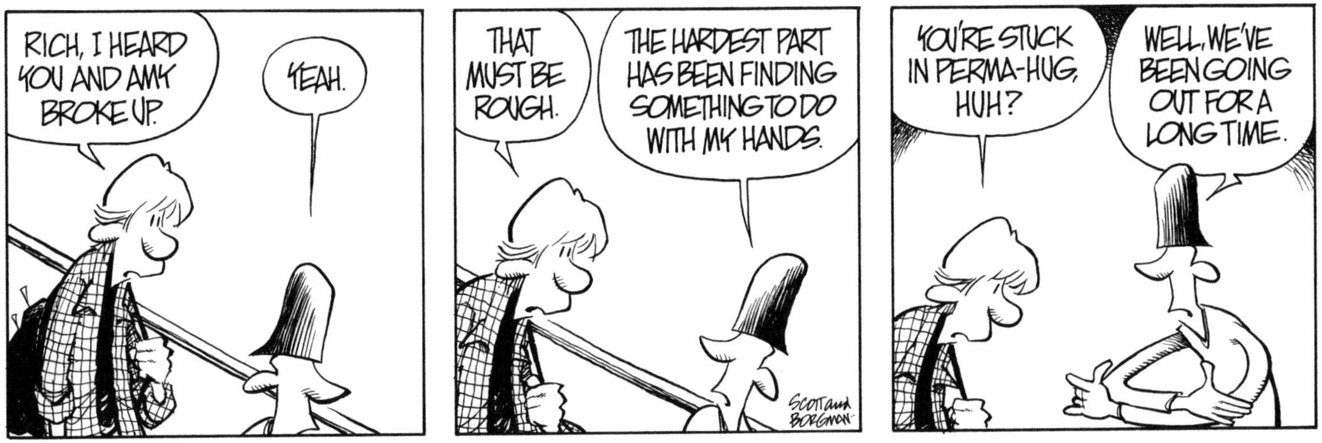
RICH, I HEARD YOU AND AMY BROKE UP.
YEAH.
THAT MUST BE ROUGH.
THE HARDEST PART HAS BEEN FINDING SOMETHING TO DO WITH MY HANDS.
SCOTT and BORGMAN
YOU'RE STUCK IN PERMA-HUG, HUH?
WELL, WE'VE BEEN GOING OUT FOR A LONG TIME.

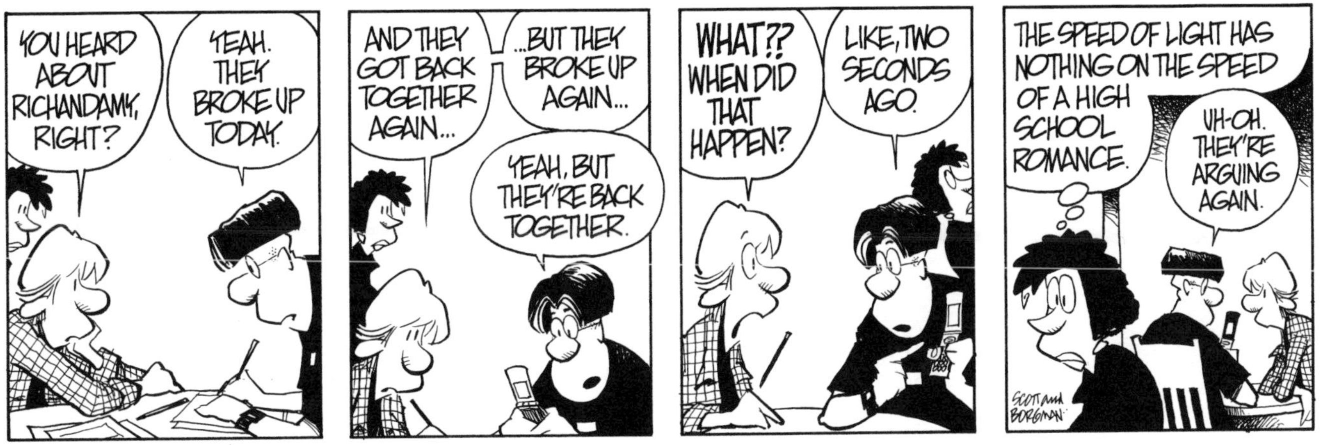
YOU HEARD ABOUT RICHANDAMY, RIGHT?
YEAH. THEY BROKE UP TODAY.
AND THEY GOT BACK TOGETHER AGAIN...
...BUT THEY BROKE UP AGAIN...
YEAH, BUT THEY'RE BACK TOGETHER.
WHAT?? WHEN DID THAT HAPPEN?
LIKE, TWO SECONDS AGO.
THE SPEED OF LIGHT HAS NOTHING ON THE SPEED OF A HIGH SCHOOL ROMANCE.
UH-OH. THEY'RE ARGUING AGAIN.
SCOTT and BORGMAN

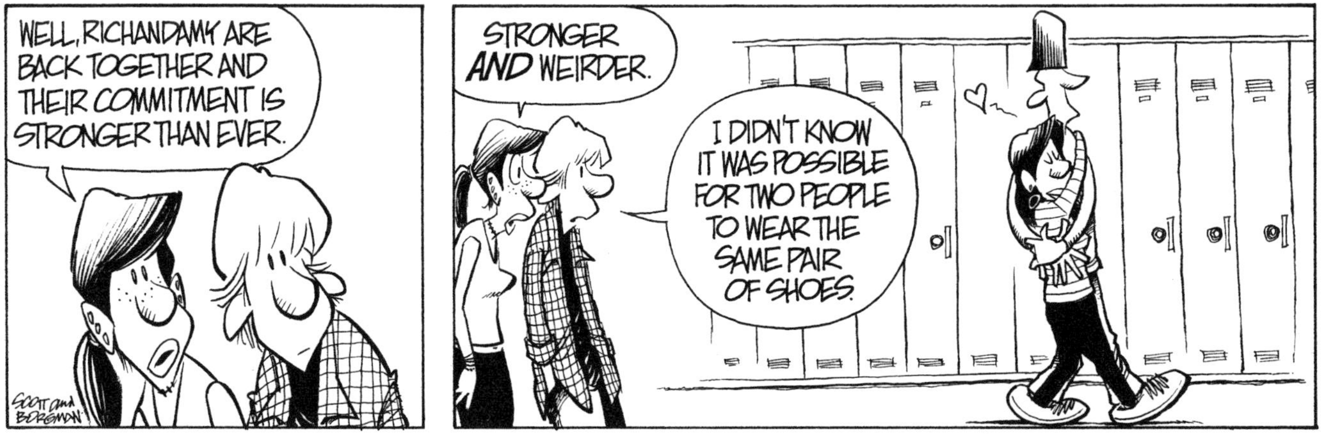
WELL, RICHANDAMY ARE BACK TOGETHER AND THEIR COMMITMENT IS STRONGER THAN EVER.
STRONGER AND WEIRDER.
I DIDN'T KNOW IT WAS POSSIBLE FOR TWO PEOPLE TO WEAR THE SAME PAIR OF SHOES.
SCOTT AND BORGMAN

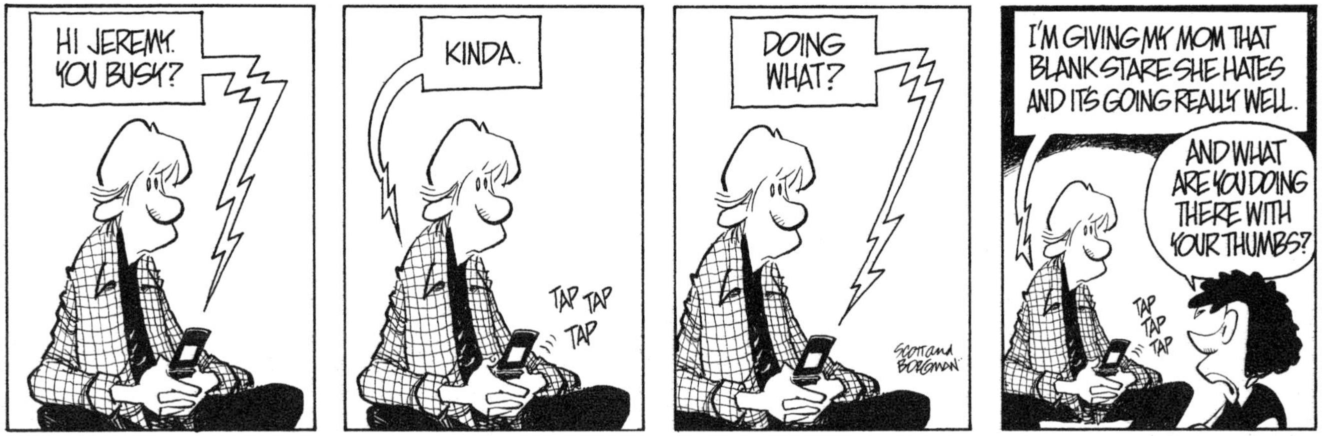
HI JEREMY. YOU BUSY?
KINDA.
TAP TAP TAP
DOING WHAT?
SCOTT AND BORGMAN
I'M GIVING MY MOM THAT BLANK STARE SHE HATES AND IT'S GOING REALLY WELL.
AND WHAT ARE YOU DOING THERE WITH YOUR THUMBS?
TAP TAP TAP

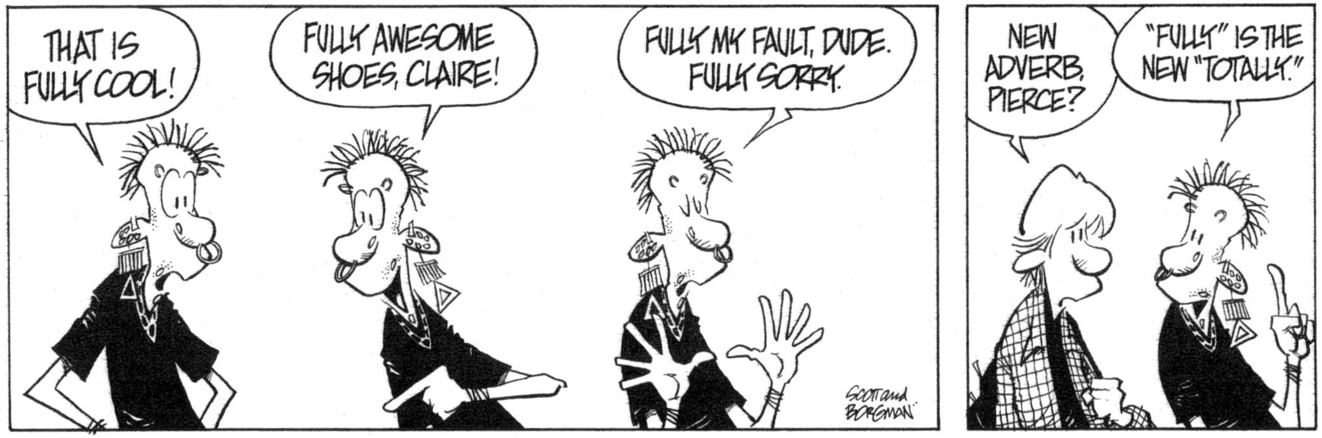
THAT IS FULLY COOL!
FULLY AWESOME SHOES, CLAIRE!
FULLY MY FAULT, DUDE. FULLY SORRY.
SCOTT AND BORGMAN
NEW ADVERB, PIERCE?
"FULLY" IS THE NEW "TOTALLY."

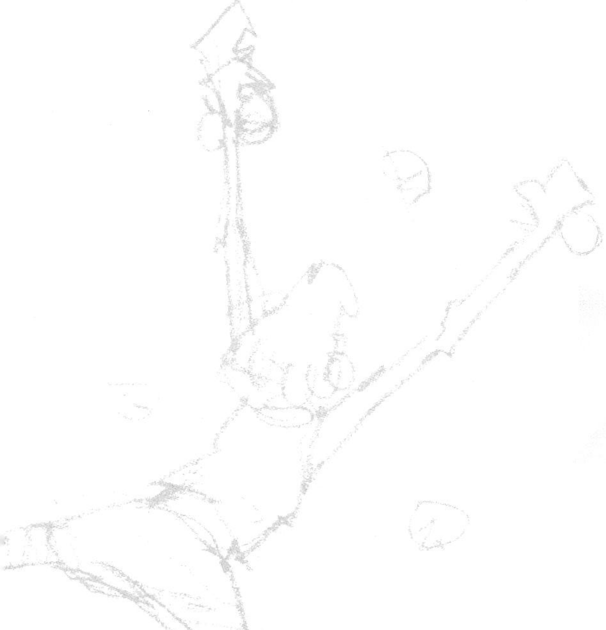

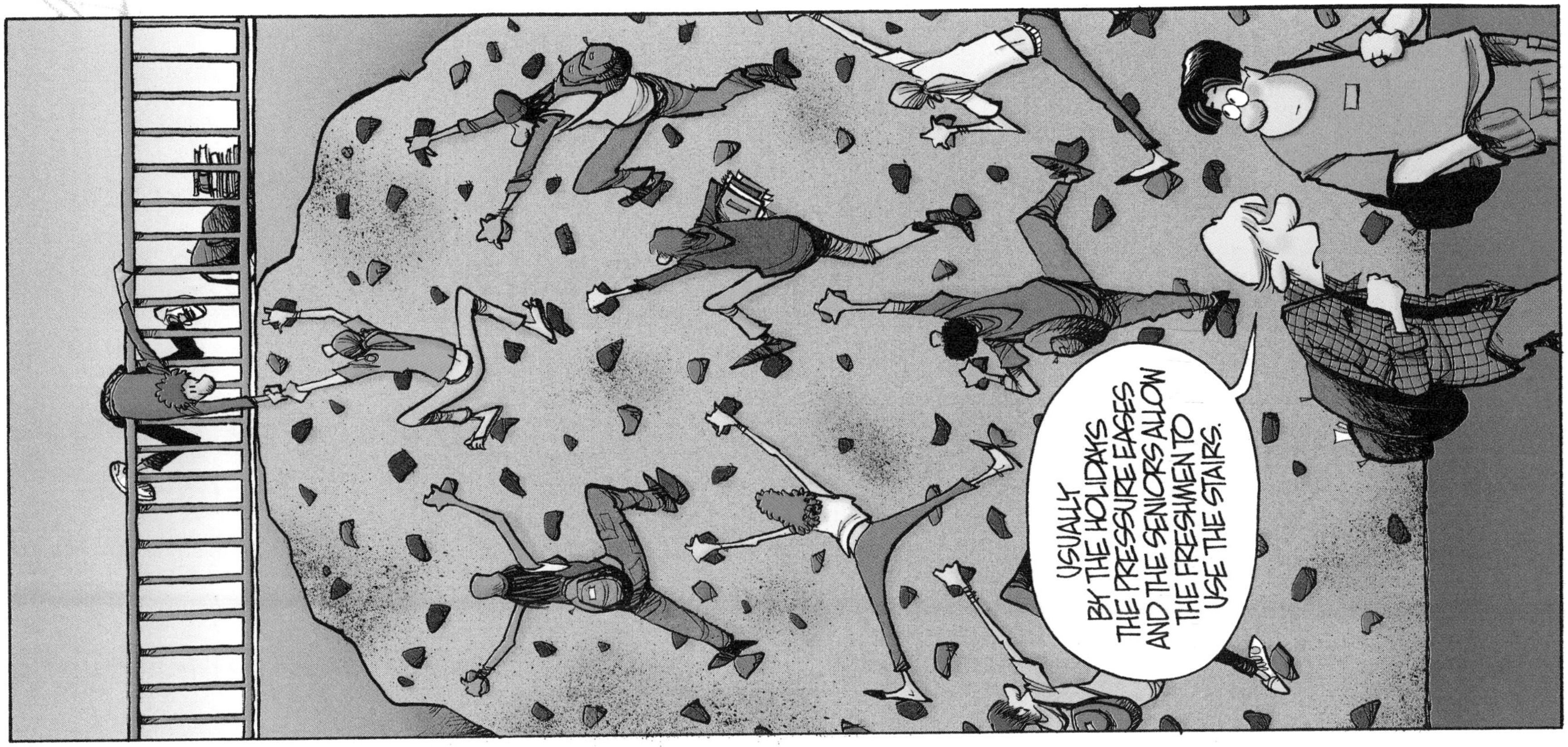

USUALLY BY THE HOLIDAYS THE PRESSURE EASES AND THE SENIORS ALLOW THE FRESHMEN TO USE THE STAIRS.

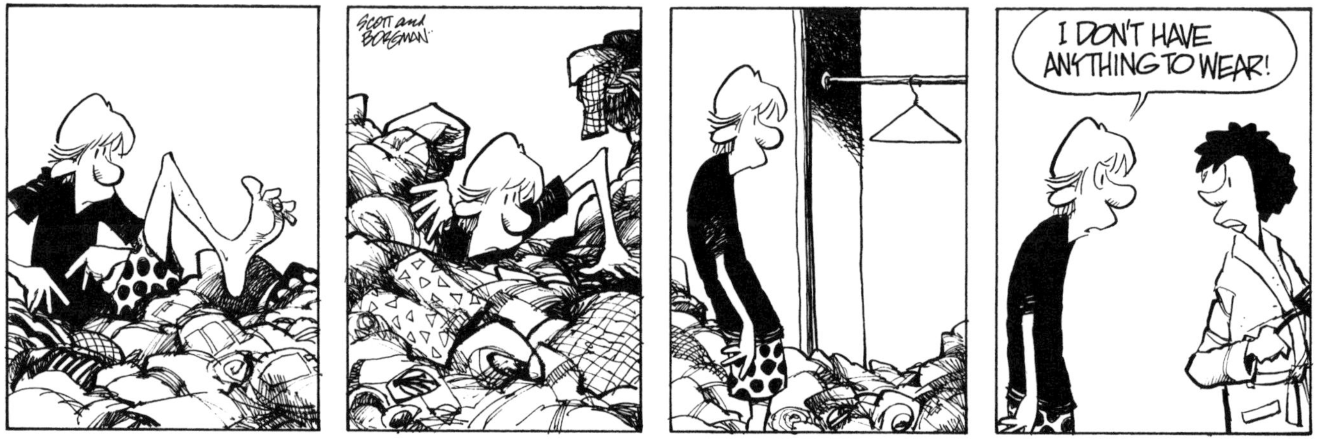
SCOTT and BORGMAN
I DON'T HAVE ANYTHING TO WEAR!

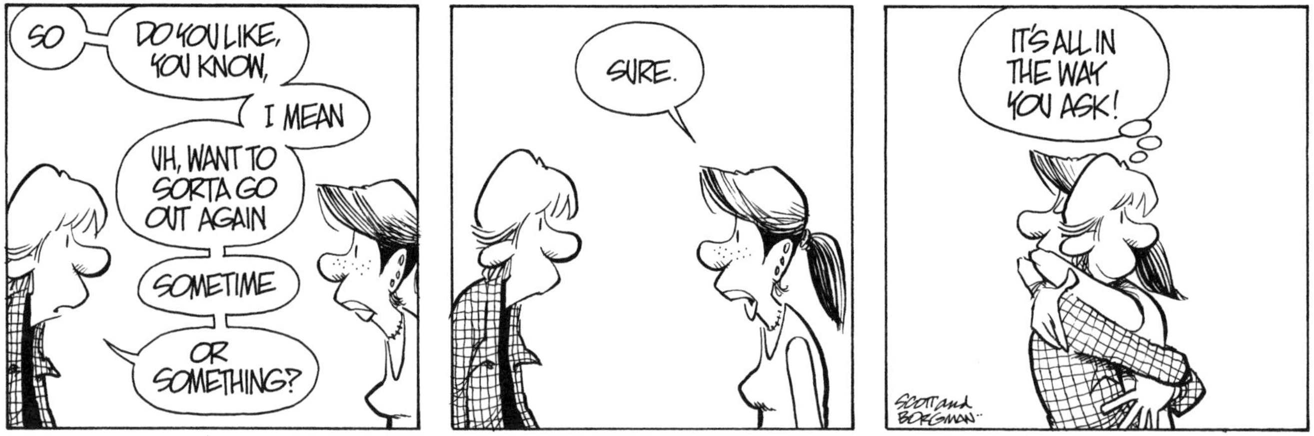
SO
DO YOU LIKE, YOU KNOW,
I MEAN
UH, WANT TO SORTA GO OUT AGAIN
SOMETIME
OR SOMETHING?
SURE.
IT'S ALL IN THE WAY YOU ASK!
SCOTT and BORGMAN

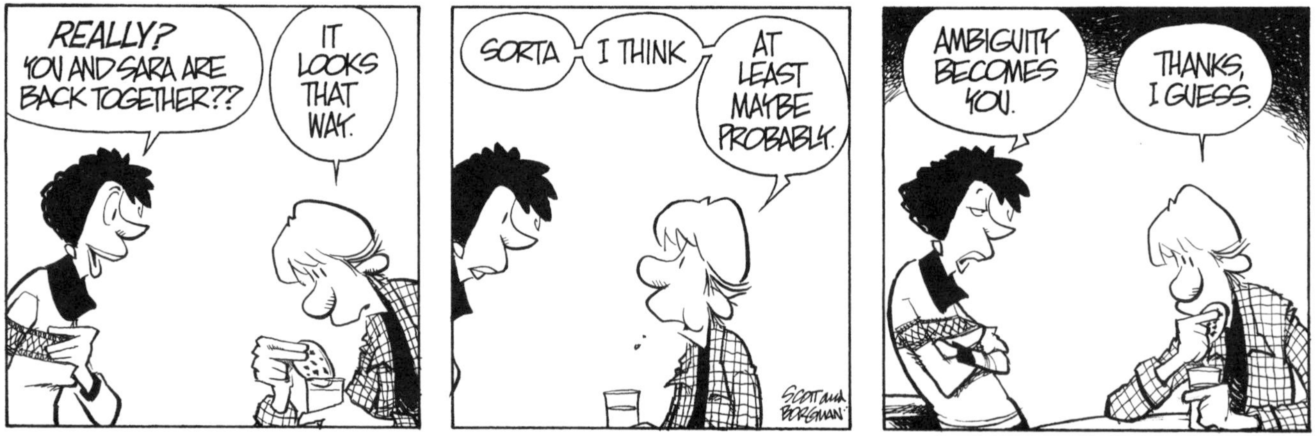
REALLY? YOU AND SARA ARE BACK TOGETHER??
IT LOOKS THAT WAY.
SORTA
I THINK
AT LEAST MAYBE PROBABLY.
SCOTT and BORGMAN
AMBIGUITY BECOMES YOU.
THANKS, I GUESS.

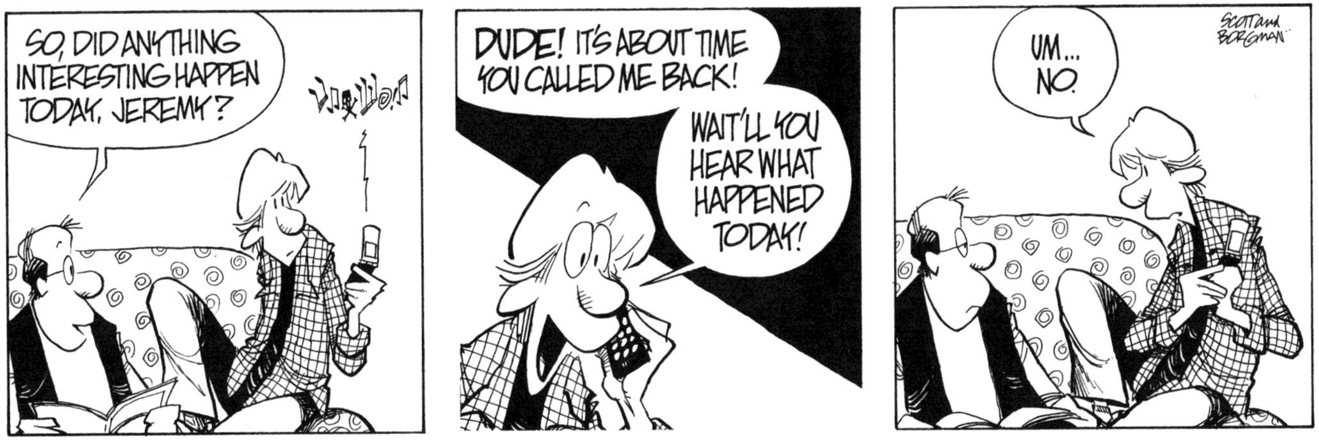
SO, DID ANYTHING INTERESTING HAPPEN TODAY, JEREMY?
DUDE! IT'S ABOUT TIME YOU CALLED ME BACK!
WAIT'LL YOU HEAR WHAT HAPPENED TODAY!
UM... NO.
SCOTT and BORGMAN

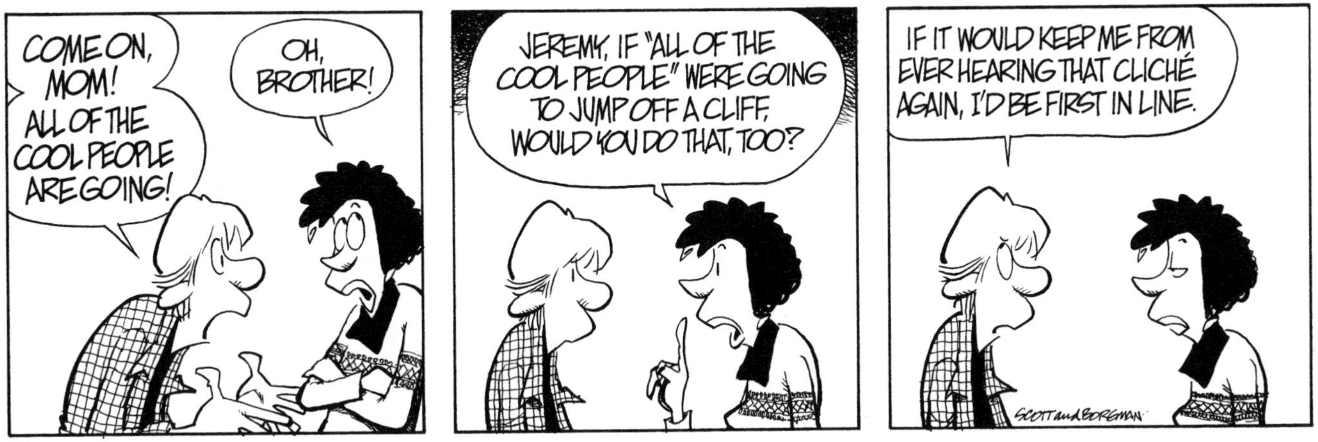
COME ON, MOM! ALL OF THE COOL PEOPLE ARE GOING!
OH, BROTHER!
JEREMY, IF "ALL OF THE COOL PEOPLE" WERE GOING TO JUMP OFF A CLIFF, WOULD YOU DO THAT, TOO?
IF IT WOULD KEEP ME FROM EVER HEARING THAT CLICHÉ AGAIN, I'D BE FIRST IN LINE.
SCOTT and BORGMAN

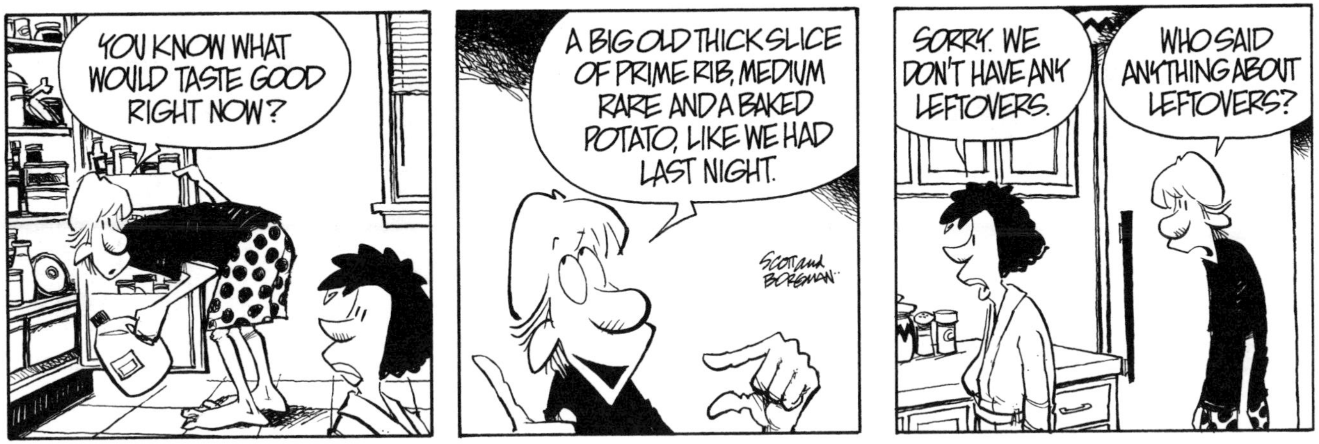
YOU KNOW WHAT WOULD TASTE GOOD RIGHT NOW?
A BIG OLD THICK SLICE OF PRIME RIB, MEDIUM RARE AND A BAKED POTATO, LIKE WE HAD LAST NIGHT.
SCOTT and BORGMAN
SORRY. WE DON'T HAVE ANY LEFTOVERS.
WHO SAID ANYTHING ABOUT LEFTOVERS?

Zits

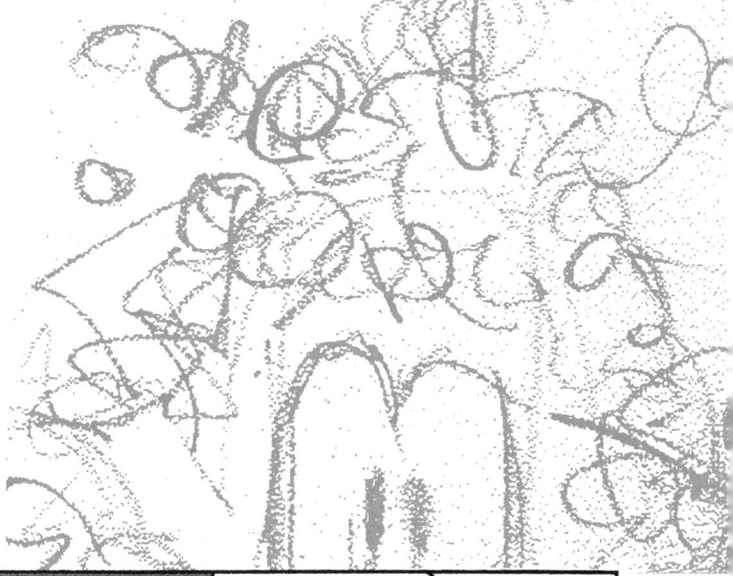

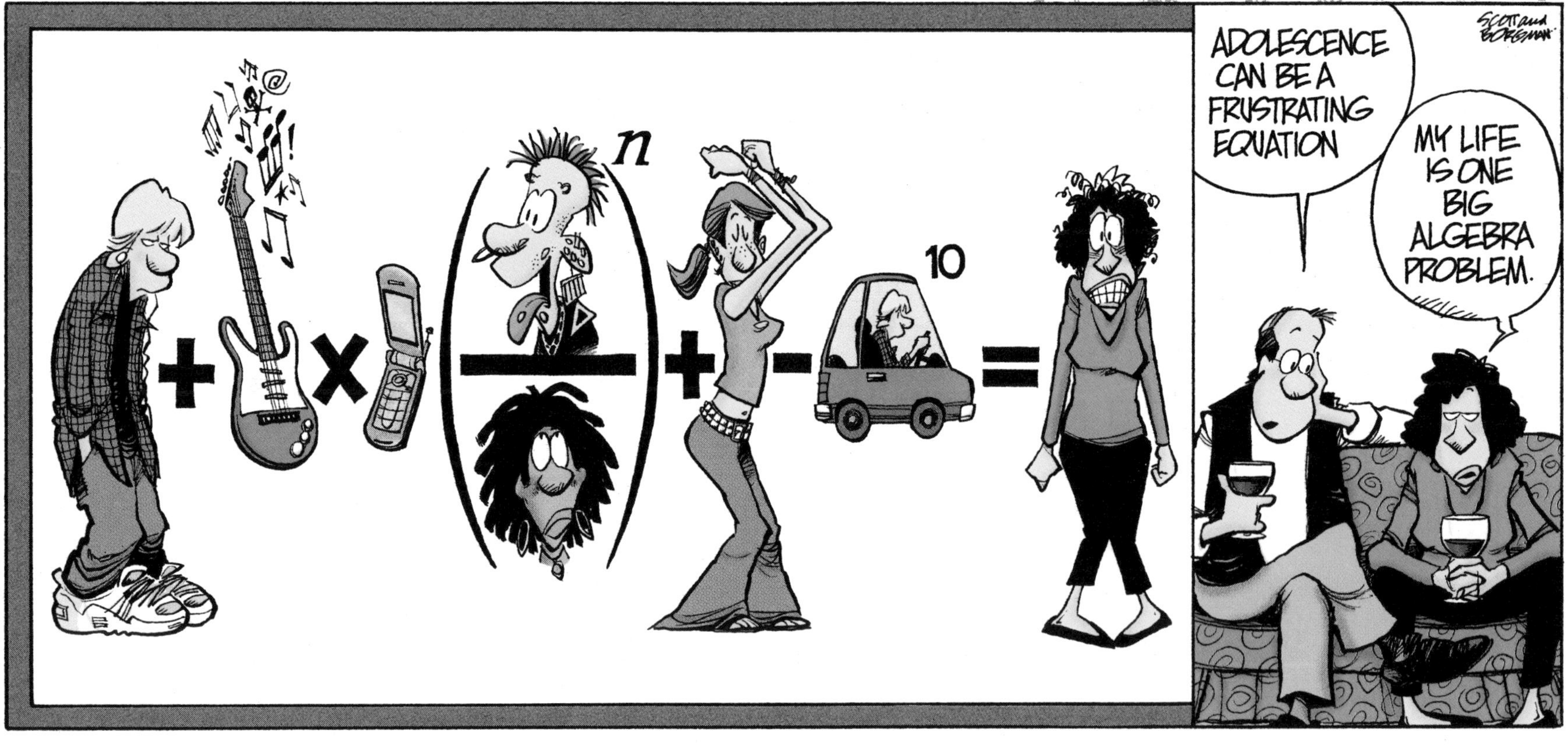

ADOLESCENCE CAN BE A FRUSTRATING EQUATION
MY LIFE IS ONE BIG ALGEBRA PROBLEM.

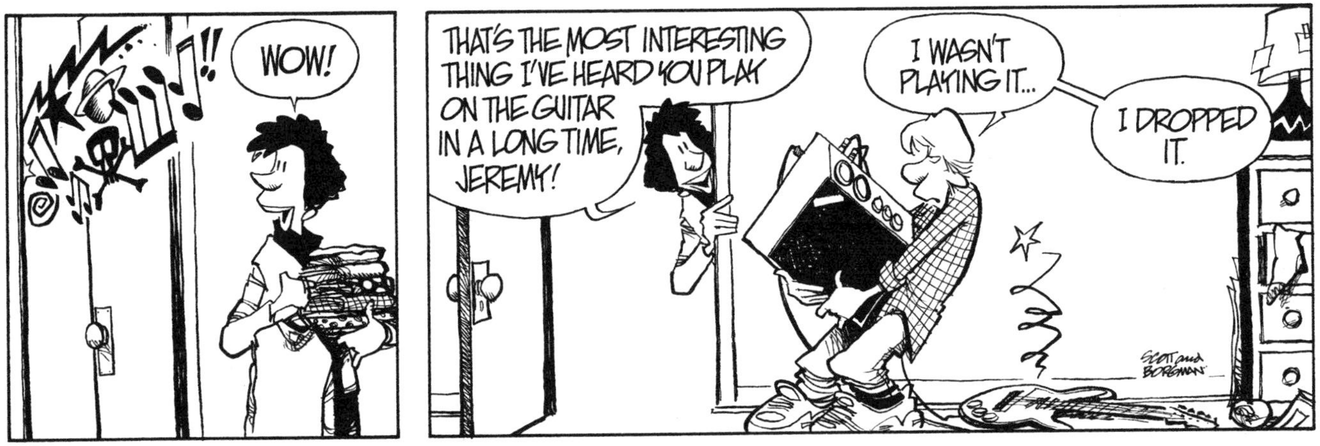
WOW!
THAT'S THE MOST INTERESTING THING I'VE HEARD YOU PLAY ON THE GUITAR IN A LONG TIME, JEREMY!
I WASN'T PLAYING IT...
I DROPPED IT.

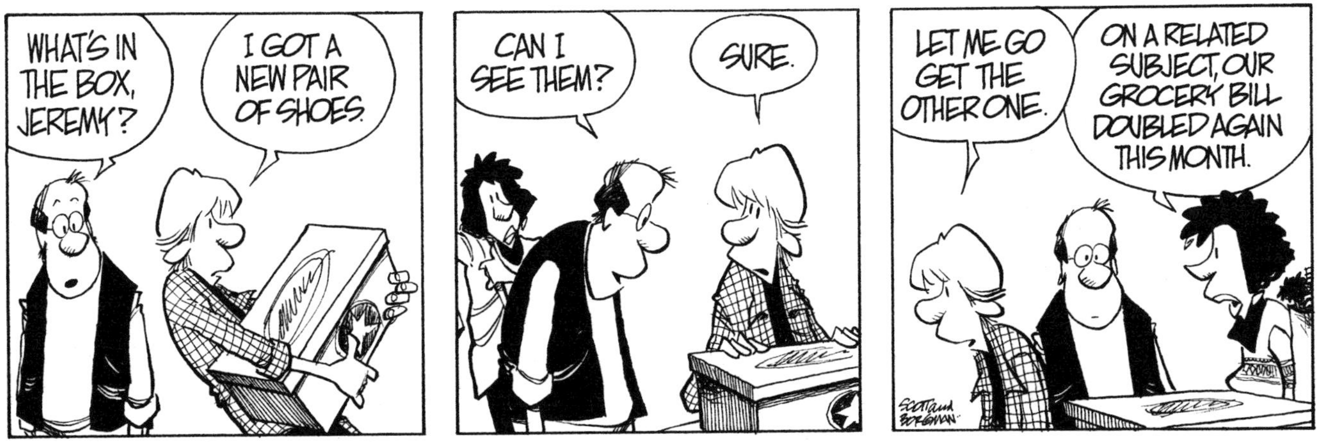
WHAT'S IN THE BOX, JEREMY?
I GOT A NEW PAIR OF SHOES.
CAN I SEE THEM?
SURE.
LET ME GO GET THE OTHER ONE.
ON A RELATED SUBJECT, OUR GROCERY BILL DOUBLED AGAIN THIS MONTH.

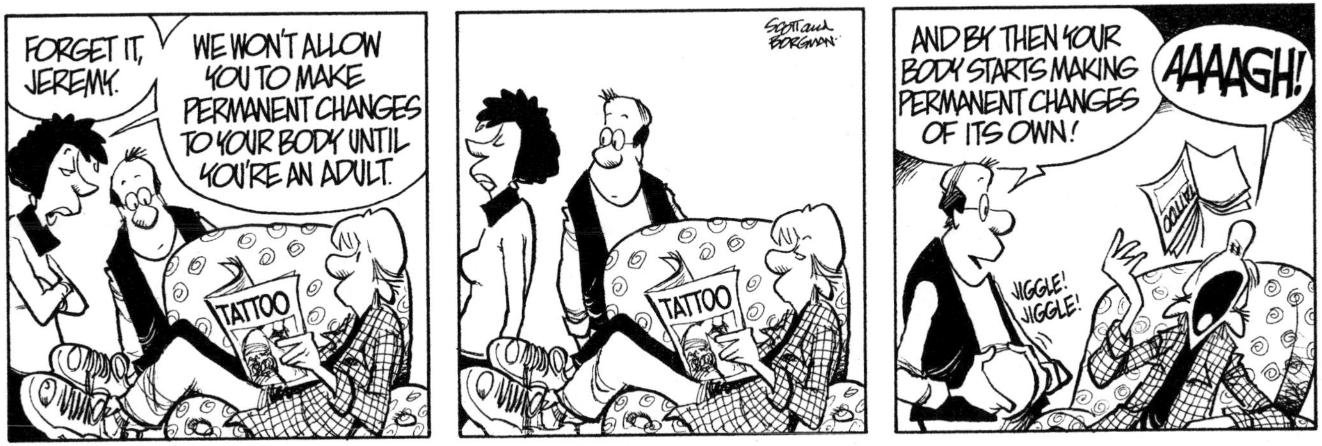
FORGET IT, JEREMY.
WE WON'T ALLOW YOU TO MAKE PERMANENT CHANGES TO YOUR BODY UNTIL YOU'RE AN ADULT.
TATTOO
TATTOO
AND BY THEN YOUR BODY STARTS MAKING PERMANENT CHANGES OF ITS OWN!
AAAAGH!
JIGGLE! JIGGLE!

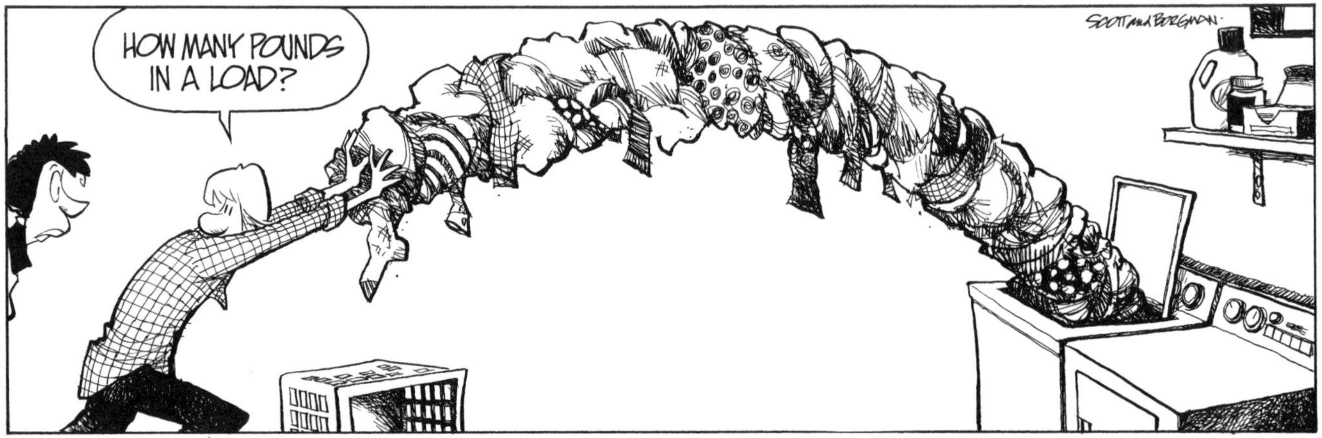
HOW MANY POUNDS IN A LOAD?

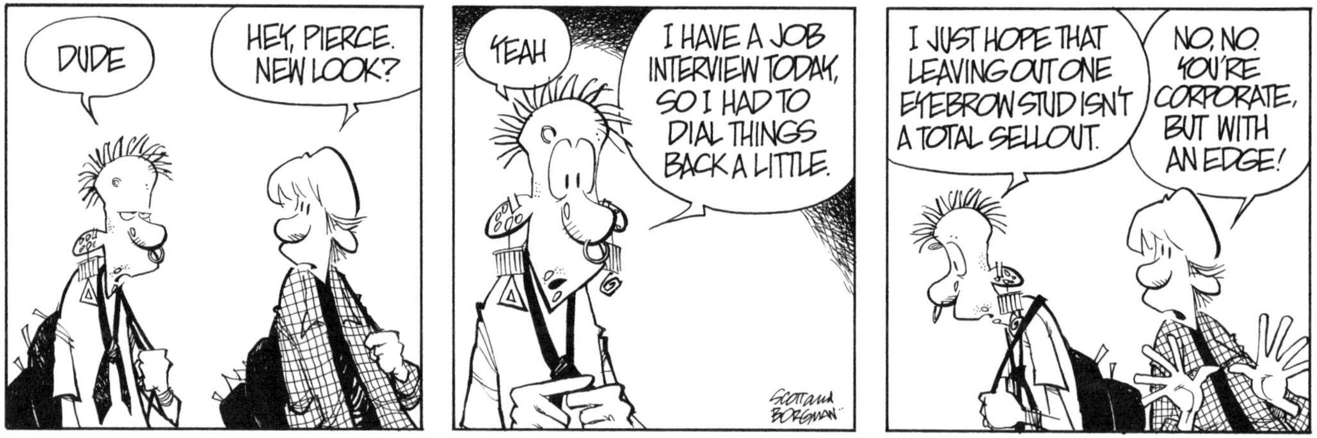
DUDE
HEY, PIERCE. NEW LOOK?
YEAH
I HAVE A JOB INTERVIEW TODAY, SO I HAD TO DIAL THINGS BACK A LITTLE.
I JUST HOPE THAT LEAVING OUT ONE EYEBROW STUD ISN'T A TOTAL SELLOUT.
NO, NO. YOU'RE CORPORATE, BUT WITH AN EDGE!

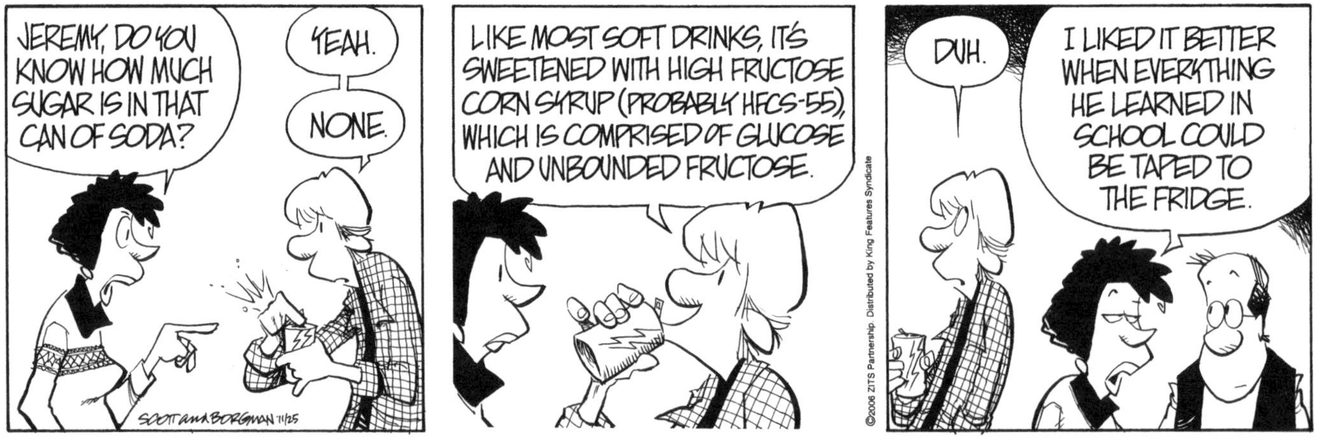
JEREMY, DO YOU KNOW HOW MUCH SUGAR IS IN THAT CAN OF SODA?
YEAH.
NONE.
LIKE MOST SOFT DRINKS, IT'S SWEETENED WITH HIGH FRUCTOSE CORN SYRUP (PROBABLY HFCS-55), WHICH IS COMPRISED OF GLUCOSE AND UNBOUNDED FRUCTOSE.
©2006 ZITS Partnership. Distributed by King Features Syndicate
DUH.
I LIKED IT BETTER WHEN EVERYTHING HE LEARNED IN SCHOOL COULD BE TAPED TO THE FRIDGE.

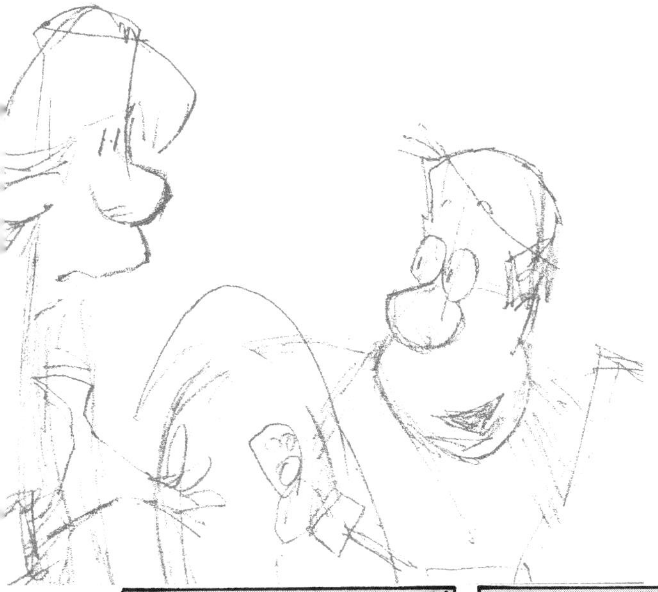

Zits

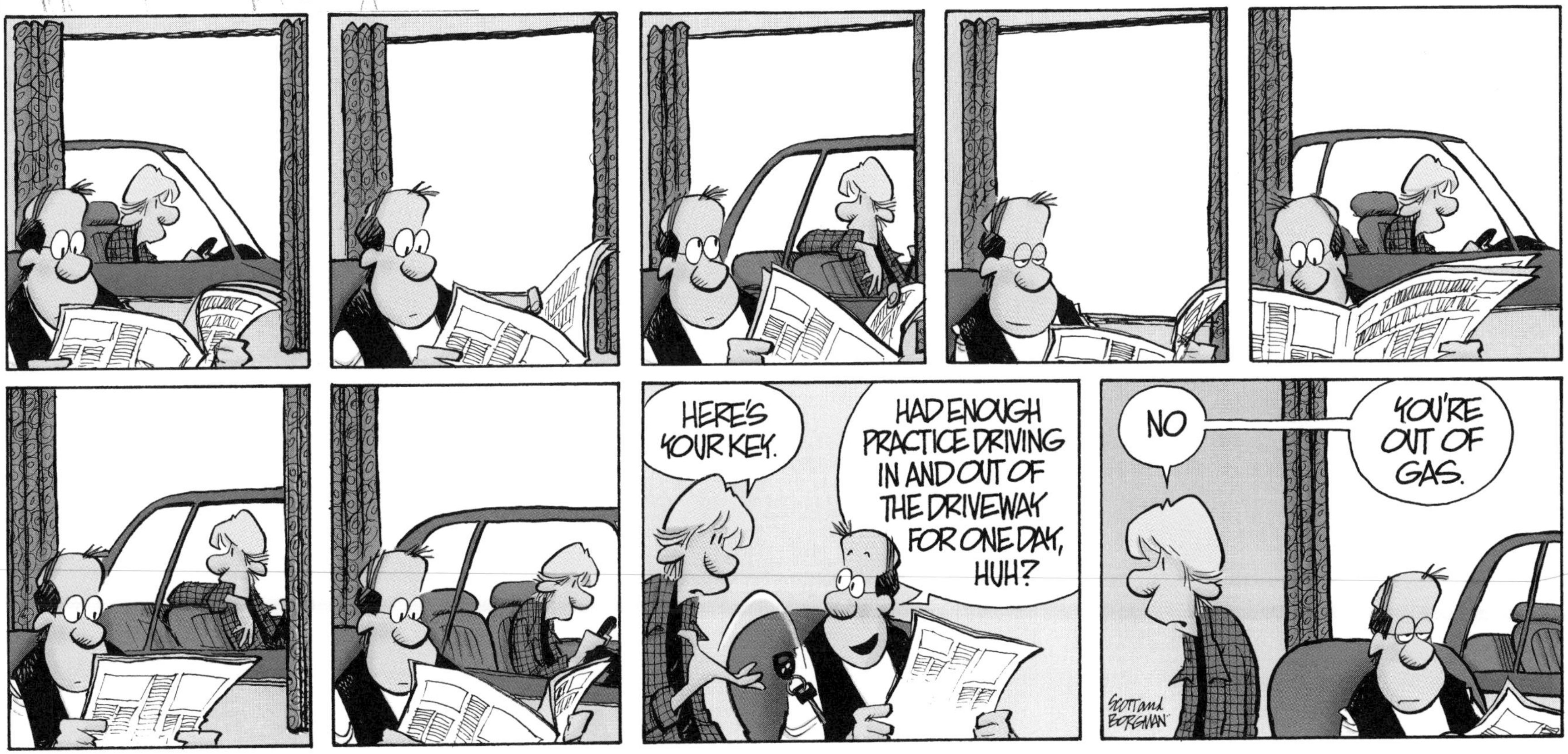
HERE'S YOUR KEY.
HAD ENOUGH PRACTICE DRIVING IN AND OUT OF THE DRIVEWAY FOR ONE DAY, HUH?
SCOTT and BORGMAN
NO
YOU'RE OUT OF GAS.

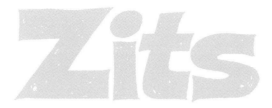